The Psychology
of Adolescence

THE PSYCHOLOGY OF ADOLESCENCE

FOURTH EDITION

John E. Horrocks

The Ohio State University

Houghton Mifflin Company · Boston

Atlanta   Dallas   Geneva, Illinois
Hopewell, New Jersey   Palo Alto   London

Material in Chapter 2 from E. B. Hurlock, "The adolescent reformer," *Adolescence* 3 (1968): 273–306, was reprinted by permission of Libra Publishers, Inc.

Material in Chapter 18 from W. W. Greulich, "Physical changes in adolescence," *Adolescence*, 43rd Yearbook of the National Society for the Study of Education (Chicago: University of Chicago Press, 1944), pp. 8–32, was reprinted by permission of the National Society for the Study of Education and the author.

Material in Chapter 18 from I. T. Nathanson, L. E. Towne, and J. C. Aub, "Normal excretion of sex hormones in childhood," *Endocrinology* 23 (1941): 851–856, was reprinted by permission of J. B. Lippincott Company.

Material in Chapters 24 and 25 from A. B. Hollingshead, *Elmtown's youth* (New York: Wiley, 1949), was reprinted by permission of John Wiley & Sons, Inc., and the author.

For Jane

Contents

PART TWO   Affective and Cognitive Development

PART THREE   Bases of Behavior

PART FOUR Motivation and Directionality of Behavior

PART FIVE   The Psychobiology of Adolescence

PART SIX   The Adolescent and Society

Preface

The purpose of the fourth edition of *The Psychology of Adolescence* is to describe the adolescent time of life, to examine adolescents in the context of their culture and their own biopsychology, and, as much as possible, to explain and make suggestions about them. Although the definition of adolescence used here extends the period over a somewhat longer span than has traditionally been the case, it does reflect newer thinking in the field. In fact, some instructors may wish to substitute the term *youth* or even *young adult* for the period the author speaks of as "late adolescence."

The fourth edition represents a thorough revision and rewriting. The sequence of topics is different from that in the previous editions. Many new studies and ideas have been added and a considerable number of studies appearing in the third edition have been dropped. New chapters have been added as old ones were eliminated. The approach, however, remains relatively eclectic, although from time to time certain theoretical positions the author believes defensible will be presented. The overall point of view is that of a psychologist, but materials from other disciplines are used as appropriate. In discussing the adolescent period, many topics of special interest could be included, but some selection must be made to keep within the bounds of the reasonable or even of the possible. Chapters on psychotherapy and on such problems of extreme deviancy as psychopathology, sociopathology, delinquency, and alcohol or drug abuse have not been included. Such areas can be highly specialized and any in-depth discussion of them would be inappropriate for a general textbook.

As was the case with previous editions, the fourth edition is research oriented. The many studies, past and present, that are cited in this text keep readers in touch with the realities of adolescent behavior and offer evidence freeing them from the necessity of having to take the author on faith. Readers may turn to each chapter's references and proceed directly to the original sources to check the validity of the points of view presented. For supplementary information, suggested readings are also provided. No attempt has been made to "talk down" to students. The treatment is that of a serious, college-level textbook written for students interested in learning about the facts and theories of the adolescent period and willing to be exposed to the actual research findings. This edition also continues the attempt to include at least a partial view of the foreign literature, on the assumption that the phenomenon of adolescence is not confined to the United States. The greater part of the literature has been cited from American and western European sources. Except for studies from Japan, India, and Israel, there is less research on adolescence being done outside Western culture than one would wish.

Instructors using this edition may wish to eliminate some chapters or change their sequence. This may be done without violating the author's overall interpretation of adolescence, since each chapter has been written so that it may stand as a unit. It is suggested, however, that Chapter 1, "Introductory Perspective," be used as a good general starting point. While this text is concerned with the *psychology* of adolescence, it draws freely on material from other behavioral, social, and biological sciences as well as from such applied fields as education. Instructors who lean toward one or another of these disciplines may wish to stress the corresponding aspects of the text. Previous courses in psychology are not essential to an understanding of the material in this textbook; an effort has been made to include all the necessary background material.

An adolescent's behavior reflects individuality as well as the general tendencies characteristic of adolescence. Conditioning and directing both individuality and stage-of-life tendency are the specifics of the time and the culture in which an adolescent lives and is reared. Each new generation is representative of its time, and when the pace of change is accelerated, it becomes increasingly difficult for succeeding generations to find a common ground of understanding. In 1969 the foreward to the third edition stated that "since 1960, the pace of change has so accelerated that many generalizations of only a few years ago are no longer valid. As we view the present generation of adolescents, we see the result of dramatic breaks with the past in attitudes, relationships, and activities." Today a new generation of adolescents has succeeded that of the late 1960s, and the generalization of dramatic difference still holds. However, while the pace of change in the 1970s remains rapid, it is in many essential ways less so than during the 1960s. There is even a noticeable tendency to return to the ways of the past in some beliefs and activities. It may well be that some of the older generalizations will regain validity as we approach the 1980s and that adolescents of 1980 will find less of a generation gap between themselves and their parents than did the adolescents of 1969. If present trends continue, they may even find that they have more in common with their grandparents.

John E. Horrocks

The Psychology of Adolescence

PART ONE

The Nature of Adolescence

Chapter One

Introductory Perspective

The Developmental Sequence

It is characteristic of the human race that a long period of growth and apprenticeship must intervene between birth and the attainment of both physical maturity and adult competence. Human young, to survive, must be carefully nurtured and protected for a number of years. They develop slowly and are endowed with a cognitive structure that does not become optimally functional during the first fifteen years of their lives. They have a great deal to learn, for of all living creatures they can learn and transmit the past, make judgments about the distant future, learn a symbolic language as a means of communicating with one another, and manipulate concepts of space-time. As the cultures they live in become more complex, they are confronted with the need to undergo long induction periods before they can take their places as fully functioning adults.

Therefore their elders must be concerned with child rearing if they are to perpetuate the species, and such concern is time consuming. That such concern is a human attribute is borne out by discussions of childhood in the written records as well as in the orally transmitted tales and traditions handed down from the past. Because man is a thinking-hypothesizing animal, he has attempted to structure his thinking about children so that he can approach their rearing and training as effectively as he feels the situation demands. As man has considered the developmental sequence of his young, it has become apparent to him that it can be viewed as a series of stages, each with

its own characteristics and problems. Such stages are, of course, artificial formulations, and there is considerable overlapping between any two adjacent stages. Since there are various ways of viewing the developmental sequence in stage terms, there has been disagreement as to the number and characteristics of the stages that can be identified and discussed. But there is one time in the developmental sequence that forms so obvious a point of demarcation, of separation from that which has gone before, that it has been commonly identified and agreed upon as the beginning of a crucial period. That point is the attainment of sexual maturity, involving the ability to reproduce one's kind. The term *puberty* has been applied to this point, and the period between the attainment of sexual maturity and the full assumption of the responsibilities and behaviors of adulthood has been commonly referred to as the adolescent period.

The Period of Adolescence

There can be no doubt that the period of adolescence is a large, significant aspect of the human developmental span, having its antecedents in the growth and developmental phenomena of the first decade of life and finding its consequents in the following years of maturity. The phenomenon of adolescence is complex, and because it is complex the many writers who have considered it have defined and interpreted it from many different theoretical points of view and have also emphasized different aspects. Naturally, one who tries to interpret adolescence does so within the limits of his own training and experience. The blind men who tried to describe an elephant come to mind. Since none of them could see the whole elephant, each was forced to describe it in terms of the sensory means available to him and within the limits of the part of the elephant he encountered. The blind man who felt only the trunk said that an elephant was like a snake. He who felt the leg said the elephant was like a tree, and so on. Yet none saw the whole elephant, and certainly none presented either a true or comprehensive picture of the whole beast. And so it is with adolescence. Only by looking at the whole phenomenon from all viewpoints can one get an integrated picture, and even then the description is static rather than dynamic, for one complication is that adolescence must be viewed in terms of structure and in terms of behavior in constantly changing cultural conditions and times in history. Over the centuries some aspects of adolescence have remained relatively constant, but others have undergone radical changes as generation has succeeded generation. The adolescent of today is not the adolescent of yesteryear, nor is he the adolescent of tomorrow. It is the task of this text to make explicit the constancies of the adolescent period, true in any century, as well as the aspects that can be considered only as contemporary.

Certainly it is incorrect to think of adolescence as a static, unchanging condition, similar for all who pass through it. The impact of adolescence and the effects of that impact vary from person to person, family to family, country to country, culture to culture, and generation to generation. In dealing with adolescents we must take them as they are and realize that they are the product of their time, their culture, and their past and present psychological and physical environment. It is important to realize that there will be individual variations and that these must be known and understood in order to do an adequate job of working with an individual. But common denominators do exist, and with proper limitations certain generalities may be applied.

Research studies and observations of adolescents have made it possible to say that under certain conditions, other things being equal, a given adolescent in a specific situation is or is not deviating from what we have grown to expect under such conditions. Deviations from expected behavior are not necessarily abnormal (as a matter of fact they may be very normal), but in any event they may serve as a significant clue to the interpretation of an individual's behavior.

Points of Reference in Viewing Adolescence

In general there are six major points of reference from which to view adolescent growth and development.

1. Adolescence is a time when an individual becomes increasingly aware of self, endeavors to test his ramifying conceptions of self against reality, and gradually works toward the self-stabilization that will characterize his adult years. During this time the individual is learning the personal and social roles most likely to fit his self-concept as well as his concept of others.

2. Adolescence is a time of seeking status as an individual. There is a tendency to attempt emancipation from childish submission to parental authority, and usually a struggle against relationships with adults in which the adolescent is subordinated on the basis of inferiority in age, experience, and skill. It is a period of emerging and developing vocational interests and striving toward economic independence.

3. Adolescence is a time when group relationships become of major importance. The adolescent is usually most anxious to attain status with, and recognition by, his age-mates. He tends to desire intensely to conform to the actions and standards of his peers. It is also a time of emerging heterosexual interests that may bring complexity and conflict to emotions and activities.

4. Adolescence is a time of physical development and growth that forms a continuous pattern common to the species, but idiosyncratic to the individual. In this period there is a rapid altering of the body, and revision of the body image and habitual motor patterns. During this time physical maturity is attained.

5. Adolescence is a time of intellectual expansion and development, and academic experience. The individual finds he has to adjust to increasing academic and intellectual requirements. He is asked to acquire many skills and concepts useful at some future time but often lacks immediate motivation. It is a time when an individual gains experience and knowledge in many areas and interprets his environment in the light of that experience.

6. Adolescence tends to be a time of development and evaluation of values. The quest for the controlling values around which the individual may integrate his life is accompanied by the development of self-ideals and acceptance of self in harmony with those ideals. It is a time of conflict between youthful idealism and reality.

Certain aspects of an adolescent's experiences and reactions are common to most of the foregoing reference points. First of all there is a continual need for adjustment to situations in which the individual is inexperienced. Coupled with this is the frequent demand that adult patterns of behavior be assumed before he is emotionally or socially ready. He is often faced with contradictory values due to culturally created dependencies, as when his parents and his high school economics teacher hold conflicting notions on the nature of economic structure or the causes of business crises. The adolescent also tends to experience frequent frustration as a result of a lack of status, cultural demands and taboos, and other restrictions. Attempts to adjust to such frustration often result in aggression or withdrawal.

In considering these reference points we must remember that while growth and development of all people follow a similar pattern, there are also individual differences within the pattern. For example, one individual may reach his maximum growth earlier than another, and one person may be heavier or possess a sturdier build than another; but such individual differences occur only within the limits allowed by their species. There is a linear height beyond which human beings do not go, and there is a body structure peculiar to human beings that is not characteristic of other members of the animal kingdom. Hence, individual variations can occur only within limits. What is true of one individual may or may not be true of another, either wholly or in part, but common trends may be postulated.

The Adolescent as a Member of His Species

Although consideration of the foregoing characteristics is of first importance in appraising or predicting an adolescent's behavior, it is also important to remember that an adolescent is a human being. As a member of the human race, he can be depended upon, in addition to his primarily adolescent reactions and preoccupations, to display behavior characteristic of the race—the kind of behavior that may be expected of any person, no matter what his age. Here the student of psychology is helped by the fact that studies in the field have established certain principles of human behavior that have proved valid to a considerable degree. These principles are applicable to adolescents as well as to persons of other ages.

For example, basic impulses to behavior, such as hunger, sex, and thirst, have been identified, and studies have revealed that the blocking or thwarting of these impulses consistently results in a limited number of alternate responses that will in turn lead to other physical, social, and personal reactions. An infant who is hungry will squirm, thrash about, and finally cry; these behaviors will continue with increasing intensity until he is fed. An adolescent who is hungry may raid the icebox, become angry with his mother for delaying dinner, find a restaurant, or engage in other, comparable behavior until he, too, is fed.

Supplementing the basic impulses to behavior are certain other needs, such as the need for approval, mastery, and security. For example, an adolescent may need the approval of his English teacher in school and so will spend long hours reading suggested literature, preparing and polishing themes, or correcting his parents' grammar. In class he may be eager to display his knowledge and mastery of the subject and so will volunteer frequently, interrupt others, or follow all discussions with alert interest. The English teacher may express approval or disapproval as a result of this behavior. Thus, these needs too may either be blocked or satisfied, and the resulting feeling of frustration (or goal achievement) will produce certain physical and social reactions that will influence the behavior not only of the individual undergoing them but, through his responses, of others. Thus, an understanding of the adolescent depends upon two things: (1) knowledge of the behavior to be expected of an adolescent as such, under given conditions, and (2) enough knowledge of human behavior in general to determine when he is acting merely as an adolescent and when he is acting like any other individual.

Adults in the Adolescent's World

It is a fallacy to assume that only an understanding of the adolescent is necessary. Frequently, the whole index to understanding a given adolescent's problems and behavior lies in a general understanding of the psychology of the adults with whom he lives and works. These important persons include not only his parents, teachers, and relatives, but also his employers and even the casual adults he meets as he grows older. The adolescent functions as a member of a community controlled by adults preoccupied with the exigencies of adult living. In addition, there is the adolescent's own personal world, inhabited only by himself, where in his dreams and his concepts of self he can

be and do anything he pleases. Hence, for the adolescent, there are two worlds: the social or three-dimensional world of reality and his own unseen world of imagination, the "fourth dimension" into which he can retreat whenever he wants to. As an individual he must accept and, in a real sense, attempt to play very different roles in both the third- and fourth-dimensional worlds. Each aspect of the social world has a different pattern of rules, restrictions, privileges, and responsibilities, and often these patterns are in direct conflict. Sometimes the different aspects of the social world are entirely separate, but even when they are not, most adolescents appear able to separate them well enough to play different and perhaps antagonistic roles in each situation.

Unfortunately, it is usually impossible to separate these worlds entirely. There is bound to be overlap as the adolescent's desire to do something approved by his peers conflicts with his parents' ideas. Overlap does not necessarily mean conflict, but a strong chance of conflict does exist, and when the adolescent finds himself having to reconcile one with the other, difficulty is bound to arise, particularly where there is antagonism or misunderstanding between the worlds. One major basis of adolescent problems begins when the child attempts to play the role of one world in one of the other worlds he inhabits. This usually causes trouble and misunderstanding on the part of everyone concerned, with resulting difficulty.

Development of Identity and Responsibility

This writer's position is that one of the most important things society can do in the educational and child-rearing practices applied to adolescents is to inculcate in these developing individuals a sense of personal responsibility, not only for themselves as individuals, but for the nation and culture of which they are a part. Such a sense of responsibility is best arrived at through facilitating the adolescent's development by giving him opportunities and help in accepting appropriate responsibility for himself and also for the daily activities of his community and his family. Obviously the extension of such opportunities has to be a gradual process, keeping step with the child's own advance toward maturity, but also preceding the advance, since responsibility fosters responsibility.

These statements form the framework upon which the discussions of the phenomenon of adolescence in this text are built. However, these statements must be seen and interpreted in a context of an overridingly important psychological view of adolescence. That view holds that the major task of adolescence is the building, integration, and consolidation of a self-concept that will lead to a real, secure identity hierarchy. Thus the idea of inculcating a sense of responsibility and facilitating its development must go hand in hand with providing a proper milieu and help where necessary for the adolescent to build such an identity. Indeed the two, a secure and stable self-identification and a sense of responsibility, are so highly related that one is virtually nonfunctional without the other except on some sort of pitiful, robotlike, conforming, "1984-ish" basis.

Yet the extension and facilitation of respon-sibility and help in the building of self-identification must not be in terms of manipulation by adults merely to serve their own ends and comfort. The adolescent's integrity as a human being and his right to privacy as a person must be preserved. We are trying to develop free, self-actualizing individuals for a democratic society, and the very essence of democracy is the integrity of man, no matter what his age. The adolescent must have an opportunity to develop along his own lines, to follow, in effect, his own star. We simply cannot raise our children to conform for conformity's sake, stifle their creativity, make them scapegoats for adult frustrations, or deny them the chance to come to grips not only with themselves as persons but with the meaning of the world in which they live. Those who rear children and those charged with their education have a fearsome and humbling responsibility as they try to steer adolescents between the Scylla of license and the Charybdis of conformity. Perhaps "try to steer" is an unhappy choice of phrase. Actually the adolescent has to learn to steer himself. We can only guide and facilitate, and we must be very sure that our guidance is really that in the best sense of the word, not just manipulation. We must remember that free men do not march in lock step nor are they strangers to themselves.

Chapter Two

Characteristics of Adolescence

The twentieth century has seen a great burgeoning of interest in adolescence. Since midcentury the interest has accelerated and is often accompanied by a concern only rarely present in previous generations. A modern-day adolescent has many characteristics in common with his predecessors but some new elements have been added. The adolescent of today has a more central role in adult affairs, his opinion is more frequently listened to and even sought, and he has much more latitude in the affairs of daily living than former generations would have deemed proper. Lowering the voting age to eighteen is only one sign of the adolescent's new role. But above all, today's adolescent is growing up in a transitional period of great uncertainty and unresolved new directions. Adults are less certain of their role or, when they become certain, find that the certainty is unacceptable to large sections of their culture. Because an air of uncertainty is abroad, adults are often unable to provide guidance in values in the present or an acceptable path into the future. The culture seems to offer more inconsistencies, and these inconsistencies are routinely brought to the attention of youth and act as further reflections of adult uncertainty. And beyond this, at least in the United States, the adolescent is being reared in a culture that worships youth, goes to great lengths to serve them, and tries to emulate them. The ultimate flattery in the United States is to tell an adult that he looks and acts younger than his age. The final accolade is for the comment to be made by a much younger person. For the first time adolescents are close to setting the national and even the international sartorial standard, and their preferences are copied by adults in many other areas. Yet, at least in early and middle adolescence, they are still dependent children, and they encounter many personal inconsistencies in the conflicts between these two roles. It is fascinating to be an adolescent today, but it is also difficult.

Descriptions of Adolescence

For all of these reasons there have been many current attempts to describe and explain the adolescent period. But there is also a long history of such descriptive and explanatory attempts, for the years of youth have consistently been of concern to mankind. And in the past, as in the present, specific conditions of the times have often accelerated the interest.

Some of the attention resulted from a direct and specific interest in adolescence. Some derived from an interest in human behavior and development that included adolescence merely as one aspect of a large developmental picture. For the latter, the issue was the nature of man, and adolescence was included only incidentally insofar as an understanding of it as a developmental stage contributed to an understanding of human behavior. The motivations of the describers varied from those of pure scientists interested in the study of behavioral phenomena apart from any application, to those of persons who wished to apply their knowledge for educational, therapeutic, or social change. Some of the descriptions were purely factual with no attempt to formulate theory, while others were efforts either to confirm or extend existing theories or to evolve new ones. Eventually enough information may be available so that a series of constructs or intervening variables may be used to formulate a truly comprehensive theory of adolescent behavior with both explanatory and predictive value. To date, no such all-encompassing theory has evolved. Existing theories are partial theories, or they deal only with special cases of adolescence. As Beley and Faure (1962) point out, we really do not know the adolescent although we have many hypotheses about him. We know that the nature of the adolescent sets him apart from the individuals in preceding and following stages. Beley and Faure are explicit in their feeling that the period of adolescence needs better conceptions and formulations than have been provided by existing theory and research.

The Problem of a Definition of Adolescence

How, then, considering all the ramifications of the term's usage, may we arrive at a definition of adolescence? As was indicated in the previous chapter, there are a great many ways of interpreting the nature and meaning of adolescence, depending upon the perceptions and purposes of the interpreter. Perceptions and corresponding definitions range from those of the man in the street or the personally involved parent, to those of persons professionally concerned with adolescents in face-to-face relationships or as subjects for theoretical study. Because these people have different backgrounds, purposes, and experiences with the adolescent, their perceptions are different. The adolescent is many things simultaneously, and he is an individual as well as a member of a general age group. He is a member of his general culture and a reflection of his culture.

He is also a member of various subgroups or subcultures within the larger culture, as well as a product of his time in history. We often find people who generalize from one adolescent they have known, or from a group of adolescents who form a subculture. Such generalizations can have only dubious validity when they are applied to the whole class, and may do injustice to the individual adolescent or may overestimate him. Professionals cannot be exempted from those who overgeneralize on insufficient grounds. Some professionals are committed to a specific theory of behavior and fit their interpretation of the adolescent to their theory's dictates.

Earlier Concerns with Adolescence

As was indicated earlier in this chapter, man has been concerned with the adolescent for a long time. Written records of this concern go back to the earliest days of recorded history and continue across the centuries of the last millennium. Even where adolescence was not actually written about, its advent was celebrated by formal acts in cultures ranging from the most primitive to the most advanced. The *rites de passage* of the primitive cultures have been described at length by anthropologists, and historians have described the recognition of the period in past civilizations by special observances and even by cults. In Rome, sixteen-year-olds are described as donning the *toga virilis* during the feast of the liberalia. Even the term *adolescent* has a long history extending through middle English and old French from the Latin *adolescere* meaning "to grow toward" or "to grow up" (*ad*, "toward," + *olescere*, "to grow or be nourished").

However, before the latter part of the nineteenth century the best source for systematic views on adolescence existed chiefly in the writings of philosophers, educators, or others interested in youth's education and behavior. Such discussions are usually speculative, but usually some attempt was made to present a unified and comprehensive point of view. It is not possible in this book to mention the names of all the early writers who dealt with the nature and education of youth, but among the more influential for their time were Aristotle, Plato, Francke, Froebel, Comenius, Rousseau, and Pestalozzi.

In the first four books of the *Odyssey* we read the story of Telemachus, the only son of Ulysses, and we find that in ancient Athens Aristotle described the physical aspects of puberty and, in some detail, the accompanying secondary sex characteristics in his *Historia Animalium.* In his *Rhetoric,* Aristotle also considered the psychological aspects of puberty. Plato included the viewpoints of youth in his *Dialogues,* one interesting example being Lysis' complaint to Socrates that he was not allowed to drive the family horses. In Rome, Plutarch, in *Moralia,* and Quintilian, in *Institutes of Oratory,* both spoke of the importance of youth's education for the assumption of adult responsibilities. We even find, as Goppert (1962) points out, the problems of the adolescent period reflected in the symbols of the fairy tales of all cultures.

Francke, in the seventeenth century, lectured at the University of Leipzig on the education of boys and pubescents (*De informatione aetatis puerilis et pubescentis*). Rousseau, in *Emile,* described at some length the events of the chronological age period from twelve to fifteen, which he called the "Age of Reason." He noted that the advent of puberty is the most crucial event in the developmental sequence and posited a series of clear-cut developmental periods, thus anticipating a long line of more modern writers. Rousseau's concept that the happiest existence and the one most conducive to the proper education of youth is a state of nature remote from civilization has been widely discussed and is the antithesis of what happens to youth in Western culture.

Froebel believed that it was the parents' function to live for their children and to sacrifice for them, but that children in turn should learn self-sacrifice and service to others, using their parents as examples. Yet Froebel saw play and work as an inseparable combination, since play was the purest and most spiritual activity of childhood and formed a basis upon which adult perceptions of the meaning of life had to be built. Pestalozzi was particularly interested in youth's cognitive capacities and approached the matter in very direct terms. His philosophy (*"keine Kentnisse ohne Fertigkeiten"*) postulated the need to decrease the interval between thinking and doing, and highlighted the importance in education of dexterity and manual skill so that satisfaction in a job well done would obtain. One outcome of his philosophy as applied in America was the interest in shop courses and the promotion of manual-training high schools. Comenius, in *The Great Didactic,* stated nine principles around which the education of youth and the fostering of their development should center.

Herbert formed the real bridge between the speculative discussions of his predecessors and the psychology that was to come, as it was influenced by both Wundt and Fechner. Writing at the beginning of the nineteenth century, Herbert saw ontogenesis[1] as recapitulating both the phylogenetic and the cultural stages in the development of the human race. He felt that the years from ten to seventeen constitute the period of greatest susceptibility to instruction, a point of view that would find some disfavor today. But this statement seems to have an implicit understanding of the growth of intellectual capacity advanced nearly a century later by Binet and those who followed him. There can be little doubt that Herbert's formulations influenced the thinking of Hall and other psychologists at the close of the nineteenth century who were concerned with the study of the phenomena of the adolescent period.

But the work of the nineteenth-century evolutionists Darwin and Haeckel gave the greatest impetus to a serious study of the developmental sequence. Today it is hard to appreciate the tremendous intellectual ferment

---

[1]Ontogenesis is the development of the individual; phylogenesis, the development of the species.

caused by the then revolutionary Darwinian hypothesis. If they did not bitterly oppose Darwin's evolutionary theories, members of the intellectual community were eager to confirm in their work the Darwinian position.[2] Among these was the psychologist G. Stanley Hall, who summarized his own thinking and the extant research on adolescence in a two-volume, 1,375-page book published in 1904. Hall's *Adolescence* was a monumental *tour de force* and set the pattern for thinking on adolescence for the next quarter-century.

In his writings on development Hall essentially restated Darwinian concepts in psychological terms as a theory of recapitulation. His position was that the developmental evolution of the human species was built into the genetic structure of each individual and that growth and development from conception to maturity was simply a sequential unfolding or recapitulation of the stages through which man had passed in his evolution from lower forms. Hence, each stage in a child's development was a mirror image of a stage through which man had passed in phylogenetic development[3] through the lower forms, and the stages were, because biologically predetermined, inevitable no matter what the environment or the culture. Hall posited four major stages as occurring during the first two decades of life: (1) infancy (first four years), (2) childhood (five through seven), (3) youth (eight through twelve), and (4) puberty (thirteen through twenty-four). Hall visualized puberty as a period of great upset and emotional maladjustment, but with certain compensating factors.

The fact that a book the size of Hall's *Adolescence* could be written as early as 1904 indicates a great deal of prior work on adolescence. Such was indeed the case, particularly following 1880, although as early as 1831 Robertson published the first of a series of studies in France and elsewhere on the advent of puberty

in girls, and most of these findings are still held as valid today. By 1889 Henry Blake, half in jest, could predict in an address to the Scientific Society of Bridgeport, Connecticut, that one day every well-constituted university in America would have its "baby chair of philosophy" to deal with rapidly burgeoning information on child development. In 1882 Hall himself had published on moral and religious training for children. In doing so, he stated what he felt to be the psychological nature of adolescence and stressed the importance of studying the period. Following this lead, Burnham wrote in 1891 that "a study of the psychology of adolescence should form a part of the education of every teacher in the higher institutions. The subject should be studied scientifically from the standpoint of physiology, anthropology, neurology, and psychology, and in its ethical, social, and pedagogical foundaions." Certainly most modern-day workers would accept the usefulness of the multidisciplinary approach, although today we would want sociology included on Burnham's list.

Typical of other early work was Daniels's (1893) description of puberty ceremonies in primitive cultures; Lancaster's (1897, 1898) administration of questionnaires, analysis of published biographies, and direct interviews with children; Starbuck's (1899) study of religion; Libby's (1901) analyses of the experience of adolescents in literature; and Swift's (1903) study of the biographies of the great, similar to the work of Lehman (1953, 1954) in the 1940s and 1950s. The work of these men was primarily descriptive and was based almost exclusively on normative surveys which used questionnaires, interviews, and analyses of writings by and about the age groups they were studying. They used the techniques and means of analysis available in their era or invented new ones for their purposes. Today these techniques and the statistics used to report their findings would be considered primitive if not naive, even as those of today will probably be thought primitive by the scientific investigators of the twenty-first century. Still, it is always surprising to find how

[2]Readers interested in obtaining a picture of the Darwinian period might like to consult a standard biography of Darwin such as that of Himmelfarb (1959).

[3]Ernst Haeckel's (1879) "bio-genetic" law that ontogeny recapitulates phylogeny.

many present-day investigators use their techniques in virtually unchanged form and seem to be fixated in their methodology at that bygone period.

However, all these men of the past had one thing in common to distinguish them from present-day investigators: they were following Hall's lead. Like Hall's, as this writer has stated elsewhere (1954), "their early work was often speculative.... There was often a tendency to attempt to fit what was observed into the pattern of evolutionary theory or to interpret data in terms of an *a priori* point of view." Necessarily such a bias led to errors of judgment and even of fact, many of which found perpetuation in the textbooks published up to the 1930s. But psychologists and educators were becoming restive at the interpretations of adolescence formulated by Hall and his school of thought, and, as Grinder and Strickland (1963) note, they centered their objections around three main issues: (1) the assumption of the overriding importance in an adolescent's development of physiological functions at the expense of cultural influence, (2) the characterization of adolescence as a period of storm and stress based upon instinctual upheavals, and (3) the assertion that the arrival of the adolescent period is abrupt, rather than the result of a continuous and gradual process.

The More Modern Era

In the present century each decade has seen an increasing amount of research and writing on the adolescent period. At the present time the amount of material written on adolescence is so large that no one is really prepared to give even an approximate guess as to its quantity. This is perhaps a natural outcome of general progress in the scientific study of man, or it may be that the times have forced attention upon this age group. There are certain periods of history in which a given age group is accentuated. This occurrence constitutes a kind of role allocation on the basis of age, which tends to emphasize the difference between the gen-

erations. When age as such becomes an issue, as it is, for example, in determining eligibility for the draft, for the ballot, or for a driver's license, we can see the impact of a deliberate use of age differences. Today, Golden Age clubs and the senior-citizen movement point up the importance of age grouping. In the early days of the American republic the age difference was de-emphasized. The family, particularly the rural family—and America was primarily rural—was a cooperative economic enterprise with everyone except babes in arms taking a productive role. On the frontiers a Golden Age club or a retirement community would have been an anomaly. An old person lived with his family and worked until the very end. An adolescent had an assigned economically productive role—a boy worked in the fields with his father and brothers, and a girl worked at the productive chores in the household. In those days an adolescent had a double role. The first was the enjoyment of adolescence, a moratorium between childhood and adulthood when one was not yet an adult; the second was that of the productive worker, which was actually a preplay of the role one would assume as an adult. In those days, the adolescent period was shorter. The role of the thirteen- or fourteen-year-old was more analogous to that of the seventeen- and eighteen-year-old of today, except that the direction in which one was going and the termination points were clearer then. Such a role does not exist at all in our cities today and probably exists only in vestigial form in our rural regions, although in some of the more specifically isolated rural sections of America and in some peasant cultures abroad it may well approach its pure form.

Definition of Adolescence

Let us begin with a definition that looks at the adolescent from the viewpoint of biology. A person becomes an adolescent when he is able to reproduce his kind. This is ordinarily known as the advent of puberty, but puberty actually begins with the action of sex hormones that results in the appearance of the secondary sex characteristics. Individual variations in the onset of hormone action are so great it is misleading to state any specific age for the beginning of puberty, but the range for most children is generally between the tenth and fifteenth years, with girls attaining pubescence on an average of from one to one and a half years earlier than boys. Puberty in a given individual is actually a gradual process, extending from the time hormonic action first begins until full sexual maturity is attained. Full puberty results in the individual's ability to reproduce. Society generally assumes that pubescence begins with the teen years, with the result that numerous children who have yet to attain puberty are called adolescents. In this sense, adolescence may be said to begin by social consensus, although a more accurate biological criterion is available.[4] There is very little room for disagreement about the advent of adolescence when it is considered in its biological aspects. The disagreement starts when we begin to discuss the less specifically biological aspects that characterize adolescence from beginning to end. We also find disagreement over when adolescence ends.

In this book it is held that adolescence ends when an individual attains emotional and social maturity and has acquired the requisite experience, ability, and willingness to assume consistently over a large range of activities the role of an adult as it is defined by the culture in which he lives. This means that for some adolescence never ends—they assume the role of an adolescent all the days of their lives. But for the most, the period may be said to end in the twenties, although for a few it ends somewhat earlier. Actually, for any given same-age cohort going through adolescence together, it will be found that after the age of twenty, there are fewer and fewer individuals each year who may still be defined as adolescents, although a few will still retain that status into their thirtieth year. So many fac-

tors—personal, cultural, and historical—are involved in the attainment of personal maturity that age citations are almost impossible. A problem is the definition of maturity. Different authors have offered various definitions. Mohsin (1960) defines an emotionally mature individual as one who is "capable of viewing his own defects and failings with a measure of objectivity and self-detachment... the emotionally mature person is relatively free from emotional involvement of the ego." Saul and Pulver (1965) speak of maturity in mental health terms as involving a dynamic equilibrium between an individual and his environment, and note the importance of a basic, constructive, responsible, giving attitude. Spivack et al. (1959) discuss the presence of a "general inhibition ability" as characteristic of adults but not of adolescence. Such approaches to an understanding of maturity are only partial views.

In any event, anyone who is going to attain adulthood may be expected to have done so by his thirtieth year. Therefore adolescence may be broadly defined as the period of the second decade and part of the third decade of life. This extends the period somewhat further at both ends than the reader may be accustomed to, but the case, especially for the later termination, will be made in subsequent discussions in this book. As a matter of fact, it would appear well to divide the term into early and late adolescence, with the physiological growth aspects of the period dominating the early stage and the social and self-concept aspects dominating the latter stage.

Some confusion in considering different interpretations of adolescence develops from the fact that different writers have used different terminology in describing the adolescent period, or even worse, have used the same word to describe different and to some extent mutually exclusive aspects of it. For example, Gesell, Ilg, and Ames (1956) speak of *youth* and define it as the period from ten to sixteen; Hall (1911) referred to this period as extending from eight to twelve; and Landis (1952) confined his use of *youth* to the late years of adolescence. The

[4]The nature and manifestations of puberty as a biological phenomenon will be discussed at length in the chapter on physiological development.

term *pubescence* is generally used as descriptive of sexual maturational aspects of adolescence (Ausubel 1954), but one team of textbook writers (Stone and Church 1957) speak of pubescence as the period of approximately two years *before* puberty.

The second point of disagreement, that of the course and nature of adolescence, is a more difficult matter to resolve than is assigning the beginning and end of the period. The following pages present typical modern descriptions of the characteristic aspects of the course and nature of adolescence.

Volatility and Exclusivity

The adolescent has been described as an emotional, highly volatile, egocentric person who is poorly in touch with reality and is incapable of self-criticism. He has also been called conservative, stereotypic, unstable, perfectionistic, and sensitive. Fountain (1961) lists the following five qualities as distinguishing adolescents from adults: (1) a special intensity and volatility of feeling, (2) a need for frequent and immediate gratification, (3) a comparatively ineffective ability to test reality, (4) lack of ability for self-criticism, and (5) an unawareness or indifference to things and events not related to oneself personally. Emma (1965) lists the gradual maturation of rational capacity and the exuberant development of the emotional life as the two prime phenomena of adolescence. Emma includes instability, uncertainty, ambivalence, and intensity as aspects of exuberant development. Agreeing with both Fountain and Emma, Friend (1970) notes that while the duration of adolescence will vary from culture to culture, the period has distinctive characteristics of drive, intensity, affect, and moods and variations in behavior. Friend speaks of the "sensitive, fluid, emotional flux" of the adolescent period.

Adolescence is often described as a period of exclusivity during which the individual makes real endeavors to set himself off from other age groups. Muzio (1970) points to this age exclusivity as the adolescent attempts to differentiate himself from younger children, but particularly from adults, whose responsibility he finds frightening. In this last sense it might be hypothesized that although the adolescent wants the privilege of responsibility and struggles for it through his emancipative efforts, at the same time he wants to hedge against its full implications. Keeping a generation difference between himself and his elders is one way of not suddenly finding himself in their world of often nonnegotiable responsibilities.

The Adolescent as Egocentric Reformer

Elkind (1967) speaks of adolescent egocentricism as a central fact of adolescence and observes that it represents a failure to differentiate between cognitive self-concerns and the concerns of others. This is a position that the reader may wish to relate to what Fountain (1961) calls the adolescent's "quality of unawareness or indifference" to things and events not related to himself. Elkind (1970), however, notes that the adolescent is an idealist-perfectionist and describes his quest for perfection as equally critical of self and others. Elkind's conception of the adolescent as an idealist-perfectionist bears an interesting relationship to Hurlock's conception of the adolescent as a reformer. Hurlock (1968) observes that adolescents typically display well-defined tendencies not only to criticize others but to attempt to reform them. It is her assumption that these tendencies are developmental phenomena, starting in childhood and reaching an extreme in adolescence. She writes, "This assumption seemed justified by the many references to criticism, name-calling, and ridiculing in studies of the content of children's speech, to the hypercritical attitude of the pubescent, and to the shift from negative to positive social attitudes in early adolescence which leads to the development of the adolescent reformer." In order to test this assumption and a set of related hypotheses, Hurlock, between the years 1955 and 1967, asked her graduate students in the courses in adolescence at the University of Pennsylvania in term-paper form to respond to the question:

Did you, as an adolescent, try to reform people or situations? If so, what were the targets of your reforms? What form did your attempts at reform take? Check your recall of your experiences with your parents, your siblings, your teachers, and your friends of adolescence to see if they can add any facts you may have forgotten.[5]

The results amply confirmed Hurlock's hypothesis. Developmentally, among Hurlock's subjects there was a pattern in elementary school of being critical of parents, siblings, relatives, and teachers, although the criticism was usually done behind the backs of the subjects rather than in face-to-face confrontation. During junior and senior high school overt attempts at reform were added to the criticisms. Hurlock writes of her subjects,

Some explained that because they felt grown-up and worldly-wise when they reached high school, they thought they knew enough about how things should be done to justify telling people specifically how to do them. Instead of the general type of reform characteristic of some children in elementary school, the teen ager gave specific and what he considered to be "helpful" advice in how to do things better. Even those brought up in homes where parental authority was strong seemed little deterred in their reform attempts.

Hurlock also wrote of her findings, "Most adolescent reformers are not specific reformers who concentrate their efforts in one area, or on one person or on a group of people they want to change." Three quotations from the subjects themselves give the flavor of their adolescent reform tendencies. One wrote, "My parents were severely taxed by my passionate reform tendencies. In particular, I felt it my

solemn duty to bring my parents up to date in speech, clothing, fashions, and social behavior." Another wrote, "After meeting with considerable success in reforming my family, the next step on my program of reforms was the political awakening of the brighter students in my school. I organized a reading club, and planned a meeting where lists of books would be distributed and plans for discussing them would be given to the members." Still another wrote, "I wrote to J. Edgar Hoover about a way to cure lawlessness in our city.... In regard to national reform, I have only to say that the President had the nerve to ignore my letters."

The reader may wonder if Hurlock's findings do not conflict with Elkind's hypothesis of egocentricism and Fountain's contention that adolescents are unaware of or indifferent to anything that does not concern them directly. There is really no conflict. Hurlock's subjects did feel personally concerned. As highly egocentric persons, their reforms became personal issues with them and they felt that matters of concern to them should become matters of concern to everyone. In their responses there is no interest in how others might feel but only in how they themselves felt. Perhaps in comparing these studies it should be remembered that adolescents are constantly testing reality and trying to come to terms with the world. In doing this they range widely, but what they discover has always to be interpreted in a very egocentric manner, usually against some criterion of perfection. As Elkind noted, the adolescent is an idealistic perfectionist.

Encounter with Reality

The adolescent's encounter with reality is at least implied in many of the writings on the characteristics of the period. Essentially an inexperienced child in increasingly adult situations, and this at a time when his self-view is unstable and still in process of formation, the adolescent is constantly testing reality without knowing what the response will be or to what extent reality will confirm or deny the tenuous

[5] Retrospective accounts place burdens of memory and of post hoc interpretation upon respondents, and as Hurlock notes, her subjects were too highly selected to ever have been representative of typical adolescents. However, the respondents were at least to some degree trained professionals with psychological insights and an understanding of the necessity for objectivity in research reporting.

self-view he has built to that time. Under the circumstances, he seeks security by denial, by apparent noninvolvement, but at the same time by cautious copying, with his lines of retreat well established. Often he falls back upon the old and familiar as a security blanket. Aquinas (1958) notes that children are copyists and tend to reflect the attitudes that adults tolerate. Heath, Maier, and Remmers (1958), analyzing high-school students' responses to a nationwide opinion poll note that teenagers seem to absorb the values of the culture and to reflect very closely in their feelings the attitude of the culture toward drinking, dating, divorce, religion, and juvenile delinquency. It is quite probable that the current adolescent interest in the drug culture is only a reflection of the permissive but quite vocal attitudes of a visible section of the adult population. However, Adelson (1964) defines "normative" adolescents as persons involved in "avoidance of inner and outer conflict, premature identity consolidation, ego and ideological constriction and genuine unwillingness to take psychic risk." In this Adelson agrees with the previously cited study by Muzio (1970). Some years ago *playing it cool* became a frequently used term and a criterion for behavior among adolescents. The idea was not to show enthusiasm, appreciation, or, ideally, any reaction at all. Even such idols of the time as the Beatles found part of their popularity in their "coolness," represented by their unruffled, really uninvolved stance, when pandemonium was going on around them. The behavioral implications of *cool* were sometimes hard for adults to understand. Adelson (1964) in one discussion of adolescence mentions the dullness of their lives. Underneath, of course, was the volatility mentioned by Emma and by Fountain and under certain selected circumstances it was permissive to "lose your cool." A dramatic example, again in the case of the Beatles, was the swooning and public frenzy of their followers who that very day might have been "playing it cool" at home, in school, or among their peer group. The term *cool* no longer has its old currency, but the behavior it stood for is still

very much present. Among adolescents it is "cool" to show lack of enthusiasm in exciting situations or in situations where one might give oneself away by appearing inexperienced, childish, or lacking in sophistication. As has been said previously, a good defense is to try nothing new and to seek refuge in the familiar.

Adolescence as a Stereotypic Period

There has been some belief that adolescence produces a tendency toward stereotypy of response, possibly resulting from some constriction of personality. There appears to be some indication that this may be true. Cotte (1958) administered the Rorschach to a group of boys and girls ranging in age from twelve to sixteen and reported an apparent age-related fluctuation to interpret the inkblots in terms of animal responses.[6] The average number of animal responses increases steadily from age seven to eleven, recedes slightly at twelve, reaches a peak at thirteen and subsequently declines until at sixteen it is approximately where it was at the age nine level. Thus, at least in Rorschach responses the advent of puberty does coincide with a stereotypic tendency that begins to decline immediately after puberty. However, Cotte reports the tendency as being clearer in the case of girls than it is in boys. Ordinarily first menstruation and physical burgeoning are more dramatic for girls than the parallel pubescent changes are for boys. It may well represent for girls a brief period of drawing-in and self-preoccupation as they endeavor to accustom themselves to their new state in life and its possible stimulus value for others.

As has been implied in the preceding section, it is a characteristic of adolescence to reject the

---

[6]The animal kingdom is an obvious response category in responding to a number of the inkblots and is believed to be one indication of stereotypy of response. Klopfer and Kelley (1942) write, "The more a subject is able to choose his concepts outside this most obvious area the less likely he is to be confined to the obvious, the stereotyped, or a narrow range of interests." Of course, another obvious content area such as geography could be substituted for the animal category with the same results.

new in favor of the security-inducing familiar. Anyone trying to introduce an adolescent to new food patterns will, for example, usually meet with surprising resistance. To do what one has previously done, and in the company and place where one has often done it, is welcome security for an adolescent trying to cope with a new self-view as well as with new conditions. It would not be surprising to find over the entire adolescent span a retreat to stereotypy or an attempt to define reality in narrowly rigid terms at the appearance of any new and threatening change. In this last connection Tooley (1972) compared the writing styles of three age groups: adolescence, late adolescence, and adult. In general she found that late adolescents were less flamboyant in writing style than were early adolescents or adults. Late adolescents in their expressive style of writing were more moderate in emotional tone and more heavily reliant on intellectualizing defenses. Tooley felt that this was "a style which facilitates the meeting of the developmental tasks of adolescence." It would appear that the late adolescents may have been displaying a need to hold close to reality.

Stress During Adolescence

It has been well over half a century since G. Stanley Hall advanced his hypothesis of the inevitability of stress during adolescence and nearly half a century since cultural anthropologists cast doubt upon the validity of the hypothesis. Today it is still to some extent a controversial issue. Writers such as Kiell (1964), in agreement with the Hall position, feel that adolescence is a time of great turmoil and external disorder. Kiell takes the position that the turmoil is universal and is only moderately affected by cultural determinants. Barnett (1970) maintains that adolescence is an anxiety-producing developmental process in which the essential tasks are the loss of childhood innocence and the achievement of personal distance from the social needs and aspirations of the family. Both tasks obviously

present traumatic possibilities at worst and difficulty in adjustment at best.

One indication that adolescence may indeed represent a stressful period in the developmental span is offered by Eysenck and Eysenck (1969). These investigators administered to persons ranging in age from ten to seventy a personality measure, the PEN Inventory, which yields scores on the extroversion, neuroticism, and psychoticism dimensions of personality.[7]

Subjects were divided into six age groups, and age comparisons were made on the basis of the three dimensions. Results are presented in Table 1. Young persons in the ten to twenty-nine age group, approximately the age span of adolescence as defined by the present writer, received higher scores than the other five age groups on all three dimensions. Within the ten to twenty-nine age group, males were higher than females on extroversion and psychoticism and lower on neuroticism. In discussing their findings, the Eysencks write that results concerning the younger age group "are in line with common sense observation and expectation; youth has always been the time of *Sturm und Drang,* and the higher scores of our young sample on the N, E, and P is in line with this observation." When, as may be seen in Table 1, the early- and middle-adolescent individuals, as represented by the ten to nineteen age group, are compared to the late-adolescent and early-adult individuals, as represented by the twenty to twenty-nine age group, the younger group are still highest on all three dimensions. Here we might hypothesize that the main stresses of adolescence fall during the second decade

[7]The dimension of psychoticism distinguishes normals from psychotics; neuroticism is a dimension on which neurotics have higher scores than normals; and extroversion represents placement along an extroversion-introversion continuum. All three dimensions simply indicate placement along a continuum from least to most, and scores must be viewed as relative standings in relation to the extreme end of the dimension. For example, a psychoticism score simply indicates relative standing on that continuum and does not necessarily imply that a person is psychotic in a legal or medical sense. In fact, his psychoticism score may place him well within the normal population range on the continuum. See Eysenck (1952) and Eysenck, Eysenck, and Claridge (1960).

Table 1 *Scores on Three Personality Dimensions by Age and Sex from the PEN Inventory*

	Personality Dimension																	
	Extroversion						Neuroticism						Psychoticism					
	Male			Female			Male			Female			Male			Female		
Age Group	N[a]	Mn[b]	SD[c]	N	Mn	SD	N	Mn	SD	N	Mn	SD	N	Mn	SD	N	Mn	SD
10–29	843	*13.46*	3.83	576	*13.02*	3.45	843	*8.34*	4.30	576	*9.71*	4.22	843	*2.60*	2.58	576	*1.92*	2.28
30–49	415	*11.81*	4.34	279	*11.72*	3.83	415	*6.68*	4.06	279	*7.62*	4.22	415	*2.15*	2.66	279	*1.73*	1.97
50–69	165	*11.55*	4.31	113	*11.40*	3.50	165	*5.79*	4.64	113	*6.50*	4.07	165	*2.90*	3.73	113	*2.33*	2.51
10–19	23	*14.65*	5.20	12	*13.92*	3.06	23	*8.37*	5.12	12	*8.79*	3.55	23	*3.56*	3.28	12	*3.42*	2.57
20–29	124	*12.28*	4.05	68	*12.15*	3.56	124	*7.72*	4.25	68	*8.52*	4.17	124	*2.11*	2.75	68	*1.41*	1.97
30–39	84	*11.27*	4.54	44	*11.63*	3.76	84	*6.19*	4.28	44	*8.64*	4.01	84	*1.65*	2.00	44	*1.46*	1.57

[a] N = number of respondents.   [b] Mn = mean.   [c] SD = standard deviation.

Source: Adapted from S. B. G. Eysenck and H. J. Eysenck, "Scores on three personality variables as a function of age, sex and social class," *British Journal of Social and Clinical Psychology* 8 (1969): 69–76. Table represents a combination of data from tables 1, 2, and 3 on pp. 71–73. Reprinted by permission of the British Psychological Society.

of life. Then, during the third decade, adolescence is gradually being phased out by most individuals, and, of course, the twenty to twenty-nine age group contains a number of persons who have entirely left adolescence behind. However, it is interesting to note that, with the exception of females on the psychoticism and neuroticism dimension, the twenty to twenty-nine age group are also higher on all three dimensions than are the adjoining thirty to thirty-nine age group. The reader should note that none of the differences shown in Table 1 are very large, but, as the Eysencks note, they are all sufficiently marked to be statistically significant. As an indication that stress conditions within the individual are not free of relationship to the environment, the Eysencks also report that middle-class persons, as compared to those from upper and lower socioeconomic classes, are lowest on all three personality dimensions.

It should be remembered that the data cited by Eysenck and Eysenck are in terms of central tendency and variability for age groups. Any given individual may depart radically from the norm established by his group, although the probability of there being such an individual has to be seen in terms of the normative situation obtaining in the group. It is

also necessary to consider that the Eysencks' study was performed in England and may not replicate in another culture. However, the similarities in the cultures of England and the United States increase the probability that a cross-cultural generalization to the United States may be made.

In marked contrast to the positions of Kiell and Barnett, and to a lesser degree to that of the Eysencks, a number of studies of normal adolescents have shown a picture of an apparent lack of problems and of stress states. Offer, Sabshin, and Marcus (1965) studied a group of eighty-four "model" adolescent boys, aged fourteen through sixteen, from two suburban high schools. These adolescents, according to the investigators, felt that they were a part of their cultural environment and were well aware of its norms and values. As a group they were characterized by flexibility of affect expression, got along well with adults, and displayed complete absence of psychopathology. Masterson (1968) studied the question of the presence of turmoil in adolescence by means of a longitudinal study of adolescent patients and their controls. As a result of his study, he concluded that less emphasis should be placed upon the turmoil aspects of adolescence. Masterson does take a different approach from most writers in warning that it is dangerous to assume that adolescence is necessarily a period of stress. He feels that such an assumption is likely to produce a tendency to neglect the appearance in an adolescent of the symptomology of psychiatric difficulty because it would be felt that the symptoms were mainly evidences of "natural" turmoil.

For an individual adolescent living in Western culture, it is probable that the actual truth lies someplace between these extremes. A number of writers take the position that the adolescent period contains potential for problems and stress reactions but that personal or cultural circumstances can serve to alleviate pressures or, in turn, can create them. For example, Levy (1969) feels that stress in adolescence comes as a result of changes demanding revision of relationships and self-image. He sees these changes centering on new perceptions of parents and other authority figures and growth in self-view following puberty. Levy sees these two changes as most stress-producing in the adolescent, and both demand considerable psychological effort as the adolescent has to revise his self-image and his relationships with adults. But, it can be assumed that many adolescents are capable of the psychological effort and should suffer little or no stress. Dragunova (1972) expresses a facilitation point of view in making the point that as a child grows older he undergoes a qualitative change in his relationships, which become more adultlike. If changes in the adolescent's personality and perception of himself as an adult occur before changes in his relationships with adults, conflicts will result. An adult who relates to an adolescent as though he were still a child is at variance with the adolescent's self-view and with his perception of rights as compared to the amount of independence he actually has. According to Dragunova, if an adult anticipates the change in the adult-adolescent relationship and takes initiative in fostering it, the transition is easier and conflict is avoided. The key here is anticipation and early facilitative activity on the part of the parent. Nevel'shstein (1969), speaking about child-rearing

practices in Russia, notes that difficult youth attitudes spring from the insufficient life experiences of the adolescent caused by his parents withholding from him appropriate adult experiences. In a similar vein, Minuchin (1969) advocates a broader approach to the treatment of adolescent problems, an approach that takes into account the social structures in which the adolescent functions and the need to change these structures. However, that facilitation of the transitional phase is often neglected is indicated by Adams (1969), who sees puberty as a paradox because it ushers in significant biosocial changes without being accorded much importance by society.

The Effect of Changing Times

Since the end of World War II, as social and economic changes accelerated and became a fact of everyday life, it was natural that there would be much speculation about the effect of these changes upon the adolescent period. Different writers discussed different aspects of the changes. For example, Bronfenbrener (1961) speculated that with more permissive child-rearing practices and the de-emphasis of the authoritarian father over the past twenty-five years, there are bound to be reflected changes. At the beginning of this chapter the writer analyzed several aspects of modern life that he expected to affect the adolescent to some degree. But the exact nature of the effects of cultural change have remained unclear. While it may be speculated that today's youth are in many ways different from those of past generations, research studies provide inadequate information to prove it. Needed are numerous studies, using comparable measures and subjects, where same-age groups of different generations can be compared. However, Greenfield and Finkelstein (1970) and Kaczkowski (1962) have performed studies that provide partial cross-generation comparisons. Greenfield and Finkelstein (1970) compared a sample of 211 children aged twelve to fifteen with a similar sample from the same school thirty years earlier. Present-day children were found to be more autonomous and outgoing, in that they were more involved in expressing themselves, with more focus on themselves. In contrast, the children of thirty years earlier were much more focused on economic matters. The investigators felt that there was an overall difference in the personal-social characteristics of the children of the two periods. The more autonomous and self-referent nature of the present-day children seemed to bear out Bronnfenbrenner's speculation on the effects of permissiveness, while the focus of the early generation of children may have reflected the fact that they grew up in the very serious depression of the 1930s. Kaczkowski's (1962) replication of earlier studies also indicated differences involving cultural changes, although there was relative stability in what could be called the basic characteristics of adolescence. Perhaps the most adequate summary of the adolescent period is made by Pasanella and Willingham (1968), who speak of adolescence as a period of transition and decision making. They note that adolescent lives are marked by fluidity and shift centering around the three major transition areas of cognitive-educational development, changes in attitudes and values, and vocational choice and career development. The writer would add physical-physiological and sex-social development as two further categories to be made explicit.

General Characteristics of Adolescence

Adolescence brings with it a multiplicity of changes in every aspect of a child's life. There is great expansion and intensification of the emotional life as the adolescent reaches out for new experiences and understanding but at the same time adopts a defensive stance against the possible consequences. It is normally a period of hopes and ideals, of longings often divorced from reality, and of passions over matters that older persons often see as being of little consequence. Emotions do tend to show greater fluctuations during adolescence than in the periods that precede and follow it. Periods of great enthusiasm and attempts at high achievement are followed by periods of languor, depression, dissatisfaction, and even of morbid self-analysis. Emotions can lead to violent attachments to members of the opposite sex and intense friendships characterized by pledges and vows.

During adolescence home often tends to become confining and to seem restrictive as the desire for movement and adventure becomes paramount and "to do and dare" seems to be the very desiderata of existence. Poetry, romance, and artistic sensibility rank high. Many adolescents are in love with love and feel that they want to reach out and encompass the universe. This becomes particularly true as enthusiasms are directed to a larger stage than the immediate surroundings and the adolescent wants to achieve great things and reform existing evils. Don Quixote's tilting at windmills and dreaming "the impossible dream" becomes a familiar outlook to many adolescents. Unfortunately the reality of the windmill may often lead to doubt and negative speculation as the adolescent attempts to assess the real world and relate himself to it.

To relate himself to others is the key to the whole stage, for such a relationship involves having a self to relate. All of his life the adolescent has been engaged in building concepts of himself, but in adolescence, as he enters the stage of operational thought and becomes able to deal with hypotheses, the building process accelerates as he attempts to answer the age-old questions, "Who and what am I," and "Where am I going?" It is fair to say that the main business of adolescence is that of building and confirming a stable concept of self. Confirmation means that reality must be tested again and again. Often the tests are negative and carefully built houses of cards come tumbling down to bury fond hopes and aspirations. Given such a negative test result, the adolescent must then resolve his problem either by retreating and perhaps fixating at an earlier stage of development or by rallying to build again.

The adolescent's approach to life is essentially inductive. His lack of experience and his preoccupation with the here and now lead him to generalize from specific cases and to believe that what is true of certain individuals, or what is true of a class of events, or what is true of a specific time will be true under similar circumstances at all times. His generalization becomes quite pervasive because he is coming to grips with the whole world and must take to that wider arena that which he knows. The evil of one man is interpreted as the evil of all men, and the adolescent tends to seek confirmation of his hypothesis by seeking examples to prove it, including the filtering-out of any refutations. That is to say, his thinking is still mystical. The logic he applies tends to insulate him from objective proof. That is his problem. Reality is antagonistic to simple insulation, and the adolescent is confronted with the need to revise, or maladjustively, to retreat from reality in the display of psychic or somatic aberrations. It is indeed easier to become an adolescent than to be one.

Adult Stereotypes of Adolescents

The view of adolescence presented by psychology does not always agree with the impressions of the man-in-the-street. Adults have grown to consider adolescents in terms of stereotypes promoted by the mass media and, to a lesser extent, by professional writers on adolescence. For example, there has been so much discussion about the conflict of generations that many adults—even parents—are convinced that at least a cold war is in progress. Anthony (1966) feels that the situation has reached the point at which a number of parents "respond to their children as though they were embodiments of negative ideas rather than real people."

These stereotypes have tended to operate in two directions. The adolescent, knowing what is said about him, believes that is either the way he is or should be and does his best to emulate the image society has held before him. He shapes his behavior to meet expectations and sometimes becomes the personification of the stereotype. At this point we witness an unfortunate circularity of behavior. The adolescent tries to behave as adults suspect him to be, and the adult witnessing the behavior receives confirmation of his stereotype. Meanwhile, society at large learns through its mass media of the behavior, reports it, and further spreads and enlarges the stereotype. All this, getting back to the adolescent, further reinforces his own stereotype of himself, and he again tries to meet expectations, creating a vicious circle.

Of course, stereotypes do not operate in a psychological vacuum. The adult's behavior in reacting to a single adolescent or to adolescents in general is dictated by what Anthony (1966) has called a collusion of three factors. First is the collective reaction called forth by the stereotype; second is a wholly personal reaction based on the people and experiences at issue; and third is a "transference" reaction "in which pre-existing factors from an earlier phase of life exert an influence, unbeknownst to the participants, on their attitudes, affects, and actions, often to the detriment of the relationship." Of course, in the case of a parent-child or other adult-child interaction in which there is fundamental dislike or rejection, the stereotype will be more severely applied and the unconscious irrational modes of reacting will be even more maladaptive.

What are some of the common stereotypes? First there is the conviction that adolescence is a period of acute disequilibrium and storm and stress, despite all the findings to the contrary. In a poll of teachers, Denny, Feldhausen, and Condon (1965) report that over 80 percent believed that adolescence could best be described as a period of "great emotional disturbance" and over 50 percent thought that adolescence brought about a complete change of personality in the child.

Second is the stereotype of the teenager as the overpampered, hedonistic individual—a nuisance, if not an enemy. For example, in *Teenage Tyranny* the Hechingers (1963) write:

Teenage, like birth and death, is inevitable. It is nothing to be ashamed of. Nor is it a badge of special distinction worthy of a continuous birth-day party ... we are not against teenagers nor are we particularly for them. It would be dishonest for us to claim that some of our best friends are teen-agers.... We are not writing this book to declare war on teenagers ... what worries us is not greater freedom of youth but rather the abdication of the rights and privileges of adults for the con-venience of the immature ... the pages that follow are not intended as a declaration of war ... we do not want to be cantankerous....

Anthony (1966) lists various other stereo-types, including the adolescent as a sexual object, as an object of envy, as a dangerous and endangered object, and as a lost object. Many more stereotypes might be isolated. How-ever, Anthony warns that the inherently dichotomous nature of the stereotype as good or bad presents a biased view. Human behav-ior, including adolescent behavior, usually rep-resents a continuum with reactions distributed in the form of a normal curve. "The 'good' adolescent although representing perhaps three quarters of the adolescent population, is so ef-fectively camouflaged by his conformity to the standards of a given culture, that he is scarcely credited with existence."

Stages in Adolescent Development

Psychologists often think of the developmental sequence as a series of stages or phases, some discrete, some overlapping. Some of the stages proposed are fairly all-encompassing, the ulti-mate example being the "adolescent period" of development. Others are more specific, as "stage of heterosexual pairing." A fair ques-tion is: To what extent can any stage theory make a valuable contribution to the under-standing of adolescence? Also, insofar as stage conceptualizations are worthwhile, what are

the characteristics of a good stage theory? Actually, the majority of those who describe adolescence in terms of stages tend to be rather vague about the exact time of beginning or ending of a stage. The discussion usually in-volves a description of the stage's characteris-tics and dynamics and its relationship to the ongoing environment. Obviously, if we look at behavior in terms of phases, we must recognize that a number of phases can occur simultane-ously, although one may be of such overriding importance that it can be called particularly characteristic or crucial. Most stage discus-sions usually say less than one would wish about the relationship or interaction of the various stages.

Another difficulty with stages is that they tend to be descriptive only—they tell us what has happened, but as Rosler (1963) points out, they do not tell us why. We may speculate, but we cannot be entirely clear on the relative con-tribution of biological and sociological causes. Henny (1961) makes the point that chronolog-ical age should not be a criterion in defining adolescence. He feels that crucial aspects of organic and psychological maturation have situational relationships that make age cate-gorization misleading. Cohen-Raz (1966) agrees, but goes further in noting the limita-tions of the application of "stage concept" as a basic construct in describing the develop-mental process. To him, explanation of the discrepancies between levels of varying organ-ismic and mental functions is more definitive. He takes the position that subtle patterns of "synchronization" and "desynchronization" seem to enhance or impede transitions from stage to stage, and he would like to interpret stages in terms of molecular development lying behind overt molar behavior. Friedenberg (1959) advances the hypothesis that the con-cept of adolescence as a stage in social and personal development is becoming less tenable. He would describe adolescence more specifically in terms of emotional development, the effect of adolescents on adults, and the impact of school upon the adolescent's experience and self-esteem. English (1957), in a survey of the responses of seventy-four fellows of the Division of Developmental Psychology of the American Psychological Association, reported that many were reluctant to accept a chronological boundary for any of the terms characteristically used to describe development. There was a general feeling among English's sample that all distinctions are arbitrary and that limits of life periods could well be shifted backward or forward. But there was agreement that it would be well if common definitions could be reached. Opposing these positions is the stand taken by Gesell et al. (1956), whose approach has normative implications and makes extensive use of age "zones." Olson (1959) takes the position that research has demonstrated the "crudity of the age criterion for most purposes" and notes that within-age differences may well be greater than between-age differences. However, he feels that consideration of

age differences does have a place and in discussing the point writes:

Age changes, correlated with maturity changes, do have much significance for the content of experience, for methods of teaching, for interpersonal relationships, and for the social and emotional life of the child. Age thus serves a fundamental purpose, as an average indication, in approaching problems of adjusting institutions.

The Number of Adolescents

Table 2 presents the distribution of the population of the United States by ages. An examination of the table indicates, taking the ages of 14 to 24 as approximately the period of adolescence, that in 1970 there were 39,536,000 persons, or 19.4 percent of the population of

Table 2 *Population of the United States by Age and Sex: 1960 and 1970*

Age (in years)	Population						Percent Distribution					
	1960 (Apr. 1)			1970 (Apr. 1)[1]			1960 (Apr. 1)			1970 (Apr. 1)[1]		
	Total	Male	Female	Total	Male	Female	Total	Male	Female	Total	Male	Female
Total	179,323	88,331	90,992	203,166	98,882	104,284	100.0	100.0	100.0	100.0	100.0	100.0
Under 5	20,321	10,330	9,991	17,167	8,745	8,422	11.3	11.7	11.0	8.4	8.8	8.1
5–13	32,726	16,640	16,087	36,647	18,670	17,976	18.2	18.8	17.7	18.0	18.9	17.2
14–17	11,155	5,646	5,508	15,839	8,063	7,777	6.2	6.4	6.1	7.8	8.2	7.5
18–20	6,998	3,443	3,555	10,815	5,337	5,479	3.9	3.9	3.9	5.3	5.4	5.3
21–24	8,607	4,205	4,401	12,882	6,240	6,642	4.8	4.8	4.8	6.3	6.3	6.4
25–34	22,818	11,179	11,639	24,908	12,217	12,691	12.7	12.7	12.8	12.3	12.4	12.2
35–44	24,081	11,756	12,326	23,072	11,223	11,849	13.4	13.3	13.5	11.4	11.3	11.4
45–54	20,485	10,093	10,393	23,203	11,191	12,012	11.4	11.4	11.4	11.4	11.3	11.5
55–64	15,572	7,536	8,036	18,582	8,789	9,793	8.7	8.5	8.8	9.1	8.9	9.4
65–74	10,997	5,116	5,881	12,425	5,431	6,993	6.1	5.8	6.5	6.1	5.5	6.7
75 and over	5,562	2,387	3,176	7,625	2,977	4,648	3.1	2.7	3.5	3.8	3.0	4.5
18 and over	115,121	55,716	59,406	133,513	63,404	70,108	64.2	63.1	65.3	65.7	64.1	67.2
21 and over	108,124	52,273	55,851	122,697	58,068	64,630	60.3	59.2	61.4	60.4	58.7	61.0
Median age[2]	29.5	28.7	30.3	28.3	27.0	29.6	x[3]	x	x	x	x	x

[1]Preliminary. [2]In thousands except as indicated. Total resident population, excluding Armed Forces abroad. [3]x = not applicable.

Source: U.S. Bureau of the Census, *Statistical Abstract of the United States: 1971*, 5th edition, Washington, D. C., 1971, table 21, p. 23.

the United States, who potentially could be classified as adolescents. In contrast, in 1960 there were only 26,760,000 representing 14.9 percent of the population. The increase in gross numbers reflects the country's population increase, but the larger percentage of the population represented by the 14 to 24 age group shows a large and significant increase over a ten-year period in the relative number of teen-agers in the population. During the decade of the 1960s the median age of the American population fell from 29.5 to 28.3. A look at the 5 to 13 age group in Table 2 indicates that this trend will continue at least into the 1980s. Because there is no way of knowing which of the individuals in the age groups listed in Table 2 actually are adolescents except by age-behavior probabilities, the reader should realize that assumptions about the number of adolescents in the United States are only approximations. Further, Table 2 excludes members of the armed services serving abroad, many of whom are in the 18 to 24 age range. However, even within the limits of probable error and with the exclusion of youth in military service abroad, one cannot escape the conclusion that adolescents represent a significantly large and potentially influential segment of the population. Insofar as it may be said that adolescents represent a group with special attributes, attitudes, and needs, then an understanding of the nature of this group should have high priority on the part of those who have to deal with them, either as individuals or as a class of persons.

Summary

The modern-day adolescent has much in common with his predecessors, but two new elements have been added. First, he is growing up in a transitional period of doubt and uncertainty when the guidance of his elders is apt to lack decision or clarity. Second, he is taking a more central role in adult affairs than was the case with previous generations of adolescents. Often he is in the position of leading adults rather than following them but at the same time is faced with the paradox that he is not an adult and is not accepted as one with any degree of consistency.

The adolescent has long been a subject for study, but modern conditions have accelerated interest in him. A great deal is known about him, and there are many excellent theories and points of view, but there is lacking a fully integrated theoretical view that has both explanatory and predictive value.

The need for a long period of growth and development before the attainment of full maturity is characteristic of the human species. During this period society must expend a great deal of effort in protecting and fostering the proper development of its younger members. Because man is a thinking animal he has endeavored to understand the phenomena of development and has found it convenient to do so by visualizing the developmental sequence in terms of stages of growth. Of these the adolescent period has been regarded as a particularly definitive stage.

Adolescence results from hormonic activity that leads to the appearance of secondary sex characteristics and eventually to the ability to reproduce one's kind. It begins earlier in girls than in boys and ordinarily occurs shortly after the child enters his second decade of life. This is a biological definition; adolescence is also a cultural phenomenon involving matters of child-rearing and emotional outlook. There has been much disagreement about the nature of adolescence as a cultural phenomenon, as well as about the time and conditions of its cessation. In general, it ends when an individual attains emotional and social maturity and has acquired the requisite experience, ability, and willingness to assume consistently over a large range of activities the role of an adult as his culture defines the adult role. While this may occur very late in the second decade of life, it is more usually an occurrence of the third decade.

Interested persons have written about the nature and education of youth from earlier times, but the hypotheses of the nineteenth-century evolutionists furnished the impetus for the scientific study of adolescence. G. Stanley

Hall stood for over a quarter-century as the foremost interpreter of the adolescent period.

The adolescent has been described in many ways. He is believed to be an emotional, highly volatile, egocentric person lacking an awareness of things not of direct personal concern. He is believed to be impatient when thwarted, ineffective at testing reality, conservative, unstable, perfectionistic, and sensitive. Adolescence is a cross-cultural phenomenon possessing distinctive characteristics of drive, intensity, affect, and moods and variations in behavior. On the whole, adolescents tend to be an age-exclusive group abounding in self-reference. In addition to such egocentricism they tend to wish to reform others, their efforts becoming more overt as they move into middle adolescence.

The adolescent's encounter with reality is one of the main features of the developmental stage, and the results are sometimes traumatic, although a stable concept of self cannot emerge until self-confirmation has been gained by reality tests over long periods of time. Because adolescents are trying to protect the selves they have constructed they seek security by retreating from the unknown, but at the same time are faced with the fact that sooner or later they must breach their own defense and seek out the new. Their defensive behavior has been variously interpreted, its characterizations ranging from stereotypy to dullness. Attempts to cling to the familiar represent a common adolescent style of behavior.

There has been considerable discussion as to whether adolescence is a stressful period, and different authorities disagree to some extent. In actuality there are numerous possibilities for stress in adolescence and there are probably few adolescents who are stress-free. But significant persons such as parents and teachers may do much to alleviate the stress conditions and may even eliminate many of them. On the whole there appears to be no inherent reason why adolescence should be a stressful period. There are only external conditions and interpersonal relationships that may trigger off stress. Parents and others would do well to consider means of facilitating the transition to adulthood if they wish to make the period less stressful.

The adolescent of today while fundamentally like the adolescent of yesterday exhibits certain differences in self-expression, self-focus, and in personal social characteristics. However, there has been relative stability in the basic characteristics of adolescence. Adult stereotypes of adolescence tend to visualize it as a period of stress and disequilibrium.

References

Adams, P. L. Puberty as a biosocial turning point. *Psychosomatics* 10 (1969) : 343–349.

Adelson, J. The mystique of adolescence. *Psychiatry* 27 (1964) : 1–5.

Aquinas, T. Youth and its psychological problems. *Journal of Social Therapy* 4 (1958) : 26–31.

Anthony, E. J. The reactions of adults to adolescents and their behavior. *Preliminary Notes for the Sixth International Congress for Child Psychiatry*, Edinburgh, Scotland, 1966.

Ausubel, D. P. *Theory and problems of adolescent development.* New York: Grune and Stratton, 1954.

Barnett, J. Abhangigkeitskonflikte beim Jugendlichen. *Fortschritte der Psychoanalyse* 4 (1970) : 189–203.

Beley, A., and Faure, H. Enquete nationale d'hygiene mentale portant sur le devenir des modes d'assistance en neuropsychiatrie infanto-juvenile. *Hygiene Mentale* 51 (1962) : 129–139.

Bronfenbrener, U. The changing American child—a speclative analysis. *Merrill-Palmer Quarterly* 7 (1961) : 73–84.

Cohen-Raz, R. Explanation of the significance of developmental stages. *Megamot* 14 (1966) : 137–146.

Cotte, S. Etude statistique sur les reponses zoomorphiques (An et And) dans le test de Rorschach des enfants de 12 a 16 ans. *Bulletin de la Groupe Francaise Rorschach* 10 (1958) : 27–32.

Daniels, A. D. The new life: A study of regeneration. *American Journal of Psychology* 6 (1893) : 61–106.

Denny, T.; Feldhausen, J.; and Condon, C. Anxiety, divergent thinking, and achievement. *Journal of Educational Psychology* 56 (1965): 40.

Dragunova, T. V. Problem konflikta v podrostkovom vozraste. *Voprosy Psikhologii* 18 (1972): 25–38.

Elkind, D. Egocentricism in adolescence. *Child Development* 38 (1967): 1025–1034.

Elkind, D. *Children and adolescents.* Oxford: Oxford University Press, 1970.

Emma, M. Characteristiche della vita affettiva dell'adolescente. *Scuola Viva LM* 1 (1965): 28–31.

English, H. B. Chronological divisions of the life span. *Journal of Educational Psychology* 48 (1957): 437–439.

Eysenck, H. J. *The scientific study of personality.* London: Routledge and Kegan Paul, 1952.

Eysenck, S. B. G., and Eysenck, H. J. Scores on three personality variables as a function of age, sex and social class. *British Journal of Social and Clinical Psychology* 8 (1969): 69–76.

Eysenck, S. B. G.; Eysenck, H. J.; and Claridge, G. Dimensions of personality, psychiatric syndromes, and mathematical models. *Journal of Mental Science* 106 (1960): 581–589.

Fountain, G. Adolescent into adult: An inquiry. *Journal of the American Psychoanalytic Association* 9 (1961): 417–432.

Friend, M. R. "Youth unrest: Reflections of a psychoanalyst." *Journal of the American Academy of Child Psychiatry* 9 (1970): 224–232.

Friedenberg, E. Z. *The vanishing adolescent.* Boston: Beacon, 1959.

Gesell, A.; Ilg, F. L.; and Ames, L. B. *Youth: The years from ten to sixteen.* New York: Harper & Row, 1956.

Goppert, S. Uber die seelische Entwicklung des Jugendlichen und ihre Krisen. *Praxis der Kinderpsychologie und Kinderpsychiatrie* 11 (1962): 161–167.

Greenfield, N., and Finkelstein, E. L. A comparison of the characteristics of junior high school students. *Journal of Genetic Psychology* 117 (1970): 37–50.

Grinder, R. E., and Strickland, C. E. G. Stanley Hall and the social significance of adolescence. *Teachers College Record* 64 (1963): 390–399.

Haeckel, E. *Das system der Medusen.* Jena, 1879.

Hall, G. S. *Adolescence.* 2 Vols. New York: D. Appleton, 1911.

Heath, R. W.; Maier, M. H.; and Remmers, H. H. Youths' attitudes toward various aspects of their lives. *Purdue Opinion Poll Report* no. 51 (1958).

Hechinger, G., and Hechinger, F. M. *Teenage tyranny.* New York: Morrow, 1963.

Henny, R. De quelques aspects structuraux et psychotherapiques de l'adolescence. *Revue Francaise Psychoanalyse* 25 (1961): 379–404.

Himmelfarb, G. *Darwin and the Darwinian revolution.* Garden City: Doubleday, 1959.

Horrocks, J. E. The adolescent. In Carmichael, L., ed., *Manual of child psychology.* 2nd ed. New York: Wiley, 1954.

Hurlock, E. B. The adolescent reformer. *Adolescence* 3 (1968): 273–306.

Kaczkowski, H. Sex and age difference in the life problems of adolescents. *Journal of Psychological Studies* 13 (1962): 165–169.

Kiell, N. *The universal experience of adolescence.* New York: International Universities Press, 1964.

Klopfer, B., and Kelley, D. M. *The Rorschach technique.* Yonkers-on-Hudson: World Book, 1942.

Lancaster, E. G. The psychology and pedagogy of adolescence. *Pedagogical Seminary* 5 (1897): 61–128.

Lancaster, E. G. The vanishing character of the adolescent experience. *Northwestern Monthly* 8 (1898): 644.

Landis, P. H. *Adolescence and youth: The process of maturing.* New York: McGraw-Hill, 1952.

Lehman, H. C. *Age and achievement.* Princeton: Princeton University Press, 1953.

Lehman, H. C. Men's creative production rate in different ages and in different countries. *Scientific Monthly* 78 (1954): 321–326.

Levy, E. Toward understanding the adolescent. *Menninger Quarterly* 23 (1969): 14–21.

Libby, M. F. Shakespeare and adolescence. *Pedagogical Seminary* 9 (1901): 163–205.

Masterson, J. F., Jr. The psychiatric significance of adolescent turmoil. *American Journal of Psychiatry* 124 (1968): 1549–1554.

Minuchin, S. Adolescence: Society's response and responsibility. *Adolescence* 4 (1969): 455–476.

Mohsin, S. M. A measure of emotional maturity. *Psychological Studies* (Mysore) 5 (1960): 78–83.

Muzio, N. R. La valutazione di alcuni aspetti della personalita in soggetti dagli 11 ai 15 anni mediante il test del Bestiaire de Zazzo-Mathon: II, *Bollettino di Psicologia Applicata*, nos. 100–102 (1970): 247–260.

Nevel'shstein, V. S. O sotsial'nopsikhologicheskom

issledovanii nekotorykh sotsial'nykh ustrem-lenlii molodezhi. In Rozhin, V. P., ed., *Filosofskie i sotsiologicheskie issledovaniya*. Leningrad, U.S.S.R.: Leningrad University, 1969.

Offer, D.; Sabshin, M.; and Marcus, D. Clinical evaluation of normal adolescents. *American Journal of Psychiatry* 121 (1965): 864–872.

Olson, W. C. *Child development*. Boston: Heath, 1959.

Pasanella, A. K., and Willingham, W. W. Testing the educational and psychological development of young adults: Ages 18–25. *Review of Educational Research* 38 (1969): 42–48.

Rosler, H. D. Sur Frage des psychischen Entwicklungswandels unserer Jugend. *Psychiatrie, Neurologie, und Medizinische Psychologie* 15 (1963): 467–478.

Saul, L. J., and Pulver, S. E. The concept of emotional maturity. *Comprehensive Psychiatry* 6 (1965): 6–20.

Spivack, G.; Levine, M.; Fuschillo, J.; and Travernier, A. Research movement responses and inhibition responses in adolescents. *Journal of Projective Techniques* 23 (1959): 462–466.

Starbuck, E. D. *Psychology of religion*. New York: Scribner, 1899.

Stone, L. J., and Church, L. *Childhood and adolescence*. New York: Random House, 1957.

Swift, E. J. Standards of efficiency in school and life. *Pedagogical Seminary* 10 (1903): 3–22.

Tooley, K. Expressive style as a developmental index in late adolescence. *Journal of Projective Techniques and Personality Assessment* 31 (1967): 51–59.

Suggested Readings

Alissi, A. S. Concepts of adolescence. *Adolescence* 7 (1972): 491–510.

Bandura, A. The stormy decade: Fact or fiction. *Psychology in the Schools* 1 (1964): 224–231.

Cohen, Y. A. *The transition from childhood to adolescence*. Chicago: Aldine, 1964.

Cottle, T. J. The connections of adolescence. *Daedalus* (Fall 1971): 1177–1219.

Cottle, T. J. On studying the young. *Journal of Youth and Adolescence* 1 (1972): 3–11.

Graff, H. The development of the adolescent. *Pennsylvania Psychiatric Quarterly* 10 (1970): 27–32.

Grinder, R. E. The concept of adolescence in the genetic psychology of G. Stanley Hall. *Child Development* 40 (1969): 355–369.

Hurlock, E. B. American adolescents of today: A new species. In Clarizio, H. F.; Craig, R. C.; and Mehrens, W. A., eds., *Contemporary issues in educational psychology*, pp. 140–155. Boston: Allyn and Bacon, 1970.

Kessen, W. Stage and structure in the study of children. *Monographs of the Society for Research in Child Development* 27, no. 83 (1962): 65–82.

Mussen, P. H., and Jones, M. C. Self-conceptions, motivations and inter-personal attitudes of late and early maturing boys. *Child Development* 28 (1957): 243–256.

Nelson, E. A., and Rosenbaum, E. Language patterns within the youth subculture: Development of slang vocabularies. *Merrill-Palmer Quarterly* 18 (1972): 273–285.

Nixon, R. E. Psychological normality in the years of youth. *Teachers College Record* 66 (1964): 71–79.

Ralston, N. C., and Thomas, G. P. America's artificial adolescents. *Adolescence* 6 (1972): 137–142.

Ross, D. *G. Stanley Hall*. Chicago: University of Chicago Press, 1972.

Salzman, L. Adolescence: Epoch or disease? *Adolescence* 8 (1973): 247–256.

Shaimberg, D. Personality restriction in adolescents. *Psychiatric Quarterly* 40 (1966): 258–270.

Shantz, D. W., and Voydanoff, D. A. Situational effects on retaliatory aggression at three age levels. *Child Development* 44 (1973): 149–153.

Shannon, P. D. The adolescent experience. *American Journal of Occupational Therapy* 26 (1972): 284–287.

Wapner, S. Developmental level, emotional involvement, and the resolution of inconsistency in impression formation. *Developmental Psychology* 8 (1973): 120–130.

Winter, G. D., and Nuss, E. M., eds. *The young adult*. Glenview, Ill.: Scott, Foresman, 1969.

Witkin, W., Goodenough, D., and Karp, S. Stability of cognitive style from childhood to young adulthood. *Journal of Personality and Social Psychology* 7 (1967); 291–300.

Chapter Three

Theories of Adolescence

The preceding chapter has provided a general picture of the characteristics of adolescence by citing a number of descriptive studies and presenting some speculative points of view. The task was to describe what various authorities had learned and thought about adolescence without reference to comprehensive theory. This chapter will describe a number of major organized comprehensive theories of adolescence. Some of the theories were formulated purely as theories of adolescence while others are overall theories of human behavior in which adolescence has been considered as an aspect of the larger theory. All of the theories are well known and have gained many followers.

Definition of Theory

A theory is a coherent and interrelated group of general propositions used as principles of explanation for a class or group of phenomena. It represents a mutually consistent and reinforcing system of related and interlocking constructs.[1] It is, in effect, a statement of the relations believed to prevail in a comprehen-

sive body of facts. A theory both evolves from and is capable of generating hypotheses. Theory formulation evolves from a consideration and integration of available evidence, which includes not only the results of various studies, observations, and practical experience, but also emotional and philosophical speculation and the possession of attitudes based upon the theorist's own training.

Psychologists attempting to build theory must make inferences or assumptions about what goes on when their direct observations do not account for what happens.

Theory Verification

Ideally every theory should be subjected to research confirmation or disproof. One approach to theory validation is to hypothesize the relationship of the constructs and then to test this relationship. It is manifestly impossible to have mutually exclusive constructs in the same theory. There might appear to be such, but the seeming inconsistency must be explained by an explanatory construct or the whole theoretical system fails. The psychological theorist must constantly guard against inconsistency in his theory and should have a quite objective basis for any explaining-away behavior in which he indulges when inconsistency is found. An inconsistency represents a research challenge as well as a possible need to reformulate or modify.

It is unfortunate that some theorists, having hypothesized a construct, become comfortable

---

[1]A construct, according to English and English (1958), is "a property ascribed to at least two objects as a result of scientific observation and comparison; a concept, formally proposed, with definition and limits explicitly related to empirical data." As used in psychology, a construct can be taken to mean a hypothetical construct, which English defines as "a construct referring to an entity or process that is inferred as actually existing (though not at present fully observable) and as giving rise to measurable phenomena, including phenomena other than the observables that led to hypothesizing the construct."

in using it and begin to conceive of it as true, forgetting or ignoring that a construct by its very nature is provisional and needs confirmatory supporting objective evidence. Others have tended to avoid research confirmation, partly because many constructs are so complex and molar in nature that it is difficult to conceive appropriate confirming research and partly because many who use theory are practitioners dealing daily with adolescents in a setting that either discourages or leaves little time for research. But whatever the reason for lack of attempts at research confirmation, a theory is held to lack "respectability" or scientific validity until it is submitted to research verification. One of the most important aspects of theory construction is that of formulating the theory in such a manner that it is susceptible to research.

Types of Theories

There have been a number of attempts to categorize existing theories of development, an example being Ausubel's (1958) categorization of theories as preformationistic, predeterministic, and tabula rasa. In this writer's opinion, both the theories and the categorizations are oversimplifications. In the developmental sequence of any one person's life, manifestations and inceptions of behavior made explicit in nearly every one of the theories may be seen, but one fails to see a complete vindication of any one theory at the expense of all. As a matter of fact, the various theories have tended to borrow from preceding theories, and research has failed to confirm the universality of any one approach as explanatory or inclusive of all that happens. Since aspects of most theories seem to fit (to some extent) practically any of the categories, it may be that the categories are more at fault than are any one of the individual theorists. However, the majority of theories can be placed, at least partially, in nearly any given category, providing the category is well conceived. For example, while Freud's theory can largely be placed under Ausubel's prede-

terministic category, few are prepared to say that Freud's formulations, particularly in his later years, and the neo-Freudian approaches and modernizations of Freud, present solely a predeterministic hypothesis.

We can identify roughly three types of approach to an interpretation of adolescence. First are those theories of adolescence that are in effect a catalog of problems faced by children as they approach and pass through the second decade of life. Such theories find their orientation in the environment, which is examined to find the problems it poses and the tasks it sets for children. The individual is incidental to the situation. These theories are of particular interest in sociology, anthropology, social psychology, and education.

Second, and distinctly different from the first, are those theories that focus upon the individual's behavior and see the environment as a stage upon which he plays his unfolding role. Such theories concentrate upon what happens within the individual, although they do not deny the environment's influence. But the environment is incidental to the individual. Such theories are of particular interest to psychologists and psychiatrists. These two approaches contrast. One group is interested primarily in how youth behave—the focus is on the individual child. The other group focus their attention on the problems society poses for youth. A theory explicitly combining these two categories might be termed *interactionist*.

The third approach is purely descriptive and is in effect atheoretical. The method is akin to that of the naturalist who observes and records what he sees without building a systematic theory. In focus, such approaches are closer to the behavior-oriented theories than to the environmentally oriented and are of particular interest to the biologist, the pediatrician, and the historian.

Of course, many approaches represent an overlap of all these positions. Probably no theory is purely any one of the three; its categorizing depends upon which of the three directions the theory appears to take. One may, of course, ask what the theorist is attempting to do with his theory, whether he is trying to describe the characteristics of the period as an impersonal scientist, facilitating youth's passage through the period of adolescence, or hoping to change the nature of adolescence to meet some social, philosophical, or moral end.

Gesell's Growth Patterning Process

Arnold Gesell, who defines adolescence as "preeminently a period of rapid and intense physical growth accompanied by profound changes which involve the entire economy of the organism" (1956), has proposed a comprehensive developmental theory in which he deals specifically with the adolescent period. Gesell conceives of development as a gradual patterning process extending over time, with each year of maturity bringing forth characteristic behaviors and trends. Gesell's formulations are supported by a longitudinal study of children at ages ranging from birth through the sixteenth year (1940, 1946, 1956).[2] His subjects, of both sexes, were of "favorable" socioeconomic status drawn from a "high to superior level" of school population in New Haven, Connecticut. His contention was that such a homogeneous sample would not lead to false generalizations because he was seeking basic human sequences and directions of development that are not fortuitous and would therefore, despite diversities in individuality, show significant relationships to chronological age and maturity levels. His contention might be challenged, but at least his premises in selecting his sample are made explicit. In the section of his research relevant to this text (ages ten to sixteen), from sixty to eighty-eight individuals were examined at each age. Data were gathered by means of observations, interviews, and various measuring instruments. Parents as well as their children were involved in the interviews. Several thousand behavior patterns classified under ten major

developmental areas were codified into longitudinal "growth gradients" in order to show the directions and sequences of development. Individual age groupings were studied to determine the outstanding behaviors occurring consistently at each age.

Gesell visualizes development as a genetically determined unfolding process proceeding over time and governed primarily by "internal" timing which he relates to more "external" universal measures, the most fundamental of which he believes to be "clock time" or "calendar time." He admits that although calendar time does not measure developmental time, it does approximate it. The significant time unit for considering adolescence is one-year intervals, but these yearly intervals are conceptualized as yearly age "zones" rather than as exact birthdays. Flexibility is provided in the zone concept by allowing for a certain amount of overlap. For example, a twelve-year-old may show aspects of thirteen-year-old behavior. The approach is normative, and the individual's status is evaluated against the norms. The premise is that every year of adolescent growth makes a distinct developmental difference.

Gesell has been accused of emphasizing normative growth at the expense of a consideration of individual differences, but he does allow for individual variations in that he notes that the development of each child is in accordance with a unique pattern of growth characteristic of him as a person. However, Gesell sees this unique pattern as merely a variation of a "ground plan of growth" to a large degree characteristic of the human species. He writes: "Into development go genetic factors of individual constitution and innate maturation sequence, and environmental factors ranging from home and school to the total cultural setting." The growing adolescent reveals his individuality in the manner in which he progresses from stage to stage of maturity. While any adolescent can be expected to approximate the human sequence pattern, he can also be expected to depart from it by showing individualities of style and timing, even when his behavior is most typical of his age group. In

[2]This study does not constitute Gesell's only work of significance for his theory. Among the basic sources is work on the embryology of behavior (1945).

Gesell's theory, experience, individuality, and normative growth are interdependent.

The core of Gesell's theory is his concept of reciprocal interweaving (1939) and spiral reincorporation (1945). Of reciprocal interweaving he writes:

Ontogenetic organization does not advance on an even front. There is a more or less periodic fluctuation of dominance in counterbalanced functions: flexors versus extensors, right and left extremities, ipsilateral and bilateral segments. The functional organization of reciprocal relationships between two sets of opposed or counteracting motor systems is manifested by shifting ascendencies of these systems during their ontogenesis. Neurologically this involves a progressive interweaving of underlying structures.

Gesell uses the metaphor of the loom to interpret the complexities of the developmental process.

In explaining spiral reincorporation, Gesell (1945) writes:

For given complexes of behavior the directional trend repeats itself at ascending levels of organization. This imparts a spiral trend to the course of growth. Thus in the patterning of locomotor behavior, the trunk has three major orientations at three successive stages: (a) prostrate, (b) elevated, (c) upright. At each stage there is a partial recurrence of previous patterns of leg activity. There are sub-cycles within greater cycles. The first cycle culminates in pivoting, the second in creeping, the third in walking. Common and closely related components are progressively reincorporated in the corpus of behavior.

Thus, we note a rhythmic development pattern in which an underlying theme repeats itself.

As Gesell extends these concepts to age sequences in his longitudinal study, he states that the human infant produces behavior patterns and modes of growth that resemble those appearing later in childhood and youth. In other words, the course of growth in its emotional, intellectual, and physical aspects is composed in rhythmic sequence of a progression of subcycles that repeat one another. The developing individual passes through a phase that is repeated later in the sequence, at a higher level of organization. Gesell et al. (1956) write:

The developmental progression repeats itself once again from Year Ten to Year Sixteen. Viewed from a distance great enough to obscure the many smaller points of difference, the panorama is very similar, the landmarks appear in the same succession. Eleven, like Five-and-a-half to Six is "loosening up," "snapping old bonds"; Twelve is more positive in mood, smoother in relationships (as are Three and Six-and-a-half); Thirteen pulls inward (comparable to Three-and-a-half and Seven); Fourteen thrusts out (comparable to Four and Eight); Fifteen specifies and organizes (comparable to Four-and-a-half and Nine); Sixteen again achieves a more golden mean (as do Five and Ten).

Where reciprocal interweaving is concerned, Gesell notes that the entire sequence of development presents opposing alternatives. Some originate in the culture, but tension and choice rest in the organism itself. The task of the developmental action system is to channel two-way tensions (conflicts) so that the individual may achieve integration, choice, and direction. As Gesell puts it, "The growth process counterbalances one extreme of behavior by offsetting or pairing it with its opposite."

Characteristics of Gesell's Age Groupings

The tenth year marks the consummation of the childhood years and, as such, presents the child with a relaxed interlude during which he may assimilate and integrate the gains he has made. Fond of home, family, and friends, heterosexual interests are at a low ebb. Assimilative, causal, concrete, he does not indulge in self-analysis. It is a period of equilibrium, of equipoise. Relatively tension-free, the child tends to accept the world as he finds it.

The eleventh year is the "epochal year of transition." Poise departs, and restless activity mounts. New forms of self-assertion, sociability, and curiosity appear. Emotional life alternates between gloom and good nature, but above all else, the child is intense. He is awkward, likes to argue, and seeks leverages to work against. The eleven-year-old becomes critical, quarrels, "messes around" with his age group, and is often rude. Problems of family relationship arise. Innocent and naive, the child begins to exhibit individuality and self-reliance. It is an age of disequilibrium, but equally of burgeoning.

The twelfth year is a return to greater equilibrium. Less insistent, more reasonable, more companionable, the twelve-year-old is less of a problem to adults. He is more objective, less naive and self-centered, and is expanding his social horizons. The peer group becomes important, and enthusiasms are high. This period favors the integration of personality, a time of empathy. The child shows signs of a capacity to mature.

The thirteenth year sees the child well into adolescence. Not as open and communicative as the twelve-year-old, the thirteen-year-old tends to be adaptable and dependable. He is a worrier, tends to withdraw from the family circle and to become introspective and reflective. There is movement toward a more mature self. He begins taking pleasure in rational thought and is sensitive to criticism. He is more discriminating in his social relationships, withdraws still further from his family, and the influence of the peer group mounts. There is a deepening and expanding sense of self. This is a time of "inner mobilization and organization of forces."

The fourteenth year is a time of robust expressiveness and of less withdrawal. The fourteen-year-old is better oriented to himself and his environment. He has joy in life and interest in people. He does some dating, but his fundamental interest is in the coterie of own-sex friends. There is deeper entrance into the ideational realms of thought and increasing self-reliance, together with enough experience of the world to begin to understand it. Fourteen is less tight and withdrawn than thirteen.

The fifteenth year is many-faceted, and the fifteen-year-old is deeply interested in self-understanding and understanding by others. There is growing appreciation of finer shades

of meaning and feeling. Fifteen is quieter but more vulnerable to subjective feelings of grudge, revenge, and violence. Family problems mount, the spirit of independence is in the ascendency, and there is much peer gregariousness. The fifteen-year-old is beginning to be future-oriented. He is, in fact, sixteen in the making.

The sixteenth year marks the end of the cycle that began at ten. Society accords sixteen more status, and there is an air of wholesome self-assurance and tolerance. Friendships are important, but broader socializing experiences lead to neglect of the family. There is more solid orientation to the future and less concentration on self-awareness. The emotions are fairly under control, there is less worry, and feelings are covered up. Here we have real intimations of maturity.

Gesell does not take us past sixteen, but he makes the point that the developmental sequence continues, although the divisions should be expressed in terms of decades rather than years. Gesell's theory is, as Baldwin (1967) points out, probably the best example of a purely maturational theory. His age sequences can be held too rigidly by those who try to apply his theory, but as an attempt to interpret the developmental sequence, it is provocative though controversial.

Freud's Developmental Theory

Sigmund Freud's biologically oriented developmental theory presents psychological development as resulting from the interaction of learning and the unfolding of the three vital organ systems of orality, anality, and genitality. Development is seen as proceeding sequentially through five stages: oral, anal, phallic, latent, and genital. Of these, the first three represent the phase of infancy Freud integrates by his doctrine of infant sexuality, which assumes the sexual nature of the sources of behavior. The infancy period is seen as particularly important in the formation of personality, for the events of these first years build

foundations that have repercussions throughout the entire subsequent life of the individual.

The oral stage, which occurs during the
first months of life, is the period when the infant experiences through his mouth and the
feeding process both satisfactions and discomforts, many of which occur in his relationships
with others, particularly his mother. He becomes overwhelmed with fear and anxiety if
he is harshly treated or deprived of food, and,
conversely, feels secure and self-confident if
his needs are satisfied appropriately. An orally
deprived baby tends to become prematurely
self-dependent and simultaneously feels uncertain and insecure. In his later behavior he
tends to accept dependency unwillingly and
untrustingly. The orally satisfied baby, on the
other hand, may in his later behavior become
unrealistically trusting of others and highly
dependent.

The succeeding anal stage, occurring between the twelfth and eighteenth months and
the fourth year, is a time of dominance of the
anal-eliminative system. During this period
the child learns the fundamentals of control
based essentially upon the giving and withholding involved in the eliminative processes.
The child's natural exploratory interests are
thought to be inhibited by overly strict toilet
training, so that, filled with shame, he may
regress to the more dependent oral stage at
the expense of the development of self-confidence and independent problem-solving behavior. During this period the child learns to
submit his will to the demands of others, even
at the expense of his own pleasure. Given
much affection and overindulgence during
this period, the individual may become fixated
at the anal stage, although overstrictness and
harshness could have the same effect. The trait
of autonomy is developed or blunted in this
period.

The phallic stage, beginning at about four
and extending through the middle years of
childhood, is a time when the child becomes
deeply involved with both his own power and
his own body. As in the first two stages there
is the possibility of overindulgence or of overly
harsh restrictive treatment. The latter produces anxiety about the body and its functions,
particularly those involving sexual behavior.
Such anxiety tends to restrict ambition and
to impair curiosity and self-confidence. In
American culture overindulgence at the phallic
stage is inhibited by society's taboos, which
the child finds implemented, if not by his parents, then by others he encounters outside his
home.

An understanding of the dynamics of the
Freudian developmental sequence depends
upon various other aspects of Freud's theory.
Perhaps the most important construct among
Freud's formulations is that of the basic drives
or urges. Behavior is seen as motivated by two
basic urges, the life urge and the death urge.
The life urge leads to the preservation of self
as well as of others and is manifested as love,
sociability, creativity, and constructiveness.
Basic to the life urge is the libido, a form of
psychological energy, which operates to draw
people together in close psychological interaction. It finds expression in all close personal
relationships, including those of friendship
and of sex. In contrast is the death urge, which
Freud saw as the expression of man's aggressive and destructive character. The death
urge may be turned inward upon oneself or
outward upon others. While these two urges
seem mutually exclusive they often interpene-
trate and result in ambivalence and conflict.

For an understanding of development, the
most important conflict resulting from the in-
terpenetration of the life and death urges is
in the Oedipus complex.[3] In this situation the
child is hypothesized as feeling hatred or hostility toward the parent of his own sex who
frustrates him as he strives for libidinal gratification. A girl, attached to her father, places
herself as her mother's competitor and resents
her mother's favored relationship with her
father. She is thus placed in the position of

[3]The Oedipus complex as an aspect of universal human
behavior has been challenged, since it is not clear that it is
applicable outside Western culture. The matter is still in
controversy, although the Oedipus complex is regarded as
basic in the Freudian system.

both loving and hating her mother. If the course of development is to be normal, girls must forgo intense relationships they are assumed to have had with their fathers, and conversely, boys must renounce the intensity of their relationship with their mothers. Ordinarily the Oedipus complex is resolved sometime between the fifth and the seventh years of life and sets the stage for the period of latency. If this complex is successfully resolved, the child identifies with the parent of the same sex and is able to assume a natural, easy, and proud acceptance of maleness or femaleness, as the case may be. If the resolution is not achieved, the child continues identification with the parent of the opposite sex, to the disadvantage of later development.[4]

As the child grows from the middle years of childhood and leaves the phallic stage behind, he enters the period of latency—a time of ego maturation. Ego maturation consists of the development of social skills and thought processes, and the establishment of object relationships beyond those of the immediate family. Such extension of object relationships involves peers, teachers, group leaders, and others outside the family sphere. Latency

represents a repression of infantile sexuality and is inspired by the child's fear of punishment for his erotic interest in his same-sexed parent. The primitive fantasies related to orality and anality are also repressed. Thus, latency emerges as the child finds a need to renounce his Oedipal strivings. Latency is characterized by orientation to reality and by seeming lack of sexuality, although clinical evidence cited by Alpert (1941) and Bornstein (1951) catalog activities indicating the presence of sexual feelings. As a period of life, latency is somewhat reminiscent of Gesell's description of the ten-year-old. Writing on latency, Blos (1961) notes: "The consequence of more stringent inner controls becomes apparent in the emergence of behavior and attitudes which are motivated by logic and oriented toward values. This general development brings higher mental functions into autonomous play." Anna Freud (1965) writes of "the postoedipal lessening of drive urgency and the transfer of libido from the parental figures to contemporaries, community groups, teachers, leaders." During this phase the developing child tends to find equilibrium of personality and to lay a foundation that enables him to withstand the oncoming onslaught of adolescence with greater stability and more security.

The genital stage marks the advent of puberty and entrance into adolescence. The sexuality repressed during latency now reappears and brings with it a whole host of problems latency had erased. Adolescence, from the Freudian view, is a time when the developing child is faced with a threat. This threat involves the dissolution of the personality he has built and stabilized during the latency period. The child is faced with the need to redefine and regroup his defenses and modes of adaptation. Jacobson (1964) states the Freudian position when she writes: "We know that during the adolescent's struggle the defenses established during latency become so badly battered that they may partly break down under the onslaught of instinctual impulses."

A characteristic of adolescence, as interpreted by Freudians, is a reawakening of Oedipal

---

[4]A picture of Freudian theory is not presented as such. Only elements with particular relevance for understanding Freudian comments upon the nature of adolescence are discussed. However, certain structural hypotheses advanced by Freud should be included in the background discussion. Particularly important are the three functionally related systems of the mind: the id, ego, and superego. The id represents the individual's original psychic apparatus, which includes the basic drives (instincts) and their derivates. Id impulses are undisciplined and subordinate only to the pleasure principle. Taken at its id source, a need demands immediate gratification. The ego and the superego develop out of the id.

The ego is the I and governs those aspects of personality responsible for choosing, perceiving, thinking, knowing, and feeling. It acts to control the id impulses and mediate between it and the environment. The ego begins its development at about the sixth month, as a result of the frustrations caused by the child's external environment.

The superego represents ideal aspirations and moral percepts and begins to emerge from the id at about five or six. Freud believed that the development of the superego came as a result of the Oedipal conflict. Although largely unconscious, the superego represents the individual's conscience as it acts to censor the id impulses and the activities of the ego. With the advent of the superego, morality can become an internal matter rather than a threat imposed from without.

and pre-Oedipal strivings with the resulting desire to maintain family bonds at a time when a developmental task is to relinquish them. Deutsch (1944) has called the child's conflict between his desires to retain and to relinquish his family bonds a clash between progressive and regressive forces. But the return to the Oedipal conflict in adolescence is not identical with the conflict the younger child faced. For the younger Oedipal child the problem is merely that of repressing or defending against aggressive and incestuous feelings toward his parents. He may do this and retain his parent, but the adolescent must truly cut himself off and move toward relinquishment if he is to retain his parent. Blos (1961) speaks of the reality of the loss and the "mourning" of separation. Root (1957) also speaks of mourning as an important psychosocial task in adolescence and mentions the related denial of inner and outer reality. Jacobson's (1964) summary is a good statement of the Freudian position:

The Oedipal child has to repress his sexual and hostile impulses in favor of affectionate attachments to his parents. In adolescence, the sexual maturation process leads to a temporary revival of the pre-Oedipal and Oedipal instinctual strivings, thus reviving the infantile struggle. But now the incestuous sexual and hostile wishes must be fully relinquished. Moreover, the adolescent's affectionate ties to the parents must be sufficiently loosened to guarantee his future freedom of object choice and to present him with a sound orientation toward his own generation and a normal adjustment to adult social reality. This is the cause of his grief reactions which have no parallel in childhood.

The Freudian position states the adolescent's task as that of turning his back upon immature relationships to his parents, of creating for himself a firm sense of worth, and of bending his efforts toward the progressive enterprise of what Blos (1961) calls "falling in love" with all that is involved in building new and consistent object relationships as he prepares to enter the adult world.

Actually Freudian theory is built primarily upon the events of the first decade of life.

Adolescence tends to be represented as an area of the developmental sequence in which Freudian theory may be applied and, perhaps, extended, but applications have not been particularly satisfactory when tested in analytic therapy. Anna Freud (1960) writes: "When it comes to adolescence we feel hesitant and accordingly cannot satisfy the parents or educational workers who apply for help to us and to our knowledge. One can hear it said frequently that adolescence is a neglected period, a stepchild where analytic thinking is concerned." Attempts to work out special techniques for working with adolescence, as reported by Fraiberg (1955), Noshpitz (1957), and Adatto (1958), confirm Anna Freud's comment.

Sigmund Freud himself did not deal with adolescence until 1905 in his *Three Essays on Sexuality,* where, in passing, he described adolescence as a time when changes give infant sexuality its final form. He saw as the main events genitality with its accompanying new sexual aims and the discovery of the new sexual objects outside the family. Ernest Jones's 1922 formulations represent the first really major application of Freudian theory to adolescence following Freud's original statement. He wrote: "The individual recapitulates and expands in the second decennium of life the development he has passed through in the first five years"; and he propounded the general law "that adolescence recapitulates infancy and that the precise way in which a given person will pass through the necessary stages of development in adolescence is to a very great extent determined by the form of his infantile development." Bernfeld (1923, 1924, 1938), Hoffer (1946), and Aichorn (1948), among others, extend the Freudian view of adolescence in some depth. But Anna Freud's contributions have been the most extensive. She sees adolescent upset as inevitable because the balance between id and ego forces achieved during latency is both preliminary and precarious. The changes in drive activity and quality brought about by puberty upset this balance, and the developing individual must set about achieving adult sexuality. The action of such internal adjustments brings about the behavioral upheavals manifested in adolescence. However, some adolescents are "reluctant to grow up" and do not display these propensities. Such children make much of family relationships and are considerate and submissive sons and daughters. They retain the ideas and ideals of their earlier background. Anna Freud believes that such "reluctance" comes from the superego rather than from the id aspects of personality. She interprets such behavior as a crippling result of excessive defenses against drive activity and believes it is a serious block to normal development.

Anna Freud takes the position that inconsistent and unpredictable behavior is normal in adolescence. The adolescent accepts his impulses and rejects them; he loves and hates his parents and alternates between dependence and revolt; he seeks a secure identity but equally tries to merge his identity with others; he is idealistic, generous, artistic, and unselfish but alternates with self-centeredness and egotism. In later periods of life such behavior would be pathological; in adolescence it is normal to the point where absence of such conflict means that the child is really in trouble. As the reader can well imagine, this viewpoint is disturbing to parents and teachers since it interprets the "good" adolescent as not developing normally, while the fluctuating, conflict-ridden adolescent difficult for adults to get along with is developing normally (A. Freud 1927, 1946, 1960, 1965). Anna Freud is not alone in her viewpoint. The conflict-ridden adolescent is a recurring theme in psychoanalytic literature, as evidenced by discussions such as those by Spiegel (1961)[5] and Harley (1961).

The many criticisms of psychoanalytic theory are too well documented to require space in this text, but the theory has wide currency and contrasts with many other theoreti-

[5]Spiegel (1951) has presented a good review of psychoanalytically oriented discussions on adolescence, and Anna Freud (1958) has summarized some of the basic literature on the same topic.

cal formulations in that it emphasizes the study of the single individual as the ultimate source of valid information about behavior. Rosenblatt (1966) affirms the importance of studying the individual when he writes, "the study of individuals generates an entirely different type of conceptualization from the type that is generated through the study of groups. The individual is, in a sense, more complex than the group can be, and the individual is related to his own history in a far more intimate way than the study of groups can fathom." Werner (1957) made the same point when he noted:

The original aim of developmental theory directed toward the study of universal genetic changes, is still one of its main concerns; but side by side with this concern, the conviction has been growing in recent years that developmental conceptualization, in order to reaffirm its truly organismic character, has to expand its orbit of interest to include as a central problem the study of individuality.

Entirely apart from the insight that Freudian theory may provide when applied to the processes of adolescence, the fact remains that the theory has encountered difficulties when used in therapy with adolescents. As Anna Freud (1960) writes, "the analytic treatment of adolescents is a hazardous venture from beginning to end, a venture in which the analyst has to meet resistances of unusual strength and variety." She notes that in meeting resistance from adults it is possible to adapt the analytic technique to the resistance, which, for the kind of mental order involved, is specific. But this is "not so in adolescence where the patient may change rapidly from one of these emotional positions to the next, exhibit them all simultaneously, or in quick succession, leaving the analyst little time and scope to marshal his forces and change his handling of the case according to the changing need." It is perhaps of interest, as Anna Freud affirms, that in many cases of adult treatment it is not possible to revive adolescent experiences in the force usual with childhood experiences that are more remote in time.

A further difficulty in psychoanalysis with adolescents is the difficulty in getting them to continue therapy after more than one or two sessions. It may be that the analyst typifies the hated adult world from which the adolescent is in full retreat and from which he tries to hide his real self. This conditioned behavior could be triggered when the analyst probes into the adolescent period either of the adolescent himself or of an adult who had found the adolescent period particularly traumatic. It may also be that adolescence is a time of such mixed and shifting roles that it is unclear, not only as one looks back upon it, but as one goes through it. It would seem obvious that adaptations of analytic techniques are required in adolescent therapy. Boenheim[6] suggests the mutually reinforcing possibilities of the group therapy session, where the therapist is in a more catalytic position.

Departures from the Freudian Position

The Freudian hypotheses have many faithful followers, but it was inevitable that, sooner or later, some would seek modifications within classical Freudian theory, while others, starting from a Freudian base, would depart radically in formulating explanations for the course and the governing conditions of the developmental sequence. Such departures have occurred, often as the result of the substitution of some other primary causal force for the sexual origins of behavior Freud postulated. Such departures were not usually the result of any fundamental disagreement with Freud's empirical methods or with his emphasis on the study of the individual.

Alfred Adler (1917, 1927, 1931) was one of the first of Freud's followers to challenge his position by rejecting the sexual origin of the neuroses in favor of a concept holding that the origins of personality are to be found in the manner in which a person adjusts to the feeling of inferiority found in everyone. This

feeling of inferiority is seen as the result of the original helplessness of infants and children and is enhanced or mitigated by parental attitudes of rejection or acceptance. Here we see the substitution of the inferiority complex for the Oedipus complex as a universal event in early childhood. The child, feeling inferior, seeks ways of feeling superior and out of this quest grows the search for power as the fundamental determinant of personality. Interpreting Adler's position, we may see adolescence as a quest for superiority as the child endeavors to attain adulthood and adequacy as a man or woman. The quest for personal adequacy is marked by various compensations, of which the most important is that of masculinity, marked by behavior described as masculine protest. In adolescence particularly, this protest encounters social reality in the form of limited personal endowment and social and economic barriers. The resulting conflict must be successfully resolved or it leads to neurotic behavior in the form of unrealistic compensations or, more seriously, to mental illness.

Adler stresses the social nature of man, which he sees as innate rather than acquired. But each person's innate social nature is unique, and as he interacts with others he develops a unique social self and manner of "striving for perfection." This Adler calls the person's "style of life." One task for an adolescent is the continuing development and implementation of his style of life.

Adler takes the position that man's development has a social rather than a biological basis and differs from Freud in emphasizing the search for power rather than the search for sex as the most important determinant of human development and behavior. In the Adlerian system, sex is simply a means by which one acquires power over others.

Adler was particularly interested in preventive approaches in the area of mental health and felt that his system had direct applications to education and to child-rearing practices in general. He founded the Child Guidance Center in the public schools of Vienna and the guiding concepts of that center have spread

[6]Personal communication from Dr. Curt Boenheim.

to other centers established in various countries of western Europe as well as in the United States. It was Adler's opinion that the mother is in a particularly strategic position to deal with children and that a child should not be turned over to others for care or treatment; the mother could serve this function instead of an outside substitute. He believed that mothers, or parents in general, should be trained by the public schools in the guidance centers to serve their child-rearing function. While this concept was specifically aimed at the younger child, it is also applicable at the adolescent level. There is no reason why training in understanding and dealing with children should be confined to occupational categories such as teaching and social work. It is indeed the parent who has daily—and nightly—face-to-face contact.

In educational practice, Adler, as Nikelly (1971) notes, recommended that authoritative imposition of knowledge be avoided, lest the learner come to feel that success stems from personal superiority. Adler would see social conscience as the most important objective of both education and therapy. There can be no doubt that the nonauthoritarian and relatively permissive Adlerian approaches are particularly palatable to adolescents. Their efficacy has been a matter of dispute, but the reader should compare the implications of Freudian as compared to Adlerian theory in working with adolescents.

A group of theorists who also depart from Freudian theory include Fromm (1955, 1956), Horney (1939, 1950), Kardiner (1939, 1945), and Sullivan (1947, 1953). These individuals, none of whom were ever coworkers of Freud, are psychologists classified generally as neo-Freudians. They take as their orientation sociology and anthropology rather than biology. Personality is seen as determined by the cultural environment rather than by biological heredity. In their view, different cultures produce different personalities and different motivations.

Harry Stack Sullivan's emphasis, in contrast to Freud's primacy of the organ system, is on the child's perception of the world and his adaptation to it. Psychological development results from the learning engendered by alternating tension and tension reduction, which build into the child patterns of anxiety and expectation. Part of the learning involves making differentiations about the behavior of others and the development of a self-concept. Development is seen as occurring in six heuristic stages, each beginning with new interpersonal needs and relationships that offer opportunities for new and more adjustive learnings. While the learnings of one stage are reflected in the behavior of the succeeding one, Sullivan believes that "everything that has gone before becomes reasonably open to influence." New stages often usher in situations that make the personality built in previous stages "somewhat acutely inadequate."

Sullivan's stages are infancy, childhood, the juvenile era, preadolescence, adolescence, and adulthood. Adolescence is divided into two eras: early and late. Infancy extends from birth to the appearance of articulate speech, however meaningless or uncommunicative. Childhood is represented by the child's ability to use speech meaningfully and ends with the appearance of a need for playmates. The juvenile era, extending through most of the elementary school years, implements the need for playmates. Preadolescence begins when the maturing child manifests a need for an intimate pairing relationship with another same-sex person of a status comparable to his own. In Sullivan's system the need for social intimacy is postulated as basic, and during the juvenile and preadolescent eras, this need is seen as developing. The periods of infancy and childhood are similarly represented as times of development of the need for security with its accompanying manifestations of anxiety. During preadolescence, as the child becomes preoccupied with his chum relationships, there is a tendency to move out from the close family relationships, although parents are still significant. However, the child does begin to make some quite astute and objective evaluations of his parents, as well as of other aspects of his environment. Sullivan writes, "The preadolescent frames of reference are, at least in our culture, about the clearest and most workable ones we have." Adolescence begins "with the eruption of genital sexuality and puberty."

Early adolescence, ushered in by puberty, is a period in which a zone of the body previously associated with the excretion of waste, "becomes newly and rapidly significant as a zone of interaction in physical interpersonal intimacy." This leads to a constellation of new needs with resulting tensions that Sullivan identifies as lust. He makes the specific point, however, that as an integrating tendency the needs culminating the lust are separate from the need for intimacy. The extent to which complexities and difficulties appear in adolescence or later in life depends upon the clarity with which the individual distinguishes among the three highly interacting but often contradictory needs: (1) the need for intimacy; (2) the need for lustful satisfactions; and (3) the need for personal security in the form of freedom from anxiety. Thus we see adolescence as characterized by three powerful motivational systems that may run collision courses. For example, there are collisions between the intimacy need and lust, between lust and security, and between intimacy and security.

Late adolescence, according to Sullivan, "extends from the patterning of preferred genital activity through un-numbered educative steps to the establishment of a fully human or mature repertory of interpersonal relations, as permitted by available opportunity, personal and cultural."[7] That is, the individual is categorized as a late adolescent when he has succeeded in discovering what he prefers in genital behavior and how it may be fitted into the remainder of his life. This is a stage some individuals never attain, no matter what their ages may be.

[7]In *Conceptions of modern psychiatry* (1953) Sullivan noted the value of distinguishing (as a separate era) middle adolescence, a period extending from the completion of voice change to the patterning of genital behavior. His major discussions, however, are in terms of the two eras, early and late adolescence.

Fundamentally, late adolescence is a time of self-formulation and of gaining experience that must be interpreted and tested against reality. The impending features interfering with the development of true maturity are anxiety and an unrealistic self-system leading to distortions of the individual's perceptions of his own experience and avoidance of much that might lead to normal development. Unfortunately the self-systems of many late adolescents show so many falsifications that proper gaining and interpretation of experience are impossible. There is, of course, the matter of whether or not opportunities exist for the adolescent to gain the experience that he needs.

If the experiential and self-personification tasks of late adolescence are successfully resolved, the individual develops competence and respect for himself as a person and is able to extend respect to others. Anxiety is under control, and coping behaviors are developed. Sullivan writes that adulthood begins when the person is able "to establish relationships of love for some other person, in which relationship the other person is as significant, or nearly as significant as oneself."

A related view is expressed by Josselyn (1971), who proposes the two instinctual drives of autoplasticism and alloplasticism. The autoplastic drive represents the urge to be loved, and the alloplastic drive the need to love others. Josselyn feels that where alloplasticism is concerned the adolescent expresses in his behavior something lacking in himself. She makes the point that some of the genuine or pseudosocial pathology found in adolescents is partially explained by the stress placed on the need to be loved, with little accompanying emphasis on the inherent urge to love. It is interesting that the term *love* has become a kind of slogan among the modern-day younger generation. It may represent on their part a conscious or unconscious effort to emphasize something missing in parent-child relations, where child-rearing practices are so often a one-way street from the parent to the child. It could be that Sullivan's last stage could be considerably accelerated, given proper cultural expectations as to the role of the child.

Erich Fromm (1955, 1956, 1964) is included here not because he has a theory of adolescent behavior but because he expresses in his theorizing—and philosophizing—a point of view that the writer has heard expressed again and again by high-school and college students over the past decade. Fromm would appear to be the adolescents' favorite theorizer in that he is expressing a feeling that, at least verbally, seems to represent the adolescent *Zeitgeist*. That the average adolescent who expresses the feeling has never heard of Fromm simply proves the concept of the spirit of the age.[8] Fromm sees all men as ultimately idealists capable of rising above reliance upon the purely hedonistic aspects of life. Man is what society makes him, but because he is capable of solving his own problems, he can rise above the strictures of society. As a member of society he has created the problems, and as a member of society he can solve them. Unfortunately man has become materialistic and has grown to worship the products of his own hand. But there is hope, because ultimately value judgments determine actions, and the great value is love. Fromm sees love as humanity's answer to its problems and notes that humanity is starved for love but warns that the need for love and to love is reciprocal. The dynamics of love are care, responsibility, respect, and knowledge. For fulfillment, according to Fromm, man must satisfy five needs: (1) he must develop a feeling of oneness with his fellow men; (2) he must eschew artificial symbols in favor of a natural way of life, and instead of merely working for money, he must seek to gain satisfaction from life; (3) he must transcend his animal nature and improve and learn; (4) he should learn to know his true self and identify with others; and (5) he should work toward creating a reasonable life in a reasoning world, a life that is aware,

responsible, and creative. Fromm makes the point that as man fulfills himself, he moves toward a humanistic, communal social order.

Developmental Tasks

As the child moves through the developmental sequence, he encounters a number of tasks set by his cultural milieu, by himself as a biological organism, or by an interaction of cultural and biological factors. Certain of these tasks are particularly crucial, since they must be accomplished or mastered if the child is to develop normally, to achieve acceptable socialization, and to be able to meet subsequent crucial tasks successfully. The developmental task approach to the analysis of development attempts to isolate and describe these crucial tasks, to place them in proper sequence, to indicate at about what ages they become an issue, and to indicate the consequences of failure to master any given task. In a real sense, developmental tasks may be taken to represent the critical periods of development. Certain of them may be attempted too early or too late, and some, if not mastered at the optimum time, may never be mastered, with a resulting lack of balance in an individual's development. Certain developmental tasks are so much a matter of cultural expectation or of economic necessity that failure to master them may result in lack of efficiency, ridicule, or the application of various kinds of cultural disapproval. One such developmental task in American culture involves learning to drive an automobile.

The developmental task concept was originally an outgrowth of psychoanalytic thinking in the 1930s, but in recent years the concept has not had any particular theoretical referents, although most of those who have used it have espoused some type of dynamic approach.[9] Havighurst, one of the leading exponents of the developmental task concept, defined a developmental task in 1953 as a task

[8]A number of persons have, from time to time, expressed the adolescent feeling about life and the world and have been identified by the adolescent peer culture as so doing. Ayn Rand is an example. It is curious that Fromm has not been so widely identified and has not been admitted to status as a cult leader. Perhaps his day will come.

[9]Relating to change or that which causes change. Dynamic psychology stresses cause-and-effect relationships and usually emphasizes drives and motives. Psychoanalysis is dynamic, but there are various other forms of dynamic psychology.

that "arises at or about a certain period in the life of the individual, successful achievement of which leads to his happiness and to success with later tasks, while failure leads to unhappiness in the individual, disapproval by society, and difficulty with later tasks." Havighurst (1956) notes that there are three sources of developmental tasks for any given group of people: (1) physical maturation, (2) cultural expectation and pressure, and (3) individual aspirations. Havighurst (1953) lists ten tasks of the adolescent period:

1. Achievement of new and more mature relations with age-mates of both sexes.
2. Achievement of a socially approved masculine or feminine social role.
3. Acceptance of one's physique and the effective use of the body.
4. Achievement of emotional independence of parents and other adults.
5. Achievement of the assurance of economic independence in the sense of feeling that one could make one's own living if necessary.
6. Selection and preparation for an occupation.
7. Preparation for marriage and family life.
8. Development of intellectual skills and concepts necessary for civic competence.
9. The desiring and achieving of socially responsible behavior.
10. Acquisition of a set of values and an ethical system as a guide to behavior.

Zaccaria (1965) notes that the concept of developmental tasks actually consists of "three unique formulations of the concept." First are the general development tasks formulated by Havighurst (1953); second, the vocational developmental tasks of Super[10] et al. (1957, 1963); and third, Erikson's (1959, 1963) psychosocial crises. Zaccaria also points out that while most writers have viewed developmental tasks as a nomothetic concept, it is important to remember that even within the same culture persons differ and there is much to be gained

[10]Super's theory is discussed in the chapter on vocational development.

in considering the ideographic dimension, particularly in face-to-face relationships with single individuals, as in guidance counseling. Zaccaria's point, of course, holds true in applying any theory to an individual's behavior, and most theoretical positions do make at least limited provision for individual differences. There can be no doubt that in considering the developmental history of a single individual in view of his own unique interests, values, motivations, and vocational-avocational decisions, certain unique developmental tasks might be set for him if the sequence of his life is to be orderly and successful for him and for society. Still, one must not forget that those developmental tasks representing social roles require behavior expected and held desirable not only by most people in a society but by the individual himself—for example, getting married, with its accompanying social roles of suitor, fiance, and groom.

A number of persons have done research using the developmental task concept either to test basic hypotheses or to identify new tasks. For example, two hypotheses about developmental tasks state that, at any given chronological age, ability to perform a given developmental task is positively related to ability to perform other tasks appropriate to that age, and that performance on a given task at one age is positively related to ability to perform tasks in that same area at later ages. Schoeppe and Havighurst (1953) tested these hypotheses with a heterosexual sample of ten-, thirteen-, and sixteen-year-olds by determining the relationships between ability to perform a given task at these three ages. Correlations between performance on a given task at two age levels ranged from .4 to above .9, and correlations between two tasks ranged from .4 to .8. As Havighurst (1956) notes, "there is not much compensation of low performance on one task by high performance on another task, although this occasionally does occur."

In another study by Schoeppe, Haggard, and Havighurst (1953) of factors affecting success in developmental tasks, the authors in their conclusions stated that their findings stressed both:

the greater importance of emotionality and its expression in outlets satisfying to the individual and acceptable to society. If the adolescent is to accomplish successfully the developmental tasks required in his society, it is imperative that he master his impulsivity and accept himself, so that he can mobilize his energy to deal effectively with the social and cultural forces which impinge upon him.

In a study of adolescents' concepts of their past, Kastenbaum (1965) writes:

Most adolescents in a normative sample had an aversive, blocking-out reaction toward their personal past. The implication might be that one of the developmental tasks which still lies ahead for many adolescents is the ability to take pastness into account in elaborating a cohesive view of life . . . neither the adolescent who ignores the past nor the aged who ignore the future could develop or maintain a genuine time perspective, according to the present line of reasoning.

Various writers have added to or revised the list of developmental tasks proposed by Havighurst in 1953, or have used other terminology. Speaking of the middle-adolescent period Angelino (1955) notes that with the advent at puberty of new needs and drives and the consequent expansion and change of "inner-directed" controls, each adolescent must:

1. Come to terms with his own body.
2. Learn the appropriate sex roles in preparation for marriage and family life.
3. Learn how to get along with age-mates.
4. Achieve independence from parents.
5. Prepare for economic independence through vocational and occupational choices.
6. Develop a system of values and ideals.

Thornberg (1970) makes the point that changing times and cultural outlooks make it necessary to revise lists of developmental tasks to fit the times. He writes:

Most tasks, including those with a strong biological basis are affected by social approvals and disapprovals. Furthermore, society has appropriate times for certain developmental tasks to be worked out by the adolescent. Inability to accomplish the task within the allotted time interval compounds the learning of such a task, sometimes to the point of non-resolution within the individual himself. Therefore, in light of (a) society's attempt to help the individual learn tasks, (b) the rapid sociological and technological changes that have been made since World War II, and (c) the continuing change within our contemporary society, it seems necessary to reevaluate adolescent developmental tasks in respect to our existing society.

For an example of Havighurst's Task 1 (which Thornberg renames "learning appropriate relationships with peers"), Thornberg notes that in the 1950s Havighurst had predicted the tasks under that heading on the assumption that the ages of thirteen to fourteen were the appropriate time for boys and girls to become immersed in social activities. Yet, by the late 1960s a number of factors had contributed to earlier adolescent socialization, and the ages thirteen to fourteen should have been moved downward. Among the socialization factors cited by Thornberg were the new public school organizational middle-school movement, earlier dating accompanied by parental pressures to date, and media "appeals to 10–11 year old femininity."

Erikson's Psychosocial Tasks

Erik Erikson (1963, 1964, 1968), who works within the boundaries of Freudian theory, describes the developmental sequence as consisting of eight stages, each of which presents the individual with a conflict that may be dealt with in one of two ways. Of these two ways, one is benign and represents successful resolution of the conflict; the other is harmful and represents failure.

As the individual passes through the eight stages of development, he acquires an ego identity, with each of the stages contributing positive or negative influences, depending upon how successfully he has resolved the conflict presented by that stage. In effect, the various stages present a series of psychosocial tasks, each of which must be mastered at the appropriate time, lest the tasks of the succeeding stages present additional difficulties. Thus,

Erikson presents two postulates. First, as an individual increases in age, the ego develops systematically in a sequential series of stages. These stages are marked by the development of psychosocial attitudes related to libidinal and maturational processes. The stage for the emergence of attitudes is the widening social environment of the child. Second, as the ego develops, it encounters psychosocial crises caused by the attitudes that emerge in each stage.

The eight stages are: (1) the achievement of trust (basic trust versus basic mistrust), (2) the achievement of autonomy (autonomy versus shame and doubt), (3) the achievement of initiative (initiative versus guilt), (4) the achievement of industry (industry versus inferiority), (5) the achievement of identity (identity versus identity diffusion), (6) the achievement of intimacy (intimacy versus isolation), (7) the achievement of generativity (generativity versus stagnation), (8) the achievement of ego integrity (ego integrity versus despair). The first three stages represent infancy and childhood, stage four represents latency, stage five is puberty and adolescence, stage six is young adulthood, and the last two stages represent adulthood and the later years.[11]

[11]The reader may wish to compare Erikson's eight stages with Shakespeare's seven ages of man. In *As You Like It* Jaques says:

His acts being seven ages. At first the infant,
Mewling and puking in the nurse's arms.
Then the whining schoolboy, with his satchel
And shining morning face, creeping like snail
Unwillingly to school. And then the lover,
Sighing like furnace, with a woeful ballad
Made to his mistress' eyebrow. Then a soldier,
Full of strange oaths, and bearded like the pard,
Jealous in honor, sudden, and quick in quarrel,
Seeking the bubble reputation
Even in the cannon's mouth. And then the justice,
In fair round belly with good capon lin'd,
With eyes severe and beard of formal cut,
Full of wise saws and modern instances;
And so he plays his part. The sixth age shifts
Into the lean and slippered pantaloon,
With spectacles on nose and pouch on side,
. . . .
 . . . Last scene of all,
That ends this strange eventful history,
Is second childishness and mere oblivion,
Sans teeth, sans eyes, sans taste, sans every thing.

In this textbook we are interested in stage five and, to some extent, in stage six, since the latter represents the barrier separating adolescence from maturity.

Erikson's fifth stage, the time of identity achievement, ushers in puberty. Then, the sameness and continuities the child has depended upon since the learnings of stage one can no longer be counted on. His focus is upon himself and he becomes concerned with how he feels he is. He is also concerned about how he may relate the roles and skills learned before puberty with the "occupational prototypes of the day." But above all, his quest is for a new assurance of sameness and continuity. In this quest the adolescent revisits the conflicts of earlier years and uses other people as adversaries as he refights the old battles.

The main business of the fifth stage is ego identity. During this time the individual tries to come to terms with himself and to build a self-concept with which he can live. But such ego identity represents an integration that grows out of social experience and the assumption of social roles. Unfortunately, the adolescent's ego is still so blurred that there is much role confusion and a tendency to overidentify with peer and ideal figures. Others are used as a means of trying out. Falling in love becomes a means of projecting one's diffused ego identity on another. Adolescents during this period are capable of great intolerance as they freely make judgments about right and wrong and about what is in and what is out. In this psychosocial stage between childhood and adulthood, when the individual can identify with neither, there is a feeling of nonbelonging, of moratorium.

In stage six, the time of achieving intimacy, the individual becomes eager to fuse the identity he has built with the identity of others, and during this period genitality of the identity-searching kind can be exchanged for "true genitality." Erikson sees the danger of this stage as that of isolation, of "the avoidance of contacts which commit to intimacy" (1963).

Erikson's eight stages may be considered as representing the presentation of a series of sequential developmental tasks to the developing individual. However, Erikson's psychosocial tasks are more comprehensive than are developmental tasks as usually defined, and while not specifically biological in nature, they are anchored in Freudian theory.

In Erikson's eight epigenetic psychosocial stages of development adolescence is seen as a stage representing a critical period, since during it the identity process either remains diffuse or crystallizes. If the ego identity remains diffuse, the adolescent, as Bronson (1959) points out, is characterized by increasing anxiety levels with repercussions in various aspects of his life. For example, Centi (1962), Irvin (1969), and Fisher (1960–1961) note the falling-off in college grades and other criteria of achievement of those who are exhibiting increasing symptoms of anxiety. But if the anxiety or its reasons are resolved, then the identity can be expected to crystallize in late adolescence. Rubins (1968) characterizes an acute identity crisis during adolescence by three traits: (1) extreme fluidity and shifting symptoms, (2) a glorified self-image, and (3) confusion about self-concept and identity.

Erikson has been accused of lack of clarity in his explanation of identity, but his general position is that identity involves selecting, testing, and integrating self-images derived from childhood psychosocial crises in reference to the adolescent's ideological climate. "Identity diffusion," in contrast to its opposite, "ego identity," refers to the lack of ability of many adolescents to commit themselves even in late adolescence to an occupational or ideological position or even to assume a recognizable station in life. The question might be raised as to the relationship between Erikson's ego-diffuse adolescent and Fromm's self-fulfilled adolescent.

Erikson's postulates of ego epigenesis have had considerable currency, and there have been numerous research attempts to test at least aspects of the theory. Ciaccio (1971) attempted to study the validity of Erikson's two postulates with five-, eight-, and eleven-year-olds, using a technique developed by Boyd (1964) for the study of ego-stage progression.

Ciaccio reports confirmation of Erikson's first postulate (see discussion above for definition of the first postulate) for stages two, three, and four but was unable to confirm postulate two, that the ego develops as it meets the different crisis aspects of the ego states. Ciaccio writes that "it might be ... argued that the first five crises outlined by Erikson are merely different levels or dimensions of the same underlying crisis." Ciaccio feels that the establishment of autonomy (autonomy versus shame and doubt) is the focal crisis of the first five stages. Howard (1960) reports a study that she claims confirms Erikson's contention that the core conflict of adolescence is identity versus identity diffusion, but states that a number of subsidiary adolescent conflicts can be subsumed under the major one. Among these are self-certainty versus identity-consciousness, time perspective versus time diffusion, anticipation of achievement against paralysis, and sexual identity versus bisexual diffusion. Santrock (1970) studied the resolution of Erikson's first four developmental crises among father-present and father-absent fifth-grade males. He writes that the results of his study support "Erikson's contention that the development of basic trust in the child's early years serves as a foundation on which ensuing stages may build."

A number of investigators have studied the characteristics and relationships of ego identity. In an investigation of the relationship between ego identity status and moral judgment Podd (1972) reports that the most mature levels of moral judgment are possessed by individuals who have achieved ego identity. In contrast, those who have achieved lesser levels of ego identity are least mature in moral judgment or show themselves to be in a transitional state. Bauer and Snyder (1972) report in a study of college undergraduates that persons showing high achievement and affiliation motivation possess a more satisfactory ego identity than persons with lower levels of motivation. These investigators feel that their subjects' levels of achievement motivation reflected the degree of success of the resolution of the achievement crisis of the latency period.

Ego identity has been related to "certainty of self-conception" and "temporal stability of self-rating" by Bronson (1959), to a subject's willingness to accept a false personality picture of himself as true by Block (1961), and to sociometric ratings of adjustment by Rasmussen (1964).

Marcia (1966), speaking of identity achievement as the polar alternatives inherent in Erikson's psychosocial theory, notes the following four status positions along the continuum between the two poles: (1) identity achievement, (2) moratorium, (3) foreclosure, and (4) identity diffusion. Marcia studied these status categories in an investigation of eighty-six college males in which he used identity status interviews, an ego identity incomplete sentences blank, a concept attainment task, and a self-esteem questionnaire. Marcia describes the moratorium-status person as being in the crisis period and struggling to make commitments, although he is rather vague as to what they should be. Of him Marcia writes, "Issues often described as adolescent preoccupy him. Although his parents' wishes are still important to him, he is attempting a compromise among them, society's demands, and his own capabilities. His sometimes bewildered appearance stems from his vital concern and internal preoccupation with what appear to him to be unresolvable questions." Marcia describes the foreclosure-status person as a person who has not experienced a crisis but is expressing a commitment which is hardly his own. He is still parent-centered, and his beliefs are theirs. Seemingly rigid in this respect, he finds childhood beliefs confirmed in present experience. The two polar status positions, as Marcia defines them, represent the standard Eriksonian description, but he does propose two different types of identity-diffuse individuals as "playboy" and "schizoid personality."

Adolescence as a Moratorium Period

An interesting concept included in Erikson's fifth stage is that of adolescence as a period of moratorium. Various writers have spoken of the "psychosocial moratorium" of youth. This phrase means that youth is a period of standing back, of analyzing, and of not having to assume the role of an adult, although free of the child's role. Thus the period may be seen, in Eisenstadt's (1962) terms, as a period of role moratorium, "a period in which one may play with various roles without definitely choosing any." Yet this seems an oversimplification. The adolescent, although he is not playing or being allowed to play the role of either child or adult, does have to play the role of the adolescent in the culture in which he is growing up. Perhaps this duality of having an assigned role—that of an adolescent—but at the same time of being free to defer the other roles of life and play many exploratory roles is one of the problem areas of adolescence. Of course, the transitoriness of the role of adolescent is apparent as it is at no other role-stage in the life sequence, except perhaps in old age. A child thinks of himself concretely as a child, and although he may speak of himself as growing up someday, he really means he will be a child grown up: he does not see himself abandoning his child's role. The adult, knowing he has attained maturity, knows also that he is playing his ultimate life role. He has, in a real sense, arrived. But the adolescent feels he has specifically abandoned the role of childhood. He recognizes that he cannot remain forever an adolescent with a permissive moratorium of role. He knows he must eventually assume the final role of adulthood and, in the meantime, finds himself playing a role without real substance, one that even he sees cannot go on. Thus, for him, this period is one of play-acting. He must often perceive himself as an actor on the stage and wonder what is behind the mask—or what should be. There is, somehow, an unreal, dreaming quality to adolescence.

Lewin's Field Theory

Kurt Lewin (1935, 1939, 1942, 1954) was interested in behavior in general and only incidentally in adolescent behavior as such.

However, he was interested in the changes that development and behavior bring about over time, and inevitably, as he discussed the dynamics of individual and group behavior, many things had direct application to the adolescent period. Essentially he was interested in the study of the individual. He wrote (1942):

As any science, psychology is in a dilemma when it tries to develop "general" concepts and laws. If one "abstracts from individual differences" there is no logical way back from these generalities to the individual case. Such a generalization leads from individual children to children of a certain age or certain economic level and from them to children of all ages and all economic levels; it leads from a psychopathic individual to similar pathological types and from there to the general category "abnormal" person. However, there is no logical way back from the concept "child" or "abnormal person" to the individual case. What is the value of general concepts if they do not permit predictions for the individual case?

Lewin hoped to represent the individual with the help of various "elements" of construction such as psychological "position," psychological "forces," and similar concepts. The foundations of Lewin's field elements go back to a gestalt-psychology past. For example, his concept of "life space" is quite analagous to Koffka's (1935) "behavioral environment."

As an interaction theorist, Lewin saw behavior as a result of interdependent variables consisting of the nature and past experience of the individual and the state of the environment in which he exists from moment to moment. Thus each individual exists in a life space consisting of his needs, motivations, and the physical stimuli that impinge on him. In effect, behavior may be seen as locomotion, either away from or toward a goal, with frustration resulting from barriers to such locomotion. Human development consists of differentiation of those areas of the life space that are unstructured or undifferentiated and proceed at different rates and different times in the life span. Lewin defines three specific periods,

childhood, adolescence, and adulthood, and notes that in adolescence particularly rapid changes occur in the structure of life space. Younger children are seen as unable to distinguish between reality and "irreality," whereas adolescents make such distinctions. That is, the child does not distinguish between truth and untruth; a wish is as good as an imminent event. A child is highly dependent upon others; the adolescent has learned to depend upon himself. Lewin cites stages of development as related to the individual's degree of life-space differentiation in terms of activities and social relations, in terms of its scope, and in terms of general fluidity.

For Lewin the social context is important, and he sees the social relationships of adolescence as one of the crucial aspects of the period. It is an ambiguous period for the adolescent, neither child nor adult, who carries on social transactions in both worlds, but actually belongs to neither. Hence he encounters considerable inconsistency of attitude, and he too becomes ambivalent, as he reflects the inconsistency about him. What people expect of him or what he expects of himself is still unstructured; hence he is in a state of social locomotion.

Lewin sees a major problem in the fact that the adolescent's life space provides goals his culture does not permit him to attain. Frustration results, leading to aggressive and withdrawal behavior or the espousal of negative causes. But the adolescent's cognitive structure is such that he cannot be sure that he will not actually attain his goals, so the period is marked by uncertainty. Self-concept is important in adolescence and depends upon body image, but many changes occur in adolescence, and it is difficult for the adolescent to attain a sense of stability and certainty. Perspective of time is also an important aspect of adolescent life, for upon it depends progress in vocational goals and eventual movement into maturity.

As a matter of fact, while he did deal with the adolescent period as such, Lewin was not comfortable with the concept. He preferred to conceive of adolescence as consisting of the area where the two regions of childhood and adulthood overlap. In that way there would be no separate region of adolescence at all. Using his own field theory and the marginality formulations of Stonequist (1937), Lewin spoke of the adolescent as marginal man, a term bearing a direct relationship to Erikson's concept of moratorium. In this view the adolescent is in a frontier state where he is neither child nor adult. Considering children underprivileged, he does not wish to be identified with them. Correspondingly, he is attracted to the privileged adult group who withhold their privileges from him.

Mann (1965), using seventy-five adolescents, endeavored to test Lewin's concept of the adolescent as a marginal man. He administered a set of questionnaires to a group of seventeen- to twenty-one-year-olds. The questionnaires were designed to elicit responses indicating the respondents' perceptions of the characteristics of the age periods of childhood, adolescence (their own), and adulthood. If the adolescent marginality hypothesis held, responses, as represented in Table 3, would clearly indicate differences in the respondents' perceptions of childhood and adulthood, but would not indicate adolescence as a distinct period. That is, the perceived characteristics of adolescence would also be included under childhood or adulthood, leaving adolescence with no traits distinctly its own.

Table 3 *Qualities Attributed by a Sample of Seventy-five Seventeen- to Twenty-one-year-olds to Three Life Stages*

The Typical Child (Aged 7 to 12)		The Typical Person (Aged 13 to 19)		The Typical Adult	
Epithet	Number Choosing Epithet	Epithet	Number Choosing Epithet	Epithet	Number Choosing Epithet
Carefree	61				
Happy	57				
Comical	38				
Contented	38				
Immature	54	Immature	48		
Healthy	52	Healthy	39		
Restless	48	Restless	61		
Self-absorbed	39	Self-absorbed	50		
		Inhibited	50		
		Awkward	49		
		Bewildered	41		
		Thoughtful	39	Thoughtful	45
				Experienced	61
				Self-controlled	59
				Understanding	58
				Knowledgeable	52
				Stable	52
				Confident	47
				Efficient	45
				Poised	41

Source: J. W. Mann, "Adolescent marginality," *Journal of Genetic Psychology* 106 (1965): 221–235, table 1, p. 225. Reprinted by permission of The Journal Press and the author.

Results indicated that in terms of their own perceptions, while indeed some adolescents can be termed marginal, traits representing marginality were not widespread throughout this sample. Thus, marginal personalities could not be clearly linked to the adolescent situation, as represented by the seventeen- to twenty-one-year-olds studied by Mann. An examination of Table 3, which presents Mann's findings, shows that the subjects perceived the three developmental age spans as distinct, with each having characteristics not possessed by the other two. There is some overlap, with childhood and adolescence sharing the characteristics of immaturity, healthiness, restlessness, and self-absorption. Adolescence and adulthood shared the trait of thoughtfulness. The unique characteristics of adolescence were perceived by the adolescents themselves as inhibition, awkwardness, and bewilderedness. The shared traits of thoughtfulness, healthiness, and self-absorption make the adolescent period more palatable, but the fact remains that at least an appreciable number of one group of seventy-five adolescents seemed to visualize their time of life in stress terms. Mann writes: "The child seems pictured as a satisfied being, the adolescent as someone tormented by perplexities. . . . both childhood and adulthood represent generally attractive states. Adolescence, on the other hand, fails to allure. One [questionnaire] shows it to be markedly repellent. Another shows that while there is no marked trend against adolescence, there is no leaning in its favor."

An examination of these data, however, shows no real indication, except on the very borders of childhood or adulthood, that adolescents have any desire either to return to childhood or to advance to adulthood, even though they find their own adolescence to be difficult. In interpreting this study the reader should refer to the percentages listed in Table 3 and understand that there was only a trend in opinion and certainly not unanimity. The small number of subjects and the restricted age range set limits upon the generality of the study. Mann's findings do indicate the possible

need for some modification of Lewinian theory as it applies to adolescents, but this is an area in which further research is required. There are indications in other developmental studies that the perceptions of Mann's group of adolescents may not be entirely unique to their own group.

S-R and Behavior Theory

In marked contrast to the theoretical positions discussed up to this point are the formulations and research strategies of stimulus-response and behavior theorists, who, while not a unified school, have a number of viewpoints in common. Their origins in America go back to the work of J. B. Watson and the primary role of learning in behavior. External reinforcement is seen as basic to learning. Their position is that the experimenter must view an organism's behavior from outside, without subjective bias, and that the best research context is provided by the laboratory, where variables can be controlled. Behavior theorists' research designs are parsimonious, in that they prefer to apply their concepts to relatively simple "chunks" of behavior rather than to more global aspects of behavior. Above all, they feel that a theory must be stated so that it is testable. Thus their explanations of behavior are arrived at through carefully controlled experiments on seemingly simple aspects of behavior.

Behavior theorists take the view that behavior is a universal phenomenon obeying universal laws, with the result that if the conditions are stipulated, behavioral laws may be applied wherever behavior and learning occur. These theorists are not interested in typical stage theories, especially not in those that substitute psychological explanations for operational definitions. While developmental approaches may be used, there is no concentration on age groupings as such. No specific literature on adolescence *qua* adolescence emanates from behaviorist sources, since adolescence is seen as merely a time in the life span when behavior occurs, and such behavior can be expected to follow the universal laws of behavior in a special context. Thus adolescent behavior as it occurs could be "explained" by defining the context and applying the pertinent behavioral laws.

A current movement in the study of development called experimental child psychology is closely related to behavior theory, although experimental child psychology is not identical with behavior theory and many of its exponents would certainly deny that they could be called S-R theorists. Those writing in the field of experimental child psychology have not usually been concerned with the period of adolescence as such. For example, in the *Journal of Experimental Child Psychology,* the term *adolescent* rarely appears, although the words *child* or *children* appear frequently and the word *infant* is occasionally used. As a matter of fact, the vast majority of research in experimental child psychology does not use adolescents at all; it tends to be confined to younger children and infants. A typical experimental child-research study was reported by Tiktin and Hartup (1965) in their investigation of sociometric status and the reinforcing effectiveness of children's peers. This study, using eighty-four elementary-school children as subjects, investigated changes in response rate on a marble-dropping test in relation to the socioeconomic status of the child, who supplied verbal reinforcement during the task. Their findings demonstrate "the enhancing effect of verbal reinforcement dispensed by unpopular peers relative to popular or socially isolated peers on performance in a simple task." A study by Odom and Coon (1966) on the development of hypothesis testing is an example of a study that did use adolescent subjects along with younger children. The subjects in this study were six, eleven, and nineteen years of age.

A departure from strict behavior theory is represented by such social-learning theorists as Bandura (1963), Dollard (1950), Mowrer (1960), and Sears (1965). These men use learning and reinforcement as explanatory principles and use S-R terminology, but they have borrowed freely from anthropology and from those aspects of Freudian theory that they feel are applicable to their approach and susceptible to testing. Sears (1965) describes their position as "a testing of a behavioral theory that was suggested by psychoanalytic observations and was then constructed within the framework of an entirely different theoretical structure." Social-learning theory has endeavored to avoid the use of psychological explanation, a position made explicit by Bandura and Walters (1963) when they state, in writing about punishment and its termination effects, that there is no "need to assume that some inner moral agent or faculty has played a role in regulating behavior."

The question of operational definition versus psychological explanation remains controversial. There are psychologists who would not be classified as behaviorists who nevertheless feel their approach to psychology is scientific and therefore behavioristic. Lewin (1942) wrote:

Many psychologists, particularly those who have followed the theory of conditioned reflex, have confused this requirement for operational definitions with a demand for eliminating psychological descriptions. They insisted on defining "stimuli" superficially in terms of physics. One of the basic characteristics of field theory in psychology, as I see it, is the demand that the field which influences an individual should be described not in "objective" physicalistic terms, but in the way that it exists for that person at that time.

Of course there are many who simply use psychological descriptions and empirical observations without scientific defense, on the assumption that such approaches are the most valid ways of explaining behavior.

In conclusion, it seems fair to say that those who study the development of behavior have to make their own decisions as to the validity of their point of view and permit others to do likewise. We have too much to do in psychology to waste time in controversy. So far, no one seems to have encountered ultimate truth.

Summary

A theory is a statement of the relations believed to prevail in a comprehensive body of facts. A theory should be capable of generating hypothesis, and if the theory is in the realm of science, it should be susceptible to confirmation or refutation. An approach to theory validation involves hypothesizing the relationships of its constructs and then testing that relationship.

Theories have been categorized as preformationistic, predeterministic, or tabula rasa, although a truly comprehensive theory usually contains within itself aspects of several different categories. Adolescent theories usually consist of catalogues of environmentally centered problems of the period, with the individual seen as incidental; of approaches focused upon the individual rather than the environment; or of relatively atheoretical descriptions of the period. A combination of the first two is known as an interactionist approach.

Gesell visualizes development as a gradual patterning process extending over time, with each year bringing forth characteristic behaviors. Calendar time does not measure developmental time; it approximates it. Gesell's system provides for flexibility by allowing for a certain amount of overlap between age groupings and by recognizing that the development of each child accords with a unique pattern of growth characteristic of him as a person. The core of Gesell's theory is his concept of reciprocal interweaving and spiral reincorporation. He sees the developmental pattern as repeating itself again and again as the individual ages. His theory emphasizes the maturational aspects of growth.

Freudian theory presents development in biological stage terms as a sequential unfolding of three vital organ systems in a learning context. To understand Freudian discussions of the adolescent period, it is necessary to understand such basic Freudian concepts as orality, anality, genitality, the phallic stage, the Oedipus complex, latency, the two basic drives of life and death, and the structural formulations of the id, ego, and superego. The genital stage marks the advent of puberty and represents the dissolution of the personality built during latency. It is a time when the child is faced with the need to define and regroup his defenses and modes of adaptation. There is a reawakening of Oedipal and pre-Oedipal strivings. Anna Freud sees adolescence as inevitably and normally a period of tension and conflict. Freudian theory's emphasis upon the individual is one of its most outstanding features.

There have been a number of departures from the Freudian position, notably that of Adler who substituted the power drive for Freud's sex drive. Other departures, classified as neo-Freudian, are those of Fromm, Horney, Kardiner, and Sullivan. Sullivan differed from Freud in his emphasis upon the child's perception of the world and his adaptation to it. Sullivan divided development into six successive stages and treated adolescence in terms of early and late development.

Developmental tasks are tasks that arise at or about a certain period in the developmental sequence. Successful mastery of the task leads to adjustive behavior and success with later tasks. Failure leads to maladjustment, societal disapproval, and difficulty with subsequent tasks. Havighurst has proposed ten developmental tasks. The psychosocial tasks listed by Erikson are forms of developmental tasks, presented sequentially to the individual as he passes through the eight stages of development. Each stage poses a conflict situation that must be resolved if the individual's course of development is to be normal and relatively problem-free. The major issue of adolescence is the quest for ego identity, a matter of considerable difficulty.

Lewin was a field theorist who felt the major problem of adolescence was the fact that the adolescent's life space provides goals his culture does not permit him to attain. As a result, he becomes frustrated and often displays aggressive or withdrawal behavior.

S-R theory is characterized by a parsimonious research design, objectivity, experimental procedures that examine relatively simple aspects of behavior under controlled conditions, a belief in the primacy of learning as the basis of behavior, and a reluctance to use subjective psychological constructs. Experimental child psychology and social learning theory are closely related to S-R theory, but are not identical to it.

References

Adatto, C. P. Ego reintegration observed in analysis of late adolescents. *International Journal of Psychoanalysis* 39 (1958).

Adler, A. *A study of organ inferiority and its psychical compensations.* New York: Nervous and Mental Disease Pub. Co., 1917.

Adler, A. *The practice and theory of individual psychology.* New York: Harcourt, Brace, 1927.

Adler, A. *What life should mean to you.* Boston: Little, Brown, 1931.

Aichorn, A. *Wayward youth.* New York: Viking, 1948.

Alpert, A. The latency period. *American Journal of Orthopsychiatry* 11 (1941): 126–133.

Angelino, H. Developmental tasks and problems of the middle adolescent period. *Education* 76 (1955): 226–231.

Ausubel, D. P. *Theory and problems of child development.* New York: Grune and Stratton, 1958.

Baldwin, A. L. *Theories of child development.* New York: Wiley, 1967.

Bandura, A., and Walters, R. H. *Social learning and personality development.* New York: Holt, Rinehart and Winston, 1963.

Bauer, R., and Snyder, R. Ego identity and motivation: An empirical study of achievement and affiliation in Erikson's theory. *Psychological Reports* 30 (1972): 951–955.

Bernfeld, S. Uber typische Form der mannlichen Pubertat. *Imago* 9 (1923).

Bernfeld, S. *Vom dichterischen Schaffen der Jugend.* Wein: Internationaler Psychoanalytischer Verlag, 1924.

Bernfeld, S. Types of adolescence. *Psychoanalytic Quarterly* 7 (1938).

Block, J. Ego identity, role variability, and adjustment. *Journal of Consulting Psychology* 25 (1961): 392–397.

Blos, P. *On adolescence, a psychoanalytic interpretation.* New York: Free Press, 1961 (paperback edition, 1965).

Bornstein, B. On latency. *Psychoanalytic Study of the Child,* vol. 15. New York: International Universities Press, 1951.

Boyd, R. Analysis of the ego-stage development of school age children. *Journal of Experimental Education* 32 (1964): 249–257.

Bronson, G. W. Identity diffusion in late adolescence. *Journal of Abnormal and Social Psychology* 59 (1959): 414–417.

Centi, P. Personality factors related to college success. *Journal of Educational Research* 55 (1962): 187–188.

Ciaccio, N. V. A test of Erikson's theory of ego epigenesis. *Developmental Psychology* 4 (1971): 306–311.

Deutsch, H. *The psychology of women,* vol. 1. New York: Grune and Stratton, 1944.

Dollard, J., and Miller, N. *Personality and psychotherapy.* New York: McGraw-Hill, 1950.

Eisenstadt, S. N. Archetypal patterns of youth. *Daedalus* 91 (1962): 28–46.

English, H. B., and English, A. C. *A comprehensive dictionary of psychological and psychoanalytical terms.* London: Longmans, 1958.

Erikson, E. H. Growth and crisis of the healthy personality. *Psychological Issues* 1 (1959): 50–100.

Erikson, E. H. *Childhood and society.* 2nd ed. New York: Norton, 1963.

Erikson, E. H. *Insight and responsibility.* New York: Norton, 1964.

Erikson, E. H. *Identity: youth and crisis.* London: Faber and Faber, 1968.

Fisher, M. B. Trends in college students' grades. *Personnel and Guidance Journal* 39 (1960–1961): 491–496.

Fraiberg, S. Some considerations in the introduction of therapy in puberty. *The Psychoanalytic Study of the Child* X. New York: International Universities Press, 1955.

Freud, A. *Psycho-analytic treatment of children.* London: Imago, 1927.

Freud, A. *The ego and the mechanisms of defense.* New York: International Universities Press, 1946.

Freud, A. Adolescence. *Psychoanalytic Study of the Child* 13 (1958) : 255–278.

Freud, A. Adolescence. In Weinreb, J., ed., *Recent developments in psychoanalytic child therapy,* pp. 1–24. New York: International Universities Press, 1960.

Freud, A. *Normality and pathology in childhood.* New York: International Universities Press, 1965.

Freud, S. *Three essays in the theory of sexuality* (1905). Standard edition of the complete psychological works of Sigmund Freud, vol. 7. London: Hogarth Press, 1953.

Fromm, E. *The sane society.* New York: Holt, Rinehart and Winston, 1955.

Fromm, E. *The art of loving,* New York: Harper & Row, 1956.

Fromm, E. *The heart of man: Its genius for good and evil.* New York: Harper & Row, 1964.

Gesell, A. Reciprocal interweaving in neuromotor development: A principle of development evidenced in the patterning of infant behavior. *Journal of Comparative Neurology* 70 (1939): 161–180.

Gesell, A. *The embryology of behavior.* New York: Harper, 1945.

Gesell, A.; Halverson, H. M.; Thompson, H.; et al. *The first five years of life.* New York: Harper, 1940.

Gesell, A., and Ilg, F. *The child from five to ten.* New York: Harper, 1946.

Gesell, A.; Ilg, F. L.; and Ames, L. B. *Youth: The years from ten to sixteen.* New York: Harper, 1956.

Harley, M. Some observations on the relationship between genitality and structural development at adolescence. *Journal of American Psychoanalytic Association* 9 (1961): 434–460.

Havighurst, R. J. *Human development and education.* London: Longmans, 1953.

Havighurst, R. J. Research on the developmental task concept. *School Review* 64 (1956): 214–223.

Hoffer, W. Diaries of adolescent schizophrenics. *The Psychoanalytic Study of the Child* II. New York: International Universities Press, 1946.

Horney, K. *New Ways in psychoanalysis.* New York: Norton, 1939.

Horney, K. *Neurosis and human growth.* New York: Norton, 1950.

Howard, L. P. Identity conflicts in adolescent girls. *Smith College Studies in Social Work* 31 (1960): 1–21.

Irvin, F. S. The relationship between manifest anxiety and measures of aptitude, achievement, and interest. *Educational and Psychological Measurement* 29 (1969): 957–961.

Jacobson, E. *The self and the object world.* New York: International Universities Press, 1964.

Jones, E. (1922) Some problems of adolescence. 5th ed. *Papers on psychoanalysis.* London: Baillière, Tindall & Cox, 1948.

Josselyn, I. M. The capacity to love: A possible reformulation. *Journal of the American Academy of Child Psychiatry* 10 (1971): 6–22.

Kardiner, A. *The individual and his society.* New York: Columbia University Press, 1939.

Kardiner, A. *The psychological frontiers of society.* New York: Columbia University Press, 1945.

Kastenbaum, R. The direction of time perspective. I: The influence of affective set. *Journal of General Psychology* 73 (1965): 189–201.

Koffka, K. *Principles of gestalt psychology.* New York: Harcourt, Brace, 1935.

Lewin, K. *A dynamic theory of personality.* New York: McGraw-Hill, 1935.

Lewin, K. Field theory and experiment in social psychology: Concepts and methods. *American Journal of Sociology* 44 (1939): 868–897.

Lewin, K. Field theory and learning. In McConnel, T. R., ed., *The psychology of learning. 41st Yearbook,* pt. II, Nat. Soc. Stud. Educat. Chicago: N.S.S.E., 1942.

Lewin, K. Behavior and development as a function of the total situation. In Carmichael, L., ed., *Manual of child psychology.* New York: Wiley, 1954.

Mann, J. W. Adolescent marginality. *Journal of Genetic Psychology* 106 (1965): 221–235.

Marcia, J. E. Development and validation of ego identity status. *Journal of Personality and Social Psychology* 3 (1966): 551–558.

Mowrer, O. H. *Learning theory and behavior.* New York: Wiley, 1960.

Nikelly, A. G. Alfred Adler's contribution to modern education and its goals. *Individual Psychologist* 8 (1971): 1–6.

Noshpitz, J. D. Opening phase in the psychotherapy of adolescents with character disorders. *Bulletin Menninger Clinic* 21 (1957).

Odom, R. D., and Coon, R. C., The development of hypothesis testing. *Journal of Experimental*

Child Psychology 4 (1966) : 285–291.

Podd, M. H. Ego identity status and morality: The relationship between two developmental constructs. *Developmental Psychology* 6 (1972) : 497–507.

Rasmussen, J. E. The relationship of ego identity to psychosocial effectiveness. *Psychological Reports* 15 (1964) : 815–825.

Root, N. N. A neurosis in adolescence. *Psychoanalytic Study of the Child* 12 (1957) : 320–334.

Rosenblatt, B. Some contributions of the psychoanalytic concept of development to personality research. *Monographs of the Society for Research in Child Development* 31 (5) (1966) : 18–35.

Rubins, J. L. The problem of the acute identity crisis in adolescence. *American Journal of Psychoanalysis* 28 (1968) : 37–47.

Santrock, J. W. Influence of onset and type of paternal absence on the first four Eriksonian developmental crises. *Developmental Psychology* 3 (1970) : 273–274.

Sears, R. R., Rau, L., and Alpert, R. *Identification and child rearing.* Stanford: Stanford University Press, 1965.

Schoeppe, A., and Havighurst, R. J. A validation of development and adjustment hypotheses of adolescence. *Journal of Educational Psychology* 43 (1953) : 339–353.

Schoeppe, A.; Haggard, E. A.; and Havighurst, R. J. Some factors affecting sixteen-year-olds' success in five developmental tasks. *Journal of Abnormal Social Psychology* 48 (1953) : 42–52.

Spiegel, L. A. A review of contributions to a psychoanalytic theory of adolescence. *The Psycho-analytic Study of the Child* VI. New York: International Universities Press, 1951.

Spiegel, L. A. Disorder and consolidation in adolescence. *Journal of American Psychoanalytic Association* 9 (1961) : 406–417.

Stonequist, E. V. *The marginal man.* New York: Scribner, 1937.

Sullivan, H. S. *Conceptions of modern psychiatry.* Washington: William Alanson White Foundation, 1947. (Paperback edition, Norton, 1953.)

Sullivan, H. S. *The interpersonal theory of psychiatry* (Edited by Perry, H. S., and Gawel, M. L., from Sullivan's 1949 lectures.) New York: Norton, 1953.

Super, D. E., et al. *Vocational development: A framework for research.* New York: Bureau of Publications, Teachers College, Columbia University, 1957.

Super, D. E., et al. *Career Development: Self-concept theory.* CEEB Research Monograph, no. 4. New York: CEEB, 1963.

Thornberg, H. Adolescence: A re-interpretation. *Adolescence* 5 (1970) : 463–484.

Tiktin, S., and Hartup, W. W. Sociometric status and the reinforcing effectiveness of children's peers. *Journal of Experimental Psychology* 2 (1965) : 306–315.

Werner, H. The concept of development from a comparative and organismic point of view. In Harris, D. B., ed., *Concept of development*, Minneapolis: University of Minnesota Press, 1957.

Zaccaria, J. S. Developmental tasks: Implications for the goals of guidance. *Personnel Guidance Journal* 44 (1965) : 372–375.

Suggested Readings

Adatto, C. P. On the metamorphosis from adolescence into adulthood. *Journal of the American Psychoanalytic Association* 14 (1966) : 485–509.

Adler, A. *What life should mean to you.* New York: Capricorn Books, 1932.

Baruch, G. K. Anne Frank on adolescence. *Adolescence* 3 (1968–1969) : 425–434.

Blos, P. *The young adolescent: Clinical studies.* New York: Free Press, 1970.

Blos, P. The child analyst looks at the young adolescent. *Daedalus* 100 (1971) : 961–978.

Boyd, R. D., and Koskela, R. N. A test of Erikson's theory of ego-stage development by means of a self-report instrument. *Journal of Experimental Education* 38 (1970) : 1–14.

Brodsky, P. Problems of adolescence: An Adlerian view. *Adolescence* 3 (1968) : 9–22.

Capps, W. H. Ideology, ego, and ethos: A comment on Erikson. *Humanitas* 5 (1970) : 255–263.

Duncan, A. D. Self-application of behavior-modification techniques by teen-agers. *Adolescence* 4 (1969) : 541–556.

Evans, R. I. *Dialogue with Erich Fromm.* New York: Harper & Row, 1966.

Friend, M. R. "Youth unrest": Reflections of a

psychoanalyst. *Journal of the American Academy of Child Psychiatry* 9 (1970) : 224–232.

Grace, H. A., and Lewellyn, L. W. The no-man's land of youth. *Journal of Educational Sociology* 33 (1959) : 135–140.

Jacobson, E. Adolescent moods and the remodeling of psychic structures in adolescence. *Psychoanalytic Study of the Child* 16 (1961) : 164–183.

Koury, M. A. Crisis: Identity. *Adolescence* 6 (1971) : 229–234.

Langs, R. J. Manifest dreams in adolescents: A controlled pilot study. *Journal of Nervous and Mental Disease* 145 (1967) : 43–52.

Muus, R. E. *Theories of adolescence.* New York: Random House, 1962.

Settlage, C. F. Cultural values and the superego in late adolescence. *Psychoanalytic Study of the Child* 27 (1973) : 74–92.

Wolf, E. S.; Gedo, J. E.; and Terman, D. M. On the adolescent process as a transformation of the self. *Journal of Youth and Adolescence* 1 (1972) : 257–272.

Chapter Four

Personality Development

It is a fascinating business to watch a child develop individuality—an individuality setting him apart from others and giving him uniqueness. As year succeeds year, the core of the individuality seems to become stronger, and if one has learned to know the child as a person, his behavior becomes both more predictable and more understandable. It is this core of individuality that is known as personality.

As a term, personality is derived from the Latin word *persona* used in the days of ancient Rome to designate a theatrical mask. From this stems the concept of the actor, or person, as a socially perceived entity. By extension, although still in theater terms, the roles he assumes on stage (*dramatis personae*) are included in this concept. Thus, personality has to do with the person and the part he is taking in the socialized drama of life. It may seem a long leap from this concept to the specific example of teenage Mary (the player) as a high-school student (the role) entering her English class (the stage). Yet Mary over her lifetime will assume many roles in many different situations. And the factor binding them together, giving them continuity and to some extent commonality, is Mary's habitual manner of behavior. It is that manner of behavior, extending across situations and roles, that is called individuality and, hence, personality.

Definition of Personality

In defining personality, psychologists, referring to the uniqueness of the individual, speak of dispositions, temperament, habitual modes of response, and defining tendencies. Some conceive of personality in holistic or integrative terms, whereas others prefer to deal with it in terms of a set of more or less independent components. Some like to stress the adaptive aspects. But underlying most definitions are the twin concepts of organization and direction. Allport (1955) defined personality as "the dynamic organization within the individual of those psychological systems that determine his unique adjustment to his environment." This writer defines personality as the organization or structure of personal meanings and habits that impart directionality to behavior. Personality, in this sense, represents an individual's personal action system. However, personality is more than a purely intra-individual matter of structure and organization. An analysis of the personality of any individual should stress both his differences and similarities in relation to other persons. It should also indicate the extent to which he fits the socialized pattern of his culture.

Description of Personality

In reality, personality is so complex a concept with so many possibilities for description and with so many implications for behavior that we are naturally faced with a multiplicity of ways of describing it. The form and extent of the description become particularly crucial when an instrument or a technique has to be devised to provide a measure of personality. In general, as may be seen from the studies that follow, in describing personality one or more personal traits, such as extroversion, are selected as descriptive. Some investigators will select few such traits for their personality description, while others will present a whole array. Varying claims will be made for the inclusiveness of the description as encompassing all of the domain of personality.

A number of personality studies are performed by persons unconcerned with the overall picture of personality, preferring to concentrate on some single aspect of the whole. The continuing problem in personality description is that of the interaction of traits. An extrovert with a low profile of anxiety is a very different person from an extrovert with a high level of anxiety. Further, personality description can be no better than both the validity and the reliability of the means of gathering personality-trait and trait-interaction information. Different data-gathering techniques and measures are not all equally valid.

In considering personality descriptions, it must also be recognized that possession of a personality trait is always a matter of degree, since amounts of the trait are distributed along a continuum. In the citation of many personality traits, it is customary to connect them with their polar opposite as, for example, extroversion-introversion. The question then becomes: Where on the continuum between the poles of maximum extroversion and of maximum introversion does the individual fall?

In attempting to interpret a continuum ranging from a "good" to a "bad" attribute or from a "low" to a "high," one should remember, as Kagan and Moss (1962) point out, the double-ended nature of the variables dealt with. Because the continuum is double-ended, statements of position can be made with either end of the continuum as a point of reference, thus changing the flavor of an interpretation that might be made. Bronson (1966), discussing this point, writes: "In the process of evaluating my own results, I was often struck by

how frequently a feeling of intuitive obviousness about a relation focusing on the deviant or pathognomic end of the continuum would become questioned when the relation was rephrased in its opposite, more 'healthy' term."

But the matter is not really quite so simple. In terms of behavior the person who fixes the point of reference is the subject himself, not the research observer. The observer simply records what he believes he sees and makes his interpretation. But where is the subject focusing? It is reasonable to suppose that in interpreting his own behavior, feelings, and attitudes an individual will focus at different times at different ends of the continuum, sometimes interpreting himself negatively, sometimes positively. Most individuals, however, will display a tendency to focus more often at one end of the continuum than at the other. Ideally, the observer's rating should at least reflect this self-interpretive tendency.

Personality Classification

Caution should be observed in accepting classifications or categorizations purporting to describe the behavior-direction structure of an individual or a group. This becomes particularly true when such a complex construct as personality is applied to the crucial stage of adolescence, characterized as it is by such a range of variables acting as limiting or conditioning factors. Science's problem is to make order out of chaos and to use the evolved order as a means of predicting events with a high order of efficiency. A most useful approach to order is the formulation of categories under which events may be classified and ordered. The difficulty is that categorization may be used in such a manner that it loses touch with reality by imposing a concrete rigidity upon events that ignores the essential interrelatedness of phenomena. This tendency is often encountered in psychology, the very complexity of the phenomena with which psychologists deal leading to an insecurity that is manifested by a need for categorization. Actually, we might take the stand that behavior is composed of a large and undetermined number of dimensions and that each of these dimensions is potentially present in any behaving organism. It is a case of the extent to which each of the dimensions is operative in any given person. For instance, the fact that an adolescent may be classified as high in dominance does not mean that he does not possess some degree of submission, and while there are larger and more molar categories than dominance-submission, the point holds for each of these as well. A complication is that behavior is situational, and while there is usually a personal consistency or pattern across situations, we must recognize the fluctuation of categorical positions within a person as he encounters different situations, and as, of course, his behavior finds reconstruction of experience through therapy, learning, and various other environmental events. We may even observe fluctuation of behavior in situations that to the observer appear identical.[1]

Two other things must be considered in attempting to classify a person or make a diagnosis, and eventually to determine what intervention is most likely to lead to acceptable reconstruction. First is the implementation behavior, the means the individual uses to operate the various dimensions he possesses. Here, in part, we could use the term *coping behavior*. Second is the picture of interrelationships that exist among the various dimensions in the behavior of *that particular person*. The sequence is: (1) to find the behavioral dimensions that appear most significant in the life of any given person; (2) to determine the degree to which they are present; (3) to determine how the individual implements his dimensions; (4) to ascertain under what conditions and situations these implementations occur; (5) and finally (as a measure of the

individual's success) to determine to what extent his implementations test reality. Ultimately some interrelationship picture of the behavioral relationship of the dimensions must be formulated.

Personality Measurement

When a personality measurement is to be performed, it is necessary to do so in terms of some defined criterion of personality. Information to meet the criterion is ordinarily gathered by techniques of varying precision and comprehension. Such techniques include anecdotal records, interviews, personal documents of the subjects, observation, performance on a simulated task, or, more usually, performance on a standard personality questionnaire. Since such measures and techniques are not of equal reliability and validity, and since the meanings of terms may vary, it is essential, in interpreting a personality study, to be familiar with both the nomenclature and the instrument or technique used. For example, Peterson (1965) notes that personality factors derived from ratings of traits that have been defined verbally might well have more to do with the perception and biases of the raters than with the actual behavior of those observed. He mentions as an illustration of his point that teacher ratings of students tend to reflect matters other than the traits being rated and can't substitute for objective behavior observations and standard tests.

Many studies of adolescent personality gather data essentially clinical or medical in nature, the subjects often coming from deviate samples of adolescents. For example, an essentially clinical instrument such as the Minnesota Multiphasic Personality Inventory yields a number of scores primarily of psychiatric interest. As Berdie (1968) states, the information derived from the MMPI is sometimes difficult to interpret for those working with typical adolescents. Even when normal subjects and nonclinical instruments are used, sampling procedures may be faulty. The

[1]The position may be taken that no two situations ever can be identical and that inconsistent or unpredicted behavior merely reflects the inconsistency of the situation. This line of reasoning would assume that, given identical situations and an individual to whom nothing had happened between situations, we could expect identical behavior.

sample may be inadequate in size, or it may be confined to a special category, such as female or middle-class children, with a resulting loss in generalizability.

Age and Factor Stability

A question often asked is whether or not the same personality factors or traits are present at all ages. That is, do some traits appear in adolescence while others disappear?[2] A number of investigations of the development of personality from a structural position have compared personality structure at different ages and generally have reported that the same personality factors are present at all ages tested. Among these investigations were those of Cattell and Gruen (1953), Cattell (1957), Cattell and Coan (1957a), Peterson (1965), and Eysenck, Easting, and Eysenck (1970), all of whom propose lists of varying numbers of factors. For example, the 16-Personality Factor Questionnaire of Cattell contains, as its name implies, sixteen different personality factors. Different investigators, while they have accepted the hypothesis that the same personality factors are present at all ages, at least after infancy, have nevertheless disagreed as to the number of factors that could be clearly and logically defended. A number of lists of various lengths have been proposed, although there is usually considerable overlap. The results of factor analysis depend heavily upon the perception of the factor analyst. There has been some feeling that several factors on one investigator's list are more properly aspects of one factor on another investigator's list.

In factor analysis, the large question has to do with the number of factors a factor analyst is willing to extract, that is, the number of factors rotated. Past a certain point there is not only the problem of descriptive efficiency but also the possibility of dealing with chance phenomena. The factor analyst has to decide when his additional factors are becoming meaningless and when he has accounted for 100 percent of the communality.[3] In one study of factor loadings reported in several different published studies, Peterson (1960) comes to the conclusion that the correlation coefficients reported are of such a magnitude that the previous authors' claims of identity cannot be substantiated. The reader should bear this possibility in mind in considering the descriptions of the studies by Sealy and Cattell (1966), Schaie (1966), and Black (1965) which follow.

Techniques for Seeking Continuity

For looking for continuity over time of personality traits and conditions, there are two techniques in common use. One, possible only with longitudinal data, involves the computation of correlations between measures taken at a specified number of different times over the developmental span included in the study. Such correlations provide measures of the chronological age relationships of the traits or conditions being studied. The second, used with cross-sectional data,[4] in which a developmental sequence is established with individuals living simultaneously at a point in time, involves the

[2]This question has nothing to do with the possibility of an individual at different ages displaying more or less of the trait. The question has to do with the possibility of either the absolute disappearance of an old trait during adolescence or of the appearance of any degree of a completely new trait.

[3]Useful general references for those wishing to gain a working knowledge of factor analysis include Thomson (1939), Thurstone (1947), Cattell (1952), and Fruchter (1954).

[4]Both cross-sectional and longitudinal studies examine changes over time by comparing the situation obtaining where a given variable is concerned at each age over a sequence of ages, as, for example, extroversion at ages twelve, fourteen, sixteen, and eighteen. The longitudinal approach does so by examining the same individuals as they progress through each of the ages included in the study. Thus, in the foregoing example, the same child is examined at twelve, again at fourteen, at sixteen, and at eighteen. The cross-sectional study, to gain its picture of change over time, examines different persons at each of the ages and does so at the same point in time. In comparison to the cross-sectional, the longitudinal study takes as long as the time span included in the study and suffers the possible loss of subjects as time passes.

compilation of age-related trend lines. The former approach is exemplified by the Fels Institute longitudinal studies described in part by Kagan and Moss (1962), and the latter by the research conducted at the University of Illinois by Cattell and his associates and reported in part in Cattell and Coan (1957b), Coan and Cattell (1958), Cattell, Coan, and Beloff (1959), and Sealy and Cattell (1966).

Let us now, in cross-sectional studies by Sealy and Cattell (1966), Schaie (1966), and Black (1965) examine some generalizations about adolescent personality to see to what extent they may be useful in defining and understanding adolescence.

Personality Structure in Adolescence

Sealy and Cattell (1966) administered the High School Personality Questionnaire and the 16-Personality Factor Questionnaire to 1,995 male and 2,409 female subjects ranging in age from eleven to twenty-three, with the below eighteen-year-olds being largely tested by the HSPQ and the above seventeen-year-olds by the 16-PF. The sample was selected from high school and college students, was diverse in socioeconomic background and was "reasonably well scattered across the United States." The HSPQ and 16-PF questionnaires measure twelve personality traits in common. The traits used for analysis in the Sealy and Cattell study, together with a description of each trait, are presented in Table 4.

The investigators performed trend analyses for each factor by age and sex to find the nature and degree of changes taking place from age eleven to age twenty-three. Significant linear regressions of score on age were reported for seven factors, and consistent slight but not significant trends were found on four others. This study demonstrates that as measured by the instruments and the factors used, major aspects of personality do change over the adolescent period, and the changes show important sex differences. Whatever adolescence may be,

it is not quite the same for a boy as it is for a girl. An examination of the sex differences shown in Table 4 leads to the conclusion that cultural dictates and female role expectations are responsible for many of the sex differences found. Certainly her role as a female becomes increasingly central in a girl's life as she proceeds through adolescence. The sharp rise in Premsia and the decline in Protension are examples in point (see Table 4). Writing on this topic, Sealy and Cattell speculate that the increasing eleven-seventeen dominance trend in women "may be connected with the experience of increasing social and sexual desirability over this period." It is hardly possible that a newly nubile girl can fail to notice that she is increasingly becoming a subject of attention to members of the opposite sex. Of course, it must be admitted that the physical composition of some girls makes them greater targets of attention than others.

A further examination of Table 4 leads to a concept of adolescence as a time of increasing sociability, of increasing self-sufficiency, of dominance, and, for the majority, of generally good adjustment. Males, at least, are becoming more tough-minded, and both sexes are increasingly aware of the demands of reality. There is a gradual decrease in worry and anxiety.

Adolescence, according to the Sealy and Cattell study, is a time of great energy and activity unlikely to be sustained far into adulthood. Stress seems to lessen as the individual grows older. It is possible, from the data of this study, to hypothesize a quite stressful early adolescence followed by an increasingly less stressful middle adolescence. Late adolescence, at least in the case of college youth, continues the trend toward less stress. Many college males appear to be increasingly less self-centered. However, it should be noted that the discussion is about trends. Movement toward less stress from a base of high stress does not necessarily mean that the individual is no longer under stress conditions. The mere fact of increasing movement toward good adjustment is a relative statement that should

Table 4 *Adolescent Personality Trends, Eleven to Twenty-three*

Cattell Source Trait	Trait Description	Findings in Sealy and Cattell (1966)
A. Affectothymia (Cyclothymia vs. Schizothymia)	The clinically known range of temperament differences. Cyclothymia is the positively loaded pole. Cheerful and adaptable as compared to depressed and rigid.	From 11 through 17 there is an increase in sociability and a reduction in aloofness. College-bound males (18+) are especially high in this factor, but during their college years there is a shift toward objectivity, scepticism, and aloofness. In contrast, college girls decline only very slightly in Cyclothymia.
B. Intelligence	As ordinarily defined. See Chapter 7.	Steep rise from 11 through 15. See chapter on intelligence for discussion of this topic.
C. Ego Strength (Ego Strength vs. General Emotionality)	Ability to maintain one's ego; in this sense ability to maintain one's adjustment in general.	Tangent plots are positive but increases are not significant for either sex.
D. Phlegmatic-Excitable	Excitability marks a picture of an impulsive, hyperactive, restless person—immaturity and "cleverness."	From 11 through 17 both sexes become more self-sufficient, deliberate, placid, and self-effacing as they become markedly less excitable and insecure.
E. Dominance (Dominance vs. Submissiveness)	Ascendance.	From 11 through 17 both sexes show increasing dominance although significantly so only for females. From 18 to 23 men continue the increased dominance trend, with women showing a slight though not significant trend toward submissiveness. Women's dominance scores are lower than men's over the entire 11–23 period.
F. Surgency (Surgency vs. Desurgency)	Surgency behaviors are cheerful, lively, responsive, sociable, trustful (*not* extroversion). Desurgency connotes depression and anxiety.	Surgency increases from 11 to 17, but flattens out at 17 to 19 and then begins to decline.
G. Superego (Superego Strength)	Implementation of conscious and unconscious motivations deriving from parental and social standards and demands.	No significant or consistent trend.
H. Parmia (Parmia vs. Threctia)	Parmia is characterized by bold equanimity and insusceptibility to threat. Threctia at the negative pole characterized by withdrawn, correct, hostile behavior arising from reactivity to threat.	Slight but nonsignificant rise except for college men. There is some evidence of a slight decline in shyness (Threctia: threat, susceptibility) during adolescence.
I. Premsia (Premsia vs. Harria)	Harria, a trait characterized by toughness and realism and in opposition to Premsia, characterized by protected sensitive emotionality.	Scores for males are considerably lower than those for females. In early adolescence, males show definite increases as they become more tough-minded, realistic, and self-reliant. A sharp rise at 15 to 18 for females. This is an area in which males and females pull far apart during adolescence.

Table 4 *Adolescent Personality Trends, Eleven to Twenty-three (cont.)*

Cattell Source Trait	Trait Description	Findings in Sealy and Cattell (1966)
J. Coasthenia (Coasthenia vs. Zeppia)	Coasthenia, a trait showing compulsive asthenic features, at one pole. At the other, Zeppia, characterized by energy, decisiveness, a ready group participation.	From 11 to 17 females decline slightly in Coasthenia as they become less idiosyncratic and more group active. Male decline is slower as they remain more idiosyncratic.
L. Protension (Protension vs. Inner Relaxation)	Opposite of calm and placid, lack of self-confidence, poor memory, aspects of paranoid trend.	There is a nonsignificant decline over adolescence for males, but for females the decline is both regular and significant.
M. Autia (Autia vs. Praxernia)	Praxernia is a trait characterized by practical concern. At the opposite pole, Autia is characterized by "Bohemian unconcern."	From 11 to 17 scores increase nonsignificantly for both sexes, representing a tendency to become more conventional, realistic, and practical. In college men, scores continue to increase nonsignificantly, but women's decline at a significant rate.
N. Shrewdness (Shrewdness vs. Naivety)	Either (a) temperamental quickness, alert, but leading readily to exhaustion, or (b) assertive, self-conscious, self-sentiment with social impatience and state of stress.	The linearity is not significant but there is a slight tendency to increase from 11 to 15 and to increase even more from 15 to 23.
O. Guilt Proneness (Guilt Proneness vs. Confidence)	Worrying, depressed, and readily guilt-ridden. Elements of free-floating anxiety.	The tendency is to decrease, with girls tending to score higher than boys. Boys become significantly less worrying, depressed, and readily guilt-prone throughout adolescence.
Q. Radicalism (Radicalism vs. Conservatism)	Radical vs. conservative sentiments.	Girls are more conservative than boys and show no trend toward radicalism at 11 to 17, but their radicalism scores increase throughout college. Boys' scores also increase during college. College youth show an increase in radicalism; noncollege youth a decline.
Q_2. Self-sufficiency	Common definition applicable.	Girls show a significant decline at 11 to 16, while boys show a slight decline. Following that period, increases are significant for both sexes.
Q_3. Self-sentiment	Extent to which a person is able to achieve the self-sentiment society approves. Considerate, relaxed when necessary, emotions under control, not distracted easily, not self-centered, etc. Will control vs. slothful undependability.	Irregular changes except for a significant increase in males over the latter part of adolescence. In college, both sexes register a nonsignificant trend of increase.
Q_4. Ergic Tension	Innate reactivity toward a goal although stimuli and means are learned.	Rise for both in early adolescence (11–15) with the rise being sustained for a shorter period with boys. A significant fall at 18 to 23 for noncollege males and for college males and females.

Source: Compiled from data in A. P. Sealy and R. B. Cattell, "Adolescent personality trends in primary factors measured on the 16-PF and the HSPQ questionnaires through ages 11 to 23," *British Journal of Social and Clinical Psychology* 5 (1966): 172–184.

not be taken to mean that good adjustment has been attained.

The value of Sealy and Cattell's study, excellent as it is, would have been increased if post-eighteen noncollege youth could have been included in numbers approximately equal to those of college youth. That they were not points up a continuing problem in developmental research. Subjects must obviously be available if they are to be tested, and out-of-school youth, whether dropouts or high-school graduates, do not form a population to be readily found in one place, as in school, and in conditions where they are likely to respond to requests to answer questionnaires. Sealy and Cattell have analyzed their data by age and sex, but there are other variables that would be enlightening, such as socioeconomic status, type of community of residence, and race. Unfortunately, the addition of each new variable in a study adds tremendously to the work involved and usually requires the addition of many more subjects, so that sufficient numbers to warrant analysis will be available for each variable. Each researcher has to make a decision as to how far his resources of time and money will permit him to go. No one, except possibly in certain molecular types of carefully controlled laboratory research, is likely to include all possible variables in one study, if, indeed, he knew what all the potential possibilities actually were. However, it should be realized that behind any study there is a background of years of research and training in the discipline it represents. Investigators sometimes do not include certain variables because other studies reported in the literature have demonstrated again and again that either it is not worthwhile to do so or that the answer as to their effect is already well known.

Schaie (1966) also studied the year-by-year course of personality development but used as subjects children aged six through eighteen. He randomly selected twenty-five boys and twenty-five girls in each grade from kindergarten through grade 12 in Lincoln, Nebraska, and had their teachers rate each one on a three-point trait-rating scale, consisting of forty-two bipolar trait descriptions. The trait descriptions were adapted from those given by Cattell (1957), and final scores were cited in terms of fifteen factors proposed by Cattell (Cattell's factors A through O as listed in Table 4). Thirty-four of the traits produced significant age differences, but only for the traits meditative-unquestioning and stable-unstable was the interaction between sex and age significant. All of the fifteen factors, except Autia versus Praxernia (Factor M in Table 4), show specific age or sex differences. Trend lines for ages six through eighteen on the personality factors were nonmonotonic,[5] and the maturational gradients coincided in shape but differed in level. Depending upon the sex of the subject, peaks as well as low points for the different factors occur at different ages. As examples, Figure 1 presents trend lines over age for the factors of Cyclothymia versus Schizothymia (Factor A), Dominance versus Submissiveness (Factor E), and Premsia versus Harria (Factor I).

An examination of the Cyclothymia-Schizothymia factor in Figure 1 finds females as compared to males, except at age fourteen, depicted as more outgoing and adaptive to their environments. A dip toward the more anxious and inflexible Schizothymia end of the pole may be seen for both sexes at age ten and for girls again at age fourteen. Following age seventeen, there is a marked upturn toward Cyclothymia for both sexes, an event continuing a trend established by females following their age fourteen dip, but reversing a downward trend for boys that had its inception at age fourteen. The trend line for this factor may indicate the existence of a prepubertal crisis at age ten for both sexes with girls recovering more rapidly, only to face a further crisis at age fourteen that may have some association with pubertal processes. While the trend line does not extend beyond age eighteen, and its nonmonotonic nature does not permit any firm extrapolation, there is some

[5]That is, the trend lines oscillated across the age range and did not present a picture of steadily increasing or decreasing trends.

Figure 1 *Trend Lines over Age for Three Personality Factors*

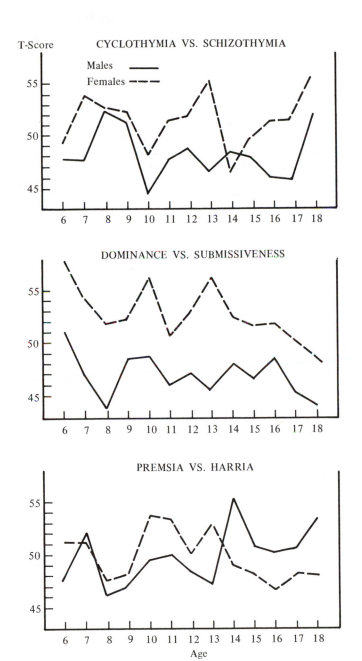

Source: Adapted from K. W. Schaie, "Year by year changes in personality from six to eighteen years," *Multivariate Behavioral Research* 1 (1966): 293–305, figs. 1–3. Reprinted by permission of the author and the editors of *Multivariate Behavioral Research*.

indication of an approach toward a calmer, better-adjusted period in late adolescence. Thus Schaie's finding is in general agreement with Sealy and Cattell's report that a more stressful early period is replaced in middle and late adolescence by one that is less stressful.

The Dominance vs. Submissiveness trend line shown in Figure 1 clearly differentiates between males and females. It depicts a gradual downward trend toward submissiveness, possibly the result of socialization and reality testing. The interesting peaking for girls at ages ten and thirteen has no satisfactory explanation for this writer in view of the dip at eleven, but the reader might wish to compare the Cyclothymia peak at thirteen for girls with the Dominance peak at the same age. The years following thirteen seem to usher in for girls some specific directional changes in personality. Their higher Dominance rating over the entire length of the trend line is not in accord with the stereotype of the more dominant male. There well may be, as Schaie suggests for all of the factors, some teacher bias in systematically viewing girls in terms of their school performance. Girls have long been regarded as generally "better citizens" in school. Somewhat different ratings might have been secured with a set of judges from a pool of playground supervisors, parents, or "interested" adults. Behavior does have to occur in a context and, within limits, will vary from context to context.

The Premsia vs. Harria trend line in Figure 1 does not show as clear an overall picture of sex differences as do the other two graphs. Following age thirteen, the trend for girls is in the direction of tender-mindedness, while boys move somewhat less clearly in the tough-mindedness[6] direction. Previous to age thirteen, girls as compared to boys appear to be more tough-minded. The sex reversal following

age thirteen may well represent culturally expected sex-role acceptance on the part of both sexes. Space does not permit further trend-line analysis of the remaining thirteen trait factors, but the three illustrations should serve to present the overall developmental picture in personality traits during adolescence. Many factors show significant year-by-year changes, the changes occurring within major periods of development as well as within subperiods. Lumping several years together or not separating the sexes in considering developmental trends may obscure the actual state of affairs. Discussing this point, Schaie (1966) writes: "The conclusion may be drawn that the concept of periods in development has had too great breadth. To quote a mean value for the whole five or six years of middle childhood with respect to emotional maturity would clearly mask two very sharp cycles of development with low points at ages six, ten, and thirteen."

A further study of personality development covering the period between the ninth and thirteenth grades was performed by Berdie (1968). As compared to the studies of Sealy and Cattell and Schaie, Berdie's study utilized the longitudinal rather than the cross-sectional method, used a personality classification system that was not based on the Cattell factors, and secured subjects by means of different selection procedures.

Berdie's sample was comprised of 148 men and 111 women entering the University of Minnesota as freshmen who, as high-school students, had taken the Minnesota Counseling Inventory (MCI) four years earlier. Forty-three different Minnesota high schools were represented in the study. Upon their entrance at the University of Minnesota the MCI was again administered to these subjects. Thus, the approximate age range dealt with was fourteen through eighteen, affording an opportu-

---

[6]The terms *tough-minded* and *tender-minded* were proposed by William James to contrast two fundamental types of persons. James described the tough-minded as materialistic, empiricist, skeptical, pluralistic, and fatalistic. The tender-minded were seen as idealistic, optimistic, monistic, dogmatic, rationalistic, and intellectualistic. Modern-day psychology sees these two categories as describing styles

of behavior and thinking rather than as descriptions of types of persons. In other words the subsumed behaviors do not constitute coherent behavior clusters of a unitary personal-trait nature.

Table 5   *Results of Administration of Minnesota Counseling Inventory to Students Tested in Grade 9 and Later in Grade 13*

Scale*	Men (N = 148)					Women (N = 111)				
	Grade 9		Grade 13			Grade 9		Grade 13		
	Mn	SD	Mn	SD	r	Mn	SD	Mn	SD	r
Validity. Degree of defensiveness.	3.63	2.31	3.41	2.36	.62	3.77	2.27	3.66	2.01	.34
Family Relations. Adjustment to family.	7.12	5.28	7.56	5.84	.50	8.50	6.73	8.46	6.08	.59
Social Relations. Nature of relations with others.	22.12	11.00	20.04	14.31	.56	19.23	10.86	17.59	11.50	.71
Emotional Stability. Extent is worried, calm or relaxed, fearful or timid, emotionally stable or unstable.	13.13	6.52	10.49	6.54	.55	15.85	6.58	13.43	6.90	.48
Conformity. Type of adjustment to situations requiring conforming or responsible behavior.	11.90	3.93	10.84	3.87	.46	12.64	3.36	11.41	3.50	.38
Reality. How one copes. How one approaches threatening situations by mastery attempts or withdrawal.	10.90	6.86	7.41	6.14	.52	11.75	7.57	8.47	6.85	.60
Mood. Mood or emotional state.	11.93	3.41	10.71	3.79	.40	12.93	4.15	12.62	4.41	.46
Leadership. Personality characteristics reflected in leadership behavior.	11.95	4.40	11.18	5.71	.49	12.65	4.89	12.15	4.90	.65

*Low scores on all scales indicate characteristics usually considered desirable.

Source: Adapted from R. F. Berdie, "Personality changes from high school entrance to college matriculation," *Journal of Counseling Psychology* 15 (1968): 376–380, table 1, p. 378. Copyright 1968 by the American Psychological Association. Reprinted by permission.

nity to observe changes from early through middle adolescence.

Table 5 presents the results of Berdie's study. An examination of the table shows that for females each thirteenth-grade mean score is lower than that received in the ninth grade, representing movement over the four-year span in a direction usually considered desirable by the adult community. Of these mean differences for females, however, the validity, family relations, mood, and leadership scales are not statistically significant. With the sole exception of family relations, all male scores show movement in a desirable direction, with only the differences for the validity and leadership scales lacking statistical significance. All of the correlation coefficients, indicating the degree of personality stability over the four-year period, are significant beyond the .01 level of probability. These changes seem to indicate slight improvements in emotional and social relationships, greater acceptance of responsibility, and better contact with reality, as well as a more extroverted attitude toward life. Perhaps the most interesting fact in these data is the difference in family attitudes of the two sexes. Girls do not change in family attitudes between the ninth and thirteenth grades, but boys display at least slightly more negative family attitudes. Speculating upon this, Berdie wrote:

Most ninth grade boys have not progressed very far into adolescent rebellion against the family and this rebellion is perhaps at its height around the time of graduation from high school or entrance to college. Many fathers will agree that the relationship the 18-year-old boy has with his family is not quite as satisfactory as it was when he was fourteen. Perhaps a larger proportion of girls, by the time they have graduated from high school, have resolved many family conflicts and this may be reflected by the slightly lower thirteenth-grade score on family relations.

The general picture presented by Berdie's study is one of steady change in personality between the ninth and thirteenth grades, but the changes tend to follow an orderly pattern. That is, the way a person responds to a personality inventory such as the MCI when he is in the ninth grade bears a substantial relationship to the way he will respond to the same inventory as he enters college four years later.

In a study using the Minnesota Multiphasic Personality Inventory,[7] Hathaway and Monachesi (1963) made a longitudinal three-year-interval survey of item-response changes on the inventory. Subjects initially consisted of over fifteen thousand Minnesota ninth-graders who were administered the MMPI. As many as possible of the same individuals were retested with the MMPI three years later. Hathaway and Monachesi cite statistically significant response changes (yes to no, or no to yes) of more than seventeen percent among boys on twenty-nine items, and among girls on thirty items. (There are 566 booklet items in the MMPI.) Of these forty-seven items representing change from the ninth to the twelfth grade, only seven were common to both boys and girls. These seven items represented, for twelfth-graders of both sexes, greater attraction to members of the opposite sex and less to one's own, more interest in sexual matters, a less proscriptive attitude, more physical stability, greater freedom from family interference, and greater confidence in the good judgment of others. Writing on their results Hathaway and Monachesi (1963) note:

[7]The Minnesota Multiphasic Personality Inventory is a more clinically oriented questionnaire than the Minnesota Counseling Inventory used by Berdie (1968). However, the MCI originally devised by Berdie and Layton (1957) contains some of the scales of the MMPI.

Changes in boys include more interest in love and in flirting and dancing. They also come to worry more over disease and general health. The girls most markedly appear to become more tolerant and to feel better rapport with others. For example, they do not so much feel that people are jealous of them; neither do they so much dislike doing favors for people, or misunderstand them so much. There is less self-consciousness about blushing.

Where the thirteen personality dimensions of the MMPI are concerned, significant changes occur for boys on all but one and for girls on all but two. Most of the MMPI changes over the four-year period were in a desirable direction, but undesirable individual changes were not uncommon. In the life of any adolescent, circumstances may intervene to modify the pattern of his personality as it is reflected in his test performance, his attitudes, and in his behavior. A new teacher, success or failure in sports or in social relationships, or changed communication with parents may constitute especially critical events in the lives of some adolescents and may effect important reversals of previous trends. Such circumstances do, of course, cause any individual to deviate from the normative state of his age-mates. In considering adolescent behavior, the possibility of either positive or negative deviation for any given individual should always be kept in mind.

In interpreting the Hathaway and Monachesi study it should be recalled that item analysis departs from an examination of personality in trait terms. Items represent the operational behavior specifics of a trait, and such specific behaviors are more subject to change than the trait they represent.

Specific Personality Traits During Adolescence

A very considerable literature describes the nature, incidence, and the behavioral effects of various personality traits and components during the adolescent years. Bendig (1960), Cattell (1957), Hallworth (1965), Pflaum

(1964), and Ramfalk (1966) have discussed anxiety during adolescence; Douglas (1965) and Rosenzweig and Braun (1970) have considered the frustration-prone adolescent. Braen and Wallen (1960), Haakenstad and Apostal (1971), and Iscoe, Williams, and Harvey (1963) have dealt with rigidity and conformity; Shaimberg (1966) has been concerned with youth who manifest a need to be free of friction and controversy; Carrier (1957), Schuerger, Dielman, and Cattell (1970), and Entwhistle and Entwhistle (1970) with those whose need for achievement is high; Booth (1958) with competitors versus noncompetitors; Minkowich and Shaked (1962) with authoritarian personalities; and Kallen (1963) with inner- and outer-directed youth. Count (1967) studied hostility in adolescents; Wallach et al. (1962) have reported on defensive youth; Iverson and Reuder (1965) on self versus extrapunitive youth; and Elliot (1972) on neuroticism. Hubmann (1957) has dealt with hedonistically inclined youth; and Callard and Goodfellow (1962), Entwhistle (1972), and Eysenck, Easting, and Eysenck (1970) have considered extroversion-introversion.

Extroversion-Introversion

Extroversion-introversion represents a personality dimension at the extrovert end of which an individual's interest and attention are directed outward to the social world about him. Introversion, at the opposite end of the continuum, represents interest and attention directed inward at the expense of outer-world social interests and relationships. An introverted person is one primarily interested in his own thoughts and feelings. The introvert tends to de-emphasize interpersonal relationships that do not feed directly into his own self-preoccupation. The picture is one of social withdrawal. In contrast, the extrovert is very much interested in others and wants to have many relationships with them. The extrovert is an essentially social animal.

Adolescence has been described as a period of introversion, and some writers speak of an "introversial crisis" appearing at about ages fourteen to fifteen. Ames (1966), in a study of Rorschach scores from ages ten to sixteen, notes that an even more complex situation in adolescent introversion exists than the single-year crisis occurring between fourteen and fifteen. She writes: "Mean scores are introversive at every age from ten to sixteen. Moreover, by far the majority of individual cases at every age are introversive." However, Ames goes on to report that any given adolescent is undoubtedly more strongly introvertive at some ages than at others. Between ages ten and sixteen, periods of greater restriction alternate with periods of more expansive behavior. She writes: "The adolescent does not simply move into and then out of an introversive, or more restrictive period. Rather he moves through a sequence of phases in which introversive or restrictive trends alternate with more expansive ones." One possible explanation is that the sequence of introversions represents periods of withdrawal as a result of encounters with situations for which the adolescent has so far failed to develop coping behaviors.

It has long been established, and recent research confirms the point of view, that extroverted children are most likely to come from families whose child-rearing practices are positive and where the family climate is one of love and acceptance. Conversely, introverted children tend to come from families where parent behavior is negative in that it is cold and rejecting. Years ago, in his study of needs, Murray (1938) noted that the "sensitive, avoidant introvert" was a person whose parents had inculcated in him fears involving rejection, lack of support, danger, ridicule, and punishment. In contrast, Baldwin et al. (1949), in a study of parental behavior, reported that socially outgoing children, whether or not their manner was hostile or friendly, came from homes characterized by warm parental behavior. Hoffman (1963) noted the attitude of nonconflict with peers and of positive affective orientation toward others among children coming from homes where there was pleasurable nondisciplinary parental interaction. Similar findings have been reported by Bayley and Schaefer (1960), Porter (1967), Siegelman (1965, 1966), and Slater (1962).

Siegelman (1968) suggests that social-learning theory stressing initiation and reinforcement may explain the relationship between child-rearing practices and extroversion-introversion status. In support of this contention is a study by Gall (1960) reporting the high affiliative need of children encouraged to maintain extensive interpersonal relations. Further support is to be found in a study by Roe and Siegelman (1964) in which the investigators reported that extroverted, as compared to introverted children, had parents whose participation in outside social activities was more extensive.

Hostility and Anxiety

Hostility and anxiety bear a reciprocal relationship to each other in that either may lead to the other. An anxious person, in order to find relief or justification for his feelings of anxiety may indulge in hostile behavior. Hostility can be satisfying because it may appear to the hostile person that he is actually doing something concrete about his anxiety. If he can find a scapegoat, he can become wrathful and blame the scapegoat for all of his problems, thereby justifying if not relieving his anxiety. The scapegoat, of course, can be a person, an institution, or even an idea. On the other hand, hostility often leads to anxiety because the hostile acts or thoughts indulged in are usually unacceptable not only to society but even to the individual himself. The whole situation may become circular as hostility leads to anxiety, leading to further or more serious hostility, which further enhances anxiety. Things may easily get out of control as the tempo of the hostility-anxiety reciprocity increases. It is interesting that both hostility and anxiety may be completely unconscious states. Many exceedingly hostile or anxious individuals would be surprised to be so identified. Equally, hostility may be overt or covert in its expression, and it may be directed at

others or at self. Some suicides can be interpreted as extreme examples of self-directed hostility. Either hostility or anxiety may find its inception in lack of coping ability, and any situation in which an individual is unable to cope, particularly if the situation endures over time, is potentially anxiety and hostility producing. For some individuals hostility and anxiety gradually become a style of life.

The conditions of growing up, of beginning to assume adulthood, or of having to deal with adults while still an adolescent—and all the new adjustments and stresses that such development potentially involves—make adolescence a sometimes difficult period of life. Many situations arise in which lack of experience or adult demands leave no possibility of effective coping behavior. Defiance of adult authority in one form or another is an almost inevitable hostile reaction due to the conditions of growing up and the questions and feelings an adolescent has about his status as a burgeoning adult. It is not surprising that many adolescents possess a basic underlay of hostility.

Fortunately for most adolescents, as Count (1967) notes, such hostility tends to remain a hidden factor. However, it can take overt forms such as daily subversion of adult authority, including truancy, drugs, destructive and delinquent behavior, displaced aggression, cheating in school, deviation in dress, sexual experimentation, espousal of offbeat causes, and violations or evasions of school rules. Such behaviors are anxiety producing, and it can be expected that adolescents indulging in them will display considerable covert if not overt anxiety. Presumably, with the acquirement of more experience, more self-security, and more adequate coping behaviors, the need for hostility will be less, leading to a corresponding drop in anxiety. By the same token, it can be hypothesized that younger, less experienced adolescents will find more in their environments to create feelings of anxiety than would be true of older more experienced adolescents. Cattell (1957) reports a decrease with age in total anxiety scores but found that females possessed a considerably higher level of anxiety than did males, although the slope of the curve was the same for both. The reader might wish to speculate upon environmental conditions that might cause this sex discrepancy.

Bendig (1960), using an older age group ranging from seventeen into adulthood, only partially confirms Cattell's finding of a general decrease in anxiety with age. Bendig, working with the Cattell IPAT Anxiety Scale, reports a linear decline in the overt anxiety subscale, but found no differences on the covert subscale. Bendig makes the point that overt responses might be more subject to the social desirability variable proposed by Edwards (1957) as an important conditioning factor in personality assessment. That is to say, as adolescents grow older, they may adopt a defensive stance as they acquire status and a self-view that makes them want to attribute desirable, in this case nonanxious, attributes to themselves. Bendig feels that overt items are more influenced by the tendency than are covert items. Adolescents might be less defensive in their anxiety-test results because they are less aware of the implications of what they are saying than adults are. There should be fluctuations in anxiety over the life span, as certain periods of life typically present, for the time being, problems with which it is harder to cope. There is ample indication that adolescence is potentially a period presenting various coping problems and that some individuals during their adolescence encounter especially severe problems.

Categorizing Personality

In personality research and theory, as has been previously mentioned, a continuing question has to do with the number and nature of the descriptive categories to be used. A study by Black (1965) is of interest in this connection. Black used a rating schedule consisting of fifty-one eight-point bipolar scales[8] (1) to ex-

amine changes in personality structure as a function of age and (2) to determine the most appropriate descriptive categories. Black's subjects consisted of seven hundred individuals, fifty in each grade, evenly divided as to sex, from nursery school and kindergarten through the last year of high school. All subjects came from two Illinois public schools or from the Child Development Laboratory at the University of Illinois. For purposes of data analysis, Black designated seven grade levels, placing two grades at each level. Thus, level 1 consisted of nursery school and kindergarten, level 2 of first and second grades, and level 6 of ninth and tenth grades. Subjects, whose ages ranged from four through eighteen were rated for personality traits on the Black schedule by their teachers.

Using a factor-analytic technique developed by Tucker, the investigator extracted two factors as being common within the age range of his sample.[9] The first factor was interpreted as General Adjustment, representing behaviors characteristic of socially well adjusted versus socially poorly adjusted persons. Black, noting the highly evaluative connotation of every variable loading on the General Adjustment factor writes:

Bearing in mind the fact that these ratings are those by teachers of students, the two poles of the variables seem to represent just the sort of behavior that teachers would, and would not, respectively, like in their students. Factor 2, less evaluative in connotation, appeared best interpretable as one of outward versus inward direction of activities or of Introversion-Extroversion.

Black also notes that these factors "do not appear to correspond to any of the factors" found by Cattell, although they do appear to cut across those found by the Cattell studies. This is possibly so, although the present writer feels

[8]Forty-four of Black's fifty-one variables were taken from "The personality sphere: Most condensed form" proposed by Cattell (1957, pp. 813–817), and four were taken from the Fels Behavior Rating Scale of Richards and Simons (1941).

[9]Black found that four factors were sufficient to account for the covariance among the original variables since the last appreciable decrease in eigenvalues occurred between the fourth and fifth factors, the fifth and beyond having apparently reached a plateau, with only small secondary decreases. Black rejected the varimax solution in favor of a binormamin one to arrive at his two factor solution.

that there is a close relationship between Black's General Adjustment factor and Cattell's Cyclothymia vs. Schizothymia, and Cattell's primary source trait number 32 is labeled Extroversion vs. Introversion.

In contrasting the three studies discussed in the preceding pages, Black presents a two-factor personality structure as compared to the multiple structure presented by Sealy and Cattell and by Schaie. The difference has to do with the number of logical categories deemed most useful in classifying the various behavior components. Black presumably is dealing with the same behaviors as Schaie and Sealy and Cattell but is using a more simplistic categorical model. Sealy and Cattell gathered their data by questionnaire self-responses of their sample, while Schaie and Black used behavioral ratings of the subjects by their teachers. Presumably the teachers ratings would be based upon a narrower sample of behaviors than would the students' own self-ratings, since the students potentially have available the entire universe of their own behaviors in making their self-ratings. All three studies took the factors proposed by Cattell as their starting point, and all three viewed personality in structural terms. The pictures of personality change during adolescence presented by Sealy and Cattell and by Schaie are not essentially in disagreement.

Behavioral Style and Orientation

Bronson (1966, 1972) also used a more unitary holistic approach to the analysis of behavior by advancing the hypothesis that any given person is characterized by a style of life consisting of sets of attitudes, abilities, and traits that, taken together, impart "a characteristic flavor to all of a person's interactions." She postulates the existence of central orientations developed early in a child's life as a result of interpersonal experiences, physical-physiological events, and possibly by the unfolding of genetic characteristics. Of these orientations she writes:

They set the broad limits on the repertoire of responses favored by the organism and are responsible for the underlying continuity of development. Within any given orientation a variety of behaviors is possible depending on temporal or environmental appropriateness, however, by being expressions of the particular orientation, such behaviors attain a conceptual or functional equivalence.

Bronson set out, in seeking research support for her hypothesis, to find the most appropriate orientation categories and to discover for what behaviors repeated measurements would be most suitable in defining an orientation. She further wished to examine developmental changes and consistencies within the framework of the orientations she found.

In carrying out her purpose Bronson analyzed, for her 1966 as well as her 1972 study, longitudinal data obtained from the Berkeley Growth Study.[10] As a result of her 1966 study, Bronson proposed the existence of three orientation dimensions: (1) withdrawal-expressiveness, (2) reactivity-placidity, and (3) passivity-dominance. However, she suggests that only the first two represented "relatively unmodifiable" orientations. Of passivity-dominance, she writes that it did not "share the 'organismic' quality of the other two; although it represents a salient and persistent type of behavior...it is best conceptualized as an orientation that is in itself a product of the interaction between 'organismic' qualities and psychosocial pressures." In her 1972 study, which was in effect a replication of her 1966 study, with a different subsample of Berkeley Guidance study subjects, Bronson proposed the two central behavioral dimensions as placidity-explosiveness and emotional-expressiveness-reserve.

[10]The Berkeley Guidance Study described by Macfarlane (1938) consisted of a longitudinal study of 124 children (chosen in 1928–1929) from the ages of 21 months through 18 years. Yearly or half-yearly tests and interviews with the children and their parents were conducted during the over 16 years of the study's duration. In 1957 when the subjects were 30 years old a follow-up was conducted to examine the coping behavior, at that age, characteristic of the individual members of the sample.

Bronson's findings offer support for the assumption that individuals do possess an enduring lifestyle and interpersonal approach that, though it is effected by environmental experience, will often serve to set up the kind of experience the environment will provide. Discussing the results of her study Bronson writes:

A large number and a wide variety of behaviors were investigated: They yielded complex, yet, I contend, convincing developmental patterns when structured from the perspective of the postulated orientations. The coherence among such a large variety of longitudinal observations demonstrates that the essential continuity of personality development will emerge if interactional and feedback processes are built into the conceptual perspective from which it is approached.

In her examination of developmental changes and consistencies within the framework of the orientations she proposes, Bronson describes her subjects in terms of the relationship between their ages at each of a series of consecutive age periods and their positions on the proposed dimensions.

Table 6 presents, for boys and girls separately, the most important behavioral age-related correlates for each of the three dimensions proposed by Bronson in 1966. Bronson's three dimensions may be conceived of as broad arenas for attitudes and behavior. Each dimension consists of a number of behavior components, each of which exists along a continuum, and each of which is related to all of the others to some degree. However, for any given individual, specific placement on the various continua making up the dimensions changes from time to time. The attitudinal placement of the individual along each of the continua will vary as a result of internal or external circumstances. While there undoubtedly is an overall correlative picture among the components, large changes along one of the continua may only be peripherally reflected (in terms of the overall correlation) in all of the rest. For example, an individual may move from a very uncompetitive placement to a competitive one on the competitive-uncompetitive continuum but remain as he originally was at the uncertain end of the uncertain-confident continuum. Obviously the quality of his new competitiveness will be reflected by his uncertainty (part of the effect of the overall relationships among the continua of the dimension of withdrawal-expressiveness). If movement had also taken place along the uncertain-confident continuum toward confidence the individual's approach toward his competitive efforts might have been very different, or at least evaluated differently by peers and others dealing with him. It follows, of course, that change along one continuum may establish a train of behavior and events that will make further moves along other intradimensional continua likely, instead of simple confinement to the continuum in question. For example, if the competitiveness is successful, we might expect positive movement along the uncertain-confident continuum and quite possibly along the cautious-adventurous and vulnerable-invulnerable continua.[11] However, it should be remembered there is individual-state persistence of continua placement within the dimension. What a child's position is in this dimension is strongly reflected over the years of his adolescence. One question that does arise is why changes take place so that "characteristic" age-related statements can be made, such as, "During late adolescence an individual is likely to be—" (other things being equal). The answer to that is situational. The culture may present an age group with a characteristic situation, such as withholding emancipation but being inconsistent and undefined in its withholding, that may give directionality to movement within a dimension. But with so many dimensions and the resulting possibility of permutations and combinations to various kinds of behavior, there is room for individual differences. We can predict

[11]The reader should be advised that these interpretations of continua within the dimensions are the sole responsibility of the present writer and should not be attributed as having been stated by Dr. Bronson. They appear to this writer to be a logical way of interpreting and expanding Dr. Bronson's findings and formulations, but she might or might not agree with them.

Table 6 *Behavioral Continua of Greatest Relevance at Various Ages and by Sex for Each of Three Dimensions of Personality*

Dimension Correlates (Behavioral Continua)	Dimension 1 Withdrawal-Expressiveness					
	8–10		11–13		14–16	
	Boys	Girls	Boys	Girls	Boys	Girls
Inner-Outer Oriented	.69 ①	.46 ②	.64 ①	.50 ①	.65 ①	.53 ①
Exhibitionistic–Socially Withdrawn	−.64 ②	−.42 ③	−.51 ③	−.49 ②	−.40 ②	−.50 ③
Anxious-Relaxed	.37 ⑥		.52 ②	.38 ⑤	.33 ④	
Restless-Inactive	−.40 ⑤	−.30 ⑥	−.32 ⑥	−.47 ③		−.41 ④
Appetite: Poor-Good						
Cautious-Adventurous	.41 ④	.47 ①				.52 ②
Body Attitude: Embarrassed-Comfortable						
Vulnerable-Invulnerable	.51 ③	.36 ④	.38 ④			.34 ⑤
Emotionally Labile–Stable			.38 ⑤			
Jealous–Not Jealous						
Competitive-Uncompetitive					−.30 ⑤	
Uncertain-Confident				.40 ④	.37 ③	
Complaining-Uncomplaining						
Disturbing Dreams: Frequent-Rare		.34 ⑦				
Emotionally Dependent–Independent						
Intellectually Inert–Inquisitive				.37 ⑥		
Sleep: Restless-Quiet						
Quarrelsome-Placating						
Tantrums: Frequent-Rare						
Grasping-Generous						
Attention-Demanding–Self-sufficient						
Attitude to Food: Finicky-Adventuresome						
Evasive-Truthful						
Destructive-Careful						
Untidy-Fastidious						
Fearful-Unafraid						

All coefficients are statistically significant.

Source: Adapted from W. C. Bronson, "Central orientations: A study of behavior organization from childhood to adolescence," *Child Development* 37 (1966): 125–155. Table contains elements from tables 5–9 in Bronson. Copyright © 1966 by The Society for Research in Child Development, Inc. Reprinted by permission of the publisher and the author.

group trends much more efficiently than individual trends on the basis of the data research made available to us. Still, if we have established a group norm and we know that a given individual is a member of that group, we are in a position to make probability statements about him as long as we are aware that in his individual case the probability may not be borne out as his personal condition and environmental circumstance force him into deviate directions. For any given individual, in addition to his past history, there is always the possibility of present fortuitous circumstances as the determiner of his behavior. Of course this circumstance has a hopeful side, for if fortuitous circumstances can be causal, then so can planned intervention, whether it is called education, counseling, or therapy.

	Dimension 2 Reactivity-Placidity						Dimension 3 Passivity-Dominance					
	8–10		11–13		14–16		8–10		11–13		14–16	
	Boys	Girls	Boys	Girls	Boys	Girls	Boys	Girls	Boys	Girls	Boys	Girls
						.30 ②	−.42 ②		−.42 ④	−.65 ①	−.37 ⑥	−.42 ④
			.44 ③	.43 ①			−.42 ①	−.60 ②	−.43 ③	−.47 ③	−.47 ③	−.32 ⑥
				.33 ④						.40 ⑥	.48 ①	.66 ①
							.29 ⑥					
							.33 ④		.40 ⑤	.43 ④		
	.37 ①		.41 ③		.29 ⑥							
	.34 ②		.35 ④							−.43 ⑤		
				.32 ⑥								
									.36 ⑥			.44 ③
		.54 ①	.29 ⑥	.46 ①	.40 ②	.30 ②			.45 ②			
		.41 ④										
									.56 ①			.48 ②
		.57 ②	.43 ②	.42 ④	.38 ③	.33 ①	−.35 ③	−.63 ①		−.58 ②	−.43 ④	
		.41 ⑤	.51 ①	.45 ②	.32 ⑤	.30 ②		−.47 ③			−.39 ⑤	
			.35 ⑤					.33 ⑤				
		.39 ⑥						.37 ④			.48 ②	
					.30 ②							
				.36 ⑤			.30 ⑤					
		.45 ③						.33 ⑥				
												.33 ⑤

Within-Age Variance in Personality

Black (1965), previously cited, also reports on variance among children within a grade level. For a given personality trait, the question was: To what extent do children vary within their age group, and how does the extent of this variation change over time? The variance for each grade level is shown in Figure 2. For Black's Factor 1, General Adjustment, a trend of increasing variance begins in nursery school-kindergarten and reaches a peak in grades five and six when the children are about ten to twelve years of age. Following the fifth and sixth grades, variation drops to its former level and remains so throughout the junior and senior high school years. The

Figure 2   *Variance of Each Grade Level for Two Factors of Personality*

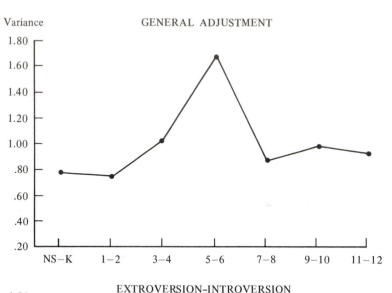

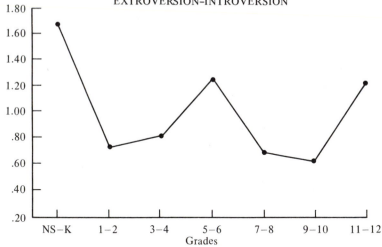

Source: Adapted from M. S. Black, "The development of personality factors in children and adolescents," *Educational and Psychological Measurement* 25 (1965): 767–785, figs. 1–2. Reprinted by permission of the publisher.

reason for the fifth- and sixth-grade variance is unclear. It is a time when some children, mostly girls, are entering puberty, but the majority are not. If puberty is causing the differentiation in the fifth- and sixth-grade group, it is surprising that the falloff comes in grades seven and eight, when it would be expected to increase or at least to maintain. The fifth and sixth grades are, of course, the time of the prepubescent growth spurt, and the accompanying physical factors may have caused the peak in variance in Black's study. A more revealing situation might have maintained if the investigator had graphed boys and girls separately. In Black's study, as may be seen in Figure 2, Factor 2 (Extroversion-Introversion) showed three peaks of considerable variance among subjects. One was at nursery school-kindergarten level, one at the fifth-to-sixth-grade level, and one at the eleventh-to-twelfth-grade level. Black wrote that the peaks seemed to coincide with transition stages in children's lives. In the first the child enters school, in the second the child enter puberty, and in the third he is beginning a transition into adult life.

It seems to this writer that while the peaks undoubtedly exist, Black's causal hypotheses are not tenable. The relationship to puberty in grades five to six has been discussed above as unlikely. If school entrance in nursery school-kindergarten were causal, then grades one to two would also show a peak, instead of a fall as Figure 2 indicates, because numbers of children enter school in the first grade rather than in nursery school or kindergarten. And finally, in the last year of high school, children are still adolescents and are not yet adults to the point where transition into adulthood would be an issue. It is true that in the last year of high school a number of adolescents are getting ready to leave school and find a job, but it is still more remote in their day-to-day thinking than one might suppose. The simple fact of leaving high school, or of getting ready to leave it, does not represent adulthood or anything more than a very peripheral transition into adulthood.

Normal Development During Adolescence

A study designed "to examine the relative influences of internal psychological and external environmental factors upon the functioning of . . . modal adolescents as they approach adulthood" was performed by Offer and his associates (1968, 1969, 1970). In carrying out their purpose these investigators conducted a seven-year longitudinal study of a group of middle-class boys, beginning in the first year of high school and extending through three to four of the post–high school years. Subjects were included in the group for study because they were average or normal (modal) adolescents and did not represent an extreme, either of psychopathology or of superior adjustment. The initial group consisted of seventy-three boys, but attrition reduced this number to between sixty-one to forty-five for the post–high school phase of the study.

In the post–high school phase of the study, Offer and his associates emphasized changes in the emotional conflicts and in the coping methods of their subjects. During his four years in high school, each subject was interviewed on six different occasions by a psychiatrist and additional information was gained through psychological testing, background data, teacher ratings, adjective check lists, and interviews with parents. During the first post–high school year, parents completed a 26-item questionnaire, and the boys completed a 56-item identity scale to assess operationally Erikson's theoretical concepts of identity. During the second or third high school year, the subjects were again interviewed by the psychiatrist who had initially interviewed them. This last interview dealt with the nature of the individual's present adjustment to his environment, the extent to which he had developed new objectives, relationships with parents, vocational-educational goals, and the extent of concern with social issues.[12]

Adolescence, as Offer (1969) interprets it from the results of his study, is a relatively long and leisurely period offering a number of different transitional routes from childhood to adolescence. Offer's modal adolescents passed through the period with relatively little turmoil, slowly mastering the development tasks with which they were confronted. Emotional fluctuations existed, but the performances depicting them were not "staccato." Offer describes the progress through adolescence of his subjects as presenting a picture of "gradualism, as contrasted to volcanic eruptions."

[12]A second follow-up phase is planned during which subjects will again be tested by instruments used in the high school phase of the study (Rorschach, Thematic Apperception Test, etc.).

Relationships to both father and mother changed during the high school years, but the changes were in the direction of acceptance and maturity, without evidence of a generation gap, and little real parent-child difficulty was encountered. In general, the subjects of Offer's study seemed to approve and share their parents' social values. There were some problems of identity conflict, ranging from mild to moderate, but there were no examples of identity crisis in the Eriksonian sense. Affective responses most often observed were anxiety, acting out, and depression, with shame, obsession, compulsion, and guilt appearing to a lesser degree. But none of these responses were of a degree or a duration to represent a picture of classic turmoil or prolonged basic maladjustment. The greatest amount of turmoil appeared during early adolescence. Offer (1969) writes: "Personality functioning among these boys is quite diverse, and it is clear that normality is not a unitary function. What we find instead is that these youngsters, using widely varying techniques hold their own." They use humor, they utilize the issues of their day, they relate to people seriously and with charm, they are self-aware of their failings, and they try to make up for their limitations. But, as Offer notes, "they do all these things in ways that are unique to each of them, even though in general their conflicts, their experience of the world and themselves in relation to the world, are common to most of them."

In the follow-up portion of the study, when the subjects are out of school and in their late adolescence, Offer et al. (1970) note that while the environmental settings have changed, characteristic individual patterns of functioning are still in evidence as they are applied to new situations. Independence is being achieved, heterosexual activity has gradually increased since high school, and conflict, insofar as it exists, is manageable. Identity consolidation has yet to be achieved, and the overall picture is still one of gradualism as these not-yet-adults are in their final transitional and inductive period. It is obvious that simple chronological age is not an index to trust in assessing psychological maturity.

Offer's group of subjects present an unusual, relatively idyllic picture as compared either to the popular stereotypes of the period or, indeed, to the findings of the majority of the research on adolescence accumulated over the years. They were picked because they were "average," possessing neither a picture of psychopathology nor of superior adjustment. In addition, they formed a cohort; there were only a few of them, and they were all white males from suburban middle-class families. In their "normality," are they really so abnormal, as most children in America go, that generalizations about the adolescent period as it really exists cannot be made from them? Offer does not think so. Much after the fashion of the squeaky wheel that gets the grease, the maladjusted, dissatisfied, rebellious, problem adolescent gets the attention and comes to seem the prototype of all adolescents. Offer (1969) writes:

In fact, we believe that we are describing a population that is larger in number and has greater influence than the sample described either in the psychiatric, psychoanalytic, or social-science literature. In other words we have come upon a sample that, in our judgment, is representative of many adolescents in suburban America. They are less visible because they share the values of their parents and society. They are less visible because they are able to communicate effectively with adults. They are less visible because, in general, they have fewer problems and move into normative social roles with relative ease and comfort.

That there are such groups of adolescents is obvious from Offer's study. That they are representative of even the middle-class white suburban adolescent population is still a moot question from the available evidence, although replication research could do much to resolve the question. Possibly the majority of adolescents described in the research literature to date have been drawn from normal or average populations, although there has seldom been an attempt, as in Offer's case, to insure modality in each subject to be included in a research project. However, the picture of Offer's normal adolescents is not particularly different in general outlines from the picture presented by the more miscellaneous samples described in the various studies cited earlier in this chapter. The difference is only in specific details. Offer's study is of particular interest because it presents a grouping of adolescents growing and adjusting well to their environment and themselves and thereby indicating that tension and difficulty during the adolescent period are not inevitable.

Cohort Differences over Time

Present-day developmental research is particularly interested (Schaie 1970, Schaie and Strother 1968, Woodruff and Birren 1972) in distinguishing among age differences, age changes, and cultural changes. Personality, at least as it is measured by personality tests, will reflect social events and the times in which an individual and his cohort of same-age individuals live. For example, in 1947 Hathaway and Monachesi (1953, 1963) administered the Minnesota Multiphasic Personality Inventory to the ninth graders in one school in a small city. In 1954 they again administered the MMPI to the ninth graders in the same school. Ninth-grade boys between these two testings registered significant changes in five of the thirteen scales of the MMPI, with the 1954 sample displaying less neuroticism and less behavioral revolt. As a group the 1954 ninth graders were more psychologically secure and less rebellious than the ninth graders of seven years before. In discussing their results Hathaway and Monachesi (1963) write: "The change in scale 4 (Pd.: Rebellious, cynical, disregards rules, socially aggressive, selfish) could mean that in general, boys are conforming with less resistance to the restraints of the social order. One could conclude that there is less evidence of reaction to stress in the later samples." Hathaway and Monachesi do not speculate as to what cultural events may have been reflected in the change, and it is difficult at this late date

to speak to the question. The change may have come as a result of some internal change in the school or local community, or it may have reflected some larger change. The 1954 responses may have had some relationship to the Korean War, since changes for boys appeared to be greater than they were for girls. The major change for girls seemed to be in the direction of less self-dissatisfaction and unhappiness, but even in this dimension (scale 2, depression: serious, low in morale, unhappy, self-dissatisfied) the change was less than it was for boys. But for our purposes the exact reasons for the change are less important than the fact that personality can and does reflect the conditions of the times. Woodruff and Birren (1972) in both longitudinal and cross-sectional comparisons of changes in personality in three cohort groups note that objective cohort differences were larger than objective age changes over a span from adolescence to middle age. They recommend that it is "useful to utilize subjective as well as objective assessments of personality."

Individual Differences in Personality

The development of any teenager is a continuing interaction of physical and psychological growth and consolidation. During this period, at perhaps an accelerated pace, the process of socialization helps an individual produce a personality structure that either will characterize him all of his life or will serve as a base from which further personality changes will develop. Personality becomes both the conditioning and the limiting factor in an individual's behavior. Normative studies of personality furnish useful guidelines for understanding the adolescent period, but in the final analysis personality is a highly individual matter. The total of an individual's personality consists of the integration, lack of integration, or partial integration of many components. The sheer number of possible components and the permutations and combinations of these components in the relationships and integrations governing behavior make for the uniqueness of each individual in the behavioral realm.

Of course, given a stated milieu including common conditions of education and child rearing, there are many common patterns in any given population of persons. The presence or absence of certain personality factors or tendencies to behavior may be expected in terms of probability at a high level of confidence. However, one must not forget that any one individual may deviate markedly, even when the normative probabilities for his group make deviation unlikely. And no individual can live apart from environmental circumstances, many of them quite fortuitous. Coincidences of time, place, and event may present conditions leading to changes in both the nature and conditions of personal behavioral tendencies. The likelihood of occurrence of such fortuitous circumstances may to some extent be predicted, but this only gives us an individual being reared in circumstances including not only the internal combinations of personality tendencies, as well as those of environmental circumstances, but also the varieties of combinations that personality may evolve. For these reasons it is impossible to say that the personality of every adolescent is alike or even to make any generalization about personality that is equally applicable to every adolescent. Still, generalizations may be made about adolescent personality based upon normative tendencies for defined populations of adolescents. Such generalizations may be useful even though it is true that individual idiosyncracies are not only possible, but likely.

It is also true that some generalizations are larger in scope than others. That is, they can include greater numbers of individuals over greater ranges of envionmental conditions. For example, one generalization might apply only to boys attending private schools in the American Midwest, another to boys and girls attending high school in Iran, another to teenagers reared in the cultures of western Europe and the Americas, or still another to teenagers of one sex or of one chronological

age. Obviously, the broader the coverage of the generalization the more universal the statement, but in psychology such universal generalizations are not only difficult to arrive at by scientific means but appear to be relatively few in number.

Viewing Individual Development

From the preceding discussions it follows that studies of trends and changes in personality during adolescence must focus upon the individual as well as upon the developmental stage if a realistic understanding of adolescence is to be gained. Trend lines based upon normative cultural, or even subcultural, data may cancel out the fact of individual deviations. While such average trend lines may be representative of the group as a whole, they may, equally, be unrepresentative of the members of the group. The fundamental question to be asked in an individual-oriented examination of personality development data is whether any group-applicable developmental generalizations can be made from an examination of individual sequential curves. Specifically, under what conditions and to what extent do people maintain stability or exhibit change in their overall patterns of personality as they move from childhood through adolescence? Two problems arise at this point. First is the necessity of acquiring developmental data based upon growth over time in the same persons. Second is the statistical problem of a summary presentation of individual curve data that will avoid or minimize central tendency (mean, median, mode) statements obscuring the picture of individual deviations.

An answer to the fundamental question can be found only in longitudinal data. It is obvious that cross-sectional data, based as they are upon age changes with different individuals used at each of the successive ages, cannot present a picture of age changes in the same persons. The reader at this point may feel that while the issue of longitudinal versus cross-sectional data collection is of hypothetical interest, the actuality of personality development is such that either method will yield results approximately similar. In actuality the issue is of more than hypothetical interest in that there are discrepancies in the results of cross-sectional as compared to longitudinal research on personality development in adolescence. In the former the picture is one of considerable personality change over the years of adolescence, while in the latter the picture is one of relatively less change.

Summary

Personality represents a person's core of individuality and determines how he adjusts to his environment. It has been defined as the structure of personal meanings and habits imparting directionality to behavior. Personality represents an individual's personal action system. There are many ways of describing personality, ranging from the atomistic description of a single trait to holistic descriptions of clusters of traits. Trait interaction is a complicating factor when realistic description is attempted.

When personality traits are cited in terms of polar opposites, a person's trait description places him someplace along the continuum between the two poles. Basic to interpretation of an individual's trait description is whether the descriptive point of reference is the negative or positive pole of the trait. A knowledge of an individual's own focus of reference is important in understanding his behavior. Even relatively objective observer ratings tend to reflect the subjective perception of the observer and may differ from the self-perception of the subject.

Personality is usually analyzed by classifying behaviors under various categories, the categories representing the dimensions of personality. Because personality is such a complex construct, it is not surprising that theorists will differ in the number and inclusiveness of the dimensions they use to describe it. Different techniques are used to arrive at the number and description of the dimensions to be selected. Factor analysis has been one productive means of trying to locate appropriate dimensions. It is generally agreed that while personality changes at least to some extent with age, the dimensions of personality, insofar as they can be identified, remain stable across ages. That is, position along a dimension continuum may change with age, but the continuum itself remains constant.

A number of different measures and techniques have been devised to assess personality, but they are not of equal precision and comprehensiveness. The questionnaire and ratings by observers are often used in research, but they often produce somewhat different results, possibly because of the subjective elements included in both. Any assessment of personality is, of course, conditioned by the dimensions inherent in the particular measure used or by the limitations of the technique adopted for gathering data.

Studies of the development of personality are either longitudinal or cross-sectional. The former follows the same individuals over a span of time, making possible the computation of correlations between measures taken on the same persons at different ages. The cross-sectional method makes age comparisons using different individuals at each age. A research difficulty with the longitudinal approach is the lengthy duration of a study and the possibility of loss of subjects from year to year.

Major changes in personality normatively occur during adolescence with some of the changes fluctuating from year to year between the negative and positive poles of certain of the dimensions of personality. Other changes follow a linear line of development, in that they progress steadily without fluctuation from one pole toward the other. A few dimensions exhibit no change, remaining stable throughout the adolescent period. Important sex differences in personality development occur during adolescence, many of them being attributable to cultural customs and sex-role expectations.

Adolescence is generally a time of increasing self-sufficiency following some dependency reactions at the beginning of the period. Stress tends to lessen with increasing age, with a consequent decrease in anxiety and hostility. Hostility and anxiety bear a reciprocal relationship, and early and middle adolescence are potentially times offering many situations leading to circular hostility-anxiety or anxiety-hostility behaviors. Fortunately, as adolescents gain in experience and effective coping behavior, there is less and less need for such defensive behaviors as hostility and anxiety if the course of development has been normal. Thus for the majority, adolescence is a time of increasing good adjustment marked by a decline in worry and anxiety. Despite this, the overall picture of the period is one of more introversion than extroversion, although for any individual, depending upon his success from time to time in coping with his problems, there will tend to be considerable fluctuation. The increase in sociability noted in middle adolescence may be a counteractivity of influence to introversion, but it is possible that the adolescent is simply using the peer culture for his own reality testing rather than because of any extrovert tendency.

Responsiveness tends to increase during adolescence, although sheer physical reactivity begins to decline. Late adolescents display a nonsignificant tendency to become more conventional, realistic, and practical. Late adolescents are increasingly shaped by their culture as they become less idiosyncratic and begin to merge into the group culture of adult society.

During adolescence girls display a fluctuating picture of submission-dominance, although following puberty there is a specific increase in dominance. In contrast to girls, boys tend to display a stronger trait of dominance at most ages. The sharp increase in tough-mindedness (more materialistic, skeptical, multisolutional) in boys during adolescence constitutes one of the largest areas of boy-girl differences in personality. As boys are becoming more tough-minded, girls are tending in the opposite direction of idealism and rationalism. In general, girls remain more conservative than boys throughout the period. Noncollege males show a tendency to become more conservative in late adolescence in contrast to the much less conservative attitude of college males.

The normative data of personality are hard to interpret not only because of the fluctuation over time of a number of personality dimensions but also because, depending on the sex of the individual, peaks as well as low points for the different factors occur at different ages. A further complication is the crucial influence of environmental conditions varying from individual to individual, from family to family, and from subcultural to subcultural group. Considerable intragroup variation has been noted at all ages and on all dimensions. Normative adolescent-stage trend lines present a useful general picture of the adolescent period but they must be used with great caution when applied to individuals or specific groups. The following chapter will consider aspects of these problems with particular reference to individual differences in personality development.

References

Allport, G. W. *Becoming*. New Haven: Yale University Press, 1955.

Ames, L. B. Changes in Rorschach response throughout the human life span. *Genetic Psychology Monographs* 74 (1966): 89–125.

Baldwin, A. L.; Kalhorn, J.; and Breese, F. H. The appraisal of parent behavior. *Psychological Monographs* 63 (4) (1949), whole no. 229.

Bayley, N., and Schaefer, E. S. Maternal behavior and personality development data from the Berkeley growth study. *Psychiatric Research Reports* 13 (1960): 155–173.

Bendig, A. W. Age-related changes in covert and overt anxiety. *Journal of General Psychology* 62 (1960): 159–163.

Berdie, R. F. Personality changes from high school entrance to college matriculation. *Journal of Counseling Psychology* 15 (1968): 376–380.

Berdie, R. F., and Layton, W. L. *Minnesota Counseling Inventory*. New York: Psychological Corporation, 1957.

Black, M. S. The development of personality factors in children and adolescents. *Educational and Psychological Measurement* 25 (1965): 767–785.

Booth, E. G., Jr. Personality traits of athletes as measured by the MMPI. *Research Quarterly of the American Association for Physical Education* 29 (1958): 127–138.

Braen, B. B., and Wallen, N. F. Measurement of rigidity in high school students. *Psychological Reports* 7 (1960): 11–17.

Bronson, W. C. Central orientations: A study of behavior organization from childhood to adolescence. *Child Development* 37 (1966): 125–155.

Bronson, W. C. The role of enduring orientations to the environment in personality development. *Genetic Psychology Monographs* 86 (1972): 3–80.

Callard, M. P., and Goodfellow, C. L. Neuroticism and extraversion in schoolboys as measured by the Junior Maudsley Personality Inventory. *British Journal of Educational Psychology* 32 (1962): 241–250.

Carrier, N. A. The relationship of certain personality measures to examination performance under stress. *Journal of Educational Psychology* 48 (1957): 510–520.

Cattell, R. B. *Factor analysis*. New York: Harper, 1952.

Cattell, R. B. *Personality and motivation, structure and measurement*. Yonkers-on-Hudson: World Book, 1957.

Cattell, R. B., and Coan, R. W. Child personality structure as revealed in teachers' behavior ratings. *Journal of Clinical Psychology* 13 (1957): 215–237.

Cattell, R. B., and Coan, R. W. Personality factors in middle childhood as revealed in parents' ratings. *Child Development* 28 (1957): 439–458.

Cattell, R. B.; Coan, R. W.; and Beloff, H. A reexamination of personality structure in late childhood, and development of the High School Personality Questionnaire. *Journal of Experimental Education* 27 (1959): 73–88.

Cattell, R. B., and Gruen, W. The personality factor structure of 11-year-old children in terms of behavior rating data. *Journal of Clinical Psychology* 9 (1953): 256–266.

Coan, R. W., and Cattell, R. B. Reproducible personality factors in middle childhood. *Journal of Clinical Psychology* 14 (1958): 339–345.

Count, J. The conflict factor in adolescent growth. *Adolescence* 2 (1967): 167–181.

Douglas, V. I. Children's responses to frustration: a developmental study. *Canadian Journal of Psychology* 19 (1965): 161–171.

Edwards, A. L. *The social desirability variable in personality assessment and research*. New York: Dryden, 1957.

Elliott, C. D. Personality factors and scholastic attainment. *British Journal of Educational Psychology* 42 (1972): 23–32.

Entwhistle, N. J. Personality and academic attainment. *British Journal of Educational Psychology* 42 (1972): 137–151.

Entwhistle, N. J., and Entwhistle, D. The relationships between personality, study methods and academic performance. *British Journal of Educational Psychology* 40 (1970): 132–143.

Eysenck, H. J.; Easting, G.; and Eysenck, S. B. Personality measurement in children: A dimensional approach. *Journal of Special Education* 4 (1970): 261–268.

Fruchter, B. *Introduction to factor analysis*. New York: Van Nostrand, 1954.

Gall, H. S. The development of affilation motivation. *Doctoral dissertation*, University of North Carolina, 1960.

Haakenstad, K. W., and Apostal, R. A. Acquiescence and nonoccupational interests. *Journal of Counseling Psychology* 18 (1971): 501–502.

Hallworth, H. J. The dimensions of personality among children of school age. *British Journal of Mathematical and Statistical Psychology* 18 (1965): 45–56.

Hathaway, S. R., and Monachesi, E. D. *Analyzing and predicting juvenile delinquency with the MMPI*. Minneapolis: University of Minnesota Press, 1953.

Hathaway, S. R., and Monachesi, E. D. *Adolescent personality and behavior*. Minneapolis: University of Minnesota Press, 1963.

Hoffman, M. L. Parental discipline and the child's consideration for others. *Child Development* 34 (1963): 573–588.

Hubmann, E. Leichtsinnige Jugendliche. *Heilpadagogik* 26 (1957): 61–71.

Iscoe, I.; Williams, M.; and Harvey, J. Modification of children's judgments by a simulated group technique: A normative developmental study. *Child Development* 34 (1963): 963–978.

Iverson, M. A., and Reuder, M. E. Personality impressions of self-punitive and extrapunitive stimulus persons. *Journal of Social Psychology* 65 (1965): 67–83.

Kagan, J., and Moss, H. A. *Birth to maturity.* New York: Wiley, 1962.

Kallen, D. J. Inner direction, other direction, and social integration setting. *Human Relations* 16 (1963): 76–87.

Macfarlane, J. W. Studies in child guidance: I. Methodology of data collection and organization. *Monographs of the Society for Research in Child Development* 3 (1938): 1–254.

Minkowich, A., and Shaked, A. Haishiyut has-amkhutit. (The authoritarian personality). *Megamot* 12 (1962): 24–47.

Murray, H. A. *Explorations in personality.* New York: Oxford University Press, 1938.

Offer, D.; Marcus, D.; and Offer, J. L. A longitudinal study of normal adolescent boys. *American Journal of Psychiatry* 126 (1970): 41–48.

Offer, D., and Offer, J. L. *The psychological world of the teen-ager.* New York: Basic Books, 1969.

Offer, D., and Sabshin, M. *Normality.* New York: Basic Books, 1968.

Peterson, D. R. Age generality of personality factors derived from ratings. *Educational and Psychological Measurement* 20 (1960): 461–474.

Peterson, D. R. The scope and generality of verbally defined personality factors. *Psychological Review* 62 (1965): 48–59.

Pfiaum, J. Nature and incidence of manifest anxiety responses among college students. *Psychological Reports* 15 (1964): 720.

Porter, J. B. The vocational choice of college freshmen women as influenced by psychological needs and parent-child relationships. In Parker, H. J. et al., eds., *Parent-child relations research status, measurement and predictive value.* Oklahoma City: University of Oklahoma Medical Research Center, 1967.

Ramfalk, C. W. Studies in personality: II. A biopsychological and experimental approach to problems of human adaptation in modern society. *Scandinavian Journal of Psychology* 7 (1966): 121–144.

Richards, T. W., and Simons, M. P. The Fels child behavior scales. *Genetic Psychology Monographs* 24 (1941): 259–309.

Roe, A., and Siegelman, M. A study of the origin of interests. *American Personnel and Guidance Association Inquiry Study* 1 (1964): 1–98.

Rosenzweig, S., and Braun, H. Sex differences in reactions to frustration among adolescents as explored by the Rosenzweig P-F Study. *Journal of Genetic Psychology* 116 (1970): 53–61.

Schaie, K. W. Year-by-year changes in personality from six to eighteen years. *Multivariate Behavioral Research* 1 (1966): 293–305.

Schaie, K. W. A reinterpretation of age-related changes in cognitive structure and functioning. In Goulet, R., and Baltes, P. B., eds., *Life-span developmental psychology: research and theory.* New York: Academic Press, 1970.

Schaie, K. W., and Strother, C. R. The effect of time and cohort differences on the interpretation of age changes in cognitive behavior. *Multivariate Behavioral Research* 3 (1968): 259–294.

Schuerger, J. M.; Dielman, T. E.; and Cattell, R. B. Objective-analytic personality factors (U.I. 16, 17, 19, 20) as correlates of school achievement. *Personality: An International Journal* 1 (1970): 95–101.

Sealy, A. P., and Cattell, R. B. Adolescent personality trends in primary factors measured on the 16 PF and the HSPQ questionnaires through ages 11 to 23. *British Journal of Social and Clinical Psychology* 5 (1966): 172–184.

Shaimberg, D. Personality restriction in adolescents. *Psychiatric Quarterly* 40 (1966): 258–270.

Siegelman, M. College student personality correlates of early parent-child relationships. *Journal of Consulting Psychology* 29 (1965): 558–564.

Siegelman, M. Loving and punishing parental behavior and introversion tendencies in sons. *Child Development* 37 (1966): 985–992.

Siegelman, M. "Origins" of extroversion-introversion. *Journal of Psychology* 69 (1968): 85–91.

Slater, P. E. Parental behavior and the personality of the child. *Journal of Genetic Psychology* 101 (1962): 53–68.

Thomson, G. H. *The factorial analysis of human ability.* Boston: Houghton Mifflin, 1939.

Thurstone, L. L. *Multiple factor analysis.* Chicago: University of Chicago Press, 1947.

Wallach, M. A.; Green, L. R.; Lippitt, P. D.; and Minehart, J. B. Contradiction between overt and projective personality indicators as a function of defensiveness. *Psychological Monographs* 76 (1962), no. 520.

Woodruff, D. S., and Birren, J. E. Age changes and cohort differences in personality. *Developmental Psychology* 6 (1972): 252–259.

Suggested Readings

Ames, L. B. Longitudinal survey of child Rorschach responses: older subjects ages 10 to 16 years. *Genetic Psychology Monographs* 62 (1960): 185–229.

Bloom, B. S. *Stability and change in human characteristics.* New York: Wiley, 1964.

Calden, G., and Hokanson, J. E. The influence of age on MMPI responses. *Journal of Clinical Psychology* 15 (1959): 194–195.

Cattell, R. B., and Warburton, F. W. A cross-cultural comparison of patterns of extroversion and anxiety. *British Journal of Psychology* 52 (1961): 3–16.

Clifford, P. L. Testing the educational and psychological development of adolescents: ages 12–18. *Review of Educational Research* 38 (1968): 29–41.

Eysenck, S. B., and Eysenck, H. J. Scores of three personality variables as a function of age, sex, and social class. *British Journal of Social and Clinical Psychology* 8 (1969): 69–76.

Felker, D. W., and Hunter, D. Sex and age differences in response to cartoons depicting subjects of different ages and sex. *Journal of Psychology* 76 (1970): 19–21.

Greenfeld, N., and Finkelstein, E. L. A comparison of the characteristics of junior high school students. *Journal of Genetic Psychology* 117 (1970): 37–50.

Holmes, D. S. Aggression, displacement, and guilt. *Journal of Personality and Social Psychology* 21 (1972): 296–301.

Jamison, K., and Comrey, A. L. A comparison of the personality factor structure in British and American university students. *Journal of Psychology* 71 (1969): 45–57.

Lewis, W. C.; Wolman, R. N.; and King, M. The development of the language of the emotions. *American Journal of Psychiatry* 127 (1971): 1491–1497.

Lief, H. I., and Thompson, J. The prediction of behavior from adolescence to adulthood. *Psychiatry* 24: 32–38.

Morgan, J. C. Adolescent problems and the Mooney Problem Check List. *Adolescence* 4 (1969): 111–126.

Moss, H. A., and Kagan, J. Report on personality consistency and change from Fels Longitudinal Study. *Vita Humana* 7 (1964): 127–139.

Murphy, L. B. Factors in continuity and change in the development of adaptational style in children. *Vita Humana* 7 (1964): 96–114.

Plant, W. T., and Telford, C. W. Changes in personality for groups completing different amounts of college over two years. *Genetic Psychology Monographs* 74 (1966): 3–36.

Sage, E. H. Developmental scales for college freshmen. *Journal of Counseling Psychology* 15 (1968): 381–385.

Schaefer, E. S. An analysis of consensus in longitudinal research on personality consistency and change: Discussion of papers by Bayley, Macfarlane, Moss and Kagan, and Murphy. *Vita Humana* 7 (1964): 67–72.

Yarrow, L. J. Personality consistency and change: An overview of some conceptual and methodological issues. *Vita Humana* 7 (1964): 67–72.

Yoshida, T. A study of the personality factors determining goal setting behavior: Experimental analysis of level of aspiration. *Journal of Child Development* 7 (1971): 22–34.

PART TWO

Affective and Cognitive Development

Chapter Five

The Development of Self-concept

Adolescence is a period when an individual is trying to come to terms with himself and his environment. It is a time of development of a set of concepts of self, the confirmation and integration of which will be crucial in determining the adolescent's personal and social behavior as well as his future status as a functionally mature individual. Normally, most adolescents find the development of an integrated, reality-tested set of self-concepts a difficult task, even though facilitative factors in the environment may ease the way for specific individuals and classes of individuals. A number of factors bear witness to the difficulty. Among these are the conditions of the individual's self-confidence, his self-esteem, nervous habits, and psychosomatic complaints, tendency to aggression or withdrawal, and affiliative behavior with peers against other persons. Certain areas in the environment become testing grounds for the development of self-concept, and during adolescence problems that arise tend to cluster around them. Among these are the areas of peer behavior and relationships, heterosexual relations, the physical self, emancipation from adult authority, perception of role and role induction, occupational choice, academic learning and experience, self-acceptance, and development and evaluation of values.

The most difficult period in resolving the problems posed by the final formulation of the self-concept appears to be between ages fourteen and eighteen, although there are individual variations. After eighteen the difficulty gradually begins to decrease until stability of self-perception is reached for most persons sometime in the twenties or early thirties.

The Importance of Self-concepts

The only reality man has is the self, and that is curious, because of all his attributes, this is the least tangible and most amorphous. Actually the self represents a duality looking both outwards and inwards. It is the mediator that presents, interprets, and explains the exterior environment as it exists at any moment and as it may be hypothesized in the past and future; equally it mediates the individual's physical interior.

From birth the human organism has the long developmental task of building a set of identities with which it can interpret and cope not only with its social and physical environment but also with itself as a functioning physical organism. This is a gradual process occurring over a long period of time, never really ending during the life of the individual, although in its formative stages the first two decades of life are the most crucial and action-fraught. During these years identities are not only hypothesized; they are related to the surrounding world of persons and things. Hypothesized identities have to be tested against reality and must be modified and changed as reality proves them to be inappropriate or ill conceived. During this period events as represented by people, things, and happenings must be understood and integrated with the individual's past experiences. The culture is assimilated in the form of symbolic organization leading to patterns of adaptation integrated to the point of permitting: (1) independence; (2) a set of identities of one's own; (3) conceptualization of a path into the future; (4) assumption of responsibility for self and for others; and as the apex of the process, (5) attainment of the capacity for selfless love.

It is not an exaggeration to say that the process of self- and identity-building is the chief developmental task in the psychic or affective-cognitive area of the human organism. To a lesser degree it is also an important developmental task in the physical-physiological domain. By this process the organism implements its humanity as it gains a mediator between itself and its environment. In the view of this writer, the task of building, rebuilding, revising, and finally of integrating a set of concepts of self is the chief and most important business of the adolescent period. An individual's concepts of self are pervasive throughout all his behavior. They are as much a product of the emotions as of the intellect. Man's undoubted ability, at least to a point, to increase in problem-solving and other cognitive abilities throughout the early and middle decades of his life always has the brake of the functionally more primitive emotions.

The Background of Self-concept

The concept of a self has a long history in the development of the human race. It has been variously defined, interpreted, and explained, but whatever the definition or manner of approach, the concept is, as a concept, ubiquitous in man's age-old effort to understand himself. To this writer's knowledge, there is no language, modern or classical, primitive or sophisticated, which has not included the words *I, me, myself,* and *mine,* or their equivalents. In the closing years of the last century, psychologists introduced the term *self-concept* and, with their interest in clarification by means of research, have endeavored to incorporate the concept in the whole corpus of be-

havior and to express it in terms susceptible to verification or refutation. As early as 1890 James in his *Principles* devoted a whole chapter to the self. There has since been no year in which more than one article on self-concept has not appeared in the psychological, psychiatric, and sociological journals, and in many years the number of articles has exceeded one hundred. Rogers, in 1947 and Hilgard, in 1949 made their presidential addresses before the American Psychological Association on self-concept. Today more articles on self-concept are being published than at any previous period in the history of psychology. The concept has of course been a preoccupation of philosophy from the earliest days when man attempted to come to grips with himself and with the universe.

Despite the interest of so many psychologists in self-concept, the reader should be aware that a good many other psychologists, particularly of the behaviorist or more traditional experimental variety, find the ideas of self and self-concept too "mentalistic" a construct for their purposes. In their view, the idea of self is a metaphysical concept of an order that makes it inseparable from metaphysics, hence inadmissible as a valid aspect of the science of psychology. However, clinical psychologists, school psychologists, and others directly concerned with children and adolescents have found the construct useful, not only as a background for conceptualizing the nature of development, but also in carrying out their day-to-day work.

This writer's view is that the construct self is necessary to an understanding of human behavior and that it can be removed from its metaphysical status and be so hypothesized that it can be a valid subject for psychological study. True, the idea of a self remains largely in the realm of metaphysics, but science has often progressed by attempting to take metaphysical concepts, state them in terms of hypotheses, and then devise research making the hypotheses susceptible to refutation. Often one has to acquire new knowledge and invent new techniques to make such a venture feasible, but that does not mean the task is necessarily impossible. It is unfortunate that many psychologists attempting to study self have given an old entity a new name, and while denying its existence as an entity, have proceeded as though they were in fact really dealing with an entity. Thus they become victims of their own nomenclature ("I call him Harvey, because that is his name.") and try to apply experimental techniques to a concept they have really left in the metaphysical domain. Psychologists studying the self should endeavor to separate the "entity" from its metaphysical base and anchor it in such a manner that statements about self would be susceptible, if not to empirical verification, at least to refutation.[1]

The Definition of Self

In defining self, it is most useful to reject those definitions that conceive of a self as an entity existing as some tangible or intangible component of the organism, and most particularly of an entity that has an existence apart from the organism. The self represents the continuing cognitive-affective organization and reorganization of the individual's experienced past, experiencing present, and anticipation of the future. It is, as Nixon (1962) notes, "the person's symbol for his own organization." R. N. Harris (1971) speaks of the self as the

active, organizing principle which is the system of coordinates, frame of reference or context, in which all isolated data and bits of experience derive their meaning. It is, further, that which is characteristic of the person, his underlying spirit with which the reception of external influences is invested with the flavor and unique spice of life.

Gordon (1969) calls self-concept "the structure of self-referential meanings available to

an individual's conscious interpretive processes."

Actually, as Horrocks and Jackson (1972) and Lifton (1971) point out, self is best conceived as a process. Horrocks and Jackson (1972) write:

Self is a process by means of which the organism derives and constructs self-products which, taken together, represent the organism's interpretation and meaning of itself. In this relationship the organism is the entity and self is the process that evolves representations of its own entity and its related mental and behavioral activities. Operationally, defining or describing one's self is a continuously evolving product of learning, structured in the form of interacting emotional and cognitive elements. Thus, self is the means by which the organism is aware of and understands itself as a corporate being with a past history and a probable or possible future.

For a self to be operative, there has to be an environmental context, a memory or storage system, an integration and differentiation of experience, internal and external interaction, and feeling-affect. A self-concept forms the parameters within which, at the level of conscious behavior, cognitive processes operate. To some extent the development of self-concept has an integral relationship to the development of ability to think, thinking being conceived of as an elaboration of awareness. In essence, the self is a symbolization of the organism and is integrally a functional aspect of it. Actually it can best be defined as a construct that has evolved from the interaction of the organism with itself and its physical environment as a result of its transactions with other organisms. It is a construct of relationship unconfined by limitations of space-time, but one that can never exist apart from the neurological substrate from which it grew. Therefore, at any point in time it must be considered a process rather than an entity.

In defining self one must also reject the idea of preformation. At birth the individual, insofar as anyone has been able to discover, has no concept of self other than whatever protoself

---

[1]The difficulty becomes clear when one considers endeavoring to refute the basic hypothesis, "There is a self." Obviously we must begin with more operational statements derived from a consideration of the developmental sequence.

may have evolved as a result of learning or adaptation during embryogenesis. Certainly the newborn organism has no way of separating itself from its surroundings. The self evolves after conception, within the parameters of the infant's physical and social environment. The individual does bring into the world a genetically coded program that has produced it to that point as a *physical* organism and that, through the directional process of physical maturation and growth, will be effected over the organism's life span; but at birth the psychic aspect is missing and has certainly not been genetically programmed. The psychic program has to be produced by the organism itself after its birth and is limited only by the physical substrate with which it has been endowed and by opportunities provided by the environment in which, initially, it is placed and in which, later, it places itself.

In the light of the foregoing discussion, the self may be further defined as a personal reference construct that involves a perceiving-interpreting action system (that is, possessing the attribute of awareness) operating on the bases of hypotheses and expectancies formulated as the result of learning and previous experience. Thus the self is a very personal concept and really represents an inner view. It is the total construction that an observing, attending organism places upon itself and its surrounding environment—or the environment's past, present, and future that the organism is able to hypothesize. In short, it represents the cognitive organization of the individual's experienced past.

From this cognitive organization, which is really a kind of dynamic process that has emerged during the development of the individual from birth on, evolves the hypothesis of a set of identities, the integration of which may be called the *self-hypothesized identity*. This is the individual's picture (concept) of himself. But this is not to say that the individual may not possess an *aspiration identity*, which is either what he is striving to become or what he wishes he could become even though he has no hope of attaining it.

But man is a social creature interacting with others who perceive his behavior, make judgments about him, and, in effect, define him by attributing to him various identities. There are also the realities of the environment and of an individual's capacities, which force him to assume various roles and to select identities that fit the roles. Equally, the individual may take a role to fit the identities that he perceives himself as having.

Is the hypothesized identity the one others perceive, or is it the one the realities of the environment will permit to operate? The answer is neither, for an individual's self-perception may be neither in accord with the perception others have of him nor with the roles the realities of economic and social life force him to assume. An individual's behavior not in accord with his hypothesized identity may be called his *elicited identity*. Thus, an individual may possess simultaneously four identities: (1) a hypothesized identity, (2) an aspiration indentity, (3) an identity perceived by others,[2] and (4) an elicited identity. The coping behavior involved in dealing with these four identities is the focal problem in the development of the self-concept, particularly during the second decade of life.

Identity and Self

The reader will have observed that this writer differentiates between self and identity and does not use them interchangeably. Identity is the result of a dynamic process that has been defined as the self. The self is the process that hypothesizes identity as the individual is able to verbalize to himself and to others who and what he is. An identity is a self-concept produced by the self-process. In this sense, the identity is the self's own construct, evolving

[2]In actuality any individual has numerous perceived identities, probably as many as there are perceivers, for different people interpret the same person differently, depending upon their relative roles and the situations in which interaction takes place. Yet an individual's pattern of behavior can be such that there may be considerable commonality in the views most persons have of him.

from the physical-physiological development of a living organism possessing awareness, hence mind. Such a construct, of course, must be based upon a series of postulates and hypotheses that have to face the test of reality. No assumption should be made that the self-process is infallible, since its product, identity, is only an hypothesis, and, like all hypotheses, may prove to be untenable when tested against reality. However, when the hypothesized identity is confirmed by reality the individual's identity is more secure and he has taken a further step toward his ultimate maturity.

The reader will find various different uses of the terms *self, self-concept,* and *identity* in the literature of psychology and sociology. For that reason he should be careful to look for specific definitions when different writers use the terms. For example, Erikson's (1963) use of the term *identity* is more global than is that of this writer, and when he uses the term *identity* Erikson does not visualize a multiplicity of identities coexisting as the structure of an individual's self-view. For the purposes of this textbook, this writer posits self as a process whose end product consists of self-hypotheses called identities. Any individual has numerous different identities[3] for use at different times as his own and society's expectations make them appropriate. Optimally, in an individual's self-view, such identities should form an integrated whole. That they do not in adolescence is one of the problems of that period of life. Identity integration is a continuing developmental task of the adolescent period.

The Hypothesized Identity

Since identity is defined as a hypothesis made by the organism about itself, it is important to examine the child's intellectual ability to hy-

pothesize. Here the formulations of Inhelder and Piaget (1958) have relevance, since they enable us to understand what approaches an individual uses at the various developmental stages as he builds his hypothesized identity. Piaget reports that during the chronological age period from seven to eleven the child exists in a concrete, simplistic world. His approach is descriptive, and he limits himself to the raw data of his perceptions. He classifies, orders data in series, and sets up correspondences. He does not isolate the factors involved or embark upon systematic experimentation. He is able to tell who and what he is, but he does not ask what or why he is. He accepts himself without question on the basis of the data at hand.

According to Piaget, the child begins a final period of operational development (propositional or formal elements) at about eleven to twelve and reaches a peak at fourteen to fifteen. During this period he develops the ability to reason by hypothesis—that is, he can now accept any sort of data as hypothetical and can reason from it. Thought no longer proceeds from the actual to the theoretical; it starts from theory so as to establish or verify relationships between things. Instead of merely coordinating facts about the actual world, hypothetico-deductive reasoning draws out the implications of possibilities. Thus the adolescent tries to discover all possible combinations so as to select the true and discard the false. He typically begins to form hypotheses about himself, which he then feels impelled to test against reality.[4] When the hypotheses so tested are found inaccurate they must be modified or dropped. A child who hypothesizes a brick wall as made of glass and tries to see through it encounters reality, even as when he hypothesizes the bricks as made of air and walks into them. It is interesting that a means of ignoring reality is to make believe and play a game that one can really see through the bricks. Children often do this, and we call it

---

[3]An individual is many things, not only to himself, but to others. He may simultaneously be a male, an American, a father, a son, a student, a photographer, a golfer, etc. In any given role situation he selects any clustering of such identities as he deems appropriate. Obviously, no person uses all of his identities in any given role situation.

[4]The problem of reality has presented difficulties for psychological theory. For an insightful discussion of the nature and meaning of reality, the reader is referred to Murphy and Spohn (1968).

play or imagination. When adolescents do it, we are less understanding and call it daydreaming or fantasy. But in either case, the matter becomes serious when, refusing to accept reality, the individual clings to his original hypothesis that the bricks are made of air and continues to act as though they were indeed air. In its more massive forms, we call this psychosis, and in its less massive forms, we call it neurosis.

Still the matter is not simple, for with the integration of experience hypotheses become integrated-related, and whole constellations of hypotheses must be depended upon as the individual builds his personal house of cards. To test one hypothesis against reality is, in effect, to test a number, and, to find one inaccurate or insufficient and in need of modification leads to the need to modify a number of others. Obviously, some tests of reality are indeed crucial and may lead to some exceedingly major changes. And when resistance is encountered, the changes may have far-reaching effects on the individual.

Actually the adolescent is in search of himself. Previously he accepted what he found and did not question it, nor did he have any particular reason to defend it. During his adolescence he hypothesizes and rejects and feels the need to explain.

However, although the adolescent is capable of trying to discover all possible combinations and to discard the false and select the true, he must still operate under certain limitations. Affect, habit, and the stereotypes engendered by previous experience exist. Defensive behavior may force him to operate at an earlier stage of his intellectual development. In everyday life one does not exist in a logical world of mathematics and physics. The individual must often use faulty or wrong data provided by his culture and his previous experience.

Self-disclosure

Measurement of adolescent self-concept is usually performed by means of questionnaires, self-ratings, personal descriptions by the respondent, or by adult raters using specified behaviors as criteria. As was indicated in the preceding chapter on personality, all such measurements are subject to error owing both to possible dishonesty, or lack of acumen of the rater, and to the possible low level of reliability and validity of the technique or instrument used. Particularly in the case of an area so personal as one's self-view, measurement of self-disclosure presents the possibility of confabulation, if not more specific dishonesty. This becomes particularly true when self-revelation is personally threatening because of real or imagined inferiorities difficult to face, or when it is due to fear of use of the results by the adult gathering the information. It is only natural for an adolescent to want to protect himself against threat as well as to want to try to look well in the eyes of others. In some situations generalized adult-adolescent hostility militates against the likelihood of truthful responses. For these reasons self-disclosures of adolescents have to be interpreted with caution. Still, with proper precautions, self-disclosure studies do yield insights into the state of adolescent self-perceptions as well as the extent of their willingness to share these perceptions with others.

West (1970), in a study of ninth graders, reports that girls tend to be more circumspect in choosing the persons to whom they extend their confidences, while in contrast boys tend to be more circumspect in what they say, but less so in the person they select for the confidence. A study made by Rivenbark (1971) agrees with that of West about the freer content of girls' self-disclosures. In addition, speaking of the targets of self-disclosure communications, Rivenbark notes that disclosures to same-age friends increase with age during adolescence, that mothers tend to be confided in more than do fathers, and that personal disclosures are more apt to be made to same-sex peers.

Where sheer willingness to yield self-disclosure information is concerned, a study of urban females aged twelve to eighteen made in India by Sinha (1972) yields an interesting U-shaped curve of change. Sinha found that twelve- to fourteen-year-olds showed most self-disclosure with seventeen- to eighteen-year-olds next and fifteen to sixteen-year-olds least. In discussing his results Sinha notes that the extent of self-disclosure varies with the advance of adolescence and writes:

This may be explained on the presumption that as girls advance in age from early to midadolescence, they become more conscious of their self and start inhibiting its expression and disclosure to others. But, when they leave midadolescence and reach the late adolescent period, their self-consciousness becomes mature and they start disclosing themselves.

Sinha's findings, of course, apply specifically to modern urban Indian females, but it may be assumed that, except for a somewhat longer span of years for middle adolescence, the picture is not materially different in America, despite the existence of obvious differences in the two cultures. Of course willingness to disclose oneself to others is a highly personal matter, and factors other than sex, age, and pubescent status have to be taken into consideration. For example, Lubin (1965), Pederson and Higbee (1969), and Halverson and Shore (1969) have indicated the relationship of self-disclosure to personality, and Jourard (1961) and Dimond and Hellkamp (1969) have cited correlations with race and culture.

Accuracy in Self-reporting

How accurate are an adolescent's self-reports? As Jones et al. (1973) report in a study of self-descriptions of three hundred males and females, persons tend to put their best foot forward in self-reports. It may be assumed that if they are not actually falsifying, many will be at least selective in what they do and do not report. This being true, a great deal depends upon the manner of eliciting self-reports and the adolescent's perception of the reason for the collection of the information. It is well known that questionnaires are subject to motivational distortion when the respondent

feels that something personally important is at stake, or even to cognitive distortion if the individual is inaccurate in his own self-view. Distortion becomes even more feasible when information is gained by means of self-essays or interviews. Jones et al. (1973), for example, note that persons making self-reports usually present themselves as nonthreatening individuals in terms of presenting themselves as non-aggressive, introverted, inhibited—even soft. One technique, while certainly not free from error, enabling an experimenter to check some aspects of self-report accuracy is to have peers rate the person doing the self-evaluation, making use of the same rating technique or instrument—such as a questionnaire—as the subject is using for himself.

In a study of children in grades five through twelve (age ranges approximately ten to nineteen), de Jung (1959) reported that as an individual proceeds through adolescence and advances in schooling, the accuracy of his self-reports tend to increase in terms of their agreement with the reports made of him by others, although in late adolescence (eighteen to nineteen) there appears to be a small decrease in such agreement. Confirming the de Jung findings, Bailey and Gibby (1971) reported that individuals in the seventeen-to-nineteen-year-old range were more realistic and less discrepant in their self-reports than were preadolescents in the eleven-to-twelve-year-old range. However, de Jung (1959) adds an interesting observation in noting that within a given grade in school chronological age is not a factor. Apparently, educational experience rather than age itself seems to be a major factor in self-report accuracy. It is quite possible that added experience, as represented by increments of schooling and related opportunities to socialize, enable a person to know himself better or rather to formulate self-statements more in accord with reality. The younger persons may have been accurate in reporting what they perceived, but the accuracy of their perceptions as judged by an outside criterion was much less than later experience would enable it to become. The point might even be raised that as long as he tells the truth as he sees it an individual cannot have an inaccurate self-view. Where he is concerned, he is what he perceives himself to be, until reality forces him to accept or abandon that self-interpretation. Even others' consensual perception of an individual is only their view—not the individual's.

Turning from general age or grade trends to matters more specifically individual in nature, we find Barrett (1968), in a study of ninth-grade boys, reporting that persons possessing high rather than low self-regard tend to make more accurate self-estimates, and that knowledge of exactly where one stands in the estimation of others tends to produce greater self-report accuracy. Where intelligence is concerned, Spaights (1965) reports that bright individuals in very early adolescence (ages twelve to thirteen) tend to rate themselves less accurately than do their less able peers. Perhaps, being bright, they are more adept at distortion, or perhaps they have imaginations providing more scope for fantasy. On the other hand, de Jung (1959) reports a lack of relationship across the years of adolescence between mental age and self-report accuracy.

The Exteriorization of Identity

As the individual's sense of identity is evolving from his self-concept, or even after the identity is well formulated, tested successfully against reality, and integrated into the behavior, the individual may exteriorize identity —give it away, so to speak—to some person or object in the actual hypothesized environment.[5] In the cartoon series *Peanuts*, Linus

carries an old blanket about with him and refuses to be separated from it. We may assume that for Linus the blanket becomes himself and, in effect, may be thought of as standing surrogate for himself. To separate him from it is to separate him from himself, and since he has given himself away (to the blanket), nothing is left when the blanket is gone.

Of course the exteriorization may only be partial, in that we may project some aspects of our identity to an object or a person and withhold other aspects for ourselves. In considering an exteriorizing individual, it would be revealing to analyze what aspects have been projected and what retained.

For most of us, the idea of projecting ourselves to an inanimate object is quite bizarre. But to make such a projection to another person seems more logical, although psychologically it is neither more nor less so. In considering exteriorization, it may well be necessary to consider the somatic and the psychic identities separately. Can one ever give away the somatic identity? Probably not, except in cases of extreme hysteria or other really deviate manifestations.

Persons who are field-independent probably exteriorize more easily than those who are field-dependent.[6] Witkin et al. (1962) note that field-independents have a greater developed sense of separate identity. It may be that field-independents have something to give away, while the field-dependents, having nothing, give nothing.

Changes in Self-concept

It is perhaps trite to say that changes bring differences, but nevertheless they do, and this fact presents a further problem during

---

[5]An individual may depart so far from reality that he is able to build for himself, and even surround himself by, a false or imaginary environment incapable of being sensed by others. The individual's degree of belief in and the completeness of his acceptance of this hypothesized environment is an index of his contact with reality. Some individuals become so immersed in their imaginary environments that nothing outside is real and they may be said to have retreated from the world in order to live in a figment of their own imagination.

[6]"The person with a more field-independent way of perceiving tends to experience his surroundings analytically, with objects experienced as discrete from their backgrounds. The person with a more field-dependent way of perceiving tends to experience his surroundings in a relatively global fashion, passively conforming to the influence of the prevailing field or context." (Witkin et al. 1962, p. 35)

the development of a conception of self. What one is today one may not be tomorrow, to the extent of losing continuity with oneself. Adults whose identities and their integration have become relatively secure can rationalize these lacks of continuity, but for the adolescent whose self-percepts are insecure at best the matter is more serious. Hence he has trouble in maintaining continuity with himself and in recognizing himself as he existed in times past as the same person he now is. The tendency is to allow a generalized term to stand for the continuity and say, *"Then* I was a child, *now* I am grown up." But one is not a child one day and a grown-up the next. There have been years of transition and living in between, so that the generalized response answers nothing if one really thinks about the difference. An adolescent in trouble will often say, "I don't know what is the matter with me. I never used to be like that. What has happened to me?"

Studies of self-concept during adolescence do indicate the occurrence of specific sequential changes.[7] Degenhardt (1971), in a longitudinal study of ten- to fourteen-year-old girls, using a semantic differential and a questionnaire, reported a continuous modification of self-image during the very early years of adolescence. Undeutsch (1959), in a study of the development of boys and girls between the ages of ten and sixteen, reported that during the years of early and middle adolescence the ability to be aware of emotions and the motivational processes in oneself is developed and becomes differentiated. Undeutsch sees such development and differentiation as the most important developmental aspect during adolescence.

[7]A problem in interpreting such studies concerns the frequently differing definitions of self used, as well as the kinds of measures used to gain self-information. A typical technique has been to ask an adolescent to rate himself in answer to various questions having to do with, "What I am like" or "My characteristic self." Difficulties with the use of self-ratings were discussed in the previous chapter on personality and there is always the question of whether what the investigator conceives to be a measure of self-concept really does provide a valid measure of anything as complex as an integration of self-views.

Long et al. (1967), discussing a self-social theory of personality, hypothesize changes in self-concept during childhood and note that grade in school is related to esteem, social dependency, individuation, power relative to the teacher, and identification with others. In a further discussion, Long et al. (1968) note: (1) a tendency for social withdrawal of girls in early adolescence and their subsequent return, (2) a tendency as age increased to place fathers in a higher and teachers in a more egalitarian position, (3) a tendency to increase in self-esteem with age, and (4) a tendency to increase in dependency in early adolescence, followed by a decrease in dependency in the later years of adolescence. Kuhn (1960), in a study of self-definitions of 1,185 persons aged seven to twenty-four, also noted marked differences and changes over the span of these years. As individuals grew older, they began to define themselves more and more in terms of group membership and categories such as age, sex, or educational attainment. For example, "I am *in* the first grade," as compared to "I *am* a sophomore." Bowers and London (1965) reported the inception of this trend in a study of children's role playing when, in terms of self-portrayal in an unfamiliar situation, they found an increase in role-playing ability with age.

Interesting contrasts in the development of self-view are to be found in studies enabling comparisons to be made between boys and girls. For example, Perkins (1958) reports on an increasing congruence of self and ideal self over time and noted that girls generally demonstrated a greater congruence than did boys. Carlson (1965) conducted a longitudinal study of changes in the structure of self-image by measuring the self-image of children in the sixth grade and then measuring them again six years later when these same children were in the twelfth grade. He reports that over the six years the girls showed an increase in social-self orientation whereas, in contrast, the boys' increase in orientation was personal rather than social. Washburn (1961), in reporting that over the years of adolescence changes in self-concept—as one might expect —were in the direction of increasing maturity, notes that while self-views of college males were more mature than those of high-school males, the differences in maturity of self-view between college and high-school females, while present, was less marked. Nawas (1971) reports research in which a group of 125 males and females were studied first as adolescents and then eight years later as adults. He notes that changes from adolescence to young adulthood indicated a significant increase for males and a highly significant decrease for females both in ego-complexity and in ego-sufficiency.

Monge (1973) reports a series of crucial differences between boys and girls in the content and development of self-view. In performing his study Monge administered a seven-point semantic differential scale to over two thousand boys and girls in grades six through twelve. The subjects rated the concept "My Characteristic Self" on twenty-one polar adjective pairs. Data were analyzed on the basis of factor analysis yielding the following four factors displaying structural similarity across grade and sex in the self-concept ratings: (1) achievement-leadership, (2) congeniality-sociability, (3) adjustment, and (4) masculinity-femininity. In achievement-leadership, Monge reports that "boys' self-ratings were higher than girls' in every grade, and that boys' means generally increased from Grade 6 to Grade 12, while girls' ratings rose from Grade 6 to a plateau in Grades 7, 8, and 9, then declined gently to Grade 11, followed by a sharp recovery to almost boys' level in Grade 12." Where congeniality-sociability were concerned, the picture was considerably more favorable for girls than for boys. On this factor in every grade girls rated themselves considerably higher than did boys. At every grade level boys' means were negative and girls' were positive. In general, however, and despite the sex differences, the trend toward sociability was upward, with ninth and tenth graders rating themselves significantly higher than sixth and seventh graders. On the adjustment factor, Monge notes a discouraging finding. He writes that there was "for each sex a significant decline in mean ratings from Grade 6 to Grade 10, with a further significant drop for girls from Grade 10 to Grade 11 with a recovery back to the sophomore level by 12th Grade." At every grade level boys rated themselves higher than girls. In discussing this finding Monge speculates, "It appears that as adolescents grow older they find it increasingly difficult to live within the social system revolving about the school." One might add to Monge's statement that the home and society in general also offer problems of adjustment to the burgeoning adolescent. Finally, on the last factor, masculinity-femininity, Monge noted a decline with age in femininity (or an increase in masculinity) for girls from Grades 7 to 12. Boys on this factor apparently affirm the continuity of the masculine role in which they were indoctrinated as small children. Girls on the other hand seem to find that the feminine role in practice is not quite as clear as early indoctrination might have led them to believe.

However, although the identities constituting the conception of self do change and develop over the entire adolescent span, the need for continuity and the security it brings are necessary to the point that the self-view does become increasingly stable, since the adolescent tends to resent change and to cling to what he has built. This is particularly true when the resolution of the self-percept has been satisfactory as it is confirmed by experience and offers the adolescent an acceptable self-view. Engel (1959) noted the relative stability of self-concept during the adolescence of better-adjusted children. She studied stability of self-concept by testing adolescents in the eighth and tenth grades, and then testing the same individuals a second time two years later when they were in the tenth and twelfth grades. Over this two-year period she found that those with an initially positive self-concept retained this status, but those whose original self-concept was negative displayed less stability and gave evidence of significantly more maladjustment over the two-year run.

Bunt (1968) also noted that constancy of self-concept during adolescence bears a direct relationship to the relative degree of ego identity attained.

Self-concept, as both Gecas (1971) and Levine (1958) note, evolves as a sequential series of levels of self-perception arising through interaction with significant others. If, in these social interactions, the individual finds that his tests of reality confirm his self-percepts, his self-concept tends to remain more stable than if he encounters lack of success. A further factor promoting self-view stability, although of a nature promoting maladjustment, is the individual's tendency to find security by resisting change. For many adolescents who seek security through stability, we find attempts to retain perceived identities that have failed tests of reality even if it becomes necessary to resort to defensive behavior to do so. Efforts by teachers, parents, and society in general to impose various standards that attack an adolescent's self-concept are bound to meet resistance and defensive behavior, particularly if the peer culture is supportive and passivity has not already been built into the child by previous child-rearing practices.

Combs and Snygg (1959), in commenting on resistance to change, write: "The stability of the phenomenal self makes change difficult by causing us (a) to ignore aspects of our experience which are inconsistent with it, or (b) to select perceptions in such a way as to confirm the concepts of self we already possess." They feel that change in perceived self depends upon three factors: (1) the clarity of experience provided by a new perception, (2) the way the revised concept fits into the existing self-organization, and (3) the relation of the revised concept to the individual's needs. Obviously, less important aspects of the self-concept are more susceptible to change than are more central ones. Still, changes come slowly, unless the experience that includes change is particularly vivid. Parents and teachers may not assume that a simple admonition is going to produce any substantial results. A child who feels inadequate in any situation is hardly likely to feel suddenly adequate on the basis of a single success experience.

In general, it may be said that development represents movement toward differentiation, and in the course of development over adolescence it may be expected that normally there will be increasing differentiation, at least in the sense of the sequential addition of more differentiated identities, permitting greater potentiality for role behavior. Fortunately, the structure of the self-concept permits many different self-views, many of which may actually be mutually exclusive. Development toward a mature self-concept involves movement toward a resolution of dissonance among self-views and the gradual emergence of an integration of self-views into a harmonious reality-tested self-system.

Identity Diffusion

In the Chapter 3 discussion of Erikson's (1963, 1964) theory of psychosocial development, the period of adolescence was presented as a time of seeking a final integrated identity in the face of complicating environmental and personal factors that promote role confusion. This leads to a situation of crisis in which the adolescent becomes involved in trying to evolve a new set of self-views from his previous identities and values; yet the new self must lead to meaningful goals and behavior compatible with those of the peer group. Erikson concluded that the core conflict of adolescence is identity versus identity diffusion. According to Erikson, the other conflicts of adolescence may be subsumed under the main conflict and include: self-certainty versus identity-consciousness, time perspective versus time diffusion, anticipation of achievement against paralysis, and sexual identity versus bisexual diffusion.

While Erikson does not see the process of identity as limited to adolescence, he does visualize adolescence as a time span during which already acquired partial identifications have to find combination with new identifications and with choosing a pattern for future role behavior. For Erikson (1964), adolescence is a time of identity consolidation. He sees, as Enker (1971) points out, the key problem of identity as one of sameness in change and speaks of identity as "the capacity of the ego to sustain sameness and continuity in the face of changing fate."

In his description of adolescence, Erikson (1955) notes that

each society and each culture institutionalizes a certain moratorium for the majority of its young people. Such a moratorium provides the adolescent with a period of delay during which he experiments with various roles and ideologies as he endeavors to find out who he is and where he belongs in the world of other persons. The result may be a period of identity confusion or diffusion leading to a syndrome of behavior representing the core conflict of adolescence.

In describing the crisis of this conflict, Erikson (1964) writes:

Like a trapeze artist, the young person in the middle of vigorous motion must let go of his safe hold on childhood and reach out for a firm grasp on adulthood, depending for a breathless interval on a relatedness between the past and the future, and on the reliability of those he must let go of, and those who will "receive" him.

An adolescent successfully resolving his identity crisis will regroup his childhood identifications into a new pattern. He will have defined himself and set up a hierarchy of expectations in which he has confidence. His interpersonal relationships will be harmonious and reciprocal, he will be secure in his self-perception, and he will have confidence that others' perceptions of him will be congruent with his own. He has evolved a secure inner identity, yet feels accepted in society.

The adolescent who has not been successful in his resolution of the conflict and whose identity is diffuse will represent the opposite picture. Bronson (1959) reports four interrelated specific characteristics of the identity-diffuse person: (1) lack of continuity between past and present picture, (2) high degree of anxiety, (3) less certainty about present dominant characteristics of self, and (4) fluctua-

tions in feelings about self. Rubins (1968) lists three traits characterizing the attitudinal state of this crisis: (1) extreme fluidity and shifting of symptoms, (2) a glorified self-image, and (3) confusion about self and identity. Rubins also notes that social conditions may aggravate identity distortions such as self-glorification. Giovacchini (1968), in a study of an eighteen-year-old male and a fourteen-year-old female with psychopathological disorders related to identity crisis, notes that both were characterized by their rebellion against their parents' compulsion to make them happy. Obviously behavior during the identity crisis will take different forms. Some adolescents will, for example, deliberately try to prolong their period of dependency (moratorium), others reject their parents, and still others go to great lengths to assume an identity that they have learned is one they should not assume.

The adolescent who is having difficulty in his development of a self-concept to the point of being identity diffuse[8] often uses the different or out-group person as a target for the attribution of his own self-doubts. This is his means of finding closer identification with the peer group and of setting up a personal defense against his own guidelines for mastery and success. Erikson (1959), writing on the conflicts of the acutely diffuse adolescent, notes:

To keep themselves together they temporarily identify, to the point of apparent complete loss of identity, with the heroes of cliques and crowds. On the other hand they become remarkably clannish, intolerant, and cruel in their exclusion of others who are different in skin color or cultural background, in tastes and gifts, and often in entirely petty aspects of dress and gesture arbitrarily selected as the sign of an in-grouper or an out-grouper. It is important to understand such intolerance as the necessary defense against a sense of identity diffusion.... Adolescents help one another temporarily through such discomforts by forming cliques and by stereotyping themselves, their ideals, and their enemies.

[8]Really true to some extent of all adolescents at some period in their progression through adolescence.

The identity-diffuse adolescent lacks inner referents to which to anchor new experiences, he lacks adaptability and tends to fluctuate between unbending resistance and easy compliance. Essentially the identity-diffuse person is dependent, often to the point of passivity, despite his occasional resistances.

Lomas (1965) notes that passivity represents an abnegation of natural authentic development. It arises in an environment that discourages action and rewards parasitism. The passive person often accepts the identity assigned to him or copies an idealized identity. Adults often tend to encourage such acceptance in their young as they lay down the rules of a "good" and a "bad" person. In Victorian times women were the victims of such passivity. The current adolescent unrest and alienated behavior may well have as its basis role assignment by elders, which, if accepted, could lead to identity confusion. Authenticity is one of the battle cries of many of our protesting youth.

In contrast to Erikson, who notes that each culture and each society institutionalizes the moratorium of adolescence, Frankenstein (1966) believes that the moratorium is a purely middle-class phenomenon and that it is to be found only in the cultures of Western society. A child growing up in poverty or, in all probability, one reared in the cultures of the East will not experience the moratorium, since in these situations adolescence is most unlikely to be a noncommitted period between childhood and adulthood. Frankenstein (1966) writes: "When social conditions require the child to participate in his adults' labors and concerns from early life on and the personalistic climate of the family is thereby being reduced to a minimum, a moratory existence, and a life with principles are *ipso facto* excluded."

Frankenstein further disagrees with Erikson in that he does not see identity formation as a normative function of adolescence. For Frankenstein, adolescence represents an interruption in the identity continuum during which the child accepts the illusion of finality rather than the reality of continuity. As Frankenstein sees it, in the absence of need for readjustment to reality there is a corresponding absence of adolescent crisis of the kind typically found in the middle-class Western-type family. In the light of Frankenstein's position, Enker (1971) makes the point that, "the possibility exists that when youth exhibit substandard performance they are only doing what is expected of them. When expected to perform well, they seem to be able to do so. Thus, the strategic act of recognition, the label or diagnosis acquired at this stage, plays a crucial role."

Negativism in Adolescence

It has been widely noted that in early childhood, usually between the fourth and sixth years, the child enters a period of negativism and self-assertion. Such negativism appears to arise as a result of the resistance the child's environment offers to his mastery motives as he attempts to manipulate it. This resistance comes primarily from the people who inhabit the immediate environment; hence the negativism is characteristically directed against the small number of persons, usually his parents and siblings, who comprise his limited social world. As the child perceives it, others are constantly attempting to impose their wills on his. Later his mastery attempts begin to succeed as he learns coping behavior and overt negativism is replaced by a seemingly more cooperative spirit. But the process of building and integrating a concept of self continues.

The advent of puberty and its demands to test reality with the self-structure he has built find the adolescent again entering a negativistic period. Two aspects of his life contribute to this return to negativism. First, the adolescent's greater mobility and new status sooner or later cause parents and other adults to impose a blocking of his mastery motive. Second, the adolescent's hypothesized identity has difficulty as it attempts to test reality; reanalysis and adaptation are uncomfortable, since they frustrate and induce anxiety. It is not pleasant to find that what one has built does not work and must be changed. It is only natural that the adolescent comes to feel that everything else is out of step except himself, that the world is not treating him either fairly or reasonably, and that it is perceiving him incorrectly. Hence the resistance and negativism that maturity with its tested and confirmed identity makes unnecessary. Many adults fail in this area because they have never worked out their problems of self-concept and identity. Even the most mature adult, finding his self-concept under attack, may for a time revisit his adolescent negativism and resistance.

Self-esteem

Having built a concept of self and constructed an identity from it, the question arises as to the esteem with which the adolescent then views himself. What value does he place upon the self he perceives? So many of the decisions he must make rest upon his evaluation of himself and of his hypothesized identity. He has to make an occupational or curricular choice and has to decide whether he is good enough to do what must be done to succeed in a given occupation. He has to decide whether he has the ability to participate in various social or athletic enterprises. Heterosexually, is he attractive enough to interest and succeed with a really desirable member of the opposite sex? Is he a good son? Is he the kind of person others like? Will he succeed in marriage? Will he make a good parent? Does he feel he has the courage, moral or physical, to carry out his convictions and those tasks and roles that have been assigned to him? Is he a coward? Does he have stamina? Could he visualize himself as a leader?

The origins and subsequent development of self-esteem are largely a matter of interaction between an individual's personality and his social experiences. Equally, as U'Ren (1971) notes, the social behaviors resulting from self-esteem are influential in the development of personality and social effectiveness. An individual's behavior in social situations is correlated at least to some degree to his level of self-esteem. For example, Mossman and Ziller (1968) make the point that self-esteem is the component of an individual's self-system most closely associated with his consistency of self-response. Ziller et al. (1969) add that self-acceptance and social acceptance are closely combined.

Research studies have shown the level of self-esteem to be of particular importance in determining an individual's receptivity to others. Walster (1965) has reported self-esteem as affecting a person's receptivity to affection from another and notes that a person momentarily low in self-esteem is more apt to like someone who is accepting and affectionate than would a person of high self-esteem. On the other hand Jacobs et al. (1971) report that persons of low self-esteem often experience difficulty in recognizing affectionate or accepting overtures even when they are being offered. A person convinced of his own lack of worth expects social validation of his own adverse self-views and tends to interpret behavior of others in terms of his own expectations. As might be expected, in a study reported by Simon (1972), persons high in self-esteem were found to perceive themselves as significantly more popular than did persons low in self-esteem. But, high self-esteem also sets social expectations of approval from others. Kimble and Helmreich (1972) found that as compared to persons of moderate self-esteem persons either of high or of low self-esteem show a greater need for approval. Here we find persons of high and of low self-esteem both displaying a need for social approval for quite different reasons. The high-self-esteem person because of approval expectations set by his evaluation of his own worth expects approval and displays need behavior when it is withheld. The low-self-esteem person has little expectation of finding social approval and for that reason is in particular need of receiving it. The person of moderate self-esteem, probably more closely in touch with reality, would appear to have the best probability of normal social adjustment.

There are, as Bruch et al. (1972) and Brissett (1972) explain, a number of complexities involved in considering self-esteem. According to Brissett (1972), self-esteem encompasses two different sociopsychological processes: self-worth and self-evaluation. Self-worth, representing a "feeling of self," has to do with an individual's sense of security and personal worth as a person. On the other hand, Brissett defines self-evaluation as a "process of making a conscious judgment of the social importance or significance of the self." Of the two, self-worth would appear to be less situation-bound, while self-evaluation, because it is directed to performance of a role in a given situation, can and does vary from situation to situation. An adolescent's feeling of self-worth might be very high, but in a given situation his evaluation of himself in that situation could well be realistically low. On the other hand, an adolescent with little feeling of self-worth might, in a situation where past experience has taught him he does well, display a high level of self-evaluation. Of course, it is also true that the two components of self-esteem are not entirely unrelated. Reality may, over a period of time, present an adolescent with such a consecutive series of situations where he is forced to evaluate himself in negative terms that the cumulative effect may be one of erosion where his self-worth is concerned. The opposite effect may occur as positive self-worth is built following a cumulation of situations where reality has fostered good self-evaluations. Parents and teachers can do much to help an adolescent find role situations in which he can arrive at positive self-evaluations. A study by Coombs (1969) is of interest in this connection. Coombs, in a longitudinal study of the dating behavior of 220 male-female pairs, investigated the relationship between social participation, self-concept, and interpersonal valuation. He reported that interpersonal success has a positive effect on self-view and that social participation in an accepting situation leads to further interpersonal success. A further finding of Coombs's study was that a favorable self-evaluation increases social participation. That it is possible to effect short- as well as long-term changes in self-esteem has been reported by such investigators as Baron, Bass, and Vietze (1971), Cooper and Duncan (1971), and Tippett and Silber (1966).

Self-esteem as an Attitude

Rosenberg (1965) has noted that "when an individual is faced with a serious and urgent decision, and when a major basis for this decision is his view of what he is like, then the self-image is likely to move to the forefront of his attention." Rosenberg (1965) further notes that people have attitudes that they apply toward objects and the self may be thought of as an object toward which one has an attitude—"there is no qualitative difference in the characteristics of attitudes toward the self and attitudes toward soup, soap, cereal, or suburbia." In discussing attitudes, Rosenberg makes the point that attitudes differ in content, direction, intensity, importance, salience, consistency, stability, and clarity, and that individuals' self-classifications are made on the basis of these eight dimensions.

We might look at these eight in terms of the adolescent's self-attitude. Where *content* is concerned, what does an adolescent see when he looks at himself? What is his gross self-description? This might include his sex, religion, attributes, school status, skills, and physical structure. Where *direction* is concerned, how favorable or unfavorable, positive or negative are his feelings toward himself? *Intensity* has to do with the strength of his self-feelings—he may feel strongly adverse to himself, or only mildly so. *Salience* of self-attitude tends to be indicated by the amount of time and effort the adolescent expends upon consideration of himself, his characteristics and attributes, in comparison to other things he does. *Importance* is indicated, as the term implies, by how important the adolescent feels he is as compared to the other aspects of his environment. *Stability* is determined by the extent to which the adolescent's self-attitudes fluctuate from time to time, while *consistency*, closely related to stability, depends upon how contradictory the fluctuating self-attitude may be. And finally, *clarity* is determined by the extent to which the adolescent's self-attitudes are sharp and well defined as compared to vague, hazy, and ambiguous. For example, George's self-esteem may stem from the fact that he is a boy of upper socioeconomic status who feels strongly favorable to himself, who spends a great deal of time thinking of himself, always in clear and unambiguous terms, as an exceedingly important person as compared to anyone else he knows.

As a matter of fact, the normally developing adolescent tends to feel, whether his self-attitude is favorable or unfavorable, that he is an important person worthy of a great deal of his own (as well as everyone else's) attention. However, if environmental circumstances and personal attributes are at all favorable, the tendency is for the self-view to be positive rather than negative. As Rosenberg (1965) states, "The distinctive characteristic of self-attitudes . . . is that everyone is motivated to hold the same attitude toward the object, namely, a positive attitude." Murphy (1947) writes: "The main self attitudes, those involving the fear of losing the self esteem . . . struggle to keep the self picture good." The adolescent typically filters out, ignores, or resists exceptions to the favorable self-postulates he holds. As Murphy (1947) further notes, "The self-picture is carried about and consolidated until the individual feels that ordinarily it will hold up pretty well against the efforts of others to penetrate or disvalue it. Any effort of others gradually to dissect or belittle it is handled with reasonable dispatch by taking countermeasures." When the self-attitudes do become unfavorable, the results in the whole adjustive picture presented by the adolescent may be quite serious. Rubins (1965) notes that disturbances in the development of self-idealization and in maturational development of the self tend to produce the following five adverse behavior tendencies in older adolescents: (1) extreme intensity and shifting fluidity of clinical phenomena; (2) intensification of pre-existing attitudinal and emotional conflicts; (3) changeableness and tentativeness of solutions in such conflicts; (4) confusion in the self-concept and identity confusion; and (5) tendency toward exaggerated self-idealization.

Rubin's fifth behavior tendency is, of course, the individual's effort, mentioned by Murphy, to keep the self-picture good. Washburn (1962) studied the mental mechanisms used as protective screening by those who perceive themselves as inadequate. He administered a forced-choice test sampling fifteen different defense mechanisms to groups of high school and college students whose self-views could be identified either as adequate or inadequate. He reported that individuals who perceive themselves as inadequate will tend to develop more hostile defenses against adverse views of themselves than will those who perceive themselves as adequate. Washburn (1962) reported that persons whose self-perception was inadequate adopted more retreating defenses. Nixon (1964) reported that, "The psychologically normal late adolescent . . . is not the average youth, but rather the one who functions in accordance with his psychological design. The normal youth shows self-regard, absence of destructive rebellious behavior, questioning of old values, and a degree of anxiety." In the previously cited study, Washburn reported that subjects in his research characteristically having more anxiety tended to have fewer defensive attitudes justifying unacceptable behavior and avoiding blame than did individuals experiencing less anxiety.

Who Am I?

The answer to the question, "Who am I?" can provide insight into an individual's identity status. There are, of course, vast individual and situational differences in adolescent's answers, but a normative developmental trend is observable. Mullener and Laird (1971) have reported the responses of seventh and twelfth graders and of college students to a questionnaire on which they were asked to rate themselves on personal characteristics such as various achievement traits, intellectual skills, interpersonal skills, physical skills, and social responsibility. Preadolescents and early adolescents, according to these investigators, tend to describe themselves in global terms, but as they grow older their self-descriptions become increasingly more differentiated and articulated. In a setting using 1,185 subjects aged seven to twenty-four, Kuhn (1960) reported that as one grows older one is more apt to define himself in terms of social group membership and categories such as educational attainment, age, and sex. Females tended to identify themselves more by sex and kinship than did males. Persons embarked upon or contemplating professional training tended to mention this affiliation early in their responses. In a study contrasting self-perceptions of males and females Rongved (1961) reported that women tend to select characteristics emphasizing motivational forces while males show a preference for descriptive words depicting regulatory activity. However, sex differences for motivational tendencies tended to decrease with age and those for regulating qualities tended to become greater.

One task of growing up is to develop a self-concept that allows ease in playing the roles set by one's own biology and physical make-up. Too, it involves the ability to play certain roles expected in the culture in which one is reared. One of the most important of these roles involves acceptance of masculinity for boys and of femininity for girls. The ability to accept and play appropriate "demand" roles appears to be partly a result of an individual's personal adequacy and emotional stability. This view was confirmed in a study by Mussen (1961) in which he reported that adolescent boys who scored highest in masculinity on the masculinity-femininity scale of the Strong Vocational Interest Blank showed greater indications of personal adequacy and emotional stability than did boys who scored lowest.

The same situations hold true in other areas. For example, Perkins and Shannon (1965) reported that ideal self-scores are related to both IQ and academic success. Pilisuk (1962) reported that self-evaluations (defined as attitudes closest to one's conception of oneself) changed in adolescents in high school in accordance with their levels of performance in school.

Self-concept and Environment

As studies by Searles (1966), Fine and Jennings (1965), and Cernik and Thompson (1966) attest, the circumstances in which a child is reared are of exceeding importance in his identity formation and in his self-esteem. Kardiner (1968) writes: "The growth of the self-image as a summary of past successes and failures adds up to a conception of oneself as a collection of selected guaranteed successes and failures." Bledsoe and Wiggins (1973), McBride et al. (1970), and Piers (1972) have indicated the importance of the family setting and parental child-rearing practices in the development of the sort of person who emerges. Bledsoe and Wiggins (1973) noted that ninth-grade adolescents who felt that their parents were understanding possessed better self-images on factors involving parent-teenage relations and academic adequacy than was true of self-perceived misunderstood adolescents. Cernick and Thompson (1966) reported that adolescents most successful in recognizing their own strengths and weaknesses presented a pattern of objectivity, organization, positive approach, and a tendency *to utilize home resources*. The mother rather than the father appears to be the key figure in the home's influence. For example, Medinnus (1965) noted that adolescent self-regard was more closely related to the mother's child-rearing attitudes than to the father's. Dignan's (1965) study supported Erikson's theory that, of the early single identifications, that with the mother is extremely significant for identity formation during adolescence.

Coppersmith (1967) studied, over a period of eight years, the antecedents and consequences of self-esteem in terms of background factors, personal characteristics, and the parental treatment associated with high, medium, low, and defensive self-esteem. He asked his subjects: "What are the conditions that lead an individual to value himself and to regard himself as an object of worth?" The answers were: parental warmth, clearly defined limits, and respectful treatment. Coppersmith's opinion was that the four best ways of altering an individual's self-esteem in a positive direction are successes, inculcation of ideas, encouragement of the individual's aspirations, and help in building defenses against onslaughts on self-perception.

It is a good question as to how far parents and other adults should go in building their children's self-esteem. Facilitation can become interference, and it can foster dependence. McBride, Eisenman, and Platt (1970) make the point that definition of self and the development of self-reliance can involve conflict problems of dependence-independence in child-parent relationships. These investigators make the point that symbiotic ties with adults, including parents or other authority figures, can stand in the way of individuation.

The social and economic circumstances under which an adolescent is reared have also been found to be related to self-esteem to some degree although individual and situational differences make generalization difficult. It might be expected that children reared in socioeconomically advantaged families would be more likely to be high in self-esteem than would those from families possessing fewer advantages. A study conducted by Collins and Burger (1969) supports this expectation. These investigators, using the Tennessee Self-concept Scale, with a sample of thirteen- to fourteen-year-olds matched for IQ and race, report that in a comparison of suburban with inner-city school youth the former had higher self-concept scores on seven of nine self-concept variables. Of these seven variables physical-self and family-self showed differences at the highest level of significance. However, the preponderance of evidence reported in other studies appears to disagree with that of Collins and

Burger. Trowbridge (1972), using a sample of 3,789 children and early adolescents, compared self-concept and socioeconomic status on the following four subscales of the Coopersmith Self-esteem Inventory: (1) general self, (2) social self-peers, (3) school-academic, and (4) home-parents. She reports that both children and early adolescents of both sexes, black as well as white, who were of low socioeconomic status scored higher in self-concept than did those of middle socioeconomic status on three of the four subscales. The sole subscale favoring those of middle socioeconomic status was that involving home and parents. In a study concerned with minority groups, Powers et al. (1971) studied the self-image of blacks, Jewish whites, and non-Jewish whites all of whom were attending an inner suburban integrated high school. Among these children, blacks, although lower in performance on various educational measures, displayed a tendency to be higher in self-image.

In a series of studies of advantaged as compared to disadvantaged children, Soares and Soares (1972, 1971a, 1971b, 1970, 1969) also reported that disadvantaged as compared to advantaged elementary and secondary school students possessed more positive self-perceptions. Although in the Soares and Soares studies the disadvantaged children were relatively lower in school achievement, they continued to feel that they would do better than the actuality of the final grade proved to be true. In contrast, advantaged children were more realistic in their appraisal of their own relatively higher achievement outcomes but at the same time maintained their significantly lower self-perceptions. In one study Soares and Soares (1970) report that teachers tended to think more highly of advantaged students, but, interestingly enough, disadvantaged students did not seem to perceive this, believing that their teachers' perception of them was congruent with their own. In summarizing their findings, Soares and Soares noted that they failed to support the widely accepted hypothesis that disadvantaged children necessarily possess negative self-concepts. They further noted that this situation held both for segregated and for nonsegregated schools.

It is encouraging to find disadvantaged children maintaining a relatively good sense of self-worth. That they frequently do is not, however, as surprising as it may seem to those having limited knowledge of the day-to-day lives of disadvantaged children.[9] The tendency is to view disadvantaged children almost solely in terms of lack of material possessions and specific opportunities considered desirable in terms of the middle-class definition of future success. But for the disadvantaged child living in warm and accepting family circumstances with significant adults and peers to whom he can relate, there is no inherent reason for low self-esteem, even though his present circumstances and future prospects are comparatively far from ideal. The encouraging point is that the educational and other efforts on his behalf seeking to improve his present as well as his future circumstances have a decent base of self-worth upon which to build. However, in interpreting the foregoing studies it should be understood that not all disadvantaged youth are high in self-esteem and that, particularly in later adolescence, circumstances may begin to present an accumulation of evidence adverse to a favorable self-view. The question might be raised as to whether the earlier high self-esteem might offer problems of adjustment to reality, especially if the self-esteem is particularly unrealistic. In considering this question, the reader might wish to consider the distinction described earlier between self-worth and self-evaluation. Another understanding necessary in interpreting the foregoing studies is that there is no implication that the self-esteem of middle- and upper-class children is necessarily low. Typically it is not. The studies simply indicate that with the particular

[9]It should be understood that the writer is referring to how the children feel about themselves, what they are doing, and where they are living. The criterion here is that of *the children's own perception at that time in their lives.* It is not that of an adult in a position to evaluate not only their future chances but their present disadvantages in health, schooling, privacy, material possessions, suitable companions, etc.

samples used the central tendency was for the lower socioeconomic class children to maintain self-perceptions relatively higher than was true of more advantaged children.

Nothing said in the preceding paragraphs should be taken to mean that educators and parents should discontinue efforts to improve adolescents' sense of their own personal worth, whether they are advantaged or disadvantaged or whether they fall into any other category. As was indicated at the beginning of this chapter, building and testing a conception of self is a chief task of adolescence. And self-esteem is a central aspect of a positive and healthy conception of self. As Zirkel (1972) has indicated, schools endeavoring to enhance students' self-perceptions have the possibilities of the regular curriculum; ancillary services; significant others, both peer and adult; and special services. Parents have the less formal possibility of building warm and understanding relationships with their adolescent sons and daughters. One difficulty in considering programs for the enhancement of self-view lies in the lack of validity of parents' and teachers' perceptions of the situation actually obtaining where their children's self-perceptions are concerned. For example, Piers (1972) has reported as one indication of lack of validity that parents of disturbed children underestimated their children's self-image while parents of normal children tended to overestimate it.

Summary

Of all man's attributes his conception of self is least tangible, but it is a necessary possession, for it is the mediator with which the individual makes sense of his interior and exterior world. Adolescence marks the crucial final stages of the development of self-concept. During this period many adolescents encounter difficulty in evolving an integrated self-view able to withstand or to adapt to the tests of reality. However, development of a functional and effective self-view must be achieved before psychological maturity may be reached. The task of building and integrating a conception of self is the most important business of the adolescent period.

The idea of a self has characterized man's long effort to understand his own nature, and modern psychology has been vigorously engaged in removing it, as a concept, from the metaphysical domain, in order to make it a proper subject for scientific study. Not all psychologists feel that a construct of self has any place in a science of psychology.

Self should not be thought of as an entity. It is an affective-cognitive process by means of which an individual derives and constructs self-products that, taken together, represent his interpretation of himself. Conception of self is the product of the self-process. An individual's self-concept represents the cognitive organization of his experienced past. To be operative it must have available a context, a memory, differentiated experience, internal and external interaction, and feeling-affect. Self-concept evolves chiefly through learning and is not preformed at birth. In actuality an individual's conception of self involves a set of identities finding exemplification in role behavior, and self-process operates on the basis of hypotheses and expectancies growing out of previous experience. From the process of self, carried on over time, emerge hypothesized identities, aspiration identities, perceived identities, and elicited identities; thus, self-concept and identity are not viewed as synonymous, nor does any individual possess only one identity. Identities should be interpreted as multiple and as products of the dynamic process that has been defined as the self. Identities begin to emerge following inception of ability to think symbolically, although identity formation can reach full fruition only when (in adolescence) an individual develops the ability to reason by hypothesis. He can then formulate his own hypothesis of identity. In some cases identity may be exteriorized to some person or object in the actual or hypothesized environment.

A great deal of the measurement of self-perception depends upon an individual's willingness to disclose personal information about himself. It cannot be expected that such self-disclosure will always be forthcoming, especially when the adolescent is threatened by exposure of his self-view. There is usually a tendency to accentuate the positive and minimize or ignore the negative. In general, younger children are more apt to provide truthful self-disclosures than are individuals in middle and later adolescence. A further problem has to do with the adolescent's accuracy in perceiving and reporting his own self-perceptions. As an individual grows older, his accuracy of self-disclosure tends to increase, even if his willingness to make such disclosures tends to decline. Early in the period of adolescence self-perceptions are often so diffuse that the adolescent is actually too unsure of who and what he is to make any reliable self-interpretations, even if he wishes to do so. Despite age trends, self-disclosure during adolescence can only be seen as a highly individual matter.

While self-concept changes and develops during adolescence, there is a tendency toward stability of self-concept that becomes increasingly strong in the later years. This is particularly true when the resolution of the self-concept has been satisfactory as it is confirmed by experience and offers a satisfactory self-view. Hypothesized identities are less stable than is an individual's self-concept. In general self-concept during adolescence should be seen as undergoing continuous modification and differentiation. As individuals grow older, they begin to define themselves more and more in terms of group membership and categories such as age, sex, or educational attainment. Such changes are reflected in the adolescent's role behavior. Crucial differences are to be found in the development during adolescence of the self-view of boys as compared to that of girls. Greatest stability of self-view is found when the resolution of the self-percept has been satisfactory as it is confirmed by experience and offers the adolescent an acceptable self-view.

According to Erikson the core conflict of adolescence is identity versus identity diffusion and the other conflicts of adolescence may be subsumed under it. The adolescent who successfully resolves his identity crisis has to regroup his childhood identifications and build and test a new identity in which he has confidence. Adolescents unsuccessful in this resolution become ego-diffuse. Erikson believes that each culture and each society institutionalizes a moratorium period during adolescence, but it has been suggested that such a moratorium is a middle-class phenomenon confined to the cultures of Western society.

The life sequence includes two major periods of negativism, one in early childhood and one in adolescence. Adolescent negativism stems from environmental blocking of the mastery motives and from the difficulty encountered by the hypothesized identity in testing reality.

Another important aspect of adolescence has to do with self-esteem. The adolescent's choices, self-evaluations, and self-perceptions depend upon his self-esteem. Self-attitudes differ in content, direction, importance, salience, consistency, stability, and clarity, and the adolescent classifies himself on the basis of these eight dimensions. Normally, self-attitudes are favorable, but when they become unfavorable the results may be quite serious. The origins and subsequent development of self-esteem are largely a matter of interaction between an individual's personality and his social experience, and an individual's level of self-esteem not only grows out of his positive and negative social experiences but in any given social situation is important in deter-

mining not only how he will react but how he will be reacted to. In considering self-esteem it is important to distinguish between self-evaluation and self-worth. Self-worth is the more fundamental of the two in that it is more intrasituational, but on any occasion an individual may be high on one and low on the other.

The answer to the question "Who am I?" is one way to gain insight into an individual's identity status. His concepts of identity are the adolescent's guide to the roles he may appropriately play and dictate the manner in which he will handle the roles he does accept for himself. Here again, age adds differentiation to self-description. Children and younger adolescents tend to describe themselves in terms considerably more global than is true of middle and late adolescents.

The circumstances in which a child is reared are exceedingly important in his identity formation. Of these circumstances, the child-rearing practices of the parents, and particularly those of the mother, are primary. Peer relationships also play an important role. Social and economic circumstances are related to self-esteem, although the relationship is conditioned by individual and situational differences. In general, counter to general expectations, self-esteem in disadvantaged children and adolescents is higher than it is among advantaged children. This self-perception is not in accord with reality but is a state of affairs to be taken into consideration when dealing with the disadvantaged.

References

Bailey, K. G., and Gibby, R. G. Developmental differences in self-ratings on intelligence. *Journal of Clinical Psychology* 27 (1971): 51–54.

Baron, R. M.; Bass, A. R.; and Vietze, P. M. Type and frequency of praise as determinants of favorability of self-image: An experiment in a field setting. *Journal of Personality* 39 (1971): 493–511.

Barrett, R. L. Changes in accuracy of self-estimates. *Personnel and Guidance Journal* 47 (1968): 353–357.

Bledsoe, J. C., and Wiggins, R. G. Congruence of adolescents' self-concepts. *Journal of Psychology* 83 (1973): 131–136.

Bowers, P., and London, P. Developmental correlates of role playing ability. *Child Development* 36 (1965): 499–508.

Brissett, D. Toward a clarification of self-esteem. *Psychiatry* 35 (1972): 255–263.

Bronson, G. W. Identity diffusion in late adolescents. *Journal of Abnormal and Social Psychology* 59 (1959): 414–417.

Bruch, M. A.; Kunce, J. T.; and Eggeman, D. F. Parental devaluation: A protection of self-esteem. *Journal of Counseling Psychology* 19 (1972): 555–558.

Bunt, M. E. Ego identity: Its relationship to the discrepancy between how an adolescent views himself and how he perceives that others view him. *Psychology* 5 (1968): 14–25.

Carlson, R. Stability and change in the adolescent's self-image. *Child Development* 36 (1965): 162–168.

Cernik, H., and Thompson, N. H. Decision-making by teen-agers in six problem areas: Response to the problem of choice of mates. *Character Potential* 3 (1966): 162–168.

Collins, H. A., and Burger, G. K. The self concept of inner city and suburban youth. *National Catholic Guidance Conference Journal* 13 (1969): 10–17.

Combs, A. W., and Snygg, D. *Individual behavior.* New York: Harper, 1959.

Coombs, R. H. Social participation, self concept and interpersonal valuation. *Sociometry* 32 (1969): 273–286.

Cooper, J., and Duncan, B. L. Cognitive dissonance as a function of self-esteem and logical inconsistency. *Journal of Personality* 39 (1971): 298–302.

Coppersmith, S. *Antecedents of self-esteem.* San Francisco: Freeman, 1967.

Degenhardt, A. Aur Veranderung des Selbstbildes von jungen Madchen beim Eintritt in die Reifezeit. *Zeitschrift fur Entwicklungspsychologie und Padagogische Psychologie* 3 (1971): 1–3.

de Jung, J. E. Measurement of accuracy of self-role perceptions. In Huddleston, E. M., ed., *The Sixteenth Yearbook of the National Council on Measurements Used in Education,* pp. 111–116. New York: NCMUE, 1959.

Dignan, M. H. Ego identity and maternal identification. *Journal of Personality and Social Psychology* 1 (1965): 476–483.

Dimond, R. E., and Hellkamp, D. T. Race, sex, ordinal position of birth, and self-disclosure of high school students. *Psychological Reports* 25 (1969): 235–238.

Engel, M. The stability of the self-concept in adolescence. *Journal of Abnormal Social Psychology* 58 (1959): 211–215.

Enker, M. S. The process of identity: Two views. *Mental Hygiene* 55 (1971): 369–374.

Erikson, E. H. Ego identity and psychosocial moratorium. In Witmer and Kotinsky, eds., *New perspectives for research in juvenile delinquency,* pp. 1–23. U.S. Children's Bureau Publication no. 356, 1955.

Erikson, E. H. Identity and the life cycle. *Psychological Issues* 1, no. 1, 1959.

Erikson, E. H. *Childhood and society.* 2nd ed. New York: Norton, 1963.

Erikson, E. H. *Insight and responsibility.* New York: Norton, 1964.

Fine, P. M., and Jennings, C. L. Coping and developmental theory. *Aeromedical Review,* no. 1 (1965).

Frankenstein, C. *The roots of the ego.* Baltimore: Williams and Wilkins, 1966.

Gecas, V. Parental behavior and dimensions of adolescent self-evaluation. *Sociometry* 34 (1971): 466–482.

Giovacchini, P. L. Compulsory happiness: adolescent despair. *Archives of General Psychiatry* 18 (1968): 650–657.

Gordon, C. Self-conceptions methodologies. *Journal of Nervous and Mental Disease* 148 (1969): 328–364.

Halverson, C. F., Jr., and Shore, R. E. Self-disclosure and interpersonal functioning. *Journal of Counseling and Clinical Psychology* 33 (1969): 213–217.

Harris, R. N. The meaning of personal identity. *American Journal of Psychoanalysis* 31 (1971): 39–47.

Hilgard, E. R. Human motives and the concept of self. *American Psychologist* 4 (1949): 374–382.

Horrocks, J. E., and Jackson, D. W. *Self and role: A theory of self-process and role behavior.* Boston: Houghton Mifflin, 1972.

Inhelder, B., and Piaget, J. *The growth of logical thinking from childhood to adolescence.* New York: Basic Books, 1958.

Jacobs, L.; Berscheid, E.; and Walster, E. Self-esteem and attraction. *Journal of Personality and Social Psychology* 17 (1971): 84–91.

James, W. *The principles of psychology.* New York: Holt, 1890.

Jones, R. A.; Sensenig, J.; and Haley, J. V. Self conception: Extraction of structure from free-response protocols. *Proceedings of the Annual Convention of the American Psychological Association* 8 (1973): 231–232.

Jourard, S. M. Self-disclosure patterns in British and American college females. *Journal of Social Psychology* 54 (1961): 315–320.

Kardiner, A. *Human adaptation.* Boston: Houghton Mifflin, in press.

Kimble, C., and Helmreich, R. Self-esteem and the need for social approval. *Psychonomic Science* 26 (1972): 339–342.

Kuhn, M. H. Self attitudes by age, and professional training. *Sociological Quarterly* 1 (1960): 39–55.

Levine, J. Representation des etapes du developpement et conscience de soi chez l'enfant. *Enfance,* no. 2 (1958): 85–114.

Lifton, R. J. Protean man. *Archives of General Psychiatry* 24 (1971): 298–304.

Lomas, P. Passivity and failure of identity development. *International Journal of Psychoanalysis* 46 (1965): 438–454.

Long, B. H.; Henderson, E. H.; and Ziller, R. C. Developmental changes in the self-concept during middle childhood. *Merrill-Palmer Quarterly* 13 (1967): 201–215.

Long, B.; Ziller, R.; and Henderson, E. Developmental changes in the self-concept during adolescence. *School Review* 76 (1968): 210–230.

Lubin, B. A. A modified version of Self-disclosure Inventory. *Psychological Reports* 17 (1965): 498.

McBride, J. W.; Eisenman, R.; and Platt, J. J. Dependence, independence, symbiosis, and therapy. *Psychology* 7 (1970): 7–14.

Medinnus, G. R. Adolescents' self acceptance and perceptions of their parents. *Journal of Consulting Psychology* 29 (1965): 150–154.

Monge, R. H. Developmental trends in factors of adolescent self-concept. *Developmental Psychology* 8 (1973): 382–393.

Mossman, B. M., and Ziller, R. C. Self-esteem and consistency of social behavior. *Journal of Abnormal Psychology* 73 (1968): 363–367.

Mullener, N., and Laird, J. D. Some developmental changes in the organization of self-evaluations. *Developmental Psychology* 5 (1971): 233–236.

Murphy, G. *Personality,* New York: Harper, 1947.

Murphy, G., and Spohn, H. E. *Encounter with reality.* Boston: Houghton Mifflin, 1968.

Mussen, P. Some antecedents and consequents of masculine sex-typing in adolescent boys. *Psychological Monographs* 75 (1961), whole no. 506.

Nawas, M. M. Change in efficiency of ego functioning and complexity from adolescent to young adulthood. *Developmental Psychology* 4 (1971): 412–415.

Nixon, R. E. An approach to the dynamics of growth in adolescence. *Psychiatry* 24 (1962): 18–31.

Nixon, R. E. Psychological normality in the years of youth. *Teachers College Record* 66 (1964): 70–71.

Pederson, D. M., and Higbee, K. L. Personality correlates of self-disclosure, *Journal of Social Psychology* 78 (1969): 81–89.

Perkins, C. W., and Shannon, D. T. Three techniques for obtaining self-perceptions in pre-adolescent boys. *Journal of Personality and Social Psychology* 2 (1965): 443–447.

Perkins, H. V. Factors influencing change in childhood self concepts. *Child Development* 29 (1958): 221–230.

Piers, E. V. Parental prediction of children's self-concepts. *Journal of Consulting and Clinical Psychology* 38 (1972): 428–433.

Pilisuk, M. Cognitive balance and self relevant attitude. *Journal of Abnormal and Social Psychology* 65 (1962): 95–103.

Powers, J. M. et al. A research note on the self-perception of youth. *American Educational Research Journal* 8 (1971): 665–670.

Rivenbark, W. H. Self-disclosure patterns among adolescents. *Psychological Reports* 28 (1971): 35–42.

Rogers, C. R. Some observations on the organization of the personality. *American Psychologist* 2 (1947): 358–368.

Rongved, M. Sex and age differences in self-perception. *Vita Humana* 4 (1961): 148–158.

Rosenberg, M. *Society and the adolescent self-image.* Princeton: Princeton University Press, 1965.

Rubins, J. L. The self-idealizing and self-alienating process during late adolescence. *American Journal of Psychoanalysis* 25 (1965): 27–40.

Rubins, J. L. The problem of the acute identity crisis in adolescence. *American Journal of Psychoanalysis* 28 (1968): 37–47.

Searles, H. F. Concerning the development of an identity. *Psychoanalytic Review* 53 (1966): 7–30.

Simon. W. E. Some sociometric evidence for validity of Coopersmith's Self-Esteem Inventory. *Perceptual and Motor Skills* 34 (1972): 93–94.

Sinha, V. Age differences in self-disclosure. *Developmental Psychology* 7 (1972): 257–258.

Soares, A. T., and Soares, L. M. Self-perceptions of culturally disadvantaged children. *American Educational Research Journal* 6 (1969): 31–45.

Soares, A. T., and Soares, L. M. Interpersonal and self-perceptions of disadvantaged and advantaged high school students. *Proceedings of the Annual Convention of the American Psychological Association* 5, pt. 1 (1970): 457–458.

Soares, A. T., and Soares, L. M. Expectancy, achievement, and self-concept correlates in disadvantaged and advantaged youths. *Proceedings of the Annual Convention of the American Psychological Association* 6 (1971): 561–562.

Soares, A. T., and Soares, L. M. Comparative differences in the self-perceptions of disadvantaged and advantaged students. *Journal of School Psychology* 9 (1971): 424–429.

Soares, A. T., and Soares, L. M. The self concept differential in disadvantaged and advantaged students. *Proceedings of the Annual Convention of the American Psychological Association* 7, pt. 1 (1972): 195–196.

Spaights, E. Accuracy of self-estimation of junior high school students. *Journal of Educational Research* 58 (1965): 416–419.

Tippett, J. S., and Silber, E. Autonomy of self esteem: An experimental approach. *Archives of General Psychiatry* 14 (1966): 372–385.

Trowbridge, N. Self concept and socio-economic status in elementary school children. *American Educational Research Journal* 9 (1972): 525–537.

Undeutsch, U. Neuere Untersuchungen zur Alter-

gestalt de Pubeszenz. *Zeitschrift für Experimentelle und Angewandte Psychologie* 6 (1959): 578–588.

U'Ren, R. C. A perspective on self-esteem. *Comprehensive Psychiatry* 12 (1971): 466–472.

Walster, E. The effect of self-esteem on romantic liking. *Journal of Experimental and Social Psychology* 1 (1965): 184–197.

Washburn, W. C. Patterns of self-conceptualization in high-school and college students. *Journal of Educational Psychology* 52 (1961): 123–131.

Washburn, W. C. Patterns of protective attitudes in relation to differentiation in self-evaluation and anxiety level among high school students. *California Journal of Educational Research* 13 (1962): 84–94.

West, L. W. Sex differences in the exercise of circumspection in self-disclosure among adolescents. *Psychological Reports* 26 (1970): 226.

Witkin, H. A.; Dyk, R. B.; Faterson, H. F.; Goodenough, D. R.; and Karp, S. A. *Psychological differentiation.* New York: Wiley, 1962.

Ziller, R. C.; Hagey, J.; Smith, M.; and Long, B. H. Self-esteem: A self-social construct. *Journal of Consulting and Clinical Psychology* 33 (1969): 84–95.

Zirkel, P. A. Enhancing the self-concept of disadvantaged students. *California Journal of Educational Research* 23 (1972): 125–137.

Suggested Readings

Avila, D., and Purkey, W. Self-theory and behaviorism: A rapprochement. *Psychology in the Schools* 9 (1972): 124–126.

Bakan, R. Academic performance and self-concept as a function of achievement variability. *Journal of Educational Measurement* 8 (1971): 317–319.

Barinbaum, L. Role confusion in adolescents. *Adolescence* 6 (1972): 121–127.

Bell, A. P. Role modelship and interaction in adolescence and young adulthood. *Developmental Psychology* 2 (1970): 123–128.

Brim, O. G. Jr., Adolescent personality as self-other systems. *Journal of Marriage and the Family* 27 (1965): 156–162.

Carlson, R. Stability and change in the adolescent's self image. *Child Development* 36 (1965): 659–666.

Cohen, H. A., and Miller, R. Mobility as a factor

in adolescent identity problems. *Psychological Reports* 25 (1969): 775–778.

Fretz, B. R. and Engle, D. A. Changes in self-concept as a function of academic test results. *Journal of Educational Research* 66 (1973): 227–229.

Gecas, V. Parental behavior and contextual variations in adolescent self-esteem. *Sociometry* 35 (1972): 332–345.

Gergen, K. J. *The concept of self.* New York: Holt, Rinehart and Winston, 1971.

Hollander, J. Sex differences in sources of social self-esteem. *Journal of Consulting and Clinical Psychology* 38 (1972): 343–347.

Jorgensen, E. G., and Howell, R. J. Changes in self, ideal-self correlations from ages 8 through 18. *Journal of Social Psychology* 79 (1969): 63–67.

Kay, R. S.; Felker, D. W.; and Varoz, R. O. Sports

interests and abilities as contributors to self-concept in junior high school boys. *Research Quarterly* 43 (1972) : 208–215.

Korman, A. K. Relevance of personal need satisfaction for overall satisfaction as a function of self-esteem. *Journal of Applied Psychology* 51 (1967) : 533–538.

Ludwig, D. J. Evidence of construct and criterion-related validity for the self-concept. *Journal of Social Psychology* 80 (1970) : 213–223.

Meltzer, M. L., and Levy, B. I. Self-esteem in a public school. *Psychology in the Schools* 7 (1970) : 14–20.

Otto, H. A., and Healy, S. L. Adolescents' self-perception of personality strengths. *Journal of Human Relations* 14 (1966): 483–491.

Paschal, B. J., and Williams, R. H. Some effects of participation in summer Upward Bound program on the self-concept and attitude of the disadvantaged adolescent. *Journal of Negro Education* 39 (1970) : 34–43.

Perez, J. F., and Cohen, A. I. *Mom and dad are me.* Belmont, Calif.: Brooks-Cole, 1969.

Schonfeld, W. A. Adolescent turmoil and the search for identity. *American Journal of Psychoanalysis* 31 (1971) : 19–34.

Sears, P. S., and Sherman, V. S. *In pursuit of self-esteem.* Belmont, Calif.: Wadsworth, 1964.

Smith, S. L. *Nobody said it's easy.* New York: Macmillan, 1965.

Snider, J. G.; Snider, J. A., Jr.; and Nichols, K. E. Active-passive social attitudes toward self and ideal-self in children in Canada and the United States. *Journal of Social Psychology* 76 (1968) : 135–136.

Soares, L. M., and Soares, A. T. Self-concepts of disadvantaged students. *Child Study Journal* 1 (1970–1971) : 69–73.

Trowbridge, N. Socioeconomic status and self-concept of children. *Journal of Teacher Education* 23 (1972) : 63–65.

Trowbridge, N.; Trowbridge, L.; and Trowbridge, L. Self-concept and socio-economic status. *Child Study Journal* 2 (1972) : 123–143.

Waterbor, R. Experiental bases of the sense of self. *Journal of Personality* 40 (1972) : 162–179.

Wooster, A. D., and Harris, G. Concepts of self and others in highly mobile service boys. *Educational Research* 14 (1972): 195–199.

Wylie, R. C. *The self-concept.* Lincoln: University of Nebraska Press, 1961.

Chapter Six

Cognition and Cognitive Development

The Definition and Nature of Cognition

To this point in our consideration of the nature of adolescence the discussion has centered primarily around general characteristics of the period, personality, and the development of self-percepts. Another important area in behavior during adolescence has to do with cognitive development and functioning.

Cognition is a generic term for all of those processes by means of which an individual apprehends and imparts meaning to an object or idea or grouping of objects and ideas. Through the processes of cognition an individual becomes aware and gains knowledge of an object. Cognition includes perceiving, sensing, recognizing, associating, conditioning, thinking, conceiving, judging, reasoning, problem solving, and remembering as relevant processes. According to Piaget (1950), cognition involves the structuring behavior that determines the various possible circuits between subject and object. He gives as examples of cognition a perception, a sensorimotor learning (habit), an act of insight, and an act of judgment. Horrocks and Jackson (1972) write that

in the cognitive process the complex of imprints of past experience upon the organismic structure are combined with the attributes of the presented stimulus object or situational event to determine how that object or event will be perceived and processed. The expectancies and assumptions that an individual makes about his internal and external world are outcomes of the cognitive process. The manner in which he sees and interrelates the various aspects of his entire environment define an individual's cognitive structures.

In the study of behavior, cognition has to do with the question of *how* behavior takes place. It does not deal with the question of *why* behavior takes place; hence is not concerned with conation or affect.[1] At the present time in developmental psychology (including, of course, the psychology of adolescence), the study of cognitive process is primarily concerned with concept formation, problem solving, and the thought processes. Recently research and speculative writings have extended the field to include learning, and a great deal has been written about cognition and the educative process.

Theories of behavior of the kind presented in Chapter 3 may be divided roughly into cognitive and noncognitive theories. For example, van de Geer and Jaspars (1966) note that in the field of learning theory a distinction may be made between cognitive positions and stimulus-response approaches, the latter offering their explanations in terms of habit acquisition, the former in terms of cognitive structure. However, the distinction between cognitive and noncognitive theories often becomes blurred because of the very nature of the cognitive process. Van de Geer and Jaspars

---

[1]Obviously cognition is influenced both by needs-goals and emotions, but influence does not mean that either conation or affection are aspects of cognition. Cognition can best be conceived as a mode of consciousness coordinate with conation and affect.

(1966) note that in actuality one distinguishes between cognitive and noncognitive theories not by their content or by the domains of psychology they include but by their approach —"the particular flavor of their approach." One could consider cognitive behavior in terms of a form of internal mapping or of a network of implicit responses. Still another approach would examine the strategies by which an individual arrives at various levels of decision by a selective collection of inputs.

Harvey, Hunt, and Schroder (1961) write that the individual's conceptual system is an "experiential filter through which impinging events are screened, gauged, and evaluated; a process that determines in large part what responses can and will occur." An individual builds a conceptual system and through it he interprets his world. The developmental issue here is the level of cognitive manipulation available to him in building his system. Obviously, if he is unable to formulate hypotheses or to manipulate space-time relationships, his cognitive view will be limited thereby and will be, in effect, less formal.[2]

The Development of Cognition

An individual's cognitive development may best be described as an ascending sequence of identifiable stages, each more complex than the preceding one. Thus, the cognitive behavior of individuals at different stages in mental development may be differentiated. Knowledge of a person's stage of cognitive development enables predictions to be made of his most probable cognitively based behavior and at the same time indicates the limits of the experiences to which he may profitably be exposed. Piaget (1960) has stated that a concept of cognitive stages must include four general characteristics. First, each stage as compared to every other should imply a qualitatively dis-

tinct method (mode) by means of which an individual thinks and solves problems. Second, the stages must be in invariant sequence. Cultural or other environmental factors may alter the rate at which the sequence proceeds, but the sequence is unalterable. Third, each stage should represent a relatively unique underlying thought organization (as level of formal operations). Such organization is best thought of as a structured whole. And fourth, each stage should represent a hierarchical integration. As one stage succeeds another, the direction is toward increasingly differentiated and integrated structures. A new stage always displaces or reintegrates the structures of the preceding stages. For example, the stage characteristic of the adolescent period (formal operations) includes all of the structural properties of the preceding preadolescent stage (concrete operations) but at a new level of organization.

It may be expected that an individual who is in a given stage will prefer to solve problems confronting him at the level characteristic of that stage. That is, his solution will be made at the highest level of which he is capable. This preference for the highest-level solution has been called hierarchical preference and imparts a certain consistency to behavior. However, personal or situational specifics may cause a violation of the operation of hierarchical preference. An individual may return in a given situation to an earlier level either because it is adequate for his purpose, because it requires too much sustained effort at that time to operate at the higher level, or because efforts at solution at the level of the higher stage have failed.

Where the developmental sequences of cognitive acquisitions are concerned, as Flavell (1971) points out, earlier appearing cognitive items such as skills, operations, and concepts appearing in given sequence will be found related to later ones. Such relationships are those of addition, inclusion, substitution, modification, or mediation, and the relationship may be explicated in terms of the

[2]Emphasis upon form or rules at the expense of matter or content, e.g., formal logic dealing with rules that define validity in thinking.

structure of the organism, the organism's operational environment, or the cognitive items themselves. Across all stages the general adaptational functions of all the cognitive structures may be assumed to remain constant in that a balance of assimilation and accommodation is maintained between the individual and the environment. Such a balance is called equilibrium.

The Sequence of the Stages

Over a considerable range of years psychologists have proposed various sequences of cognitive development. Some of the sequences are expressed in terms molecular enough to be called stage sequences, while others, descriptively more molecular, are simply listings of the temporal progressions of specific aspects of cognitive functioning or of the sequential unfolding of a single stage.

Vygotsky (1934) identified three stages of cognitive development of which the last, concept formation, emerges in adolescence, although preliminary forms appear earlier. Vygotsky wrote: "A concept emerges only when the abstracted traits are synthesized anew and the resulting abstract synthesis becomes the main instrument of thought." Werner (1940) was also interested in the mind's structural properties. As he saw it, a basic principle of development is a constantly increasing differentiation and centralization or hierarchic integration of function within the developing organism. Werner hypothesized cognitive development as a sequence of increasing differentiation that, as it moved toward discrete thinking, served to displace syncretic thinking.[3] As Werner saw it, each succeeding and higher level of cognitive development is new. An earlier level of development may not be reconstructed by a subtraction of single qualities from the later level. Any level, even

the most primitive, is a relatively closed, self-subsisting totality. Werner (1940) wrote, "In general the more differentiated and hierarchically organized the mental structure of an organism, the more flexible or plastic its behavior." Hence, as the developing child learns to differentiate, he assumes an increasing ability to subordinate and integrate ideas—that is, he develops the ability to think hierarchically. It may then be assumed that the adolescent is well into the hierarchical thinking stage, which means that he is able, within a considerable range, to adapt to numerous situations with varying demands. An adolescent's chief limitation in cognitive behavior is his lack of information and experience. Harvey, Hunt, and Schroder (1961) relate cognitive and personality development in a system comprising four developmental levels. The first level, *unilateral dependence,* is characterized by external control and acceptance of absolutistic, externally derived controls. The second level, *negative independence,* is characterized by the beginnings of internal control and resistance to authoritarian control. The third level, *mutuality,* is one in which other persons are viewed less subjectively and in terms of others' standards. Mutual relationships are possible, and alternative views may be held simultaneously. In the fourth level, *mutuality* and *autonomy* are integrated and functioning is characterized by abstract standards, the availability of alternative conceptual schema, and the ability to hold a strong view without distorting incoming information. Between these four levels are various transitional stages. A child who encounters a relatively new environmental demand situation is likely to begin an entirely new developmental cycle. Level four is most likely to appear during adolescence and not before age nine.

Elkind (1971), speaking of general cognitive realization cycles, writes that "every mental ability seeks to realize itself in action and goes through a characteristic growth cycle in the process." Growth-cycle data may be related to accelerating mental growth, critical periods, and intrinsic motivation in learning

[3] A mentality can be called syncretic when the objects, meanings, or acts recognized as separate or discrete in an advanced state of maturity are fused together.

and performance. Elkind (1967–1968) notes that various aspects of adolescent behavior may be due to the appearance of new cognitive capacities. Among these are the adolescent's tendency to introspect and evaluate himself from the perspective of other people; his stance of idealism and a tendency to reason about contrary-to-fact principles; his perception of alternate social-choice situations with a resulting difficulty in arriving at social decisions; and his ability to deal with problems in which many factors operate at the same time. In this connection Elkind (1967) notes that the cognitive structures of a given developmental stage can provide insights with respect to personality characteristics typically to be found in individuals at that developmental level. As an example he cites typical adolescent egocentricism as represented by failure to differentiate between the cognitive concerns of other persons and those of the self. Quadrio and Peri (1970) have also noted the inception of an egocentric attitude in preadolescence and the early years of adolescence.

Elkind (1966) also states that an adolescent's thought is not only more logically complex but also more flexible and mobile. A middle-childhood individual tends to stay with his initial strategy, whereas an adolescent, who may start out with a quite complex strategy, is more ready to shift to a simpler one. Children are not as able to distinguish between their own thought products and reality as are adolescents. Elkind writes: "The adolescent is well aware of the arbitrariness of his hypotheses and their necessary lack of connection with the facts." In an earlier study Morris (1958) made a somewhat similar point. Writing on the adolescent period he noted:

Normative expectations become more liberal, responses more flexible and qualified. There is greater tendency for respondents to be unwilling to give an answer to situations as they stand and to say, "well, it depends on a number of different things. For instance, if . . . ," and to specify modifying conditions. Self-interested elements also show a change from selfishness to more independent, autonomous responses.

But this differentiation brings the problem of personal guilt, since the adolescent is able to recognize the sins of both omission and commission as he operates in a world of opposing values. To do what one "should" is oftentimes to reject something that one also "should," and so often in real life the "shoulds" are mutually exclusive. The implications for self-concept are obvious. For example, Katz and Zigler (1967) see self-image disparity as a function of developmental level, which involves two factors tending to increase with maturity: (1) capacity for guilt and (2) ability for cognitive differentiation.

Gardner (1962) presents a picture of development on an uneven front and notes that some cognitive functions move toward greater differentiation while others move toward greater synthesis, and that many functions related to each other in adulthood are statistically unrelated at earlier ages. Leskow and Smock (1970), in a study of developmental changes in problem-solving strategies as reflected in children's solutions to permutation problems, noted differential developmental trends (age levels twelve, fifteen, and eighteen) in the usual product score as compared to the strategy score. These investigators concluded that stimulus variables had a complex effect on strategy selection and that sex and age bore a significant relationship to the selection process. Adelson and O'Neil (1966) have reported changes in political ideas as representing a shift toward integration and future-oriented concepts. Before age thirteen it is difficult for a child to imagine the consequences of a political action; before five they cannot visualize the government as a whole. Adelson and O'Neil suggest that because preadolescents have an undifferentiated view they cannot grasp the community's legitimate claims on the citizen. The retarded or the socially deviating adolescent, such as a delinquent, is a similar case, although in the majority of the latter we may assume that attitudinal factors interfere with the cognitive processes of which the older adolescent is presumably capable. In this connection it is interesting to note Kohlberg's (1963) finding that younger children are insensitive to individuality and are more authoritarian in their interpersonal relationships than are adolescents.

Fischer and Leder (1961) report that older teenagers are less stereotyped in their conceptual judgments than are younger ones, and boys tend to be less stereotyped than girls. Using younger subjects DiVesta (1964) reports that as these children become older their answers in a complex word task become more stereotyped, possibly as the result of cultural factors. Increasing stereotyping in the earlier years is replaced by decreased stereotyping as the individual grows older. Freed (1965) reports that as adolescence proceeds there is increasing individuality, as compared to the clustering of similar responses leading to the conformity and stereotyping that characterize the ninth year.

Development from Concrete to Abstract

It is well understood that during the course of cognitive development the direction is from concrete to abstract. The potential cognitive behavior of the individual acquires the capacity to become increasingly complex as he becomes capable of an ascending level of abstraction. Harvey, Hunt, and Schroder (1961) note that as an individual grows older his movement is toward greater abstractive behavior: "As progressive development occurs, a person orders his world more realistically ... he operates more in terms of multiple alternatives rather than in terms of bifurcated black-white categories." Wolfe (1963) also characterizes conceptual level as ranging from the concrete to the abstract. At the highest levels the child can adopt the conditional attitude and function at a maximally abstract level with a high developmental power of differentiation. Such persons can infer beyond the perceptually given. Lunzer (1965) reports that ability to perform verbal and numerical analogies depends upon the ability to establish

second-order relations, an ability that increases with age.

Penk (1971) studied age differences in conceptual behavior, using as subjects children aged six to fourteen. He noted shifts in levels of abstraction as a function of age as well as a progressive increase in enculturation effects. Among the younger children global concepts predominated, but at age eight there was a substantial increase in differentiation. Older children were characterized by hierarchically integrated conceptual responses. In a study of the growth of the idea of law in adolescence, Adelson, Green, and O'Neil conducted in-depth interviews enabling them to compare the responses of children at ages eleven, thirteen, fifteen, and eighteen. Response directionality as a function of age was from concrete to abstract. A tendency at younger ages to stress the restrictive aspects of the law was replaced at later ages by a tendency to stress the positive aims of the law and to consider its intrapsychic effects. As adolescence progressed the tendency was to view law less in absolutistic terms and more in functional terms, visualizing it as a tool to achieve community objectives. Bourne and O'Banion (1971), in a study of conceptual-rule learning from childhood through adolescence, also reported a transition from concrete to abstract thought between the eleventh and the thirteenth year.

Linhart and Exner (1971), using a sample of four hundred seven- to fifteen-year-olds, studied developmental changes in problem solving and corresponding changes in differentiation, generalization, and thinking abilities. Subjects were asked to differentiate between similar or related pictures presented simultaneously or successively. Successful solutions increased with age, accelerated periods occurring at ages seven and eleven. But even after eleven most of the tasks were solved by simple strategies indicating that complex cognitive processes depend upon a specific level of cognitive development. Elkind, Medvene, and Rockway (1970) studied concept production in children and adolescents using both pictorial and verbal matched pairs of stimuli, with the subjects being asked to tell the ways in which the various stimuli were the same or different. They reported that the number of concepts produced by the younger children, but not by the adolescents, was in inverse relation to the level of abstractness of the stimuli. For adolescents, but not for children, the percentage of total perceptual responses displayed a significant variation with the level of stimulus presentation. From this study it appears that, when confronted by a concept-production study, adolescents are more ready than children to shift from their dominant conceptual orientation. Tyszkowa (1971), in a study of the solving of difficult mathematical problems by nine- to thirteen-year-olds, reported that the elements of orientation expanded during the process of problem solving. The younger subjects displayed a tendency to return to the earlier orientation phase as they persevered in attempting trial-and-error solutions where the older subjects tried to form and internally evaluate ideas on how the solution should go. Older children tended to abandon attempts at solution of problems that their evaluation led them to believe they could not solve, while the younger children persevered in their trial-and-error attempts long after the time the older children, believing their impossibility evaluation, would have given up. Wohlwill and Lowe (1962), following Witkin's (1962) lead, feel that a decreasing dependence upon information in the immediate stimulus field yields a better conception of cognitive development than does an increase in either powers of abstraction or intervention of symbolic processes. Anchoring the process more directly to the environment, Bruner (1966) visualizes cognitive development in terms of "the internalization of technologies from the culture, language, and the more effective technology available."

Piaget's Formulations

Jean Piaget, in his formulation of a four-stage sequential theory of cognitive development, has added new dimensions to our understanding of cognitive function and its development over the years of childhood and at least the early years of adolescence. Piaget's theory and its accompanying research are very popular among American psychologists and educators, inspiring a large volume of research endeavoring to confirm or disprove the theory. His point of view has even attracted attention in popular press and magazine outlets.[4] This present popularity, which is certainly well deserved, constitutes an American rediscovery, following a long period when his work was largely ignored, although it was available to American psychologists in English-language translations.[5]

Piaget (1950) writes that intelligence is "only a generic term to indicate the superior forms of organization of cognitive structurings . . . behavior becomes more 'intelligent' as the pathways between the subject and the objects on which it acts cease to be simple and become progressively more complex." Further, "intelligence constitutes the state of equilibrium towards which tend all the successive adaptations of sensorimotor and cognitive nature, as well as all assimilatory and accommodatory interactions between the organism and the environment." The problem of intellectual growth, particularly as the child passes through the middle years of childhood and enters adolescence, is accommodation rather than assimilation. Accommodation is the higher intellectual hurdle.

As with the work of any scientist, Piaget's work had to have some relation to that of those who had gone before. Among American psychologists, James M. Baldwin's thinking may have been influential. Baldwin's roots were as much in philosophy as in psychology, and he was not primarily an experimentalist, although he did define various basic concepts found in Piaget's formulations. Among these were

---

[4]For example, the May 20, 1967, issue of *Saturday Review* carried his portrait on the front cover and included an article that was in effect a character sketch ("Jean Piaget: Notes on Learning").

[5]A translation of *Judgment and reasoning in the child* was available in 1928 and of *The language and thought of the child* in 1926. See the references at the end of this chapter.

"assimilation," "accommodation," "schemata," and the "stage" concept, included in his three-volume *Thought and things or genetic logic* in 1906 to 1911. In 1925, Baldwin and Stecher reported a study of time and number concepts in children in the Piaget tradition. Most of Baldwin's work was either originally published in French or translated into that language, and Baldwin collaborated with Binet, Flournoy, and Janet when Piaget was assisting Binet's associate, Simon. Both Baldwin and Piaget spoke of their theory as "genetic epistemology."

Piaget postulates four sequential major stages of cognitive growth[6] through which every intact child passes in his progress toward maturity. The first two are the sensorimotor stage and the stage of preoperational thought. Following in succession and comprising the period of operational thinking is the stage of concrete operations and the stage of propositional or formal operations.

In the first stage, the sensorimotor period (birth to age two), the child begins life with a few inherited reflex-type schemata, and as his environment requires it, he develops more complex motor responses and habits. During this period cognitive functioning is highly event-specific. Piaget (1950) likens it to a "slow motion film in which all of the pictures are seen in succession but without fusion." Actions have yet to be internalized so they can be formed into representations or thoughts.

At the beginning of the second or preoperational thought stage (ages two to seven), symbolic or thought functions begin to appear. To immediate sensorimotor space is added the complexity of actions remote in space and time. Cognitive classes of objects are being developed, although they lack the generality that will characterize a later stage of development. The child at this point is handicapped

by the lack of a logical system to which he can fit classes so that he can "operate" on them. This stage may be subdivided into two recognizable substages, the preconceptual and the intuitive. The preconceptual substage (ages two to four) is the transition period during which the child's previous, highly individual event perception is being overlaid with a more general concept of events. Insofar as reasoning occurs, it is event to event, based on direct analogies but lacking either reversibility or generality. The second substage, that of intuitive thought (ages four to seven), moves the child from intuitive thought characterized by immediate relations between events toward an event-and-relations perception characterized by generality and reversibility. Piaget (1950) describes this as a period of gradual "coordination of representative relations and thus a growing conceptualization, which leads the child from the symbolic or preconceptual phase to the beginnings of the operation."

During the third, or concrete operations, stage (ages seven to eleven), the child develops operations implicitly based on the logic of classes and relations, although the operations lack the combinational possibilities characteristic of the succeeding stage of formal operations. During this period the child's operations are concrete in that they are concerned with reality itself, as exemplified by real objects that can be manipulated and "subjected to real action." In the concrete period the child including the preadolescent, deals only with the real things of his environment. The hypotheses he makes depend upon his own experience of reality and to this extent represent what might be called an extension of personally experienced reality. Concrete structures are based on the operations of classes and relations organized according to defined laws. Piaget calls these operations "elementary groupings," as contrasted to the logical groups and lattices that come later. At this time in the developmental sequence, tangible reality objects not present can be replaced by more or less vivid representations that stand for

[6]Piaget's writings are in French, and American psychologists know them primarily through the various English-language translations available, a situation that can lead to occasional misinterpretations, as the translation of often complex statements distorts original meanings. Flavell (1963) has written a standard general discussion of Piaget's work.

reality. The child cannot yet deal in the verbal domain with reasoning involving simple hypotheses; he has to rely upon the prelogical intuition of the early stage if forced into a situation demanding hypothetico-deductive reasoning.

During the fourth stage, that of propositional or formal operations (ages eleven-twelve to fourteen-fifteen), the child no longer must confine himself to perceived data from his immediate temporal and spatial environment. The period of formal operations, ushered in by disequilibrium, which disrupts previous cognitive balance, takes the adolescent beyond personal experience and enables him to base his hypotheses upon the nonobserved and the nonexperienced. He can now deal with information across the barriers of space and time in probabilistic terms and is free, if he wishes, to reconstruct reality. Thus the adolescent in the formal operations period has extended his world and may philosophize and otherwise range freely outside his own immediate circumstances and past experiences. He may see the possible as containing the real and has acquired the capacity for hypothetico-deductive thinking. That is to say that his thinking has become propositional, and he can interrelate propositions. In order to achieve this status of formal thought construction, the adolescent must be able to apply operations to objects by mentally executing various actions on them, and he must be able to "reflect" these operations on pure propositions, which have replaced objects. Piaget (1967) writes that "concrete thinking is the representation of a possible action, and formal thinking is the representation of a representation of possible action," and in this sense is "thought raised to the second power." Thus formal operations are applied to hypotheses or propositions, while concrete operations are applied to tangible objects. This is their crucial difference. Piaget (1967) notes: "Formal operations engender a 'logic of propositions' in contrast to a logic of relations, classes, and numbers engendered by concrete operations." Piaget (1972) notes that the processes of formal operations provide

the essence of the logic of cultured adults and the basis for elementary scientific thought.

In describing the fourth stage Piaget (1967) writes: "At the age of eleven to twelve years, formal thinking becomes possible, i.e., logical operations begin to be transposed from the plane of concrete manipulation to the ideational plane, where they are expressed in some kind of language (words, mathematical symbols, etc.), without the support of perception, experience, or even faith." Thus the child who has entered Piaget's fourth stage is able to draw conclusions from pure hypothesis without having to rely on actual observation.

There are four interrelated characteristics of formal operations: (1) the relationship of the real to the possible, (2) the ability for combinatorial analysis, (3) ability for propositional thinking, and (4) the ability for hypothetico-deductive thinking. In the concrete stage the child or preadolescent deals with multiple variables in a given situation with one-many correspondences or with unsystematic other possible correspondences. But as an adolescent, employing combinatorial analysis, he can deal in a systematic way with the variables in all possible combinations; that is to say that the adolescent has the potential of dealing successfully with problems and situations in which a number of factors are simultaneously operating.

In the propositional-thinking aspect of formal operations the adolescent makes use, not of raw data itself, but of propositional statements about raw data. Piaget calls this aspect of thinking second-degree thinking operations. An example of second-degree thinking operations is provided by Lunzer (1965), who notes that numerical as well as verbal analogies demand the application of formal reasoning.

In hypothetico-deductive thinking, the adolescent's approach is more in terms of, "If this *were* true it would follow that . . ." than of "If this *is* true it would follow that. . . ." Of course younger children make use of "If, then" thinking, but they differ from adolescents in that they are limited to their own immediate experience. Inhelder and Piaget (1958) make the point that in formal thinking, necessity is an important characteristic. The adolescent is not content with sufficient causes; he looks for necessary ones. The result is that the adolescent is a better perceiver of relationships than is the concrete operations child.

Adolescents can symbolize symbols. Words are now multipotential in that they can symbolize other symbols. For example, the adolescent can deal with metaphor, something beyond the child, and he spends considerable time and derives much more or less innocent pleasure from playing with double meanings, both in words and in jokes. The adolescent may now go about the business of self-construction, using aspects of himself as symbols for other aspects or even using himself as a symbol for himself.

His entrance into the formal structures period enables the adolescent to become an idealist, and this he indeed becomes. The result is that he often takes positions that will present him with difficulties in personal adjustment and social acceptance when he encounters the realities of everyday living. As was indicated before, the adolescent, unlike the child, can accept premises and argue as if they were true. One would not get very far if one said to a child, "Rain is dry." He knows that rain is wet and that the premise is in error. An adolescent can accept the premise and argue for the dry rain assumption. An adolescent can accept the premise of the future and behave proactively in terms of the assumptions of the premise, whereas the child is limited in his concepts of future time.

Because he is increasingly multipotential the adolescent finds it harder to make decisions and is constantly perceiving alternatives to things that teachers and parents suggest he should do, although in some emotional states, frightened of where the alternatives lead, he retires to the security of rejecting alternatives and of docile dependency on adult directions. During such a phase an adolescent may actually reject hierarchical preference and revert, in some cases, to the previous stage

of concrete operations. Of course, even when the adolescent continues the alternatives approach, he sometimes finds it difficult to decide among alternatives and may return to acceptance of directions for a reason very different from fear of alternatives.

From the foregoing discussion we may gain a picture of how the adolescent thinks as he makes use of the operations of the formal period in his cognitive processes. When an adolescent encounters a new situation, and if in his behavior he exemplifies the formal operations period, he makes a classification or ordering of the concrete elements he finds. He then handles these elements simply as propositions, divorcing them from their ties with reality, and by combinatorial analysis arrives at hypotheses that are susceptible to acceptance or rejection.

It should now be clear that central to an understanding of the fourth stage is the picture of the adolescent as an hypothesizing, system-building organism. In contrasting the thought processes of adolescents and preadolescents, Piaget (1967) observes: "By comparison ... an adolescent is an individual who constructs systems and theories." Certainly the child, bound as he is to concrete thinking, does not build systems, nor does he abstract theory-based common principles from data. He deals with each problem in isolation. Insofar as children may be said to have theories, they are unconscious or unformulated. In contrast, the adolescent, with his facility for elaborating abstract theories, is constantly engaged in hypothesis and theory formulation frequently unrelated to everyday realities. How do adolescents handle their theoretical formulations? Some write and some talk, but as Piaget (1967) notes, "The majority talk about only a small part of their personal creations and confine themselves to ruminating about them intimately and in secret. But all of them have systems and theories that transform the world in one way or another." Equipped with the ability to think formally, the adolescent can now reflect and theorize spontaneously and, characteristically, will be found to play with his new-found power as he finds before him new worlds that he tries to incorporate into himself by egocentric assimilation.

Adolescent Egocentricity

Piaget (1967) writes:

Adolescent egocentricity is manifested by belief in the omnipotence of reflection, as though the world should submit itself to idealistic schemes rather than to systems of reality. It is the metaphysical age *par excellence;* the self is strong enough to construct the universe and big enough to incorporate it.

Gradually, as the individual moves through adolescence, he increasingly is able to gain control of his formal thinking capacity and put it to work rather than treating it primarily as a unique new toy. Formal thought and reality become reconciled and, as Piaget points out, the adolescent comes to perceive that the proper function of reflection is to predict and interpret experience, not merely to contradict. This is attainment of a new equilibrium that omits the metaphysical egocentricity of early adolescence.

Thus it appears that the egocentric and narcissistic stance tends to occur in immature individuals (or those not fully mature) whenever the system receives input that causes them to appraise, analyze, and cope with ideas not previously in their thinking. An adolescent first learning about social action, political action, or other like matters tends to become quite egocentric and narcissistic in his approach. During this phase we speak of idealism and the intolerance of adolescents, and also of their strongly expressed belief that they have somehow tapped the springs of eternal truth and that those who oppose are, in the adolescent's own terms, "not with it," out of touch, possibly venal, and perhaps simply perverse, if not stupid. This egocentric tendency can well, as Scarlette (1971) notes, bring the younger generation into direct conflict with the older generation, who may also hold strong convictions but who are mature enough to hold their own egocentricity in check. The writer feels that

such adolescent egocentricity is neither good nor bad—it is simply a developmental fact of life. If anything, aside from the conflict it causes, it is a good thing because it gives the adolescent an opportunity to become acquainted with all kinds of current and past issues and to engage in cognitive restructuring. If nothing else, it gives him an interest in life, and adults should be as tolerant and understanding as they can.

However, in considering adolescent egocentricity we are once again confronted with individual differences and situational idiosyncrasies. Adolescent egocentricity is conditioned by the situation in which it occurs and the subject matter upon which it is operating. The same individual can show egocentricity in some matters and not in others, depending upon when each input occurs and the extent to which it represents a new cognitive field of action. Performances typically measured by the Piaget experiments usually appear earlier than do the more social-action-oriented matters of later adolescence. All we can say is that, as maturity is approached and achieved, the areas of egocentricity tend to lessen, although before maturity any newly introduced area will tend to some extent to elicit egocentric behavior, whether in the area of sexual behavior, political action, or "higher aspects of ratiocination." Piaget (1967) notes that every transition from one stage to another is likely to provoke temporary oscillation" with the result of "provisional disequilibrium."[7]

We can say that, individual differences and specific special situations aside, as adolescence proceeds greater egocentricity is displaced by greater selflessness, but the advance is on an uneven front, as Gardner and Schoen (1962) note of development in general.

The Validity of Piaget's Formulations

It was inevitable that so provocative a formulation as Piaget's stage theory of cognitive

[7]Piaget made this statement with reference to movement from stage to stage of his four developmental stages, but it applies equally well to movement within a stage.

development would generate a considerable amount of critical discussion and research. Criticisms have included the fact that (1) the theory is not fully applicable to American children because the data were gathered on European samples from a different educational and cultural milieu; (2) the experiments were conducted without rigorous experimental controls; (3) matters of individual differences and personality were frequently ignored; (4) the experiments concentrated on intellectual growth applicable primarily to mathematics and physics; (5) generalizations were made on inadequate data; and (6) Piaget assumed children knew the meaning of adult words used in his experiments.[8]

Where adolescence is concerned, research findings indicate, confirming Piaget's hypothesis, that significant changes in cognitive performance occur sometime during the twelfth and fifteenth years. Such changes appear to be the result of experience and maturation, and although they are associated in time with the advent of puberty, there is no evidence that the physiological changes of adolescence are causal. However, there is evidence that in other cultures and with other subjects the age at which the various operations appear will vary somewhat from the ages Piaget cited. There is no evidence that the sequential stages he hypothesizes are in error. Space does not permit a complete account of the supporting research findings, but a selected few will furnish an overview.

The actuality of the existence of the processes of a concrete and of a formal operations stage in human development has been mas-

sively confirmed in psychological research. Typical of such confirmation attempts is a study reported by Elkind, Barocas, and Johnsen (1969). These investigators administered a concept-production task to 180 children under conditions of perceptual set, functional set, and no set as well as under two levels of stimuli consisting of objects and object labels. When the presentation stimuli were object labels rather than the objects themselves, children, as compared to adolescents, produced a significantly smaller number of concepts. Further, concept production to objects, but not to object labels, was significantly reduced by the introduction of functional set. The investigators partially replicated their study using a further group of 90 children and adolescents. Elkind et al. discussed their results in terms of concrete and formal operational thought. Brainerd (1971), in a cross-sectional attempt to validate Inhelder and Piaget's statements about proportionality, tested 72 eight- to fifteen-yearolds. The Piaget statements being tested were that the concepts of proportionality are acquired between ages eight and fifteen, that the volume index of the proportionality is acquired earlier than is the density index, and that concepts of density and volume are indices of the same cognitive. Brainerd's reported confirmation of Piaget's statements includes evidence that the concept of density was more easily learned by the older children than the younger children, who suffered the predicted difficulties in handling the density concept. Lunzer (1965), using a sample of 153 English children between the ages of nine and seventeen, conducted research on the nature of formal as compared to concrete operations. He reports that formal operations were clearly second-order relations and were qualitatively distinct from concrete operations.

A number of investigators have endeavored to replicate the Inhelder-Piaget (1958) experiments involving formal operations as one of the phenomena of adolescent development. Lovell (1961), using as subjects two hundred English children, simulated ten of Inhelder and Piaget's 1958 experiments. Lovell reports

---

[8]The majority of Piaget's experiments have been performed with preadolescent subjects, although the implications for the adolescent period have been made explicit, particularly in Inhelder and Piaget (1958) and in Piaget (1967). The experimentation itself has been chiefly concerned with the products of classes and relations and with the development of conceptions of conservation, number, time, space, and quantity. Piaget has been chiefly interested in the means by which children acquire and use knowledge, and his theory may be said to be one involving the development of knowledge and the processes by which it is utilized. Piaget's theory stands outside the classical theories of ability and psychometrics so characteristic of theories of intelligence.

confirmation not only of the actual existence of the stages but of their sequence. Noelting (1961) and Hotyat (1961) also report studies confirming Piaget's cognitive stages and their sequential development. However, Lovell (1961) did note in his study that a number of his subjects still seemed unable to deal with logical thought as late as their fifteenth year. Elkind (1961) reported the same situation, taking successful volume conservation as one indication of formal operational ability, noting that 27 percent of seventeen-year-olds, 36 percent of sixteen-year-olds, 53 percent of fifteen-year-olds, 54 percent of fourteen-year-olds, and 64 percent of thirteen-year-olds were unsuccessful at volume conservation. By 1965, investigators such as Jackson (1965) were able to state the consensus that there were not only wide variations in logical thinking in children of similar mental and chronological ages, but there seemed also to be considerable intraindividual variation from situation to situation. In general, Piaget's original estimates had to be revised upward, and variations caused by individual differences had to be made explicit. For example, Yudin (1966), using a sample with an IQ range from 80 to 130, reports that the average dull children completed formal operations between fourteen and sixteen, average children between twelve and fourteen, and bright children by twelve. Obviously more difficult aspects of formal operations were achieved at later ages. Neimark (1970) reports that ability to cope with disjunction is usually not achieved until late adolescence. In this same connection Wolfe (1963) reports that none of the subjects used in his research did well in formal thinking until age fourteen, although subjects between eleven and thirteen categorized as abstract thinkers did better than those categorized as concrete thinkers. Wolfe takes the position that large differences exist between eleven-to-thirteen-year-olds and fourteen-year-olds. Relevant to Lovell and Wolfe's advent of formal operations findings is Leake's (1965) report that mental age is more important in concept formation than is chronological age. Lunzer (1965), using a sample of above average intelligence, notes that formal operations appeared earlier than thirteen and fourteen, as Piaget hypothesized. In Lunzer's sample formal operations seemed established between the eleventh and twelfth years. In discussing how soon formal thought is possible in a variety of subject matters, Stone and Ausubel (1969) note that the degree of generality manifested is at least in part positively related to intelligence.

However, the fact of individual differences does not negate the further fact noted by Piaget, that as an individual proceeds into adolescence there is a continuing tendency for his thought processes to gain in elaboration and complexity. Elkind (1966) reports that adolescents are more successful than children in their ability to shift conceptual orientation in resolving a concept-formation task. Elkind suggests that his findings confirm Inhelder and Piaget's (1958) statement that an adolescent's thought processes are more logically elaborate than a child's.

Osler and Kofsky (1965) report that cognitive processes become more complex and differentiated with age, and as a result, the older child is able to deal with numerous dimensions simultaneously and to select relevant cues. Undeutsch (1960), using as subjects ten- to sixteen-year-olds given the task of interpreting literary and motion-picture material, reports that with increasing age more attention is paid to the psychological content of the material and less to the frame in which it appears, indicating a developmental progression from concrete to more abstract operations. Undeutsch also reported that education has some influence upon the course of this progression. Peel (1966), in a study of British adolescents, reported that in general children to the age of thirteen and one-half years judged circumstantially, and a firm tendency to make comprehensive judgments involving the production of possible explanations appeared only in the fourteenth year. Bakker (1965), using a German sample of 1,090 boys aged seven to seventeen, reported that an action quotient (ratio of activity verbs to qualitative words) steadily decreased while the use of qualitative words steadily increased in frequency. There was no trend in the use of activity verbs.

The Inevitability of the Use of Formal Operations

The discussion in the last section has dealt with evidence of an adolescent's ability to utilize formal operations. However, this does not mean that every adolescent capable of formal operations thinks in that fashion all of the time or, in the case of some, even most of the time. Shaimberg (1970) writes: "The process of cognitive development does not proceed necessarily with an ontogenetic finality. Frequently adolescents are involved in concrete operational forms of thinking supposedly characteristic of the middle years child." Dufoyer (1969–1970), Kessen (1962), and Higgins-Trenk and Gaite (1971) all report research to remind us that the analytic thinking of adolescents still leaves something to be desired, reminding us that what they may be conceptually capable of in theory and what they actually do are not necessarily congruent. For example, Dufoyer (1969–1970), in a study of adolescents (ages 12 to 16.3) as compared to adults, asked his subjects to identify characters, represented by stick figures, using a series of propositions such as "Larry is as heavy as Paul; Larry is as tall as Mark; Mark is taller than John; Paul is heavier than John." Dufoyer reports significant differences between adolescents and adults in identifications made. Errors in identification by all of the adolescents and by half of the adults led to the conclusion that they had underestimated the implied equality in "A is as ——— as B," relying instead upon the adjectives *heavy, tall,* etc. It would appear that the subjects in the study, despite their ages and the possibility of hierarchic preference, often did not recognize the fact that "Larry is as tall as Mark" has nothing to do with whether both men are in actuality either tall or short. In this study we observe not only that every adolescent in the study at least occasionally operated below

his presumed level of cognitive development, but that even among the adult subjects there was a tendency for half of them occasionally to perform at a level they should have left behind with their preadolescence.

A similar picture, where adolescents are concerned, is presented by Higgins-Trenk and Gaite (1971), who investigated the incidence of formal thinking in adolescents ranging in mean age from 13.4 to 17.7 years. Subjects were presented with two kinds of situations, both requiring formal thinking. One was a typical Piaget-type task, while the other was a situational problem judged by the investigators as more relevant to the everyday interests of adolescents. It was found that in the solution of these tasks formal operations were infrequently used by the adolescent sample. The investigators speculated that such absence of formal operational thought may well have been due to the egocentricity of adolescence.

Of course, the possibility of situational reversion to earlier stages is always possible because the advent of formal operations does not eradicate earlier stages, which are simply integrated into later stages. In any event, an adolescent's occasional failure to operate at the level of formal operations does not deny Piaget's stage concept of formal operations as characteristic of the adolescent period. It does, however, make explicit the point that one should not necessarily expect that any given adolescent will inevitably be cognizing at the formal operational level in the case of every problem he encounters.

The Mechanisms Underlying Growth and Change in Cognition

Inhelder and Piaget (1958) note that the transition to formal operations stems from cultural pressures and the adolescent's need to take on adult roles and to exemplify adult modes of thought. As this occurs, the adolescent's conceptual range is extended to the hypothetical and the future. They also note that a maturation of cerebral structure coincides with the type of ability required by formal thinking.

However, Ausubel and Ausubel (1966) criticize Piaget's position by pointing out that it does not account for experiential and intellectual potential factors within the child, and they further note that Piaget's position postulates neurophysiological changes that are still unproven.

Ausubel and Ausubel (1966) speak of the importance of experience and postulate three trends as accounting for the transition in cognitive development: (1) acquisition of a vocabulary of transactional terms; (2) growing fund of stable, higher-order concepts and principles; and (3) greater facility in manipulating relationships with the aid of concrete props so that these operations may eventually be performed without the props. Shaffer, Sundberg, and Tyler (1969), in a study comparing American, Dutch, and Indian adolescents, emphasized the existence of intercultural differences in the manner in which adolescents in different cultures interpret their environments. Darbyshire and Scott (1970), in a study of Australian primitive and modern cultures, make a similar point. Okonji (1969), in a research investigation of Nigerian adolescents and college students, in which he compared their performance with American norms on various perceptual tests (Embedded Figures, Rod and Frame), noted that cultural factors are most important in developing visual perceptual field independence. Bruner et al. (1966) note that the more technical the culture, the greater the impetus toward hierarchical connection.

Bruner (1960, 1966) also takes the position that there is a means of communicating ideas to children that is appropriate to a particular age. He feels that it is educationally futile to wait passively for a child to grow into readiness. Elkind (1966) writes (and here he differs from Piaget), "What is significant about the growth of the mind in the child is to what degree it depends not upon capacity but upon the unlocking of capacity by techniques that come from exposure to the specialized environment of the child." Langer (1971) notes the tendency of family environment to influence some aspects of concept thinking, particularly summarizing, in a task requiring children to classify and interpret written articles. It is interesting that this tendency seemed to depend on general family climate since socioeconomic status, as represented by father's occupation, had no significant effect.

Elkind (1961) notes that only those adolescents who have adopted social roles conducive to the formation of quantity conceptions will form them at any acceptable level. Braham (1965) feels that peer groups account for the emergence of thinking operations in the adolescent. In this connection a pertinent comment based on a cross-cultural study by Maccoby and Modiane (1966) is: "Even at the age of sixteen or seventeen the Mexican adolescent seldom abstracts even formally, while the North American develops increasing facility with abstract functions and formal equivalences." In Mexico the peer group does not have the status and function it has in the United States.

Cognitive Acceleration

The question of intellectual acceleration has often been raised. Piaget's stages have offered explicit statements of status that have enabled investigators to manipulate the environment and measure amounts of acceleration that have taken place. In development, an individual's ability to react and to perform is a combination of his experience, his stage of maturation, and the inherent efficiency and intactness of his neurological system. Chronological age or sheer passage of time is not significant—it simply is an expression of passage of time. If, within time, experiences have not occurred, or if for some reason, neurological or otherwise, the individual is incapable of profiting by the experience, then sheer passage of time is not significant, since the individual has not been influenced by it. For example, Keasey and Charles (1969) report on differing amounts of natural experience in concept formation and development of concept as a function of mental age. In their study they tested retarded and normal subjects (matched on mental age by an average of 11.41 years in chronological age) for understanding of the concept of conservation of substance. They found no significant differences in performance between groups. The determining factor was the mental age of the subjects. Mental age and understanding of conservation of substance were significantly correlated. Chronological age, however, was not.

Smedslund (1961a) found that it was possible to instill the concept of conservation of weight in children who did not appear to possess the concept before the experiences provided by his experiment. However, Smedslund (1961b) subsequently reports that such artificially accelerated children, when confronted with evidence at variance with what they had learned, tended to revert to nonconservation status. In contrast, children who acquired the concept "naturally" tended to be much more resistant to the experimenter's attempts to extinguish the concept. Apparently experience alone does not necessarily lead to stable concepts. Wohlwill (1959, 1960, 1962, 1966) reports that training can accelerate attainment of concepts of conservation of number and weight, providing the instructional methods and conditions are reasonably optimum. Wallace (1965) reports similar findings for number concepts. Tomlinson-Keasey (1972) reports some success through training sessions, using flexibility problems, to improve cognitive-level performance.

While much of the research on cognitive acceleration has dealt with younger children, the lesson seems clear. Acceleration under controlled conditions is possible. However, the educator concerned with the learning process must answer further questions. To what extent is acceleration desirable, and at what expense in other matters must it be attained? There is reason to believe that the American high school curriculum, and for that matter, American child-rearing practices for those in the second decade of life, do not pose any great intellectual challenge, nor do they typically provide experiences that tend to accelerate adolescent cognitive growth for the majority of children. Perhaps we should provide grist for the mill. The adolescent is a hypothesizing animal. Cognitively he functions by means of hypotheses, and his attitudes, beliefs, and knowledge consist of hypotheses. Even his reaction to himself as a functioning organism consists of a series of hypotheses. But his environment, and especially his school, must broaden his horizons so that he has rich sources of material about which to make hypotheses —sources that present a challenge. Actually adolescents want to be challenged intellectually. To understand one of the most puzzling and exasperating aspects of the adolescent period—their insurgence, "unreasonableness," rebellion, contrariness, espousement of peculiar (to adults) causes and activities—one must realize that they have attained a period of life characterized by great idealism and a quest for something to which they can be true that will not let them down. At the same time this something must be meaningful in their own terms, must not stand for the past, and must represent to them the wave of the future. Erikson (1962) speaks of this aspect of youth as the "capacity for fidelity." He sees it as a strength of youth, although, equally, the quest for fidelity can bring youth and society to a confrontation difficult for both. Erikson's position is that, given the cognitive and interest structure of younger children, fidelity could not develop earlier than adolescence but "must not, in the crises of youth, fail its time of ascendance."

Summary

Cognition is a process whereby an organism becomes aware or obtains knowledge of an object. In developmental psychology cognition is primarily considered in terms of concept formation, problem solving, and the thought processes. Behavior theories may be divided into cognitive and noncognitive theories, although the distinction often blurs. Any individual builds a conceptual system, through which he views his world. Developmentally the issue has to do with the level of cognitive manipulation available to the individual as he builds his system. An individual's cognitive development is an ascending sequence of identifiable stages, each more complex than the preceding one. Thus, as the individual grows older, his movement is toward greater abstract behavior while he passes through various cognitive stages. Each of the stages is qualitatively different from the others, the stages are in invariant sequence, and each new stage always displaces or reintegrates the structures of the preceding stage. When confronted by a problem, an individual, following the principle of hierarchical preference, will tend to solve the problem at the highest level of which he is capable. Across all stages the general adaptational functions of the cognitive structures may be assumed to remain constant, in that a balance of assimilation and accommodation is maintained between the individual and his environment. Such a balance is called equilibrium.

There have been a number of stage theories, among them that of Vygotsky, who posited three stages of cognitive development. Werner advanced a theory that depended upon a concept of increasing differentiation and centralization or hierarchic integration of function within the developing organism. In its development the organism moves from syncretic to discrete thinking. The adolescent's thought is not only more logically complex; it is also more flexible and mobile. Development proceeds unevenly, with some cognitive functions moving toward greater differentiation and some toward greater synthesis. There is also a movement, as the individual enters adolescence, from selfishness to more independent, autonomous responses. Elkind has pointed out that various aspects of adolescent behavior may be due to the appearance of new cognitive capacities. Among these are the adolescent's tendency to introspect, to be idealistic, to evaluate himself from the perspective of others, to consider alternate possibilities, and to deal with multifaceted situations. Others have noted, citing relationships to cognitive stages, the adolescent's increasing individuality, decrease in stereotyping, decrease in authoritarian behavior, greater ability to differentiate, and

increasing flexibility. In general, directionality in cognitive development is from the concrete to the abstract.

Piaget has advanced a currently popular sequential theory of cognitive growth consisting of four stages: (1) the sensorimotor, (2) the preoperational, (3) the concrete operational, and (4) the propositional, or formal operations. During the concrete operations stage the child's cognitive operations are concerned with reality itself, as exemplified by real objects that can be manipulated and subjected to real action. The child has yet to deal in the verbal domain with reasoning involving simple hypotheses. During the fourth stage the child, now an adolescent, no longer must confine himself to perceived data from his immediate temporal and spatial environment. His thinking becomes propositional, and he possesses the capacity to interrelate propositions. Thus the formal operations of the fourth stage are applied to hypotheses or propositions, while the concrete operations of the third stage are applied to tangible objects. Central to an understanding of the fourth stage is the picture of the adolescent as a hypothesizing, system-building organism. The four interrelated characteristics of formal operations are (1) the relationship of the real to the possible, (2) the ability for combinatorial analysis, (3) the ability for propositional thinking, and (4) the ability for hypothetico-deductive thinking. When an adolescent encounters a new situation, if in his behavior he exemplifies the formal operations period, he makes a classification or ordering of the concrete elements he finds. He then handles these elements simply as propositions, divorcing them from their ties with reality, and by combinatorial analysis arrives at hypotheses that are susceptible to acceptance or rejection.

As he enters the fourth stage he displays considerable egocentricity, but with increasing maturity he leaves this egocentricity, as he comes to perceive that the proper function of reflection is to predict and interpret experience, not merely to contradict. But obviously, any generalizations made about the adolescent period must be interpreted in terms of individual and specific situational peculiarities.

There have been a number of criticisms of Piaget's formulations, but research has confirmed that significant changes in cognitive performance do occur sometime between the twelfth and fifteenth year, although there are wide variations in logical thinking in children of similar mental and chronological ages as well as considerable intraindividual variation from situation to situation. In general, Piaget's original estimates had to be revised upward, and variations caused by individual differences had to be made explicit. However, neither the existence of individual differences nor of cultural differences negates the fact that as an adolescent proceeds into adolescence there is a continuing tendency for his thought processes to gain in elaboration and complexity as the result of experience and maturation.

The transition to formal operations results from cultural pressures, need to assume adult roles, maturation of cerebral structures, and new learning and social experiences. It appears that, given optimum conditions, considerable cognitive acceleration is possible. Adolescents desire intellectual stimulation and tend to react favorably to it when it is offered. However, not every adolescent capable of formal operations thinks in that fashion all of the time or, in the case of some, even most of the time. It often happens that an adolescent capable of formal operations regresses to concrete operational forms. In general, it may be assumed that neither chronological age nor the sheer passage of time is significant in cognitive development. If, within time, experiences have not occurred, or if for some reason the individual is incapable of profiting from the experiences he has had, then it may be expected that he will be retarded in his cognitive development. On the other hand, environmental enrichment does make possible an opportunity for cognitive acceleration.

References

Adelson, J.; Green, B.; and O'Neil, R. Growth of the idea of law in adolescence. *Developmental Psychology* 1 (1969): 327–332.

Adelson, J., and O'Neil, R. The growth of political ideas in adolescence. *Journal of Personality and Social Psychology* 4 (1966): 295–306.

Ausubel, D. P., and Ausubel, P. Cognitive development in adolescence. *Review of Educational Research* 36 (1966): 403–413.

Bakker, F. J. Untersuchungen zur Entwicklung der Aktionsquotienten *Archiv fur die Gesamte Psychologie* 117 (1965): 78–103.

Baldwin, B. T., and Stecher, L. I. *The psychology of the preschool child.* New York: Appleton, 1925.

Bourne, L. E., and O'Banion, K. Conceptual rule learning and chronological age. *Developmental Psychology* 5 (1971): 525–534.

Braham, M. Peer-group deterrents to intellectual development during adolescence. *Educational Theory* 15 (1965): 248–258.

Brainerd, C. J. The development of the proportionality scheme in children and adolescents. *Developmental Psychology* 5 (1971): 469–476.

Bruner, J. S. *The process of education.* Cambridge: Harvard University Press, 1960.

Bruner, J. S.; Olver, R. R.; Greenfield, P. M. et al. *Studies in cognitive growth.* New York: Wiley, 1966.

Darbyshire, M., and Scott, P. M. Some cultural factors related to cognitive functioning: I and II. *Australian Journal of Mental Retardation* 1 (1970): 40–45.

DiVesta, F. J. The distribution of modifiers used by children in a word-association task. *Journal of Verbal Learning and Verbal Behavior* 3 (1964): 421–427.

Dufoyer, J. P. Role de certaines habitudes verbales dans la conduite du raisonnement chez des adolescents et des adultes. *Bulletin de Psychologie* 23 (1969–1970): 526–532.

Elkind, D. Quantity conceptions in junior and senior high school students. *Child Development* 23 (1961): 551–560.

Elkind, D. Conceptual orientation shifts in children and adolescents. *Child Development* 37 (1966): 493–498.

Elkind, D. Egocentricism in adolescence. *Child Development* 38 (1967): 1025–1034.

Elkind, D. Cognitive structure and adolescent experience. *Adolescence* 2 (1967–1968): 427–434.

Elkind, D.; Medvene, L.; and Rockway, A. S. Representational level and concept production in children and adolescents. *Developmental Psychology* 2 (1970): 85–89.

Elkind, D. Cognitive growth cycles in mental development. *Nebraska Symposium on Motivation* 19 (1971): 1–31.

Elkind, D.; Barocas, R.; and Johnsen, P. Concept production in children and adolescents. *Human Development* 12 (1969): 10–21.

Erikson, E. H. Youth: Fidelity and diversity. *Daedalus* 91 (1962): 5–27.

Fischer, H., and Leder, A. Untersuchungen uber die Begriffsauffassung bei Jugendlichen. *Zeitschrift fur Experimentelle und Angewandte Psychologie* 8 (1961): 23–41.

Freed, E. X. Normative data on a self-administered projective question for children. *Journal of Projective Techniques and Personal Assessment* 29 (1965): 3–6.

Gardner, R. W. Cognitive controls in adaptation: Research and measurement. In Messick, S. and Ross, J., eds., *Measurement in personality and cognition.* New York: Wiley, 1962.

Gardner, R. W., and Schoen, R. A. Differentiation and abstraction on concept formation. *Psychological Monographs* 76 (1962).

Harvey, O. J.; Hunt, D. E.; and Schroder, H. M. *Conceptual systems and personality organization.* New York: Wiley, 1961.

Higgins-Trenk, A., and Gaite, A. J. The elusiveness of formal operational thought in adolescence. *Proceedings of the Annual Convention of the American Psychological Association* 6 (1971): 201–202.

Horrocks, J. E., and Jackson, D. W. *Self and role: A theory of self-process and role behavior.* Boston: Houghton Mifflin, 1972.

Hotyat, F. L'Enseignement des mathematiques au niveau secondaire. Les recherches dans les pays europeens de langue francaise. *International Review of Education* 7 (1961): 235–246.

Inhelder, B., and Piaget, J. *The growth of logical thinking from childhood to adolescence.* New York: Basic Books, 1958.

Jackson, S. The growth of logical thinking in normal and subnormal children. *British Journal of Educational Psychology* 35 (1965): 255–258.

Katz, A., and Zigler, E. Self-image disparity: A developmental approach. *Journal of Personality and Social Psychology* 5 (1967): 186–195.

Keasey, C. T., and Charles, D. C. Conservation of substance in normal and mentally retarded children. *Journal of Genetic Psychology* (1969).

Kessen, W. "Stage" and structure in the study of children. *Monographs of the Society for Research in Child Development* 27 (1962): 65–82, whole no. 83.

Kohlberg, L. The development of children's orientations toward a moral order. *Vita Humana* 6 (1963): 11–33.

Langer, S. Beitrag zur Bestimmung des Altersfaktors in Denkprozessen bei 9–15 jahrigen Kindern auf Grund der Dispersionsanalyse. *Psychologia a Patopsychologia Dietata* 6 (1971): 43–52.

Leake, L., Jr. The status of three concepts of probability in children of seventh, eighth and ninth grades. *Journal of Experimental Education* 34 (1965): 78–84.

Leskow, S., and Smock, C. D. Developmental changes in problem-solving strategies: Permutation. *Developmental Psychology* 2 (1970): 412–422.

Linhart, J., and Exner, J. Towards a theory of cognitive development. *Psychologia a Patopsychologia Dietata* 6 (1971): 27–42.

Lovell, K. A follow-up study of Inhelder and Piaget's *The growth of logical thinking.* *British Journal of Psychology* 52 (1961): 143–153.

Lunzer, E. Problems of formal reasoning in test situations. In P. Mussen, ed., *European research in cognitive development. Monographs of the Society for Research in Child Development* 30 (1965): 19–46.

Maccoby, M., and Modiane, H. On culture and equivalence. In J. S. Bruner, ed., *Studies in cognitive growth.* New York: Wiley, 1966.

Morris, J. F. Symposium: The development of moral values in children: II. The development of the adolescent value judgments. *British Journal of Educational Psychology* 28 (1958): 1–14.

Neimark, E. D. A preliminary search for formal operations structures. *Journal of Genetic Psychology* 116 (1970): 223–232.

Noelting, G. Quelques aspects de la genese du raisonnement mathematique chez l'enfant. *International Review of Education* 7 (1961): 197–205.

Okonji, M. O. The differential effects of rural and urban upbringing on the development of cognitive styles. *International Journal of Psychology* 4 (1969): 293–305.

Osler, S., and Kofsky, E. Stimulus uncertainty as a variable in the development of conceptual ability. *Journal of Experimental Psychology* 2

(1965) : 264–279.

Peel, E. A. A study of differences in the judgments of adolescent pupils. *British Journal of Educational Psychology* 36 (1966) : 77–86.

Penk, W. E. Developmental patterns of conceptual styles. *Psychological Reports* 29 (1971): 635–649.

Piaget, J. *The language and thought of the child.* New York: Harcourt, Brace, 1926.

Piaget, J. *Judgment and reasoning in the child.* New York: Harcourt, Brace, 1928.

Piaget, J. (1947) *The psychology of intelligence.* New York: Harcourt, Brace, 1950. (First published in France in 1947.)

Piaget, J. The general problems of the psychobiological development of the child. In Tanner, J. M., and Inhelder, B. eds., *Discussions on Child Development, Proceedings of the World Health Organization,* vol. IV, pp. 3–27. New York: International Universities Press, 1960.

Piaget, J. *Six psychological studies.* New York: Random House, 1967.

Piaget, J. Intellectual evolution from adolescence to adulthood. *Human Development* 15 (1972): 1–12.

Quadrio, A., and Peri, G. L'utilizzazione dei concetti di caso e di fortuna nel pensiero del pre-adolescente. *Contributi dell'Instituto di Psicologia* 30 (1970) : 190–209.

Scarlette, G. Adolescent thinking and the diary of Anne Frank. *Psychoanalytic Review* 58 (1971): 265–278.

Shaffer, M.; Sundberg, N. D.; and Tyler, L. E. Content differences on word listing by American, Dutch, and Indian adolescents. *Journal of Social Psychology* 79 (1969) : 139–140.

Shaimberg, D. "It really blew my mind": A study of adolescent cognition. *Adolescence* 5 (1970): 17–36.

Smedslund, J. The acquisition of conservation of substance and weight in children: External reinforcement of conservation of weight and of the operations of addition and subtraction. *Scandinavian Journal of Psychology* 2 (1961a) : 71–84.

Smedslund, J. The acquisition of conservation of substance and weight in children: Extinction of conservation of weight in children: Extinction of conservation of weight acquired "normally" and by means of empirical controls on a balance. *Scandinavian Journal of Psychology* 2 (1961b) : 85–87.

Stone, M. A., and Ausubel, D. P. The intersituational generality of formal thought. *Journal of Genetic Psychology* 115 (1969) : 169–180.

Tomlinson-Keasey, C. Formal operations in females from eleven to fifty-four years of age. *Developmental Psychology* 6 (1972) : 364.

Tyszkowa, M. Analiza rozwiazywania trudnych zadàn (problemow przez dzieci szkolne). *Przeglad Psychologiczny* 1 (NS) (1971) : 71–86.

Undeutsch, U. Neuere Untersuchungen zur Altergestalt der Pubescenz. *Zeitschrift fur Experimentelle und Angewandte Psychologie* 6 (1960): 578–588.

Van de Geer, J. P., and Jaspars, J. M. F. Cognitive functions. In P. R. Farnsworth et al., eds., *Annual Review of Psychology,* vol. 17, pp. 145–176. Palo Alto: Annual Reviews, Inc., 1966.

Vygotsky, L. S. *Thought and language.* Cambridge, Mass.: M.I.T. Press, 1962. (Note: This is a translation from the Russian. Vygotsky's book appeared in 1934.)

Wallace, J. G. *Concept growth and the education of the child.* Sussex: National Foundation for Educational Research in England and Wales, 1965.

Werner, H. *Comparative psychology of mental development.* New York: Harper, 1940. (See also Science Editions, New York, 1961. A 1948 edition is also available.)

Witkin, H. A., et al. *Psychological differentiation.* New York: Wiley, 1962.

Wohlwill, J. F. Un essai d'apprentissage dans le domaine de la conservation du nombre. *Etudes d'epistemologie genetique* 9 (1959) : 125–135.

Wohlwill, J. F. A study of the development of the number concept by scalogram analysis. *Journal of Genetic Psychology* 96 (1960) : 347–377.

Wohlwill, J. Vers une reformulation du role de l'experience dans le developpement cognitif. In Bresson, F., and de Montmollin, eds., *Psychologie et epistemologie genetiques: themes piagetiens,* pp. 211–222. Paris: Dunod, 1966.

Wohlwill, J. F., and Lowe, B. C. Experimental analysis of the development of conservation of number. *Child development* 33 (1962) : 153–167.

Wolfe, R. The role of conceptual systems in cognitive functioning at varying levels of age and intelligence. *Journal of Personality* 31 (1963): 108–123.

Yudin, L. W. Formal thought in adolescence as a function of intelligence. *Child Development* 37 (1966) : 697–703.

Suggested Readings

Bynum, T. W.; Thomas, J. A.; and Weitz, L. J. Truth-functional logic in formal operational thinking: Inhelder and Piaget's evidence. *Developmental Psychology* 7 (1972) : 129–132.

Cohler, B. J. Psychoanalysis, adaptation, and education: II. Development of thinking. *Psychological Reports* 30 (1972) : 719–740.

Das, J. P. Cultural deprivation and cognitive competence. In Ellis, N. R., ed., *International review of research in mental retardation:* VI. New York: Academic Press, 1973.

Eimas, P. D. A developmental study of hypothesis behavior and focusing. *Journal of Experimental Child Psychology* 8 (1969): 160–172.

Elkind, D. *Children and adolescents: Interpretive essays on Jean Piaget,* New York: Oxford University Press, 1970.

Evans, R. I. *Jean Piaget: The man and his ideas.* New York: Dutton, 1973.

Farrell, M. A. The formal stage: A review of the research. *Journal of Research and Development in Education* 3 (1969) : 111–118.

Flavell, J. H. *The developmental psychology of Jean Piaget.* Princeton: Van Nostrand, 1963.

Flavell, J. H. Stage-related properties of cognitive development. *Cognitive Psychology* 2 (1971) : 421–453.

Freides, D.; Fredenthal, B. J.; Grisell, J. L.; and Cohen, B. D. Changes in two dimensions of cognition during adolescence. *Child Development* 34 (1963) : 1047–1055.

Ginsburg, H., and Opper, S. *Piaget's theory of intellectual development.* Englewood Cliffs, N. J.: Prentice-Hall, 1969.

Halford, G. S. The impact of Piaget on psychology in the seventies. In Dodwell, P. C., *New horizons in psychology.* Harmondsworth, England: Penguin, 1972.

Hartigan, R. R. A temporal-spatial concept scale: A developmental study. *Journal of Clinical Psychology* 27 (1971) : 221–223.

Inhelder, B., and Sinclair, H. Learning cognitive structures. In Mussen, P.; Langer, J.; and Covington, M., eds., *Trends and issues in developmental psychology.* New York: Holt, Rinehart, and Winston, 1969.

Jahoda, G. Understanding the mechanism of bicycles: A cross-cultural study of developmental change after 13 years. *International Journal of Psychology* 4 (1969) : 103–108.

Murray, F. B., ed. *Critical features of Piaget's theory of the development of thought.* New York: MSS Information, 1972.

Muus, R. E. Jean Piaget's cognitive theory of adolescent development. *Adolescence* 2 (1967): 285–310.

Odom, R. D., and Guzman, R. D. Development of hierarchies of dimensional salience. *Developmental Psychology* 6 (1972): 271–287.

Peel, E. A. *The nature of adolescent judgment.* New York: Wiley-Interscience, 1971.

Penk, W. E. Developmental patterns of conceptual styles. *Psychological Reports* 29 (1971) : 635–649.

Pollio, H. R., and Gray, R. T. Change-making strategies in children and adults. *Journal of Psychology* 84 (1973) : 173–179.

Rimoldi, H. J.; Aghi, M.; and Burger, G. Some effects of logical structure, language, and age in problem solving in children. *Journal of Genetic Psychology* 112 (1968): 127–143.

Rimoldi, H. J., and VanderWonde, K. Aging and problem solving. *Archives of General Psychiatry* 20 (1969) : 215–225.

Roberge, J. J., and Paulus, D. H. Developmental patterns for children's class and conditional reasoning abilities. *Developmental Psychology* 4 (1971) : 191–200.

Sieveking, N. A. Effects of age on incongruity viewing. *Journal of Genetic Psychology* 119 (1971) : 251–257.

Vickers, M., and Blanchard, E. B. The development of preference for cognitive balance. *Journal of Genetic Psychology* 122 (1973) : 189–195.

Wachs, T. D., and Gruen, G. E. The effects of chronological age, trials, and lists characteristics upon children's category clustering. *Child Development* 42 (1971) : 1217–1227.

Yudin, L. W. The nature of adolescent thought. *Adolescence* 2 (1967) : 137–151.

Chapter Seven

Intelligence: Nature and Development

In the preceding chapter we discussed cognitive functioning and development. The discussion centered around the manner in which intellectual functioning changes as an individual becomes capable of increasingly higher levels of cognitive activity. Such a way of looking at intellectual functioning is based upon a consideration of its qualitative-dynamic aspects. In contrast, Chapter 7 considers a quantitative approach to intellectual functioning, giving particular emphasis to the measurement of capacity. As Guilford (1967) points out, the main question characterizing the quantitative approach is that of how much ability exists. In contrast, the qualitative approach asks how and in what order changes in ability take place.

Traditionally in psychology and education, when one speaks of intelligence and its measurement, the reference is to the quantitative approach and the special and general psychological aptitude tests upon which it is based. Actually there are two quite different quantitative approaches. One is unitary, viewing intelligence in holistic terms as a general function. The other is factorial, viewing intelligence more atomistically as composed of a number of different and not highly related components each of which is susceptible to separate measurement. Another term for the quantitative approach which is perhaps more meaningfully descriptive is the *analytical-psychometric approach*.

The Nature of Intelligence

The capacity to behave intelligently is one of man's most precious possessions. It is the attribute that makes his behavior uniquely human. It enables him to learn, to reason, to take advantage of the past, predict the future, manipulate his environment, and transcend in his thinking the barriers of time and space. Backman (1971) emphasizes the interaction of experience and the social environment when he defines intelligence as a gradually accumulated group of skills greatly affected by social interaction. Yet it is difficult to formulate a wholly satisfactory definition of intelligence because intelligence is really a series of exceedingly complex behaviors grouped under the common term *intelligence*. For this reason different theorists have emphasized different aspects and have defined intelligence in different ways, although as Cassell (1969) notes, the definitions can generally be categorized under one or the other of two categories: first, definitions emphasizing the ability to learn and to manipulate objects; second, definitions emphasizing individual adaptivity and ability to adjust to the environment. Cassell himself defines intelligence as being cognitive and as including ability to learn and to manipulate objects. He also sees intelligence in terms of adaptability in the sense of adjusting to one's environment. Various investigators such as Irvine (1970) and Chateau (1967) insist that intelligence must be evaluated in terms of affect, values, and attitudes, not solely in terms of traditional mental abilities.

Certainly intelligence is not an entity that can be isolated and examined in any physical sense. Measures of intelligence are indirect and merely examine an individual's ability to perform the behaviors that we agree to call representative of intelligence and that enable us to predict the probable future intellectual level of an individual's behavior. The problem lies in agreeing upon the significant behaviors to be classified as representative of intelligence, in finding satisfactory measures for those behaviors upon which there is agreement, and in deciding whether there is one overall general factor of intelligence or whether intelligence can only be seen as a composite of relatively independent abilities or traits. Of course if we accept a multiple-trait theory we must recognize that in a complex behavioral situation these traits will interact. A further complication is that an individual's intellectual functioning at any given time will depend, as was previously indicated, upon his past experiences, upon his personality and affect, upon his needs and motivations, and upon the specifics of his environmental situation.

Some writers have felt it expedient to identify several different kinds of intelligence as, for example, verbal intelligence, quantitative intelligence, and social intelligence. Lately some investigators have included creativity as a separate kind of intelligence. Cattell (1963, 1968) advances the idea of fluid and crystallized intelligence. He defines fluid intelligence as a "general relation-perceiving capacity, independent of sensory area ... determined by the individual's endowment in cortical, neurological-connection count development." Fluid intelligence is a broad factor because it represents an integrating power operative in practically any perceptual or reasoning situation. Cattell defines crystallized intelligence as a "related circle of abilities— verbal, numerical, reasoning ... that normally are taught at school ... [and] reflects both the neurological integrative potential of the individual and his fortune in cultural experience." In examining the distinction between fluid and crystallized intelligence, Horn (1972) notes that the distinction may be seen most clearly at the trait level of intellective description.

Unitary and Multiple-factor Approaches

Unitary theorists' definitions may be grouped, according to their emphasis, under three headings: (1) intelligence as the ability to adapt or adjust, (2) intelligence as the ability to learn, and (3) intelligence as the ability to think abstractly. Unitary theorists assume a general intelligence basic to all problem solving. They further assume that an individual's intelligence remains relatively constant from situation to situation.

There are essentially two major factorial approaches to intelligence,[1] the two-factor theory of Spearman (1914, 1927) and the multiple-factor theory of Thurstone (1938). The two-factor theory postulates that all cognitive behavior may be accounted for by a general factor, *g*, common to every cognitive reaction, and an indeterminate number of special factors, *s*, each independent of *g* and relatively independent of one another. Factorial theorists in the United States generally reject Spearman's two-factor theory and espouse either Thurstone's multiple-factor theory or a variation of it.

Multiple-factor theory postulates a number of distinct factors and dispenses with *g* as an

---

[1] All factorial approaches stem from a technique originally proposed by Spearman, known as factor analysis. Factor analysis is a rational, mathematical solution to an examination of a table of intercorrelations such that the data trends in the matrix may be determined. A factor analysis of a group of test scores, by examining their interrelationships, tries to find unitary elements or traits in surface relationships that may exist among the tests being considered. The analysis might reveal that the surface relationships among the tests were due to a single factor common to them all, or it might be found that several factors could be isolated and described.

important component of intellectual functioning. Thurstone (1938) initially isolated eight major factors ("primary mental abilities") as follows: Verbal (V), Perceptual Speed (P), Number (N), Inductive Reasoning (1), Rote Memory (R), Deductive Reasoning (D), Word Fluency (W), and Space (S). Following his original study Thurstone modified his factors, but on the whole they have remained relatively stable. Ahmavaara (1957) analyzed thirty-one different factorial studies and attempted by transformation analysis to isolate those factors that had been strongest and most commonly found. He cited nine "first certainty" factors. He listed six of Thurstone's factors (N, W, S, V, D, P) but did not list Inductive Reasoning and Rote Memory. He added to Thurstone's list a Reasoning factor, a Visualization factor, and a Speed and Strength of Perceptual Closure factor. Guilford (1967) has advanced an interesting structure of the intellect theory involving a matrix of cognition factors.[2]

A Workable Definition

For those readers who wish a workable definition of intelligence, one by Wechsler (1958) is suggested. Wechsler defines intelligence as "the aggregate or global[3] capacity of the individual to act purposefully, to think rationally, and to deal effectively with his environment." He notes that "intelligence is global because it characterizes the individual's behavior as a whole; it is an aggregate because it is composed of elements or abilities which, though not entirely independent, are qualitatively differentiable." One would wish, however, to extend Wechsler's definition to include the fact that the elements are also quantitatively differentiable. While Wechsler is essen-

tially a unitary theorist his statement that intelligence is an aggregate composed of "elements or abilities" is not incompatible with multiple-factor theory. Nor is Wechsler's definition necessarily incompatible with the general trend of psychometric thinking in the United States, as represented by writers such as Levinson (1964), which visualizes the eventual abandonment of any unidimensional index of intelligence.

Adolescence and Intelligence

The function of development, acting within the individual organism over time, is to prepare it to operate at increasing levels of complexity in such cognitive functions as deduction, induction, perception, spatial and number manipulation, and verbal facility. Adolescence is part of the developmental sequence during which these increasingly complex levels of cognitive function are being carried to fruition. Adolescence is a time of intellectual development during which the organism becomes increasingly able to interpret and cope with its environment and with itself.

Mental growth and development are important in the study of adolescence not simply as developmental phenomena, but because intellectual status is a limiting factor in assessing an individual's capabilities. Adolescence is a time of academic training and ever-broadening experience; therefore, it is essential for those interested in youth to form some estimate of teenagers' intellectual potentials. Such an estimate, if accurately made, will indicate the kind of experience most likely to be profitable to adolescents, as well as those experiences which should be withheld until later. This is particularly true for educators, who have the task of providing an effective curriculum for the education of youth. Vocational choice is a paramount consideration for adolescents, and vocational counselors must discuss future plans in terms of the individual's abilities if sound vocational planning is to ensue. The most accurate possible estimate of an adoles-

[2]A detailed discussion of Guilford's structure of intellect theory may be found in Guilford (1970, pp. 70–249). For a shorter account, see J. J. Michael (1968).

[3]The Oxford Dictionary defines *global* as "pertaining to or embracing the totality of a group of items or categories."

cent's intellectual ability also helps parents and the various agencies that hope to provide learning and other experiences for youth so that their upbringing may make them better individuals and better citizens.

It is known that intellectual ability is an aspect of growth and development that is related to other factors of physical growth. It is also known that an individual's ability to function in an intelligent manner at any given time is a combination of his stage of neural development and the past experiences to which he has been subjected. At any given time, an individual's intellectual growth and his prior experiences may be insufficient for him to profit or learn from present experiences and intellectual demands made upon him. There are also periods in a person's intellectual development when a given experience is more appropriate than it would be earlier or later. Hence the educator and others working with youth must determine what kinds of experience a child will find most profitable at any given point in his development and provide him with the preliminary knowledge and skills that are necessary if he is later to profit from learning experiences of a broader or more complex character.

The Measurement of Intelligence

Intelligence is ordinarily measured by individual or group tests that endeavor to estimate how intelligent a person is by one or more of three devices: (1) the level of difficulty of the problems a person can solve, (2) the range or number of problems he is able to solve at that level, and (3) the speed with which he can solve the problems.

Children's performance on measures of intelligence is indicated by raw scores that may be expressed in terms of mental age (MA). Mental age is defined as the amount or degree of general mental ability possessed by an average child of corresponding chronological age. It is an index of the developmental level in intellectual function a child has reached at a given time. For example, a child has a mental age of twelve if his mental development is exactly equal that of a normal child with a chronological age of twelve. Hence a child with a chronological age of twelve and a mental age of ten is of less than average intelligence for his age. A child with a chronological age of twelve and a mental age of fourteen is above average. Thus, mental age is an index of a person's level of performance on an intelligence test.

Performance on an intelligence test may also be expressed in terms of an intelligence quotient (IQ). The IQ is a means of expressing the relationship between a person's mental age and his chronological age. The formula for computing IQ is $IQ = 100(MA/CA)$. Thus, the IQ is a ratio of a person's ability, while the MA expresses what he is capable of at any moment. Two children who, on the same test, receive MAs of fourteen may be said to be capable of the same performance. But two children with IQs of 120, while both are above average for their ages, may not be capable *at that time* of the same performance, since one could be eight years old and the other fifteen.

The best-known individual intelligence tests suitable for adolescents in use today are the Stanford Revision of the Binet and the Wechsler Bellevue scales.[4]

For teenagers, the items of the Stanford-Binet largely call for verbal manipulation— an understanding and use of word or number concepts. Youngsters of these ages are also asked to show how they would find a purse lost in a large field, make connected sentences out of separated words or mixed-up words, recognize absurd stories and pictures, and so on. The variety of tasks is appealing, and although some of the items are reminiscent of schoolwork to the youngsters, most call for what the layman refers to as common sense. The score on the Stanford-Binet makes possible an estimate on individual's mental age.

[4]The Wechsler Adult Intelligence Scale (WAIS) was developed for adolescents as well as adults, but young adolescents may also be measured by the Wechsler Intelligence Scale for Children (WISC).

Figure 3   *Sample Profile of an Eighth-Grade Girl on the California Test of Mental Maturity*

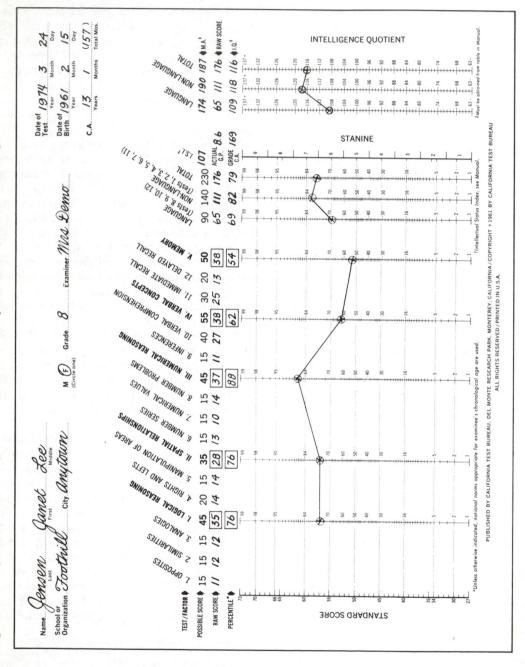

Source: California Test of Mental Maturity, Level 3, devised by E. T. Sullivan, W. W. Clark, and E. W. Tiegs. Copyright © 1961 by McGraw-Hill, Inc. Reproduced by permission of the publisher, CTB/McGraw-Hill, Del Monte Research Park, Monterey, CA. All rights reserved.

The Wechsler-Bellevue combines verbal features as in the Stanford-Binet and performance features by having verbal subtests and performance subtests. An IQ is quoted for each section. On the Wechsler scale the point score is converted directly to an IQ without the MA. A teenager taking the Wechsler is given some general information questions, arithmetic problems, items of comprehension about things like theater fires or being lost in the woods, similarities between objects; and, on the performance part of the test, he must put pictures in logical sequence, assemble cut-up pieces to form a whole (as in a jigsaw puzzle), make designs from blocks, and so on. The scores on the two halves of the test may be combined to form an IQ for the whole.

The difficulty with individual tests of intelligence is that they can be given to only one person at a time and must be administered by a well-trained tester. Hence, they are expensive and time-consuming. Many institutions are unable to afford either a Binet tester or the time required to test large groups of subjects one at a time. The group test of intelligence was devised to meet the demand for a comparatively inexpensive test that could be administered simultaneously by one tester to large groups of persons.

A good many group tests of intelligence are suitable for adolescents, but the California Test of Mental Maturity is representative of those available.[5] Figure 3 shows the profile of an eighth-grade girl on the CTMM. Subscores are obtained for logical reasoning, spatial relationships, numerical reasoning, verbal concepts, and memory. Three final scores are provided: language, nonlanguage, and total, all of which may be converted to mental ages or IQs. Many mental tests do not provide such a breakdown into part scores, only a single score that may be converted into mental age or IQ. Ordinarily, when an IQ is cited, the total score in its converted form is indicated.

[5] A discussion of other available group tests may be found in the current *Buros Mental Measurements Yearbook* or in a standard textbook on psychological measurement.

Various mental tests vary in their content and comparability, and the same individual will perform somewhat differently on one as compared to another. However, correlations are comparatively high, and IQ differences will not be great. But in view of their lack of strict comparability it is good practice to cite the intelligence test used when an individual's IQ or mental age is given. For example, IQ 95 (CTMM), or IQ 105 (Binet).

In deciding whether to administer an individual or a group intelligence test, or in interpreting results, it should be remembered that the individual mental test is a more sensitive indicator of mental level and also provides an opportunity for the tester to observe the examinee's reactions and methods of attack as he attempts to answer the questions posed by the test. At the present time, the Stanford Revision of the Binet is recognized by many competent authorities as the standard American measure of intelligence, and it is the custom in introducing a new intelligence test to cite its correlation with the Stanford-Binet.

But in the final analysis, an individual's general ability must be viewed and interpreted in terms of what he can do at any given time. Since his behavior is not his actual intelligence, but the product of it, our only present method of measuring intelligence is an indirect one. It is not possible to measure a person's potential directly, as we would measure his height or his weight; we must set him a number of tasks to perform, then rate his performance compared with others of the same status.

In designing a test of intelligence the test maker has to decide upon his definition of intelligence and select the tasks best calculated to measure it according to his definition. Here is a source of differences among tests as persons with different definitions of intelligence attempt to construct tests of mental ability. Since, as has been noted earlier, opinions differ on exactly what intelligence is, test contents differ. Moreover, even though their definitions of intelligence agree, two different test makers may disagree on the kinds of tasks that are most apt to implement their concept of intelligence on a test; or when similar tasks are used, they may disagree upon the relative weight to give the various tasks. Despite disagreements, tests of intelligence have many elements in common, though not enough to allow test users to assume that any two tests are equivalent. Hence, developmental studies of mental growth that use different tests may be expected to show different results, although the differences may not be radical.

Culture-fair Tests of Intelligence

It is unfortunate that many tests of intelligence tend to be weighted in favor of background experiences common to one subgroup of the culture, such as children reared in middle-class homes. Such weighting becomes particularly pernicious when the tests are used indiscriminately for purposes of group comparison or for certain kinds of selection and elimination. A child reared in an inner-city, an ethnic, or a rural environment usually does not have the kinds of experiences, values, and opportunities characteristic of those reared in a suburban, middle-class environment. Even vocabulary and speech forms may be crucially different. The existence of differences, however, should not be taken to mean that the inner-city, ethnic, or rural environment is necessarily inferior or that it lacks intellectual stimulation. It is simply that a test that will give an adequate assessment of the present intellectual status and future potential of an individual from one kind of environment will not necessarily do the same adequate job for an individual from a contrasting environment. Such being the case, four possibilities exist to prevent misuse of intelligence tests. The first possibility is not to use intelligence tests at all, thus avoiding any likelihood of misuse. This possibility is not really acceptable because intelligence tests do appraise an important aspect of human behavior and to throw them out simply because they present

certain problems is analogous to throwing the baby out with the bath water.

A second possibility is to use different tests with different subgroups of the population when it has been established that essential differences do exist and are reflected in test performance to the detriment of obtaining an accurate view of intellectual potential. The use of multiple tests, however, is a difficult solution because of the large number of different tests potentially needed and the difficulty in making valid comparisons. Third is the possibility of using present tests, even though it is recognized that they are heavily weighted in favor of academic learning and middle-class experiences and values, but to use test results with caution and with full understanding of their bias. This is the most commonly taken approach at the present time, although there is always a question as to the extent of the "full understanding" of many test users. The fourth possibility is that of devising tests designed to minimize environmental differences to the greatest degree possible. Such tests, which attempt to measure intellectual power and attitude relatively free of special environmental influences, are called culture-free or culture-fair tests of intelligence.

It would appear that the fourth approach is the most adequate solution to the problem. Equally, it appears to be a particularly difficult solution in that it seems almost impossible to separate special influences from universal environmental ones. While a number of attempts have been made, success to date has been limited.[6]

Theoretically, the culture-fair test provides a measure of the same things with the same results as the more traditional test of intelligence but does so with a minimum or a total lack of use of language and in a somewhat different task format. Alzobaie et al. (1968),

[6]Four tests that have been used with varying degrees of success are the Raven Progressive Matrices, the Cattell IPAT (Institute for Personality and Ability Testing) Culture-Free Intelligence Test, the Davis-Eells Games, and the Leiter International Performance Scale.

testing disadvantaged tenth-grade adolescents, noted that measures of divergent production[7] provided an alternate way of predicting traditionally assessed school performance of disadvantaged children with receptive and expressive language function disabilities.

Individuals of any subculture within a larger general culture should, in terms of inherent ability, be distributed along the same curve of normal distribution, and their various aspects of intellectual functioning should fall into the same domain. The assumption underlying the culture-fair test is that the members of any subculture can generalize, abstract, draw analogies, and manipulate numbers. Consequently the function of the culture-fair test is to enable them to display these capacities in a format that is fair to their particular environment.[8]

Ways Intelligence Tests Are Used

Intelligence tests are used in today's schools chiefly for three purposes: (1) determining what level of school work is best suited to the child, (2) vocational advisement and planning, and (3) research. The first purpose may involve the child's grade placement, the presentation of special materials within the work of any grade, or the subjects in the curriculum that he should pursue or avoid. The second purpose, vocational advisement, may include consideration of specific subjects in the curriculum, the years of education the child might plan for, and future occupations open to him. The third purpose, research, is an attempt to gain a picture of intellectual growth, development, and performance as a means of understanding their cause and nature and of discovering those things to which they are most closely related. Research also becomes a

[7]Guilford's nonverbal tests: Making Objects, Utility Test, and Figure Production.

[8]The culture-fair test format discussed here refers to one suitable for the peoples of modern and particularly Western cultures. When primitive peoples are to be measured, the best recourse is to use different tests as suggested in the second possibility previously discussed.

means of providing a direct practical answer to questions pertinent to the school's everyday operation.

Most tests used for any of the above purposes are group intelligence tests. Ordinarily a school will administer an individual test to a child only when his behavior or achievement seems not to be in accord with the rough measure the group tests provide. Many school systems have not adopted the policy of schoolwide intelligence tests; however, many school administrators have adopted the additional policy of not allowing the classroom teacher to have access to the students' records. The assumptions underlying the latter policy are usually that intelligence test results may be badly misinterpreted by the inadequately informed teacher, and the teacher might, unconsciously or not, use them in a manner adverse to the pupils' best interests. A further point is that frequently it is tempting to pin a label on a student and expect him always to behave according to that label. Such remarks as "With your brains you should be better prepared for this class," or "You probably couldn't get this anyway" are indicative of such attitudes; unfortunately they are occasionally heard. But these comments should not be taken to mean that the able student should not be expected to maintain a high level of performance. It is simply a matter of how the teacher goes about motivating a student to function at the level at which, *all things considered,* he is able.

The subject matter of most courses in the school curriculum is planned with a view to the achievement of the average child in the class. Knowledge of this average ability should be considered essential in planning work for the group. When certain students in the classroom seem not to be meeting the group's average achievement, an intelligence test is indicated to discover possible reasons for the discrepancy. Frequently a child's intellectual inability to pursue a given field of study has been obscured by an air of alertness and eager interest. Conversely, many a bright child ceases trying to achieve even at the average level, out of boredom and impatience with those who do not understand explanations as readily as he does.

The Development of Intelligence

For a good many years it has been a common theoretical assumption that the course of development proceeds from relative globality toward increasing differentiation and hierarchization. According to this assumption, intellectual ability should become increasingly differentiated in its progression in an individual from infancy through adolescence into adulthood. Koffka (1925), representing the Gestalt school, spoke of intellectual, social, and perceptual development as a process of differentiation progressing from an initial base of organized structure. For Koffka intellectual development was an elaboration or differentiation of already existing mental structures, rather than an addition of new functions. Lewin (1935) theorized that intellectual development occurred as a gradual differentiation of the cognitive field. As Lewin saw it, as a person grows older the boundaries among the differentiated areas of the cognitive field become less flexible and increasingly rigid. For example, a younger child as compared to an adolescent would have a smaller number of cognitive regions, and the boundaries of these regions would be relatively more fluid and less specific. Werner (1948) advanced as a fundamental law of development the postulate that development proceeds toward an increasing differentiation of parts and hierarchization. He wrote: "The fundamental law of development ... may logically be applied to the mental functions *per se*. An increasing differentiation and refinement of mental phenomena and functions and a progressive hierarchization may be accepted as a basic principle." Piaget (1950) discussing the "hierarchy of operations and their progressive differentiation" wrote that "each of the transitions from one of these levels to the next is therefore characterized by a new differentiation of the

systems constituting the unit of the preceding level." Speaking of the developmental aspects of a schema, Piaget (1952, 1958) points out that a necessary intellectual progression is repetition, generalization, and differentiation. And finally, Gesell (1954) speaks of a sequential patterning expressing itself in progressive differentiation within a total action system.

An early influential statement of the application of the differentiation hypothesis to the development of intelligence was made by Garrett (1938). Later, in an expansion of his original statement, Garrett (1946) wrote:

Abstract or symbol intelligence changes in its organization as age increases from a fairly unified and general ability to a loosely organized group of abilities or factors.... Over the elementary school years we find a functional generality among tests at the symbol level. Later on this general factor or "g" breaks down into the quasi-independent factors reported by many investigators.... At high school and college levels ... it would seem to be theoretically more defensible, therefore, practically more useful, to measure verbal, numerical, perceptual or spatial ability, and perhaps other factors at these ages, than to give the subject a single over-all score.[9]

Typical of the research attempts to test the differentiation hypothesis was one conducted by Dye and Very (1968). These investigators administered a battery of twenty tests to 556 subjects (258 males, 298 females), constituting the entire ninth and eleventh grades of an urban-fringe New England high school and a group of volunteers from a college course in introductory psychology. Mean ages of the sample were 14.0 years for the ninth-grade group, 16.2 for the eleventh graders, and 19.8 for the college group. The twenty tests included five reasoning ability measures, and tests of verbal ability, perceptual speed, numerical facility, and mathematics achievement. Dye and Very report an increasing number of factors at succeeding age levels, with more factors

[9]Among Garrett's "many investigators" reporting on the independent mental factors were Thorndike (1926), Schneck (1929), Garrett (1930), Anastasi (1932), Bryan (1934), Schiller (1934), Garrett, Bryan and Perl (1935), Thurstone and Thurstone (1938), Clark (1944), and Reichard (1944).

appearing for males than for females. Major sex differences were found in the development of several reasoning abilities, with females showing verbal ability to a greater extent than males. However, male reasoning factors appeared more specific, particularly in the areas of inductive, arithmetic, and general reasoning. The clearest evidence in favor of the age-differentiation hypothesis to emerge from the Dye and Very study was the differentiation of a single general factor combining tests of numerical facility and perceptual speed in the ninth-grade group into two separate factors, Numerical Facility and Perceptual Speed, in the eleventh-grade and college groups. It would appear that the ninth-graders applied the same ability to both types of tests while, in contrast, a distinct ability was applied to each area by eleventh graders and college freshmen.

In another examination of age and differentiation, Nguyen-Xuan (1969), using a sample of French youth nine through eighteen years of age, reports that the processes of differentiation and hierarchical integration occur in cyclic succession by the emergence of higher-level integrative ability. Such integrative ability seems to appear as a limited ability, becoming increasingly more important, until it becomes a general ability characterized by both quantitative and qualitative development in the factorial model.

Quereshi (1967) also reports research substantially validating the differentiation hypothesis for mental development. However, in a later study in which Wechsler test materials were used, Quereshi (1973) was unable to find corroboration for the hypothesis. Of this last study he writes:

One may conclude that the type of test materials involved have definite bearing on the trends in patterns of intellectual development. Thus, one can state with a high degree of confidence—since none of the studies with WISC/WAIS scales have yielded data in support of the differentiation hypothesis—that Wechsler scales do not constitute those samples of the cognitive and psychomotor domains that are suited for testing the differentiation hypothesis.

It is true that investigators other than Quereshi and including Balinski (1941), McNemar (1942), Doppelt (1950) and Cohen (1957, 1959) have reported results inconsistent with the differentiation hypothesis, but it appears reasonable to assume that such adverse results are due more to problems of research design and instrumentation than to the untenability of the differentiation hypothesis itself. Quereshi (1973) notes that such research and instrumentation problems include (1) inappropriate selection of subjects and lack of control of sex presentation at various age levels; (2) inadequate representation of the spectrum of human abilities due to certain test selection procedures; (3) noncomparability of tests at different age levels and inappropriate methods of analysis; (4) nonequivalence of reliability, even when the tests are the same, at different age levels; and (5) differences in educational, cultural, occupational, ethnic, and socioeconomic backgrounds as well as group differences in heterogeneity (since most of the studies are cross-sectional).

The Age of Cessation of Mental Growth

Following World War I considerable study was devoted to the subject of mental growth and development. At that time it was the consensus, based upon the results of mental testing, that the average Caucasian adult in the United States possessed a mental age of thirteen years and that mental growth was usually complete by the time an individual had attained the age of thirteen or fourteen.

From 1921 through 1924, however, considerable further research upon the age of cessation of mental growth indicated that earlier estimates should be revised. It then became generally accepted that sixteen rather than thirteen or fourteen was a more likely age for cessation. The later point of view was based upon the results of studies such as those by Baldwin and Stecher (1922) and Brooks (1921). Using the Stanford-Binet on normal and superior children, Baldwin and Stecher showed growth continuing until sixteen, the highest age they tested. Brooks found mental age was still increasing at fifteen, the highest chronological age included in his study. Of course, learning continues after mental growth stops, but the *rate* of learning does not improve after such growth stops.

The trouble with such studies is their limited upper age range and the fact that many of them found that mental age was still increasing in the highest year they tested. Had young adults been included, the results would probably have been similar to those reported by present-day investigators, some of which indicate mental growth continuing into late adolescence and early maturity (the twenties) and, in some aspects of intelligence, even into late maturity. Another fault with the earlier studies was that they did not allow for the effect of practice on their retest runs, although this can hardly be regarded as a particularly serious criticism. Thorndike (1926a) reran Brooks's (1921) study, allowing for retest practice, and got similar results. On the other hand, Thorndike (1923) retested 8,564 high school students after twelve months and found mental growth continuing until eighteen, the highest age he tested. He then ran a second study (1926b) on a random sample of students used in his original study (1923), allowing for practice effect. This time he reported that mental growth continued "beyond eighteen."

A number of studies indicated that differential chronological cessation points were characteristic of various classes of intelligence. Kuhlmann (1921) tested 639 feebleminded children every year for ten years and reported mental age increasing until around fifteen for idiots, fifteen to sixteen for imbeciles, seventeen for morons, and eighteen for borderlines. Thurstone and Ackerson (1929) reported that "the mental growth curve for bright children approaches the level of test-maturity sooner than that of dull children."

Studies of mental growth after 1924, with few exceptions, have continued to raise the estimates for age of cessation upward toward the early twenties and even beyond. Hart (1924), using the Army Alpha, found mental growth approaching a point of cessation at sixteen or seventeen. Dearborn and Cattell (1930) found mental ages and point scores on the Dearborn test greater at eighteen than at any previous age. Some studies indicated even higher levels. For example, Sudweeks (1927), with a sample of 1,800, found scores on the Terman group test increasing to age nineteen, although results that were statistically significant did not appear with the small number of cases included at that age.

An interesting communitywide study of the growth and decline of intelligence was made by Jones and Conrad (1933), who tested 1,191 rural New Englanders with the Army Alpha. They found that the curve of mental growth rose to about sixteen, displayed a negative acceleration[10] following sixteen, and reached its highest point between nineteen and twenty-one. After twenty-one a long slow decline began, so that scores regressed to about the fourteen-year age level in the middle fifties. Wechsler (1958) depicts intelligence performance as increasing until the early twenties, although after about fifteen the acceleration of the curve of increase rapidly decreases. Ghiselli (1957) hypothesizes, however, that with an intelligence test measuring the higher intellectual functions and putting no premium on spread of response, adults who have achieved higher levels of intelligence would show little or no decline in performance with increasing age. He designed two tests to measure the higher aspects of intelligence and administered them to groups of 628 and 795 persons ranging in age from twenty to sixty-five who had completed at least one year of college. On neither test was there a downward trend in scores with increasing age. Thus, in Ghiselli's study no relationship was found between age and intellectual ability.

Cattell (1968) notes that the curves of growth of the two types of intelligence (crys-

[10]A curve becomes negatively accelerated when, from a period of comparatively rapid rise (positive acceleration), its rise becomes markedly slower.

tallized and fluid, cited earlier in this chapter) he postulates differ. The crystallized curves show increases to ages sixteen and eighteen and beyond, while the fluid curve, following a generalized biological growth curve, appears to reach a plateau at about age fourteen. Fluid intelligence appears to decline steadily after age twenty-two, but the crystallized curve seems not to decline until middle age or slightly thereafter. Obviously, fluid intelligence is more dependent upon hereditary factors than is crystallized intelligence. Horn and Cattell (1967) studied 297 subjects from fourteen to sixty-one years of age, divided into five age groups. They reported that: (1) the mean level of crystallized intelligence was systematically higher for older adults, while the mean level of fluid intelligence was systematically higher for younger adults; (2) the mean of the twenty-one to twenty-eight age group in general visualization function was highest for all age groups with the means on either side of the high values systematically dropping; and (3) there appeared to be no systematic age trends for the factors of fluency, speediness, and carefulness. Horn (1968) also noted that measures of fluid intelligence are more sensitive indicators of brain malfunction in that fluid intelligence declines with brain damage and aging in adulthood.

Jones (1955) reported a gain in mental age for a sample of 83 tested in the ninth grade and again at age thirty-three. He reported retest correlations of .84 for men and .90 for women. However, he felt that the gains may well have been based largely on vocabulary and on the general mental growth in the years immediately after sixteen. Owens (1953) reported similar results for a group of 127 college graduates who were tested as freshmen and again at age fifty. As with the Jones study, the Owens results may have been due largely to gains from nineteen to twenty-two, rather than in the later years of the life span.

Some of the disagreements over the age of cessation of mental growth may be accounted for by the operation of a selective factor. A comprehensive communitywide sample such as that obtained by Jones and Conrad in the study previously cited will show more generally representative results than will a more confined study limited to the rural public schools. Most generally representative to date have been the results of the Army General Classification Test used during World War II, although even there the younger population is missing and the female scores available represent a highly selected sample.

It is particularly true that when serial or cross-sectional records of mental test scores are obtained from an institution, such as a school, where there are continued dropouts as children grow older and where those who remain constitute a selection on the basis of intelligence, different results appear than would come from a comprehensive sample including individuals of all categories. Other things being equal, longitudinal studies wherein children are tested at one age and then retested a number of times after intervening periods of time yield more sensitive results than do cross-sectional studies. When possible, testing in longitudinal studies is done with the same form or an alternate form of the same test.

Another problem in determining the time of cessation of mental growth arises from the fact that various individual mental factors may show different cessation levels. Ordinarily, mental level is computed from the total score received on an intelligence test, but the tests are usually composed of various subtests or at least of different types of items. Standings on individual subtests or performance on different kinds of items are obscured when they are summed together. There is thus a question as to whether or not all the various components of intelligence rise and decline together. Some light is thrown on this problem by studies made by Woolley (1926) and by Jones and Conrad (1933). Woolley, in a study of two groups of children, one of which left school to work at fourteen while the other remained in school, administered various tests (including tapping, card sorting, cancellation, rote memory, substitution, and completion) on an annual retest basis. He reported: "The easier the mental task, the earlier an approximate adult status is reached. Thus in memory an adult status is attained for the seven-place series (digits) at fifteen, for the eight-place at sixteen, and for the nine-place at seventeen years." That schooling did not cause gains on these tasks was manifested by the fact that development of the functions measured continued equally long for both groups.

Scores for increasing ages on the subtests of the Army Alpha are shown in Figure 4 from the previously cited community study made by Jones and Conrad. There is considerable difference in growth and decline of the eight tests measured: Oral Directions, Arithmetical Problems, "Common Sense," "Opposites" (Vocabulary), Dissected Sentences, Numerical Completions, Analogies, and General Information. Some tests find adolescents surpassing adults; some show adults surpassing adolescents. Some note sharp declines in maturity, while others show either gradual declines or none at all. The years of peak performance tend to vary from test to test. However, Jones and Conrad draw the conclusion that native capacity of "sheer modifiability" tends to suffer most greatly with advancing age.

Bayley and Odeon (1955), in a longitudinal study extending into the adult years, report a correlation of .88 between two forms of a concept-mastery test administered at twelve-year intervals. This study reported a performance increase with age during adult life. Thurstone (1955), in a study of adult asymptotes[11] for the seven primary mental abilities tested by his Primary Mental Abilities Test, reported that earliest maturing occurs in the perceptual speed factor, which reaches adult level at age twelve, and that verbal comprehension and word fluency mature relatively late. Space and reasoning factors attain adult level at age fourteen, and number and memory factors at about age sixteen. In a series of learning experiments with adults, Kay (1955) reported diminishing efficiency with age, particularly as the tasks became more complex. He hypothesized that such losses were probably due more to a loss of flexibility in adapting to new conditions and data. Lehman (1953) has reported that in most intellectual occupations the highest quality work is ordinarily accomplished before age forty.

The implication of age of mental-growth cessation for the education of adolescents is that the adolescent is nearing his peak in terms of mental ability or power. By the time he is eighteen he has either already reached his peak or, except for a few mental functions, will show only a slight increase from that point on. Under the circumstances, his learning ability is potentially nearly as great as it will be during his adult years, and he may profitably be subjected to learning experiences that will challenge his capacities. The reason for withholding certain types of learning experience from an adolescent is not that he is not potentially capable of profiting from them, but that he may have had insufficient previous experience or training. Thus, an intelligent eleventh grader would be capable of learning calculus providing he had previously studied preliminary mathematics. The process of curriculum development is that of providing essential preliminary learning experiences to children so that they can profit from advanced learning experiences as soon as they are capable of being subjected to them. The curriculum maker will remember that individuals differ in intelligence and that an effective school program is one that individualizes its instruction on the basis of the intellectual capacities of the various children in the school. The problem is partly that of endeavoring to provide everyone with at least a minimum of learning experiences so he may live an effective and productive life *in terms of his abilities.*[12]

[11]An asymptote is a straight line that a regular curve constantly approaches but never reaches, or reaches only at infinity.

[12]Effective learning by an adolescent has, of course, prerequisites other than that of preliminary learning and an adequate mental level. Included in these are motivation and readiness, good teaching, physical well-being, and good emotional adjustment.

Figure 4 *Growth and Decline of Ability in the Individual Subtests of the Army Alpha. Note: The T-score values for each test are given at the left; chronological age is given at the bottom; original data for total group are plotted as dots.*

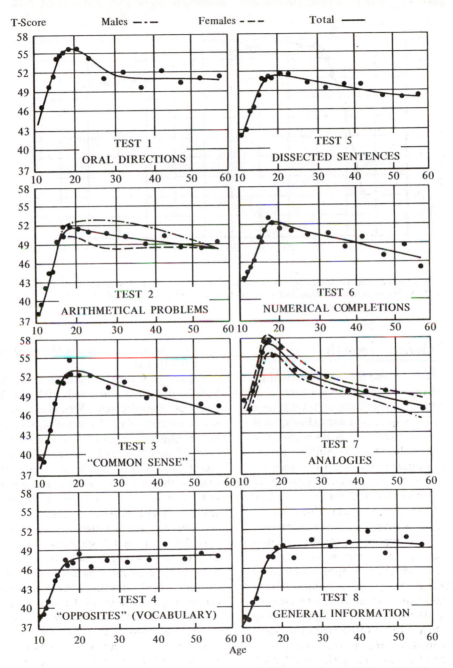

Source: Adapted from H. E. Jones and H. S. Conrad, "The growth and decline of intelligence," *Genetic Psychology Monographs* 13 (1933): 223–298. Reprinted by permission of The Journal Press.

Figure 5 *Curve of Mental Growth and Decline—Bellevue Full Scale, Ages 7–65*

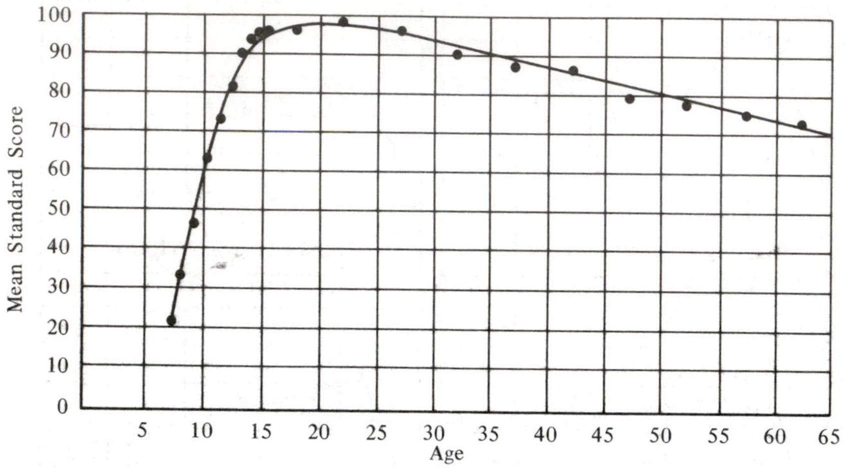

Source: Adapted from D. Wechsler, *The measurement and appraisal of adult intelligence*, 4th ed. (Baltimore: Williams and Wilkins, 1958), p. 31. Reprinted by permission of the author.

The Rate of Mental Growth

The rate of mental growth has been studied by numerous investigators, and the consensus of their findings is that the growth of intelligence does not proceed by equal amounts throughout its period of development, nor is its course the same for every child. Mental ability grows rapidly during childhood and begins to decelerate in adolescence. Ljung (1965) tested four groups of Swedish boys and girls (nine to ten, ten to eleven, twelve to thirteen, fourteen to fifteen) on verbal comprehension and mathematics factors. She reports a mental growth spurt for girls at ages twelve to thirteen, with a lesser one for boys at ages fourteen to fifteen. According to Ljung, a comparatively slow growth rate seems to be characteristic of the period immediately before the spurt. These findings indicate a difference between the sexes in mental maturation and a tendency for a more rapid growth rate for girls in all four groups studied. For any given factor, level and growth rate appear to be positively correlated.

In other words, the higher the level, the faster the growth rate.

Figure 5 shows a curve of mental growth based upon data obtained with the Wechsler-Bellevue Intelligence Examination for ages seven to sixty-five. In general, curves of rate of intelligence growth show a much greater rate of development in early than in later years. The curve tends to diminish in rate from eight to fifteen with a greater reduction following fifteen, resulting in negative acceleration in the middle or late teens. The rate appears to vary unpredictably at different ages but it is not highly variable or erratic, despite the fact that each child tends to show a distinctive growth pattern. On the basis of Ljung's (1965) findings there appears to be a common developmental time relationship between the onset of puberty and acceleration in rate, but there is no evidence of a causal relationship. In an early study Stone and Barker (1937) found intelligence test scores and IQs of post- as compared to prepubescent girls somewhat higher.

Bayley (1955), in discussing individual differences in growth rates, writes:

Relative scores tend to make us forget that intellectual growth is a dynamic ongoing process, in which both averages and standard deviations in scores are related to the age of the subjects. It is worthwhile, therefore, to try to present individual curves of growth in units that will emphasize a child's change in relation to himself. Growth curves will enable us to observe a child's periods of fast and slow progress, his spurts and plateaus, and even regressions, in relation to himself.

The reasons for deviations and differences from point to point in an individual's intellectual growth may be due to passing conditions of health, motivation, and emotional adjustment. They may also be due to genetic factors or prolonged environmental deprivation or emotional upset. It has been hypothesized that a number of intellectual attributes appear to have accelerated over the past several generations on the basis of cross-generation scores on such measures as the WAIS, Raven Progressive Matrices, and the Army Alpha Intelligence Test. Support for this hypothesis has been advanced by Koppen-Thulesuis and Teichman (1972), who compared the scores of 343 East German school children on old and new standardizations of the Pauli Test with those made by children in 1925, 1937, and 1946. The modern German children showed marked improvement on the older averages. Elley (1969) in a New Zealand study using the Otis Intermediate Test of Mental Ability compared the performance of 6,000 nine- to fourteen-year-olds tested in 1936 with that of 6,000 of the same age tested in 1968. The resulting comparative analysis indicated performance differences between 1936 as compared to 1968 in sex, age groups, rural-urban residence, occupational groups, and geographical location in New Zealand. There was an overall improvement over the span of the study in verbal reasoning skills. At each age level, girls showed a significantly greater increase than did boys.

Interpretation of the reasons for changes such as those described in the studies by Elley (1969) and Koppen-Thulesuis and Teichman (1972) should be embarked upon with considerable caution. Although, as Bloom (1964) notes, the general pattern of intelligence develops in an exceedingly lawful way, the effects of time and situation are absorbed into the developmental sequences to be observed. For that reason, in considering curves of mental growth gradients in children, it should be borne in mind, as Schaie (1972) points out, that such curves may be "highly specific for the particular time and circumstances when the data were collected and that such specificity, moreover, is likely to operate differentially for boys and girls."[13]

The Constancy of the IQ

In the early days of intelligence measurement it was assumed that the IQ changed very little, with variability chiefly due to inaccuracies of measurement. Much of the early research upon which this assumption rested was based upon cross-sectional data and upon short-term retests of the same children over a period ranging from a few days to a time span usually not exceeding a year. Longitudinal research began to present a different picture, and the position today is that significant changes may and do take place in many children during their developmental period. Today predictions as to a child's intellectual potential must be made with considerable caution. Bradway (1944, 1945) reported on a sample of 138 children who were tested when they were from two to six years of age and were then retested ten years later. Four- and five-year-old children tested ten years later had IQs correlated .67

[13]Baltes (1968), Baltes and Reinert (1969), Schaie and Strother (1968), and Schaie (1970) have noted that a more parsimonious explanation for age differences found in longitudinal studies can be found in the assumption of actual differences in levels of performance between successive generations rather than in the assumption of inherent changes. That is, the age changes can be attributed in large part to the impact of environmental rather than developmental factors.

with the original testing and two- and three-year-olds produced correlations of .66. About one-fourth of the two- and three-year-olds and one-third of the four- and five-year-olds changed less than five points, and about half the children changed less than ten points. According to the Bradway study, about one child in three or four who is under six will show IQ changes of fifteen or more points in the ten following years. Studies by Honzik (1938), Bayley (1949), and Goodenough and Maurer (1942) point to the danger of predicting intellectual capacity during the later years of development from nursery-school mental-test scores. As Sontag, Baker, and Nelson (1958) note, "From the various longitudinal studies . . . it has become evident that cycles or patterns of change in IQ do occur among children. Not only does the amount of change in IQ differ from individual to individual, but also the age periods at which various kinds of changes occur differ in individual cases."

Distribution of Ability

Generally speaking, the intellectual level of any large unselected sample of the population of the same chronological age will be found to be normally distributed.[14] The larger the sample and the greater the extent to which selective factors have been ruled out in selecting the sample, the more likely it is that the ensuing distribution of intellectual status will be in the form of the normal bell-shaped curve. However, when a selective factor enters the picture,

[14]If a normal distribution were presented in the form of a curve, the curve would appear in a bell-shaped form known as the normal or Gaussian curve. The area under the curve represents the number or percent of cases. The median is that point above and below which one-half of the cases occur. If the distribution is not normal the curve will be skewed; that is, it will not be bell-shaped, with the majority of cases clustered around a median located on the base line directly under the highest point on the curve. The cases in the skewed distribution will tend to pile up at the high or low end of the distribution. Sometimes the nonnormal distribution is depicted in the form of a rectangle or a square. Or the curve shows two or more humps with valleys between; then the distribution is said to be bi- or trimodal, depending upon the number of humps.

the curve will tend to be skewed either to the right or left, depending upon the nature of the sample. For example, in an institution for the feeble-minded or in a slum area one would expect the distribution of intelligence depicted by test scores to show a majority below the median for a distribution composed of the whole population. By the same token, the distribution of intelligence of college students or of professional men and women would be expected to show a preponderance on the upper end of the intellectual scale. Where two very diverse groups come together a bimodal distribution may be found, as in a very bright and a very dull group who for some selection reason were included in the same sample.

Stroud and his associates (1960) conducted a survey of the intelligence of fifth-grade children in 10 percent of the public elementary schools in Iowa, and classified them on the basis of seven intelligence-score categories. The children were further classified by the size of the communities in which they lived. Two assumptions were made by the investigators. First, they assumed that the tested 10 percent were representative of the entire fifth-grade population of Iowa and that it would be possible to generalize what was true of the sample's 10 percent for the remaining 90 percent of fifth graders. Second, they assumed that the estimated percentage distribution of IQs for all fifth-grade public school pupils in Iowa would accurately represent the percentage for all elementary school children in all grades in Iowa. Table 7 presents the distribution of intelligence for Iowa fifth graders on the basis of the size of the community in which they lived (stratum), together with an Iowa overall and a national comparison. The Lorge-Thorndike Intelligence Test, Verbal Battery, was the measure of intelligence used. Figure 6 presents a comparison of the performance of Iowa children with national norms at each IQ level from 50 to 150.

If teachers of adolescent groups will ascertain the intellectual status of their groups, they may be more effective in adapting their instruction as well as their program to provide for individual differences in intellectual

Table 7 *Estimated Percentages* of Iowa Public Elementary School Children in Each of Seven Intelligence-Score Categories; By Stratum and Overall Intelligence-Score Category*

Stratum	1** 50–84	2 85–92	3 93–103	4 104–114	5 115–124	6 125–132	7 133–150
I	3.0	7.5	24.6	28.4	22.5	8.4	5.7
II	5.9	7.7	17.0	33.6	22.9	7.4	5.6
III	4.6	7.4	20.0	30.9	21.4	9.0	6.7
IV	3.0	8.7	19.3	33.7	23.0	8.7	3.7
V	4.2	5.1	19.0	30.7	22.7	11.2	7.0
VI	4.6	7.1	18.8	32.0	22.7	8.7	6.1
VII	4.4	5.3	12.8	34.3	23.7	11.7	7.8
VIII	3.7	7.2	21.3	28.1	21.8	10.2	7.8
IX	6.6	7.5	20.5	26.4	18.9	11.2	9.0
X	9.5	11.8	22.5	26.5	17.6	6.9	5.2
Iowa Overall	5.0	7.5	19.6	30.6	21.7	9.3	6.4
Assumed Nat'l	15.9	15.0	26.7	25.1	10.7	4.4	2.3

Description of Strata

Stratum	Community Population	Remarks
I		Schools in this stratum could not be identified with communities. This stratum actually includes all 1-teacher schools and all 2- to 5-teacher non-high-school-district schools having eight or fewer 5th-grade pupils.
II	Under 500	Each of these strata includes as distinct "communities" 3- to 7-teacher, non-high-school-district schools having total elementary enrollments similar to the total elementary enrollments in communities of the specified size.
III	500–1,000	
IV	1,000–3,000	Each of these strata includes as distinct "communities" non-high-school-district schools with eight or more teachers having total elementary enrollments similar to the enrollments in communities of the specified size. Schools in suburban communities were grouped with the schools of the associated metropolitan community.
V	3,000–8,000	
VI	8,000–15,000	
VII	15,000–27,000	
VIII	27,000–45,000	
IX	45,000–100,000	
X	Over 100,000	

*Estimates of percentages have the following approximate probable errors:

Categories	Individual Stratum	Overall
1 and 7	±1.5%	±.5%
2 and 6	±2.5%	±.7%
3, 4, 5	±5.0%	±1.0%

**Educable children enrolled in classes for the mentally retarded and in the two state institutions are not included in these figures. It is estimated that this group would represent about 1.5 percent of the total, and if placed in category 1, the Iowa overall total would be raised from 5.0 to 6.5 percent.

Source: J. B. Stroud et al., "Distribution of intelligence scores of Iowa public school children," *Testing Today*, no. 3 (1960): 4. Reprinted by permission of Houghton Mifflin Company.

Figure 6   *Distributions of Lorge-Thorndike IQs in Iowa and in the Nation*

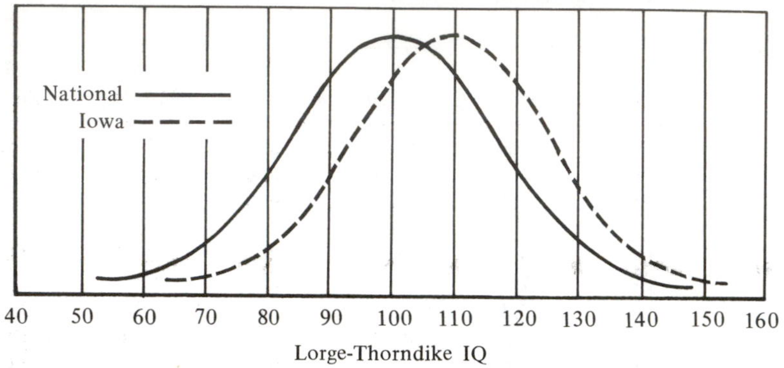

Lorge-Thorndike IQ

Source: Adapted from J. B. Stroud et al., "Distribution of intelligence scores of Iowa public school children," *Testing Today*, no. 3 (1960): 4. Reprinted by permission of Houghton Mifflin Company.

ability. The teacher of a more complex or difficult subject will usually find a selected group of rather highly intelligent boys and girls in her classes. But sometimes she will find individuals of lesser ability who are there because of poor guidance and overoptimism, mistakes of scheduling, parental or school requirements, or some other reason. Such individuals should either be tactfully guided out of the class and into something more in accord with their ability, or they should receive special attention; sometimes it is possible to provide a lower standard more nearly equal to their capacity. What is actually done is a matter of school policy, but teachers and others should keep constantly in mind the frustration, the hopelessness, the embarrassment, and, frequently, the overt problem behavior of the child who has to sit day after day in a classroom where the material taught is beyond his grasp and where he must continually account for a lack of understanding and achievement not properly his fault.

It is true that many children do not try nearly so hard as their ability would permit. On the other hand, many children do work up to their level of ability and, in some cases, work too hard for their level of ability. A teacher should be very certain of causes before she takes action against a student. It is her job to

help students. To do this she must find where they are and help them, always in terms of their own capacity, to the place where she would like them to be. A teacher, or anyone else who works with youth, should always remember that an individual can never do more than his capacity permits, no matter how hard he tries. If he is continually driven to attempt to excel his capacity, the results are likely to be unfortunate for him as a person as well as for all he comes in contact with. Luckily for the mental welfare of many children who find school beyond their capacities, there are usually compensations outside school and even in the extracurricular school program. But if all sources of satisfaction are closed, the situation for the child may become extremely serious.

Heredity and Environment

There has been considerable discussion over the years as to the relative contribution of heredity and environment to intellectual capacity and functioning, with some theorists emphasizing the primacy of genetic factors and others emphasizing the environment. The hereditarian position, sometimes referred to as the polygenic theory of inheritance, takes the position that given an initially low IQ an individual is unable to acquire higher cognitive skills, such as those involved in abstract thinking and problem solving. It is further held by some but not all hereditarians that inherent or genetic components are at the heart of ethnic and racial differences in IQ. Leading proponents of the hereditary position are Shockley (1972a, 1972b) and Jensen (1969, 1970, 1971a, 1971b). Jensen argues that prenatal factors are of greatest relevance and that racial and social-class differences reported in the literature can not be accounted for solely by environmental differences. Correspondingly, Jensen feels that while environmental deprivation can make it unlikely that a child will live up to his genetic potential, an enriched or a compensatory education program cannot push him above that genetic potential. According to Jensen, mental development occurs in qualitatively different but hierarchically related stages. These stages exhibit species, subpopulation, individual, and ontogenetic differences, with the social system tending to stratify persons on the basis of the differences. Both Shockley and Jensen cite twin studies in support of their views.

In contrast, the environmentalist position takes the stand that current mental tests now basically reflect socioeconomic differences and do not per se reflect differences in capacity to learn. For example, Wienke (1970), noting that intelligence tests originally were devised to measure capacity, hypothesizes that the socioeconomic effect on learning will be mostly nullified by the time a person gets to college, and that his performance on tests there will indicate his capacity to learn. To test his hypothesis Wienke compared the course-of-study test performance of 33 black and 113 white students taking the same course at adjacent universities. He reported that neither the mean scores nor the variances of the two groups differed significantly. Feuerstein and Krasilowsky (1972) take the position that even after deprivation in childhood an adolescent can achieve significant cognitive modification during his second decade of life. These writers suggest that such learning may be at-

tained through mediated learning experiences and by direct exposures to sources of stimuli. Meuris (1970), in a factorial study of mental abilities in Belgian youth between the ages of twelve and eighteen, noted that academic specialization improves performance in the mental abilities most necessary to those specializations. Harris and Loevinger (1967) also report research that provided groups of disadvantaged youth with special educational procedures over a three-year period. Resulting increases in the mean Verbal and Full Scale IQs of the experimental groups exceeded those of the control groups with group difference reliabilities at the 1 percent level of significance.

The foregoing studies indicate that improvements in mental performance may be effected even when there is a background of environmental deprivation and that such an achievement can occur even as late as the high school years and beyond. This should not, however, be taken to indicate in any way that deprivation may not lead to serious deficiencies in cognitive efficiency if environmental intervention is not attempted. For example, in a training program of Indian and white Canadian adolescents in the use of strategies for solving Wechsler Similarities and Block Design tests, Schubert and Cropley (1972) made a detailed analysis of reactions and of the verbal regulation of behavior scores of subjects from a remote Indian reservation. As a result of this analysis, Schubert and Cropley contend that the low IQ of that group was the result of an environment that did not encourage reflective verbal thought.

A great deal of research on environmental effect has been performed in the areas of family status and structure. It appears well established that composition of family and family socioeconomic status appear to bear some relationship to an individual's intellectual functioning. Chopra (1966), using a sample of fourteen- to seventeen-year-old boys, reports a gradual decline in mean intelligence-test scores and mean high school marks as family size increased, although ordinal position within the family appeared to have no effect. Dandes and Dow (1969) report negative correlation coefficients between family size and density index and measures of intelligence. The larger and more closely spaced the family, the lower the tested intelligence. Migliorino (1971–1972), using an Italian sample of nearly 4,000 children reports results similar to those of Dandes and Dow, while Mehryar (1972), using an Iranian sample of 1,008 seventeen- to nineteen-year-olds, reports a decrease in intelligence test scores with an increase in number of siblings. Schoonover (1959) analyzed sibling performance on intelligence and achievement tests, utilizing longitudinal data, and he reports that either girls or boys who had brothers consistently had higher mental achievement ages than those who had sisters.

There appears to be a positive relationship between the socioeconomic position of adolescents and their level of intelligence. IQ differences have been found among children from different socioeconomic levels at all ages from nursery school through college, with the relationship between intelligence and socioeconomic status tending to increase as the individual grows older. Tamhanker (1968), in a study of tenth-grade urban boys, using Raven's Advanced Progressive Matrices, reports significant differences in the mean scores of higher and lower income groups. Migliorino (1971–1972) also reports significant differences between socioeconomic status groups on the basis of their intelligence-test performance with the significance holding for each of the ages included in his study. Schnake (1972) in a study of Chilean children notes that children's IQs bore a direct relation to the occupational level of the parents. Upper- and middle-class children performed better than lower-class children.

But the reader should not assume that children from lower socioeconomic groups are inevitably less intelligent and those from higher socioeconomic groups, more intelligent. Many children from lower socioeconomic groups are of markedly superior intellectual ability, and numerous children from upper socioeconomic levels are of inferior ability. The studies simply indicate that, given large

numbers from the various socioeconomic backgrounds, children from higher socioeconomic levels will tend to receive higher scores on the intelligence tests currently available. Goodenough (1954) writes that the fact that

performance on intelligence tests varies according to the social class from which the subjects are drawn has been recognized since the days of Binet. That the relationship is not one of simple cause and effect is demonstrated by the fact that every level of intelligence can be found within each social level, though not in equal proportion. A greater percentage of the very bright come from families of superior socioeconomic status, whereas the frequency of backward children is proportionately greater among the lower social classes. The relationship is sufficiently marked to bring about a difference of 20 to 30 IQ points in the mean test standing of children of college professors and those of day laborers.

It is impossible to predict what level of intelligence may be found in any given individual or small group. It may be assumed that the child from the upper socioeconomic group is the product of a selective process that may have been going on for years. He also has the added advantage of a better material environment. Whether or not the upper socioeconomic adolescent's home is a psychologically good one depends upon factors other than material possessions. Certainly the environment in which a child is reared is more important than structural or status aspects of the environment. For example, in a study by Marjoribanks (1972), 185 eleven-year-olds were given two mental ability tests and their parents were given environmental interviews. Results indicated that the environment measure accounted for more of the variance in ability scores than did a set of social status indicators and family structure variables. McCall and Johnson (1972), in a study of changes in IQ during high school, report that the changes observed were unrelated to family size, birth order, or occupational level. In a similar finding Harnquist (1968) reports that relative changes in intelligence from age thirteen through eighteen are specifically related to educational and, to a lesser extent, to home background.

During the last several years the tempo of the nature-nurture controversy has increasingly been marked by the publication of frequently vehement articles on the topic. A considerable amount of space has been devoted to exchanges between Jensen and his environmentally oriented opponents. For example, Layzer (1972), writing as a physical scientist, claims the implicit assumptions underlying Jensen are scientifically untenable. He makes the point that the polygenic theory of inheritance, like any quantitative scientific theory, applies only to measurements that satisfy certain formal requirements. Layzer contends that measurements resulting in an IQ do not satisfy the requirements and hence any application of them to the polygenic theory is both unreliable and meaningless. Layzer makes the point that genetic differences in intelligence are untenable by present methods. He also believes that current ideas and data about cognitive development lend little support to the belief that children with low IQs or those whose parents have low IQs are necessarily limited in their capacity for acquiring higher cognitive skills. In an even more frontal attack Brace and Livingstone (1971) examine Jensen's argument that blacks are genetically inferior in intelligence and conclude that levels of complexity may be negatively related to the IQ—a position exactly the converse of Jensen's. Biesheuvel (1972), making the point that genetic determinants of race differences do not justify categorical statements, offers four criticisms of Jensen's thesis: (1) use of IQ as a behavioral entity and not as a relative statistical index, (2) discounting of the results of lower levels of motivation on black's test performance, (3) a too coarse treatment of environment, making it difficult to establish the full range of causal relationships, and (4) use of cross-sectional rather than longitudinal data.[15]

[15]Others making direct replies to Jensen have been Kagan (1969), Humphreys and Dachler (1969), Burgess and Jahoda (1971), Gregg and Sanday (1971), and Gage (1972).

What is the truth of the matter? It is obvious that the question has great social and political significance, but on the evidence we have we can say only that both heredity and environment are important and no definitive statement can be made about their relative importance. Where environment is concerned research findings leave no doubt of its great and ubiquitous importance. But what is the role of heredity? Is the genetic program overriding? Layzer's (1972) statement that genetic differences in intelligence are untenable by present methods seems to be a fair statement. It does not imply that methods may not someday be developed, but it is very explicit in that such a day has not yet arrived. Patin (1965) sums up very well when he writes that present evidence

appears to favor a concept of interdependence of genetic potential and environment...no significant statement concerning the relative contribution of these variables in the development of measured intelligence can be made at this time...although intelligence unquestionably has a physiological basis that may eventually be discovered and that may permit its direct measurement without the need of performance tests, intelligence is, nevertheless, a form of knowledge.

Attribution of Causality

Research studies have endeavored to measure the relation to intelligence of various personal and social conditions, including sex, racial and national background, geographic area, socioeconomic status, social and emotional adjustment, heredity, accelerated maturity, nutritional status, and other variables of less popular appeal. An examination of these studies and their implications reveals several areas of general agreement, taking into consideration differences in the measuring instruments, research techniques, samples, and methods of statistical analysis used. It is pretty well established that an intellectually stimulating environment will serve to improve an intact individual's performance on mental tests, as well as his everyday intellectual functioning.

With older children, however, at least a modicum of willingness to be receptive to such stimulation becomes increasingly operationally facilitative. Communities, schools, and homes may do much to provide successful experiential enrichment for a child of any age. And it should not be believed that the possibility of profiting from intellectual stimulation is confined to any one socioeconomic class or personal background.

Descriptive and comparative studies of the mental ability of various racial and ethnic groups have produced different and often conflicting results. Some have failed to find differences, while others have reported highly significant levels of difference. An analysis of the studies made leads to the conclusion that reported differences were often due to previous or existing conditions under which the children lived, the kinds of tests used, or the conditions of testing, rather than to inherent attributes of those being tested. Some studies, in selecting two groups to contrast, have used sampling procedures that may well have biased the results obtained. Existing objective evidence can enable a teacher or other youth worker dealing with children of any race or ethnic group to approach his charges with an open mind. He should not assume that any child or group of children is inevitably of inferior intelligence because it comes from any given race or nationality, or that differences revealed are inherently due to that race, nationality, or ethnic group. If a teacher or youth worker is confronted with adolescents who come from starved environments or from other cultures, he should expect to use somewhat different techniques and materials of instruction and to set different, though not necessarily lower, standards.

Sex Differences in Intelligence

There are no validly consistent sex differences in general mental ability, although various studies have shown differences on various types of intellectual tasks and on different types of tests. In a critical review of comparative studies of sex differences using a large number of different mental tests, Kuznets and McNemar (1940) reported that of fifty-six sex and age comparisons, three showed no differences, twenty-eight were in favor of boys, and twenty-five were in favor of girls. Terman (1954), in his review of the literature of sex differences in general intelligence, wrote that although many sex-difference studies have been made, even when large samples are used,

they can never be viewed as strictly random samples of the general population, since a number of factors affecting school enrollments are known to operate differentially for the sexes. In general, however, the sex differences found were so small and so inconsistent in direction that no positive claim could be made for the superiority of either sex at any age.

Ljung (1965) reports an adolescent growth spurt as more marked in females than in males. She believes that this spurt comes from greater efficiency in processing information and handling abstractions that characterize the shift to formal operations. This finding is in line with the earlier general developmental acceleration of females. Bradway and Thompson (1962) reported a greater gain in IQ between adolescence and adulthood for males than for females. Females tend to be ahead in verbal areas (word fluency, rote memory, reasoning), and males excel in quantitative and spatial categories. Here, apparently, is evidence of the environmental effects of the sex role in which boys are expected to do well in quantitative matters but girls are not.

In general, girls during the adolescent years appear to excel in the more verbal type of tests and boys appear to excel in quantitative and scientific-content tests. Such differences might be attributed to cultural stereotypes that have conditioned the interests of girls and boys. Performance in school academic subject matter might well be a more profitable comparison of sex differences in intellectual ability and function than intelligence tests themselves.

The Problem of Bias

In dealing with people it is always tempting to categorize, and almost inevitably in popular thinking the basis of categorization becomes some easily observed external characteristic such as color, shape of head, height, or weight. Failing such a criterion, the layman is apt to seize next upon some easily learned fact as the basis of his categorization, such as race, nationality, section of origin, or political beliefs. When some such basis of categorization is found, the next step is to assume that people in a given category also have a whole list of associated traits or abilities. For example, in a previous generation, women, merely because they were women, were supposed to lack the ability to generalize or to think accurately, although the record shows, even under the restrictions of the period, that sometimes women of exceptional ability were able to arrange matters so that they could play a role "unexpected in their sex." In Hitler's Germany, people of Jewish origin were accused of a whole series of stereotypes. In America, people of non-Caucasian ancestry are commonly believed to have certain attributes dealing with thrift, intelligence, sincerity, and so on. One often hears that persons of a given build are ipso facto kind, jolly, or generous. This tendency becomes most vicious when, for political or other scapegoating reasons, easily identifiable portions of the population are popularly supposed to have a long series of disagreeable attributes purely because they are representatives of a given type, origin, or point of view.

Anyone who has dealt with groups of adolescents cannot fail to be aware of their tendency to scapegoat members of their group who deviate in one way or another from the norm, and to attribute to them all sorts of disagreeable traits. An adolescent who comes to a city school from a country one, who is a member of a minority group, who is overstudious, or who possesses some anomaly of physical form or development is quite likely to face such a problem. Adults are not free from such scapegoating, or from a sincere belief that certain attributes go hand in hand, as will be understood when one hears parental admonitions to adolescents about whom among their peers they should and should not associate with and why. Nor are teachers entirely free from such proclivities. It is much easier to feel that a well-dressed, clean child from the right side of town has more intelligence and better motives than does his more poorly dressed, obviously foreign, none-too-clean opposite number from the wrong side of town.

As educated persons we are able to realize the dangers of blanket attributes and unfounded assumptions and try our best to ignore or combat them, although this is not easy when we become prejudiced or emotionally involved. On the other hand, it is known as the result of scientific experimentation that some attributes are associated with others, and that their relationship may be one of cause and effect, or perhaps merely one of contiguity. The task of the psychologist dealing with human behavior is to determine by the most adequate scientific means at his disposal the exact relationship of attributes, as well as the characteristics of a person who is placed in any type of category. One may neither affirm nor deny the truth, or the likelihood of any such relationship, without scientific proof. The procedure is to formulate a hypothesis, then to test it fairly, and finally, to reject or accept it at a given level of confidence. Finally, once the hypothesis has been tested, one should not overgeneralize beyond the sample represented in the testing.

Summary

Theory and research in intelligence have tended to emphasize either a quantitative or a qualitative approach. It has been the endeavor of the quantitatively oriented theorists to isolate and identify the various components of intelligence and, especially, to ask: How much ability exists? In contrast, qualitative theorists are primarily interested in how and in what order changes in ability take place. One classification speaks of fluid and crystallized intelligence. Unitary theorists may be classified as those who see intelligence as the ability to adapt, those who see intelligence as the ability to learn, and those who see it as the ability to think abstractly. Modern factor theory postulates a number of distinct factors and identifies various lists of primary mental abilities considered basic to intellectual functioning.

Intelligence or mental ability increases with age throughout childhood and well into adolescence. There is some disagreement as to the exact year at which mental growth reaches its peak, but the consensus is that it is sometime in the late teens or early twenties, with relatively small additions occurring after the sixteenth year. Curves of mental growth, as reported in the literature, are usually composites of many individual curves and tend to conceal the wide individual differences characteristic of mental growth.

Since adolescence is a period during which the individual encounters many new experiences and learning situations, it is essential that he profit from them as much as he possibly can if he is to be a useful member of society and if he is to lead a personally satisfying life. What the individual will get out of any experience depends largely upon his level of mental ability and the experience from which he has profited in the past. It is important that youth workers attempt to determine the kind of experience to provide for an adolescent at any given point in his development, and to make certain that he receives necessary preliminary learning. Such an attempt presupposes an adequate understanding of mental growth in general, particularly of the level of mental ability, of each adolescent the youth worker is attempting to guide. In school the curriculum and the instructional procedures should be based upon the capacities of the children who are subjected to them.

Intelligence has been defined as the ability to profit from experience, to think rationally, and to deal effectively with one's environment.

It is sometimes thought of as related to the speed with which an individual can learn. Intelligence is measured by means of paper-and-pencil group tests or clinical-type individual tests. One type of intelligence test, called culture-free, is designed to obtain an estimate of the ability of those for whom a regular test would be unfair because of its loading in favor of the experiences common only among a given subclass of the culture, such as those coming from middle-class homes. A culture-fair test achieves its purpose by minimizing special environmental influences.

An individual's level of ability is computed in terms of mental age derived from his intelligence-test score. Most intelligence tests are composed of a number of subtests containing various types of tasks judged to be basic to intellectual functioning. The overall score of an intelligence test is the sum of the scores received on the various subtests or tasks included in the test.

It is generally accepted that the course of development of intellectual ability proceeds from relative globality toward increasing differentiation and hierarchization through adolescence and into adulthood. Research efforts have generally, though not entirely, confirmed the validity of the differentiation hypothesis.

There is considerable difference in the growth and decline of ability to cope with these different tasks. Some subtests show adolescents surpassing adults; some show adults surpassing adolescents. Some show sharp declines in maturity, while others show either gradual declines or none at all. The years of peak performance also tend to vary from test to test.

The implication of age of cessation of mental growth for the education of adolescents is that, in terms of mental power or ability, the adolescent is nearing his peak. By the time he is eighteen, he has either already reached his peak or will show only a slight increase from that point on, except for a few mental functions. He will, of course, grow in knowledge but not in the rate by which knowledge can be acquired. It has been observed by some researchers that a number of intellectual attributes appear to have accelerated over the past several generations; however, such changes may, though not necessarily, represent differences in circumstances when the various arrays of data were collected, rather than actual across-generation changes in intellectual power or altitude.

Environmental conditions are reflected in a child's mental performance. In a number of individuals after about age four, the IQ presents a relatively stable picture, although individual cycles or patterns of change in IQ do occur in many children. Sometimes IQ constancy depends as much upon test inadequacy as upon actual changes within the individual. Predictions as to a child's intellectual potential must be made with considerable caution.

Considerable controversy has obtained over the relative influence of heredity and environment, with the hereditarians holding that the inherent or genetic components are the prime determiners of ability, with environmental factors playing only a limited role. The environmentalists take the opposite position. Present techniques cannot provide an objective and definitive answer to the polygenic theory of inheritance, but psychological research has demonstrated the very great importance of the environment. It is well established that an intellectually stimulating environment will serve to improve an intact individual's performance on mental tests as well as his everyday mental functioning. It is established that composition of family and family socioeconomic status bear at least some statistical relationship to an individual's level of intellectual performance, although it is important to remember that the psychological climate in which a child is reared is more important than the structural aspects of his environment. It appears that improvements in mental performance can be brought about even when there is a background of deprivation. Studies comparing mental capacities of various racial and ethnic groups have produced conflicting results, but because of problems of sampling and methodology, it is impossible to make definitive statements. In terms of what is known today, it should not be assumed that any child or group of children is inevitably of inferior intelligence because it comes from any given race or nationality, or that differences revealed are inherently due to that race, nationality, or ethnic group. Similarly, it should not be assumed that these differences are due to a child's sex.

References

Ahmavaara, Y. *On the unified factor theory of mind.* Helsinki: Suomalaisen Kirjallisienden Kirjapaino, 1957.

Alzobaie, A. J.; Metfessel, N. S.; and Michael, W. B. Alternative approaches to assessing the intellectual abilities of youth from a culture of poverty. *Educational and Psychological Measurement* 28 (1968): 449–455.

Anastasi, A. Further studies on the memory factor. *Archives of Psychology* no. 142 (1932).

Backman, C. Social psychology and innovations in education. In Reynolds, M. C., ed., *Proceedings of the conference on psychology in the next decade: Alternative conceptions.* Minneapolis: University of Minnesota Press, 1971.

Baldwin, B. T., and Stecher, L. I. Mental growth curve of normal and superior children. *University of Iowa Studies in Child Welfare,* vol. 2, no. 1. Iowa City: State University of Iowa, 1922.

Balinski, B. An analysis of the mental factors of various age groups from nine to sixty. *Genetic Psychology Monographs* 23 (1941): 191–234.

Baltes, P. B. Longitudinal and cross-sectional sequences in the study of age and generation effects. *Human Development* 11 (1968): 145–171.

Baltes, P. B., and Reinert, G. Cohort effects in cognitive development in children as revealed by cross-sectional sequences. *Developmental Psychology* 1 (1969): 169–177.

Bayley, N. Consistency and variability in the growth of intelligence from birth to 18 years. *Journal of Genetic Psychology* 75 (1949): 165–196.

Bayley, N. On the growth of intelligence. *American Psychologist* 10 (1955): 805–818.

Bayley, N., and Odeon, M. H. The maintenance of intellectual ability in gifted adults. *Journal of Gerontology* 10 (1955) : 91–107.

Biesheuvel, S. An examination of Jensen's theory concerning educability, heritability and population differences. *Psychologia Africana* 14 (1972) : 87–94.

Bloom, B. S. *Stability and change in human characteristics.* New York: Wiley, 1964.

Brace, C. L., and Livingstone, F. B. On creeping Jensenism. In Brace, C. L., and Bond, J. T., eds., *Race and intelligence.* Washington, D.C.: American Anthropological Association, 1971.

Bradway, K. IQ constancy on the revised Stanford-Binet from the pre-school to the junior high school level. *Journal of Genetic Psychology* 65 (1944) : 197–217.

Bradway, K. P. An experimental study of the factors associated with Stanford-Binet IQ changes from pre-school to the junior high school. *Journal of Genetic Psychology* 66 (1945) : 107–128.

Bradway, K. P., and Thompson, C. W. Intelligence at adulthood: A twenty-five year follow-up. *Journal of Educational Psychology* 53 (1962) : 1–14.

Brooks, F. D. Changes in mental traits with age: Determined by individual retests. *Teachers College Contributions to Education,* no. 116 (1921).

Bryan, A. I. Organization of memory in young children. *Archives of Psychology,* no. 162 (1934).

Burgess, J., and Jahoda, M. Reply to Professor Jensen. *Bulletin of the British Psychological Society* 24 (1971) : 199–200.

Cassel, R. N. Historical review of theories on the nature of intelligence. *Psychology* 6 (1969) : 39–46.

Cattell, R. B. Theory of fluid and crystallized intelligence: A critical experiment. *Journal of Educational Psychology* 54 (1963) : 1–22.

Cattell, R. B. Are IQ tests intelligent? *Psychology Today* 1 (1968) : 56–62.

Chateau, J. Pour une psychopedagogie de profondeurs. *Bulletin de Psychologie* 20 (1967) : 626–630.

Chopra, S. L. Family size and sibling position as related to intelligence test scores and academic achievement. *Journal of Social Psychology* 70 (1966) : 133–137.

Clark, M. P. Changes in primary abilities with age. *Archives of Psychology,* no. 291 (1944).

Cohen, J. The factorial structure of the WAIS between early adulthood and old age. *Journal of Consulting Psychology* 21 (1957) : 238–290.

Cohen, J. The factorial structure of the WISC. *Journal of Consulting Psychology* 23 (1959) : 285–299.

Dandes, H. M., and Dow, D. Relation of intelligence to family size and density. *Child Development* 40 (1969) : 641–645.

Dearborn, W. F., and Cattell, P. The intelligence and achievement of private school pupils. *Journal of Educational Psychology* 21 (1930) : 197–211.

Doppelt, J. E. The organization of mental abilities in the age ranges 13 to 17. *Teachers College Contributions to Education,* no. 962 (1950).

Dye, N. W., and Very, P. S. Growth changes in factorial structure by age and sex. *Genetic Psychology Monographs* 78 (1968) : 55–88.

Elley, W. B. Changes in mental ability in New Zealand school children, 1936–1968. *New Zealand Journal of Educational Studies* 4 (1969) : 140–155.

Feuerstein, R., and Krasilowsky, D. Interventional strategies for the significant modification of cognitive functioning in the disadvantaged adolescent. *Journal of the American Academy of Child Psychiatry* 11 (1972) : 572–582.

Gage, N. L. Replies to Shockley, Page, and Jensen: The causes of race differences in IQ. *Phi Delta Kappan,* March 1972, pp. 422–427.

Garrett, H. E. A study of the CAVD intelligence examination. *Journal of Educational Research* 21 (1930) : 103–108.

Garrett, H. E. Differentiable mental traits. *Psychological Record* 2 (1938) : 259–298.

Garrett, H. E. A developmental theory of intelligence. *American Psychologist* 1 (1946) : 372–378.

Garrett, H. E.; Bryan, A. L.; and Perl, R. The age factor in mental organization. *Archives of Psychology,* no. 176 (1935).

Gesell, A. The ontogenesis of infant behavior. In Carmichael, L., ed., *Manual of Child Psychology.* 2nd ed. New York: Wiley, 1954.

Ghiselli, E. E. The relationship between intelligence and age among superior adults. *Journal of Genetic Psychology* 90 (1957) : 131–142.

Goodenough, F. L. The measurement of mental growth in childhood. Chapter 8 in Carmichael, L., *Manual of Child Psychology.* 2nd ed. New York: Wiley, 1954.

Goodenough, F. L., and Maurer, K. *The mental growth of children two to fourteen years of age.* Minneapolis: University of Minnesota Press, 1942.

Gregg, T. G., and Sanday, P. R. Genetic and environmental components of differential intelligence. In Brace, C. L.; Gamble, G. R.; and Bond, J. T. *Race and intelligence.* Washington, D.C.: American Anthropological Association, 1971.

Guilford, J. P. *The nature of human intelligence.* New York: McGraw-Hill, 1967.

Harnquist, K. Relative changes in intelligence from 13 to 18: II. Results. *Scandinavian Journal of Psychology* 9 (1968): 65–82.

Harris, A. J., and Loevinger, R. J. Quelques donnees longitudinales sur les modifications de IQ dans l'intelligence d'adolescents noirs. *Enfance* 2 (1967): 171–174.

Hart, H. The slowing up of growth in mental test ability. *School and Society* 20 (1924): 573–574.

Honzik, M. P. The constancy of mental test performance during the pre-school period. *Journal of Genetic Psychology* 52 (1938): 285–302.

Horn, J. L. Organization of abilities and the development of intelligence. *Psychological Review* 75 (1968): 242–259.

Horn, J. L. State, trait and change dimensions of intelligence. *British Journal of Educational Psychology* 42 (1972): 159–185.

Horn, J. L., and Cattell, R. B. Age differences in fluid and crystallized intelligence. *Acta Psychologica* 26 (1967): 107–129.

Humphreys, L. G., and Dachler, H. P. Jensen's theory of intelligence: A rebuttal. *Journal of Educational Psychology* 60 (1969): 432–433.

Irvine, S. H. Affect and construct: A cross-cultural check on theories of intelligence. *Journal of Social Psychology* 80 (1970): 23–30.

Jensen, A. R. How much can we boost I.Q. and scholastic achievement? *Harvard Educational Review* 39 (1969): 1–123.

Jensen, A. R. IQs of identical twins reared apart. *Behavior Genetics* 1 (1970): 133–148.

Jensen, A. R. The phylogeny and ontogeny of intelligence. *Perspectives in Biology and Medicine* 15 (1971): 37–43.

Jensen, A. R. Can we and should we study race differences? In Brace, C. L.; Gamble, G. R.; and Bond, J. T., eds., *Race and Intelligence.* Washington, D.C.: American Anthropological Association, 1971.

Jones, H. E. The analysis of age decrements in mental performance. *Proceedings,* Bethesda Conference on the Problems of Aging. Washington, D.C.: American Psychological Association, Division 20, 1955.

Jones, H. E., and Conrad, H. S. The growth and decline of intelligence. *Genetic Psychology Monographs* 13 (1933): 223–298.

Kagan, J. S. Inadequate evidence and illogical conclusions. *Harvard Education Review* 39 (1969): 274–277.

Kay, H. Some experiments on adult learning. *Old age in the modern world.* Report of the Third Congress of the International Association of Gerontology in London, 1954. Edinburgh: Livingstone, 1955.

Koffka, K. *The growth of the mind.* New York: Harcourt, Brace, 1925.

Koppen-Thulesius, L. K., and Teichmann, H. Accelerative trends in intellectual development. *British Journal of Social and Clinical Psychology* 11 (1972): 284–294.

Kuhlmann, F. The results of repeated mental examinations of 639 feeble-minded over a period of ten years. *Journal of Applied Psychology* 5 (1921): 195–224.

Kuznets, G. M., and McNemar, Q. Sex differences in intelligence test scores. *Thirty-Ninth Yearbook,* National Society for the Study of Education 39.1 (1940): 211–220.

Layzer, D. Science or superstition: A physical scientist looks at the I.Q. controversy. *Cognition* 1 (1972): 265–299.

Lehmann, I. J. Curricular differences in selected cognitive and affective characteristics. *Journal of Educational Measurement* 2 (1965): 103–110.

Levinson, B. M. Quo vadis IQ? Some reflections on the current psychological scene. *Mental Hygiene* 48 (1964): 108–113.

Lewin, K. *A dynamic theory of personality.* New York: McGraw-Hill, 1935.

Ljung, B. O. *The adolescent spurt in mental growth.* Stockholm Studies in Educational Psychology. Uppsala, Sweden: Alinquist and Wiksell, 1965.

McCall, J. N., and Johnson, O. G. The independence of intelligence from family size and birth order. *Journal of Genetic Psychology* 121 (1972): 203–207.

McNemar, Q. *The revision of the Stanford-Binet Scale.* Boston: Houghton Mifflin, 1942.

Marjoribanks, K. Environment, social class, and mental abilities. *Journal of Educational Psychology* 63 (1972) : 103–109.

Mehryar, A. H. Father's education, family size and children's intelligence and academic performance in Iran. *International Journal of Psychology* 7 (1972) : 47–50.

Meuris, G. The structure of primary mental abilities of Belgian secondary school students. *Journal of Educational Measurement* 7 (1970): 191–197.

Michael, J. J. Structure of intellect theory and the validity of achievement examinations. *Educational and Psychological Measurement* 28 (1968) : 1141–1149.

Migliorino, G. Relations entre l'intelligence des enfants, milieu social-economique des parents et la dimension de la famille. *Bulletin de Psychologie* 25 (1971–1972): 986–994.

Nguyen-Xuan, A. Etude par le modele factoriel d'une hypothese sur les processus de developpement: Recherche experimentale sur quelques aptitudes intellectuelles chez des eleves du premier cycle de l'enseignement secondaire. *Bulletin de l'Institut National d'Etude du Travail et d'Orientation Professionnelle*, serie 2, vol. 25 (1969).

Owens, W. A., Jr. Age and mental abilities: A longitudinal study. *Genetic Psychology Monographs* 48 (1953) : 3–54.

Patin, H. A. Intelligence and education. *School Review* 73 (1965) : 359–373.

Piaget, J. *The psychology of intelligence*. London: Routledge and Kegan Paul, 1950.

Piaget, J. *The origins of intelligence in children*. New York: International Universities Press, 1952.

Piaget, J. Assimilation et connaissance. In Jonckheere, A.; Mandelbrot, B.; Piaget, J., La lecture de l'experience. *Etudes d'epistemologie genetique*, vol. 5. Paris: Presses Universitaires de France, 1958.

Quereshi, M. Y. Patterns of psycholinguistic development during early and middle childhood. *Educational and Psychological Measurement* 27 (1967) : 803–810.

Quereshi, M. Y. Patterns of intellectual development during childhood and adolescence. *Genetic Psychology Monographs* 87 (1973) : 313–344.

Reichard, S. Mental organization and age level. *Archives of Psychology*, no. 295 (1944).

Schaie, K. W. A reinterpretation of age-related changes in cognitive structure and functioning. In Goulet and Baltes, *Life-span developmental psychology*. New York: Academic Press, 1970.

Schaie, K. W. Limitations on the generalizability of growth curves of intelligence. *Human Development* 15 (1972) : 141–152.

Schaie, K. W., and Strother, C. R. The effects of time and cohort differences on the interpretation of age changes in cognitive behavior. *Multivariate Behavior Research* 3 (1968): 259–293.

Schiller, B. Verbal, numerical and spatial abilities in young children. *Archives of Psychology*, no. 161 (1934).

Schnake Ayechu, H. Relacion entre los dos padres ocupacion y los ninos intelectual coeficientes. *Revista Latinoamericana de Psicologia* 4 (1972): 197–220.

Schneck, M. R. The measurement of verbal and numerical abilities. *Archives of Psychology*, no. 107 (1929).

Schoonover, S. M. The relationship of intelligence and achievement to birth order, sex of sibling, and age interval. *Journal of Educational Psychology* 50 (1959) : 143–146.

Schubert, J., and Cropley, A. J. Verbal regulation of behavior and IQ in Canadian Indian and white children. *Developmental Psychology* 7 (1972): 295–301.

Shockley, W. Dysgenics, geneticity, raceology: A challenge to the intellectual responsibility of educators. *Phi Delta Kappan*, January 1972, pp. 297–307. (a)

Shockley, W. A debate challenge: Geneticity is 80% for white identical twins' IQs. *Phi Delta Kappan*, March 1972, pp. 415–419. (b)

Sontag, L. W.; Baker, C. T.; and Nelson, V. L. Mental growth and personality development. *Monographs of Society for Research in Child Development*, vol. 23 (1958).

Spearman, C. The theory of two factors. *Psychological Review* 21 (1914): 101–115.

Spearman, C. *The abilities of man*. London: Macmillan, 1927.

Stone, C. P., and Barker, R. G. Aspects of personality and intelligence in postmenarcheal and pre-menarcheal girls of the same chronological ages. *Journal of Comparative Psychology* 23 (1937): 439–455.

Stroud, J. B., et al. Distribution of intelligence scores of Iowa public school children. *Testing Today*, no. 4. Boston: Houghton Mifflin, 1960.

Sudweeks, J. Intelligence of the continuation

school pupils of Wisconsin. *Journal of Educational Psychology* 18 (1927): 601–610.

Tamhanker, V. S. Norms for the X grade on advanced progressive matrices (1962) and some correlates of intelligence. *Journal of Psychological Researches* 12 (1968): 85–89.

Terman, L. M. Psychological sex differences. Chapter 19 in Carmichael, L., ed., *Manual of child psychology*. 2nd ed. New York: Wiley, 1954.

Thorndike, E. L. On the improvement of intelligence scores from fourteen to eighteen. *Journal of Educational Psychology* 14 (1923): 513–516.

Thorndike, E. L., et al. *The measurement of intelligence*. New York: Teachers College, 1926.

Thorndike, E. L. On the improvement of intelligence scores from thirteen to nineteen, *Journal of Educational Psychology* 17 (1926): 73–76.

Thurstone, L. L. *Primary mental abilities. Psychometric Monographs*, no. 1. Chicago: University of Chicago Press, 1938.

Thurstone, L. L. *The differential growth of mental abilities*. Chapel Hill: University of North Carolina Psychometric Laboratory, 1955.

Thurstone, L. L., and Ackerson, L. The mental growth curve for the Binet tests. *Journal of Educational Psychology* 20 (1929): 569–583.

Thurstone, L. L. and Thurstone, T. L. *Factorial studies in intelligence. Psychometric Monographs*, no. 1. Chicago: University of Chicago Press, 1938.

Wechsler, D. *The measurement and appraisal of adult intelligence*. 4th ed. Baltimore: Wilkins, 1958.

Werner, H. *Comparative psychology of mental development*. Chicago: Follette, 1948.

Wienke, R. Are there racial differences in educability? *Journal of Human Relations* 18 (1970): 1190–1203.

Woolley, H. T. *An experimental study of children at work and in school between the ages of 14 and 18 years*. New York: Macmillan, 1926.

Suggested Readings

Barber, L. W. Decision-making and level of intelligence. *Character Potential* 4 (1968): 85–86.

Caldwell, M. B., and Smith, T. A. Intellectual structure of Southern Negro children. *Psychological Reports* 23 (1968): 63–71.

Cancro, R., ed. *Intelligence: Genetic and environmental influences*. New York: Grune and Stratton, 1971.

Crano, W. D.; Kenny, D. A.; and Campbell, D. T. Does intelligence cause achievement?: A cross-logged panel analysis. *Journal of Educational Psychology* 63 (1972): 258–275.

Cunningham, M. *Intelligence: Its organization and development*. New York: Academic Press, 1972.

Droege, R. C. GATB aptitude intercorrelations of ninth and twelfth graders: A study in organization of mental abilities. *Personnel and Guidance Journal* 46 (1968): 668–672.

Eaves, L. J., and Jinks, J. L. Insignificance of evidence for differences in heritability of IQ between races and social classes. *Nature* 240 (1972): 84–88.

Elkind, D., and Tuddenham, R. D. Two approaches to intelligence: Piagetian and psychometric. In Green, D. R.; Ford, M. P.; and Flamer, G. B., eds., *Measurement and Piaget*. New York: McGraw-Hill, 1972.

Eysenck, H. J. *The IQ argument: Race, intelligence and education*. New York: Library Press, 1971.

Fitzgerald, J. M.; Nesselrode, J. R.; and Baltes, P. B. Emergence of adult intellectual structure: Prior to or during adolescence? *Developmental Psychology* 9 (1973): 114–119.

Handel, A. The D48 as a measure of general ability among adolescents in Israel. *Journal of Cross-Cultural Psychology* 4 (1973): 302–313.

Hannon, J. E., and Kicklighter, R. WAIS versus WISC in adolescents. *Journal of Consulting and Clinical Psychology* 35 (1970): 179–182.

Horn, J. L. Intelligence: Why it grows, why it declines. In Hunt, J. M., ed., *Human intelligence*. New Jersey: Transaction Books, 1972.

Kennedy, W. A. A follow-up normative study of Negro intelligence and achievement. *Monographs of the Society for Research in Child Development* vol. 34. 2 (1969).

Klonoff, H. I.Q. constancy and age. *Perceptual and Motor Skills* 35 (1972): 527–534.

Lunneborg, P. W. Sex differences in aptitude maturation during college. *Journal of Counseling Psychology* 16 (1969) : 463–464.

Norden, K. The structure of abilities in a group of deaf adolescents. *Educational and Psychological Interactions*, no. 32 (1970).

Rowland, T., and McGuire, C. The development of intelligent behavior: IV. Jerome S. Bruner. *Psychology in the Schools* 5 (1968) : 317–329.

Rowland, T., and McGuire, C. The development of intelligent behavior: VI. J. McV. Hunt. *Psychology in the Schools* 6 (1969) : 123–133.

Shields, R. V.; Gordon, M. A.; and Evans, S. H. Schematic concept formation in relationship to mental ability in adolescents. *Psychonomic Science* 17 (1969) : 361–362.

Stephens, B.; McLaughlin, J. A.; Miller, C. K.; and Glass, G. V. Factorial structure of selected psychoeducational measures and Piagetian reasoning assessments. *Developmental Psychology* 6 (1972) : 343–348.

Tulkin, S. R. Race, class, family, and school achievement. *Journal of Personality and Social Psychology* 9 (1968) : 31–37. See also–Gallo, P. S., and Dorfman, D. D. Racial differences in intelligence: Comment on Tulkin. *Representative Research in Social Psychology* 1 (1970) : 24–28.

Vernon, P. E. *Intelligence and cultural environment.* London: Methuen, 1972.

Weinberg, S., and Rabinowitz, J. A sex difference in the Wechsler IQ vocabulary score as a predictor of strategy in a probability-learning task performed by adolescents. *Developmental Psychology* 3 (1970) : 218–224.

Wesman, A. G. Intelligence testing. *American Psychologist* 23 (1968) : 267–274.

Youniss, J., and Furth, H. G. Reasoning and Piaget. *Nature* 244 (1973) : 314–315.

Chapter Eight

Creativity and the Gifted Adolescent

That a form of behavior called creative actually exists is an assumption that few would deny. Nearly everyone can cite examples of creative behavior or can name persons believed to be highly creative in some area of endeavor. Some occupations are commonly believed to be particularly representative of the creative act. But consensus fails when it comes to defining the term or to explaining what creativity actually is. Is creativity learned or inherited? Is it a general trait, or are there many kinds of creativity? Is it something more than technique or proficiency? What, in particular, is its relationship to intelligence and personality? What is the ontogenesis of creativity over the life span of a given individual? Specifically, for the interests of this textbook, how does creativity relate to the adolescent years?

A number of psychologists have endeavored to measure creative ability. Among them Guilford (1967), Torrance (1965), and Getzels and Jackson (1962) have been prominent. The approach typically has been to construct a test designed to measure and predict creativity, the assumption being that creativity is something quite different from whatever is measured by standard intelligence or aptitude tests. Obviously without this assumption there would be no need to construct separate creativity tests, since the regular measures of intelligence would suffice. The common difficulty faced by all test constructors is the lack of essential agreement about either a definition of creativity or the conditions that promote it. It has not been fully established that the present measures of creativity actually measure anything not already handled at least to an appreciable extent by regular intelligence tests. Thorndike (1963) notes that available creativity measures correlate as highly with standard intelligence tests as they correlate with each other. However, Wallach and Kogan (1965), Lasswell (1959), Rogers (1959), and Dentler and Mackler (1964) have experimented with approaches to the measurement of creativity outside the traditional intelligence testing model and have presented preliminary evidence that creativity tests presented in a gamelike, relaxed, and task-oriented atmosphere yield results in which creativity tests do correlate highly and are substantially unrelated to intelligence-test performance. However, Nicholls (1971) advances arguments against favoring gamelike rather than testlike creativity measurement.

The Nature of Creativity

Torrance (1963) defines creative thinking as "the process of sensing gaps or disturbing missing elements; forming new hypotheses concerning them; testing these hypotheses and communicating the results, possibly modifying and retesting the hypotheses." At a "creativity" panel held at the 27th International Psychoanalytical Congress (Kligerman 1972), Sterba noted that creative imagination consists of breaking old established patterns of relationships and establishing new ones. However, Sterba felt that it is a mistake to generalize creativity or creative personality as being of only one kind. In this same panel, De Levita proposed that creativity is almost a defining characteristic of humanity. Man as a creative being elaborates inventively on innate strivings and external stimuli. For panel member de M'Uzan, the creative process was seen as essentially a movement toward other people as a means of resolving one's own inner conflicts.

Zisulescu (1967) studied the creative act among adolescents, making clear-cut distinctions between reasoning and imagination as well as between memory and imagination. He reports three distinct phases in the adolescent creative act: (1) a sensation of void, which is actually a time of selecting material, (2) the appearance of a dominant idea, and (3) the final shaping of the material into a new or novel creation. Zisulescu proposes that inspiration and hard, consciously sustained work are also aspects of the creative process. Schaefer (1971), in a projective technique (thematic stories in response to pictures) study comparing creative and noncreative high school girls, found creative girls exhibiting greater primary-process thinking than their less creative peers. The stories of the creative girls were characterized by comparatively more fluid transformations, a greater proportion of unlikely combinations, and by more contradictions and magic occurrences. In short, the creative girls were more imaginative than their noncreative peers.

Creativity is sometimes defined in terms of the emergence of originals, that is, upon the basis of an individual's ability to produce something new or to display divergence in his thinking and productions. Further, it is believed that flexibility is an important condition permitting divergent production. In this connection, Carlier (1971) administered tests of verbal and nonverbal flexibility to a group of 78 boys whose average age was eighteen. A factor analysis of the responses yielded four kinds of flexibility: general, associative, ideational, and graphic. Carlier's finding of four flexibility factors lends some support to a concept of creativity as multidimensional. Adcock and Martin (1971) administered a battery of

sixteen tests of closure to 188 tenth graders and factor-analyzed the results. Adcock and Martin report six oblique factors, two being flexibility of closure factors, which they interpreted as representing factors of creativity. It is interesting that Peal and Lambert (1962), basing their view on the superior performance of bilinguals as compared to monolinguals on both verbal and nonverbal intelligence tests, note that bilinguals seem to have a "more diversified set of mental abilities than monolinguals." These investigators feel that bilinguals have greater mental flexibility and, as a result, greater facility at concept formation.

In contrast to Carlier's and Adcock and Martin's views, Moerdyk (1971) makes the point that divergency relates more to an individual's interests than to his creativity and, therefore, the convergence-divergence dichotomy is not an accurate index of creativity. The fact that interests may produce divergence is apparent enough to the writer of this textbook, but it seems equally apparent that deviating interests themselves may be the product of creativity. Moerdyk's attempt to make such a clear distinction between interest and creativity appears less than satisfactory.

Personal Attributes of the Creative Individual

One way of approaching an understanding of creativity is the operational one of asking what a creative person is like and what he characteristically does and thinks. It appears that various motivational and personality variables interact with situational variables in producing creative behavior. There is some reason to believe that there is a positive relationship between anxiety and creativity, but empirical results have not been uniform in confirming this point. In his study of high school males Pearce (1968), for example, reports his more creative group to be both less anxious and less guilt-prone. Leith (1972), in a study of nine-, eleven-, and thirteen-year-olds, administered three verbal creativity tests in both a relaxed and in a moderately stressful atmosphere and reports that the number and originality of responses was greater in the stressful condition. Apparently moderate, but certainly not severe, stress tends to have a motivating and focus-of-attention aspect, leading to greater situational productivity on the part of those with the capacity to perform creatively. This finding is counter to the popular impression that creativity comes best under optimum conditions, usually interpreted as stressfree. However, Wallach and Kogan (1965) do state that defensiveness has an inhibitory effect on creativity. Zimbardo, Barnard, and Berkowitz (1963) report that novel, permissive situations disturb defensive individuals because they tend to interfere with the defense patterns they have built up to handle situations in which they are being evaluated.

There seems to be some difference of opinion as to the extroversion-introversion status of the creative individual. Pearce (1968) reports his creative group as more introverted and self-sufficient, much in accord with the reputation creative individuals have, but, in contrast, Kurtzman (1967), comparing three groups of adolescents, found the highest level of extroversion among his most creative group. Borod, Grossman, and Eisenman (1971) report similar results, although their findings may well have been confounded by the common relationship of both creativity and extroversion to a third variable. Kurtzman also reports his most creative group as being more intelligent, more adventuresome, and, unfortunately, less favorable in their attitude toward school. Wade (1971), reporting a study of high school sophomores in two upper-middle-class communities, notes that the leisure time of the middle-class adolescent was filled with activities ranging from an assortment of hobbies to membership in a number of organizations. Wade writes that the creative adolescent "reads about as much, watches TV less, and generally exposes himself to more highly diversified activities than his less creative peers." Wade's picture of the creative adolescent as a highly active person in both social and solitary enterprises presents him as a mul-

tifaceted person who alternately displays extroverted or introverted behavior as the situation demands.

Self-concept and self-actualization research findings indicate that creativity or its absence does not operate unilaterally either upon self-view or upon self-actualization. A creative individual's self-view and his feelings of self-actualization may be high or low depending upon the presence or absence of various personal environmental factors. In a study of both creative attitude and creative production, Taft and Gilchrist (1970) report that creative late adolescents and young adults see themselves as more unconventional, more willing to take risks, and more impulsive. They also see themselves as observant, imaginative, concerned with beauty, and subject to emotional conflict. Persons making high scores on creative attitudes only also scored high on traits associated with self-actualization. In contrast, those who received high scores on creative productivity but not on creative attitudes were more apt to display neurotic symptoms and lack of self-control. A study by Maw and Maw (1970) is of interest in relationship to Taft and Gilchrist's finding about creative attitudes. Maw and Maw, assuming a relationship between curiosity and creativity, administered various measures of self-concept to a group of high-curiosity boys and to a group of low-curiosity boys, equating the two groups for intelligence. These investigators reported a higher level of self-concept among the high-curiosity boys. These boys, in contrast to the low-curiosity group, participated in more activities indicating curiosity and tended to exhibit better interpersonal attitudes. Damm (1970), in a study of the relationship among creativity, intelligence, and self-actualization among 208 high school students noted that the adolescents high in both creativity and intelligence made significantly higher self-actualization scores than those high only in either creativity or intelligence. In discussing his results, Damm contends that schools should stress both intellectual and creative abilities to achieve the highest level of psychological well-being in students.

A major difficulty faced by the exceptionally creative adolescent is the very fact of his exceptionality, an exceptionality sometimes unrecognized by others or, if it is recognized, often rejected or misunderstood. The creative adolescent's ability enables him to march to a different drummer than his peers do—or even most of the adults with whom he has to deal. Schaefer (1969a) using an adjective check list to measure the self-image of eight hundred high school students divided his sample into the four hundred most and the four hundred least creative. He reported that, regardless of sex, the self-concepts of the creative adolescents as compared to the less creative showed a pattern of complexity and reconciliation of opposites, of impulsivity and craving for novelty, and of autonomy and self-assertion. The situation being what it is, gifted or highly creative children often tend to have, as Torrance (1971) points out, serious difficulty in evolving a stable concept of self. Such children usually seek a satisfactory self-view by one of three means—conformity and concealment of their creative side, rebellion leading to conflict and problem behavior, or continuation of creative expression. The last is, of course, the most positive solution, but it is undoubtedly the most difficult solution, unless the adolescent is fortunate enough to have understanding and facilitative parents and teachers who do not suppress new ideas or adopt negative attitudes. But whether facilitation is present or not, the creative adolescent has to learn, as Parloff et al. (1968) point out, to exercise discipline and to be circumspect in his dealings with others.

In an interesting study Hare (1972) reports that low authoritarianism and creativity are two aspects of a preference for complex experience resulting in a tolerance for novelty, contradiction, and information that could be personally threatening. Her subjects consisted of 119 fifteen- to eighteen-year-olds to whom she gave a measure of authoritarianism and a personal-opinion type personality test. She then administered a test designed to section at random her subjects into a "success" or a "failure" group. Finally, everyone was given a moral-judgment test. Hare reported that adolescents high in creativity and low in authoritarianism were more flexible (asocial) in their moral judgments, while success or failure had little influence on low-authoritarian adolescents. On the other hand, adolescents high in authoritarianism reacted in a different manner to failure, depending on their level of creativity. After failure, low-creative, authoritarian adolescents became more conforming while high-creative authoritarian adolescents became more flexible. Hare's results are presented in Table 8.

Table 8 *Mean Moral Judgments and Standard Deviations for Adolescents Classified by Creativity, Authoritarianism, and Success or Failure*

| | Creativity | | | |
| | High | | Low | |
Group	High authoritarian	Low authoritarian	High authoritarian	Low authoritarian
Success (N = 60)				
Mean	4.44	5.17	5.75	4.94
SD	2.13	2.40	3.04	1.84
Failure (N = 59)				
Mean	6.55	5.20	3.71	5.18
SD	1.69	2.22	2.11	1.40

Source: R. T. Hare, "Authoritarianism, creativity, success and failure among adolescents," *The Journal of Social Psychology* 86 (1972): 219–226, table 1, p. 223. Reprinted by permission of The Journal Press and the author.

In discussing her results Hare writes:

Failure for creative high authoritarian subjects seemed to move them more toward complexity: that is, to influence them to be freer of conventional restraints and to be more nonjudgmental in their values.... It is possible that the low self-esteem attributed to highly creative individuals is in part what drives them to creative endeavors. The frustration represented by failure in the experiment led to greater flexibility, measured in this case in terms of moral judgments, as a possible compensation for lack of acceptance. If this is so, then the possibility should be considered that the motivation for creativity may come from a sense of dissatisfaction in persons who are cognitively complex.

The Relationship of Intelligence and Creativity

Although intelligence and creativity do involve some similar behaviors and abilities, it is generally recognized that they are not uniformly related, in all probability representing different dimensions of aptitude. Rossman and Horn (1972) suggest that it is appropriate to think of creativity and intelligence as the outgrowth of distinct although overlapping sets of influences. In agreement with Rossman and Horn, Mattalia (1970), utilizing test results of a group of secondary students in Turin, Italy, reports the processes of creative potential as appearing to develop along lines different from those characteristic of logical intelligence. She is of the opinion that the operational differences between the two processes lie in the originality of mental elaborations of the creative process as compared to the productivity of the logical processes. Murphy (1973) administered the Wallach-Kogan creativity tests and an intelligence test to male high school students and examined the relationship of their test scores to their grades in mathematics, science, English, and social studies. He reports that while creativity in his sample was significantly related to school grades, there were present distinctly different factors of intelligence, creativity, and achievement. Murphy

notes that intelligence and creativity were independent dimensions in the performance of his subjects. Eisenman and Robinson (1967) also report a low correlation between creativity and intelligence as measured by the Stanford-Binet.

Other investigators who have reported modest correlations as existing between creativity and intelligence include Callaway (1969), Hauck and Thomas (1972), Olive (1972), and Schlict (1968). Hauck and Thomas report a correlation of .29 between the Lorge-Thorndike Intelligence test and the Torrance Test of Creative Thinking. An interesting outcome of this study, however, was a correlation of .89 between creativity and a sense of humor and .91 between intelligence and a sense of humor.

Olive (1972), using 434 ninth to eleventh graders, studied the relationship between intelligence and divergent thinking, utilizing the Otis Quick Scoring Mental Ability Test to measure the former and the Guilford tests of divergent thinking to measure the latter. She reports a significant but modest relationship between divergent thinking and both intelligence and achievement. Relationships reported by Olive are displayed in Table 9.[1]

While the preponderance of research evidence continues to indicate the low relationship between intelligence and creativity, there is also evidence that the magnitude of the relationship varies in terms of level of intelligence. Schubert (1973) administered a creative imagination test to 176 males with high and low scores on the Army General Classification Test and reported closer correspondence of creativity in persons with low rather than with high intelligence ratings. Intelligence was statistically unrelated to creativity in Schubert's sample only when a relatively high intelligence, above an IQ of 111, was considered. Schubert interpreted his results to mean that while intelligence allows the development of creativity it by no means insures it. At upper levels of intelligence it appears, from

[1]The reader may be interested in looking at the correlations among the different components of creativity as well as between each of these components and intelligence.

Table 9 *Correlation Matrix for Tests of Divergent Thinking and IQ*

Test	EF	AF	IF	AU	C-O	C-R	IQ
Word Fluency	.46	.52	.52	.45	.45	.36	.35
Expressional Fluency		.46	.40	.45	.24	.44	.42
Associational Fluency			.55	.49	.38	.41	.50
Ideational Fluency				.45	.43	.33	.31
Alternate Uses					.38	.48	.42
Consequences-Obvious						.19	.13
Consequences-Remote							.39
Otis: IQ							

Source: H. Olive, "The relationship of divergent thinking to intelligence, social class, and achievement in high school students," *Journal of Genetic Psychology* 121 (1972): 179–186, table 3, p. 182. Reprinted by permission of The Journal Press and the author.

Schubert's data, that personality and environmental factors assume greater importance. On the other hand Maier and Janzen (1969) report that subjects superior in solving difficult problems having objectively correct solutions also achieve solutions rated "creative" or superior for a problem with several possible answers.

The Development of Creativity

Research indicates the importance of environmental factors, particularly parental child-rearing practices and educational experiences, in the development of creativity. Dewing (1970) reports that the most important family variables in producing highly creative children are nonauthoritarian discipline, the presence of relatively intellectual interests in family members, and a child-parent relationship that is not overly dependent. Wade (1968) notes the importance in the development of creativity of environmental factors associated with psychological safety and personal freedom leading to independence of cognitive functioning. Heilbrun (1971) asked ninety-six male undergraduates to fill in the Parent Attitude Research Instrument and the Parent-Child Interaction Scale as they believed their mothers would. He then administered the Smith-Schaefer Creativity Scale to the entire group. It was found that maternal low nurturance and high control was associated with low creativity exhibited by males in their early twenties. Domino (1969) studied the behavior of a group of creative high school males in contrast to the behavior of the mothers of a control group. In particular, the mothers of the creative group valued autonomy and independent behavior. They were more likely to prefer unstructured behavior and change, were more insightful of the behavior of others, and they exhibited greater initiative, self-assurance, and interpersonal competence. In contrast to the control group the mothers of the creative males were less nurturant and obliging toward others, less dependable, less conscientious, less inhibited, and less concerned about creating a favorable impression. In other words, they provided their children a stimulating but unstructured environment in which the child was given considerable recognition and autonomy as an individual. Siegelman (1973), using 144 male and 274 female undergraduates, studied the association of basic dimensions of parent-child relationships and later creativity. Undergraduates possessing personality traits usually associated with creativity tended to describe their parents as more rejecting than loving, whereas the less creative undergraduates tended to describe their parents as loving.

Casual, as compared to demanding, parent behavior seemed to have little relationship to creative potential. Protecting fathers seemed to be particularly associated with females of low creative potential.

In a study of the influence of school upon creative thinking, Ogletree (1971) administered the Torrance Test of Creative Thinking to 1,165 schoolchildren in England, Scotland, and Germany. He reported that the less intellectually-oriented school system produced more creative children. Walberg (1971) reported that involvement in school activities has a positive although not particularly strong relationship to creative interests. However, it would be a mistake from the available evidence to draw any firm conclusions about the kind of school curriculum most likely to promote creativity. It is less a matter of what is studied and more of how it is studied and the personal relationships involved. As with the home, a stimulating environment is essential if the school is to promote rather than impede creative interests and productivity. It would also appear that the inculcation of work habits and attitudes of perseverance are important. Zisulescu (1967) in a study of creative adolescents, proposes that in addition to inspiration, hard, consciously sustained work is an important aspect of the creative process. Walberg (1971) also points to the association of perseverance in spite of difficulties. Torrance (1972), in a summary of 142 approaches to teaching children to think creatively, writes that the most successful approaches provide both cognitive and emotional functioning, permit interaction both with teachers and other children, provide adequate structure and motivation, and provide opportunities for involvement and practice. Passive learning is not the best approach to the production of creative potential. Torrance suggests that while motivating and facilitating conditions are important, best results will follow when deliberate teaching for creative behavior is involved. Guilford (1972) notes that education should be multivariate in nature and should afford creative children an opportunity to develop their diverse talents. He suggests that a child should be given information regarding his mental resources, including the creative, as soon as he can make use of the information. One way in which the schools can do this is to provide him with participative experiences giving him firsthand knowledge in the use of his own abilities. The adolescent by his very nature is potentially a fruitful subject for an educational program designed to inculcate creative behavior. The adolescent has only recently acquired the ability to think in hypothetical terms and to manipulate ideas logically, attributes which give him the potential to range more freely over the world of complex ideas and imaginative invention. As an individual proceeds into adolescence, his increasing sense of maturity should, given the proper stimulus, furnish him the perseverance and dedication that sustained creative endeavor requires.

An example of an approach to training in creativity is reported by Parnes and Noller (1972). These investigators made a random selection of 150 incoming freshmen and organized them into six groups to receive a one-semester course in creative study. A control group of 150 was given no such instruction. At the end of the semester, test results on the Guilford Structure of Interest Test indicated that those who had received the creative-study course were superior in cognition and in convergent and divergent thinking. They were also significantly superior on two of six English tests. Parnes and Noller present some evidence to indicate that the gains persisted a year later. In a series of studies, Torrance (1970) presents evidence to indicate that working in pairs facilitates creative endeavor, although increasing age through the school years appears to enhance the effectiveness of this dyadic relationship.

Measurement of Creativity

The main question in the measure and prediction of creativity is the extent to which measures of creativity should include intelligence as it is traditionally measured. The answer, apparent from the preceding sections, is that while factors of intellectual functioning cannot be ignored, creativity exists on another dimension. Certainly creativity measures should not be identical with those designed for the measurement of intelligence.

Dellas and Gaier (1970), summing up their review of creativity research, report that despite differences in age, cultural background, area of operation, or eminence, a consistent constellation of traits emerge as characteristic of the creative person and that such persons appear distinguished more by interests, attitudes, and drives than by intellectual ability. For that reason, measurement and prediction of creativity should include singular intellectual characteristics, cognitive styles, and personality variables. Klein and Evans (1969) obtained predictor data consisting of academic skills and past creative achievements in the seventh and ninth grades as well as criterion data on 2,337 students in the twelfth grade. They reported that the best predictors of creative achievements in high school (and probably beyond) were past creative achievements. A combination of academic skills and past achievements predicted the criterion between .40 and .50, although the magnitude of the relationship was moderated by sex and the area of the criterion, such as science or art. Torrance (1972) reports, as the result of a twelve-year follow-up study of 392 high-school students identified as highly gifted, that the creative achievements of females were significantly less predictable than those of males, and that creative achievements in leadership, writing, medicine, and science were more easily predicted than were creative achievements in business and industry or in music and the visual arts.

Findings of a study by Thacker and Rosenbluh (1972) are of particular importance for school programs. These investigators measured teachers' ability to select creative and noncreative students as well as to observe differences in the behavioral patterns of creative and noncreative individuals in their classrooms. Results of the study indicate that teachers were not adequate judges in their selection of creative students and tended to perceive the more passive individual as the more creative. In a related study, Merz and Rutherford (1972) report only a slight positive relationship for creativity measures and teacher ratings. They note that factor analysis suggests that teacher judgment and measures of creativity sample different dimensions.[2]

The Gifted Adolescent

Giftedness, in contrast to creativity, traditionally has been defined in terms of the altitude of an IQ received as a result of performance on a standard test of intelligence. The Educational Policies Commission (1950) reserved the term *gifted* for the upper 1 percent of the population. In the studies of genius conducted by Terman and his associates (1925), individuals who had attained an IQ of 130 or above represented the gifted group. Gifted adolescents represent a capacity group of the intellectually able in academic and other kinds of learning. But beyond this fact of intellectual adeptness, what is the gifted child like? What are his prospects of eventually becoming an adult who achieves notable success in one or more of a variety of personal, social, and occupational endeavors? Modern educational and psychological thinking increasingly stresses the importance of personality and social factors in the life and education of children both in and out of school. Is it true that the bright

[2]Of the various measures of creative ability available, the Torrance Tests of Creative Thinking are among the widely used and, hence, most widely criticized. These tests, which purport to measure four aspects of creative thinking, consist of measures of fluency, flexibility, originality, and elaboration. Two scores, verbal and figural, are available for each of these measures. Various forms are available for kindergarten through graduate school. Persons interested in this and other tests of creativity should consult the various editions of *Buros Mental Measurements Yearbook* for descriptions and critical reviews.

child or adolescent is equally able in his personal life and in his interpersonal relationships? What other behaviors and aptitudes are commonly found to be associated with being gifted? Many years ago, in another era that now seems very remote, Terman (1925), in his epochal study of the mental and physical traits of a thousand gifted children, reported that in social interests, social intelligence ratings, and play activities gifted children as a group were either normal or superior. Later than the Terman study, but still remote from the present time, Davidson (1943) and Pignatelli (1943) reported that mental functioning and personal adjustment appear to have little if any correlation. At about the same time Doll (1946) spoke of the "social insufficiency" of those at the lower end of the intelligence continuum as being "manifest in subnormal personal dependence, self-direction, social responsibility and self-support." Taken together the implication of these four studies is that while personal and social adjustment bear little relationship to traditional intellectual ability over the middle ranges of intelligence, there is a relationship at the lower and higher ends of the continuum of mental ability. Is this still true today? It is essentially true today, although modern thinking about adaptive behavior and the educable mentally retarded would be more optimistic than was Doll's. Correspondingly, there are some persons today who would disagree with Terman and rest their case upon the findings of Davidson and Pignatelli that there is little correlation between mental functioning and personal adjustment. In actual fact, any statement of relationship between nonintellectual attributes and level of intelligence made with reference to any capacity group has to be made with certain reservations. People as people are characterized by their differences, one from the other. It is necessary to recognize that the permutations and combinations of influences making for the state of mind and behavior of any individual at any given time are almost infinite. Intelligence, however measured, is only

one set of attributes in a complex whole of sets, and its influence may or may not on any given occasion be an overriding factor. We may report general trends for any given group, but it must be understood that any individual, or even on some occasions every individual, in the group, may constitute an exception to the generalization. Of course, not every gifted adolescent is necessarily either normal or above normal in social and personal adjustment, any more than a person of lower ability is necessarily maladjusted in any way. While it is important for us to know general group trends, it is essential that we understand that for any individual our interpretation must depend on what we know of his past history of behavior and environmental influences as well as on a knowledge of his present circumstances and how he interprets them.

A number of studies have been performed comparing various personal and social attributes of groups of bright and of average adolescents. Ages of subjects have ranged from twelve-year-olds in the sixth or seventh grades to college-age adolescents in their late teens and early twenties. Schlichting (1968), in a contrast of a group of bright male high school students (average IQ 140) with a similar but average group (average IQ 110), comments upon the relatively greater breadth of interest characteristic of the brighter students. Palmer and Wohl (1972) compared honors and non-honors university men and women using an adjective check list, the Edwards Personal Preference Schedule, and the Morris Way of Life Test. Honors students of both sexes as compared to the nonhonors students were higher in autonomy and need for independence but lower in affiliation, extrovertive orientation, and feelings of abasement. Members of the nonhonors group tend to be more socially oriented and had less difficulty in visualizing themselves as subordinate to the social group. On the whole, nonhonors males placed a greater value on the Protestant ethic of discipline and hard work, although honors females ranked highest in need for achievement. The honors females ranked lowest in personal adjustment nurturance and interest in members of the opposite sex. Groth and Holbert (1969) asked 281 ten- to fourteen-year-olds in a summer camp program for gifted children to write three wishes upon a blank sheet of paper and followed a similar procedure with matched controls from a public school. In scoring the answers, wishes were categorized on the basis of Maslow's hierarchy of needs. Gifted children were more concerned with self-actualization than were the controls, with more gifted girls being more concerned with self-actualization than gifted boys. The latter showed a comparatively greater concern with security and self-esteem.

Mason, Adams, and Blood (1968) tested bright college freshmen with the Allport-Vernon-Lindzey Study of Values and the Adjective Check List. As compared to their peers, bright students were lower in economic and higher in aesthetic values. The intellectually more able students received lower scores on the Adjective Check List for affiliation, personal adjustment, nurturance, self-control, defensiveness, and deference, but higher scores on autonomy. The investigators noted that the bright students when compared with the norm group were less well adjusted but more independent. In a further study, Adams, Mason, and Blood (1970) administered a personality test to students in three American colleges and one English grammar school. Again they reported that brighter students are more independent but are characterized by more personal-adjustment problems. Sontag, Baker, and Nelson (1958) take a somewhat different approach when they hypothesize that to some extent a child whose personal-social adjustment is good will tend to learn more adequately, hence will tend to secure higher scores on mental tests than will a less well-adjusted child. Under this hypothesis it is not true that more intelligent children are more likely to be well adjusted merely because they are more intelligent, but rather the reverse, that well-adjusted children will do well intellectually because they are well adjusted.

In general, it may be assumed that neither low nor high intelligence is important in an adolescent's social or personal adjustment, unless he is placed in a situation in which his level of intelligence is a continuing source of frustration, insecurity, unpleasantness, and ridicule, and there are no other sources of security, approval, and satisfaction available. A dull adolescent in school is usually bound to encounter failure and, all too often, censure and even ridicule because of inability to perform at a level that is completely beyond his capacity. If the adolescent is particularly sensitive, or if he has no other resources—such as specific skills in art, manual training, athletics—there is good reason to assume that he may encounter serious personality difficulties. If, in addition, his parents have too high aspirations for him and continually make an issue of his failure or let him see their disappointment, the results may be even more serious. A child in such a situation has the option of withdrawing and beginning to live in a world of his own, or of fighting back by embarking on a career of overt problem and antisocial behavior. Of the two responses the more disastrous for him personally and for his future welfare is withdrawal. Overt aggressive or problem behavior may be more antisocial and may eventually lead him to legal or other difficulty, but from the purely psychological point of view such behavior, though unfortunate and certainly in need of remedy, represents a real attempt at adjustment on his part. His conduct may be more immediately disagreeable, but it offers greater hope that something can be done for him.

In contrast consider the adolescent who finds little satisfaction in school, is even frustrated there, but who has interests and successes outside school: he may well adjust to school by ignoring it. If, in addition, he has a happy home environment and understanding parents, there is no reason why he should not find a satisfactory personal adjustment. The school can assist in the process by helping him find the things he can do well, by encouraging him and providing success experiences for him, and by refraining from setting standards he cannot possibly attain; the least it can do is guide him away from classes and situations in which his failure and possible humiliation are inevitable.

Sex Differences and the Gifted

A given level of ability, whether high or low, does not mean that all persons at that level will be identical. It may mean that their performance on the test items indicating their level is identical, but when it comes to the application or use of the ability, individual and group differences become important. For example, Gottsdanker (1968) reports that significant characteristics of gifted persons are masked when the descriptive data for the two sexes are combined. She writes that gifted women "show a different pattern of intellectual interests than do men, and they are often more divergent from average students than gifted men. They are outstandingly interested in independent thought." Gottsdanker suggests that separate norms for the sexes for intellectual interests and educational needs should be used in advisement and placement. A study whose results supported Gottsdanker's point of view about need for new norms, but not their direction, was performed by Werner and Bachtold (1969), who administered personality questionnaires to 367 eight- to fifteen-year-olds participating in a program for the gifted. They reported that gifted boys differed significantly more often from the norm groups for this age and sex than did gifted girls. Bachtold (1968), in a study of gifted twelve- through fourteen-year-olds, reports that both gifted and average boys set less value on support and benevolence and more upon leadership than did gifted and average girls.

Accomplishment and Giftedness

The discussion to this point has been confined primarily to associated personal and emotional attributes of giftedness. What of actual accomplishment? There is no doubt that high intelligence is a specialized set of attributes of great value in academic and conceptually related matters including entry into certain professional or highly technical occupations. However, given a basic level of intelligence, nonacademic accomplishment and altitude of intelligence seem largely to be independent of one another. In this connection Baird (1968) performed two studies. In his first study he compared the nonacademic and creative achievements during their first year in college of a group of 5,695 students attending 35 different colleges with those of a group of 525 National Merit Finalists attending 219 different institutions. The National Merit finalist group had an average SAT verbal score of approximately 665, placing them in the top 2 or 3 percent of college freshmen. In contrast the group of 5,695 had an American College Testing Program average score of 20 (equivalent to an SAT verbal score of 450), placing them close to the national mean for college-bound high school seniors. Table 10 presents Baird's results. An examination of this table indicates that there was very little difference between the groups in nonacademic areas of college achievement, including leadership, scientific endeavor, dramatics, literary accomplishment, music, and art. In general, the intellectually more gifted group seems to have achieved slightly more frequently in the literary area, while the average college group seems to have achieved slightly more frequently in the artistic area.

In Baird's second study a comparison was made of the number of high school achievements of 14,424 high ACT scorers as compared with those of 10,680 low scorers. The mean score of the high-scoring group was 25.5, placing them at approximately the 86th percentile on national norms, while the low scoring students mean score was 18.2, placing them at approximately the 35th percentile on the national norms. Results, showing the number of high school achievements for the two groups, are presented in Table 11. In spite of the

Table 10 *Nonacademic College Achievement of Gifted as Compared to Average College Freshmen*

College Achievement	% of Sample Indicating Achievement	
	National Merit Finalists	American College Survey
A. Leadership		
1. Was elected president of my class.	1.0	0.5
2. Initiated or organized a student movement to change institutional rules, procedures, or policies.	2.3	2.4
3. Organized a college political group or campaign.	3.7	2.1
4. Received an award or special recognition for leadership of any kind.	8.7	5.2
5. Actively campaigned to elect another student to a school office.	21.7	24.3
6. Initiated a business enterprise of any kind.	4.9	4.2
7. Participated in an off-campus political campaign.	3.7	4.0
B. Science		
1. Received a prize or award for a scientific paper or project.	0.8	0.4
2. Gave an original paper at a scientific or professional meeting sponsored by a professional society or association.	0.2	0.2
3. Had scientific or scholarly paper published (or in press) in a scientific or professional journal.	0.2	0.1
4. Invented a patentable device.	0.6	0.7
5. Member of student honorary scientific society.	1.8	0.6
6. Built a piece of equipment or laboratory apparatus of my own (not as part of course).	3.8	2.9
7. Appointed a teaching assistant in a scientific field.	1.6	0.7
8. Entered a scientific competition of any kind.	1.5	1.4
C. Dramatics		
1. Won one or more speech or debate contests.	2.8	0.8
2. Was regular performer on radio or TV program.	2.6	1.1
3. Received an award for acting, playwriting, or other phase of drama.	0.4	1.1
4. Had minor roles or leads in plays not produced by a college or university.	1.6	3.3
D. Literary		
1. Had poems, stories, essays, or articles published in a public newspaper, magazine, anthology, etc. (not a college publication).	2.0	1.9
2. Wrote one or more plays (including radio or TV plays) which were given public performance.	0.5	0.3
3. Did news or feature writing for a public newspaper.	1.7	0.8
4. Had poems, stories, essays, or articles published in a college publication.	7.1	4.9
5. Won literary award or prize for creative writing.	0.9	0.4
6. Was editor or feature writer for collegiate paper, annual, magazine, or anthology, etc.	5.4	2.6
7. Wrote an original but unpublished piece of creative writing on my own (not as part of course).	21.6	16.4
E. Music		
1. Composed music that has been given at least one public performance.	1.2	1.1
2. Had one or more musical publications.	0.1	0.3
3. Performed with a professional orchestra.	2.6	2.0
4. Gave a recital (not collegiate).	0.9	3.3

Table 10   *Nonacademic College Achievement of Gifted as Compared to Average College Freshmen (cont.)*

College Achievement	% of Sample Indicating Achievement	
	National Merit Finalists	American College Survey
F. Art		
1. Won a prize or award in an art competition (painting, sculpture, ceramics, etc.).	0.2	0.6
2. Exhibited or published at my college a work of art (painting, musical composition, sculpture).	2.2	2.7
3. Exhibited or performed (not at my college) a work of art (painting, musical composition, sculpture).	1.5	2.2
4. Entered an artistic competition or contest of any kind.	1.3	2.3
5. Finished a work of art on my own (not as part of a course).	9.5	12.0

Source: L. Baird, "The achievements of bright and average students," *Educational and Psychological Measurement* 28 (1968): 891–899, table 1, pp. 893–894. Reprinted by permission of the publisher.

enormous differences in academic aptitude the high school achievements of the two groups are essentially the same. The high ACT students had slightly more achievements in three areas, including science and writing; and the low ACT students had slightly more achievements in the artistic area. From his two studies, Baird concluded that high verbal intelligence and nonacademic achievement are independent, and it is impossible to predict from intelligence-test data whether an individual at any level of intelligence would or would not achieve at any given level in the arena of nonacademic activities.

Baird's findings are in accord with the general picture presented by previous studies. Hoyt (1966), in a review of forty-six studies, investigated the relation of college grades to adult success and noted that the consensus is that academic achievement does not have a correlation with success in later life. The lack of relationship between academic and nonacademic accomplishment has been commented upon by MacKinnon (1960), Holland and Astin (1962), Roberts (1965), Wallach and Kogan (1965), Nichols (1966), and Taylor and Ellison (1967). Results such as those reported in the studies just cited may be genuinely due to differences in abilities involved in nonacademic

as compared to academic endeavors. They may also be due at least in part to the failure of many high schools to present a stimulating atmosphere of learning and accomplishment for their brighter students. Too often the problem of the dull child is emphasized at the expense of the bright child. For many children of high intelligence, school is a completely and utterly boring place where teachers elaborate the obvious and provide "experiences" that are totally unnecessary for efficient learning. Sometimes teachers who realize this provide enrichment material that is, in reality, merely tedious busywork. There is little point in reading two books instead of one when both say the same thing, which was adequately understood the first time it was read. It is little wonder that some bright children feel that making them do extra work just because they are bright is unfair.

On the other side of the picture is the bright child who has always received high grades and copious praise for doing work that is ridiculously easy for him. He is seldom challenged intellectually and comes to assume that "sloppy" work (still superior when compared to the efforts of the less bright) is all that is required of him. He comes to feel that he has

Table 11   *Percentage of High and Low ACT Groups with Number of High School Achievements*

Area of Achievement	0	1, 2	3–5	6–8	F	ω²
			Number of High School Achievements			
Leadership						
High ACT	16.0	38.1	38.9	7.0	83.4*	.003
Low ACT	19.8	39.3	35.4	5.5		
Science						
High ACT	55.1	32.8	11.1	1.0	119.0*	.005
Low ACT	62.3	28.7	8.3	0.7		
Speech and Drama						
High ACT	42.5	41.2	15.4	0.9	1.3	.000
Low ACT	42.1	41.1	16.0	0.9		
Writing						
High ACT	40.7	43.8	14.8	0.8	192.7*	.008
Low ACT	47.9	41.9	9.8	0.5		
Music						
High ACT	41.3	31.6	22.7	4.4	1.2	.000
Low ACT	40.2	32.0	23.6	4.2		
Art						
High ACT	70.3	24.0	5.0	0.7	17.0*	.001
Low ACT	67.8	25.8	5.4	1.0		

Total Number of Nonacademic High School Achievements All Areas Combined

Group	0–1	2–3	4–5	6–7	8–9	10–11	12 or more	F	ω²
				Number of Achievements					
High ACT	6.6	12.6	16.6	17.2	14.2	11.7	21.7	82.1*	.004
Low ACT	9.0	14.6	18.0	15.8	14.2	10.3	18.2		

*Indicates significant beyond the .01 level.

Source: L. Baird, "The achievements of bright and average students," *Educational and Psychological Measurement* 28 (1968): 891–899, table 2, p. 895. Reprinted by permission of the publisher.

a right to receive high grades and high praise, although in terms of his true ability he has done little to merit them. When he enters college and has to compete against his intellectual peers, he often finds himself totally unaccustomed to the effort required of him. Many such individuals are unable to adjust to these new demands and grow resentful, feel inferior, and often leave college, or seek frantically for snap courses or curricula in which they may again shine with their accustomed luster without making any serious effort.

The fate of the bright child is of serious importance to society, for from this group the leaders, statesmen, scientists, thinkers, and creative workers of tomorrow must come. Society owes it to itself to do a good job with them. A nation, particularly in times such as these, can ill afford to neglect the best it has. Judging by the amount of literature beginning to appear on the topic of the gifted child and the need to do something for him, there is growing concern for his fate as an individual and for his potential role in the society in which he will spend his life.

But concern does not necessarily equal action. Some things are being done, but more are not. In Conant's (1959) survey of 103 schools in twenty-six states he reports that only eight were meeting the comprehensive high school objectives of (1) providing a general education for all future citizens, (2) supplying adequate electives for those who wish to use their acquired skills immediately upon graduation, and (3) offering satisfactory programs for those whose future vocations demand college training. In a survey of 254 California schools, Trimble (1955) reports that few made any provision for the gifted other than some curriculum enrichment. Forty-seven percent of these schools felt that no special program for the gifted was necessary. Typical of programs for the gifted that are being tried is one at the Hamden–New Haven Cooperative Education Center, described by Bennett et al. (1971), where an independent study program has been developed for talented and gifted students. In this program a suitable pace is established for each student, and students themselves decide what kind of tests will best indicate their accomplishments. A student's own personal goals serve to structure his program. Bennett reports that students who have been through the program claim a sense of accomplishment and a more highly developed sense of identity. Such a program can give gifted students the autonomy they seem to need, although it is particularly necessary that teachers in such a program do not abdicate their role as teachers and guides. Lack of structure can be as deadly for the gifted child as the overimposition of structure. One interesting approach to the design of educational programs is reported by Rice and Banks (1967), who interviewed 119 gifted secondary-school students in order to obtain their recom-

mendations for academic program change. The assumption was that since the gifted adolescent is potentially in the best position to profit from the academic program of a school, it is of interest to know what kind of academic experiences he would like to see as part of his education. Rice and Banks reported that their gifted sample wanted: (1) greater freedom in selecting courses; (2) more emphasis upon a general education philosophy; (3) French, German, humanities, creative writing, general mathematics, chemistry, physics, psychology, and economics courses; (4) more recognition for their work; (5) more intellectual criticism and discussion of controversial issues; and (6) some type of academic segregation or homogeneous grouping.

In the area of teacher preparation, despite the pioneer efforts of Pennsylvania, Delaware, and Indiana in providing special certification for teachers of the gifted, there remains relatively little interest. A study by Jacobs (1972) indicates one of the results of this neglect. Jacobs developed a measure of teacher attitude toward the gifted and administered it to the entire kindergarten and first-grade faculty of a school district. He reported more negative than positive attitudes toward the gifted on the part of the faculty and speculated that at any early age the gifted child is taught that his inquisitive behavior is less acceptable than that of other children. There is considerable interest in exceptionality on the part of teacher educators today, but it is concentrated, probably following the availability of federal funding for the purpose, almost entirely upon the problem of mental retardation.

Pressey (1955) attributes some of the indifference to problems of parental and peer expectation and the general antiintellectual climate of the nation, as well as to intraschool program planning. He writes:

There is a general belief . . . that intellectual precocity is somehow not quite healthy, is almost always a hazard to good social adjustment, and should be slowed down rather than facilitated. In the home, the early reading precocious child causes anxiety, in spite of the usualness of such precocity in Terman's gifted group and in the biographies of famous men. The schools oppose entrance before the standard age of 6, in spite of the evidence from some half-dozen experiments that gifted tots admitted earlier have done well, both academically and adjustment wise. The general public tends to regard the intellectually gifted small child as a freak. In short, there is usually none of the initial encouragement in the family, early fostering, and favorable general social climate that got many musical and athletic prodigies off to a flying start. As a result of mass education and indifference to the needs of the gifted, there is almost none of the individualized guidance and instruction for excellence.

Still, efforts have been made. The United States Office of Education has provided funds for research for projects such as that by McGuire and associates (1960) on talented behavior in junior high schools and by Flanagan and associates (Project Talent 1960) on development of an inventory of the aptitudes, abilities, and background characteristics of 450,000 high school students. In the McGuire study, answers to the following questions were sought in a three-year study of all boys and girls who entered the seventh grade of four medium-sized Texas communities:

What kinds of indicators or variables combine most effectively to explain and forecast talented behavior among boys and girls in the junior high school years? Are abilities relatively fixed or do some of them transfer and produce different outcomes from one stage of learning to another and from one kind of valued performance to another? To what extent can school people modify and enrich the educative process so as to foster and influence these changes? Which boys and girls respond to such opportunities and what are the characteristics of those who react negatively? In what ways are the learning experiences of students in junior high schools influenced by various kinds of groupings and by enrichment of certain courses? How are different kinds of abilities and types of performance affected by variations in personality makeup and motivation, or by pressures imposed by age mates, parents, and men and women teachers?

Answers to such questions must not only be sought by research and various other means, they must be translated as quickly as possible

into school curricula and teaching methods. The next years will see increasing efforts in these directions as new research is attempted and as the lag between what is known and what is applied is diminished. Here is a challenge.

Homogeneous Grouping

One technique for providing for the mentally adept, the average, and the mentally inept is the device of homogeneous grouping. In its early form it was the practice to segregate in a group persons of similar intellectual level. The difficulty with this procedure has been that human behavior in any given situation depends upon a good many things besides mental capacity or potential. Learning is partly a function of a person's level of intelligence, but it is also a function of a person's level of motivation, his past experience and preparation, and the facilitation offered him. A highly motivated adolescent of average intelligence may learn more effectively than may an unmotivated adolescent of superior intelligence. If motivation is equal, it is reasonable to assume that the superior person will excel. Homogeneous grouping on the single variable of intelligence also assumes that all school learning is of a high-level academic type, when, as a matter of fact, school learning may be at all levels of complexity, and sometimes, in a given situation, social intelligence or good adjustment is more important than high intellectual potential.

Nor should special abilities, such as some form of aesthetic talent, dexterity, nonverbal aptitude, or ability to discriminate, be overlooked. Many special abilities, which show low correlations with intellectual ability, are the ones most needed in subjects such as physical education, art, and manual training. Present practice, insofar as homogeneous grouping is concerned, is to group students together on the basis of several variables, such as intelligence, interest, and social competence for some specific task or subject. The variables to be selected for homogeneous grouping depend upon the task or the subject. Later, for another task or another subject, the children could be regrouped to meet the requirements of the new situation. The day of the static homogeneous group, formed on the basis of one variable, differing widely in all other respects but fated to remain together no matter what the task and the abilities required, is rapidly drawing to a close.

On the other hand, some educators prefer to avoid homogeneous grouping and teach unselected groups, endeavoring to individualize instruction. There are many techniques of instruction whose objective is to enable a teacher to individualize the learning situation with an unselected class before her. Among them are various committee and socialized learning techniques, various contract and special task plans such as the Winnetka and Dalton plans, and various work capacity plans such as the Oneida plan.[3] The student interested in the methodology of instruction is urged to read one or more of the excellent textbooks that are now available.

From the viewpoint of the psychologist interested in learning during the adolescent years, the most efficient learning will be that which is attempted in the light of what is known about the individuals to be taught, and which proceeds in terms of their interests, abilities, and previous preparation. In addition, one would hope for the learner's active cooperation.

Summary

Creativity is a controversial construct. It is believed by some that creativity is an aspect of general intelligence and is adequately measured by general intelligence tests. Others hold that it is a separate ability requiring special measures, although there has been disagreement as to the most appropriate content for such special measures.

Creativity is usually defined as multifaceted ability involving imagination, divergent thinking, various kinds of flexibility, and inventive elaboration. As a process it involves sensing gaps or missing elements, forming new hypotheses concerning them, communicating the results, and modifying and retesting the hypotheses.

It appears that creativity occurs at its highest level when an individual is under mild stress, but in a situation in which the stress does not elicit defensive and other inhibitory behavior. While there has been some difference of opinion as to the creative person's introversion-extroversion status, it is most probable that the creative person is an individual who alternately displays extroverted or introverted behavior as the situation demands. By the same token a creative individual's self-view and feelings of self-actualization may be high or low depending upon environmental factors, although, given optimum conditions of challenge and encouragement, the creative person is typically a self-actualizing person with a good self-view. The self-concepts of creative as compared to less creative persons generally tend to show a pattern of complexity and reconciliation of opposites. It is probable that the strongest motivation for creativity may come from a sense of dissatisfaction in persons who are cognitively complex.

Although intelligence and creativity do involve some similar behaviors and abilities, it is generally recognized that they are not uniformly related, in all probability representing different dimensions of aptitude. It is appropriate, however, to think of creativity as the outgrowth of overlapping sets of influences. The originality of the mental elaborations involved is a major distinction between the creative and the logical processes. Most studies reporting on the relationship between creativity and intelligence have indicated that only modest correlations may be obtained between measures of creativity and intelligence,

[3]The Winnetka and Dalton plans were methods of instruction used to provide for individual differences so that students who were intelligent and motivated would be able to work at a level more in accord with their capacity. The Oneida plan was a grading system by which students were graded on their achievement in terms of their capacity. Thus a less intelligent child, trying his best, would receive a higher grade than a more intelligent child who was not trying very hard—even though the actual level of achievement of the more intelligent child was higher than that of his less intelligent classmate.

although the magnitude of the relationship varies with the level of intelligence.

Research indicates the importance of environmental factors, particularly parental child-rearing practices and educational experiences, in the development of creativity. The most important family variables in producing highly creative children are nonauthoritarian discipline, relatively intellectual interests, and absence of overdependency. Autonomy is important to the creative person.

School has an important influence in the development of the creative person, although, as long as a stimulating environment for learning is provided, it is a mistake to draw any firm conclusions about the kind of school curriculum most likely to promote creativity. It is less a matter of what is studied and more of how it is studied and the personal relationships involved. A specific effort to teach for creativity seems highly advisable. As an individual enters the period of adolescence, his acquirement of the ability to think in hypothetical terms and to manipulate ideas furnishes him the potential of ranging more freely over the world of complex ideas and imaginative invention. The high school should capitalize upon this new capacity.

Measures of creativity should not be identical with those designed for the measurement of intelligence. Measures of creativity should include singular intellectual characteristics, cognitive styles, and personality variables. Past creative achievement is a good predictor of future creative achievement, although it is unwise to use a single predictor variable. Teachers in particular tend not to be adequate judges when it comes to identifying their most creative students.

Giftedness, in contrast to creativity, has been defined in terms of performance on a traditional test of intelligence. Gifted individuals constitute the upper 1 to 2 percent of the population. They are a capacity group of the intellectually able in academic and other kinds of learning. While personal and social adjustment bear little relationship to traditional intellectual ability over the middle ranges of intelligence, there is a relationship at the lower

and higher ends of the continuum of mental ability.

Intelligence, however measured, is only one set of attributes in a complex whole of sets, and its influence may or may not be an overriding factor on any given occasion. Individual differences must always be considered in making generalizations about the effects of intelligence. In general, brighter adolescents are characterized by a greater breadth of interests, the possession of a greater need for autonomy and independence, and a tendency to be more concerned with self-actualization. As compared to their more average peers, bright children tend to be less socially oriented, although individual differences limit the generality of such a lack of interest in social matters. Bright students often encounter interpersonal-relationship problems as a result of their interests and high level of intellectual ability, and it is in this area that parents and teachers can be of help. Unfortunately many bright students do not find school a rewarding experience.

A given level of ability, whether high or low, does not mean that all persons at that level will be identical. Gifted females appear, for example, to show a different pattern of intellectual interests than males, to the extent that some researchers have suggested that separate norms for the sexes be used in placement and educational advisement.

Given a basic level of intelligence, nonacademic accomplishment and altitude of intelligence seem largely independent of one another. It is virtually impossible to predict from intelligence-test data whether an individual at any level of intelligence would or would not achieve at any given level in the arena of nonacademic activities. It is not completely clear why this is so, but it is possible that the school curricula and methods of teaching may be contributing factors. Anything that may be done to make the schools more challenging to the gifted individual would represent a real educational advance. A first step would be to include in curricula for the preparation of teachers a specific program for teaching the gifted.

References

Adams, H. L.; Mason, E. P.; and Blood, D. F. Personality characteristics of American and English, bright and average college freshmen. *Psychological Reports* 26 (1970): 831–834.

Adcock, C. J., and Martin, W. A. Flexibility and creativity. *Journal of General Psychology* 85 (1971): 71–76.

Bachtold, L. M. Interpersonal values of gifted junior high school students. *Psychology in the Schools* 5 (1968): 368–370.

Baird, L. L. The achievements of bright and average students. *Educational and Psychological Measurement* 28 (1968): 891–899.

Bennett, F., et al. Potentially gifted and talented high school youth benefit from independent study. *Gifted Child Quarterly* 15 (1971): 96–108.

Borod, J.; Grossman, J. C.; and Eisenman, R. Extroversion, anxiety, creativity, and grades. *Perceptual and Motor Skills* 33 (1971): 1106.

Callaway, W. R. A holistic conception of creativity and its relationship to intelligence. *Gifted Child Quarterly* 13 (1969): 237–241.

Carlier, M. Flexibility, a dimensional analysis of a modality of divergent thinking. *Perceptual and Motor Skills* 32 (1971): 447–450.

Conant, J. B. *The American high school today.* New York: McGraw-Hill, 1959.

Damm, V. J. Creativity and intelligence: Research implications for equal emphasis in high school. *Exceptional Children* 36 (1970): 565–569.

Davidson, H. H. *Personality and economic background.* New York: King's Crown Press, 1943.

Dellas, M., and Gaier, E. L. Identification of creativity: The individual. *Psychological Bulletin* 73 (1970): 55–73.

Dentler, R. A., and Mackler, B. Originality: Some personal and social determinants. *Behavior Science* 9 (1964): 1–7.

Dewing, K. Family influences on creativity: A review and discussion. *Journal of Special Education* 4 (1970): 399–404.

Doll, E. A. The feeble-minded child. In Carmichael, L., *Manual of child psychology*, ch. 17. New York: Wiley, 1946.

Domino, G. Maternal personality correlates of son's creativity. *Journal of Consulting and Clinical Psychology* 33 (1969): 180–183.

Educational Policies Commission. *Education of the gifted.* Washington, D.C.: Educational Policies Commission, 1950.

Eisenman, R., and Robinson, N. Complexity-simplicity, creativity, intelligence and other correlates. *Journal of Psychology* 67 (1967): 331–334.

Getzels, J. W., and Jackson, P. W. *Creativity and intelligence.* New York: Wiley, 1962.

Gottsdanker, J. S. Intellectual interest patterns of gifted college students. *Educational and Psychological Measurement* 28 (1968): 361–366.

Groth, J. J., and Holbert, P. Hierarchical needs of gifted boys and girls in the affective domain. *Gifted Child Quarterly* 13 (1969): 129–133.

Guilford, J. P. *The nature of human intelligence.* New York: McGraw-Hill, 1967.

Guilford, J. P. Intellect and the gifted. *Gifted Child Quarterly* 16 (1972): 175–184.

Hare, R. T. Authoritarianism, creativity, success, and failure among adolescents. *Journal of Social Psychology* 86 (1972): 219–226.

Hauck, W. E., and Thomas, J. W. The relationship of humor to intelligence, creativity, and intentional and incidental learning. *Journal of Experimental Education* 40 (1972): 52–55.

Heilbrun, A. B. Maternal child rearing and creativity in sons. *Journal of Genetic Psychology* 119 (1971): 175–179.

Holland, J. L., and Astin, A. W. The prediction of the academic, artistic, scientific, and social achievement of undergraduates of superior scholastic aptitude. *Journal of Educational Psychology* 53 (1962): 132–143.

Hoyt, D. P. The relationship between college grades and adult achievement: A review of the literature. *The Educational Record* 47 (1966): 70–75.

Jacobs, J. C. Teacher attitude toward gifted children. *Gifted Child Quarterly* 16 (1972): 23–26.

Joesting, J., and Joesting, R. Future problems of gifted girls. *Gifted Child Quarterly* 14 (1970): 82–90.

Klein, S. P., and Evans, F. R. Early predictors of later creative achievements. *Proceedings*, 77th Annual Convention A.P.A. 4 (1969): 153–154.

Kligerman, C. 27th International Psychoanalytical Congress: Panel on "creativity." *International Journal of Psychoanalysis* 53 (1972): 21–30.

Kurtzman, K. A. A study of school attitudes, peer acceptance and personality of creative adolescents. *Exceptional Children* 34 (1967): 157–162.

Lasswell, H. D. The social setting of creativity. In Anderson, H., ed., *Creativity and its cultivation*, pp. 203–221. New York: Harper & Row, 1959.

Leith, G. The relationships between intelligence, personality and creativity under two conditions of stress. *British Journal of Educational Psychology* 42 (1972) : 240–247.

McGuire, C. Talented behavior in junior high schools. Final report, Project no. 025. Austin, Texas: Cooperative Research Program of the U.S. Office of Education and the University of Texas, 1960.

MacKinnon, D. W. What do we mean by talent and how do we test for it? In *Search for Talent*, pp. 20–29. New York: CEEB, 1960.

Maier, N. R., and Janzen, J. C. Are good problem solvers also creative? *Psychological Reports* 24 (1969) : 139–146.

Mason, E. P.; Adams, H. L.; and Blood, D. F. Further study of personality characteristics of bright college freshmen. *Psychological Reports* 23 (1968) : 395–400.

Mattalia, C. S. Studio comparativo dei processi mentali in un gruppo di studenti di scuola media. *Rivista di Psicologia Sociale e Archivio Italiano di Psicologia Generale e del Lavoro* 37 (1970) : 139–172.

Maw, W. H., and Maw, E. W. Self-concepts of high- and low-curiosity boys. *Child Development* 41 (1970) : 123–129.

Merz, W. R., and Rutherford, B. M. Differential teacher regard for creative students and achieving students. *California Journal of Educational Research* 23 (1972) : 83–90.

Moerdyk, A. Divergency and creativity. *Journal of Behavioral Science* 1 (1971) : 107–108.

Murphy, R. T. Relationships among a set of creativity, intelligence and achievement measures in a high school sample of boys. *Proceedings of the 81st Annual Convention of the American Psychological Association, Montreal, Canada* 8 (1973) : 633–634.

Nicholls, J. G. Some effects of testing procedure on divergent thinking. *Child Development* 42 (1971) : 1647–1651.

Nichols, R. C. The origin and development of talent. *NMSC Research Reports*, vol. 2, no. 10. National Merit Scholarship Corporation, 1966.

Ogletree, E. A cross cultural examination of the creative thinking ability of public and private school pupils in England, Scotland, and Germany. *Journal of Social Psychology* 83 (1971) : 301–302.

Olive, H. The relationship of divergent thinking to intelligence, social class, and achievement in high school students. *Journal of Genetic Psychology* 121 (1972) : 179–186.

Palmer, A. B., and Wohl, J. Some personality characteristics of honors students. *College Student Journal* 6 (1972) : 106–111.

Parloff, M.; Datta, L.; Kleman, M.; and Handlow, J. Personality characteristics which differentiate creative male adolescents and adults. *Journal of Personality* 36 (1968) : 528–552.

Parnes, S. J., and Noller, R. B. Applied creativity: II. Results of the two year program. *Journal of Creative Behavior* 6 (1972) : 164–186.

Peal, E., and Lambert, W. The relation of bilingualism to intelligence. *Psychological Monographs* 76, no. 546 (1962).

Pearce, C. Creativity in young science students. *Exceptional Children* 35 (1968) : 121–126.

Pignatelli, M. L. A comparative study of mental functioning patterns of problem and non-problem children, seven, eight, and nine years of age. *Genetic Psychology Monographs* 27 (1943) : 69–162.

Pressey, S. L. Concerning the nature and nurture of genius. *Scientific Monthly* 81 (1955) : 123–129.

Project Talent. News of Project Talent, Bulletin no. 2. Washington, D.C.: University of Pittsburgh Project Talent Office, 1960.

Rice, J. P., and Banks, G. Opinions of gifted students regarding secondary school programs. *Exceptional Children* 34 (1967) : 269–273.

Roberts, R. J. Prediction of college performance of superior students. *NMSC Research Reports*, vol. 1, no. 5. National Merit Scholarship Corporation, 1965.

Rogers, C. R. Toward a theory of creativity. In Anderson, H. H., ed., *Creativity and its cultivation*, pp. 68–82. New York: Harper & Row, 1959.

Rossman, B. B., and Horn, J. L. Cognitive, motivational and temperamental indicants of creativity and intelligence. *Journal of Educational Measurement* 9 (1972) : 265–286.

Schaefer, C. E. The self concept of creative adolescents. *Journal of Psychology* 72 (1969a) : 233–242.

Schaefer, C. E. Primary-process thinking in thematic fantasies of creative adolescents. *Personality: An International Journal* 2 (1971) : 219–225.

Schlicht, W. J. Jr., et al. Creativity and intelligence: Further findings. *Journal of Clinical Psychology* 24 (1968) : 458.

Schlichting, V. V. Einige Personlichkeitszuge von Gymnasrasten mit hoher Testintelligenz. *Archive fur die gesamte Psychologie* 120 (1968): 125–150.

Schubert, D. S. Intelligence as necessary but not sufficient for creativity. *Journal of Genetic Psychology* 122 (1973): 45–47.

Siegelman, M. Parent behavior correlates of personality traits related to creativity in sons and daughters. *Journal of Consulting and Clinical Psychology* 40 (1973): 43–47.

Sontag, L. W.; Baker, C. T.; and Nelson, V. L. Mental growth and personality development. *Monographs Society for Research in Child Development*, vol. 23 (1958).

Taft, R., and Gilchrist, M. B. Creative attitudes and creative productivity: A comparison of two aspects of creativity among students. *Journal of Educational Psychology* 61 (1970): 136–143.

Taylor, C. W., and Ellison, R. L. Biographical predictors of scientific performance. *Science* 155 (1967): 1075–1080.

Terman, L. M. et al. *Genetic studies of genius, vol. I:* Mental and physical traits of a thousand gifted children. Stanford: Stanford University Press, 1925.

Thacker, B. T., and Rosenbluh, E. S. Creativity as a reflection of teacher pupil relationships. *Psychology* 9 (1972): 23–26.

Thorndike, R. L. Some methodological issues in the study of creativity. In *Proceedings of the 1962 Invitational Conference on Testing Problems*, pp. 40–54. Princeton: Educational Testing Service, 1963.

Torrance, E. P. *Education and the creative potential*. Minneapolis: University of Minnesota Press, 1963.

Torrance, E. P. *Rewarding creative behavior*. Englewood Cliffs: Prentice-Hall, 1965.

Torrance, E. P. Dyadic interaction as a facilitator of gifted performance. *Gifted Child Quarterly* 14 (1970): 139–143.

Torrance, E. P. Identity: The gifted child's major problem. *Gifted Child Quarterly* 15 (1971): 147–155.

Torrance, E. P. Can we teach children to think creatively? *Journal of Creative Behavior* 6 (1972): 114–143.

Torrance, E. P. Career patterns and peak creative achievements of creative high school students twelve years later. *Gifted Child Quarterly* 16 (1972): 75–88.

Trimble, V. E. Special provisions for the gifted in California public secondary schools. Doctoral dissertation, Stanford University, 1955.

Wade, S. Differences between intelligence and creativity: Some speculations on the role of environment. *Journal of Creative Behavior* 2 (1968): 97–101.

Wade, S. E. Adolescents, creativity, and media: An exploratory study. *American Behavioral Scientist* 14 (1971): 341–351.

Walberg, H. J. Varieties of adolescent creativity and high school environment. *Exceptional Children* 38 (1971): 111–116.

Wallach, M. A., and Kogan, N. *Modes of thinking in young children*. New York: Holt, Rinehart and Winston, 1965.

Werner, E. E., and Bachtold, L. M. Personality factors of gifted boys and girls in middle childhood and adolescence. *Psychology in the Schools* 6 (1969): 177–182.

Zimbardo, P. G.; Barnard, J. W.; and Berkowitz, L. The role of anxiety and defensiveness in children's verbal behavior. *Journal of Personality* 31 (1963): 79–96.

Zisulescu, S. Imatinatia creatoare la adolescent. *Revista de Pedagogie* 16 (1967): 46–55.

Suggested Readings

Anastasi, A., and Schaefer, C. E. Biographical correlates of artistic and literary creativity in adolescent girls. *Journal of Applied Psychology* 53 (1969): 267–273.

Bachtold, L. Changes in interpersonal values of gifted adolescents. *Psychology in the Schools* 6 (1969): 302–306.

Cashdan, S. Social participation and sub-cultural influences in the study of adolescent creativity. *Adolescence* 6 (1971): 39–52.

Dacey, J. S., and Madans, G. F. An analysis of two hypotheses concerning the relationship between creativity and intelligence. *Journal of Educational Research* 64 (1971): 213–216.

Dacey, J., and Ripple, R. Relationships of some adolescent characteristics of verbal creativity. *Psychology in the Schools* 6 (1969): 321–324.

Datta, L. E. Family religious background and

early scientific creativity. *American Sociological Review* 32 (1967): 626–635.

Finney, B. C., and Van Dalsem, E. Group counseling for gifted underachieving high school students. *Journal of Counseling Psychology* 16 (1969): 87–94.

Gowan, J. C. The relationship between creativity and giftedness. *Gifted Child Quarterly* 15 (1971): 239–243.

Gowan, J. C., and Bruch, C. B. *The academically talented student and guidance.* Boston: Houghton Mifflin, 1971.

Halpin, G.; Payne, D.; and Ellett, C. D. Biographical correlates of the creative personality: Gifted adolescents. *Exceptional Children* 39 (1973): 652–653.

Hermanson, D. One hundred recommendations for a senior high school gifted program. *Gifted Child Quarterly* 15 (1971): 249–255.

Hutson, T., and Osen, D. A multi-media approach to the gifted in a high school group psychology-counseling seminar. *Gifted Child Quarterly* 14 (1970): 186–190.

Isaacs, A. F. Giftedness and careers. *Gifted Child Quarterly* 17 (1973): 57–59.

Khatena, J. Production of original verbal images by children between the ages of 8 and 19 as measured by the alternate forms of onomatopeia and images. *Proceedings of the Annual Convention of the American Psychological Association* 6 (1971): 187–188.

Khatena, J. Something about myself: A brief screening device for identifying creatively gifted children and adults. *Gifted Child Quarterly* 15 (1971): 262–266, 292.

Olive, H. A note on sex differences in adolescents' divergent thinking. *Journal of Psychology* 82 (1972): 39–42.

Pang, H. Undistinguished school experiences of distinguished persons. *Adolescence* 3 (1968): 319–326.

Payne, D. A.; Halpin, W. G.; and Ellett, C. D. Personality trait characteristics of differentially gifted students. *Psychology in the Schools* 10 (1973): 189–195.

Raia, J. R., and Osipow, S. Creative thinking ability and susceptibility to persuasion. *Journal of Social Psychology* 82 (1970): 181–186.

Schaefer, C. E. Imaginary companions and creative adolescents. *Developmental Psychology* 1 (1969b): 747–749.

Schaefer, C. E. A psychological study of 10 exceptionally creative adolescent girls. *Exceptional Children* 36 (1970): 431–441.

Shouksmith, G. *Intelligence, creativity, and cognitive style.* New York: Wiley, 1971.

Torrance, E. P. Prediction of adult creative achievement among high school seniors. *Gifted Child Quarterly* 13 (1969): 223–229.

Williams, F. E. Models for encouraging creativity in the classroom by integrating cognitive-affective behaviors. *Educational Technology* 9 (1969): 7–13.

Wilson, J. B. Is the term "adaptive behavior" educationally relevant? *Journal of Special Education* 6 (1972): 93–95.

PART THREE

Bases of Behavior

Chapter Nine

Fundamental Processes

In the chapters up to this point the discussion has centered on the normative characteristics of the adolescent period with particular reference to personality, affect, and cognition. In this chapter, the governing and direction-imparting bases of human behavior will be considered.

An array of factual information about adolescence has been presented in the preceding chapters. The considerable amount and scope of that information raises the problem of interpretation. Fortunately, theory exists as a means of interpreting and ordering facts so that an integrated view will emerge. Using theory as a base one can consider the implications of a given fact and help in relating it to other facts. Theory imparts meaning to facts, providing a frame of reference in which to consider and apply information. For that reason a description of the bases of human behavior has been presented in the chapters of this section as a means of providing a theoretical background for an understanding of the adolescent period.

Behavior is orderly and follows fundamental general laws. A knowledge of these laws is most helpful in understanding the elaborated behavior that both stems from them and is governed by them. All of the processes of behavior, including those having to do with cognitive activity and the development of personality, obey inherent governing, directional, and maintenance forces known as drives. Such drives impart order to behavior. They govern,

direct, and set parameters to its processes. No living individual can escape the governance of its inherent drives and, once it acquires them, of its learned needs. Consequently an understanding of the nature and operation of drives and needs is the foundation upon which an understanding of the processes of behavior is built. If adolescents were considered in the framework of human behavior expounded in this chapter, there would be considerable progress in understanding them as individuals and as representatives of a stage in human development.

An adolescent is a human being before he is an adolescent, and much of his behavior is *human* behavior rather than *adolescent* behavior. In this sense, adolescence is only a special case of human behavior. An adolescent undergoing an emotional upset is experiencing the same physiological events as a person of any age who is emotionally upset. His reactions to thwarting or to success may be expressed in terms of the same psychological symbols. He differs in the kind of stimulus that may cause him to be joyous or emotionally disturbed and frustrated, but the fact of emotional disturbance or joy is a human rather than an exclusively adolescent phenomenon. The individual adolescent may also differ from an adult or a younger child in the specific course of action he will take following thwarting, but the need for a course of action of some kind in such a situation is, again, human rather than an adolescent behavioral reaction.

Diagnosis and Prediction

Human behavior occurs either as a product of an interaction between an individual and his environment or as the result of a physiological intrapersonal reaction. Behavior may be overt or covert, and insofar as it is overt, it may be observed and interpreted by someone who has the requisite knowledge and skill. A trained observer may predict a given sequence of behavior in advance of its occurrence provided he knows enough of the history of the case he is observing. For while individual differences can be taken for granted, there are also behavioral similarities that pursue an orderly and predictable course. Prediction and, before prediction, understanding of an individual's behavior come as the result of a diagnosis made possible by an appropriate knowledge of psychology and physiology.

For the traditional scientific point of view, one must rely upon that which may be observed and quantified. Unfortunately, in dealing with human beings, one is continually presented with qualitative evidence and must frequently rely upon assumptions made as the result of likely possibilities. Much that causes behavior is unseen and often unrealized, even by the person who displays the behavior. It is far from uncommon for a person, when confronted with the underlying causes of his behavior, to repudiate them vigorously in all sincerity. To complicate matters even further, some behavior itself is, as a matter of record, unconscious on the part of the person so behaving. To this is added the difficulty that behavior must be interpreted through the medium of an observer who is himself fallibly human and possibly beset with his own psychological problems that make interpretation difficult.

In making a diagnosis one may start with the encouraging assumption that no behavior, no observable situation, exists without an underlying cause that, with proper knowledge and skill, may be identified. Thus the heart of diagnosis is the search for a cause, since, psychologically, no really lasting cure or fundamental behavior change can take place until the fundamental cause is discovered and treated. There is considerable danger that a symptom may be thought to be a cause and be treated as such. Medical as well as psychological literature has often indicated that treatment of symptoms is only a palliative remedy whose effects tend to be short-term. Treating a symptom may be likened to stopping the spout of a steaming kettle. Inevitably, the steam will escape by blowing off the lid or by some other means. A true cure or behavior change does not come through treating causes. And the ability to diagnose correctly the causes of psychological behavior and to treat them adequately and properly must rest on a solid foundation of psychological knowledge.

The Basic Drives

Underlying and governing all human development and behavior is the presence of four basic and interacting drives characteristic of all living matter. Throughout the life span these drives remain compelling forces in originating and guiding behavior. And for every person learning produces a set of idiosyncratic and relatively stable psychological needs together with the activity- and object-oriented goals that implement them. When a psychological need is once learned, the behavioral processes and outcomes resulting from its presence are directed and limited by the action of the drives. For all practical purposes, every manipulation of behavior is need- and goal-oriented, or is at least symptomatic of the individual's striving toward a goal.

The four basic drives are equilibrium, motility, completion, and organization-cohesion. *Equilibrium* represents a striving for an intraorganism steady state in which a constancy of relations is maintained by balancing opposing forces, processes, and tensions. When any variation within or without the organism interferes with the stability engendered by the steady state, there automatically follows readjustment to restore or maintain balance. In the cognitive domain, during periods of reassessment and of analysis when implementation behavior is being blocked or held in abeyance, an individual can be said to be in a state of disequilibrium (unbalance) imparting directionality toward a return to equilibrium. Equally, when an individual's conscious or unconscious goals and needs are being blocked or when progress is not satisfactory, he is in a state of disequilibrium.

Discussing such disequilibrium in terms of adolescent adjustment, Benimoff and Horrocks (1961) write:

Individual adjustment may be hypothesized to represent a state of equilibrium-disequilibrium between the exigencies of personal needs and situational demands. Good adjustment represents the interaction of a constellation of individual needs and a series of situations appropriate to the expression of those needs. An individual's entire life represents a series of attempts to reach equilibrium by need reduction through the attainment of goals consciously or unconsciously present. An unsatisfied need represents disequilibrium. When a need is unsatisfied and closure is withheld there must be a continuing effort to achieve equilibrium through need satisfaction.[1]

Motility represents a basic state of motion and unrest characteristic of all life from a simple mass of protoplasm to the most complicated organism nature has evolved. At the level of psychological process, motility historically has been known as *conation* and serves to drive the organism forward, placing it in a constantly renewed state of becoming. Motility as an intrinsic "unrest" of the organism is almost the opposite of balance or equilibrium. Behaviors and psychological states such as volition, impulse, desire, and purposive striving all emphasize conation. Herrick (1956) writes: "It seems probable ... that conscious participation in any action arises within an inhibitory state, a stage of uncompleted movement expressed as an attitude, an active tonus which

first blocks overt expression. This is followed by release of some particular activity directed toward the object of regard." The manifestations of the motility drive may be seen at a molar level in the small muscle movements continually taking place in any person as well as in a cognitive state of unrest sometimes eventuating in boredom behavior. One is tempted to speculate about the modern adolescent male in his ceaseless questing in his automobile as an elaborated aspect of motility.[2]

Completion is the drive to complete that that has started. In nature and its products, as in mathematics and music, there is order leading to directionality, impelling events once set in motion to run their course. This is true whether one is considering a cognitive-affective process, a body in a speeding car that has just hit a tree, a mathematical equation, a musical sequence, or the components in a perceptual field that one has just entered. In human behavior the completion principle provides forward thrust, continuance, perseverance, and irreversibility. Completion is a form of sequential association in which one element leads inevitably to the next until the final member is attained. Dynamically, as in reintegration, there is even a tendency to telescope the sequence to arrive at the end. Of completion we could paraphrase an old saw and say that a train of psychological events once started is bound to run its course. A homely extension of the completion principle is provided by the apartment dweller waiting for the man in the bedroom of the apartment overhead to drop the other shoe.

In the field of biology it is commonly accepted that *organization* is a fundamental life principle. When organization is destroyed or impaired, a living organism will malfunction

[1]In place of *equilibrium* Cannon (1932) used the term *homeostasis*, but the connotation is narrower than equilibrium as used here and has been confined to certain physiological conditions. *Equilibrium* includes both psychological and biological states.

[2]Such speculation flirts with psychologizing, an activity frowned upon by science. Actually it is important to understand that the drives are simply directional and governing forces that should not, apart from limited explanatory discussion for didactic purposes, be equated with specific observed behavioral acts. The drives direct and govern behavior; they themselves are not the actual behavior. Note the discussion, later in this chapter, on goal-directed behavior.

and eventually will cease to exist as a living entity. Writing about this principle Horrocks and Jackson (1972) note: "The very life of the organism as an entity depends upon the maintenance of the reciprocal relationship of its components. Organization itself depends upon two factors. One is cohesion and the other is reciprocity." *Organization-cohesion* may be postulated as a life drive resulting not only in directionality to maintain biological intactness and functional reciprocity but, equally, directionality to maintain wholeness and reciprocity in the psychological realm. Specifically, any psychological process will be initiated and will proceed under the governance of maintenance of organization, and its directionality will be defined and limited by the fundamental drive for such maintenance. As an example, one may find a crucial application of the organizational principle in the internal cognitive processes involving meaning.

A fifth drive, an attribute not of all living organisms but only of those that have evolved into highly complex cognizing organisms, is synthesis-integration. *Synthesis-integration* involves only the cognitive aspects of behavior and has been defined by Horrocks and Jackson (1972) as "a drive to utilize retained cognitive products and to create new meaning relationships." They interpret it as "a drive to find meaning and to experience closure when the human organism is confronted by the inputs from interior and exterior sources with which he is continually bombarded." Specifically, when a stimulus is introduced into an individual's attentional field, the drive for synthesis-integration leads to an immediate attempt to deal with it. Initially this requires that it be related to previous experience so that it becomes meaningful to the perceiving person. Once in the attentional field the stimulus events cannot be ignored. The result of the attribution of meaning may be recognition leading to ignoring behavior, or it may set in motion a whole sequence of cognitive processings. For example, an adolescent sitting in his room sees something entering his doorway, and the inevitable series of process questions, usually not consciously enunciated, begins. What is it—man, animal, or other? Familiar or not? Threatening or nonthreatening? Requiring action or not? And so on. Curiosity and the need to find meaning in the environment are inherent in man. They find scope in behavior ranging from simple object recognition to the curiosity exhibited by such scientists as Einstein when confronted by the presumed existence of space. The operation of the synthesis-integration drive in any given person is limited by the intactness and relative excellence of his neurological system and is, of course, conditioned by affective states.

The Interaction of Drives

Drives do not exist in isolation without affecting each other. Their relationship is a dynamic one of interaction and reciprocity. The drives may be viewed as the components of a total life-force drive. For example, the equilibrium drive leads to a state of balance and stasis, which, once attained, encounters the motility drive of unrest imparting directionality toward disequilibrium. Disequilibrium attained leads to new directionality toward balance. The situation is one of disequilibrium $\longrightarrow$ balance $\longrightarrow$ disequilibrium $\longrightarrow$ balance. Here the relationship is antagonistic, setting the stage for conflict and possible stress. However, the drive interrelationship is not always antagonistic. It is through the process of completion that an organism attains equilibrium. Still another example of relationship is cited by Horrocks and Jackson (1972): "A conditional factor on the operation of the synthesis-integration drive is the functional demand of the equilibrium drive that synthesis will eventuate in a state of accord with the self concepts an individual has developed to that point as well as with his world concepts."

Organ Tension States

Coexisting with the basic drives is a set of impulses to behavior based upon the functioning of certain organs and related endocrine systems having a special task in the body's functional economy. Horrocks and Jackson (1972) describe these impulsions to behavior as "simple physiological tension states characterized by sensations accompanying localized muscular activity and strain. As with all tension states they place the organism in a condition marked by uneasiness and unrest and by pressure and readiness to act." Some of the tension states have to do with hunger, temperature regulation, thirst, sexual release, sleep and elimination.[3] The tension state is simply a readiness to act and a state of directionality for the action. Organ tensions, as is also the case with drives, should not be thought of as behavior. They are only directional tendencies, based on the structure of the organ, leading to behavior.

Needs and Behavior

At birth an individual possesses the endowment of a genetic program, already in progress, to provide biological direction, limits, and guidance to his growth and development as a member of his species. In addition, as has been explained, he is characterized by the action of five basic drives and by a set of functional organs developed *in utero* in response to his genetic program. With these and upon his interactions with his environment he must evolve what he is to be as a person over the entire span of his life. Developmentally his first task is to begin evolving concepts of self and to acquire and elaborate through the processes of socialization a hierarchy of psychological needs. Thus at birth the individual possesses neither psychological needs nor concepts of self. Essentially he is a dynamic action mechanism ready to learn and build.

[3]The organ tension states have sometimes been referred to as physiological or biogenic needs, but the term *organ tension* is more descriptive of the biological situation involved. Organ tension states may lead to socialized elaborations that eventuate in needs and associated goal objectives. This is especially true in the cases of hunger and sex.

As a preliminary it may be assumed that every manifestation of behavior observed, other than initial random movement and structural-physiological activity, is need- and goal-directed or is at least symptomatic of the individual's striving toward a goal. The motivating need may or may not be known and accepted by the individual, but this factor is unimportant. The importance rests in the needs existence and in the individual's endeavors to attain it.

The Psychological Needs

Psychological needs are learned after birth as socialized elaborations of the basic drives and organ tensions. Thus, an adolescent acquires over his life a set of psychological needs evolved as the result of socialized elaborations of the basic drives and organ tensions. These need-producing elaborations grow out of exposures to learning experiences, many of which have occurred in a socialized context. The needs are in turn elaborated and socialized as behavior is organized and given directionality by their existence. By the time an individual has reached adolescence, the behaviors implementing the evolved psychological needs have been so ramified and socialized that the biological origins of the behaviors have become obscure, even though the directionality and limitations of the basic drives still condition every behavior act. All during adolescence, as well as during the years of adulthood, the psychological needs will continue to act as motivators. However, the intensity of the motivations engendered by the various primary goals will not be of equal strength. Each individual over the course of his development will organize for himself through learning and experience a hierarchy of needs ranging from needs of little motivating power to those that are so overriding that an individual could be said to structure his life around their attainment.

Figure 7 presents the molar behavioral situation in useful but somewhat oversimplified

Figure 7   *Sequence of Behavioral Events*

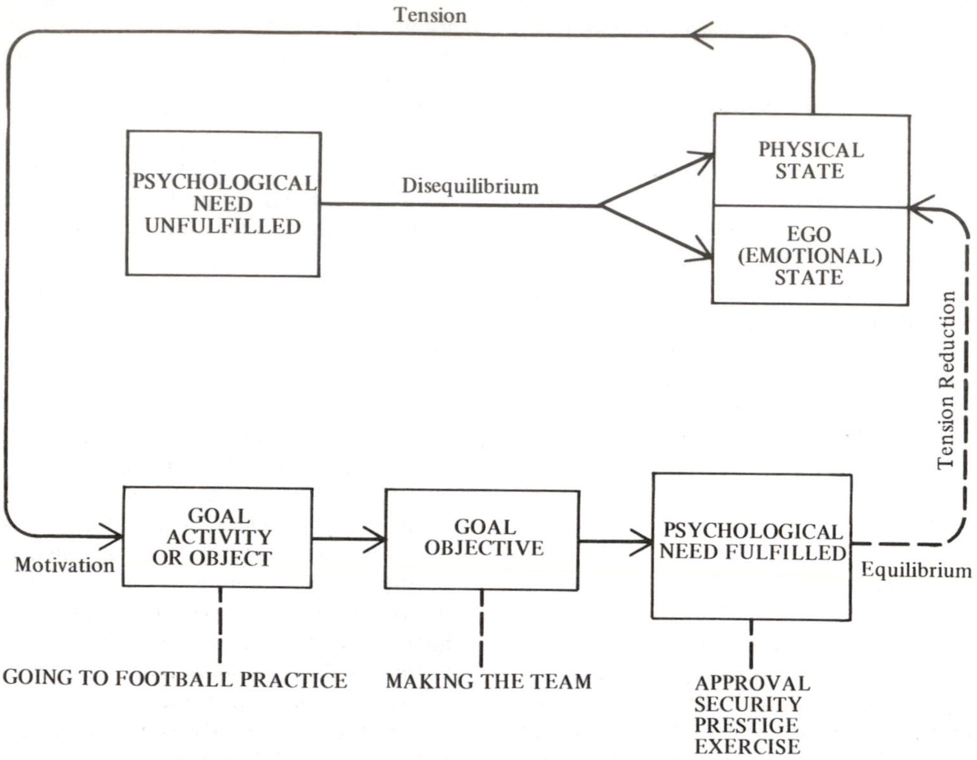

form, in which the psychological need is seen as the center of behavior, a center that could trigger a whole series of events. Nature appears to specialize in states of balance, which ideally lead to an individual's arrival at a state of equilibrium in which all goals are fulfilled. This is, of course, a hypothetical state, and if it were ever fully attained, there would be nothing to do but follow the example of the well-fed, comfortable newborn baby and go to sleep. However, it never is quite attained, and an individual is impelled to seek equilibrium amidst the disequilibrium that is his usual state. Therefore, when one or more of his needs is unfulfilled, a person exists in a state of tension, the degree of such tension being directly in proportion to the importance he attaches to the need in terms of emotional, physical, or habit state. Motivation arising out of unresolved tension and previous learning

impels the individual to action in attaining his goals and satisfying his needs, or what he perceives them to be. When goals are attained and needs satisfied, tension is reduced and a state of equilibrium exists, leading to a cessation of activity until a state of disequilibrium again exists. Lewin (1935) writes:

Needs are closely related to valences. What valences a certain object or activity has depends partly upon the nature of that activity (G), and partly upon the state of the needs of the person at that time. An increase in the intensity of a need (e.g. need for approval) leads to an increase of the positive valence for such activities (such as wearing the right clothing, having the proper attitudes) and to an increase in the negative valence of certain other activities (such as avoiding certain people). Any statement about a change of needs can be expressed by a statement about certain positive and negative valences.

Psychological goals and the behavior that results from them have two major characteristics, direction-tendency and tension reduction. Thus, every act of behavior is conceived of as providing a tension directed to the achievement of a goal, the successful attainment of which results in need reduction (see Figure 7). A definitive categorization of all the psychological goals that may be hypothesized to underlie human motivation has yet to be made, but it is probable that any classification system will contain a considerable number of general "major" and "minor" needs. Of course, for any given individual, as was pointed out previously, the relative strength of the various needs may deviate from any normative picture characteristic of most individuals in a given culture.

It is important to distinguish between needs, goal objectives, and goal objects or activities. As Figure 7 indicates, even as a goal activity or object is based upon a goal objective, so the goal objective is in turn based upon a need or a set of needs. A need itself may be based upon a need higher in the motivational hierarchy or even upon a series of such needs.

Behavior, in a molar sense, is a function of individual psychological needs and situations appropriate for their expression. Whether, in the etiology of any behavioral event, the situational demand or the individual need assumes priority is a moot question. Behavior represents reciprocity between the two, and neither may be ignored in the analysis of behavioral acts. For the individual, the situation must be interpreted in terms of his own needs, which are in turn modified and conditioned by the situation.

Individual adjustment may be hypothesized to represent a status of equilibrium-disequilibrium between the exigencies of personal needs and situational demands. Good adjustment represents the interaction of a well-integrated constellation of individual needs and a series of situations appropriate to the expression of those needs. An individual's entire life represents a series of attempts to reach equilibrium by goal attainment. An unattained need represents disequilibrium. When a need is not satisfied and its related goals are unattained, there must be a continuing effort to attain at the goal level. An individual who refrains, consciously or unconsciously, from making some effort to seek equilibrium is displaying maladjustive behavior that may well have serious emotional and social implications. Adjustment in the sense used here is relative, since at no point in his life will any person be likely to find simultaneous satisfaction of all of his psychological needs.

Therefore it becomes clear that any person possesses a multiplicity of needs and that these needs are of various degrees of importance to any individual. As Murray (1938) notes: "No therapist, or indeed anyone, can get along without some notion of motivational force (instinct, need, drive, impulse, urge, inclination, desire, or what not)." Needs are interrelated, exist in hierarchies, and differ both in the degree to which they compel satisfaction and in their manner of implementing one another. The extent to which needs may be instrumental to other needs depends upon the role of learning. As the individual grows up, various stimuli take on meaning and become activators of behavioral sequences leading to the attainment of goals, as various learning theorists including Tolman (1948), Skinner (1953), and Hull (1951) indicate.

Causal Factors in Behavior

Each morning in homes all over the world, as people read their morning newspapers, they ask, "Why did he do it? What made him behave the way he did?" Often they make a layman's guess and find an ostensible reason that may or may not contain the seeds of truth. This is nothing new. Those who have been concerned with the behavior of others have attributed to them all kinds of explanatory motivations and conditions. Psychologists are no exception, although their attributions are more likely to be based upon research or clinical judgment, or upon hypotheses founded on the available knowledge that the science of psychology has amassed about man's behavior.

For a long time psychologists and others have been trying to isolate the causes of behavior, to order them in some hierarchical fashion, to trace them back to their ontogenetic and phylogenetic origins, and to arrive at definitive basic, or fundamental, causes. Various lists have been compiled, and there is usually an attempt to posit a single primary cause or perhaps a small group of causes. Adler (1927) hypothesized the primacy of power or some form of mastery growing out of the infant's original position as an inferior, powerless person dominated by older and biologically more powerful persons. Freud (1933, 1935) discussed the primacy of the libido and its several extensions, and spoke of primitive physical needs occurring as tensions in the tissues of the organ systems. He saw needs as the reduction of these tensions. McDougall (1908) proposed twelve basic "instincts" and posited behavior as purposive goal-striving. Allport (1955) substituted six "prepotent reflexes" for McDougall's instincts. Buytendijk (1958) speaks of the importance of the desire for security, Frankl (1959) of the quest for meaning, Krakovskii (1962) of the concern for self-assertion, and Buhler (1958) of the patterns of mastery-adaptation and of activity-passivity.

Lewin (1935) stressed the influence of needs on life space and views them as organizing behavior. He believed that the attainment of a desired or a substitute goal represented need satisfaction, with behavior in any given situation resulting from a combination of needs. Murphy (1947) hypothesized that the elements of personality consist of needs or tensions. Tension-reduction is an individual's first need, and an individual may be characterized by the manner in which he reduces his tensions. Sullivan (1953) also saw the organism as a tension system ranging from absolute relaxation to absolute terror. Unsatisfied organic needs, such as hunger, give rise to tensions. Anxiety, the primary motivator and

educator of the organism, evolves through the manner in which other persons meet the individual's needs.

Goldstein (1940) proposed three dynamic concepts: (1) equalization, (2) self-actualization, and (3) coming to terms with the environment. Equalization is the average state of tension of the organism, and the process of equalization is the return to the average state when it has been disturbed. The organism's goal is equalization, rather than discharge of tension. Self-actualization represents the creative trend of human nature and is the master motive. Coming to terms with the environment is the average organism-environment interaction resulting in the individual's self-maintenance. The outer world with which the individual must cope is both a source of disturbance and the means by which he fulfills his destiny. As Goldstein saw it, the self-actualization tendency comes from within and is the means by which the individual comes to terms with the environment and endeavors to master it. When the realities of the environment are such that the individual's goals cannot be effected, the individual breaks down or reassesses and has to abandon or revise his goals and actualize on a lower level.

Self-actualization is also important in Maslow's (1954) theory of the bases of behavior. Maslow views self-actualization as man's search for self-fulfillment. In self-actualization the individual becomes what he is potentially. The need for self-actualization sets man upon the task of becoming everything he is capable of becoming. Maslow writes:

Even if all . . . needs are satisfied, we may still often (if not always) expect that a new discontent and restlessness will soon develop, unless the individual is doing what he is fitted for. A musician must make music, an artist must paint, a poet must write if he is to be ultimately at peace with himself. What a man *can* be, he *must* be.

Thus both Maslow and Goldstein hypothesize an inner self-actualizing tendency. One must do more than survive; one must be creative in coping with and mastering the environment. For Maslow, gratification is as important as deprivation, since through gratification the individual frees himself of the press of the purely physiological needs and can explore the more social goals.

One important misconception about the well-adjusted person is that he is self-satisfied, no longer strives, and tends to be neither creative nor productive. People who hold this misconception also hold that it is good to be neurotic, since only the neurotic or the anxious accomplish things and that we can therefore expect creative effort only from neurotic striving. This fallacy stems from the viewpoint that motivation is essentially deprivation, that is, that a lack of something is the only source of motivation. When needs are satisfied, when empty places are filled, nothing new remains to be done. This denies motive as a positive striving toward something and does not take into account the motility drive and the related equilibrium-disequilibrium phasing. It is also counter to Maslow's need to know and to be more and more aware and to Rogers's (1951) position of striving for greater and greater growth (improvement). Neurotic anxiety in an adolescent, or in anyone else, interferes with real progress instead of being primarily responsible for its appearance.

A comprehensive and widely accepted listing of needs has been proposed by Murray (1938) as an aspect of his analysis of the bases of personality. According to Murray, a need is an inner force to action, but he is careful to emphasize that it is also "a hypothetical process the occurrence of which is imagined in order to account for certain objective and subjective facts." He divides needs into primary (viscerogenic) and secondary (psychogenic), but only the psychogenic need formulations are relevant to the theoretical position outlined in this chapter.[4]

[4]Murray's viscerogenic needs have to do with physical satisfaction and the maintenance of life. They include "needs" for air, water, food, sex, lactation, urination, defecation, harm-avoidance, noxavoidance, sentience, and passivity. The reader will recognize these not as "needs" in the sense discussed in this chapter but as organ tensions previously discussed. Others, such as passivity, seem more closely related to a drive such as equilibrium.

The secondary needs, Murray observes, have no "subjectively localizable bodily origins" and result mainly from tensions caused by various external conditions or by images that represent such conditions. They may be said to concern emotional satisfactions and are dependent upon and derived from the primary needs (that is, more properly, from physiological and drive-action sources). The first five secondary needs have to do mainly with actions associated with inanimate objects:

1. *Acquisition* To acquire possessions and property by any available means.
2. *Conservance* To preserve, collect, clean, and protect against damage.
3. *Order* To be precise, neat, and to organize possessions.
4. *Retention* To hoard and hang on to possessions. Frugality and miserliness.
5. *Construction* To build and put things together.

The next four needs involve ambition, the quest for prestige, will-to-power, and the desire for accomplishment.

6. *Superiority* To be ambitious. The superiority need is actually composed of needs 7 and 8.
7. *Achievement* To accomplish the difficult, exercise power, and overcome obstacles.
8. *Recognition* To be respected, praised, and singled out for distinction. To boast.
9. *Exhibition* Dramatization of self and attraction of attention.

The next four needs are complementary to needs 7 and 8 and involve preservation of status and avoidance of humiliation:

10. *Inviolacy* Sensitivity and pride leading to protection of the self. Inviolacy includes needs 11, 12, and 13.
11. *Infavoidance* To avoid exceeding one's power and to avoid any denigration of the self by others.
12. *Defendance* To justify oneself.
13. *Counteraction* To retaliate, overcome defeat, and to assume the hardest tasks.

The next five involve human power resisted or exerted:

14. *Dominance* To lead, direct, restrain, control others singly and in groups.
15. *Deference* To cooperate and to follow willingly.
16. *Similance* To identify and empathize with others.
17. *Autonomy* To gain emancipation and resist being influenced. To defy.
18. *Contrarience* To be different and unique. To oppose others.

The four needs having to do with interpersonal relations are:

19. *Affiliation* To join, form friendships, and to love.
20. *Rejection* To remain aloof, snub, and to discriminate.
21. *Nurturance* To help, sympathize, and protect the helpless.
22. *Succorance* To plead, seek aid and protection, and be dependent.

And finally, various miscellaneous needs include:

23. *Aggression* To punish, injure, blame, accuse, ridicule.
24. *Abasement* Self-depreciation. To surrender, apologize, and confess.
25. *Blamavoidance* To behave well, obey the law, and avoid criticism or ostracism.
26. *Play* To avoid tension through relaxation and entertainment.
27. *Cognizance* To inquire, explore, and seek knowledge.
28. *Exposition* To explain and give information.

In discussing his listing of needs, Murray divides them into those that involve approach behavior (positive) and those that involve separation behavior (negative). He further divides positive needs into adient needs, which involve approaching a liked object, and contradient needs, involving approach to a disliked object with the purpose of mastering or destroying it. Negative needs are also defined as abient needs. Murray also classifies his needs as overt or covert, focal (fixated) or diffuse (generalizable), and proactive (internally determined) or reactive.

Following the appearance of the Murray list of needs, various attempts were made by other investigators to measure them and perform research relating to them. Barron (1959) writes: "This or that 'need' has also been taken into camp by individual investigators, so that scales bearing such names as 'deference,' 'dominance,' 'abasement,' 'orderliness,' and 'achievement' have appeared in inventory type tests both of the factor-analytically based sort and the empirically based kind." Of these last, the Edwards Personal Preference Schedule has received particularly wide use, although there have been some questions about its validity.[5]

Problems in Causal Classifications

Essentially, most of the classifications and theories of needs discussed in the previous section go back to a physical-physiological base, as indeed they must in the long run. But most theorists move out from the physical base into all kinds of derived needs, motives, and impulsions, usually explaining the derivation as evolving from the process of socialization or some other learning model. One mistake is to endeavor to use one construct, such as needs, to explain both derived and basic physiological processes and thus to assume that the processes involved at two different ends of a developmental continuum are identical. Such an assumption makes no real operational distinction between antecedents and consequents. For example, Maslow (1954) notes that the most prepotent of all needs are the physiological needs, but then writes that when these are satisfied "other (and higher) needs emerge and these rather than the physiological needs dominate the organism." Murray, in particular, who

[5]The EPPS provides scores for achievement, deference, order, exhibition, autonomy, affiliation, intraception, succorance, dominance, abasement, nurturance, change, endurance, heterosexuality, and aggression.

wished to separate his psychogenic needs from any "subjectively localizable bodily origins" complicated his theoretical position by using the needs terminology *(viscerogenic needs)* for the very thing he wished to separate from needs. Both men would have been on sounder ground if they had endeavored to handle the internal organ processes and tensions with a construct other than the one they used for their nonphysiological needs. Neither seemed to conceive of the possibility of background-governing forces such as the directional action discussed earlier in this chapter under the name of basic drives. As a matter of fact, deterred by the initial metaphysical status of the hypotheses about such forces, the majority of psychological theorists tend to avoid discussion of fundamental directional and limiting forces that regulate the formation and action even of motivators that are as presumably basic as needs.[6]

Of course those who are not developmentally oriented tend to avoid discussion of physical-physiological origins and of fundamental laws-of-life processes, saying that it may be intellectually interesting but in practical terms is essentially useless and a waste of time. Such persons often enunciate a very general concept, arrived at by assumption or fiat, and claim that as their base. This is not to say that physical-base theorists do not also operate by fiat and assumption, but at least they are closer to the organism as a functioning entity (biological), for whatever that is worth.

[6]Some theorists have avoided using a needs concept as such. Hull (1951) substitutes the concept of drive level for needs, giving it the operational definition of number of hours of deprivation, usually of food or water. Skinner (1953) avoids needs by speaking in terms of stimulus and reinforcement control of behavior, reinforcement being anything that increases the probability of a behavior. Kelly (1955) ignores needs and drives by assuming that motion is the natural state of the living organism and he therefore requires no concept of pushing and pulling forces. Kelly is interested in how persons construe their surroundings and the events they encounter. Tolman (1932) also believed that learning arises out of natural activities and uses the concept of exploratory drive. We could, of course, say that Tolman has posited an exploratory need, but he did not handle exploration as a need, saying merely that in the absence of other known drives the animal will tend to explore.

One problem faced by those who read theoretical discussions of the origins of behavior is the difference in concepts and terminology used by different writers. While most are talking about essentially the same processes, their descriptive terminology may disagree, and two different theorists may assign different meanings to the same term. Some writers have used the terms *needs* and *drives* interchangeably, and others have disagreed as to whether or not one could properly use the term *physiological need.* Some have used the term *drive* for the same construct that others term *motivation,* and others equate goals and needs. Disturbed by this, Cattell (1957) coins the term *erg* and writes:

Up to this point we have used indifferently such terms as drive, need, propensity . . . but all of these terms come encumbered with theoretical and popular connotations for which there is no adequate research evidence. Accordingly the term erg has been specialized to mean precisely a pattern found among dynamic manifestations by factor analysis and hypothesized to be an innately determined goal-directed entity.

It is true that wherever they enter the causal and sequential chain of the origins of behavior, all theorists have the same problem. They all start with an assumption or a hypothesis that is largely metaphysical in nature, and the structure they rear thereafter is no better than the metaphysical assumption with which they started. As psychology has moved away from philosophy and as it has tried to assume its place as a science, there is a desire to analyze what is being done and to identify where postulates are metaphysical and where they are not. When a metaphysical base is discovered, psychologists have one of two obligations as scientists: first, to abandon the hypothesis as scientifically inadmissible; or second, to try to make it admissible by removing it from the metaphysical realm. The second possibility can best be approached by reanalyzing the hypothesis in such a manner that it is susceptible to refutation or even to verification, although the former is all that is needed

Figure 8   *Goal-directed Behavior. I. The approach*

$$\longrightarrow \qquad \text{G}$$

to remove it from the metaphysical realm. This involves first the problem of reanalysis and then the problem of measurement that can be expressed as nearly as possible in quantitative terms.[7]

The Position Taken in This Textbook

The position taken in this textbook is that there are basic or governing process forces called drives and that these give directionality and set limits to all behavior at all levels, both molar and molecular. As part of the internal functioning of the body there are specialized organs whose functional tasks create tensions leading to reduction activity. Upon the foundation of these drives and upon the organ tensions and their propensity for action is built all of the psychological behavior of the developing individual. As socialized elaborations of the drives and of the organ tensions' reduction propensities, there gradually emerges, through contact with the environment and solely as the result of postnatal learning, an undetermined number of directional tendencies to behavior that can be called psychological needs. Inevitably some of these become prepotent over others, and operationally they will interact with each other. Accordingly, the needs assume over time a relatively stable

hierarchic order that is at least to some extent idiosyncratic to each individual. The needs themselves become socialized and elaborated and are implemented, consciously or unconsciously, by the assumption of goal objectives achieved by means of goal activities and the attainment of goal objects. At birth every individual is faced with the double developmental task of evolving a set of needs and a set of appropriate concepts of self. Thus it is viewed as incorrect to think of needs as existing before socialization. Certain behaviors and behavior propensities exist, but not psychological needs.

Goal-directed Behavior

Drives and organ tension directionality become elaborated in various forms of socialized and environmentally based behavior as the result of the conditioning of an external stimulus to operate in place of an internal one. When confronted by an external stimulus, the individual develops with experience habitual modes of response or mechanisms of behavior that enable the external stimulus to set off a series of goal-directed activities.

Goal-directed behavior may be schematized as indicated in Figure 8, where G represents the goal and the arrow symbolizes the individual's motivation and directionality in his efforts to attain the goal. The speed, intensity, and persistence of the approach to the goal may be taken to represent the strength of the motivation. The greater the value an individual places upon the attainment of a given goal, the greater will be the strength and persistence of the behavioral reactions by means of which he approaches the goal.

During adolescence, peer approval and emancipation from adult authority and controls are goals important to children. Conse-

---

[7]Psychologists should not be afraid of making initial hypothetical or even metaphysical statements simply because they are not immediately subject to proof or to disproof, although obviously one cannot build a science of psychology wholly on unproven speculations treated as proven. However, if speculative statements are never made, they can never be subject to proof or to disproof, and certainly no one will be involved in seeking methodology that will make the speculations subject to disproof. The history of psychology is a record of increasingly sophisticated methodology. Things routinely measured today were inaccessible to measurement only yesterday. Science thrives on speculation—to avoid it is to make science a static enterprise. The problem for the student of psychology is simply to try to be aware of the present proof-disproof status of the statements he encounters.

quently the motivation of most adolescents is such that a great deal of their behavior is directed toward attainment of these goals. An observer watching an adolescent's behavioral reaction is continually surprised at the persistance and scope of activity he appears willing to exert to attain his ends of peer acceptance and personal emancipation.

A difficulty in interpreting this phase of behavior lies in the possible confusion between an individual's psychological needs—love, security, power, approval, prestige—and the objects, activities, and attainments that represent these needs to him. A psychological need is not a concrete entity that can be directly attained. It is, instead, a cognitive-affective motivational state that can only be satisfied symbolically by something such as a job, a promotion, or a graduation that has come to represent the need. In the terminology of goal behavior, such a symbol is called a *goal objective*. However, a goal objective is not usually attained immediately but only through participation in a series of goal activities and through the attainment of goal objects. Thus progress toward attaining a goal objective and ultimately of obtaining need satisfaction and its attendant tension reduction usually necessitates initial participation in lesser goal activities and the attainment of various goal objects. An adolescent whose objective is to make the school basketball team will, among other things, have to watch his diet and attend many practice sessions (goal activities), and secure proper gym clothing (goal object). Sustained need satisfaction may necessitate attaining a continuing series of goal objectives and goal objects. As a matter of fact, attain-

ment of one object goal represents progress toward a goal objective, as well as toward psychological need satisfaction, and hence results in greater motivation in attaining a related series of object goals. Successful goal-directed behavior tends toward ramification as well as cumulation.

Figure 9 depicts the goal object–goal objective–need relationship. Frequently the goal objective may represent a combination of several needs. Figure 9 indicates a goal objective based upon three needs. For an adolescent boy, the goal activity might represent meeting a girl, and the goal objective, having a date with her. Need 1 might represent sex satisfaction, Need 2 might represent seeking peer approval, and Need 3 might represent a prestige motive if the girl is popular and in great demand. Various other needs higher or lower in the boy's need hierarchy might also be postulated for this dating situation, and some might be more directly related to their drive and physiological origins than others. For example, behind sex satisfaction might be organ tensions, and behind prestige might lie various security needs. Any higher-order behavioral act is complex indeed, and its antecedents may constitute several interrelated series of motives and drives of different primary levels. The diagnosis of behavior often involves looking behind the object goal for the more basic primary goals it represents. Reeducation or remediation often consists in helping an individual find new object goals that will enable him to attain his primary goals.

In the course of events, however, it becomes impossible to attain every goal. When progress toward a goal is slowed, impeded, or made

Figure 9 *Goal-directed Behavior. II. Goal Objects, Goal Objectives, and Needs*

Figure 10 *Goal-directed Behavior. III. Frustration*

impossible, the goal path is said to be blocked and goal attainment interrupted. As a result, depending upon his past experiences and the strength of motivation involved, the individual becomes thwarted or frustrated to some degree. This may be diagrammatically represented as in Figure 10.

The origin of a block may be environmental, or it may occur within the individual. For an adolescent, environmental blocks may include lack of money to do something he wishes, forbidding of some desired act by parents or teachers, an obstacle of time or of distance, or the disapproval of the peer group. Blocks that originate within the individual may be caused by a personal defect, imagined or real, that prevents the adolescent from attempting or attaining his preferred goals. Such blocks, for the adolescent, include the lack of the physical condition or coordination necessary to participate effectively in games, a physical anomaly such as poor hearing or lameness, lack of physical attractiveness to members of the opposite sex, and awkwardness. If such a state of affairs continues, an individual's experience with previous blockings may cause him to develop personality difficulties, including pronounced insecurity or inferiority feelings, which often prevent him from attempting to attain his goals.

For the adolescent, there are two other sources of thwarting or blocking. One lies in his immaturity and lack of experience, which make him unable to cope adequately or effectively with his environment. The other is the problem of opposing values or conflicting motives. This last may take either of two directions. Often in life an individual is confronted with an object he desires, but which is closely associated with another object he dislikes. Therefore, attainment of the desired object means attainment of the undesired one too. For example, an adolescent boy who wishes to play football well also must accept hard knocks, possibly injury, and the necessity of training or keeping in condition. Or a younger adolescent who wishes to take a girl to the movies must face the catcalls and jeering of his peer group. The second direction conflicting motives may take presents the individual with two highly desired but mutually exclusive goals. For example, an adolescent girl is asked to go to a dance by two boys she likes, or an adolescent boy in the spring wants to go out for either track or baseball. This introduces a new element, since both goals are acceptable; the conflict lies in deciding which to accept. If the goals possess equal valence, the individual is indeed hard put to make a selection or, having made it, to be entirely satisfied with it. Fortunately, other associated elements are taken into consideration, and the choice is made easier. For instance, in the case of the girl who must decide which boy will accompany her to the dance, one of the boys may have more money to spend, may live nearer, or know more people. However, there is no assurance that a choice once made will be permanent or that the individual may not regret his choice. As a matter of fact, there is evidence that a goal when attained often seems less desirable than a previously competing goal that, at the time of competition, seemed to have a decidedly lesser valence. Or the individual may find that the goal object does not fit the need he is experiencing as well as he thought it would. In such a case there will be dissatisfaction with the goal and a consequent lessening of the motivational force that impels behavior designed to reattain or to keep the goal object. Some goal-directed behavior, particularly among children learning to cope with their environment, is purely exploratory and serves an information-seeking purpose. There is also the often perverse human attribute of feeling that unattained fields are greener than those attained. An attained goal tends to be less challenging than an unattained one, particularly in the exploratory phases of development.

On the other hand, an attained goal object, activity, or objective may be so reinforcing that the individual is strongly motivated to keep attaining it, particularly when the goal behavior really supplies an important need. In this case a circular action is instituted in which the satisfactions derived from the goal activities lead to even greater motivation to keep them in process. In this case the goal (usually a specific goal object or goal activity) is sought for intrinsic reasons and may even attain the status of a psychological need. Figure 11 depicts such a circular action.

For example, an adolescent who makes a team, originally for prestige reasons, may find such intrinsic satisfaction from the team activity *for its own sake* that he is even more motivated to make—or to stay on—the team. In diagnosing behavior it is well to remember that some goal objects for the individual in question are really psychological needs and must be handled as such.

Blocking and opposed choice are, of course, common in all aspects of life; they are not confined to the adolescent. The adolescent differs from the adult in the nature of the events in his environment that constitute blocks. There will be considerable overlap with adults, but some elements will be present that are characteristically adolescent. This is partly a question of values, and it goes back to those things an adolescent, as compared to an adult, considers important and essential in life. Put in more sociological terms, in describing a cultural category of persons as adolescents, an attempt must be made to distinguish between those acts that are characteristic of the category *adolescent* and those characteristic of the various other cultural categories of which the adolescent may be simultaneously a member.

Perhaps one approach to this could be in terms of how the adolescent colors and conditions his role as well as his perception of his role in nonadolescent cultural categories of which he is a member. This approach could act in reverse as well—the manner in which his role in his nonadolescent categories influences his role in his adolescent category. In one case, as maleness, it would simply be an activity and interest determiner. As a wage earner, it might lead to the rejection of the adolescent role. The whole problem of emancipation is one of the gradual ascendance of nonadolescent roles over the adolescent role, or at least a new and often dissatisfied perception of the adolescent category.

As previously stated, an individual who is blocked in the attainment of a goal suffers frustration. Dollard et al. (1939) have defined frustration as the condition that exists when a goal response suffers interference. Whatever its definition, the important thing is the result—being frustrated. Normally, that result

Figure 11 *Goal-directed Behavior. IV. Circular Motivation*

GOAL SATISFACTION

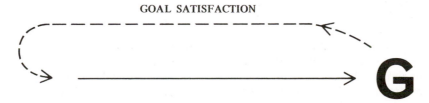

Figure 12   *Goal-directed Behavior. V. Alternate Solution*

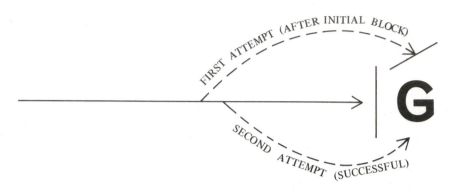

leads to increased activity; in a normal person, activity of some kind will follow thwarting. It is therefore possible to diagnose frustration by observing certain symptoms in an individual's activity. When an individual is frustrated by blocking of his goal, several things may happen, most of them pretty much dependent upon the individual's past experiences and the habits he has acquired. First, he may attempt to overcome the barrier to the goal directly, and thus abolish or surmount it. Second, if that proves unsuccessful, he may try to circumvent the block and attain the goal by other means. However, the means he selects may in turn be blocked and the individual may have to attain his goal by a still different method. This procedure is diagrammed in Figure 12.

Unfortunately for a subject's psychological well-being, every substitute means of attaining a given goal may be blocked in turn, and it may become apparent to him that success is impossible. When this occurs, the reaction to be expected will vary from individual to individual, depending upon what kind of person he is, what experiences he has had in the past, and what kind of behavior patterns have become part of his whole personality organization. We may be certain that something will happen, because blocking leading to frustration will inevitably elicit some kind of response as the individual seeks to reestablish the psychological equilibrium and sense of well-being, which have been impaired. The violence, per-

sistence, and force of what is done will depend directly upon the strength of the drive or motivation that impels the individual to seek fulfillment of his goal. In other words, in dealing with a thwarted individual whose access to a given goal has been blocked, one must recognize the valence of the goal—one must determine what the goal means to him and how greatly he is impelled or motivated to attain it.

The thwarted individual may follow several separate courses, or a combination of courses. First, he may attempt to replace the original goal with some substitute and related goal as depicted in Figure 13. When that happens, the entire process starts again: the goal is either attained or blocked, with the subsequent behavior reactions characteristic of the individual. At this point in understanding and diagnosing a given behavioral reaction, it is important to distinguish between a goal object or activity and the more fundamental goal objectives and psychological needs toward which they lead. Since blockings ordinarily tend to occur in relation to object goals that represent more important or basic underlying goal objectives and psychological needs, those which occur in an object goal are not generally of first importance, as long as the individual adopts a substitute goal object in order to attain the important goal objective or satisfy the psychological need involved. For example, a high school adolescent has acceptance and approval as his psychological needs. His sub-

Figure 13   *Goal-directed Behavior. VI. Substitution*

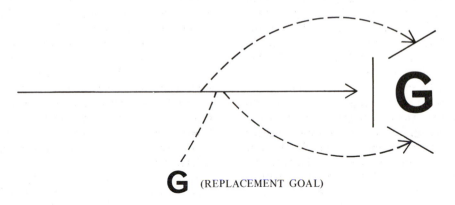

G   (REPLACEMENT GOAL)

stitute goal becomes that of achieving fame on the football field. But in trying out for the team, he is found to be too light in weight. He may then try out for the baseball team during the winter and become an extremely valuable player for his school.

The best diagnostic approach is always to ask: "What is the subject getting out of this particular piece of behavior?" Nothing happens without definite and specific causes, and the heart of psychological diagnosis rests in identifying these causes. One difficulty is that the subject may be genuinely unaware of the existence of the causes; he may not recognize or even be willing to accept the existence of the primary goals that motivate his behavior. As a matter of fact, it usually is much easier for the trained observer to identify and catalogue an individual's psychological needs than it is for the individual himself to do so.

From the viewpoint of human behavior, then, an individual selects his goals either consciously or unconsciously, and the strength and persistence of his efforts to attain them is an index of their importance to him. If, due to internal or external reasons, his goals are blocked, the individual either becomes frustrated and tries to attain them by other means, or he may seek substitute goals. In some cases he may show nonadaptive behavior by repeating over and over the activity that is failing to attain the goal for him. In any event, an

individual who is blocked is in a state of tension until such time as the attainment of the goal or the acceptance of a substitute goal leads to the reduction of tension. This period of tension is one of great activity and unrest.

An individual, adolescent or adult, who is frustrated because his goals are blocked will tend to display aggressive behavior, the amount and strength of the aggression being a direct function of the amount of frustration. Aggressive behavior is attack behavior in which an individual tries to do something to his environment in order to attain his goals or find release from his tensions. In this sense, aggressive behavior tends to be positive and is psychologically much more desirable than is withdrawal behavior.

However, aggressive behavior must be viewed in terms of its effects upon others as well as in terms of its effects on the individual displaying it. If the aggressive behavior promotes socially undesirable ends, then it is disapproved. Aggression in some individuals takes the socially approved form of ambition, hard work to prove a point, or a high competitive spirit. An individual whose aggression takes such a form may make many useful and significant contributions to society. In other persons aggression takes the socially disapproved forms of problem behavior, including delinquency, destruction, and antisocial attitudes. Aggression may be directed toward the object that blocks attainment of the goal or toward some unrelated object, or it may not be directed toward any specific object, but may instead take the form of a generalized reaction to the environment. Thus, an adolescent whose blocking agent is some parental act may display aggression against his parent or against his teacher when he gets to school, or he may just be aggressive to everything or everyone who gets in his way. Generally speaking, overt aggressive behavior is usually inhibited by fear of punishment or discomfort, and the greater the amount of anticipated punishment, the greater the inhibition of the aggressive behavior. However, if the aggressive reaction is strong enough, aggressive behavior will occur despite fear of punishment. An adolescent in school or at home may rebel and brave the displeasure of teachers or parents if frustration and the ensuing aggression become great enough to overcome the inhibition caused by fear of punishment.

Like all other behavior, aggression tends to be cumulative in its effects. An individual who has attained his ends by aggressive behavior or who has grown into the habit of such behavior will tend to repeat it. Success often leads to a repetition of the situation which led to success. Aggression also tends to have the effect of catharsis. An individual who is able to display aggression successfully feels less immediate need to act aggressively in other directions for the time being.

There are other varieties of aggressive response to frustration which are called *defense mechanisms*. These typically include *rationalization, identification, projection,* and *compensation. Compensation,* or the substitution of object goals, has already been discussed. *Rationalization* is the giving of socially approved or 'face-saving' reasons for one's behavior instead of the real reasons, which would place the individual in a poor light in his own eyes or in those of others. The individual sincerely believes his rationalizations are true. For example, an adolescent who is not doing well in geometry may rationalize by saying that ge-

ometry will be of no use to him in his future vocation and is consequently something he doesn't have to do well. The implication here is that he could do well if he wanted to. Parents, teachers, and youth workers should recognize the frequency of rationalization among adolescent youth. While rationalization may represent undesirable or immature behavior, it should also be remembered that there are times when it serves a useful purpose in helping an individual preserve his own security or in protecting him from accepting hopeless inferiority.

Identification is another mechanism that may preserve the individual's security or protect him from a feeling of inferiority. Here the individual identifies himself with other people, groups, activities, or ideals that will add to his prestige. For instance, an adolescent will feel that his school is the best school in town and his team the best team in the league, and he will bask in their reflected glory. In such cases the object identified with must be good or achieve distinction. If it fails to do so, the individual will cease to identify himself with it. For example, when an athletic team is winning, one often hears the statement, "We won last night." But when the team loses, the statement becomes "They lost last night," or "The team lost last night."

Projection is a mechanism by which an individual feels that others possess his faults or are operating with his motives. An adolescent who customarily acts dishonestly or who has selfish motives will tend to feel that others are acting in a similar manner or are actuated by the same motives. It has been said that a person who is sorely tempted is prone to feel that others are equally tempted. A common adolescent projection is that of criticizing another for being too critical.

Aggressive behavior is not the only type of behavior that follows thwarting; hand in hand with aggression goes *withdrawal.* When confronted by a block, a person may act aggressively, or he may withdraw and refuse to attempt to cope with or to overcome the block.

Psychologically, withdrawing behavior is much more serious than aggressive behavior. An individual who withdraws tends to admit defeat, and if continued blocking and frustration cause frequent withdrawing, a habit of withdrawal may be built up that will make it more difficult for him to face reality and find success in everyday life. Withdrawal behavior will frequently follow aggressive behavior that has failed. An adolescent who is placed in a series of situations where he has failed, where substitute goals have been denied him, and where aggression is either unsuccessful or inhibited because of the fear of punishment will tend to withdraw and seek his satisfactions elsewhere. Daydreaming is often an outcome of failure or lack of interest in one's present environment, and is certainly a retreat from reality.

Summary

Five basic drives govern human behavior, giving directionality and setting limits to all behavioral processes. The drives are motility, completion, equilibrium, organization-cohesion, and synthesis-integration. In addition, as part of the internal functioning of the body, there are specialized organs whose functional tasks create tensions leading to the inception of reduction activity. As socialized elaborations of the drives and of the organ tension reduction propensities, there gradually emerges a further set of directional tendencies to behavior known as psychological needs. The emergence of needs comes solely as a result of postnatal learning. An individual does not possess psychological needs before he is born.

A psychological need is a cognitive-affective motivational state that may only be satisfied indirectly through some object, activity, or objective that symbolizes the need. Sustained need satisfaction may necessitate attaining a continuing series of goal objectives and goal objects and activities, the goal objective involving more long-term planning and sequences of behavior than is true in the case of goal objects. Young children tend to confine their goal-seeking behavior to goal objects and activities, but as an individual proceeds through adolescence, he becomes increasingly capable of setting realistic and selective goal objectives for himself.

Need is the center and instigator of behavior. When a need is unfulfilled, the individual is in a state of disequilibrium and is driven to activity either to fulfill the need or find a substitute for it. When a need is fulfilled, the individual regains equilibrium, a state toward which normally functioning organisms strive. Needs assume over time a relatively stable hierarchic order idiosyncratic to each individual. Needs themselves become socialized and elaborated, and are implemented consciously or unconsciously by goal activities and the attainment of goal objects.

Various writers have postulated the primacy of a single need or a limited system of needs, but no definitive listing has evolved in the sense of having received universal acceptance. One of the more complete listings of needs was proposed by Murray, who categorized needs as secondary or primary and further divided them as approach-separate, positive-negative, and liked-disliked. Too often, statements of needs have little scientific support. It is the duty of scientists to endeavor to make statements susceptible to proof-disproof, although there is a place in science for speculation provided it is labeled as such and efforts are made to develop methodology capable of eventually submitting the speculations to proof-disproof.

In this chapter we have presented a discussion of the most typical varieties of adolescent motivation, together with a delineation of common adolescent goals. We have seen how tension and the need for activity are produced by the various ways in which these goals may be thwarted. The more common or usual ways of responding to frustration by aggression, defense, or withdrawing have been discussed.

It is from the elements of behavior outlined in this chapter that characteristic methods of responding or characteristic personality traits are formed. In the early stages of responding to frustration, individuals characteristically exhibit what has been called trial-and-error behavior. An individual may try to achieve his goal by various means. If his first attempts are thwarted, he may make several trials before he succeeds in reducing tension and achieving his goal. One of the fundamental characteristics of human behavior is that those mechanisms that have succeeded for the individual will tend to be repeated when further frustration is met. The building-

up and establishment of these reaction patterns form the individual's basic personality characteristics.

In view of the fact that no two individuals will be faced with identical frustrating situations, and in view of the infinite variety of possible reactions to frustration, it is easy to see why no two personalities are alike. Thus, many of the problems of adolescence may be interpreted against a background of knowledge of human behavior, and diagnoses may be made that will take into account the basic causes of the behavior under consideration.

References

Adler, A. *The practice and theory of individual psychology.* New York: Harcourt, Brace, 1927.

Allport, F. H. *Theories of perception and the concept of structure.* New York: Wiley, 1955.

Barron, F. Review of the Edwards Personal Preference Schedule. In Buros, O.K. *The fifth mental measurements yearbook,* pp. 114–118. Highland Park, N.J.: Gryphon Press, 1959.

Benimoff, M., and Horrocks, J. E. A developmental study of the relative needs satisfaction of youth: Equilibrium-disequilibrium. *Journal of Genetic Psychology* 99 (1961): 185–208.

Buhler, C. Earliest trends in goal setting. *Zeitshrift fur Kinderpsychiatrie* 25 (1958): 13–23.

Buytendijk, F. Unruhe und Geborgenheit in der Welt des jungen Menschen. *Universitas* 13 (1958): 721–730.

Cannon, W. B. *The wisdom of the body.* New York: Norton, 1932.

Cattell, R. B. *Personality and motivation structure and measurement.* Yonkers-on-Hudson: World, 1957.

Dollard, J.; Doob, L. W.; Miller, N. E.; Mowrer, O. H.; and Sears, R. R. *Frustration and Aggression.* New Haven: Yale University Press, 1939.

Frankl, V. E. *From death camp to existentialism.* Boston: Beacon Press, 1959.

Freud, S. *New introductory lectures on psychoanalysis.* New York: Carlton House, 1933.

Freud, S. *The ego and the id.* London: Hogarth Press, 1935.

Goldstein, K. *Human nature.* Cambridge: Harvard University Press, 1940.

Herrick, C. J. *The evolution of human nature.* Austin: University of Texas Press, 1956.

Horrocks, J. E., and Jackson, D. W. *Self and role.* Boston: Houghton Mifflin, 1972.

Hull, C. L. *Essentials of behavior.* New Haven: Yale University Press, 1951.

Kelly, G. A. *The psychology of personal constructs,* vol. 1. New York: Norton, 1955.

Krakovskii, A. P. Psychological bases of an individual approach to the young adolescent. *Doklady Akademii Pedagogicheskikh Nauk RSFSR* 23 (1962): 173–175.

Lewin, K. *A dynamic theory of personality.* New York: McGraw-Hill, 1935.

McDougall, W. *Introduction to social psychology.* Boston: Luce, 1908 (20th edition, 1926).

Maslow, A. H. *Motivation and personality.* New York: Harper, 1954.

Murphy, G. *Personality: A biosocial approach to origins and structure.* New York: Harper, 1947 (Basic Books edition, 1966).

Murray, H. A. et al. *Explorations in personality.* New York: Oxford University Press, 1938.

Rogers, C. R. *Client-centered therapy.* Boston: Houghton Mifflin, 1951.

Skinner, B. F. *Science and human behavior.* New York: Macmillan, 1953.

Sullivan, H. S. *The interpersonal theory of psychiatry.* New York: Norton, 1953.

Tolman, E. C. *Purposive behavior in animals and men.* New York: Appleton-Century, 1932.

Tolman, E. C. Cognitive maps in rats and men. *Psychological Review* 55 (1948): 189–208.

Suggested Readings

Berkowitz, L., ed. *Roots of aggression.* New York: Atherton Press, 1969.

Black, R. On the combination of drive and incentive motivation. *Psychological Review* 72 (1965): 310–317.

Brown, A. Decision-making by teenagers in six problem areas: Characteristics of effective goals. *Character Potential* 3 (1966): 186–193.

Buss, A. H.; Plomin, R.; and Willerman, L. The inheritance of temperaments. *Journal of Personality* 41 (1973): 513–524.

Butt, D. S. Aggression, neuroticism, and competence: Theoretical models for the study of sports motivation. *International Journal of Sport Psychology* 4 (1973): 3–15.

Byrne, D. Response to attitude similarity-dissimilarity as a function of affiliation need. *Journal of Personality* 30 (1962): 164–177.

Byrne, D., and Clore, G. L., Jr. Effectance arousal and attraction. *Journal of Personality and Social Psychology* 6 (1967): 1–18.

Crowne, D. P., and Marlow, D. *The approval motive: Studies in evaluative dependence.* New York: Wiley, 1964.

Erickson, G. M. Maslow's basic needs theory and decision theory. *Behavioral Science* 18 (1973): 210–211.

Fishman, C. G. Need for approval and the expression of aggression under varying conditions of frustration. *Journal of Personality and Social Psychology* 2 (1965): 809–816.

Good, L. R.; Good, K. C.; and Golden, S. R. An objective measure of the motive to avoid powerlessness. *Psychological Reports* 33 (1973): 616–618.

Locke, E. A., and Bryan, J. F. The directing function of goals in task performance. *Organizational Behavior and Human Performance* 4 (1969): 35–42.

MacMahon, C. E. Images as motives and motivators: A historical perspective. *American Journal of Psychology* 86 (1973): 465–490.

Mander, G. The interruption of behavior. *Nebraska Symposium on Motivation* 12 (1964): 163–219.

Malmo, R. B. Activation: A neuropsychological dimension. *Psychological Review* 66 (1959): 367–386.

Markey, V. K. Psychological need relationships in dyadic attraction and rejection. *Psychological Reports* 32 (1973): 111–123.

Rao, K. U., and Russell, R. W. Effects of stress on goal setting behavior. *Journal of Abnormal and Social Psychology* 61 (1960): 380–388.

Rodgers, C. W. Relationship of projective to direct expression of selected needs for nonpsychotic Ss. *Perceptual and Motor Skills* 36 (1973): 571–578.

Ross, M., and McMillan, M. J. External referents and past outcomes as determiners of social discontent. *Journal of Experimental Social Psychology* 9 (1973): 437–449.

Talkington, L. W., and Riley, J. Comparison of retarded and non-retarded adolescents on need approval. *Psychological Reports* 33 (1973): 39–42.

Veroff, J. Theoretical background for studying the origins of human motivational systems. *Merrill-Palmer Quarterly* 11 (1965): 3–18.

Van Fleet, D. D. The need-hierarchy and theories of authority. *Human Relations* 26 (1973): 567–580.

Willington, A. M., and Strickland, B. R. Need for approval and simple motor performance. *Perceptual and Motor Skills* 21 (1965): 879–884.

Wilson, J. P., and Aronoff, J. A sentence completion test assessing safety and esteem motives. *Journal of Personality Assessment* 37 (1973): 351–354.

Youngelson, M. L. The need to affiliate and self-esteem in institutionalized children. *Journal of Personality and Social Psychology* 26 (1973): 280–286.

Chapter Ten

Need-Goal Behavior in Adolescence

In the previous chapter the discussion centered on the action and interaction of the basic drives as well as on the acquisition and development of psychological needs. Needs, consciously or unconsciously perceived by the possessor, were viewed as representing socialized elaborations of the drives and impulsions to behavior aroused by functional organ tensions. It was made explicit that needs originate only as postbirth products of learning and always operate on the terms and within the parameters set by the basic drives. As the result of an individual's experiences, his needs assume a hierarchical order peculiar to himself, finding implementation through goal-directed behavior involving long-term goal objectives and shorter-term goal objects and activities. In general, needs promote differential behavior while drives promote commonality. It was proposed that the psychology of adolescence is simply a special case of general human psychology involving focus upon a specific age group and their age-related behaviors.

The present chapter is concerned with selected aspects of need and goal behavior during adolescence with particular reference to limiting and facilitating aspects. The relationship of self and needs is considered.

Studies of Adolescent Needs

Over the years there has been considerable discussion of psychological needs and related topics in the literature of psychology and education,[1] although actual developmental or theory-based research directly relevant to the construct has been relatively sparse. Studies on needs typically have tended to compile new or recombine older lists of needs or to isolate general areas of behavior in which needs function. Some have tried to express the action of needs in "life" situations in terms of striving for goal objects, activities, and objectives, often by asking adolescents about their problems, wishes, and needs. Others have simply discussed the relationship of education and needs. As such, they have added relatively little to existing knowledge, to the confirmation of theories of the kind discussed in the previous section, or to formulation of new theory. The literature on adolescent needs, if not merely general discussions, usually consists of studies of the normative survey type using questionnaires, personal documents, interviews, and, less frequently, observation. Age and various demographic conditions are often rejected as variables, probably because many researchers

[1] For example, Albou (1973–74); Archambault (1957); Bartlett and Smith (1966); Boder and Beach (1937); Bruckman (1966); Cattell, Sealy, and Sweeney (1966); Doane (1942); Douglass (1937); Evans and Anderson (1973); Gibbs (1966); Graham and Balloun (1973); Hertzler (1940); Irvin (1967); Johnson and Smith (1965); Kissel (1967); Kolb, Winter, and Berlew (1968); Levine (1973); Locke, Cartledge, and Knerr (1970); Miller and Miller (1973); Monahan, Kuhn, and Shaver (1974); Prescott (1938); Raban (1965); Sampson and Hancock (1967); Spangler and Thomas (1962); Welford (1965); White and Wash (1966); and Whiteley and Hummel (1965).

feel that the relationship of such variables to behavior is so uncertain and so situationally determined.

However, sex differences are often included, although the emphasis tends to be upon males. In contrast to the psychoanalytic literature, psychological studies, because of the normative techniques used, tend to ignore the individual case and state their findings in terms of group norms. Part of the problem is undoubtedly in the use of the normative survey, which ordinarily neglects explanatory constructs and fails to derive general principles. While normative surveys can study interdependent variables, the usual approach is that of working with discrete, unrelated variables. Consequently, the results are usually limited to the specific data obtained. The net results are a sparsity of generalized constructs that can be elaborated and retested, as well as failure to codify empirical findings. A further problem is that since needs are learned in a socialized context and since they are influenced in their etiology and operation by the culture, normative and descriptive surveys involving them become quickly dated, particularly in times when the culture is undergoing dramatic changes.

At the present time, need research is concentrated either on the need for affiliation or on the need for achievement, with the latter receiving the greater share of attention. Considerable interest is beginning to be shown in the processes of goal-directed behavior in industry and in organizational settings. It would appear that the majority of need research would best be classified under the headings of personality or social processes, with psychological need as a motivational dynamic taking a decidedly minor role.

In any event, where research in the area of adolescent needs is concerned, with the exception of the hypothesized need to achieve, and possibly of the need for affiliation, there has been a tendency to mark time, largely because of the difficulty in setting up meaningful or definitive research in this area.

It would be helpful to add experimental approaches to normative surveys in the study of psychological needs during adolescence, to consider the interrelationship of variables, to make specific attempts to confirm or build theories, to be more imaginative in the variables selected for research, and to use such techniques as factor analysis. New instruments for measuring need states are badly needed. Some of the questions that might be asked are: (1) What are the characteristics of the needs of adolescence? (2) What is the relation between age and needs under varying conditions? (3) What social situations influence the development and expression of needs? (4) How are needs related to one another in transition? and (5) What is the validity of the various major theoretical positions on development of needs?

Habit as a Determinant of Behavior

Any understanding of the bases of human behavior must of necessity include a recognition of the importance of habit. Habit may be defined as an individual's tendency to react in a certain way when confronted by a stimulus. The strength of the habit is expressed in terms of the likelihood of its occurrence when confronted with a stimulus.

The stronger the habit is (that is, the greater its reaction potential), (1) the more likely and consistent is its occurrence when the proper stimulus occurs, (2) the less is the latency of its evocation, (3) the greater is the amplitude or intensity of the reaction, and (4) the greater is the resistance to extinction.

There is an obverse side to the coin. Habit is usually thought of in terms of overt, positive performance. In reality, covert performance and the negation or inhibition of performance also have to be included. For example, an adolescent could be said to have developed a habit of not responding.

A curious consideration about habit is its existence when it is not occurring or being used; that is, when no stimulus is present to elicit it. It is something like strength, which is a matter of leverage and muscle action when it is being applied, but which, when not being applied, does not exist in any measurable performance sense. There is only potential based upon the presence and intactness of the musculature and its tonicity, as well as the bony structure to which the musculature is attached. Psychologists have called a concept such as habit an intervening variable. An intervening variable is an event that takes place —in the case of habit, within the organism— between stimulus and a response. It has also been called a construct. It is tempting to try to speculate on what habit actually is, the extent to which it is physical, and how it operates as a physical entity. But this is an unsolved mystery of behavior. The neurological operation—if that is what it is—that makes up a habit is not observable and can only be speculated upon.

The occurrence of a habit in an adolescent, or in any human being, for that matter, is dependent upon the situation. For that situation, various exterior aspects may increase or decrease habit potential. Presence or absence of a need or an organ tension may increase or decrease the potential or strength of the habit for that occurrence. For instance, hunger may make a habit more likely to occur if the habit will reduce hunger or if it will lend to the general activity common to persons in the first stages of hunger.

Habits presumably retain and even increase their strength and potential when satisfaction (or reward, although the term is often a misnomer in this connection) follows their occurrence. Lack of satisfaction leads to decreased strength and eventually to the extinction of the habit.

Certain habits, characteristic of a cultural category of persons, are usually said to be characteristic of a "typical" member of that category, such as an adolescent. Here we have simply a special case of a habit. It is still an individual matter, but its roots, sanctions, and impulses may be sought in the culture. Such

a habit, occurring in a typical member of a cultural category of persons, is known as a custom. As with habits, we may speak of a custom potential.

An adolescent's life is composed of many personal habits that are his as a unique individual. He possesses various additional habits, known as customs, which, as a member of a culture and simultaneously of various subcultures within that larger culture, he shares with other persons. But these habits and customs do not exist in isolation from one another. They are interrelated and interact and influence one another both positively and negatively. One habit may lead to and facilitate the acquiring of another habit. Or it may inhibit the potential of an already existing habit by changing reward values, by causing it to operate only with difficulty (latency), or by decreasing its tendency. A new habit may change or alter an existing habit. When it becomes apparent that a child possesses an undesirable habit or set of habits, the possibility of habit substitution as well as of goal redirection should be considered. Goal redirection, of course, has more widespread behavioral effects than does habit formation. Ultimately, in attempting to effect fundamental behavioral changes, the problem of an individual's needs and goals have to be dealt with.

The influence of habits extends beyond the individual, as the habits and customs of one individual (or their results) influence those with whom he comes in contact, even as theirs influence him. The action of habits and customs is therefore both an individual and a group matter.

Habit replacement causes difficulty for adolescents in Western culture. In children, certain habits are acquired and are even promoted by adults. Many of these habits represent security and approved ways of socialization. But, with the advent of adolescence, these childhood habits have to be replaced by habits more appropriate to older children and adults. Such replacement often happens under pressure from parents and other adults, from peer groups, and from the examples found in reading and other experiences. Some of the habits may lead to a habit complex, and in some cases they are an integral part of the child's self-concept. Here replacement could represent a very severe problem of adjustment and reevaluation of role.

There is an interesting parallel between this period of habit replacement following the advent of puberty and the time when the small child is passing from the period of initial habits to the period of socialization. One difference is that the adolescent brings to replacement the experience of his previous transition, which may have been good or bad. It is a reasonable hypothesis that transition to adolescence is easier when the earlier transition was favorable and difficult when the early transition was difficult.

Activities Versus Needs

It is a common mistake to believe that any activity indulged in by an adolescent represents the presence of a need. Such is not the case. An activity may be the performance of a developmental task set not by the organism, but by parents, school, or society. Or it may be an activity, less major than a developmental task, imposed upon an individual without his need or acceptance. The fact that nearly all children in America from six to sixteen attend school does not mean that they have a need to go to school. Going to school is what they are expected or forced to do. Of course, some aspects of school are undoubtedly need satisfying, but presence in school itself is not representative of a need, except perhaps that of escaping punishment or finding a setting in which one can conveniently perform an activity that will fulfill a need, if only at the ostensible level—playing football, reading a book, or meeting a member of the opposite sex. Joining the armed forces is another example of a common activity for an age group of males that does not in itself meet or represent a need. Having a date

is still another example. It is common to mix up activities and needs. Acceptance and security probably are representative of needs that can take quite elaborate forms as we observe them in practice.

Need Equilibrium and Development in Adolescence

Personal adjustment may be viewed largely as a matter of equilibrium-disequilibrium in the satisfaction of psychological needs. An individual's whole life may be seen as an attempt to gain and retain equilibrium in his physical as well as in his social and emotional functioning. When he is subject to the unrest and tension of an unsatisfied need, an individual is in a state of disequilibrium of which the seriousness depends upon the valence of the denied need. Given such a state of disequilibrium, the individual is impelled to institute, and to continue efforts to achieve, equilibrium. There is a paradox here, however. In another context this writer (1965) notes:

Just as there is a straining toward equilibrium, so, once attained there is a straining toward disequilibrium. The functioning organism avoids a static state—and so there arises the counter-need for a movement away from the attained equilibrium. This, of course, is in turn followed by the return quest for equilibrium again as the circle completes itself. Robert Frost speaks of the expansion and contraction of the biological aspects of the universe. Another problem arises in the person who attains equilbrium and then adjusts his needs system so that his equilibrium lessens, or at least becomes something that must be renewed and added to. For example, a person may attain success, but then discount the first success and strive for further success. One would presume that some persons go through life attaining or trying to attain goals, never being satisfied with an attained goal, but always striving for an even greater one. Others no sooner reach their goals than they relinquish or modify them, and in a sense never go ahead, but always have to start over again. There are, of course, goals that are never attained. Here we have a matter of reality testing and of self-concept in the goals that are established. There are also people who deliberately avoid goal attainment —those who are . . . abnormal.

Actually it is probably never possible to attain complete equilibrium or complete disequilibrium. Perhaps life for the adolescent, as well as for his elders, is a matter of being midway between these two poles, with each exerting its pull simultaneously. In such a situation we have ambivalence. Under some conditions, as the individual is unable to cope with ambivalence or is unable to see some future reconciliation, we find the bases of many neuroses and psychoses.

An unsatisfied need, hence a state of disequilibrium, is not necessarily bad so long as the individual continues to strive to attain his goal and does so effectively, or finds adjustment by accepting a substitute goal. One problem of growing up is that of discovering that many goals may be obtained only slowly, over a period of time, and that in many cases substitute goals have to be accepted. Youth is impatient, and it is frequently difficult for adolescents to cope with delays and the realization that all their goals may not be simultaneously served. To what extent do adolescents have difficulty in satisfying their needs, and to what extent is adolescence a period characterized by disequilibrium?

In an attempt to explore this important area of adolescent adjustment Benimoff and Horrocks(1961), using a sample of children in grades 7 through 12, attempted to answer two questions: (1) What changes take place during adolescence in need-satisfaction versus need nonsatisfaction as the needs are manifested in various environmental situations? and (2) What are the crucial areas of equilibrium-disequilibrium?

The results of the study showed a general developmental trend for youth to experience-varying amounts of disequilibrium during the early teens and the middle grades between the seventh and twelfth years of school. There was a decided trend for greater need-satisfaction to occur at either extreme of the age and grade span included. The concepts of environmental demands, psychological needs, and skill in learning new tasks could well account for this phenomenon. When a child is preadolescent, from about ages eleven to thirteen and when he is in grade seven to eight, the demands of the situations he meets are such that childish patterns of behavior may still be successful in achieving basic need-satisfaction. The environmental situation of the preadolescent may actually foster this childish pattern during this period. For example, consider the environmental situation of the child's relationships with adults. Here the preadolescent may be successful in obtaining his need-satisfactions if he continues with the same childish kind of behavior he used earlier in his life. However, upon entering adolescence he may be faced with a slightly different situation, namely, that adults now demand of him certain behavior for which he has little background of experience. Therefore, during adolescence the youth is learning those skills that will make for better adjustment, from the point of view of both environmental demand and his own need to obtain basic satisfactions.

It is important to note that essentially the same relationship existed in the environmental situation of heterosexual pairs. During preadolescence, a child may reject intimate associations with the opposite sex and still satisfy his own needs and environmental pressures. But upon entrance into adolescence he experiences changes in his needs (puberty) and his peer culture that demand that he become more skillful and resourceful with members of the opposite sex. Until he reaches the point at which he can be truly skillful in his relationships with the opposite sex, a child needs to be more or less in a state of need-nonsatisfaction. When those skills necessary for adjustment to various situations have been learned, the adolescent is capable of meeting the demands of his own needs and those of environmental situations. Need-satisfaction thus appears to be fairly well established after age sixteen and around the tenth grade. This does not mean that all adolescents possess complete need-satisfaction after sixteen and the tenth grade; there are always individual differences.

The foregoing discussion implies that the school and other community resources should concentrate more effort during early adolescence on aid in furthering youth adjustment. Social programs and curricula could be adapted to the needs of youth of this period in such a manner that they would have an opportunity to learn more quickly and efficiently skills that will help them in meeting the demands of their present and future situations. It may well be that part of the general better adjustment with advancing age and grade reflects a selection factor in which poorly adjusted students leave school in the earlier grades.

In the needs categories of achievement and mastery-dominance, Benimoff and Horrocks (1961) found that, in general, girls had greater equilibrium, whereas boys had greater disequilibrium. Thus it appears that girls are better able to obtain need-satisfactions in these two areas. The concepts of social role and opportunity to experience success may be relevant here. Apparently boys may experience a change in their social role as they progress from preadolescence through puberty. Girls may not experience a drastic change in their social role, and they may experience more success for their achievement needs, especially if teachers tend to react more favorably toward them. Therefore, boys have the added adjustment problem of a changing social role (from the dependent childish role to the dominant male role) and a lack of background experiences of learning how to react to a newer role. Until boys learn social skills that will make them more effective in achieving status, they apparently experience disequilibrium of needs of achievement and mastery-dominance.

Horrocks and Weinberg (1970) also attempted to study psychological needs of adolescents at various age levels and to examine changes in these needs over the course of the adolescent period. They also investigated the extent to which needs characteristics of the various age groups were satisfied. This study included 654 boys and girls ranging in chronological age from twelve through twenty. Indices of needs were compiled by means of a need questionnaire that required the respondents to indicate a desire or lack of desire to assume various roles. Comparison of these indices with the extent to which adolescents actually see themselves in social roles served as a measure of need-satisfaction. The most enduring needs during adolescence for the population studied were:

1. To conform to approved behavior, values, and standards designed by reference individuals or groups seen as important (parents, teachers, peers).
2. To be the special recipient of unqualified and deep expressions of affection.
3. To work hard, endeavor, and to attain worthy goals.

Horrocks and Weinberg also note greater degrees of need-satisfaction as adolescence progresses, with girls reporting greater satisfaction of needs than do boys. The transition in degree of need-satisfaction is much sharper for girls and centers around age fifteen. In evaluating efforts expended toward attaining their goals, the majority of adolescents see themselves as doing their best and commonly expressed satisfaction with their own general competence and success in activities.

For girls, there is a definite age trend toward greater attainment of affection. No such trend is indicated for boys. Throughout adolescence, the most common area of receiving affection is in unisexual peer relationship. After fifteen, unisexual group relations become the most commonly consistent source of affection. For boys, the most common area for satisfaction of affection needs is in the home.

Girls after fifteen tend to perceive themselves as playing adult roles and being accepted as adults, but boys have no such perception. Both sexes show an age trend toward greater heterosexual adjustment. In general, the school appears as a key area of conflict and nonadjustment for both sexes.

If emergence of needs may be deemed a dimension of growth, then there is a definite pattern of needs for both boys and girls that identifies a transition to adulthood. In girls this transition takes place at an earlier age and more extensively than in boys. The goals that become significant after the onset of adolescence overwhelmingly relate to the assumption of dominant adult roles and adequate heterosexual adjustment.

The early existence of values centering on work and productivity has important social significance.[2] How are such drives channeled in the world of academic and vocational activity? Are these true values or does their large incidence reflect an area of highly socialized attitudes that promote lip service? Furthermore, the existence of such an internalized pattern would suggest a higher level of maturity at pubescence, or at least the presence of a strong nucleus of values essential to maturity. One of the main differences between the child and the adult is a process of socialization or indoctrination that enables the child successfully to express any previously existing drives.

Sex Differences in Need Development

There are interesting sex differences as well as similarities in the expression of needs during the adolescent period. While girls as they grow older display less interest in group membership than do boys, they seem more anxious to maintain a favorable personal status in the in-groups they respect or wish to join. They seek equal prerogatives normal to their reference groups and tend to find their closest identification with a group that has a code of values and a standard of behavior lending personal prestige. In their group relationships girls appear more egocentric than do boys and more apt to use the group for personal aggrandizement. Girls express a wider range of emotional

needs in peer relationships than do boys, and girls have traditionally expressed a stronger need for conformity that at times borders on dependence.

In contrast to girls, boys display interest in groups more for organization than for personal aggrandizement reasons. Most boys like to see themselves as integral members of a group and want to be accepted and sought after by the group, but a great deal of their interest consists in maintaining the group's identity and in carrying out its activities. While in social matters boys conform less than girls, they do like to be proper, correct, and adept. It is a rare boy who does not actively try to avoid being the object of blame and who does not seek to become the special recipient of approval. In these years of adolescence the foundation is laid for the roles to be assumed in the years that follow, and the world of group and interpersonal relationships appears to be one training ground for such roles. In past years the group role for boys has typically seemed to lay the foundation for the traditional role of doer of the world's work that the culture has allotted the male. Girls, on the other hand, have tended to assume the more independent but stereotyped personal reference. However, cultural expectations are changing, and it may be assumed that adolescent and group roles will conform to that expectation. In future years, as females assume more and more the breadwinner and equal-partner role, and as they enter into new areas of activity, the changes in cultural expectations will accelerate to an even greater degree. At the present time the tendency is for male group roles to be somewhat less stereotypically "masculine" and female group roles to be somewhat less stereotypically "feminine." Whether the changing sex-role cultural expectations eventually will make adolescent females more likely to accept regimentation and adolescent males more likely to view the world in personal reference terms is moot at this point.

In general, as of now, boys and girls are group centered, but boys characteristically display a need for leadership or implementing

[2]Note that one of the three most enduring needs during adolescence reported by Horrocks and Weinberg was "to work hard, endeavor, and to attain worthy goals."

roles, as compared to girls' more passive interest only in membership. Girls visualize the group as important for the prestige, the personal security, and oneness it brings; boys value the group for participative purposes. Boys appear to need to display proficiency and are less tolerant of criticism in matters where their proficiency is questioned. For both boys and girls, the most significant change in needs as adolescence progresses is a developing need for social relations that are increasingly dominated by one's own capabilities, mastery, and self-expression. With approaching maturity and self-sufficiency, some adolescents find that such mastery and self-expression can best be achieved outside the group context, and, for these individuals, the group becomes less important. Dropping out of group membership occurs, particularly among girls after the age of fifteen. The late teenage girl begins to recognize her own worth as a person and become more self-sufficient. As a group, girls appear less regimented than do boys, although they face many culturally engendered and enforced pressures for conformity.

Among older adolescents of both sexes (ages sixteen through nineteen for girls, from age seventeen for boys) there is an especially strong need to play self-assertive roles characteristic of adults, to assume increasingly adequate relationships both with opposite-sex peers and with adults, and to display competence and effectiveness in activities of most personal concern, such as driving a car, dancing, and occupational endeavor.

Behavior Style Attributes

In the development of his need system and in his attempts to satisfy his needs the child, and later the adolescent, learns to assume certain behavior style attributes that exemplify in his everyday behavior the needs he possesses. Gradually an individual's behavior style attributes come to characterize and define him as a person. Edwards (1953, 1954) has formulated a group of such attributes based upon the list of manifest needs proposed by Murray (1938) as part of his theory of personality. Edwards's list of attributes is broken down as follows:

1. *Achievement (Ach)* Doing one's best, succeeding with the difficult, accomplishing something outstanding.
2. *Deference (Def)* Following rather than leading, accepting and praising others, conforming.
3. *Order (Ord)* Need for neatness, order, organization, advanced planning, and a systematic approach.
4. *Exhibition (Exh)* Need to be the center of attention and use of verbal statements and appearance to achieve that end.
5. *Autonomy (Aut)* Independent, unrestricted, unconventional, critical of authority, avoidance of obligations.
6. *Affiliation (Aff)* Friend centered, loyal, helpful, gregarious.
7. *Intraception (Int)* Analytic of others' behavior and motives. Understanding through analysis of the self and others.
8. *Succorance (Suc)* To be helped, encouraged, and liked by others. To be the recipient of sympathy and attention if things go wrong.
9. *Dominance (Dom)* To assume leadership, mediate arguments, supervise, direct, influence, make decisions for others.
10. *Abasement (Aba)* Blame accepting, feelings of timidity and inferiority, need for punishment, need to confess errors.
11. *Nurturance (Nur)* To help friends and unfortunates, to forgive, to be generous and sympathetic, to show affection.
12. *Change (Chg)* To do new and different things including travel, fads, experimenting, breaking routine, and meeting new people.
13. *Endurance (End)* To work hard, finish jobs, to stay up late and work long hours, to avoid interruptions. Not to be distracted.
14. *Heterosexuality (Het)* Participation in all levels of activity with the opposite sex.

To be interested and involved in matters having to do with sex.

15. *Aggression (Agg)* To disagree, criticize openly, get revenge, blame others, make fun of others, to become angry.

Edwards's list by no means exhausts the possible major attributes. Many others might be added, some focused in the social and some in the inner life of the individual.

Over time each person works out for himself a behavior style representing these attributes, none of which exist or operate in isolation. Actually clusters or patterns of these attributes occur, consisting of two or more acting in concert. Presumably, for any given situation, there are clusters of behavior style attributes that are complimentary and lead to integrated behavior on the adolescent's part. When a person characterized by a given cluster meets a situation in which the cluster is non-applicable or when his behavior attributes include mutually exclusive and conflicting attitudes, stress results.

Mutually Exclusive Needs and Goals

A source of disequilibrium in adolescence is uncertainty and conflict arising from mutually exclusive needs and goals. Ideally an adolescent's needs would complement and reinforce each other. Correspondingly, the goals he selects to implement the needs would be both complementary and appropriate as specific need implementors. Unfortunately, however, some of an adolescent's needs tend to be mutually exclusive, and many of his goals are unrealistic and inappropriate as well as impossible to achieve simultaneously. For example, an adolescent endeavoring to attain independence from adults is also driven to conform to adult expectations—and these very expectations may well represent the area in which he is trying to act independently. Such an adolescent may wish to follow the advice of several of his peers and engage in antisocial behavior to show his independence. Opposed to this is his desire to

be thought of by adults as a good son, a good citizen, and a good member of his school.

When a situation of opposed goals arises, and when the goals are both the objects of highly motivated behavior, a conflict situation exists. An adolescent faced by such a conflict either must choose between the two goals or reject both in favor of a substitute goal. In a free choice between two mutually opposed goals, an individual, insofar as he makes a choice, will select the one toward which he is most strongly motivated; and such a choice is usually made in terms of the needs the object goals and activities represent. An adolescent faced with taking Mary or Erika to a party will presumably select the girl he likes best or the girl who best supplies some need of high valence, such as prestige. But the choice is not always so simple. Mary may be the best liked and even be the more prestigeful of the two, but there may be obligations to Erika and parental expectations that Erika will be taken. Here we have a summation of goals that interact in the making of the final choice. It is little wonder that the adolescent often experiences difficulty as he faces the problem of conflicting goals, particularly since he does not have past experience or advice to guide him. Some persons whose motivations are not particularly strong, or whose past experience in making choices has been unfortunate, will refuse to make choices or will go to great lengths to avoid a conflict of goals. When one girl was questioned about her refusal to have dates, she observed that she never knew what to do when a boy wanted to make love to her. She was attracted but didn't want to go against her parents' wishes and so solved the problem by refusing to put herself in situations in which she would have to make a choice.

A study by Abrams (1965) is an example of needs research with interesting theoretical implications for goal-need substitute behavior. This investigator studied the fantasy life of 181 college males and 143 females (64 of the subjects were under twenty-two and 79 were over thirty-two) and reported that the most frequent fantasy was associated with achievement. Fantasies involving financial matters increased with age, but more so in the case of females than of males. The blacks in the sample displayed more interest, as evidenced by their fantasy life, in professional and financial success than did whites. Obviously, the generalizability of Abrams's study is limited by the fact that he used a limited number of college students from a specific college and the relative percentages of his sample fantasizing in any need area was not great. However, his study is productive of hypotheses that do have theoretical implications and that are susceptible to testing in other studies with other samples. For example, Abrams states: "When needs can not be gratified, indirect methods of drive reduction must be attempted. Daydreaming is one of the techniques that is employed to attain partial need satisfaction." Perhaps Abrams's college students displayed fantasies about things that as college students they were so far denied, and the black-white and male-female differences showed blacks and females as fantasizing more than white males did about things that in our culture would be easier for white males to attain. Other studies could verify or disprove the universality of Abrams's statement quoted above. A more major hypothesis involved in Abrams's study (although not stated by him) is that the situation sets the nature of the need. In science one means of evaluating a study is by the possibilities for further resarch to which it points.

The Conflict of Attributes

It is difficult to imagine a person who does not encounter in his everyday life situations that make external or internal conflict unavoidable. Certainly any adolescent finds many occasions when he is faced with the problem of conflicting attributes and needs. Sometimes the conflict is not serious or is easily resolved, but sometimes such conflicts hold the seeds of disorganization of the personality encountering them. In separate studies Trehub (1959) and Nakshian and Wiener (1964) both note that

the amount of need conflict is inversely related to the degree of adjustment. Trehub (1959) selected from Edwards's fifteen attributes four need pairs (aggression-deference, succorance-nurturance, autonomy-abasement, and order-change) that he felt would logically lead to conflict if the joint strength of the two need pairs was high in an individual. Using as his subjects persons with varying degrees of adjustment, Trehub found that "ego disjunction"[3] (need conflict) increases with the degree of psychopathology. For example, adult schizophrenics exhibited more ego disjunction than did adults with character disorder, adult neurotics, or adolescents. But the last three showed more ego disjunction than did college students, who were presumably well at the end of their adolescence and could be characterized as "normal" adults with no special problems of character disorder, neurosis, or psychopathology. Trehub obviously assumed that adolescents were a more stress-laden class than are normal adults.

Nakshian and Wiener (1964) selected from the Edwards attribute list ten need-conflict pairs[4] and obtained need-conflict scores from four different groups of subjects: thirty-three veterans in a Veteran's Administration mental hygiene clinic being treated for behavior disorders, thirty-three normal veteran controls, thirteen college fraternity members (aged seventeen to twenty-two) rated high or better than average in adjustment, and thirteen fraternity members rated low or worse than average in adjustment. Their results showed a greater similarity in the ordinal position of need-conflict scores and need-strength scores for groups with similar life-situation variables (both nonpsychiatric veterans and psychiatric

[3]Trehub uses *ego disjunction* to stand for a conflict between incompatible needs. He defines it as "the concurrence in any individual of two or more relatively long enduring needs or characteriological dispositions with mutually incompatible objectives and with a relatively high level of joint strength."

[4]Achievement-affiliation, achievement-nurturance, deference-autonomy, deference-aggression, autonomy-affiliation, autonomy-nurturance, affiliation-aggression, succorance-endurance, dominance-abasement, nurturance-aggression.

veterans), but different levels of adjustment, than for groups with similar level of adjustment (nonpsychiatric veterans and combined college groups) but with different life-situation variables.

In discussing their findings, Nakshian and Wiener speculated that the relative intensity of conflict resulting from any given need pair could be due to education, age, socioeconomic status, or some other similar situational or demographic variable. They believed that there would probably be differences in the relative importance adolescents, as compared to adults, placed upon the various need-conflict areas. Writing on this last point they noted, "If this latter reasoning is correct, the possibility then exists that a rationally derived index might include need pairs which are biased for a particular population and be differentially reliable in assessing ego disjunction in different populations." Following their line of reasoning, the four-need-pair ego-disjunction index obtained by Trehub, instead of being an index of the total ego disjunction found in all populations, may be simply more sensitive in one population than it is in another.

In any case, the reader should not assume that the presence of a need-conflict pair, or even of several pairs, in any given individual inevitably leads to maladjustment. Many individuals have worked out ways of either resolving the conflict or coping with it. Judicious assistance may help an adolescent resolve any adjustment problems that are involved. Further, it may well be that ability to cope with conflict of attributes is in itself a behavioral attribute. Cameron (1963) writes:

We have all acquired techniques for reducing the impact of conflict, for avoiding it, and for choice and decision-making which actively accept one thing and give up the other. Conflicts may be resolved in different ways. Some of them are never settled; yet they wane and disappear with time as conditions change and as new interests make them no longer important. Many of these are suppressed before they disappear, often with the help of consciously adopted reaction-formation attitudes; and some of the most important disappear from consciousness and preconscious through the defensive action of repression, but remain with all their power in the unconscious. Many conflicting desires are sublimated. . . . Many external conflicts are displaced, or their mode of expression is tamed. The . . . child may attack an adversary with flailing fists . . . in time, however, he learns to attack an adversary verbally, to argue with him, tease or belittle him, or to compete with him in games.

A further list of conflicting attribute areas, expanding those Edwards suggested, includes:

1. Tolerance for ambiguity vs. need for structure.
2. Ability to withhold closure vs. propensity for fast closure.
3. Alienation vs. need for involvement.
4. Accepting vs. rejection.
5. Dominance vs. submission.
6. Activity vs. passivity.
7. Rigidity vs. flexibility.
8. Focused vs. diffuse.
9. Inner- vs. outer-focused.
10. Altruistic vs. selfish.
11. Hedonistic vs. spartan.
12. Manic vs. depressive.
13. Acquisitive vs. nonacquisitive.
14. Possessive vs. nonpossessive.

Needs and Cognitive Style

In the preceding sections the directional and motivational operations of psychological needs have been presented as basic to human behavior. Are there conditioning factors for the acquirement and subsequent operation of psychological needs? How do adolescents differ from other persons with respect to the operation of their needs? It has already been pointed out that experience, including education, constitutes the format necessary for the acquirement of needs. But opportunities for experience, as well as the quality and quantity of experiential content, differ not only among persons and among groups but also at different times in history. For example, most adolescents growing up in a period of severe economic deprivation would be much more apt to develop security needs than those reared in more affluent times.[5] The quality of child rearing an individual encounters would also have much to do with the kinds of needs that might take precedence in his hierarchy. But even more important than environmental opportunity or exposure is an individual's ability to learn and to relate his learnings to past experiences and future expectations. This is a matter of cognitive functioning. It is only to be expected that the needs learned by persons of quite different levels or types of cognitive function would be quite different. For example, the needs structure of a highly intelligent person would, other things being equal, be more elaborated and complex than that of a much less intelligent person of the same age. By the same token, a child, at an earlier stage in cognitive development than an adolescent, would possess a less complex needs structure.

Equally as important as intellectual capacity in a person's acquirement and use of psychological needs is the manner in which he sees himself and the world. Where self is concerned, there is a continuing problem of congruence of personal needs and self-perceptions with development and experience, particularly in adolescence, moving the individual toward a resolution of conflicts between self-percepts and needs.

The way in which an individual perceives and cognitively deals with his world influences and limits all of his learning experiences, including his acquisition and implementation of needs. In that connection, work accomplished on perceptual field dependence-independence by Witkin and his associates is relevant. These investigators[6] hold that each learner has a special individual learning situation or format best adapted to the kind of person he is. Such a situation is visualized largely in terms of an individual's response to problems as he establishes a field of perception. Specifically, Witkin takes the position that an individual's location on a scale of field dependence-independence,[7] which indicates his most characteristic manner of seeking visual balance or of finding a hidden pattern, is highly related to his nature as a cognizing organism and hence to the kind of learning situation from which he is most likely to profit. To date, Witkin and his associates have used two tests, the Embedded Figures, and the Rod and Frame as the primary means of assessing the mental performance or cognitive style involved in field perception.[8]

Witkin, Goodenough, and Karp (1967) have reported a general trend toward increasing field independence during development, with the rate of increase slowing down and reaching a plateau in late adolescence or early maturity. Figure 14 presents developmental curves for the Rod and Frame Test, the Embedded Figures Test, and the Body Adjustment

---

[5]An adolescent who acquires an unusual need for security during a period of economic depression and growing up, and becoming a parent in affluent times could be expected to retain his unusual need for security and even to implement it in his child-rearing practices. His adolescent daughter, a product of affluent times with a deemphasis of security needs, might well encounter conflict and misunderstanding in her relationships with her father. Or, she might acquire her father's needs and find herself out of step with her peers and her times.

[6]Witkin (1965, 1967, 1969); Witkin, Faterson, Goodenough, and Birnbaum (1966); Witkin, Dyk, Faterson, Goodenough, and Karp (1962); and Witkin, Goodenough, and Karp (1967).

[7]In field-dependent perception the organization of the field as a whole assumes domination over perception of its parts. The observer in the field-dependent mode of perception experiences an item within the field as being fused with the organized ground. In field-independent perception the observer experiences parts of the whole field as being discrete from the holistic organization of which they are a part. The dimension of field dependence-independence extends along a continuum, with most persons finding a location someplace between the two extremes of field dependence and field independence.

[8]For the Rod and Frame Test an individual sits in a completely darkened room and is presented with the task of adjusting a luminous rod contained within a tilted luminous square frame to a position he perceives as upright. While he is doing this, the luminous frame retains its original position of tilt. In the field-dependent performance, the rod is adjusted close to the axis of the tilted frame; in a field-independent performance, the individual, referring to his own body position, brings the rod to true upright without being influenced by the frame.

For the Embedded Figures Test, the individual has the task of locating a previously seen simple geometric figure in a complex field in which it has been embedded. Field-independent persons quickly break up the organized field and locate the embedded figure, whereas field-dependent persons take much longer to break up the field and "find" the simple embedded figure. A further test places the individual in a tilted room with the task of adjusting his own body upright while the room remains tilted. The reader will recognize the gestalt origins of these tasks.

Figure 14   *Developmental Curves for Field Independence During Development*

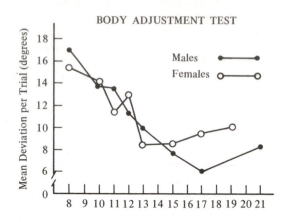

BODY ADJUSTMENT TEST

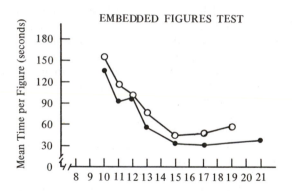

EMBEDDED FIGURES TEST

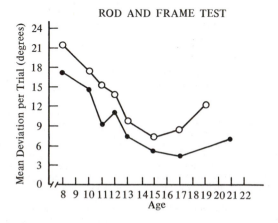

ROD AND FRAME TEST

Source: Adapted from H. A. Witkin, D. R. Goodenough, and S. A. Karp, "Stability of cognitive style," *Journal of Personality and Social Psychology* 7 (1967): 291–300, figs. 1–3. Copyright 1967 by The American Psychological Association. Reprinted by permission.

Test. In considering the implications of the curves presented in Figure 14, it is necessary to understand that while in normal development differentiation does increase with age, it is also true that *level* of differentiation remains relatively stable during development. That is, a child who is less differentiated at a given age than his fellows will also tend to be less differentiated as an adolescent and as a young adult. It is interesting, as Witkin notes, that from the standpoint of differentiation, people exhibit considerable constancy in their psychological functioning across such ostensibly diverse areas as perception, nature of defenses, sense of separate identity, and body concept. And to Witkin's list may be added structure of psychological needs.

There can be little doubt, on the basis of research reported,[9] that environmental experiences play an important part in the development of field independence and that of these experiences those of the child with his parents, particularly the mother, and other significant figures are of great importance. However, at early ages, as Wachs et al. (1971), White (1971), Hunt (1961, 1965), and Watson (1971) point out, attempts at enrichment may actually retard development or should at least be embarked upon under specified circumstances. By the time a child has reached adolescence, however, there can be little reason to observe the precautions standard in dealing with younger children. Specifically, as is indicated in the chapter on moral development, there is no reason why proper environmental experiences may not be planned to effect desirable changes in his need structure.

The Origins and Elaboration of Self

In the previous chapter it was stated that an individual is faced at birth with two major developmental tasks, namely, to learn and elaborate a set of psychological needs, and to

evolve appropriate concepts of self. Over the individual's entire life span, his psychological needs and his concepts of self interact as they govern his perceptions and his responses to his world. If the interaction of these two basic attributes is complementary, the prognosis for the personal adjustment of the individual is favorable. If, in addition, the results of their interaction leads to behavior in accord with the expectations of society, the social adjustment and social efficiency of the individual is favorable. On the contrary, if self and needs have not been integrated and are in conflict, the individual faces a lifetime of emotional tension and stress unless the conflict can be resolved. And if the interaction places the individual in conflict with the expectations of society, then even though the interaction is complementary where the individual is concerned, his life will be one of social deviation and social inefficiency.[10] For these reasons it is important to consider the developmental relationship of self and needs.

How does an individual go about the developmental task of self-construction? In answering this question, let us turn, as in the case of the origin of the psychological needs, to the time of the individual's birth. He is at birth a biological organism differing from other members of the animal kingdom only in potential and structure and in the possession of a genetic program passed on from previous generations that, within limitations, will chart the future course of his biological development. The drives possessed by this individual at birth are entirely in the physical-physiological area. The motivating force of these drives, as previously explained, is directionality leading to motility, organization-cohesion, completion, equilibrium, and cognitive synthesis-integration. At birth the individual has responses rather than needs; the needs are still to be learned. Because the

[9]Bieri (1960); Witkin et al. (1962); Corah (1965); Dyk and Witkin (1965); Berry (1966); Dawson (1967).

[10]Expectations of society as used here means avoidance of behavior and attitudes personally and socially harmful to self and society in favor of more positive and facilitative approaches. It should not be taken to include socially and personally useful and positive deviations such as creativity.

individual is a functional biological organism, he also possesses organ function responses manifested in the form of organ tensions ready for reduction. At this point the physical environment offers experience, and the developing physical system, using the base of the five drives and of the organ tensions, begins to program into itself psychological needs. These needs provide expectancies, sets, and directionality, leading to the rudimentary beginnings of a perception of a somatic self. The first task in building a somatic self involves the organism's gradual perception of itself as an entity separate from its surroundings. The next tasks are those of locating, of articulating, and of controlling the parts of this entity and of developing responses and coordinations leading to the organism's control and manipulation of the environment to serve its own directionality and stimulus hunger.

Almost simultaneously, the culture, in the form of people, begins to provide culturally engendered experiences. The action is still on the physical side, and while the infant now learns to respond to significant others as facilitative—that is, functionally—there is as yet no beginning of a psychic self, although the somatic self is becoming fairly well formulated.

While this is going on, a whole group of elaborated needs are developing, although their initial focus is upon physical function and tissue preservation. From the continuing socialization and elaboration of these needs, particularly as they become more cognitively focused, the individual's concepts of a psychic self must evolve. As the concepts of psychic self begin to emerge, a gradual change is effected, with the motivating force for the self-needs becoming major and the tissue needs becoming minor in the need hierarchy.[11]

Two self-needs develop. One is the exemplification and perpetuation of the self-view; the other is the indulgence of the self. Developmentally, the former appears later than the latter. But the transition from a major focus on tissue needs to self-needs provides a conflict, and throughout life there is a fluctuation as these need areas strive to gain the ascendency. Here, in this conflict area, we find the basis of neuroses and psychoses. This same conflict forms the raison d'etre of the mental mechanisms that form our ego defenses. But developmentally, the socialization battle is lost, as in late old age and in senescence the tissue needs tend to regain ascendency and the circle is complete.

One of the most dramatic demarcation lines in the development of the self is crossed when the developing organism becomes capable of symbolization leading to all the complexities of speech. This is rudimentary at first, but at this point there is the beginning of what may be called psychic self-hypothesis ("I want...," "Give me...," "I won't..."). In the early stages of symbolization, the somatic self and the psychic self are not really distinguished by the organism. The analogy is the child's difficulty at birth in separating himself as an entity from his surroundings.

But the separation continues, and we now have a duality of selves, a psychic self and a somatic self, related but separate. These two selves are often in conflict, and the integration of these selves into a combined self (personal self) is the task of development and a major source of neuroses, psychoses, problem behavior, and maladjustment generally.

In the early stages, the selves (that is, concepts of self) are very diffuse—even amorphous—and at this time there is a tendency to exteriorize or extend the self outside

----

[11]But the tissue needs are always there, even though they are incidentally served by the elaborated self-needs. Let these elaborated needs cease to serve the tissue needs, and the tissue needs reassume their primacy in all of the individual's behaviors. Quite possibly the elaborated self-needs, if they have really denied the tissue needs, may wage a battle for primacy, but it is a losing one. There are records of those who have apparently won the battle

over the tissue needs, as in the case of certain ascetics, but if the victory is carried too far, the result is death. The forces of nature will not be completely denied, even by the mind of man. Of course, everyone has won a minor skirmish, as in temporarily resisting fatigue, or in losing weight under a sustained diet, but these are only minor victories and do not upset the ultimate primacy of the physiological.

Figure 15   *Process of Socialization-Humanization: Self-needs*

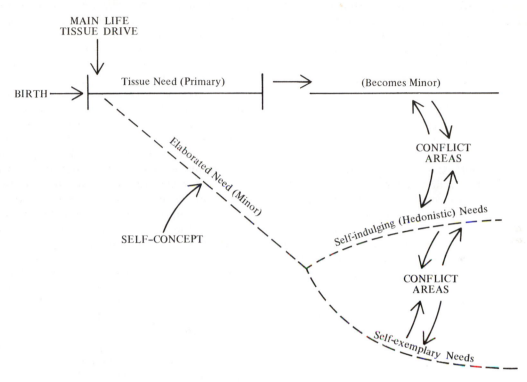

the organism. This is incompatible and is resisted to the point that the individual becomes very egocentric to others as he enters the negativistic periods of early childhood and of middle adolescence. As the self becomes less diffuse—that is, with the appearance of greater self-security—the developing child is able to return to exteriorization, but in the earlier stages the exteriorization is a means of engulfing that which is exteriorized. Later the exteriorization is more a matter of giving away and is in reality a "selfless" reaction. This is true maturity and will seldom occur until the thirties.

In any event, by the time basic needs have been socialized and elaborated, and as the individual symbolizes and distinguishes between his somatic and psychic selves, we can formulate a concept of purposive behavior based on directionality engendered by a hierarchy of needs. We can also start conceptualizing profit-

ably about the relationship of goal-directed behavior to needs and can postulate the development of a hierarchical order of needs with referents in the psychic and the somatic realms.

At first, the needs system in the psychic realm (see Figure 15) is hedonistic, and this develops the hidden and often unconscious impulses of the psychic apparatus. These impulses develop only as a defense against the evolving conscience, which has been guided by the agents of socialization and cultural mores. Later the self-exemplary needs appear, with their intimate relationship to the conscience. Of these, altruism and capacity for selfless love represent examples of the highest and most mature level.

As this constellation of psychically engendered needs is developing, its progress is paralleled in the somatic realm by the same hedonistic and, though to a lesser extent, exemplary needs. A parallel somatic unconscious and conscience forms, although in all probability the somatic conscience is more permissive. In the effort to integrate the psychic and the somatic selves, the psychic conscience tends to engulf the somatic conscience.[12]

Therefore, by the middle years of adolescence, each individual has evolved a personal self that includes both a somatic and a psychic self, as a result of the developmental process. One problem of development is that this personal self actually tends to rest upon two quite opposed concepts, the ideal self and the operational self. The individual has also evolved a concept of his environment, which also may be divided into a concept based upon experience and a concept based upon supposition. Both these environmental concepts may be described in general terms, although within the parameters of both are various subclasses and deviations. However, where personal concept of self is concerned, most normally developing persons tend to visualize themselves in terms of the self-exemplary motivations.

Summary

Discussions of psychological needs have been current in psychology and education but have resulted in relatively little developmental or theory-based research directly relevant to the construct. Research studies usually compile new or recombine older lists of needs or attempt to isolate areas of behavior in which needs function. Some studies have examined life-situation action of needs, basing their data collection on questionnaires. Present research is particularly interested in the study of affiliation and achievement needs and in goal behavior in industrial settings.

[12] In this writer's use of *conscience* and unconscious, the reader may have been reminded of the terms *superego* and *id*. These terms could equally well have been used, but the writer's placement of these concepts in the developmental sequence and his interpretation of their origin differs so markedly from psychoanalytic usage that it seems inadvisable to use terms so specifically defined by psychoanalytic theory.

Habit, defined as an individual's tendency to react in a certain way when confronted by a stimulus, is basic to an understanding of human behavior. Habit is situation bound, with various exterior aspects of the situation increasing or decreasing the habit potential. Presence or absence of a need or an organ tension may increase or decrease the potential or strength of the habit for a need-related situation. As with needs, habits often increase their strength and potential when satisfaction follows their occurrence. Habit replacement often represents a severe problem of adjustment and reevaluation of role in adolescence.

Not all activities of adolescents are goal activities representing a psychological need. Such nongoal activities may represent the performance of a developmental task or a demand set, not by the adolescent, but by parents, school, or society. However, even a nongoal activity may involve need elements having nothing to do with the activity itself but with the adolescent's relationship to the person or persons who set the activity.

There appears to be a general developmental trend to experience varying amounts of disequilibrium during the early teens and the middle grades of junior-senior high school. There is a decided trend for greater need-satisfaction at either extreme of the high school age and grade span. In general, girls appear better able to obtain need-satisfaction; hence they display a greater amount of equilibrium than do boys. Much disequilibrium in boys may be based on the greater change they experience in social role as they progress from preadolescence through puberty. Girls also have greater success in school in meeting their achievement needs than is characteristically true of boys.

Throughout the entire span of adolescence, the most enduring needs are conformity, affection, and achievement, although there are very specific sex differences in the way needs develop and in their importance to the individual. There is a definite pattern of needs for both boys and girls that identifies transition to adulthood.

In the development of his need system and in his attempts to satisfy his needs, the child, and later the adolescent, learns to assume certain behavior style attributes that characterize and define him as a person. Edwards provides such a list. Over time, each person works out for himself a behavior style representing these attributes. However, various of these attributes are mutually opposed or incompatible and lead to conflict.

A source of disequilibrium in adolescence is uncertainty and conflict arising from mutually exclusive goals and needs. An adolescent faced with such a conflict either must choose between the two goals or reject both in favor of a substitute goal. While conflict is not always serious in its behavioral repercussions, it can lead to maladjustive behavior and sometimes even to the disorganization of the personality encountering them. Assistance may help an adolescent resolve any adjustment problems involved in conflict resolution, although it should be remembered that ability to cope with conflict may be a behavioral attribute. A number of need-related conflicting attributes are listed and discussed.

There are certain conditioning factors for the acquirement and subsequent operation of psychological needs. Among these are time in history, child-rearing practices, self-perceptions, and manner of perceiving and cognitively dealing with the environment. One aspect of the latter is the individual's response to problems as he establishes a field of perception. Witkin takes the position that an individual's location on a scale of field dependence-independence, which indicates his most characteristic manner of seeking visual balance or of finding a hidden pattern, is highly related to his nature as a cognizing organism, and hence to the kind of learning situation from which he is most likely to profit. There is a general trend toward increasing field independence during development, with the rate of increase slowing down and reaching a plateau in late adolescence or early maturity. However, while in normal development differentiation does increase with age, it is also true that comparative level of development remains constant.

Self and needs interact as they govern an individual's perceptions and his responses to his world. If the interaction is complementary, the prognosis for good adjustment is excellent. If it is not, the prognosis is poor. Needs and self-percepts develop in parallel from the time an individual is born, and their etiology and relationship to the drives is similar. Self develops over time as the culture, in the form of people, begins to provide culturally engendered experiences. A somatic self emerges before a psychic self. With the emergence of the psychic self, a gradual change is effected as the motivating force for the self-needs becomes major and the tissue needs become minor in the need hierarchy.

Two self-needs develop, one an exemplification and a perpetuation of the self-view, and the other the indulgence of the self. Developmentally the former appears before the latter. Eventually an individual develops a personal self consisting of an ideal and an operational self, although most individuals define themselves more in terms of the more exemplary personal self.

References

Abrams, S. The need system of college students. *Journal of Social Psychology* 66 (1965): 227–239.

Albou, P. A contribution to the history of economic motives: The concepts of Keynes and Pareto. *Bulletin de Psychologie* 26 (1972–1973): 941–953.

Archambault, R. D. The concept of need and its relation to certain aspects of educational theory. *Harvard Educational Review* 27 (1957): 38–62.

Bartlett, E. W., and Smith, C. P. Child-rearing practices, birth order, and the development of achievement-related motives. *Psychological Reports* 19 (1966): 1207–1216.

Benimoff, M., and Horrocks, J. E. A developmental study of the relative needs satisfaction of youth: Equilibrium-disequilibrium. *Journal of Genetic Psychology* 99 (1961): 185–208.

Berry, J. W. Temne and Eskimo perceptual skills. *International Journal of Psychology* 1 (1966): 207–229.

Bieri, J. Parental identification, acceptance of authority, and within-sex differences in cognitive behavior. *Journal of Abnormal and Social Psychology* 60 (1960): 76–79.

Boder, D. P., and Beach, E. V. Wants of adolescence. I. A preliminary study. *Journal of Psychology* 3 (1937): 505–511.

Bruckman, I. R. The relationship between achievement motivation and sex, age, social class, school stream and intelligence. *Journal of Social and Clinical Psychology* 5 (1966): 211–220.

Cameron, N. *Personality development and psychotherapy.* Boston: Houghton Mifflin, 1963.

Cattell, R. B.; Sealy, A. P.; and Sweeney, A. B. What can personality and motivation source trait measurements add to the prediction of school achievement? *British Journal of Educational Psychology* 36 (1966): 280–295.

Corah, N. L. Differentiation in children and their parents. *Journal of Personality* 33 (1965): 300–308.

Dawson, J. L. M. Cultural and physiological influences upon spatial-perceptual processes in West Africa, parts I and II. *International Journal of Psychology* 2 (1967): 115–128; 171–185.

Doane, D. C. The needs of youth, an evaluation for curricular purposes. *Teachers College Contributions to Education.* New York: Columbia University Press, 1942.

Douglass, N. R. *Secondary education for youth in modern America.* Washington, D.C.: American Council on Education, 1937.

Dyk, R. B., and Witkin, H. A. Family experiences related to the development of differentiation in children. *Child Development* 30 (1965): 21–55.

Edwards, A. L. The relationship between the judged desirability of a trait and the probability that the trait will be endorsed. *Journal of Applied Psychology* 37 (1953): 90–93.

Edwards, A. L. *Manual for Edwards's Personal Preference Schedule.* New York: Psychological Corporation, 1954.

Evans, F. B., and Anderson, J. G. The psychocultural origins of achievement and achievement motivation: The Mexican-American family. *Sociology of Education* 46 (1973): 396–416.

Gibbs, D. N. A cross-cultural comparison of needs and achievement of university freshmen. *Personnel and Guidance Journal* 44 (1966): 813–816.

Graham, W. K., and Balloun, G. An empirical test of Maslow's need hierarchy theory. *Journal of Humanistic Psychology* 13 (1973): 97–108.

Hertzler, A. E. Problems of the normal adolescent girl. *California Journal of Secondary Education* 15 (1940): 114–119.

Horrocks, J. E. Adolescent attitudes and goals. In Sherif, M., and Sherif, C. W., eds., *Problems of youth: Transition to adulthood in a changing world,* pp. 15–27. Chicago: Aldine, 1965.

Horrocks, J. E., and Weinberg, S. A. Psychological needs and their development during adolescence. *Journal of Psychology* 74 (1970): 51–69.

Hunt, J. McV. *Intelligence and experience.* New York: Ronald, 1961.

Hunt, J. McV. Intrinsic motivation and its role in psychological development. In Levine, D., ed., *Nebraska Symposium on Motivation* 13 (1965): 189–282.

Irvin, F. S. Sentence-completion responses and scholastic success or failure. *Journal of Counseling Psychology* 14 (1967): 269–271.

Johnson, T. J., and Smith, L. M. Achievement, affiliation, and power motivation in adolescents. *Psychological Reports* 16 (1965): 1249–1252.

Kissel, S. Anxiety, affiliation, and juvenile delinquency. *Journal of Clinical Psychology* 23 (1967): 173–175.

Kolb, D. A.; Winter, S. K.; and Berlew, D. W. Self-directed change: Two studies. *Journal of Applied Behavior Science* 4 (1968): 453–472.

Levine, E. L. Problems of organizational control in microcosm: Group performance and group-member satisfaction as a function of difference in control structure. *Journal of Applied Psychology* 58 (1973): 186–196.

Locke, E. A.; Cartledge, N.; and Knerr, C. S. Studies in the relationship between satisfaction, goal setting, and performance. *Organizational Behavior and Human Performance* 5 (1970): 135–158.

Miller, T., and Miller, P. McC. Some fantasy correlates of experimentally aroused aggression. *British Journal of Social and Clinical Psychology* 12 (1973): 378–383.

Monahan, L.; Kuhn, D.; and Shaver, P. Intrapsychic versus cultural explanations of the "fear of success" motive. *Journal of Personality and Social Psychology* 29 (1974): 60–64.

Murray, H. A., et al. *Explorations in personality.* New York: Oxford University Press, 1938.

Nakshian, J., and Wiener, M. Need strength, need conflict, and adjustment. *Journal of Social Psychology* 62 (1964): 29–43.

Prescott, D. A. *Emotion and the educative process.* Washington: American Council on Education, 1938.

Raban, R. Need achievement in college women: The effects of success or failure. *Connecticut College Psychology Journal* 2 (1965): 24–48.

Sampson, E. E., and Hancock, F. T. An examination of the relationship between ordinal position, personality, and conformity: An extension, replication, and verification. *Journal of Personality and Social Psychology* 5 (1967): 398–407.

Spangler, D. P., and Thomas, C. W. The effects of age, sex, and physical disability upon manifest needs. *Journal of Counseling Psychology* 9 (1962): 313–319.

Trehub, E. Ego disjunction and psychopathology. *Journal of Abnormal and Social Psychology* 58 (1959): 191–194.

Wachs, T. D.; Uzgiris, I. C.; and Hunt, J. McV. Cognitive development of infants of different age levels and from different environment backgrounds: An explanatory investigation. *Merrill-Palmer Quarterly* 17 (1971): 283–317.

Watson, J. S. Cognitive-perceptual development in infancy: Setting for the seventies. *Merrill-Palmer* 17 (1971): 139–152.

Welford, A. T. Stress and achievement. *Australian Journal of Psychology* 17 (1965): 1–11.

White, B. L. *Human infants: Experience and psychological development.* Englewood Cliffs, N.J.: Prentice-Hall, 1971.

White, W. F., and Wash, J. A., Jr. Preception of teacher effectiveness as a function of the students' need for social approval. *Perceptual and Motor Skills* 23 (1966): 711–717.

Whiteley, J. M., and Hummel, R. Adaptive ego functioning in relation to academic achievement. *Journal of Counseling Psychology* 12 (1965): 306–310.

Witkin, H. A. Psychological differentiation and forms of pathology. *Journal of Abnormal Psychology* 70 (1965): 317–336.

Witkin, H. A. Cognitive styles and cross-cultural research. *International Journal of Psychology* 2 (1967): 233–250.

Witkin, H. A. Social influences in the development of cognitive style. In Goslin, D. A., *Handbook of socialization theory and research,* pp. 687–706. Chicago: Rand McNally, 1969.

Witkin, H. A.; Dyk, R. B.; Faterson, H. F.; Goodenough, D.R.; and Karp, S. A. *Psychological differentiation.* New York: Wiley, 1962.

Witkin, H. A.; Faterson, H. F.; Goodenough, D. R.; and Birnbaum, J. Cognitive patterning in mildly retarded boys. *Child Development* 37 (1966): 301–316.

Witkin, H. A.; Goodenough, D. R.; and Karp, S. A. Stability of cognitive style from childhood to young adulthood. *Journal of Personality and Social Psychology* 7 (1967): 291–300.

Suggested Readings

Allard, M., and Carlson, E. R. The generality of cognitive complexity. *Journal of Social Psychology* 59 (1953): 73–75.

Barclay, A., and Cusumano, D. R. Father absence, cross-sex identity, and field dependent behavior in male adolescents. *Child Development* 38 (1967): 243–250.

Baumeister, A.; Hawkins, W. F.; and Cromwell, R. Need states and activity level. *Psychological Bulletin* 61 (1964): 438–453.

Bing, E. S. Effect of child-rearing practices on the development of differential cognitive abilities. *Child Development* 34 (1963): 631–648.

Cohen, L., and Scaife, R. Self-environmental similarity and satisfaction in a college of education. *Human Relations* 26 (1973): 89–99.

Cross, H. J. Conceptual systems theory-application to some problems of adolescents. *Adolescence* 2 (1967): 153–165.

Crowley, F. J. The goals of male high school seniors. *Personnel and Guidance Journal* 37 (1959): 488–492.

Finlayson, D. S. Expressed achievement motivation in relation to the achievement motive, neuroticism, and school success. *British Journal of Educational Psychology* 42 (1972): 65–70.

Fiske, D. W. Can a personality construct be validated empirically? *Psychological Bulletin* 80 (1973): 89–92.

Gjesme, T. Sex differences in the connection between need for achievement and school performance. *Journal of Applied Psychology* 58 (1973): 270–272.

Haronian, F., and Sugarman, A. A. Fixed and mobile field independence: Review of studies relevant to Werner's dimension. *Psychological Reports* 21 (1967): 41–57.

Heckhausen, H. *The anatomy of achievement motivation.* New York: Academic Press, 1967.

Hoffman, L. W. Early childhood experiences and women's achievement motives. *School Psychology Digest* 2 (1973) 18–23.

Immergluck, L., and Mearini, M. C. Age and sex differences in responses to Embedded Figures and Reversible Figures. *Journal of Experimental Child Psychology* 8 (1969): 210–211.

Iscoe, I., and Carden, J. A. Field dependence, manifest anxiety, and sociometric status in children. *Journal of Consulting Psychology* 25 (1961): 184.

Jessor, R.; Liverant, S.; and Opochinsky, S. Imbalance in need structure and maladjustment. *Journal of Abnormal and Social Psychology* 66 (1963): 271–275.

Katz, P., and Zigler, E. Self-image disparity: A developmental approach. *Journal of Personality and Social Psychology* 5 (1967): 186–195.

Konstadt, N., and Forman, E. Field dependence and external directedness. *Journal of Personality and Social Psychology* 1 (1965): 490–493.

Linden, W. Practicing of mediation by high school children and their levels of field dependence-independence, test anxiety and reading achievement. *Journal of Consulting and Clinical Psychology* 41 (1973): 139–143.

Maehr, M. L., and Stallings, W. M. Freedom from external evaluation. *Child Development* 43 (1972): 177–185.

Phillips, B. N. Age changes in accuracy of self-perceptions. *Child Development* 34 (1963).

Richards, J. M., Jr. Life goals of American college freshmen. *Journal of Counseling Psychology* 13 (1966): 12–20.

Sah, A. P. Perceptual suggestibility as a function of age, sex, and education. *Indian Journal of Experimental Psychology* 7 (1973): 21–25.

Seyfried, B. A., and Hendrick, C. Need similarity and complementarity in interpersonal attraction. *Sociometry* 36 (1973): 207–220.

Teichman, Y. Emotional arousal and affiliation. *Journal of Experimental Social Psychology* 9 (1973): 591–605.

Chapter Eleven

A Case History:
Diagnosis and Remediation

The preceding chapters have explained that an understanding of adolescent behavior might be gained by studying the characteristic responses and problems of adolescents against a framework of the basic elements of human behavior. The following case presents the history of an adolescent girl who encountered and attempted to solve several specific problems. Following the case, a number of question statements of diagnostic and remedial import are listed. Readers may wish to react to these in terms of what they know about adolescent and human behavior to this point so that they may better assess their knowledge and insight. Notes interpreting the case follow the questions. It is suggested that the questions be covered *before* reading the case notes.

The Case of Mary Marlowe

Mary Marlowe was referred to the University Psychological Clinic by the community juvenile court after she had attempted to commit suicide. A case history was made so that the clinician assigned to work with Mary would have the necessary background upon which to base his therapy.

At the time of referral Mary was seventeen and in the last half of her senior year at Central High School. She came from a lower-middle-class section of Central City, where her parents had lived since Mary was nine. Both parents were high school graduates, and the mother had completed two years at the local State University College of Education. Mr.

Marlowe was employed as an accountant in the National Machine Company. From Mary's fourth to her ninth year the family, because of her father's poor health, had been forced to live on a somewhat isolated farm. Mr. Marlowe's main recreational interests consisted of gardening, fixing things around the house, and attending the Masonic Lodge once or twice a week.

Mrs. Marlowe confined most of her activities to her home and children and a small circle of friends living in the immediate neighborhood. There were three children in the family —Mary and two younger boys. Both parents were interested in religion, and as members of the Second Methodist Church prided themselves upon their church activity. They attended church regularly and insisted that the children do likewise.

The Marlowe home was comfortable and quite large. It was well and tastefully furnished, although there were few books or other outlets for cultural interests. Mary occupied a room by herself and was allowed considerable freedom in furnishing it according to her own tastes, which the high school art teacher considered were good but apt to be changeable.

Mary's relations with her brothers were generally friendly, although the boys both felt that Mary tried "to boss us around" too much and was always wanting her own way. Birthdays and other special occasions were always made much of in the Marlowe home, with a family party and an exchange of presents.

Mr. and Mrs. Marlowe were an affectionate couple whose universe revolved pretty much around their home and their children. Company was seldom invited to the home, the parents feeling that their own closely knit family circle was a sufficient recreational outlet. Mrs. Marlowe had been an officer of the local child-study group several times and was generally considered to be an ideal mother. In talking with the case worker after the suicide attempt, Mary appeared to be particularly concerned lest she hurt her parents, for whom she expressed great affection. Mary said she knew that her mother wanted her to "make something of herself," but that her mother did not really understand her. She said that Mrs. Marlowe was always trying to get her to do things she didn't want to do or blaming her for things that she couldn't help. Mary seemed particularly annoyed at the fact that her parents were always holding a cousin, Alice Allen, up to her as an example of the way a girl should behave and get along with others. Mary said she disliked Alice because she was "insincere" and had snubbed her whenever Mary tried to be friendly. Mary felt that Alice was laughing at her and "talking about me to the other girls." Mary said that she could not understand why Alice was so popular when she was such a snob. She appeared to resent particularly the fact that Alice had been asked to join one of the high school sororities while she had not been asked. Mary asked the case worker to say nothing to her mother about her feelings toward Alice because, "Ma is only trying to help me. She wants me to be popular like Alice and thinks if I act like her I'll be popular too. But I won't act like her. I hate her."

Mary's academic record was poor in Central High School, although she had done better than average work in junior high, where she seemed much better liked than she was after she reached senior high. The junior high school teachers remembered her as "lively," although apt to be shy and not very popular with the other students. The principal felt that her shyness was due to her early life on the farm, where there had been few opportunities to meet and play with other children. Mrs. Marlowe said that Mary had always been shy, particu-

larly with strangers, and seemed to be by herself a lot.

As a child she had a particularly rich imaginative life and had a whole series of imaginary friends whom she used to order around. She still does a lot of daydreaming. This last two or three years it is growing worse. It is getting so I can't get her to do any work around the house at all. She resents whatever I tell her to do and seems to grow more and more irresponsible and forgetful. I can't even trust her to dust, so I've just been letting her alone and doing the work myself. I really believe she is living in a dream world. She is forever trying to act like some actress, although in these last few months she has given that up and spends all her time up in her room when she isn't in school. She never brings any of the other girls to our home, and they never invite her to theirs. I asked her why she didn't invite some nice girls to come and see her, and she did ask several but they wouldn't come. Mary cried about it, but I guess now she doesn't care. I wish she would try to be with people more, but she says they don't like her. She used to be very self-reliant and gay, but now she can never make up her mind about anything. She just refuses to make choices of any kind and bursts into tears when we try to make her. Her work at school is suffering, and I think she is afraid she is not going to graduate with her class. Every time there is an examination she gets ill. If only she had some friends. She has never had a date and has not been asked to a party since we moved back here to Central City.

Mary's seventh-grade homeroom teacher characterized her as:

a dear child—so much fun and yet quite serious and often more quiet than one would expect in a child of her age. She was always making careful plans and carrying them out. She was very imaginative and had lots of original ideas. I could always depend upon her to take a responsible part in any work the class did. I don't believe she was very well liked by the other children, and she did seem more restless than most of them. She was looking forward to going to senior high school and wanted to become a teacher.

Mary's early record at Central High School formed a contrast to her previous school record. She did poor work in the ninth grade and grew steadily worse each year. Her teachers felt that she was not trying. Competition seemed to bother her, and examinations appeared to be an ordeal. She missed school frequently and complained of being tired and not feeling well. The ninth-grade homeroom teacher couldn't remember her very clearly, but felt that she had been "average as a person, although she was having trouble with her school work." The other teachers remembered more of her. The ninth-grade social studies teacher remembered her as overassertive and bossy: "She tried to tell everybody what to do and was forever annoying the other children. It was hard to get anyone to work on a committee with her. I think she tried hard enough, but she just couldn't get along in a socialized situation." The mathematics teacher said that she seemed "preoccupied and not very interested." He thought she was "prone to daydream in class, although her assignments were usually done on time." He felt that she didn't like to try "challenging problems" and seemed to want to "avoid having to do very much work." He noticed that she seemed interested in the boys in her class, although they did not appear to pay any attention to her.

Miss Buxton, Mary's tenth-grade homeroom teacher, said she never could understand Mary: "Sometimes she was very aggressive, and at other times she was just the opposite. She was definitely unpopular with the other children both in the homeroom and out. She wasn't in any extracurricular activities, although I believe she had tried to join two or three and hadn't been accepted." Miss Buxton felt that Mary's behavior fluctuated much more than that of most girls her age: "She was flighty and never seemed to know what she wanted, and she resented any kind of criticism. She was really a nice girl but was having a hard time adjusting to school. She could be very agreeable when she wanted to, but spoiled it all by her outbursts and her undependability. She daydreamed a lot and seemed to think it smart to appear cynical." Most of Mary's tenth-grade teachers seemed to agree with Miss Buxton. The French II teacher said:

Nice enough sometimes, but she seems to be up and down a lot. I don't think she knows her own mind. One day she seems to want to be friendly and the next day won't have anything to do with anyone. One day in class she was impudent because I didn't call upon her when she volunteered, and two or three days later she did everything she could to keep me from calling on her, although she knew the assignment well enough. She seems to lack self-confidence, although she talks about wanting to go on the stage.

The eleventh-grade homeroom teacher said:

Mary was a real problem. She seems to be a very disagreeable person. She was continually criticizing the other boys and girls, and she was forever making cynical remarks. I don't believe that she was a good influence in Central at all. Her grades were failing or only fair, and she was either aggressive and mean or in a fit of sulks. She was blackballed by one of the sororities, and that seemed to make her more stubborn and sulky than ever. It also seemed to make her more quiet. I guess it was a good thing for her to see how other people really felt about her. I noticed last spring that she seemed to have more and more days when she was especially quiet. She told me once that she sometimes feels she isn't worth very much and won't ever be able to accomplish anything in life. She was having trouble making up her mind about what she wanted to be. I got her to try out for the junior play, but she failed to receive a part. She was quite religious and I heard that she was taking an active part in the religious work program at the YWCA.

The world history teacher said that he was surprised that Mary was able to do as well on examinations as she did.

Her mind never seemed to be on her work and she just sat and stared off into space. I had to speak to her on a number of occasions and I told her she would have to leave class if it occurred again. She seemed unstable. I was never sure just how she was going to react in class. It never seemed to be the same twice except for this business of woolgathering, in which she certainly seems consistent.

The twelfth-grade homeroom teacher said that she had been worried about Mary, although she felt that she was the most annoying and disagreeable person in the senior class.

Half the time she is in open rebellion and the other half of the time she sulks and is sullen. Lately there is less open rebellion and more stubborn resistance. She cried a lot last winter and never seemed to know her own mind, yet she gets indignant if any suggestions are made to her. She seems suspicious of the other children and feels they talk about her. I think she feels the same way about her teachers. She doesn't seem to have made any clear-cut vocational decision but seems to have new ideas every other week, and then after a while she seems to be back on the same vocational choice that she made several weeks before. She changes her mind the same way about everything. I've talked to her mother, and her mother is just as puzzled as I am.

The English IV teacher said:

I'm disgusted with Mary. I've certainly done everything I could do to help her, but she is completely unreasonable and won't take any kind of advice. I knew her fifth-grade teacher, who said that she was such a lovely little girl, but something seems to have happened to her since the fifth grade. I suppose it is just growing up too fast, but I'm glad it does not affect the rest of them like that. I've sent her to the principal's office for not paying attention in class or for reading movie magazines in study hall. I'll be glad when she is out of my class.

The principal reported that Mary seemed to become more and more of a discipline problem the longer she stayed in school. He said that for the few months prior to the suicide attempt she must have spent more time in the office waiting to be reprimanded than she spent in class. He said:

Mary is a rather unusual case. I don't believe she is mean or mischievous exactly, but she is unreasonable. She has constantly been getting into personal difficulties with her teachers this past year or two. She seems intolerant of criticism, is by turns sarcastic or sulky, and is forever changing her mind or trying some new idea with no regard whatsoever for the personal feelings or convenience of others. She has come down here sometimes with a chip on her shoulder, and other times has blamed herself bitterly and said that she didn't know what was the matter with her— that she wished she did. Her parents seemed even more mystified than I and said that they just did not know what to do with her; she was acting

the same way at home as she was at school. She seems to have lost all her friends, insofar as she ever had any. About the only one she really seemed to want to be friends with was Miss Wheat, the Latin teacher. Miss Wheat is a quiet, mousey sort of person and does not appear to have any more friends here than Mary does. We are not going to renew her contract for next year. Mary spends most of her spare time hanging around Miss Wheat's homeroom. I told Mary that perhaps she might find someone a little more social for a friend, and she flared up and became very indignant—not for herself, but for Miss Wheat. I wish we could have done something for Mary, but we are so crowded here. I certainly never thought it would come to suicide. Why, we have any number of kids who cause much more real trouble here than Mary ever did. They seem much worse to me. Her parents should have clamped down long before things came to such a head as this.

The guidance counselor said:

I think I know Mary as well as anyone else in the building. Ever since she came to Central City High she has been trying to make up her mind about her vocational future. She seems to have narrowed it down to three things: actress, teacher, or missionary. Unfortunately she keeps changing from one to the other. I think when she decides on one of them for a day or two she tries to play the part. When it is a missionary, she becomes very religious and wants to lecture all the kids about how bad they are, and she begins to worry about how bad she is. All the time the idea that she wants to go on the stage is in the back of her mind, and she fights the idea from the religious point of view. Then a few days later she shifts over to being an actress, and she sort of tries to act like some movie actress or other. It's always a different actress, I guess. During the actress phase she is forever reading movie-star magazines. The kids don't know what to make of it. One day she lectures them, and the next tries to act like some glamour star. It was quite a blow to her when she didn't make the junior play. When she isn't being an actress or a missionary, she thinks she would like to be a teacher. I don't believe she really wants to be a teacher. I think she is just sort of imitating that quiet little Miss Wheat. She even tries to fix her hair like Miss Wheat's. I suppose that it is one of those girlish crushes that most kids go through. I've talked to her and showed her that the stage and religious work don't pay off very well, but she won't listen.

I think this past year she has completely stopped listening to anyone. She just moons around the corridors and seems to be living in a world all her own. This past two months it seems to have reached a crisis. She has gotten so she won't even speak to people.

Miss Wheat said that she did not like Mary.

She is such a queer child, but she does follow me around a lot. I don't mind as long as she doesn't get in the way too much. At least she is friendly, and that is more than anyone else in Central City has been.

Mary's minister said that he was horrified at Mary's suicide attempt.

She is such a fine young woman. Always interested in church work and such a hard worker. She has lots of ability, but is very modest and unassuming about it. She never hung around with the crowd after Sunday school, but helped in the building, straightening it up, or went home with her parents. She wanted to be a missionary, you know, and we had many long talks about her "call." Unfortunately, she was exposed to many temptations and used to think she might like to be an actress instead. She said that she couldn't help it and felt very guilty about it. I wish that there were fewer magazines, television, and moving pictures to unsettle young people these days. I do think that Mary did feel too guilty about herself and her state of grace. She used to think about it a lot and come in and talk to me about it. As a matter of fact, many a time she sat in my study crying as though her heart would break.

The YWCA secretary in whose program Mary was working said that Mary came to the "Y" full of enthusiasm and was put to work several afternoons in one of the settlement houses on the south side.

Mary was not popular at all. Some days she would do well, but most of the time she was just flighty or preoccupied, and once in a while she acted as though the settlement house was far below her dignity. She seemed to run the whole range from self-depreciation through cynicism to smart-alecky overassertion. We finally had to dispense with her services.

Mary herself said:

I don't know why I did it. Or I guess I don't. Things just seemed to pile up and pile up. I didn't feel as though I could go on any longer. I didn't know what to do with myself—there were so many things that I wanted, but none of them seemed right, somehow. I was always feeling guilty and I began to think I just plain wasn't any good and that no one liked me anymore except Ma and Pa, and even they didn't understand me. I used to say things to people I didn't mean, and then afterwards I was sorry. I couldn't make up my mind what to do with my life. I was all confused, and the more I thought about it the more I got confused. I used to daydream and make believe a lot. Sometimes I could forget myself that way, but after a while it wasn't any fun anymore, although I just couldn't stop. I'd sit down, and the first thing I knew I'd come to with a start. First I used to see myself doing all sorts of interesting things, but this last year I imagined everything was against me and got to thinking how bad people would feel if something happened to me. Sometimes I'd imagine myself being a failure while other people succeeded and made fun of me. I used to imagine myself in all kinds of situations where that happened. The funny part of it was that I found myself being glad that I failed in something I wanted to do very badly. Like not getting in the sorority or getting a part in the play. I got so I didn't sleep well either. In the daytime it was hard to make up my mind about anything. I just didn't care, and it didn't seem worth doing all the things I had to do every day. It was just torture to go on. No one really understood me. I used to lash out at the other kids. I really wanted to be friends, but somehow I couldn't let myself go. I was all tense inside. And even when I tried to make friends, people wouldn't have anything to do with me or want me around. And the teachers—they acted awful. Just as though I had done something terrible. I got so I couldn't even study anymore, and then the woman at the YWCA told me I wasn't fit to work with people and I thought that it just wasn't any use anymore. I had such fun when I was a kid.

Questions About Mary

Read each of the following statements and decide, on the basis of the evidence presented in the case, whether you agree or disagree with the statement, or whether you are uncertain or feel that there is no evidence.

Diagnostic

1. Mary Marlowe presents a problem that, aside from the suicide attempt, is typical of the average adolescent girl.
2. Mary's early life before entering high school was thoroughly normal and lacked symptomatic indications of her later behavior.
3. The Marlowes' interest in the church made it more difficult for Mary to adjust to everyday life.
4. Mary's daydreams, in which she placed herself in an undesirable or failing role, were serious symptoms of psychological difficulty.
5. Mary's reaction of being more quiet after being refused sorority membership was an example of improved adjustment on her part.
6. The difference between Mary's work in junior as compared to senior high school resulted from the fact the level of difficulty of the work in senior high was getting beyond her capacity.
7. The sorority and the play episodes were severe blows to Mary's sense of security.
8. In her senior year Mary began to avoid people because she had grown to dislike them and would not have accepted friendship if anyone had offered it.
9. Mrs. Marlowe was too overpossessive for Mary's own good.
10. Fluctuation in occupational plans and desires is typical of the adolescent period.
11. Mary's fear of examinations was primarily due to lack of preparation on her part.
12. Mary's early evidence of shyness was a danger signal.
13. Mary was extremely sensitive to other people's opinions of her.
14. Mary lacked any qualities by which she could gain status in the eyes of her peers.
15. Mary tended to be afraid to place herself in a competitive position.
16. The fact that Mary daydreamed as much as she did could be taken to mean that her daily life failed to interest her or to offer her the necessary satisfactions.
17. Mary's resistance to criticism was an indication of feelings of inferiority on her part.
18. Mary's inability to decide on her vocation was less a matter of trying to find an occupational future than it was an attempt to work out some concept of herself that she could accept.
19. As the case progressed, there was a trend toward retreat into a world of fantasy and daydreaming.
20. In Mary's case, when aggressive behavior failed to obtain results it was followed by a period of withdrawal.
21. Situations at Central City High School were continually impairing Mary's confidence in herself.
22. The Marlowe home situation promoted Mary's feelings of isolation and insecurity.
23. Mary's aggressive tendencies and behavior were more serious psychologically than were her withdrawal tendencies.
24. This case presents well-defined symptoms of insecurity on the part of an individual who found her feelings of security being continually undermined.
25. Mary was having great difficulty in finding an acceptable and suitable role to play in life.
26. Mary's daydreaming tendencies were a cause rather than a symptom of her difficulties.
27. The progression of Mary's case indicated increasing disorganization and inability on her part to accept a choice situation.
28. Mary probably attempted to commit suicide because she preferred death to uncertainty and thwarting.
29. The major issue in this case is one of vocational choice.
30. The major problem in this case is physical difficulty and lack of vitality.
31. A major problem in this case is social maladjustment.
32. This is a case of excessive conflict on the part of an individual trying to find herself.
33. In making a diagnosis of Mary's case one basic cause may be assigned as the basis of her problems.

34. This is probably a manic-depressive case.
35. This is probably a case of incipient schizophrenia.

Remedial

1. Behavior such as that presented by Mary will usually adjust itself after adolescence. No particular remedial action is indicated.
2. Mary's case was one that should have been referred to the school psychologist or to a psychiatrist.
3. The eleventh-grade homeroom teacher's point, that Mary's being turned down by the sorority was good for her because it let her know how other people felt about her, was well taken.
4. Mary should have been placed in a series of situations where she would have been forced to make choices and decisions.
5. The problem here was one of teaching Mary a number of skills so that she would have some basis for winning status with her peers.
6. The YWCA secretary was ill advised to speak to Mary in such a pointed fashion.
7. When the children in the ninth grade did not like to serve on committees with Mary, she should have been permitted to work by herself.
8. Mary should have been made to give up her room in favor of sharing one with her parents or brothers in order to eliminate the possibility of her being alone whenever she wanted to.
9. A summer camp some distance away from Central City where Mary would not meet any of her schoolmates would have been a good idea.
10. Mary needed to have considerable responsibility placed on her shoulders.
11. Mr. Marlowe was right in his opinion that he had been overindulgent with Mary. He should have been more strict.
12. The principal should have insisted that Mary be permitted to join the high school sorority.
13. Mary should have been institutionalized some time during her senior year.

14. The guidance counselor should have shown Mary some of the possibilities in interior decoration, art, or some other allied occupational field.
15. Mary needed more rebuffs to "toughen" her so that she could get along in typical social situations.
16. At almost any point in the progression of Mary's case, an understanding and sympathetic person would probably have eliminated much of her difficulty.
17. It was important that the parents should have taken some pains to see that when Mary was a child she met and played with other children.
18. The school authorities, that is, a homeroom teacher or the principal, should have talked to dependable, trustworthy girls in the high school in an attempt to persuade them to be nice to Mary and include her in their activities.
19. The Marlowes should have made a point of having company in their home, particularly during the family parties.
20. Mrs. Marlowe's attempts to set Alice Allen as an example for Mary were wise on the grounds that Mary needed as an example someone who was well adjusted socially.
21. The school should have concerned itself with promoting Mary's social adjustment even at the expense of her academic success.
22. The occupational counselor was well advised to indicate quite definitely to Mary the impossibility of her vocational desires.
23. Mary should have been removed from school and given a full-time job.
24. Mary should have been removed from her parents and placed in a foster home.
25. The best way to have eliminated Mary's daydreaming tendencies would have been to give her greater means of satisfaction with real-life situations.
26. The family insistence that Mary attend church regularly was a precipitating factor in her maladjustment.
27. Central High School should make a general rule that no one in school who wishes to join may be excluded from any school club.

28. If Mary could be graduated and sent to a college some distance from her hometown, her problems would probably clear up.
29. Mary should not have been allowed access to movie magazines.
30. The school authorities and Mary's parents should have cooperated in an effort to force her to cease daydreaming.
31. The school principal should try to encourage the vocational guidance director to take a friendly, sympathetic attitude toward Mary.
32. In school faculty meetings the teachers who have a special interest in Mary should discuss ways to help her.
33. Mary's homeroom teachers would have done well to find out how Mary felt about her problems.
34. It would have been a good idea to try to interest Mary in a correspondence club so that she could make some pen pals to whom she could write regularly.

Case Notes: An Interpretation[1]

The case of Mary Marlowe shows a socially maladjusted adolescent who is striving to gain status in the eyes of her peers and who is at the same time undergoing severe conflict in an effort to establish a satisfactory and acceptable self-concept. The case presents a continual picture of thwarting with a series of events that tend to impair Mary's confidence in herself and to establish feelings of insecurity and inferiority. Her behavior is marked by unusual fluctuation as she fights an unfriendly environment in her desire to be accepted and in her efforts to find herself. Incidents of aggression and overassertion are followed by spells of withdrawal characterized by daydreaming and fantasy, which become more serious as she proceeds through senior high school. There is evidence of increasing disor-

ganization and inability to meet a choice situation. In her senior year in high school her behavior is definitely prepsychotic, with good prospects of eventual institutionalization for schizophrenia if circumstances are not improved. She tries to end her uncertainty and frustration by attempting suicide in her seventeenth year.

Mary's early childhood was fairly normal. She did well in school, and while she was not popular, she was not disliked. There were, however, certain danger signals in her shyness and frequent desire to be alone. An early life on an isolated farm denied her the opportunity of meeting and playing with other children and thus of developing in normal social situations. In junior and senior high school there was gradual evidence of increasing unpopularity by an absence of friends of either sex, and by the fact that she belonged to no school clubs, including the potent status-building sorority. In her desire to be accepted, she reacted to rebuffs from her peers in a manner that accentuated and added to her difficulties. As she fought back, her behavior was variable and was misunderstood by her teachers, the other children, and her parents. When aggressive behavior did not get results, she retreated further from reality. Daydreams, which at first gave her satisfaction, began to tend toward fantasies in which she saw herself being deprived of something. She began to turn more and more from people and to become suspicious of their motives, but underneath it all there was still an intense desire to find acceptance.

Complicating the whole picture was Mary's inability to find and accept a role that she could play in life. She was trying to find herself and was having more than the average adolescent's difficulty. Her fluctuating and antagonistic occupational interests were attempts to find and accept a role. A great deal of her daydreaming took the form of trying to act out the role of a missionary or a glamorous theatrical star, but she was misunderstood by the other children. Mary gradually built up feelings of guilt and characterized herself as being "no good." Unfortunately at this stage almost any situa-

[1]The reader is urged to cover the preceding question statements before reading the case notes, which are typical of those a psychologist might have made.

tion that tended to impair Mary's confidence in herself, or to cause unusual uncertainty, impeded her progress in finding herself, which means that her social maladjustment became particularly serious. There was also a picture of low physical vitality and frequent minor illnesses and indispositions.

Mary's home is physically adequate and her parents are affectionate but overprotective. There is an undue amount of family-circle recreation and no opportunity for Mary to increase her social horizons. The family minister was undoubtedly an unfortunate influence because he failed to understand Mary or what she really wanted, and his discussions with her built up her feelings of uncertainty and guilt. The school was large and busy, and there is no evidence of understanding or sympathy on the part of any of her high school teachers. The principal, the homeroom teachers, and the guidance counselor were in particularly strategic positions, but did nothing. The guidance director does not appear to have given Mary any impression at all of the vocational opportunities open to her.

Essentially it appears that if at almost any point in Mary's high school career she could have had access to a sympathetic and understanding person who would have tried to help her, much might have been accomplished. The desire for social acceptance, an effort to find oneself, and a certain amount of daydreaming are some of the usual characteristics of the adolescent. In Mary's case it was a matter of greater degree and of continual blocking and frustration, which naturally elicited aggressive and withdrawing reactions. If Mary could have gained social acceptance, she would, in all probability, have had less difficulty in finding her own role, and there would have been no need for a retreat from reality, for reality would have been satisfying and confidence-inspiring. In the beginning, although there were certain predisposing factors present, Mary's behavior was not abnormal. It became increasingly deviate, however, when she failed to receive any help from others in working out her problems.

From a therapeutic point of view it was important to place Mary in a situation where she would find social acceptance among her peers so that she could build up feelings of confidence and security. Unfortunately Mary apparently did not possess attributes or skills that made it possible for her to do this without assistance. At this point two remedial alternatives present themselves. First would be the possibility of working with a group of reliable and dependable boys and girls in Central High School with the purpose of getting them to include Mary in their activities so that her confidence and feeling of acceptance could be built up. There are, of course, certain dangers in this technique. Careful selection of the boys and girls involved, however, would probably obviate that danger. Second would be the possibility of teaching or helping Mary attain certain skills that would make it possible for her to gain acceptance in her own right. This could range all the way from instruction in social behavior to specific training in some skill or activity esteemed by people of Mary's age group. There would also, of course, be the problem of furnishing her with opportunities to display those skills. Probably a combination of the two techniques would be best.

It would also be well if the guidance director could give Mary an adequate and interesting picture of the vocational possibilities open to her in terms of her abilities and interests. The minister and Mary's parents could be taken into the confidence of the people working with Mary; when her case and her problem were explained to them, they could offer considerable help. There should also be one or two sympathetic and understanding adults to whom Mary can go with her problems. If a school or clinical psychologist were available, it would be an appropriate part of his regular duties to work with Mary along these lines and help her to gain self-insight and personal and social adjustment. If no psychologist were available, an interested teacher or other adult could function excellently. In any event, the cooperation of the school authorities would be essential. In Mary's case the most important thing that Central City High School could do for her would be to promote her personal and social adjustment, even if it were at the expense of any other aspect of their educational program. In the event that enough had not been accomplished by the end of the senior year, it is suggested that Mary might be persuaded to take an additional, postgraduate, year.

The Value of Case Studies

The case of Mary Marlowe has given readers an opportunity to apply what they have learned in the first ten chapters of this textbook as they try their hand at diagnosis and remediation. For those who wish to learn more about human and adolescent behavior and to gain practice in thinking about and working with problems of behavior, the reading of case studies offers good training. If one does not have an opportunity to work with people, the case study is an excellent substitute. Making a case study is also good practice. If readers do not have an opportunity to make a study of someone else, they might find it good practice to write a personal case study—possibly in the third person as an aid to greater objectivity.

Suggested Readings

Barker, R. G., and Wright, H. F. *One boy's day: A specimen record of behavior.* New York: Harper, 1951.

Copeland, J. *For the love of Ann: Based on a diary by Jack Hodges.* New York: Ballantine, 1973.

Dreikurs, R. Family counseling: A demonstration. *Journal of Individual Psychology* 28 (1972): 207–222.

Dreikurs, R. Counseling a boy: A demonstration. *Journal of Individual Psychology* 28 (1972): 223–231.

Goethals, G. W., and Klos, D. S. *Experiencing youth: First-person accounts.* Boston: Little Brown, 1970.

Hawkey, L. Case study of an adolescent girl. *Journal of Analytical Psychology* 15 (1970): 138–147.

Horrocks, J. E., and Horrocks, W. B. *A study of Murray Mursell.* Columbus: Charles Merrill, 1960.

Horrocks, J. E.; Horrocks, W. B.; and Troyer, M. E. A study of Sam Smith; A study of Connie Casey; A study of Barry Black. Columbus: Charles Merrill, 1960.

Horton, P., and Miller, D. The etiology of multiple personality. *Comprehensive Psychiatry* 13 (1972): 151–159.

Jones, H. E. *Development in adolescence.* New York: Appleton-Century, 1943.

Kiell, N. *The adolescent through fiction.* New York: International Universities Press, 1959.

Kline, P., and Grindley, J. A 28-day case study with the M.A.T. *Journal of Multivariate Experimental Personality and Clinical Psychology* 1 (1973): 13–22.

Legeitner, C. W., and Berks, H. M. Behavioral counseling with a mentally retarded client: A case study. *Michigan Personnel and Guidance Journal* 4 (1973): 49–55.

Lorber, R., and Fladell, E. *The gap.* New York: McGraw-Hill, 1968.

Mosak, H. H. Life style assessment: A demonstration focused on family constellation. *Journal of Individual Psychology* 28 (1972): 232–247.

Perkin, G. J.; Rowe, G. P.; and Farmer, R. G. Operant conditioning of emotional responsiveness as a prerequisite for behavioral analysis: A case study of an adolescent school phobic. *Australian and New Zealand Journal of Psychiatry* 7 (1973): 180–184.

Pivetta, R. Obsessional neurosis: Etiology and biopsychological presuppositions: A comparative study involving Freudian and Piagetian theory. *Genetic Psychology Monographs* 88 (1973): 287–304.

Tars, S. E., and Appleby, L. The same child in home and institution: An observational study. *Environment and Behavior* 5 (1973): 3–28.

van Amerongen, S. T. The psychoanalysis of a young adolescent girl. *Journal of the American Academy of Child Psychiatry* 10 (1971): 23–52.

Witham, W. T. *The adolescent in the American novel, 1920–1960.* New York: Ungar, 1964.

PART FOUR

Motivation and Directionality of Behavior

Chapter Twelve

Interests and Activities

The Nature and Importance of Interests

An interest is an attitudinal set to give selective attention to a class of objects or activities that are of self-concern. The behavioral outcome of an interest is cognitive-affective activation leading to activity that may be intellectual, sympathetic, emotional, or merely personal in nature, such as an interest in philosophy or science, an interest in sports, an interest in human welfare, or an interest in looking well. Most interests are positive in that their expression involves a relatively large component of gratification, but there are also negative interests of avoidance and rejection. Larcebeau (1967), in a longitudinal study of the interests of children between ages of nine and seventeen, reports three general types: (1) social and personal interests (including ideas and comprehension of reality), (2) interest toward physical and concrete activities versus intellectual interests, and (3) interest toward pleasureful versus dutiful activities. Larcebeau also reported that the general interests of the children in his study remained relatively stable from the eleventh year on. In general, an individual's interests may be taken as an indication of his motivational structure. Group interests provide one means of defining the group.

A background knowledge of the most characteristic interests and preoccupations of teenagers is helpful in understanding and predicting adolescent behavior. We are in the best position to understand present behavior and to predict what will happen in the future when we know, within the limitations imposed by individual differences, what to expect an adolescent to think or like—in short, when we know the things upon which he bases his interests.

Certainly the most effective road to motivation and control of a person's behavior is through the things that interest him. However, the study of interests is complicated by the fact that the specific expressions of children's interests vary so much from year to year and from community to community—and are so greatly affected by individual differences, availability of interest media, and economic factors—that it is very difficult to present any highly valid or reliable picture. What is true in 1975 is surprisingly different from what was true in 1965, or will be true in 1985. A catalogue of studies of specific interests has the currency of a daily newspaper, but the basic attributes underlying interests are relatively stable. Manifestation of an interest is a passing thing varying with the times, but the psychological elements underlying the interest remain. For any particular year we may not be able to predict the form the interest will take in its manifestation, but we can predict the major direction children will take in expressing their interests.

Although it is impossible to be absolutely certain of the individual case, there are common biological and cultural things underlying all behavior. For example, we can know what things are most likely to be characteristic of a given sex at a given age. Therefore, it seems reasonable to approach the study of adolescent interests by considering those things that are ordinarily common to all adolescents. We may assume tentatively that a boy or girl who deviates seriously from the norm of his time may well be displaying crucial symptoms of maladjustment.

This does not imply that all deviation is abnormal or undesirable. In some cases, deviate behavior is not only desirable; it may even be essential. Thus, an understanding of any given individual's interests must be arrived at in terms of the interests common for his age and cultural status, along with his own personal idiosyncrasies and past experiences. Insofar as groups are concerned, the problem is easier because the norm is more apt to apply, although there are individual differences among groups as well as among individuals. This discussion will endeavor to ascertain who is interested in what and to trace the effects of that interest.

In considering interests two aspects must be taken into account. First, what interests does an individual of a given status generally have? Second, what does he do, or fail to do, about that interest? In psychology, the word *interest* is generally defined in positive terms. One is interested in those things that give pleasure or satisfaction, that compel and hold attention, or that offer a welcome challenge. Interest may be thought of in goal-need and tension-reduction terms. Some objects, activities, or sensations appear to have a positive valence for some individuals—the stronger the attraction; the greater the interest. This implies that when a person is interested, when he perceives a goal-object as desirable, activity will ensue as tension reduction; the reader may accept this implication with the understanding that, as is usual with behavioral phenomena, the activity may be covert as well as overt.

The individual's opportunity to do something about his interests is a function of his environment, his abilities, status, cultural relationships, the roles in life he habitually plays, his inhibitions, the time in history during which he lives, and the actual amount of interest-drive he has. Some adolescents are interested in games but do not know how to play. They may be unable to participate because they are isolated from other children by physical distance, by barriers of race or religion, or by social rejection on some other basis. Often a child who would like to participate in games, dancing, softball, or some other sport, but who lacks skill, will refuse to participate because he is afraid of being laughed at or ridiculed. Parental objection and lack of money or intellectual capacity are obvious reasons why an individual will refrain from doing things that interest him. Bledsoe and Brown (1965) note a decreasing interest in number of activities as children grow older, but they attribute the change to a crystallization of interests rather than to a decrease in interests as such.

There is also the question of success. Some adolescents have failed so often when they have attempted to do things that they have accepted the habit of refusing to participate. In arousing a person's interest, few things are more important than providing success experiences. We tend to do those things that we do best, at which we have been successful, and to avoid those things that cause us to fail or feel inadequate. Unfortunately, as competitive games are organized in our culture, the emphasis tends to be upon successful competition, and a premium is placed upon the successful competitor. Too often the game is not the most important thing.

But sports are not the only activities in which success is crucial. A boy or girl who reads poorly, for whom reading is a slow and painful process, will usually endeavor to read as little as possible. If a child has had a bad experience with mathematics in elementary school, he will often be uninterested in high school mathematics. He may even become emotionally upset when he is confronted with the need for numerical calculations. Another example is the boy who is interested in a girl but is uncertain how he should act. He may prefer to avoid her rather than submit to embarrassment. On the other hand, if he has summoned up his courage and been rebuffed, he may refuse to place himself in such a position in the future.

Interests,[1] apart from certain fundamental organ tensions, which soon become culturally conditioned in any event, are not innate. One is not congenitally interested in anything; one is interested because immediate environment and one's experiences and cultural milieu have engendered interest. It is difficult to separate interests from needs, attitudes, and motivation. General and specific abilities will enable an individual to derive certain satisfactions or success experiences from some kinds of activities, but this merely means one is able to make the most of one's environment because of physical structure or neural organization. In this case, socioeconomic position is comparable to physical endowment, because it accords privileges to some and withholds them from others.

In diagnosing a given individual's interest, the psychologist must realize that he cannot always proceed on the basis of what the individual is actually doing. Sometimes, as previously indicated, there are obstacles in attempting to satisfy certain interests. A frequency distribution of a given adolescent's daily activities may reveal that the activity in which he most frequently indulges is far from being the one he most prefers. In trying to determine the appropriateness of an adolescent's activities in the light of his real interests, the youth worker must fall back upon what he knows as most likely to be characteristic of youth and use that as a starting point in assuming the interests of the person with whom he is concerned. Later, as opportunity affords, he may be able to learn enough about the person involved to understand his interest status more fully.

---

[1] In relating the discussion of adolescent needs in Chapter 10 to the discussion of interests in this chapter, it should be recognized that an interest is usually manifested by a goal object or a goal activity and that *goal* and *interest* are not merely synonymous terms. An interest is served and satisfied by a goal object or a goal activity. The interest selects and makes the goal attractive. In this sense, interest is a very important aspect of motivation.

It is also important to realize the place of opportunity in interest formation. People with specific interests have them because they have had an opportunity to develop them. One cannot be expected to be interested in something one has neither seen nor heard about.

The intermediary task of the youth worker is to provide his charges with opportunities to develop desirable interests by helping to make available the necessary raw materials and skill. This he must do in a way that will make the boy or girl want to participate and to enjoy it.

Play Activities as Interests

Play is a spontaneous and voluntary activity performed for immediate gratification without ulterior motives. It represents an individual's free self-expression carried on for the sheer pleasure of the expression. Play as an activity is both highly motivated and self-sustaining. An individual at play is one who at that moment is doing what he finds most pleasurable. Play may be thought of as the implementation of interest. It is the activity expression of an interest and becomes a means of demonstrating interests through actually doing something about them.

A good many years ago, in a comprehensive objective study of play activities of children, Lehman and Witty (1927) defined play as doing what one wants to do. Of course this is an oversimplification, because there are degrees of "doing what one wants to do." The adolescent may go out for the football team because he likes to play football. But he may do so also because of the social approval and prestige accorded to a varsity member, the need to keep in shape, and perhaps other reasons. Slobin (1964) notes that in answering the question, "Why do children play?" we must consider the source of play energy, the biological functions of play, preference over other activities, continuance of games, and relationships of play to child development. Thus any child's or adolescent's play goals may be multiple and, almost inevitably, are a mixture of intrinsic and extrinsic ends.

One may regard play in terms of its content "activity" or, ignoring content, in terms of its antecedents and consequents. Some theorists have considered play primarily in developmental terms, that is, as a necessary part of the developmental process leading to the possibility of further development. Others have considered play primarily as an arena for behavior that serves to fulfill an individual's existing psychological needs. The former see play primarily as a characteristic of childhood, while the latter do not see play as being confined to any one age, although its incidence is recognized as greatest during the early years.

It is a problem for all concerned that play is ordinarily thought of as the occupation of childhood with resulting reluctance to admit that it extends beyond childhood even into adolescence, let alone adulthood. Yet whatever our station in life, whatever our prestige or lack of it, we all play throughout our life span. If we are lucky we are able to play a great deal. The fact that we give it another name—hobby, activity, avocation, interest, vocation, relaxation, or recreation—does not negate the actuality and purpose of the play activity in consideration.

Because play traditionally has been assumed to be confined to childhood, most of the theories of play deal only with its occurrence during the first decade of life and confine their interpretations to that period. Piaget (1951), for example, divides the development of play into three stages corresponding to those of cognitive development, and visualizes it merely as a process of thinking needed by a child to achieve movement from his early egocentric to his later objective and rational outlook. Piaget feels that an adult's mastery of reality makes it unnecessary for him to resort to play except in dreams and in certain types of incidental behavior such as doodling. Here Piaget misses the point. It is because as adults we occasionally need to retreat from or to reshape reality that we indulge in play behavior. Play can also be symbolic of reality as well as nonreality states. An adolescent or an adult will use play to meet the needs of his particular stage of life and will adapt it to meet intellectual and emotional demands. Play becomes particularly important during adolescence when an individual is testing reality and endeavoring to build adequate and satisfying concepts of self. The long period of moratorium permitted the adolescent when he is neither a child nor an adult and when he is not yet a member of the regular work force permits the adolescent ample opportunity for *play*, as long as he does not use the term. As a matter of fact, there is reason to believe that an adolescent tends to bring the moratorium with him to his first jobs and will often behave accordingly—sometimes to the annoyance of his employer, who feels that he should be paying wages to an adult rather than to an adolescent.

In the study of adolescent interests, play activities can be a useful means of showing the kinds of things that appeal to an adolescent when he is on his own, not under an adult's direct supervision. Play activities may also provide insight into an adolescent's efforts to cope with reality and to test his own self-view.

Play is sometimes defined as *useless behavior*. This definition clearly negates what play really is. Uselessness depends upon one's point of view; what is considered useless will vary from individual to individual, and from group to group. Bridge for an expert could hardly be called useless, but for someone unfamiliar with or opposed to the game it would most certainly be a useless activity. Public reaction to baseball or to a traditional holiday is part of the same contrast in viewpoints. Not only will the idea of usefulness vary from individual to individual, but the individual will himself change his mind about what is useful from time to time. Culbertson, once a famous bridge teacher, became less interested in bridge when he developed an interest in world government. An adolescent who played marbles or collected stamps as a child may contemptuously observe his younger brother indulging in the same activity and term it *useless*.

As a matter of fact, play may best be described as something interesting one does primarily because one wants to. In this sense, work, as ordinarily defined, may be play for a given individual. For this reason the high school vocational counselor should determine his counselee's interests so that he may help him enter a field of work that will, in effect, allow him to play as he works.

Probably the great difference between actual work and play is the more intermittent nature of the latter. When we grow tired of playing, we turn to something else. In vocational life such fluctuation is usually impossible. Of course, a person who has chosen his occupation as the result of sound vocational counseling may more often be able to "play" on his job than may one whose vocational selection has been less well advised. Therefore, activity described as play is a matter of the individual's point of view. There is no reason why play cannot be both play and work at the same time. In any event, an activity becomes play as the individual feels that it is, no matter what anyone else may think. Young children tend to be more unselective in their play than are adolescents, who are more likely to choose play activities more in line with their abilities. Nugent (1961) reports that eleventh-grade children whose interests and aptitudes were similar showed better personality scores than did those who showed a discrepancy between interests and aptitudes, but this relationship did not hold true for ninth graders. However, children's interests do tend to display a pattern of similarity that transcends even national boundaries, particularly when the cultures of the countries involved are not too different. For example, Tyler (1956), in a comparative study of English and American preadolescents, reports interest correlations of .84 and .89 (answers to a questionnaire) with samples drawn from the two countries. It is interesting that Tyler found sex differences more important than national differences, in that the interests of boys as compared to girls in either the United States or Great Britain were considerably less similar than were those between boys and boys and girls and girls across the boundaries of the two countries.

For the teacher or youth worker, play can be an extremely powerful device with which to motivate activity in learning. When an event or an activity is interesting enough to a person—when he considers it play—he will participate in it much more willingly, more effectively, and for longer periods of time. The teaching of any school subject will be most effective when approached via the interests of the class enrolled, with special recognition of individual interests that may depart somewhat from those of the group. The power of play may be illustrated by Jimmie's case. He can find all kinds of excuses to avoid digging a hole in the backyard for his mother's new plant. But the same Jimmie will spend hour upon hour, day after day, digging an elaborate system of trenches and fortifications with his friends on a neighboring hillside so they can play at war. Equally familiar is the case of Tom Sawyer, whose aunt assigned him the disagreeable task of whitewashing the fence. Tom, using the "proper psychological approach," persuaded a passing friend who really wanted to go fishing that whitewashing a fence was just about the most wonderful job in the world. As a result, the friend paid Tom to let him take over the job of whitewashing.

In a former day, and in some groups today, work as contrasted to play is supposed to have great virtue. "Work" is supposed to build character, while "play" is regarded as demoralizing. The approach is summed up in the biblical quotation, "When I was a child, I spake as a child, I understood as a child: but when I became a man, I put away childish things" (1 Corinthians 13:11). This point of view was particularly compatible with a rural economy where everyone living on a farm was required, no matter what his age, to pitch in and help. It was not uncommon for a boy to be working alongside his father doing a man's work long before he had reached his fifteenth year. In rural America until well into the twentieth century, schools were simply closed during harvest periods so that everybody could go to work. Girls were no exception. There were always heavy expectations for them in the work of the kitchen as well as in the plethora of chores to be done about house, barn, and garden. The inception of the Industrial Revolution and child labor in the factories, including children as young as ten, was a fact of life for many decades in the industrial economies of Europe and the United States.

The modern viewpoint fortunately rejects this approach for children on the basis that "good character" is not a direct result of self-denial and boredom. It is believed that a child will be better off if he can explore and develop his interests. This does not imply that interests may not or should not be guided; the implication is that if we know the things in which an individual is or may become interested and use those interests as a starting point, we may in time gradually induct him into experiences more nearly in line with what we would like to have him do and can help him succeed in his new ventures. This is particularly important; to quote an old saying now grown trite, "Nothing succeeds like success."

Of course the modern viewpoint is not confined to children. Early retirement, the world of hobbies, and expectations that adolescents will engage in play activities, indicate an implicit admission that indivduals may still play after their twelfth year, although there is still a feeling that the play ought somehow to be justified. As a matter of fact, there seems to be an unwitting attempt to turn piay into work as a way of making it respectable. If an adolescent wishes to play a sport while he is in school, his first encounter is apt to be with a professional coach who instructs him not only in rules and techniques of play but introduces him to the world of competitive sports where the job is to win. He is told that keeping in condition so that he can play is "good" for him. If he wishes to take up photography, he is inducted into a club where he can "learn" to take pictures and presumably enter them in contests. If he wants to travel abroad, he is told that he should learn a language and study history so that he may "meet the people" and "profit" otherwise from his trip. When an adolescent has learned to disassemble and assemble the engine of his automobile and keeps doing it over and over again, adults justify it by saying that he is learning and may someday put it to vocational use. The fact that play

ideally involves creation, is often symbolic, and allows one to test reality, as well as to leave the world of restraint and reality, seems to have been forgotten.

The Use of Interests in Learning

The youth worker should constantly be on the alert to seek out his charges' interests and to use those interests as a springboard into new activities and experiences. One method of setting up exploratory programs in high school might be in terms of a skill quest. Under the skill-quest plan the school institutes a series of exploratory hobby courses so that each pupil has an opportunity to sample a wide variety of hobby and recreational experiences over a period of time. Since a course can die from lack of interest if it continues too long, each exploratory course should be limited to a period not exceeding ten weeks (ten meetings), after which it can be discontinued in favor of another. During this period an overview of the hobby involved could be provided and preliminary attempts made to develop the skills that are needed.

A wide selection of courses should be offered and publicized by mimeographing the list, with course descriptions. Descriptions and discussions could be given in the school paper and in the assembly. The whole aim should be to arouse interest and popularity. Each student would be expected to register for one such course a semester, or in some cases, perhaps for more than one. If real interest were aroused, the student could reregister the second time the course was given and perhaps help in presenting the material, as older Boy Scouts do in their group operation. If a group seems really interested, an advanced course might be arranged for them after they have completed the preliminary course.

The students' expressed interests may well serve as the final guide to the number of such courses to give and the hobbies and recreations to include. The faculty, after a survey of their own interests, might offer some usable suggestions based upon their knowledge of the particular school and community and of the likes and dislikes of high school children in general. Some of the courses offered would be so popular that it would probably be necessary to hold more than one section. Examples of possible courses include dressmaking, singing, photography, sketching, hiking, social dancing, tap dancing, stamp collecting, camp cookery, first aid, wood finishing, bookbinding, gardening, and public speaking. In fact, anything that people may profitably do in their spare time could become the basis of study for a group of interested boys and girls. How practical or theoretical each course is should depend entirely upon the group taking it. Such courses have more than a recreational significance; they may also serve as leads into possible vocations or may help the student in his choice of school electives.

The skill-quest approach may be applied in situations other than the school. It is useful in a summer camp, a club, a community house, a YMCA or YWCA, or in any of the numerous other places where young people gather to participate in some kind of organized program. The skill quest need not be as highly organized or formalized in terms of course content as the above example seems to imply. The whole idea is to expand the possibilities of old interests and to explore new ones.

The Junior Achievement Program is an interesting attempt to give adolescents an opportunity to explore an interest that may have vocational possibilities and to simultaneously engage in a business-educational venture that would give them experience and some financial return. Under this program groups of adolescents of both sexes, aged fifteen to twenty-one, are set up in small companies operated and managed by the boys and girls themselves. A sponsor is provided for each junior business by the local business concern or civic or professional group sponsoring the idea in that particular community. The local sponsor group also arranges for the services of advisers who are recognized experts in production, business, and sales. Each junior achievement company is composed of boys and girls who have their sponsor's advice and technical assistance. They

sell stock at fifty cents a share for working capital with which to start their business.

The classroom teacher may take the class interests as a starting point in teaching her subject matter. A teacher of literature or of history has rich motivational resources in the ever-present interests of high school boys and girls in heterosexual relations, manners and ways of doing things, competitive activity, and striving against difficulty. It is not a big step from action stories to historical novels, and from historical novels to biography and non-fiction works.

Differences and Similarities of Interests

The previous discussion has considered the nature of interests and their importance as a motivating factor in human activity. Play was defined and introduced as an implementation of interest—a way of putting an interest to work and of getting something out of it. The following discussion will examine kinds of interests and activities and try to answer a number of questions: Who does what? Are certain interests and activities characteristic of adolescents in general? Are certain ones particularly accentuated or missing during the teens? Are sex differences present and, if so, to what degree? What other variables make for interest differences during adolescence, from one adolescent to another and from adolescents to older and younger people? How is it possible to know what an individual's interests are? Are there ways to ascertain an individual's interests other than by finding out what he actually does? How constant are interests—that is, do they fluctuate from person to person and from time to time, and if so, to what extent?

What do young people do? What do they like to do? The answer must at best be provisional since we must immediately ask the question: What youth and where? Some of the variables which make for differences in interests during the adolescent period range all the way from the obvious differences (age, sex) through the differences caused by the less obvious factors of intelligence, socioeconomic status, place of residence, physical endowment, opportunities and experiences, period of history, and parental restrictions and taboos.

A good many studies have been made categorizing the various interests of youth and listing the categories in order of popularity. The difficulty with such studies is the ephemeral nature of the findings, which often makes them out of date before they are published. Of course, some adolescent interests are permanent, universal, and perennially popular, but more are not. Times change rapidly in the adolescent world, and the interest of today may well be of no interest tomorrow. Too, restricted sampling in a large and diverse country can lead only to extremely limited generalizations. The chief values of lists of interests are that they enable the investigators to relate his findings to the variables of individual differences and furnish raw materials for the formulation or hypotheses about adolescence that could lead to further research.

Intellectual Differences

Various studies have investigated children's activities in relation to level of intellectual capacity. In such studies, which usually relate intelligence of children to their hobbies, extracurricular activities, in-school and out-of-school activities, several trends appear: (1) children with higher IQs tend to have a wider range of hobby interests and to be more mature in their interests than do children of lesser intelligence; (2) children who participate in extracurricular activities are of higher average intelligence than are nonparticipants; and (3) extracurricular activities emphasizing social activities tend to attract a lower IQ group, while activities such as drama and school publications draw the children of higher IQ. In general, brighter children tend to be less interested in more active competitive games, while children of lesser intelligence have a greater interest in social activities. There are individual exceptions, particularly where the school policy encourages such exceptions.

In a comparative study of 359 children in grades seven through twelve (176 with an IQ of 111 or above and 183 with an IQ of 90 or below), Gross (1957) reported that boys of low intelligence showed greater interest in solitary out-of-doors activities such as hunting, fishing, and hiking. They also showed greater interest in more aggressive activities such as fighting, football, and roller-skating. Both girls and boys of higher intelligence were more interested in going to school affairs than were those of lesser intelligence. In discussing his results, Gross noted that for both the high- and the low-IQ groups of boys as they advanced in school, the activities in which they indicated greatest interest cost more money. The activities of older boys became less outdoor and less aggressive than was characteristic of the younger adolescent. A similar pattern of increasing interest in sedentary activities with increasing age was also found in girls.

Both intelligence and academic achievement have been shown to have some relation to the kinds of interests held by adolescent boys and girls. Contrary to the popular view that intelligence has a low correlation with the number of activities indulged in, it has been found that intelligent people tend to be "all-around" people. They frequently participate in a greater number of activities of a more diverse nature than do the less intelligent. Despite the number of sedentary and intellectual activities in which he indulges, the intelligent child's focus of interest does not seem to show undue emphasis upon such activities, although they are undoubtedly more within the grasp of intelligent children in terms of comprehension and success. It may be that the more intelligent person is more alert, hence is alive to more aspects of his environment. He may be more efficient and therefore may have more time to indulge in a wide variety of activities, although it might be expected that the quality of some of his activities would exceed those of less intelligent children. Retarded children often show relatively more social participation, mostly because success experiences with other types of activity are more difficult. Whenever an individual finds the possibility of success blocked in one field of endeavor, he is very apt to pick some substitute activity by which to gain success. If he continues an activity in which his success is impossible, his mental health and personal adjustment may suffer, particularly if he is deeply involved emotionally. In school, much problem behavior results in children whose academic success is blocked and who must look elsewhere for satisfaction. Group or social activity offers an excellent substitute, provided it is constructive. Unfortunately, the substitute social activity too often takes the form of antisocial or problem behavior in a group banded together to resist the status quo. Every juvenile court calendar is filled with such cases.

Any school with a child who regularly fails in his studies and who lacks success experiences has a potential problem behavior case, which may fall short of juvenile delinquency but which may cause trouble unless substitute activities and experiences are provided to help the child adjust better to his environment. Unfortunately, many schools take the opposite approach. A child who fails in his academic work is not allowed to go out for the team, is not allowed to participate in extracurricular activities, is placed on public probation, or is kept after school. If, because of his mental endowment, an emotional difficulty, or poor counseling, he is unable to succeed at his studies, the very sources he needs to gain his substitute satisfactions are officially denied him by the school. Under the circumstances, his only recourse is to seek them where he can; that may well be in some form of delinquent activity. Resentment builds up against the school and the teachers who deny him his activities, and this in turn may lead to further problem behavior, which will result in further restrictions as a vicious circle is set in motion. However, submission and withdrawal are psychologically even worse than overt resistance, because they are more likely to wreck the good adjustment and personality structure of the individual involved. The youth worker is thus faced with a challenge. How best to define an adolescent's needs and desires and then to serve those needs and desires in a way that will help the boy or girl attain optimum social and emotional adjustment, as well as achievement to the level of his capacity?

Sex Differences

Both popular thinking and scientific research have long recognized sex differences in interests. There are many reasons for such differences, ranging all the way from boys' physical structure, which gives them the greater potential strength required by some activities, to cultural preconceptions, which arbitrarily assign contrasting roles to the sexes. As was noted earlier, there are some things boys are permitted to do—indeed, must do—if they are to retain the approval of those around them. By the same token, the fact of being a girl has usually entailed the requirement of indulging in certain "feminine" activities and vigorously refusing certain "masculine" prerogatives. Bledsoe and Brown (1965) report that girls are significantly more interested in art, music, and home arts and boys express greater preference for manual arts and active play. In a survey of the home interests of early adolescents, Amatora (1962) reports that girls expressed highest interest in things involving the mechanics of running a home, while boys' interests were more along the lines of hobbies, pets, and animals. Girls are more interested in the home as a home than are boys, thus assuming early the role assigned females in the culture. In Amatora's study both boys and girls expressed interest in reading and in the spectator activities of radio and TV. In a study of French adolescents, Bernard (1965) noted girls' interest in individual sports, as compared to boys' predilection for team sports. The greatest audiovisual interest of French adolescents was TV, with relatively little interest in motion pictures. Music was of great importance, mostly modern of the yé-yé type. Both boys and girls tended to own large collections of records and a record player. Both sexes did a fairly extensive amount of reading, although boys were less interested in reading than girls were. In general, one could conclude from Bernard's study that French and American adolescents are quite alike in their major interests. Perhaps one crucial difference is French adolescents' preference for family vacations, which many American parents have found entirely lacking in their teenagers.

As adolescents become interested in the opposite sex and begin dating, boys and girls tend to find many interests in common. However, the existing sex differences may often cause trouble when younger boys and girls are thrown together. Girls' social interests mature earlier than do those of boys, and boys often find themselves being corralled—particularly in school or by parents—into activities and programs that they would prefer to avoid.

The culture assigns to each sex what it considers to be the appropriate sex role and tends not to sanction deviations from these roles. Some interests are assigned to males and excluded from females, and vice versa. Yet some adolescents have interests that are more usual in members of the opposite sex.[2] This may cause the deviating adolescent some real problems of acceptance by his peers and his elders, but it may also bring advantages. Mussen (1962) studied the personality and social characteristics of male late adolescents who were classified either as highly masculine or as relatively feminine in interests. He wrote, "As adolescents, the highly masculine-interest Ss were socially successful and apparently emotionally well adjusted, but failed to develop attributes of sociability and outgoingness." The relatively feminine-interest males showed

more of the "emotional-expressive" role characteristics ordinarily found in adulthood, rather than at their age level.

As times change, behavioral sex differences change with new mores and new customs. Such changes are usually slow in taking place, but at some periods in history they accelerate, usually to be followed by a period of little change while gains are being consolidated. The period of the 1960s represented a period of acceleration that has continued in the 1970s. The result seems to be a narrowing of sex differences, entirely apart from "liberation" or fair-practices legislation, that seems to have moved both sexes from extremes of masculinity and femininity closer to a common base. Both boys and girls during the adolescent years are free—and accept the freedom—to do things that a generation ago would have been frowned on as unwomanly or unmanly. Here is an area where the generation gap shows, because previous generations have difficulty in accepting ways radically different from the ones under which they were reared. Yet the climate of today is generally more permissive than previously, and the gap is certainly not uniform. In some cases members of the older generation are somewhat ahead of their adolescent progeny not only in accepting but in promoting new ways. It is interesting that while adolescents are usually seen as harbingers of change —the new generation in being—they are essentially at a conservative stage in their life span when too apparent change becomes emotionally upsetting. Many an adolescent has remonstrated with his parents when he has seen them becoming too different, and hence conspicuous, where community expectations are concerned.

Youth workers can make a mistake in overemphasizing sex differences. Obviously sex differences in interest patterns do exist, but there are activities common to both sexes that transcend the differences. When really conspicuous differences are found, they tend to be the exception rather than the rule. Girls generally are more apt to engage in sedentary activities in which little vigorous action is required. Boys tend to be interested in com-

[2]There are personality and interest measures yielding masculinity-feminity scores. A median position or even a standard deviation in the direction of the opposite sex is appropriate today on the basis that any male or female needs some leavening with the interests of the other sex. Deviation toward an interest in activities appropriate to the opposite sex would classify a boy as having a masculinity-femininity index more on the femininity side than would the majority of his sex, while a girl deviating on the side of boys' interests would have a masculinity-femininity index tending toward the masculine side. It should be emphasized that masculinity-femininity indices are measures of interests, not of homosexuality or tendency toward homosexuality. For example, male interior decorators could be expected to have a higher than ordinary femininity index simply because their occupation involves values and interests in areas the culture usually assigns to females.

petitive games requiring muscular dexterity and skill. As a group they do not resist organized activities as much as girls do, and their recreations are usually somewhat more active and vigorous. Girls are also less variable in their interests and activities and will fluctuate less from age to age.

Differences with Age

It is interesting to note that there are fewer sex differences in interests with advancing age. This may be due in part to a greater number of intersex activities as one grows older. One specific fact seems to be the existence of reversals. At one age, boys will be interested in a given activity while girls are not. A few years later, girls will be very much interested in the same activity while boys are not. The conclusion, as far as sex differences in inter-

ests during adolescence are concerned, appears to be that generalizations are unwise, and that although dramatic differences do exist, they tend to be the exception rather than the rule. In any event, most of the differences, insofar as they exist, are culturally caused or are due to physical limitations in girls.

In a comprehensive 1959 study of changes in interest with age, Pressey and his coworkers asked 4,187 individuals from grade six through college to indicate on a check list of ninety amusements and recreations those in which they were most interested. Some of the more dramatic changes are shown in Figure 16. Social matters like dancing, of little interest at the earlier ages, become increasingly important as the adolescent grows older. At the same time, the more physically active interests are replaced by interests of a more sedentary nature.

Figure 16 *Changes in Interest with Age. Note: Changes are shown by number of checks for each interest per 100 students.*

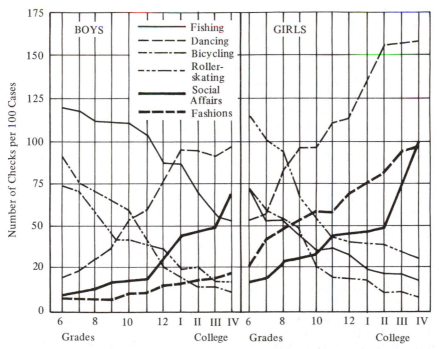

Source: Adapted from S. L. Pressey, F. P. Robinson, and J. E. Horrocks, *Psychology in education* (New York: Harper & Row, 1959), p. 88, fig. 4.1. Reprinted by permission of the publisher.

Physical Differences

The type of activity that is definitely determined on physical grounds, either for boys or girls, is one which requires strength, physical health, or coordination. The ability to play is partially determined by a person's physical endowments. Among junior high school boys the quality of their muscular tissue determines the extent of their participation and the type of activity they indulge in. Low or deficient muscular strength can be a limiting factor in boys' play activities. However, it should be remembered that lack of participation is not necessarily an index of lack of interest. Many a nonparticipator may be vitally interested. If interest exists without participation, it is the youth worker's task to help the youth redirect his interests or find outlets within his capacities. This is particularly important for the physically handicapped.

Differences Between Rural and Urban Youth

And what of the recreational activity of the adolescent in the many small towns scattered across the face of America—such towns as those with a gas station or two, a short-order restaurant, and, if the town is larger, a movie theater and perhaps a gathering center where pool may be played or drinks served? There are, of course, the local school activities and, for some, the church or the Grange. Still, for the teenager who does not want to stay home in the evening to look at TV, listen to the radio, or read, there is very little to do. For boys a gas station is a common meeting ground where bull sessions about girls, engines, and sports take up most of the time. As a matter of fact, the automobile is the real focus of an adolescent's activity. In it he can escape the narrow confines of his town; he can "park" with his date unhampered by adults; he can tinker with its engine, race it, use it to prove his manhood and sophistication, use it as a status symbol, and continually use it as a conversation piece. It is little wonder that their automobiles are dear to the adolescents of

rural America, and little wonder that the teenage boy without a car (or access to one), or the teenage girl without a boy friend with a car faces a whole host of problems.

This discussion also presents the situation of the farm youth who is even more isolated and for whom a car is a virtual necessity when he wishes to get away from the farm. One difference is that the farm boy is often a "working man" on his parents' farm and his participation is an economic necessity. The responsibility, skill, and adult acceptance his working role involves tends to make his existence more satisfying and less aimless than that of his small-town age-mate. There are also activities such as Four-H and the Grange to engage his interest. For both small-town and farm boys the church can also provide a social as well as a religious outlet and often becomes more of an activity focus than it does in the urban community.

It is in the area of interest and activity opportunities offered in school that the gap between urban and rural youth has narrowed to the greatest extent over the past generation. The old one-room school, except for the very early grades in some rural areas, has virtually disappeared. The rural adolescent of today is bussed or drives himself to the large centralized school, which has enough children of any age or sex to make it possible to form groups that can indulge in activities for specific ages and interests without shaping them to the interests and abilities of a wide age range.[3]

With the advent of the large rural centralized school and the continued urbanization of country life, urban and rural differences are lessening, although some aspects of rural living remain relatively unchanged in the more isolated regions of even such industralized countries as Canada and the United States. There is still the comparative isolation of

[3]In the one-room school, there were about forty children of both sexes ranging in age from five years through the late teens. The tendency was for the children to play together regardless of sex or age distinction. During recess and at noon hour they played red rover, tag, volleyball, or some other group game in which all could join and which was, for the most part, played so that even the younger members could participate.

country life, which often makes group activity, outside the brief interlude of going to school, something that simply does not occur. As Lehman and Witty (1927) point out, rural life permits the child reared in the country much freer expression, whereas city life, despite its occasional provision of greater opportunity for group activity, tends to be restrictive. A child reared in a small city apartment misses countless opportunities to exploit interests that commonly absorb his country cousin.

Socioeconomic Differences

A long series of studies have reported the importance of socioeconomic status as a determiner of the nature and direction of children's interests and activities. But as the technological nature of our society changes standards of living and as the mass media need-promotion succeeds, some of the former interest differentiations between the classes become blurred. In American culture most adolescent boys want to do things pertaining to cars, entertainment, dressing to conform, sexual relationships, social contacts with girls, companionship with those of like interests, and sports. But although the goals are common, the economic facts of life are present and make for differential facilities and resources in attaining the goals. For example, in the upper socioeconomic brackets a boy may have a car, but the very fact of having it limits his activity because typically a lot of time is spent in caring for the car, giving friends a ride, and thinking and talking about the next car. On the other hand, the car permits many freedoms, particularly in the heterosexual domain. The lower socioeconomic class adolescent who does not have a car really gains many freedoms thereby, but it would be exceedingly difficult to convince him of their value when they are seen as the price for not having "wheels." Probably one thing adolescent boys of all classes have in common, as Sherif and Sherif (1964) note, is that they want to do on their own those things that adults do, but without adult interference or programming.

Still it is difficult to find definite interest and activity statements that can be widely generalized. Socioeconomic status is conditioned by many variables such as race, urban-rural locale, subcultural group, and geographical location.

Interests as Represented by Group Activity

Informal groups play a much more important part in the adolescent's life than do formally organized groups. They may be thought of as a focal area of experience in the process of coming of age. The activities of the members of such informal groups may be seen as one way of examining adolescent interests. Such an examination may be made with particular reference to those attitudes and activities that contrast one group to another, as well as to the commonalities that bind them all together as part of the larger adolescent peer society.

Phelps and Horrocks (1958), in a study of the activities of informal adolescent groups in a Midwestern town of 9,500, were able to categorize the informal groups that existed in the community on the basis of nine different factors. Although this study was conducted in the 1950s and specific activities of youth have changed to some extent, periodic checks on the nature of the various groups in that community indicate that the groupings described in the Phelps and Horrocks study have remained unchanged over the intervening years.

Phelps and Horrocks reported that each informal adolescent grouping in the community focused its interest and had its reasons for being in one specific constellation of attitudes and interests that set it off from other groups. There were nine such constellations, and each informal group could be identified as primarily exemplifying one of them. The kinds of groups identified were as follows.

1. A group exhibiting a pattern of pressures leading to assumption of the adult role, emancipation from home, and assumption of heterosexual interests. None of the activities

that interested this grouping of children were home centered or home influenced to any degree. Associated with their extrahome interests appeared a need for ranging about and going some distance from the community for social participation. For the most part, these children were older adolescents of lower socioeconomic status and average or less than average intelligence. Having an automobile was very important. There was considerable interest in "hanging around" local restaurants, driving to a nearby city, just driving around, and dating. The grouping was heterosexual; movies were popular (particularly a drive-in about three miles out of town); the group liked to walk around town and window-shop; and they were often found in the local bowling alley or picnic grounds, where there was not ordinarily much supervision.

2. A group governed by a pattern of pressures in the form of a moral code approved by the school and upper socioeconomic home. These children were younger adolescents from upper socioeconomic homes. They disapproved of behavior and attitudes generally considered socially unacceptable and exhibited a moralistic point of view that seemed to indicate a need to conform to certain social standards. Many of their activities were connected with school, and there was an emphasis on family loyalty. The group's attitude judged as undesirable people who smoke, tell off-color jokes, "park," "neck," ride motorcycles, are noisy, swear, play cards, and race cars. Their favorite gathering places included school assemblies, noon movies at school, high school sport events, the city swimming pool, and a local hamburger joint. They liked to go to movies together but avoided the drive-in and (in general) places frequented by children whose attitudes and activities were unacceptable. Bicycle riding and hiking were favored physical activities. These children sometimes watched television together.

3. A nonemancipated group exhibiting home-, school-, and community-centered activity patterns. Children in this type of grouping were younger adolescents and usually were all-girl groups. Ordinarily the groups would consist of seven or more persons, all of middle-class socioeconomic status. Most of their activities were ones that would generally be approved by parents and teachers. In contrast to Group 1 above, all their activities could be carried on within a relatively short radius of home. Very prominent was going to stores where ice cream and other dairy products could be purchased. This grouping had many activities, including having picnics, listening to the radio and to records, bicycle riding, making candy, roller-skating, playing cards, playing volleyball, having parties, going swimming, and playing tennis. Activities related to school life, such as going to school affairs, studying together, going to the public library, the school lunchroom, and assemblies, were of particular interest.

4. A group exhibiting a pattern of activities and values deriving from a very low socioeconomic status. Children in groupings of this type lived in the poorest housing in the city's poorest section. There was a general trend for them to have IQs of less than 89. They liked to form their groups from people who lived in their neighborhood and were of about the same age. They rejected people from the "best" part of town and preferred children whose fathers were laborers, although they were quite accepting of the social class value of "getting ahead" and of going to college. Their groupings were sometimes biracial; physical strength was seen as an important attribute; and many of them worked after school. Church was important to them; they felt that group members should be in early at night; and they particularly liked persons who were agreeable and "always kidding." Movie attendance was not popular, nor were more elaborate or expensive eating places. One restaurant of very poor appearance, located in the business district, was popular (as it also was for Group 1 members), as were three dairy bars. Roller-skating was a favored activity. About groups of this type, the investigators noted:

Perhaps they sensed the social and economic differences between themselves and other adolescents and were trying to make up for them by having higher ideals as manifested by their attitude toward church attendance and their somewhat unrealistic aspiration of going to college. Lack of financial means must not have been the sole determiner of the kinds of activities they participated in for they were able to patronize several restaurants and dairy bars.

5. A group exhibiting a pattern of pressures leading to the assumption of an upper socioeconomic, quasi-adult social role. Such groupings were usually large and consisted of middle- and upper-class boys and girls of above-average intelligence from better homes. Members were usually eleventh or twelfth graders. Many of their activities depended upon being a member of a family in average or better socioeconomic circumstances. These groupings exhibited the members' need to satisfy heterosexual interests and to participate in activities away from home and community. However, many of their activities, such as slumber parties, listening to records, and having picnics, suggest that family approval and ability of parents to provide certain facilities were important influences. Girls in such groupings liked to dance, make candy, date, play tennis, and swim. The boys tended not to participate in organized school sports or in activities such as hunting. They preferred to have members of the group recognize the importance of good manners and liked to date. There was considerable use of automobiles and going out of town to have a good time. Two higher quality restaurants in town and one about three-fourths of a mile away, on the outskirts, were popular. In general, the group liked to eat and talk in restaurants but shunned establishments popular with Groups 1 and 3. Many activities were school-centered, and group members of the type who would not quit school were preferred.

6. Groups showing pressures toward social conformity manifested by a concern for good appearances and rejection of a noisy, "show-off" type of behavior. Adolescents in such groupings rejected persons who "park," make wisecracks, want to quit school, ride motorcycles, race cars, smoke, and are too noisy.

They felt that good clothing and manners were essential, that good looks were very important, that their members like school and have jobs after school, that they not disagree among themselves, and that they "stick up" for their family. Most of their activities were associated with the school and a small dairy bar.

7. Groups exhibiting patterns of pressures and needs involved in playing a masculine role. Favorite activities were golf, football, basketball, swimming, tennis, wrestling, fishing and hunting, pool, and hiking. A water gym with picnicking facilities about three miles outside the city and the city swimming pool were favorite gathering places. Restaurants were favorite places to congregate, and they liked to sit and talk there. They were to some extent school-centered, liked their members to be popular in school, and were interested in obtaining after-school jobs. They did a lot of "hanging around" outside school. Most members were boys, but there was a fifty-fifty chance that any such group would contain some girls. This suggests that the females involved were having difficulty in establishing their roles as feminine members of society and found the masculine participative groups a good social outlet. Socioeconomic variables were not important in such groupings.

8. Groups characterized by a pattern of pressures resulting from adult domination and lack of emancipation from the home. Groups of this type consisted of persons who strive to please parents and teachers. Group members wanted their friends to be good students, to plan on going to college, to stay out of trouble with teachers, and to mind their parents. What other people thought was considered important, and good manners were appreciated. The groups were willing to maintain their standards at the expense of sometimes being thought peculiar by their peers. Most of the group members were ninth and tenth graders.

9. Groups manifesting need for approval and status growing out of pressures applied by the middle-class family. These groupings were mostly middle-class older girls whose need for approval and status was expressed in maintaining the very best of appearances, having

good intentions, associating with the right people, and avoiding activities that might mark one as an uncouth or unladylike person. School itself did not play an important role in this group's interests, despite the fact that many of the things school stands for were within the value system of the group. Members attempted to maintain status by appearing to be as different as possible from those in a lower socioeconomic classification. The expression of a feminine role was emphasized, with rejection of masculine activities. In selecting places to go, the focus was more on where not to go than where to go.

In discussing their findings, Phelps and Horrocks note that the same activity may have different meanings for different adolescents, and hence may represent different interests and attitudes, depending upon the participant's needs. For example, members of groups such as Group 1 may find dancing a means of assuming an adult role and a means of satisfying heterosexual interests, whereas for members of Groups 3 and 5 it might be merely an activity by which relatively uncomplicated needs are satisfied.

Socioeconomic factors and adult pressures appear important in group activities, particularly for girls. The adolescent seems either to be very school-centered in his activities, or more rarely, in revolt from its influence. In general, degree of emancipation from adult control appears to be a most important influence in the formation of patterns of informal adolescent group attitudes and activities.

Adolescent Wishes

It has been hypothesized that an individual's wishes may be symptomatic of interests that will eventually be exploited or that have not been implemented because of circumstances beyond the wisher's control. It has also been hypothesized that an individual's wishes are an index to his general pattern of personality organization, and it may well be that the characteristic wishes of adolescents offer a clue to the generalized pattern of adolescence. It is a common occurrence of daily life to hope for wishes to come true. But for this to happen there must be either an actual effort on the wisher's part or a combination of more or less fortuitous circumstances that permit the fulfillment of the wish. The student of psychology will recognize the fallacy of the "good fairy" and realize that the consummation of a wish must be environmentally generated.

Studies of children's wishes are usually conducted by asking a child either to list those things he would most like if he could have anything he wished or by having him check items off on a prepared list. The form of the question has a good deal of influence on the kind of wishes children will admit having. For example, a question asking for a list of "anything you want" usually results in a list strong in personal possessions, but the question can be so phrased that the child will submit wishes that are less self-centered. One technique is to have the child wish for something for someone else on the assumption that answers would really be projections of their own desires. Cobb (1954) submitted to his subjects questions, "I wish I were ———," "I wish more than anything that ———." In discussing his results he writes:

When the statement is restricted by strong self-reference (I wish I were ———), wishes tend to be more introverted than when the reference is general (I wish more than anything that ———). In the former case, wishes for looks, stature, age, identity and smartness are prominent; in the latter these tend to be absorbed in the more general and less introverted categories of personal achievement and personal-social relations, while general welfare on the one hand, and material possessions on the other, become prominent.

Cobb reported that the most popular adolescent wishes are for those things that promote personal adequacy, such as skill in school or athletics, happiness, or health, and for those things that have display or prestige-building value, such as wealth, an automobile, and clothes. Family welfare ranks high on the list, but the welfare or good adjustment of others, or service functions, appear to be comparatively unpopular. Wheeler (1963) reports that adolescent males made more wishes concerned with money, vocations, and marriage, and that female wishes were more concerned with social relationships and benefits to parents, relatives, and others. As adolescents became older, their wishes for possessions and activities decreased in favor of wishes concerned with money, marriage, vocations, and physical and psychological benefits for self. For boys in particular, some objects served to represent symbols of adolescent striving for maturity or the working out of a masculine role. Zazzo (1962) found social success, marriage, and vocation the adolescent's foremost wishes. He also reported that girls made wishes about being loved and having friends more often than boys did.

It is to be expected that children's wishes will reflect the values of the culture in which they are reared, and as the culture's values change, so will the things its children deem important enough to be wished for. In a study of four hundred adolescents made in 1932, Washburne reported the five most common wishes to be for wealth, an automobile, clothing, skill in school, and happiness. In a developmental study of wishes made nearly thirty years after the Washburne study, Horrocks and Flory (1960) asked one hundred students in

two high schools of different socioeconomic levels and sixty college students to list three wishes in order of preference, and then compared their results with those obtained by Washburne. They report that (1) socioeconomic factors influence wishes more than does chronological age; (2) wishes are related to specific experiences one has encountered in his environment; (3) environmental conditions are important in shaping any given individual's wishes, as Washburne contends; and (4) mature students' wishes are more general and altruistic than are immature students' wishes.

In the years between the Washburne and the Horrocks and Flory studies children's wishes did not change to any great extent, although Washburne's adolescents tended to wish for material possessions such as money, an automobile, and clothes more than did the later sample, who were more interested in the general categories of health, happiness, and serving humanity. The Washburne emphasis upon material possessions may well have been a result of the depression of the 1930s. Table 12 lists the five most common wishes for the groups in the Horrocks and Flory study, as compared with the Washburne study.

Some thirteen years after the Horrocks and Flory study, Horrocks and Mussman (1973) asked a random sample drawn from five different age groups to respond to the question, "If you could have any three wishes come true, what would they be?" Subjects were further

Table 12 *Five Most Common Wishes of Persons in Two High Schools of Contrasting Socioeconomic Status, in a College, and in a Study Conducted by J. N. Washburne*

High School 1 (Higher socio-economic status)	High School 2 (Lower socio-economic status)	Ohio Wesleyan University	Washburne Study
1. Happiness	1. Wealth	1. Marriage	1. Wealth
2. Health	2. Education	2. Serve Humanity	2. Automobile
3. Wealth	3. World Peace	3. World Peace	3. Clothes
4. Success	4. Automobile	4. Success	4. Skill in School
5. World Peace	5. Job Now	5. Health	5. Happiness

Source: Adapted from W. B. Horrocks and E. Flory (1960).

asked to place plus and minus signs in front of the wishes that had the most and the least chance of coming true as well as to indicate which of the wishes they could do something about through their own efforts. The five age groups used were students in elementary school, junior high school, senior high school, early college (ages eighteen to twenty-four), and late college (ages twenty-five to fifty). Respondents' wishes were placed in appropriate categories and into subcategories including wishes having to do with possessions, activities, maintenance, achievement, and altruism. Results having to do with wishes are presented in Table 13 and in Figure 17. In Figure 17 wishes for possessions may be seen to decrease from the elementary years to the eighteen to twenty-four group and then increase during the middle years, with the category "Wealth" accounting for the change, as may be seen in Table 13. The decreasing interest in activities after junior high school may be observed and

Table 13   *Percentage of Wishes by Age Groups*

Category	Age Group					
	Elem.	Jr. High	Sr. High	18–24	25–50	All
Possessions	39	18	18	6	11	18
Wealth	10	8	11	6	11	11
Sports etc. equipment	9	4	1	0	0	3
Motor vehicle	5	3	4	0	0	1
Pets	9	2	0	0	0	1
Clothes	3	1	1	0	0	1
Activities	8	8	3	1	2	4
Sports-games-music	4	5	2	0	1	2
Maintenance	22	31	37	44	36	34
Happiness-satisfaction	2	3	6	10	10	6
Health–long life	1	2	3	8	9	5
Love–have lover	4	8	7	4	2	5
Marriage	1	2	7	11	6	5
Peer relations	3	2	2	2	1	2
Own family relations	2	4	1	1	0	2
Living conditions	3	3	3	1	0	2
Achievement	18	12	15	18	23	17
Vocation	6	6	3	6	7	5
Ability	4	2	4	6	8	5
Education	6	4	6	2	3	4
Success-recognition	2	0	2	4	4	2
Altruistic	4	24	20	28	27	21
World peace	2	12	10	10	5	8
Improve humanity	1	10	7	14	8	8
Welfare of loved one	1	2	3	5	14	5
Miscellaneous	9	7	7	2	1	6
More wishes	2	3	1	2	1	2
School avoidance	4	2	3	0	0	2
Other avoidance	2	1	2	0	0	1

N = 300 wishes for each age group and 1,500 wishes for the "All" column.

Source: J. E. Horrocks and M. C. Mussman, "Developmental trends in wishes, confidence, and the sense of personal control from childhood to middle maturity," *Journal of Psychology* 84 (1973): 241–252, table 1, p. 246. Reprinted by permission of The Journal Press.

Figure 17 *Percentage of Wishes in Major Areas by Age Groups*

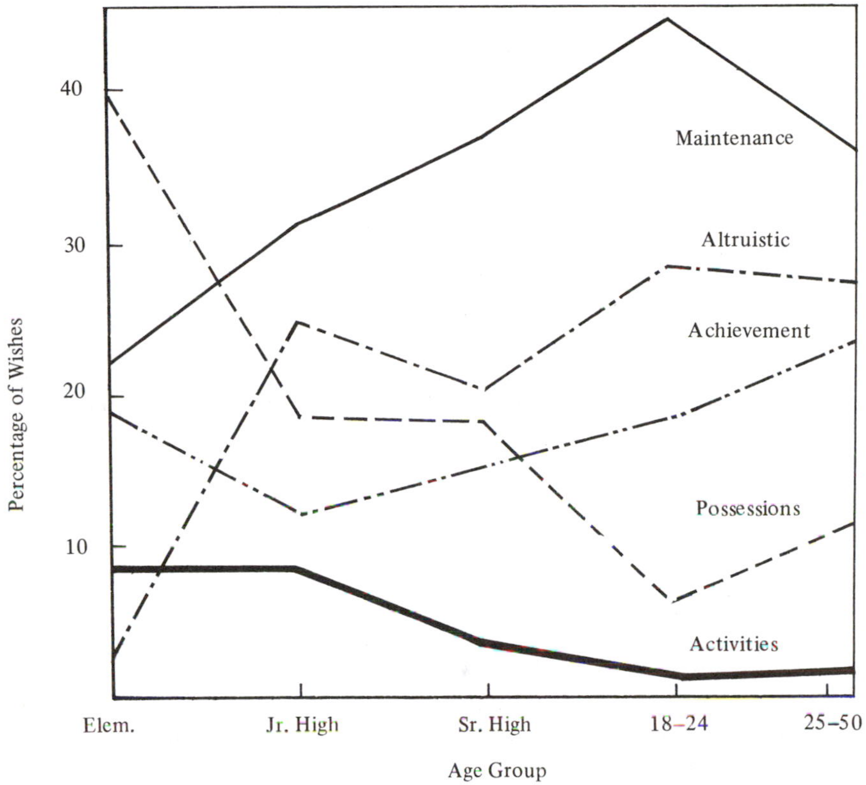

Source: Adapted from J. E. Horrocks and M. C. Mussman, "Developmental trends in wishes, confidence, and the sense of personal control from childhood to middle maturity," *Journal of Psychology* 84 (1973): 241–252, fig. 1. Reprinted by permission of The Journal Press.

may at least be partially accounted for by the principle of increasing generality with age, although it may be that activities do not provide the same satisfaction for adults that they do for children and adolescents. Wishes for maintenance, achievement, and altruistic experiences may in general be seen to grow with age, although some exceptions may be observed. Maintenance categories involving wishes for adequacy, security, acceptance, problem reduction, and so forth, are of considerably less concern to the older groups in comparison to the older adolescents and younger adults. Wishes for achievement are relatively low in junior high school compared to the levels of the elementary and senior high

groups. Altruism in senior high is lower in frequency than either in junior high or in the eighteen to twenty-four college group, the difference being found in the "Improve humanity" category. The difference between the senior high and the college group is significant in the area of altruism. These findings have some implication for age trends from early through late adolescence. The trends shown in the general areas thus support earlier data on increasing generality, increasing altruism, and decreasing materialism with age, with some specific variations.

Comparisons with previous studies raise the possibility that achievement orientations of adolescents may have lessened since the period

Table 14 *Percentages at Various Ages Indicating High Confidence and a High Sense of Personal Control*

Attribute	Age				
	Elem. (6–11)	Jr. High (12–14)	Sr. High (15–17)	Early Coll. (18–24)	Late Coll. (25–50)
High Confidence	49	45	50	55	58
High Sense of Personal Control	62	50	66	84	79

Source: Adapted from J. E. Horrocks and M. C. Mussman, "Developmental trends in wishes, confidence, and the sense of personal control from childhood to middle maturity," *Journal of Psychology* 84 (1973): 241–252, table 2, p. 247. Reprinted by permission of The Journal Press.

of the 1950s. In general, adolescents seem to be wishing for what their predecessors wished for. A comparison of the Horrocks and Flory 1960 study and the Horrocks and Mussman 1973 study follows.

1960 High School: wealth, happiness, health, success, world peace.
Early College: health, marriage, success, world peace, serve humanity.
1973 High School: wealth, marriage, love– have lover, world peace, improve humanity.
Early College: happiness, health, marriage, world peace, improve humanity.

It will be observed that the 1960 and 1973 listings differ in two respects. The presence of "Marriage" and "Love–have lover" in 1973, and the absence of "Success," does suggest that the decade of the 1960s has produced some movement for middle-class adolescents away from achievement and toward maintenance-oriented desires.

Table 14 shows the results of the Horrocks and Mussman (1973) study relative to age changes in confidence and sense of personal control. None of the changes in confidence is significant, although a slow trend toward increased expectations of success with age may be observed to occur past the junior high school group. Significant increases in the sense of personal control may be observed from junior high and from senior high to the eighteen to twenty-four group, suggesting that this construct and like constructs, such as

internal locus of control, may indeed be significantly influenced by age. It is of interest to note the depressed percentages for the junior high group in comparison to the other groups. It could be inferred that this age group does tend to lack personality characteristics often associated with personal competence and may reflect findings of other investigators relative to the high stress conditions often faced in early adolescence.

Interests of Avoidance

If wishes provide an index of interests that attract children, their reverse—fears, worries, and anxieties—provide the picture of the things children want to avoid. Although fears and worries are not ordinarily thought of as falling under the category of interests, and studies of them in this context are rare, there can be no doubt that they do provide a basis for behavior and the channeling of a fair amount of an individual's time and energy. His fears and worries not only cause a child to take on certain activities; they also prompt him to avoid others. Hence, the interests of avoidance may have just as important an effect upon an individual's activities as those of acceptance, and a knowledge of them would help in interpreting that individual's behavior.

Rubin et al. (1968) administered the Geer Fear Survey Schedule II to a group of male and female college students, most of whom would be classified as late adolescents. They factor analyzed responses and reported four factors that were confirmed in a larger replication (N = 270 and 1,098).

Factor 1 Fears relating to water including swimming alone, deep water, and boating. There was some indication that this factor had some relationship to superstitious fears.

Factor 2 Fears relating to illness including suffocation, death, death of a loved one, untimely or early death, illness or injury, auto accidents.

Factor 3 Fears relating to interpersonal events including looking foolish, being criticized, being a leader, being self-conscious, meeting authority, and speaking before a group.

Factor 4 Fears of discrete stimuli including rats and mice, snakes, cemeteries, and dark places.

Rubin et al. report that Factors 1 and 2 remained relatively constant over the original study and the replication for both sexes but for females Factor 3 separated into two separate factors: social competence and social interaction. Factor 4 did not emerge for females as a discrete factor. Apparently there

was a tendency for females to express their fears of such things as mice and snakes as parts of a particular context rather than as discrete objects.

Miller et al. (1972) asked the parents of 179 children aged six to sixteen to rate their children on the Louisville Fear Survey. A factor analysis of responses yielded three factors: (1) fear of physical injury, (2) fear of natural events, and (3) psychic stress fears. Of these, Factors 1 and 3 appear to run throughout the life span, while fear of natural events mitigated with maturation.

In a study of the self-expressed fears and worries of some 1,100 children aged nine through eighteen, Angelino, Dollins, and Mech (1956) classified expressed fears into ten categories: safety, school, personal appearance, natural phenomena, economic and political, health, animals, social relations, personal conduct, and supernatural. Children participating in the study were classified according to chronological age and socioeconomic status and were asked to list the fears and worries they thought were common in their own age group. Table 15 shows the mean number of fears and worries indicated by both boys and girls from

Table 15 *Summary of Means for the Total Number of Fears and Worries Indicated by Both Boys and Girls from Two Differing Socioeconomic Levels in Each of Ten Categories*

	Boys		Girls	
Category	Upper S-E (N = 179)	Lower S-E (N = 383)	Upper S-E (N = 178)	Lower S-E (N = 390)
1. Safety	1.07	1.05	.87	1.30
2. School	1.32	1.06	1.39	1.14
3. Personal Appearance	.04	.02	.06	.17
4. Natural Phenomena	.28	.13	.25	.35
5. Economic and Political	.49	.44	.40	.27
6. Health	.26	.16	.34	.20
7. Animals	.20	.51	.22	.64
8. Social Relations	.43	.37	.63	.58
9. Personal Conduct	.28	.22	.27	.28
10. Supernatural	.04	.04	.09	.04

Source: H. Angelino, J. Dollins, and E. V. Mech, "Trends in the 'fears and worries' of school children as related to socioeconomic status and age," *Journal of Genetic Psychology* 89 (1956): 263–276, table on p. 265. Reprinted by permission of The Journal Press.

Figure 18   *Mean Number of Fears and Worries in Four Categories for Boys and Girls Divided on the Basis of Age and Socioeconomic Status*

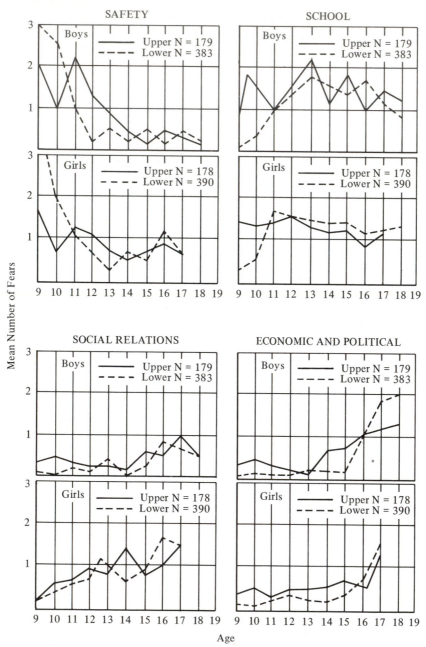

Source: Adapted from H. Angelino, J. Dollins, and E. V. Mech, "Trends in the 'fears and worries' of school children as related to socioeconomic status and age," *Journal of Genetic Psychology* 89 (1956): 263–276, figs. 1, 2, 4, and 5. Reprinted by permission of The Journal Press.

two differing socioeconomic levels in each of the ten categories. Figure 18 shows age changes in mean number of fears and worries for the four categories safety, school, social relations, and economic and political. Fears about personal safety are a phenomenon of the preadolescent rather than of the adolescent period proper. Angelino et al. note that boys of lower socioeconomic status were more concerned with matters of violence—including robbers, guns, knives, and whippings—and were also more afraid of their parents than were upper-class boys. Upper-class boys worried more about being hurt, being killed, delinquency, accidents, and disaster in general. Upper-class girls worried about personal safety factors involving ship and train wrecks, being hurt while playing hockey, and about their pets' safety. Lower-class girls expressed fear of strangers, animals, acts of violence, and drunks. Croake (1969) has also indicated that lower socioeconomic children have more fears than those coming from upper-class homes and that girls express more fear than do boys.

From the Angelino et al. study it may be gathered that school fears, not uncommon during the entire adolescent period, are perhaps of greater concern to boys, although differences are probably not significant. Such matters as stage freight, tests, teachers, grades, and schoolwork bother both upper- and lower-class boys and girls. At fifteen, upper-class boys seem to be more concerned about getting into the college of their choice, while lower-class boys are more concerned about getting into any college, or about even finishing high school. Girls seem most concerned about school between eleven and twelve and boys at around age twelve. The realm of political and economic affairs seems not to be a matter of much worry until later adolescence, although upper-class boys show a bit more concern at earlier ages. Upper-class boys are less worried about money than are lower-class boys, and their worries centered on their allowances. Lower-class boys worry more about such things as paying for college, paying the rent and debts, having to sell the family furniture, and obtain-

ing money to pay traffic tickets. In political affairs upper-class boys find their worries in the general and more global areas of war, world conditions, and national affairs, while lower-class boys have the more immediate personal concerns of the draft, police, and jobs. Girls follow a pattern quite like that of boys.

As girls grow older problems of social relations increasingly become a subject for worry, and they list twice as many worries in this area as do boys. Girls are more worried about problems of dating and their reputations than are boys. Angelino notes that the data on social relations "are not particularly illuminating except for the fact that a small but steady rise in concern over social relations is exhibited by girls." He further notes that "the main finding . . . appears to contain the rough generalization that school children, regardless of socioeconomic status, have about the same number of problems in each of the ten fears and worries categories." Qualitatively the picture is different. Within any category the socioeconomic variable reveals very specific differences in focus. One cannot escape the conclusion that the outside world has given more reason for apprehension to the lower socioeconomic class youngster than to his more fortunate upper-class opposite number. There is quite a difference in being worried that one's family will cut one's allowance and being worried that one's family will be dispossessed of its furniture.

In a study of Hungarian high school students aged ten to eighteen (N = 1,992) Gereb et al. (1968) asked his subjects to write an essay on one side of a sheet of paper and to make a drawing about fear on the reverse side. They report that older adolescents reported more fears caused by situations such as medical treatment, strangers, personal attacks, and family dissolution. A great many "didactogenous" fears were listed—fears about examinations, questions in class, and possibilities of war. Comparisons of the Hungarian results with those of a study in Germany revealed the existence of a qualitative similarity of the contents of fears reported in these two quite different countries.

Solitary Activity

One type of activity common to both boys and girls of all ages is self-entertainment carried on as a solitary, unaccompanied activity. But that such activity would be preferred is doubtful in view of the greater number of group activities participated in by most youth, although, again, the choice of activity may be based on past experience, present opportunity, and ability. Group activity requires the presence of other children; a satisfactory level of participation also requires certain skills in each participant, and acceptance of the individual by the group members.

There are many reasons why a child may engage in solitary activities. A child who lives in a rural section or in an apartment in a great city may lack opportunities for free participation. Parental restrictions and the need to work may deny him a proper social life. A more intelligent child who gains great satisfaction from reading may be tempted to spend more of his time in that activity than will his less-well-endowed age-mates. Fortunately, the superior child, while he does read more, also tends to participate in group activity.

Solitary activities may be classified as watching (movies, games, contests), listening (radio), reading (books, magazines, comic strips, or comic books), or indulging in some other activity that may be carried on alone, such as loafing, whistling, or whittling. Reading books appears to be a popular activity at all ages during adolescence in terms of both preference and activity. Looking at the comics is an activity often engaged in by both sexes at all ages, but after fifteen there is an increasing tendency to ignore this as a "most-liked" activity, even though it continues to hold its position as an activity frequently indulged in. Reading newspapers and short stories becomes increasingly popular with boys and girls after the age of fifteen.

Among older adolescent boys, particularly after fourteen, "just loafing" or "just hanging around" appears to be an often-mentioned pastime, although the loafing is not always a solitary activity, since it sometimes involves a group who range aimlessly about or stand on street corners with no apparent end in mind. Probably the true reason for loafing as a manifestation of later adolescence is the loss of interest in more childish activities, plus a lack of new activities to take their place. Too, graduation from or dropping out of high school leaves a large gap in an adolescent's life, which even a full-time job cannot fill at first. Perhaps older youth no longer have the necessary energy to participate in physical sports. Here is a crucial area in adolescent development that constitutes a vital challenge to youth workers. An idle young person may undertake undesirable activities and friendships from boredom. The corner gang is a group-loafing situation that too frequently leads to delinquent or other problem behavior. It is especially interesting that girls seldom mention loafing as something they either do or want to do.

One distinctive interest of younger girls, which is lacking in older ones and is apparently of little importance to boys at any age, is looking at pictures. The movie magazine is a rich source of material, and it is almost inevitable that a normally reared girl in our culture will collect movie stars' pictures some time between eight and fourteen.

Closely related to solitary self-entertainment is the type of activity in which one is entertained by someone else. This activity requires only the physical presence of the participant. His role is entirely passive. He sees, he hears, but his reactions for the most part are not translated into overt physical activity, unless, perchance, he happens to boo the umpire, cheer, or turn the dial of his radio or TV. The similarity between passive entertainment and solitary self-entertainment lies essentially in the fact that both activities are individual rather than group oriented. The individual, in a sense, depends upon himself. Insofar as sports are concerned, a person may go to a game with a group of people, but once there his role is primarily a solitary one, relieved from time to time by some aspects of group interaction. But with activities such as listening to the radio or record player, going to the movies, listening to stories, attending lectures or concerts, or riding in an auto, the role is usually nongroup and differs from solitary self-entertainment only in that the individual depends upon someone other than himself to provide the entertainment.

One of the most consistently popular activities, more so with boys and men than with women and girls, is that of watching athletic sports. Girls under thirteen express little if any interest, perhaps because of unfamiliarity with the possibilities for fun inherent in the activity. Going to the movies is also a popular activity with both sexes; and even apart from their availability as a place to take a date, the movies appear to hold great appeal in and of themselves. They become particularly popular with girls during middle adolescence and tend to decline somewhat thereafter in terms of girls' expressed liking for them, although attendance does not seem to be seriously affected. On the whole, the movies tend to be somewhat more popular with girls than with boys.

Some concern has been expressed from time to time about the effects of spectator activities. American youth have been accused of being afflicted with "spectatoritis" and abandoning the desire to do things themselves in favor of watching or listening to paid entertainment. This seems to be a rather pessimistic view based only partly on truth. True, youth tend to rely less on themselves than they formerly did for entertainment, but changing times and technological improvements have worked vast changes for both children and adults. In the old days people had to rely on themselves more than at present because there was no opportunity for anything else. While youth today do obtain much of their amusement from watching sports, going to the movies, and listening to the radio, they also do many other things in which their role is a great deal more active. Any consideration of the spectator activities should include the great teaching function they

can and do assume. The vast increase in the use of visual aids in our schools is an indication of the faith educators have in the efficacy of some of these media for learning and teaching purposes.

The danger in spectator activities is that some individuals may fall into the habit of getting all their experiences vicariously. When an individual, finding fewer and fewer satisfactions in the realities of everyday living, begins to rely upon spectator activities as a refuge and to retreat from reality, then their effects may indeed be pernicious. If such a poor balance is observed in an adolescent, substitute activities should be provided; but it would be unfortunate to curtail an addict's spectator activities without providing adequate scope for something that will give substitute satisfactions. It is always well in a case of suspected overindulgence to ask oneself: What is this person getting out of this activity and what need does it fulfill for him? And further, is there any other adequate way to satisfy those same needs and desires?

At the other end of the pole from solitary activity is the kind of activity that requires group participation. In any given day an adolescent is apt to spend more time in solitary or spectator amusements than in group amusements, but the different kinds of activities requiring group participation seem to have a wider range and variety. Group activity tends to require either a great deal of hard physical exercise, or comparatively no physical activity. Among the nonphysical group activities, adolescents list going to parties and picnics, telling or guessing riddles, having dates, visiting or entertaining, meeting in social clubs or being with the gang, teasing somebody, and playing card games.

The group activities that are physically more active may be classified as either competitive or noncompetitive. Competitive activities listed include team games such as football and baseball, wrestling, boxing, tennis, running races, and various other games. Noncompetitive activities include social dancing, roller-skating, and playing catch. Of course, these categories are not mutually exclusive. Social dancing may occur on a date, and being with the gang may lead to a wrestling match or a game of baseball, but on the whole the categories serve as a useful means of classifying activities.

As previously explained, girls are less apt than boys to indulge in organized activity, and they seem especially uninterested in competitive or team activities. Both boys and girls tend to become less and less interested in actual participation in team sports, or in excessive physical endeavor, with increasing age. Two examples will serve to point up girls' reluctance to participate in organized activity. Every high school principal is aware of the difficulty in trying to require adolescent girls to attend or to like gymnasium classes. There is significantly more unexcused absence, lack of cooperation, and actual dislike of the physical education program among girls than among boys, and the school authorities must make a consciously greater effort to "sell" the gym program to girls than to boys.

The second example concerns service in the armed forces by women during World War II. Women were not drafted, but many were needed in the WAC, the WAVES, the SPAR, and the Women Marines. It was hoped that adequate numbers of volunteers would be found. Many did volunteer, but the percentage of those potentially eligible who actually volunteered was extremely small. Many factors were operating, of course. Parental permission was not easy to obtain, service in the armed forces was counter to woman's traditional role, and many had responsibilities at home, but it is still a reasonable hypothesis that a great deal of the reluctance to volunteer could be attributed to antagonism to the more or less regimented and organized life that service in the armed forces required.

The Appeal of "Wheels"

In a discussion of adolescent interests, it is impossible to overlook the ubiquitous appeal of "wheels" to both sexes, although the love affair of the American adolescent male with his automobile appears to be one of the most intense aspects of his life. Female interest in cars seems more confined to their use as a means of transportation, but boys add to this an interest in why automobiles run and how. But, more important for the male, the automobile becomes a weapon with which he can prove his masculinity and his skill. More, it becomes a concrete manifestation of his emancipation from adult restraints. On the open road everyone is equal, and an adolescent finding the principal of his high school going too slowly ahead of him is free to take whatever action he wishes to show his scorn, his impatience, and his superior skill. The automobile also has the great advantage of getting an adolescent out of sight of supervising adults. It also gives him an opportunity to indulge in one of his favorite occupations—roaming aimlessly about "making the scene." At a local drive-in restaurant that is popular with teenagers, it is interesting to see how many times in a single evening the same teen-driven car pulls in and out of the parking lot.

As a driver the teenager is not nearly as good as he usually believes he is. He tends to visualize the tire-burning start and turn as an indication of skill, and his level of maturity and responsibility is such that he is much more apt to put himself and others in danger than is the more mature and responsible driver. Klein (1972) notes that deviant driving is to be expected of the younger driver because he is a member of a deviant population. It is Klein's position that the typical adolescent is not likely to drive in an adult manner unless broad changes are made in his social environment. The ratio of automobile accidents involving teenage boys, as reflected in their auto-insurance rates, indicates the need for social action. It is, of course, a mistake to assume that all adolescents are necessarily bad drivers. Some are more accident-prone than others. In a study of younger accident-prone motorcyclists, Nicholi (1970) notes the presence of an accident-proneness syndrome. Characteristics of the syndrome include (1) unusual preoccupation with motorcycles (dreams, fantasies, and free associations with various aspects of cycling); (2) a history of accident-proneness extending to childhood; (3) poor impulse control; (4) persistent fear of bodily injury; (5) conflict-ridden relationships with father and strong identification with mother; (6) extreme passivity and inability to compete; and (7) defective self-image.

The bicycle has also been gaining in popularity with teenagers, not as a substitute for the automobile but as an adjunct to it. Confined for many years primarily to younger adolescents who were too young to drive automobiles, the bicycle's new popularity is part of a present-day adolescent interest in sport activity involving cycling and walking that has led many communities to build cycling and walking paths frequently linked to a statewide and even a trans-state network. Such activities, popular in the 1930s, seem once again, some forty years later, to have appeared on the scene. It is interesting that bicycling seems as popular with girls as with boys. Unlike the automobile the bicycle is primarily an instrument of transportation and physical exercise. Certainly it lacks the combustion engine and the proof-of-masculinity power that made the automobile appealing to boys and less so to girls.

The Usefulness of Communications

In the study of adolescent interests, it is appropriate to consider various literary, visual, or aural media of communications—books, magazines, motion pictures, radio, TV, comic books, comic strips, and newspapers. These media play a triple role: they provide adolescents with an outlet through which to express their interests; they act as a means of introducing new interests; and they develop old interests. From the practical viewpoint of the psychologist, educator, or other youth worker, the communications media become vehicles for introducing youth to new ideas, knowledge, ideals, and skills. If skillfully used, they may

be powerful motivating factors. But it is equally true that such media may serve as a means of propaganda and information for agencies whose interests are sometimes inimical to the work the schools are trying to do. And finally, from the viewpoint of the youngsters themselves, these media are the companions of their leisure, often the basis of their recreation, and play an important part in building their understanding and experience, vicarious though the latter may be. Under the circumstances, it behooves those who would understand and work with youth to become familiar with the whole interrelationship of these media and the youth who experience all of them.

Probably in no other single aspect of human behavior have there been so many surveys of likes and dislikes, what is done versus what is not done, as in the field of the communications interests. A perusal of the voluminous literature, comprising literally hundreds upon hundreds of investigations and experiments, is both encouraging and discouraging: encouraging because so much has been attempted and because so many facts have emerged; discouraging because it is difficult to perceive a clear or consistent pattern, and because there has been so much disagreement among the findings of the various studies. This does not imply that the disagreement is either unexpected or unexplainable—it would be contrary to everything known about human behavior and change if the studies' findings were consistent. What is discouraging is the difficulty for the youth worker, wanting to make use of what is known, who is confronted by a multitude of conflicting and unintegrated studies.

Why do the studies disagree? A number of factors, none of them operating in isolation, are responsible. Studies have been made at different times in history, at different seasons of the year, with samples from rural or small-town communities as contrasted to samples from large cities, and with samples in which the possibilities for local differences were or were not cited (sex, race, creed, family upbringing, opportunity, instruction, intelligence, aptitude, and experience, to mention only a few possibilities).

For example, a study made during the 1920s might yield results contrary to those of samples surveyed during later decades. Studies made during wartime would afford interesting contrasts to those made during a major depression; depression studies would in turn differ from those made during prosperous times. One would not wish to compare the reading habits of youth in isolated rural districts without benefit of library facilities with those of youth who had access to ideal library facilities where use was encouraged and promoted. One study made during the early 1920s showed that youth did not listen to the radio with any frequency; a later "investigator," in comparing this finding with a 1943 survey showing great radio popularity, made the point that youth are changing. As a matter of fact, youth had not changed; the number of home-owned radios had increased. Ninety or more out of a hundred families owned radios in 1943 as compare to four or five families in a hundred in 1921.

The conclusion is that a normative survey of adolescent interests may impart information that is peculiar to a given time, group, or location, and therefore may not be universally applied in considering adolescent behavior in general—even within the limitations of a comparatively homogeneous culture.

What is the best approach for one who wishes to understand adolescent behavior, and perhaps to guide it along proper or desirable channels through proper use of communications media? The answer is, in part, a consideration of the nature of the adolescent himself as he exists in his own peculiar environment, which may differ considerably from the environment of other adolescents. Certain drives exist, certain interests also exist, or at least, in terms of the individual himself, they can be made to exist or can be promoted. For example, with puberty, we know that normally there will be an interest in members of the opposite sex. We know that in our culture the late adolescent tends to strive for emancipation from adult controls so that he may himself

assume the role of an adult. We know that physical activity becomes less with increasing age. We know that there is a desire to appear well to others, and that there is probably an instigation, if it may be called such, to gain mastery over one's environment. These are typical drives and interests during the adolescent years. Many more could be cited. Normally, these can be expected to be present to some degree in most adolescents in our culture. True, deviates do exist, and there are numerous subversions of what we regard as normal, but in studying human behavior we must know and work with the norm, even if only for a better understanding of deviates. Hence, there is little mystery about the subject of communications interests. If one is familiar with adolescents as such, and with the cultural milieu and with a specific person's environment in particular, then it is obvious that communications media may be useful.

Before surveying the media it might be well to consider their interrelationships. Sterner (1947) found that there appears to be comparatively little relationship among the media as such. She notes that the knowledge of a child's activity with one medium of communications gives no indication of how little or how much time he will devote to other media; interest rather than source appears to be the child's criterion. Thus a given medium might be less important than the type of interest that causes an adolescent to utilize it. This is true up to a point, but habit or availability may cause a given medium, such as a radio, to be used because it is a radio, not because of what is heard. Certain media become fashionable or "in" for a time, only to be discarded later. There are also media whose use is sometimes indirect—that is, they are used neither because of themselves nor because of the interests they may attempt to serve. An example is the movies, which at certain ages become a place to take a date, possibly the only available place in the community.

An interesting question is: What kind of people use a given medium? It has been common fallacy to assume that the medium selected was a function of intelligence. Sterner makes the point that "one cannot condemn a medium by sneering at its followers" or, conversely, approve a medium by pointing to the superior quality of the youth most interested. All socioeconomic classes use the various media as they are available. The good student is as likely to attend the movies as is the failure.

Reading

Reading, given favorable circumstances, can be a popular activity among adolescents intelligent enough and with adequate reading skills to be comfortable with words and ideas. Favorable circumstances include opportunity as well as encouragement and example from significant adults at home and in school. In larger cities, although not always in smaller communities, public libraries can do much to extend opportunities for those from home backgrounds where reading materials are not available. For those adolescents who do read, it would appear that the influence of reading is considerable. Fehl (1968), for example, studied the influence of reading on the personal development of high school students. She reported that only 16 of the 420 reported that reading does not influence their concepts, attitudes and behavior. Of the 1,184 influences reported, 45 percent were concepts, 40 percent were attitudes, and 15 percent were behavioral responses, although influences were reported as greatest when the adolescents selected their own reading matter. The number of influences for any individual was reported by Fehl to be related more to the reader's level of intelligence and reading proficiency than to whether the material read was fiction or nonfiction.

In general, adventure is popular in all grades, though more so in the earlier than in the later school years. Girls read more fiction and are more interested in sentiment than are boys, while boys tend to be more interested in biography. Boys do read a great deal of fiction, but they do not start to do so until somewhat later than girls, who are also more apt to read adult fiction all through the later school years. Girls are particularly fond of romantic stories, which become exceedingly popular with them

in the tenth grade and thereafter. Boys are less interested in romantic stories than are girls, and their interest tends to develop about a year later. When boys do read romantic stories, they tend to read them more in quest of information than for the interest of the story or the sentiment involved. In a study of the reading interests of 100,000 French adolescents Levy-Bruhl (1957) reports that social novels were popular with about a quarter of the sample, with girls somewhat more interested in them than boys. Boys liked novels of humor, mystery, and adventure more than girls did, while girls were more interested in novels of character. On the whole, girls were more avid readers than boys. It is interesting that little interest was shown by either sex in short stories or in legends.

Some investigators tend to evaluate the "worth" or "value" of the reading done by the subjects they select for their studies. Such a value judgment depends, of course, upon the investigators' adult frame of reference, which may well be unrealistic and completely divorced from the viewpoint or the needs of the adolescents under discussion. It appears to be an unfortunate fallacy to attempt to judge the value or worth of an adolescent's reading wholly by an adult standard or from an adult point of view. A more adequate and realistic approach would be to look at an adolescents reading from his point of view. What is he getting out of that particular material or general type of material? What needs is it fulfilling for him? There is no reason why an adult standard may not be kept in mind so the adolescent may eventually attain it when the time is ripe, providing always that the standard does not merely set assumed literary excellence or maturity as an end in itself. In any event, there is always a question as to the validity of any "best" standard. Standards are so often a function of the times or of an unthinking acceptance of something that has prestige because people say it is "good," that an adult in a position of authority over children should be exceedingly careful of the standards he wishes to impose on others. In the last analysis, how can he really be sure he is right?

Also to be considered is the fact that a communications medium supplies an adolescent with something that is satisfying to him, something that meets his psychological or emotional needs or fulfills his desire to learn something he feels he needs. To forget this is to misuse the motivating power of books and to make instruction in literature a sterile process. We are all familiar with the literature-appreciation program that exposes the student to the so-called best without attempting to relate it to his real interests and desires. The all-too-frequent result is that the student comes to associate the "best" with a boring and uncomfortable school situation. He refuses to read any more "literature" than he has to and carries from school an enduring hatred for the whole process. The misuse of Shakespeare in our schools is an example in point. How many high school graduates actually read Shakespeare? Surely most of them have been exposed to Shakespeare in school and told it was good. This they believe wholeheartedly and more or less gladly render lip service, but with the internal reservation that it is not good for them. Yet Shakespeare contains much that is pertinent to any adolescent's interests, provided Shakespeare is approached via those interests, at an appropriate time.

The result of any literature-appreciation course comes long after it is over, and may be evaluated on the basis of the graduate's public library card or his bookstore purchases. What does he read after graduation, when he is perfectly free to read anything he wishes? If the so-called best literature could have been presented in such a manner that it fulfilled a real need, then possibly one of the accompanying benefits might have been a better level of literary appreciation. The best technique in building literary appreciation appears to be to find a given individual's or group's interests, to start where they are, and to give them things that will attract their attention and fulfill their needs. For example, one could find out what the group is already reading and point out titles they may have overlooked. Then, gradually, always keeping pace with the individual's interests and level of maturity,

one could use his present interests to induct him into cognate interests that may be at a "higher" level and that may have more breadth. It is not as far from Dick Tracy to Lord Peter Wimsey, and from Lord Peter to the scientist's quest, as might be supposed. It is not improbable that an adolescent reading sea stories might become interested in geography or the problems of wind and tide, or that a historical novel originally read for its love interest might lead to an interest in history or perhaps in architecture or costume design.

The point here is that great care must be exercised in guiding an adolescent's reading, for it may become an important factor in shaping not only his daily activities and thinking, but his future as well. Properly used, reading may be one of the most powerful motivating devices in the youth worker's repertoire. Reading must be recognized as a means to an end, an induction, which must be approached in such a manner that it will satisfy an adolescent's needs, and subtly lead (perhaps) to better things. For the adolescent, reading should seldom be thought of as an end in itself, completely divorced from the adolescent as a person at the time he is actually doing the reading. There is no implication that teenage reading must serve only narrow day-to-day needs or that reading the classics is necessarily inappropriate. Today's child is a part of the stream of history, and it is highly desirable that he recognize the ramifications of his position. If properly presented, the great books of the Western world do aid in such recognition, but the presentation must take into account the interests and motivations of the child as he is.

A study of adolescent reading interests that lists only titles read is so much a function of a given time that many of the books listed are outdated in a few years, at least, current or nonclassical books. Classic and perennial favorites are another matter. But for most studies that list titles read, a more valuable approach is one that inquires into the nature of the books read. An interest in love may be universal down through the centuries. In late Victorian times Katherine Cecil Thurstone's *The Masquerader* might have fulfilled the desire to read about love; in the early 1930s it might have been Stella Benson's *The Faraway Bride;* in the early 1940s, D. L. Murray's *Tale of Three Cities;* in the early 1950s, Shellabarger's *Lord Vanity;* or in the 1960s, Moore's *I am Mary Dunne.* Probably none of the five would appear on any current list submitted by an adolescent, but he might submit a title that would share a common denominator with the other five—that is, it would satisfy his need or interest in reading about love.

Adolescents seem to read books for three main reasons. First, because they are made to do so by their parents or teachers; second, to answer their own problems; and third, to gain information. The adolescent is typically a person with "a need to know." An inexperienced child in an adult world, he has to learn the rules of the road, and often books are the only sources of the information he seeks. He can learn technical information, the rules of social conduct, and information about the world of work and of adults. Books can also provide heroes and ideals as well as outlets for feeling or sentiment.

Hence, reading seems to help adolescents achieve personal and social adjustment, it provides recreation, and it is, of course, a definite aid to academic success. As an example of the value of a good background of reading experience as an aid to academic success, we might take the case of James Benton, who came from a relatively superior socioeconomic background. His parents were both interested in books and over a period of years had built up a carefully selected library of considerable scope. James read well, and his parents and teachers had always encouraged him to read widely. He read a great deal, with the result that his knowledge and interests were considerably wider than those of most boys his age. When he entered high school, he discovered he had already read for fun all the collateral reading required in the first year. He had read the required novel for the first-semester English class five times. With proper handling, school for James would become an opportunity to expand the foundations he had already built.

Certainly the organized curriculum would offer few problems in his first year, and would give him many extra opportunities to establish himself and enrich his abilities. As a matter of fact, James spent only one semester in the freshman curriculum and then moved on as a full sophomore. Of course, in a poorly organized school where teachers were more interested in subject matter than in children, James would have been sentenced to a full year of boredom during his freshman year, marking time in the, for him, lock-step progress of his less fortunate contemporaries.

In contrast to James was Bertha Newall. Bertha was as intelligent as James and had the same socioeconomic background, but, unfortunately for her, she came from a culturally starved home where books were unknown and the family reading consisted of the evening newspaper and *Good Housekeeping* magazine. Bertha had built up some resistance to reading and had done no more than school had absolutely required. In high school everything she was given to read was new to her and difficult to understand. She did not find English or history at all interesting and was bored and frustrated with the whole educational process. When asked to write a composition, she had only her own meager and poorly interpreted experiences to fall back on, and she disliked writing in general. (James, on the other hand, could take to his composition writing a good background of vicarious experience and considerable familiarity with literary materials.) In a properly conducted school, Bertha's status could have been ascertained and an effort made to induct her gradually through an exploitation of her own interests into a liking for and a real interest in school. The point is that, given equal opportunity, James's background of reading experience would not only make almost any experience provided him more meaningful, it would also make his progress through school more interesting, considerably easier, and more successful.

The foregoing discussion implies that a school would do well to adjust its curriculum (where possible) to the needs and interests of its students, and then, using those interests as a base, to attempt to expand them. A knowledge of adolescent interests in general will help build such curricular procedures, but it is important to remember that individual differences still exist and individual adjustments will have to be made. The matter of sex differences is a case in point. With boys and girls in the same classes, and with their known differences in interests, it becomes a matter of considerable ingenuity to teach a common core. Fortunately, there are techniques for solving such a problem.

Radio and TV

Listening to radio is one of youth's most popular recreational outlets. After suffering a temporary decline some years back, radio is once again occupying a firm place in the hearts of adolescents. In the past few years radio has devoted itself increasingly to the almost continuous playing of a type of music that appears to have universal appeal among teenagers. The more than 2,500 disc jockeys who play records over the American radio, accompanying them by a series of running comments, have become important public figures and have a substantial following among the younger people of both large and small cities. Add to this, the staggering popularity and adulation given to prominent popular-music singers by adolescents, particularly girls, and it is small wonder that radio is so popular. Radio has the added virtue of relative inexpensiveness, so the average adolescent can have a set in his room, always available as a companion during periods of studying, loafing, talking, or other activities. One might say that radio forms a background to the adolescent's daily life. The transistor type is carried wherever one goes, and the radio's presence in the dashboard of most automobiles makes it indeed ubiquitous. For many an adolescent, his radio is his most prized possession and acts as an adjunct to his record player.

In comparison, as Murray et al. (1970) and others have pointed out, TV plays an insignificant role. Adolescents do watch TV, but it tends to be too static a form for an individual

who has so many things to do. It requires attention, even if of a hypnotic nature, and adolescents appear unwilling to sit in front of a set for long periods, except, of course, during the first days of having a new set. Too, TV does not cater to adolescent interests as does radio, and the limited number of channels in most communities preclude "dialing around," as on a radio.

Not so many years ago, radio and TV were still products of the future, and the time children now spend with them necessarily had to be devoted to other things. The question often arises as to whether radio and TV have had a good or bad influence upon children. On the one hand, proponents point out their great educative value and the good things, such as music, that they bring to every home. It has been pointed out that TV and radio have done much to make the home more important as a recreational center, and have, in a sense, combated the influence of the many factors in modern living that make the home less and less important, except as a place to eat and sleep. On the other hand, opponents point to the low educational and cultural level of programs, to overadvertising, and to the media's unwillingness to accept major "uplift" responsibilities. They also claim that radio and TV tend to promote a national "spectator complex" and to cause people to become more and more dependent upon paid entertainment and less upon their own ingenuity and devices. This is as it may be, but there seems little if any objective evidence to indicate that their influence is really bad, and some to indicate that they are a positive factor in American life, despite their shortcomings.

Other Communications Media

As might be expected, adolescents make at least some use of all the communications media that are available to adults. In common with the majority of American adults, adolescents are avid readers of newspapers and magazines and spend many hours with them. But it is sometimes difficult to know to what extent actual

use is a matter of real interest or just plain availability, coupled with the boredom of having nothing better to do. Probably children tend to read the magazines and newspapers available in their homes or the school library without selecting them themselves. What they actually would select if they could choose their own at the newsstands, or if, indeed, they would buy them at all, is another question. If adult magazine or newspaper purchases vary from community to community, or from socioeconomic bracket to socioeconomic bracket, as they undoubtedly do, then what is available for their children to read would vary correspondingly. This fact may partially explain some of the discrepancies or differences observed in the numerous studies made of adolescents' newspaper and magazine reading habits. Once again it is well to remember that understanding adolescents' reading habits must be in terms of why they read, not of what they read. Of course some magazines are aimed directly at the teenage market, and insofar as they are familiar with the needs and interests of their clientele, they attract a substantial following. *Seventeen* answers many questions teenage girls have and serves the adolescent female as a kind of junior edition of *Vogue*. Winick (1962) reported that the typical *Mad* reader was a high school student who read the magazine because its satire was close to his own attitudes. Adolescents from higher socioeconomic backgrounds showed the greatest interest in *Mad,* possibly because of their greater awareness of the standards violated by reading the magazine.

In the years following World War II, comic books became immensely popular with junior and senior high school students, although somewhat more so for the junior high-schoolers. But since 1955, comic book reading has decreased markedly, and while younger children are still quite fond of them, adolescents are less and less addicted. This is not to say that adolescents do not read comic books —they simply do not occupy the favored position they did at midcentury. Apparently they were a fad, and like most fads, are passing, to be succeeded by others. Adults, too impressed by the adolescent fad of the moment, would do well to remember that an issue will often take care of itself—if it is not kept green by adult overreaction and protest.

In their heyday, comic book opponents were seriously disturbed about their effects, to the point where several states or single communities either forbade or restricted their sale. A number of pressure groups and educational or parents' organizations went on record as opposing comics. There were even several sponsored attempts to present "good" comics in an effort to combat "bad" comics, on the assumption that children would read comics in any event and that a "good" type might compete with the disapproved type. Of course, comics have not disappeared as yet, and their opponents still press the attack.

Opponents of the comics insist that they are overstimulating and tend to incite youth to immoral or socially disapproved actions. They point out that, even when overt activity does not occur, the viewpoint represented is undesirable and might arouse interests and desires that would not be good for young people. Comics are seen as encouraging a retreat from reality and, especially for younger children, as causing fundamental feelings of fear, insecurity, and dissatisfaction. It is believed that the vocabulary and the literary style are the antithesis of good literary practice, and that time spent reading the comics is time stolen from more desirable activities.

Proponents of the comics deny these accusations. They point out that comics are a form of literature and that a child who reads the comics is broadening his knowledge of geography, of people, and of scientific innovations, as well as improving his reading ability. They point out that time spent reading the comics might be spent in much less desirable ways. They insist that those who allege unfortunate emotional effects do so on insufficient evidence and a priori assumptions. They contend that the comics advocate health and clean living and make a definite effort to present a crime-does-not-pay point of view.

Whether the general effect of the comics is psychologically or morally injurious has yet to be proved. There is some evidence that they have had some influence in promoting delinquent behavior, but when cases of such behavior are closely studied, a number of other factors are found operating at the same time, and so far no one has been able to isolate the comics as the sole cause. Nor have they been able to isolate the degree of their contribution. Obviously, their effect would be greater on an emotionally unstable adolescent than on one who was more stable, but then so would any other stimulating environmental aspect.

Stability of Interests

To what extent may one expect to find stability of interests at a given age, or continuity of interests from age to age? The answer, at least partly, is that basic needs tend not to change, but the organism's behavior in attempting to satisfy or fulfill these needs does change. This behavioral change is less a biological function of increasing age than a learning and cultural function of what the environment permits and what society expects of persons in certain categories. This point of view, which appears basic to any understanding of many phases of adolescent behavior, has been advanced at some length in other sections of this book.

It appears that the changes in behavior by which a person endeavors to satisfy his needs and arrive at the goals he accepts are a function of his personality pattern, the permissiveness of his environment, and the status or category that his age, sex, and socioeconomic position in society accord him. Certain individuals in a given category will, and must, display less continuity and stability than others. It is particularly hard to make generalizations in this area.

Examination of the figures included in the earlier part of the chapter indicates certain specific changes and continuities based upon age and sex. It might be more profitable, in studying interest stability and change, to ex- amine changes in some of the basic attitudes that underlie interests.

Summary

An interest is an attitudinal set to give selective attention to a class of objects or activities that are of self-concern. The behavioral outcome of an interest is cognitive-affective activity of an intellectual, emotional, or personal nature. An important key to an understanding of adolescents' behavior is a knowledge and appreciation of their activities and interests. In considering adolescent interests, it will be found that individuals vary, but similarities do exist; deviations from group references are often significant.

Activity is partly a result of interest, but the nature and the direction of the activity are functions of the environment, which may inhibit activity even where strong drives and interests exist. On the other hand, interest is itself directly dependent upon the environment and upon cultural factors, for both its inception and its sustenance. Thus, any interest is environmentally or biologically engendered and is not innate. One of the most important factors in the sustenance and arousal of interest is successful experience, and since skill results in success, training for skills is an important method of broadening an individual's interest horizons.

Interests are motivating factors to activity and are an important means of guiding and directing the activities of an individual or a group. Properly used, they may become a springboard into many activities.

Play is a spontaneous and voluntary activity performed for immediate gratification without ulterior motives. It may be regarded in terms of its "content" activity or, ignoring content, in terms of its antecedents and consequents. While play is ordinarily believed to be confined to the period of childhood, it is actually an activity that extends over the whole span. It is of particular importance in adolescent development. However, because play has

been assumed to be a childhood occupation, most theories of play are confined to early childhood.

Play during adolescence is an important means of testing reality, manipulating new elements of self-behavior, and assuming new roles. In the study of adolescent interests, play can be a useful means of showing the kinds of things that appeal to an adolescent when he is on his own, or not under the direct supervision of an adult.

A survey of interests and activities reveals certain general patterns and differences based upon age, sex, grade placement, geography and climate, socioeconomic background, and time in history. However, despite such patterns, individual differences, often dramatic, do exist. We must also remember that a survey of an individual's activities is not necessarily an index of his real interests. It is not always possible to do those things one would most like to do, and convenient substitute activities are frequently accepted. Interests need opportunity to be implemented if they are to result in activity. Overgeneralization is dangerous when discussing or forecasting the nature and direction of adolescent interests.

Surveys of interests reveal crucial differences between adolescents of different intellectual capacities, and between physical and nonphysical activities. Sex differences appear to become less distinct with increases in age, and the number of activities indulged in appears to decline, although people who had many interests as children tend to have a greater number of interests as adults than do those whose childhood interests were few.

The activities of groups often exemplify the interests of the children who compose them. A study of informal groups reveals a number of distinct categories under which such groups may be identified, each category representing a constellation of attitudes and activities that govern the group's behavior.

Wishes are an important index to a person's interests and seem to reflect both his attitudes and his social adjustment. In general, interests tend to fluctuate with age and with time and history, girls being somewhat more stable than boys. Dislikes appear to decrease with age and experience; likes appear to increase. A radical change in environment will effect a radical change in attitudes, although breadth of experience tends to lead to liberalization of attitude. In general, younger children tend to be more interested in gaining personal and material possessions, but as they grow older, their wishes become more general and less self-centered. The form of the question in which individuals state their wishes is important in determining what kind of wishes will be listed.

Worries may be considered as an obverse index of interests, indicating, as they do, the things an individual wishes to avoid. Sex, age, and socioeconomic differences appear in the things worried about and feared as well as in the things liked.

Solitary activity fills an important part of any adolescent's life. Some persons feel that youth should cultivate the capacity for self-entertainment, but the direction seems to tend toward "spectatoritis" rather than toward participative activity in later adolescence. The communications media are an important source of self-entertainment.

The place of the various communications media in adolescent behavior is most profitably viewed not in terms of the effect of isolated media, but in terms of their focused impact upon an adolescent living in a world in which he has contact with all the media and in which they join together in influencing his behavior. A typical teenager of either sex reads, sees, and hears for the most part to learn, to obtain pleasure, and to satisfy his needs and desires. No one of the media may be thought of as being the most universally popular. Any medium of communications is popular with a given adolescent when it meets his need of the moment. The following minute, day, or hour may find him equally interested in some other medium as it happens to fit that moment's need. If one were to ask an adolescent which communications media he most preferred, he would probably be at a loss for an answer, for in truth he probably would have no preference, only needs and interests, and would be quite willing to accept nearly any vehicle that would satisfy him. Hence, knowing the things in which an adolescent boy or girl may usually be expected to show interest; having some appreciation of their needs, desires, likes, and dislikes; and then utilizing this knowledge form an effective approach to the guidance of adolescent behavior. In this way books, newspapers, comics, magazines, movies, radio, TV, drama, and lectures become not an end in themselves, but a means to an end.

References

Amatora, M. Home interests in early adolescence. *Genetic Psychology Monographs* 65 (1962): 137–174.

Angelino, H.; Dollins, J.; and Mech, E. V. Trends in the "fears and worries" of school children as related to socioeconomic status and age. *Journal of Genetic Psychology* 89 (1956): 263–276.

Bernard, D. Les loisirs de l'enfant à l'age scolaire. *Enfance* 1–3 (1965): 339–353.

Bledsoe, J. C., and Brown, I. D. The interests of preadolescents: A longitudinal study. *Journal of Experimental Education* 33 (1965): 337–344.

Cobb, H. V. Role-wishes and general wishes of children and adolescents. *Child Development* 25 (1954): 161–172.

Croake, J. W. Fears of children. *Human Development* 12 (1969): 239–247.

Fehl, S. L. The influence of reading concepts, attitudes, and behavior. *Journal of the Reading Specialist* 8 (1968): 50–57.

Gereb, G.; Zzabo, E.; and Oestreich, G. Angstvorstellungen ungarischer Mittelschuler. *Praxis der Kinderpsychologie und Kinderpsychiatrie* 17 (1968): 59–70.

Gross, F. P. Recreational mobility of in-school youth in relation to level of intelligence. Master's thesis, Ohio State University, 1957.

Horrocks, J. E., and Mussman, M. C. Developmental trends in wishes, confidence, and the sense of personal control from childhood to middle maturity. *Journal of Psychology* 84 (1973): 241–252.

Horrocks, W. B., and Flory, E. Wishes of high school and college students. Unpublished data, 1960.

Klein, D. Adolescent driving as deviant driving. *Journal of Safety Research* 4 (1972): 98–105.

Larcebeau, S. Interets et education. *Bulletin de Psychologie* 20 (1967): 827–833.

Lehman, H. C., and Witty, P. A. *The psychology of play activities.* New York: Barnes, 1927.

Lévy-Bruhl, O. Les adolescents et la lecture. *Enfance* 5 (1957): 561–567.

Miller, L. C.; Barrett, R. L.; Hampe, E.; and Noble, H. Factor structure of childhood fears. *Journal of Consulting and Clinical Psychology* 39 (1972): 264–268.

Murray, R. L.; Cole, R. R.; and Fedler, F. Teenagers and TV violence: How they rate and how they view it. *Journalism Quarterly* 47 (1970): 247–255.

Mussen, P. H. Long-term consequents of masculinity of interests in adolescents. *Journal of Consulting Psychology* 26 (1962): 435–440.

Nicholi, A. M. The motorcycle syndrome. *American Journal of Psychiatry* 126 (1970): 1588–1595.

Nugent, F. A. The relationship of discrepancies between interest and aptitude scores to other selected personality variables. *Personnel and Guidance Journal* 39 (1961): 388–395.

Phelps, H. R., and Horrocks, J. E. Factors influencing informal groups of adolescents. *Child Development* 29 (1958): 69–86.

Piaget, J. *Play, dreams, and imitation in childhood.* New York: Norton, 1951.

Pressey, S. L. Changes from 1923 to 1943 in the attitudes of public school and university students. *Journal of Psychology* 21 (1946): 173–188.

Pressey, S. L., and Jones, A. W. 1923–1953 and 20–60 age changes in moral codes, anxieties, and interests as shown by the X-O tests. *Journal of Psychology* 39 (1955): 485–502.

Rubin, B. M.; Katkin, E. S.; and Weiss, B. W. Factor analysis of a fear survey schedule. *Behavior Research and Therapy* 6 (1968): 65–75.

Sherif, M. and Sherif, C. W. *Reference groups.* New York: Harper & Row, 1964.

Slobin, D. I. The fruits of the first season: A discussion of the role of play in childhood. *Journal of Humanistic Psychology* 4 (1964): 59–79.

Sterner, A. P. Radio, motion picture, and reading interests: A study of high school students. *Teachers College Contributions to Education,* No. 932, 1947.

Tyler, L. E. A comparison of the interests of English and American school children. *Journal of Genetic Psychology* 88 (1956): 175–181.

Washburne, J. N. The impulsions of adolescents as revealed by their written wishes. *Journal of Juvenile Research* 16 (1932): 193–212.

Wheeler, D. K. Expressed wishes of adolescents. *Journal of Genetic Psychology* 102 (1963): 75–81.

Winick, C. Teenagers, satire, and "Mad." *Merrill-Palmer Quarterly* 8 (1962): 183–203.

Zazzo, B. Representations of success among adolescents. *Enfance* 3 (1962): 275–289.

Suggested Readings

Amatora, M. School interests of early adolescents. *Journal of Genetic Psychology* 98 (1961): 133–145.

Barclay, J. R. Interest patterns associated with measure of social desirability. *Personnel and Guidance Journal* 45 (1966): 56–60.

Berkowitz, L. Sex and violence: We can't have it both ways. *Psychology Today* 5 (1971): 18–23.

Blumenfeld, W. S. and Remmers, H. H. Research notes on high school spectator sports preferences of high school students. *Perceptual Motor Skills* 20 (1965): 166.

Bryan, J. H. and Schwartz, T. Effects of film material upon children's behavior. *Psychological Bulletin* 75 (1971): 50–59.

Chaffee, S. H.; McLeod, J. M.; and Atkin, C. K. Parental influences on adolescent media use. *American Behavioral Scientist* 14 (1971): 323–340.

Cernik, H. C.; Mueller, N. J.; and Williams, H. J. Purpose for your life. *Character Potential* 6 (1972): 27–39.

Cole, M.; Fletcher, F. M.; and Pressey, S. L. Forty year changes in college student attitudes. *Journal of Counseling Psychology* 10 (1963): 53–55.

Crane, A. Actions and reactions to reading in the public and parochial schools. *Training School Bulletin* 64 (1967): 62–65.

Croake, J. Adolescent fears. *Adolescence* 2 (1967–1968): 459–468.

Fehl, S. Case studies of the influence of reading on adolescents. *Reading Horizons* 9 (1969): 77–83.

Fingarette, H. All work and no play. *Humanitas* 5 (1969): 5–19.

Freeberg, N. E. and Rock, D. A. Dimensional continuity of interests and activities during adolescence. *Human Development* 16 (1973): 304–316.

Gilmore, J. B. Play: A special behavior. In Haber, R. N., ed., *Current research in motivation.* New York: Holt, Rinehart and Winston, 1966.

Gratton, C. Summaries of selected works on personality and play. *Humanitas,* 5 (1969): 101–108.

Herron, R. E., and Sutton-Smith, B. *Child's play.* New York: Wiley, 1971.

Lapouse, R., and Monk, M. A. Fears and worries in a representative sample of children. *American Journal of Orthopsychiatry* 29 (1959): 803–818.

Liebert, R. M.; Neale, J. M.; and Davidson, E. S. *The early window: Effects of television on children and youth.* Elmsford, N.Y.: Pergamon Press, 1973.

Olson, A. V., and Rosen, C. L. A comparison of reading interests of two populations of ninth grade students. *Adolescence* 1 (1966): 321–326.

Pierce-Jones, J. Social mobility orientations and interests of adolescents. *Journal of Counseling Psychology* 8 (1961): 75–78.

Rabinovitch, M. S. Violence perception as a function of entertainment value and TV violence. *Psychonomic Science* 29 (1972): 360–362.

Seagoe, M. V. A comparison of children's play in six modern cultures. *Journal of Social Psychology* 9 (1971): 61–72.

Siegel, H. B. Cultural information components of adolescents. *Psychological Reports* 30 (1972): 894.

Ward, S., and Wackman, D. Family and media influences on adolescent consumer learning. *American Behavioral Scientist* 14 (1971): 415–427.

Witty, P. A study of pupils' interests: Grades 9, 10, 11, 12. *Education* 82 (1961): 39–45, 100–110, 169–174.

Chapter Thirteen

Attitudes, Values, and Ideals in Adolescence

Attitudes and Ideals in Adolescence

Since an adolescent is continually subjected to new experiences, since his knowledge is growing and expanding, and since he is leaving childhood and nearing adulthood with its new points of reference, it is inevitable that significant changes in attitudes and ideals will occur. Konopka (1973) notes that while value formation is a birth-to-death process, the intellectual and emotional aspects of values and value formation come to a peak of activity during adolescence. To what extent there can be said to be "characteristic" adolescent values is not fully agreed upon, but there is no doubt that any given adolescent's attitudes and ideals are an expression of his personality. As such, they emerge from his past and are the results of a long series of events, internal and external, that he has previously experienced. He interprets each new situation partly in terms of the attitudes and ideals he brings to it. The new situation, in its turn, becomes part of his past experience and, as such, plays its part in shaping and modifying his future attitudes and ideals.

Since individuals and their environments differ, it is difficult to believe that there is any universally applicable adolescent attitude or group of attitudes. Nor can one believe that any given ideal is exclusive to the adolescent period or that it inevitably begins at that time. There will certainly be vast individual differences, and it appears doubtful whether any consistent or reasonable set of norms may be established. Further, an attitude or an ideal lacks concrete existence until it is applied or becomes manifest through activity, verbal or physical. It seems reasonable to assume that even though two individuals have the same attitudes and ideals, their methods and their opportunities for expressing them may differ considerably.

A problem arises from the stereotyped attitude or ideal that receives cultural sanction and is expected of an individual at a given period in his development. So pervasive is the "sanctioned" attitude or idea that the ordinarily intelligent adolescent will give lip service to it to avoid censure and perhaps to gain approval and acceptance. His actual attitudes and ideals may often be another matter altogether.

It is pernicious fallacy to attribute to adolescents ideals and attitudes the adult feels that they ought characteristically to have or that he has heard they have. Many adults like to think that their own experiences, attitudes, beliefs, and ideals when they were adolescents are common to all or most of today's adolescents. Such a generalization is obviously not very fruitful when one considers the extent of individual differences in personality, environment, and opportunity. Also, it is a rare individual who can recall with any accuracy what he actually did believe, think, and feel when he was an adolescent. Even if he can remember, he has gained new points of view as an adult, interpretations and experiences that have become part of himself, and he must look back at his own childhood through his own adult self, as through a translucent screen. In recalling their own childhood, adults tend to be oversentimental and to see things through a rosy haze, or to overreact in the opposite direction and see the period as a bleak and often horrible one. As a matter of fact, for most adolescents the period of adolescence seems neither particularly horrible nor particularly wonderful, just as the adult period of life seems neither outstandingly horrible nor outstandingly good for adults passing through it. As laymen, we tend to think of our own past and future, and perhaps of the lives of other people, too rigidly in terms of periods or stages.

However, adult concepts of the adolescent's attitudes and ideals or what they should be are important for the adolescent himself, for he must live with them in his daily life. He encounters them in his parents, in his teachers, in his spiritual guides, and in other adults. Insofar as the adults have direction over him, and insofar as they possess punitive power, he must consider their point of view and take the consequences of accepting or rejecting it. This is why many adolescents have such a difficult time in establishing their own values and ideals. Most of them respect their parents, and to a lesser extent, their teachers, religious counselors, and other directing adults; and they tend to feel guilty when they find themselves at variance with these adults. Such feelings of guilt may be entirely separate from the fear of reprisal; rather, they are likely to be based on respect for parents and other adults, as well as a feeling that something must be wrong because they disagree. Many an adolescent will make extreme efforts to mold himself into the form his parents and others have set for him.

The Relationship of Attitudes and Values

An *attitude* is a learned and consistent directional state of readiness to respond (habit, predisposition) toward a given class of objects, activities and concepts not as they necessarily

are but as they are believed to be. Operationally an attitude is an expression, by word or deed, of one's reaction to or feeling about a person, a thing, an idea, or a situation. It is impossible to consider an attitude in any meaningful way without making at least the implicit assumption that attitudes stand surrogate for underlying values. Hollander (1972) makes the point that attitudes are best interpreted as parts of a system of moral values and may be taken as expressions of the system. An adolescent who expresses an attitude of distaste or rejection toward a person who advocates a given course of action, such as stealing or clandestine lovemaking, may be assumed to have a system of values that motivates him.

A *value* is a defining process enabling an individual or a social group to make decisions as to what end (need), or means to an end (goal) are desirable. Dynamically, values are learned social products imposed on an individual and slowly internalized to the point of being accepted by him. Values may be taken to be relatively stable conceptual standards, explicit or implicit, which guide an individual in his selection of goal objects, activities, and objectives to implement his psychological needs. They are also the criteria against which an individual evaluates his system of needs. A value may, up to a point, seem to act as a need, although in reality a value is a function of the valuing transaction, not of the object. A goal object or activity does not "possess value," since value is only a criterion of selection or rejection. It is proper to say that an individual values an object or activity, but it has to be remembered that the valuing is done by the individual and is an internal process of selection or rejection. The object or the activity is simply rejected or selected. As such it "possesses" nothing.

A *value judgment* is an assessment of an individual or an activity in terms of its worth based on a system of values rather than its objective characteristics. To say that an adolescent is five foot ten is an objective fact. To say that he is pleasingly tall is a value judgment. The individual's moral judgments are his attitudes and beliefs on justice, ethical behavior, rules, and so on. Hogan and Dickstein (1972), using a brief semiprojective task, rated the moral judgments of ninety-two undergraduates. They report that those whose judgments were rated as mature tended to be sensitive to injustice, well socialized, autonomous, empathic, and based their judgments on intuitive notions of "goodness." Lorr et al. (1973) identified four higher-level dimensions involved in personal value statements, each of the four dimensions being interpretable as a specific ethic or organized set of rules guiding conduct. The four ethics of value dimensions were labeled: (1) acceptance of authority, (2) work ethic, (3) humanistic orientation, and (4) hedonistic orientation.

Definitions of an Ideal

An *ideal,* as the word is ordinarily used, is an attitude or a series of attitudes toward one's own or others' behavior and motives that endeavors to have such behavior and motives embody perfection, or at least represent the highest examples of their type—the ideal parent, the ideal school, the ideal way of behaving. Ideals are an attempt on the individual's part to build for himself, and to expect from others, values on a high moral and service plane. As compared to an attitude, an ideal is an end result. As it relates to the attainment of an ideal, an attitude is a way of looking at things that will permit one to do the things needed to achieve the ideal. For example, to achieve the ideal world, attitudes to sanction activities directed toward that end would be needed, and they would have to be considered right and acceptable.

The idealistic person is one who emphasizes ideals over reality. A person who is idealistic about human social relations tends to accept altruism and self-abnegation as standards of behavior. A person of high ideals will think of himself as honest, loyal, and interested in the common good. What is more, he will expect the same attitudes and behavior in others. The idealistic person often will tend to discount reality and expect people to "rise above themselves" and to have "good" motives. Unfortunately, many people are neither uninterested in promoting their own material welfare nor interested in helping others. The idealistic person often has severe adjustments to make when confronted by reality. The validity of one's ideals also needs consideration. No one could possibly question the value and desirability of possessing fine ideals, but as a human being, one must live with others. Standards that are so high, so unreasonable, or so capricious that they are impossible of fulfillment are unfortunate for both the individual holding them and those obliged to associate with him.

Ordinarily, in speaking of the idealistic person or the person who possesses high ideals, one means ideals that society would approve of and recognize as good. On the other hand, an idealistic person can be subverted or mistaken in his moral values. For him, behavior that is the antithesis of socially approved or moral behavior may represent perfection; yet in his way and in terms of his values, he may be an exceedingly idealistic person. For example, the juvenile delinquent may think of the ideal criminal and may exemplify in his behavior and attitudes great loyalty toward criminal ways and persons. Society would hesitate to think of such a person as an idealist, yet in his own subverted way he is. It should be remembered, in dealing with adolescents, that one will occasionally have to work with children whose ideals are of this nature. With them the task is that of redirecting their outlook on life so their ideals may be more wholesome and of a more socially approved nature. Understanding and help are needed rather than harsh censure. An idealistic person, whether his ideals are good or bad, will tend to resist and resent attempts to change their nature and direction. He is usually sure he is right and that the person trying to change the ideals is unreasonable, if not amoral.

The Adolescent as an Idealist

The adolescent as a person tends to be highly idealistic. He is likely to adopt a high standard of values and to think about them a great deal. Unfortunately, he is immature and inexperienced and his values may be exceedingly unrealistic. As a person, he is also highly critical of others, particularly as they deviate from that which he accepts as right or proper. Hence, it is not unusual to find an adolescent exceedingly intolerant and censorious of those who do not conform to his point of view.[1]

Because of his lack of experience, the adolescent is also likely to forget the important fact of individual differences and to generalize on the basis of one case or situation. That is, an adolescent who believes in a particularly high standard of moral conduct may witness a lapse by some other person and come to feel that "everyone is like that." If the person who lapses happens to be well known to him, or even idealized by him, the adolescent's disillusionment may be severe. In some cases it may lead to various kinds of problem behavior on his part. Therefore, one problem in working with an idealistic adolescent is that of protecting him from disillusionment until he gains the experience and ability to understand behavior that does not always meet his own standards. This does not mean that the adolescent should be sheltered. Instead, he should be educated and guided to see and accept people as they are and to maintain a high personal standard of values while he works out an acceptable relationship between his values and the realities he encounters in daily living.

Changing Times and the Acceptability of Attitudes

Changing times have considerable influence upon the acceptability of various attitudes. The value content of moral orientation is subject to much historical and cultural specificity. It is in constant change over the generations. The ideals of today, our conceptions of what constitutes good and bad, right and wrong, may not be the same or entirely the same as they were previously. Indeed, in a mobile and highly technical culture, it would be surprising if they did display any great stability. As generation succeeds generation new things become possible, acceptable, and even expected that in former years would have been unthinkable. The adolescent may, in his attitudes and values, be more in tune with his times than is the adult who tries to change these attitudes. The use of facial cosmetics by women has been one case in point. During the late Victorian period a woman who painted her face placed herself in a most dubious position, and a girl reared during that period tended to avoid cosmetics for that reason. Her daughter, growing up in the later generation of the first world war and the early twenties, usually encountered definite opposition if she attempted to "paint"; her granddaughter, growing up in the thirties and forties, sometimes met opposition, but much less than her mother had encountered. Presumably her daughter, growing up in the sixties, encountered less opposition than her mother did. Yet in any generation the trend may be reversed, and in the eighties there might be as much opposition to women's "painting" as there was in Victorian times, in which case the mother who uses cosmetics might find herself severely censured by her daughter. But whatever the trend, there is usually a lag from generation to generation, and within any generation there are always those who are at variance with their own times. Even in the Victorian era some women used cosmetics extensively.

It is difficult for the members of any generation, steeped as they are in the attitudes and habits of their own times, to appreciate the views of those whose point of reference is

---

[1]Such a reaction is not unique to the adolescent period; it is simply more common in the adolescent, who typically tends to be intolerant and harsh in his judgments. On the other hand, his sympathy and support may often be won by appeals that would be rejected by a more mature or experienced person.

that of an earlier generation. The reader of this discussion who smiles at the Victorian prejudice against cosmetics and who perhaps feels that it was not very serious, should consider his own reactions if the men and boys of today were to begin an elaborate use of rouge and face powder after shaving and before going out. As a matter of fact, adolescent male hair styles, wearing of beads, and fanciful ways of dressing are a step in a direction that would have appalled an earlier generation, although if one were to go back to medieval times the modern adolescent's approach to dress and hair style would be quite in the mode.

Changing Attitudes

One of the jobs of growing up is that of learning the social norms that characterize the culture in which one is reared. This is the process of socialization, and it is through this process that the individual acquires both attitudes and psychological needs. Such learned social norms gradually become for each individual his criterion of what is desirable and what is undesirable. Once acquired, such criteria become relatively stable across an individual's entire life span. Klieger and Walsh (1967) have reported that judgments of what is and of what is not desirable made by college students and children aged four, five, six, and eleven intercorrelate from 0.85 to 0.96.

But although attitudes may remain relatively stable over individual life spans, and although there may be attitudes characteristic of all individuals living at a given time in history, to what extent can we anticipate stability of attitudes across history? Specifically, to what extent are the attitudes of today's youth materially different from those of yesterday's youth? Today's world is not yesterday's—the play has changed, but what of the players? It is a difficult question, for we have little real basis for comparison; the youth of yesterday were not confronted with the problems of today —their times had problems of their own, and we do not know how those of the past would have acted today. Yet it has been possible to

make limited comparisons in a number of different areas. It would appear that the past two decades have witnessed considerable attitude change among the youth both of the Americas and of western Europe. The trend, although not uniform, is definitely in the direction of greater permissiveness and freedom as well as in the direction of greater emphasis upon personal fulfillment.

Jones (1960) compared the interests of ninth graders (about fourteen years of age) in 1935, 1953, and 1959, with samples of similar age, IQ, and social status. The more recent generations indicated greater maturity of heterosexual interests, more serious purpose, and a more tolerant attitude toward social issues. Englemann (1962) studied 4,457 German youth aged nine to seventeen by means of essays they had written on "Who I would like to be most (least) like and why." He then compared the responses of these adolescents to similar previous studies dating back to 1901, and reported that today's youth show acceleration in the realm of practical intelligence, but retardation in the ethical realm. Englemann's feeling is that the gap between practical intelligence and critical control leads to increased tensions in today's youth and may well explain their proneness to misbehave or indulge in adult-disapproved activities. In these two studies we see the contrast of Jones's more optimistic assertion that youth are becoming more serious in purpose and Englemann's point that they are more retarded in the ethical realm. Of course, we are dealing with noncomparable samples drawn from different cultures, but the discrepancies may not be as marked as would at first appear. Englemann's increase in practical intelligence may well mean that these children are really trying to do something with their lives, hence may well be, in Jones's terms, more serious. Perhaps Englemann's ethical retardation may relate to Jones's statement of a more tolerant attitude toward social issues and perhaps even to her "greater maturity in heterosexual interests." All this is really speculation, of course, and each study must stand on its own to be placed in the mosaic of existing studies from which generalizations may be drawn.

The generalizations here are that changes in children's attitudes have been occurring from generation to generation and that each generation has in some areas attitudes different from those of its predecessors, while, in other areas, attitudes remain relatively constant. And this drift in change occurs whether we are comparing 1960 to 1970, 1940 to 1950, or 1900 to 1910. For example, Horton and Remmers (1954), in a study of values extending over a span of thirty-five years, report little change in major moral values, although children's attitudes are changing to reflect a definite tendency to adjust to changing cultural sanctions and technological changes. Ramsey and Nelson (1956) report a more stable picture in at least one area when, in a study of changes in values and attitudes over a twelve-year period, they note no significant changes in family adjustments and in values and attitudes toward specific family relations except in girls, who in 1952 expressed less sense of obligation to their families than did those of 1939. Ramsey and Nelson's finding is in interesting contrast to Eames's (1965) later statement that today's adolescent is witnessing the deterioration of strong obligations to the family unit. There are many other cross-generation comparisons, each with its limited sample, but these seem to be matters for the historian and of limited help in our consideration of adolescence, directed as it must be to the present era.

In a study comparing college youth of twenty years ago with those of today, Kleiber and Manaster (1972) found in today's youth a general trend toward less conservatism and traditionalism. Comparing activist and nonactivist youth, these investigators noted that activist youth were more oriented toward the present while the orientation of the nonactivist group was toward success and prestige in the future. In a replication of a 1963 survey of the moral beliefs of English boys and girls, aged seventeen to nineteen, Wright and Cox (1971) report greatest changes for beliefs about sexual behavior, but there were also large changes in beliefs about race relations and gambling. In general, the change was away from the uncompromising condemnation of behavior toward a more qualified, permissive, or undecided position. Over the seven-year period girls' beliefs had changed more than boys'. McKinney, Connolly, and Clark (1973) report a greater increase in severity of judgments to prescriptive ("ought to") items than to proscriptive ("ought not to") items. In a study of changes in theoretical, economic, aesthetic, social, political, and religious beliefs of 284 undergraduates over their four years of college, Huntley (1967) reports fourteen changes in average value scores, six of the changes being in increases in aesthetic values and five being in decreases in religious values.

Gorsuch and Daly (1970) report changes in how college students judged the "wrongness" of fifty behaviors in 1969 as compared to 1958. The average severity of the judgments decreased slightly in 1969, with females becoming more like males. Individual items showing the greatest decrease were concerned with premarital sex and religion. However, students with different backgrounds differed widely in their judgments. Gorsuch and Daly, somewhat at variance with other studies, make the point that college students today are not more critical of unethical behavior than previous generations of college students. Extending the Gorsuch-Daly study back to 1929, 1939, and 1949, Gorsuch and Smith (1972) report that only in the area of sexual behavior were definite shifts to be found. Gorsuch and Smith suggest that it may be misleading to confound differences across years with differences across universities or dissimilar environments. In a study of German youth of today as compared to those of forty years ago, Weinert (1967) reports an acceleration of about two years in their moral standards.

Ahammer (1971) investigated attitudinal judgments of four different age groups (eleven to twelve; fifteen to eighteen; thirty-four to forty; sixty-four to seventy-four) on the personality dimensions of affiliation, achievement, autonomy, and nurturance. For statements

Figure 19 *Personal Desirability Attitudes of Four Age Groups Toward Various Personality Dimensions*

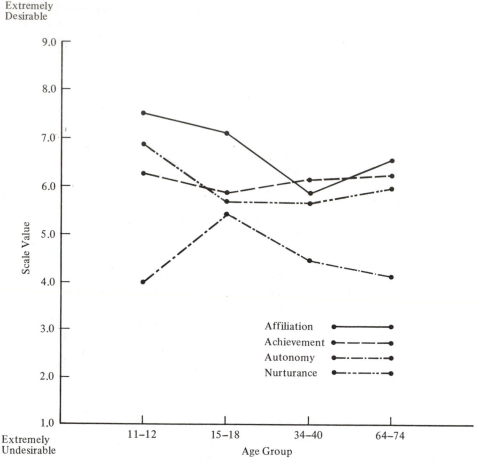

Source: Adapted from data in I. M. Ahammer, "Desirability judgments as a function of item content, instructional set, and sex: A life span developmental study," *Human Development* 14 (1971): 195–207, figs. 1–4. Reprinted by permission of S. Karger AG, Basel, Switzerland.

having to do with each of the dimensions (ten different statements for each dimension), the subjects were asked, "Indicate how desirable or undesirable you personally would consider such a statement," and were requested to answer in the form of a rating on a nine-point scale ranging from extremely desirable through neutral to extremely undesirable. Scores for each scale were obtained by adding the desirability scale values of all ten items in

each scale. Results are presented in Figure 19. Changes occurred on all dimensions for all age groups but the overall changes from preadolescence to adolescence were greater than they were between any other age groups, although large negative changes in affiliation and autonomy occurred between adolescence and adulthood.

Perhaps more meaningful for one trying to understand the process of development in the second decade of life are those studies that endeavor to present a developmental picture of attitudinal changes within an individual during his progress from early through late adolescence. Such studies are not interested in changes from one generation to the next, as were Jones's and Engelmann's studies, but rather in what happens to a given individual over the period of his adolescence. Typical of this kind of study is one by Douvan (1960). She reports that girls show less concern with values and the development of behavior controls than do boys, for whom character development is more rapid during adolescence. In looking at the development of girls' values over adolescence, Douvan notes that internalization of independent standards is not an effective prediction of ego organization or ego strength, the critical variable being a girl's progress in developing interpersonal skill and sensitivity.

Lehmann (1963) investigated changes in critical thinking ability, stereotypic beliefs, dogmatism, and values. In doing so he administered a battery of cognitive and affective measures to 1,051 individuals as college freshmen and then again when they were seniors. During this four-year period Lehmann found a significant decrease in stereotypic beliefs and lack of receptivity to new ideas, while at the same time critical-thinking ability increased significantly. Seniors were more "outer-directed" than they were as freshmen, although they tended to be less homogeneous in certain attitudinal traits than were freshmen. Most of the changes took place in the freshman and sophomore years. Morris (1958), using a sample of British children, notes that with increasing age there is a change in the direction of greater autonomy and equity in moral judgments, and such changes seem to bear no relationship to the respondent's sex. However, Morris points out that moral development reveals wide individuality variation and reflects many social influences. Eppel and Eppel (1967) note that adolescents' moral concerns seem to focus mainly on their problem of establishing good social relationships. Durkin (1959) studied a sample of seven- to twelve-year-olds in order to test Piaget's theory of moral development, and reports support for the conception of relationship between age and justice concepts, but not between age and acceptance of reciprocity. Gilen (1965), studying the evolution of conscience during puberty, reports that a majority of three hundred fifteen-year-old German adolescents reported feelings of guilt, distress, and pangs of conscience.

Using as their sample 120 children, 30 each at ages eleven, thirteen, fifteen, and eighteen, Adelson and O'Neil (1966) endeavored to trace the growth of a sense of community during the adolescent years. They report that children before thirteen are rarely able to rise above personalized modes of discourse in the political realm. These youngsters find it hard to imagine the social consequences of political action. Children below fifteen find it difficult to conceive of the community as a whole. They see government in terms of specific and tangible services. In early adolescence the idea of future is incompletely developed, and long-range effects of government are usually beyond their ken. Younger adolescents tend to advocate authoritarian solutions to political problems and are usually insensitive to individual liberties. Because they are unable to achieve a differentiated view of the social order, they have difficulty in understanding and accepting the legitimate claims of the community upon the citizen. And finally, Adelson and O'Neil note that as adolescents increase in age they increasingly begin to use philosophical principles in making their political judgments.

Causal Factors in Change

When attitudes across a broad cultural front first begin to change, analysts seek causes within the culture to explain the new attitudes. However, as time passes and the attitudes become entrenched, these same attitudes then become an exceedingly important factor not only in causing the perseveration and enhancement of the attitudes among members of new generations entering the culture, but in serving to create even more severe forms of the attitudes. Often times the new attitudes will persist long after the original cultural reasons for them have vanished or have been mitigated, and in this sense the attitudes have only themselves to feed upon. But times do change, and new attitudes gradually, or sometimes suddenly, replace old ones as new problems appear with the appearance of new generations.

One problem in social relationships has to do with attitudinal lag; that is, when one group within an advancing or changing culture perseverates in holding the old attitudes well into the time when the attitudes have become an anomaly in a culture advancing in a new direction. Of course, some attitudes are adjustively current for generations, while others are only passing fancies or temporary attempts at meeting some current problem.

Two age groups in the culture seem most apt to perseverate—those past forty and adolescents. For many older persons it becomes more difficult to adjust to change, and for those who see themselves as successful in the culture there is an added impetus to maintain the status quo. For the adolescent with the future before him the situation is different but psychologically more compelling. With his lack of experience and his great dependence on those cultural elements, such as the peer group, that he knows best, and especially with his identity structure still in process of formation and testing, the adolescent has to rely on what he hears from his surrounding associations. And such associations, as immature as the adolescent himself and as unable to make judgments comprehensive of all pertinent elements, continue the perseveration and carry forward outdated attitudes that sometimes bring adolescents into conflict with cultural expectations. It is perhaps a paradox to say, on the other hand, that adolescents often foster changes as they try to adjust to the conditions and times in which they pass their years of adolescence. In the first half of the present century and perhaps for a decade beyond, the formative forces for an adolescent's attitudes, except for such adult influences as teachers and parents charged with his upbringing were able to bring

to bear, were primarily a within-adolescent-subculture matter. But by midcentury, as the American culture moved to greater focus upon and imitation of youth, youth attitudes began to have an impact on the culture capable of creating rather massive changes in adult attitudes, especially as youth attitudes appeared to deal with issues ordinarily thought to be outside the scope of their interests.

A number of specific factors have been found to be important in attitude formation during adolescence. When an adolescent feels that he is an integral and contributing part of some enterprise his attitude will tend to be more favorable. For example, Wicker (1968) asked children from large and small high schools to provide subjective attitudinal accounts of their experiences in six kinds of extracurricular activities. Comparisons between and within large and small schools indicated that experiences such as being needed, feeling challenged, having an important job, and developing self-confidence are associated with activities where participants are not overcrowded. Most of the variations in experience were attributable to whether or not subjects held responsible positions in the activity. Sharples (1969) also studied the attitudes of preadolescents toward extracurricular activities. Expressive activities were held in higher esteem than more reproductive skills, and girls on the whole held more favorable attitudes than boys toward school activities. Older children, in particular, bore less favorable attitudes to school activities.

Negative reinforcement is a further situation giving rise to negative attitudes. Rousson (1970) measured the influence of the school environment on attitudes related to schoolwork. He reported that every negative reinforcement (blame, low grade), as well as a bad physical environment, has a cumulative discouraging effect and leads to increasingly adverse attitudes. However, Kniveton (1969), in a study of boys and girls aged fourteen to fifteen, noted that any child's attitude toward school is seldom unitary. In Kniveton's study, boys on the whole tended to be more interested in the subject matter presented in their courses than were girls. It may well be that the traditional curriculum of the average high school with its emphasis upon math, science, and history does concentrate on subject matter better fitting the stereotype of masculine interest, a stereotype to which most adolescent females will tend to conform.

Bengston and Lovejoy (1973) note covariation of attitudes with both objective experiencing (social location) and subjective experiencing (affect states). According to Rim (1970), they also vary with factors of personality. He reported systematic differences in rankings of attitudes between subjects high or low in dogmatism, authoritarianism, Machiavellianism, and intolerance and ambiguity. Podd (1972), in an interview study of 112 male undergraduates to assess relationships between ego identity status and level of moral judgment, reports that subjects undergoing an identity crisis were unstable and inconsistent in their attitudinal reasoning. Hjelle and Clouser (1970) write, "Externally controlled subjects will show more attitude change when exposed to standardized communications advocating a change in their preestablished positions than will internally controlled subjects."

O'Donnell and Brown (1973), using a sample of third through twelfth graders, report that susceptibility to attitude conditioning increased with age. The investigators speculated that the increase appeared to be a function of contingency awareness and also a function of older subjects having greater facility in transferring symbolic meaning. The changes were interpreted as being not changes in affect but cognitive changes in the symbolic reference to affect. Thus, developmental aspects of attitude change may differ, depending on whether the attitude components are primarily cognitive or affective.

Parents and other adults often fail to realize the great gap between many of their own attitudes and prejudices and those of modern youth. An adolescent and his parents often misunderstand each other's attitudes and fail to appreciate the lack of understanding with which they view each other. In such cases, parents tend to want to impose their views upon the adolescent.

From the psychologist's point of view it is less important to determine the normative picture of adolescents' ideals, values, and attitudes than it is to learn about the effect the attitudes, ideals, and values held by any given adolescent have upon him and his adjustment to his environment. It also is important to find ways and means by which any given adolescent may be guided to accept attitudes and values that are acceptable to others and satisfying to him, but will still permit him to adjust to his environment and be a useful part of the society in which he must live.

In a real sense, attitudes and values are an individual, not a group matter, and the most profitable approach appears to be that of studying each person as a separate entity and considering him in terms of his own peculiar needs, adjustments, opportunities, and background. Present research and writing in this area are moving more and more in that direction. Studies that trace the longitudinal development of a single individual in comparison with group norms are instances of this approach.

Factors Affecting Moral Development

To what extent may an individual's moral development during childhood and adolescence be delayed or accelerated by factors other than cognitive development and the passage of time? A number of investigators have made the point that an individual's opportunities for social expression and interpersonal activity exercise a facilitating and even an accelerating effect. Some go further and maintain that active social participation is essential to normal moral development. Selman (1971), in a study of the relationship between role-taking ability and moral development, administered the Peabody Picture Vocabulary Test to three groups of boys and girls aged eight, nine, and ten, as well as the Kohlberg Moral Judgment Scale for role-taking tasks. He reports the development of reciprocal role-taking skills to be related to the development of conventional moral judgments, although in a year-later follow-up of those children whose role-taking and moral-judgment levels were low in the original study, Selman notes that the ability to understand the reciprocal nature of interpersonal relations is a necessary but not sufficient condition for the development of conventional moral thought. Using children older than those in Selman's sample, Keasey (1971) also administered the Kohlberg Scale but related performance on it to the number of social organizations each of his subjects admitted belonging to, either as a member or leader. Subjects were also rated for popularity by peers and by teachers. Keasey reports that the stage of moral development was positively related to the extent of social participation, whether judged by self, peers, or teachers.

Family relationships and parental child-rearing practices have also been considered to be of major importance in their effects upon children's moral development. In a study of the relationship between moral attributes and parental identification in terms of admiration, desire to emulate, and perception of similarity, Hoffman (1970) gathered data from 664 seventh graders (age range twelve to fifteen), using structured and semiprojective items, as well as ratings by parents and teachers. He reports identification with the father as being positively related to internal moral judgment in lower- and middle-class boys, rule conformity in both middle-class boys and girls, and moral values in middle-class boys. Identification with the mother related to rule conformity in middle-class boys. Identification with the parent appeared to bear no relationship to guilt, confession, or blame-acceptance. Hoffman concluded that identification may contribute to the recognition that moral principles and not external sanctions form the basis of right and wrong, but not to the application of those principles to a child's own behavior in the ab-

sence of authority. Kuranuki (1968) correlated the attitudes toward punishment of Japanese children with the child-rearing practices of their mothers. He reports that while there was a general trend for younger children to select expiatory punishment and for older children to select punishment by reciprocity, children reared in a democratic climate were more apt to select reciprocity, while those reared in an authoritarian atmosphere were more apt to select expiation. Kuranuki concluded that the domestic climate, the attitude of the mother, and the mother's role in the family all interact in the formation of children's moral judgments. In a study of the value systems of French boys aged eight to fourteen, Borelli and Perron (1967) note that children have a value system that becomes progressively closer to that proposed by the mother. LaVoie (1973), in a study of fourteen- to sixteen-year-old boys, notes that socialization practices with individual children may be more valid predictors of moral conduct than various personality traits. LaVoie also notes that first- and early-born children tended to be less deviant than later-born children.

Stein (1972) studied the effects in a high school population of sex, grade level, and occupational groups on personal and interpersonal values. She reports that all values do not develop on an equal front but are differentially effected by a person's age, sex, and occupational group. Grade effects were stable for personal but varied for interpersonal values, while sex and occupational groups showed variation for both kinds of values.

A certain portion of adolescent attitudes are inevitably due to imitation of those held by adults. For example, Berger (1962) reports that behavior patterns approved and structured by the adult world are unconsciously subscribed to by adolescents. An adolescent who lives within the confines of a subcultural grouping, whether ethnic, religious, or racial, is quite likely to adopt at least a modification of the subculture's attitudes. For example, in a study of Jewish youth, Simon (1962) reports that "suburbia has helped develop in our youth a feeling of belonging to the Jewish group." This is all very well, but as Simon points out, such in-group attitudes make it more difficult to participate effectively in other-group life. Isolated in-groupness in adolescents tends to perpetuate itself in the adult world of affairs, where it may be quite inappropriate. Of course attitudes can change, but as the concept of self is developed and as an individual lives in a setting that reinforces his attitudes, it becomes harder to change, even when he desires to do so. Wilson (1963), in a study of 821 Boston high school students, reports that ethnic attitudes become increasingly static during adolescence. Certainly attitudes picked up within the ethnic groupings do tend to bias judgments of other groups. As a further illustration, Peck and Galliani (1962) note the biased judgments of adolescents living in mixed Texas communities.

However, there is hope, for as Livson and Nichols (1957) write, "social attitudes are less expressive of deep-lying personality factors than they are of boys' (and girls' too, for that matter) individual subcultural milieus. Sometimes a real effort to change bias has worked if there is a proper reinforcement followup." In a report on the interracial experiences of black youth in Baltimore since the 1954 desegregation, Bradley (1963) notes the increased noncompulsory association of white and black youth.[2]

What happens to an individual who holds a well-defined set of values and attitudes when he enters a unique sociocultural system (a college) with its own values and orientations as compared to those of the larger outside culture? The answer is that the individual by a principle of cognitive consistency tries to combine his own values and those of the new social milieu. The result, as Gottlieb and Hodgkins (1963) note, is the appearance of various subcultures within the major subculture. In American colleges, for example, we find the subcultures of Nonconformist, Academic, and Collegiate, battling sometimes for ascendancy where their spheres of activity overlap, but in ordinary affairs ignoring one another with some affect of dislike and even contempt.

Naturally, any adolescent has to build his attitudes upon his past experiences. Success and failure, reward and punishment are important determiners of attitudes. Fonzi (1959) reports that success tends to determine a more stereotyped frame of reference, while failure develops stronger attitudes toward criticism. Kerron (1962) reports that rejected adolescents displayed a weak ego, restricted in its integrative capacity by either impulsive demands or superego limitations. Jones, Gergen, and Davis (1962) studied individuals' reactions to being approved or disapproved as a person and noted that subjects' impressions from a disapproving source were more negative in tone than were those attained from an approving source; subjects became more self-deprecatory after negative than after positive interviews; and those receiving approving feedback felt themselves more accurate in self-presentation than those receiving negative feedback.

An adolescent's attitudes are much influenced by his family, a great deal depending upon the psychological climate of the home, its aspirations, and economic condition. Unfortunate conditions within the home can lead to attitudes in all concerned that may lead to adverse action. Rousselet (1962) reports that school dropouts are often influenced by a desire for immediate financial gains stimulated by overcrowded home conditions that gives them a short-term outlook for their future.[3]

In general, studies of the effect of institutions such as the church, the school, youth organizations, and the home on adolescents'

---

[2]In interpreting this study, the reader should be aware that it represents only an observational trend, since Bradley admits that no baseline survey was made to support the validity of her findings.

[3]Other studies on factors that shape adolescent attitudes include those of Prince (1960), Sprinthall (1964), McCue et al. (1963), Glasson (1965), and Thompson (1966).

attitudes appear to indicate that such environmental factors have considerable effect when their methods and procedures are good and take into consideration the psychology of the children with whom they are dealing. When such is not the case, effects opposite to those intended may occur. Many factors other than those of physical or social environment are instrumental in shaping an adolescent's attitudes. Among these are the vicarious experiences he encounters in books, movies, radio, and other communications media.

Attitudes Characteristic of the Adolescent Period

Descriptive catalogues of values and attitudes of adolescents have been a popular outcome of investigation; for example, Thompson (1961), Gilen (1965), Garrison (1966), Fleming (1960), and the polls of the Purdue Opinion Panel Poll (Blumenfeld et al. 1962). But the results, like the catalogues of interests cited in Chapter 12, are either ephemeral and apt to change from time to time or are specific to some relatively idiosyncratic sample. The reader should interpret such studies with caution. Cattell (1943) notes the problem of even short-term fluctuations in views over a twenty-four-hour period. However, Cattell did find less fluctuation of views in persons with highly integrated personalities. Adolescents, still in process of building a realistic and stable concept of self, lack the integration, at least during the years of early and middle adolescence, to display any great amount of attitude stability. However, there are some areas where long-term consistency seems to be the rule. In general, the adolescent admires the individual who is "with it," who is able to deal effectively with himself and with others. Morrison and Hallworth (1966) make the point that good adjustment, conscientious attitude, and personal control are highly regarded by adolescents. Beech and Schoeppe (1970), Horowitz (1967), and Hallworth and Waite (1966) also make the point that proficiency is highly

thought of during adolescence. For example, intelligence and related attributes such as logicality, competence, and intellectuality are especially admired as long as the adolescent is able to handle them in a socially acceptable manner. However, an adolescent using his intellectual ability as a means of denigrating his peers usually encounters quick rejection. The game of adolescence is to "play it cool," to use one's ability but to do so inconspicuously. Erikson (1962) speaks of youth's quest for fidelity—something to be true to, but something that in their own terms is worthwhile.

Wittenberg (1959–1960) makes the general observation that the largest number of adolescents tend to avoid concern with socially, economically, and culturally significant factors and prefer play to work. He sees this group as the mass media's particular target in attitude formation. However, he identifies two other groups of adolescents. First, a group he calls more sophisticated, alert, and informed, who tend to cope with the social environment by more or less open rebellion and defiance, criticizing social injustice, racial discrimination, poverty, disease, and other social ills. Wittenberg writes that "the interest of this group in the outside world is often a very reasonable rationalization of their own unresolved inner conflicts.... Their values are sharp and, for all their sophistication and awareness, oversimplified and primitive." The other group are conformists who defend and to some extent idealize the status quo.

Wittenberg's more sophisticated and alert group is composed of individuals who can "discuss the social and economic situation ... they are informed of what is going on, but they protect themselves from making connections between events (that is, seeing cause and effect relationships) which might make them panicky or turn into avoiders or defiers." This group, small in numbers in the 1950s, increased steadily in size during the 1960s, possibly reaching its numerically highest point during the late 1960s. Since then this group appears to have reached an asymptote, or to be decreasing somewhat in numbers if not in influence.

Of course, this group has attracted a great deal of attention because it is newsworthy and its members tend to do or say things that call them to the mass media's attention. The result is that adults tend to generalize and assume that this is the trend of American adolescents, but there is no evidence that this is the majority picture. The rebelliousness of the majority of American adolescents—insofar as they are rebellious at all—is usually directed toward personal problems of emancipation from adult controls rather than toward areas of social and political action. True, in the political campaigns of 1968, many college students did become involved, as in the various campus protest and action movements, but the vast majority showed only passing interest. And, of course, college students, whatever the divisions of their attitude, are far from comprising the majority of adolescents, who are not in college and have no intention of going.

In a study made in 1965, Trenfield confirms the presence and size of Wittenberg's "avoider" group, and adds that many adolescents show a preference for activities that seem to require comparatively little effort or preparation, being inclined to avoid activities that demand a high degree of skill and training. Thompson (1968) notes that those students most accepted by their peers were hedonistic. Less-accepted students tended to be more future oriented than their more popular peers.

Here we have an apparent discrepancy between youth's desire for fidelity and proficiency and the attitude of avoidance, the easy way out, and the hedonistic approach. The discrepancy, however, is more apparent than real. The avoidance group is only one among several different categories of groups, and it is not clear how generalized avoidance is, even among the avoidance group. It may well be that the avoidance occurs more in adult-sponsored and imposed areas than in the areas set by themselves. It is also possible that in those cases where the avoidance is generalized there may well be conflicts between tendencies for proficiency and avoidance, leading to problems of personal adjustment. This is an area of adoles-cent behavior that requires considerable further study.

Political Attitudes

A preadolescent's ideas on politics are at best vague and erratic, depending largely on what he chances to hear others saying. Adelson and O'Neil (1966) note that such ideas represent "a curious array of sentiments and dogmas, personalized ideas, randomly remembered names and party labels, half-understood platitudes." But by the time of the advent of the adolescent years, the individual's cognitive development has been such that he is potentially able to adopt, with his new capacity of operational thinking, a more reasoned or rational approach. Whether he makes use of his potential is another matter. As was indicated in the chapter on cognitive development, few individuals operate at their highest level of cognitive capacity on all occasions, and some appear to operate there infrequently, if at all.

Adelson and O'Neil (1966) conducted depth interviews with 120 adolescents, 30 each at ages eleven, thirteen, fifteen, and eighteen for the purpose of studying the growth of political ideas or concepts during adolescence. They reported, first, that before children are thirteen, they are usually unable to pass beyond highly personalized thinking about political matters. Social consequences of political action are something they simply do not take into account in forming their attitudes. Second, before they are fifteen, children visualize government in terms of concrete and specific services without any conception of the community as a whole. Third, only in the post-fifteen years do children take into account long-range goals and effects of political action. Fourth, in their earlier years, adolescents seek authoritarian solutions without being able to grasp the differentiated nature of the modern community—and of affairs in general—to the point of being able to opt for differential solutions. They can neither grasp the idea of legitimate claims of the community upon its citizens nor of the individual freedoms the community is contracted to honor. And fifth, as the adolescent passes fifteen, he begins increasingly to make use of philosophical principles in making political judgments. As Adelson and O'Neil (1966) indicate, the developmental patterns that emerge in their study are all quite in accord with Inhelder and Piaget's (1958) findings on the shift from concrete to formal operations. The eleven-year-olds in the Adelson and O'Neil study were still at the stage of concrete operations. The authors note of their eleven-year-old subjects that their thinking is "concrete, egocentric, tied to the present." Long-range consequences are beyond them, reasoning does not follow from premises, and the hypothetico-deductive mode of analysis has yet to be attained.

The thirteen-year-olds in the study were moving beyond the eleven-year-olds in that their thinking was less concrete, less tied to the present, less egocentric, the future was being perceived and hypothetico-deductive reasoning was becoming a possibility. But the process was incomplete, and it was not dependable. Depending upon circumstances, they might act either more maturely or less maturely than their age expectation. Of their thirteen-year-olds, Adelson and O'Neil comment, "They often involve an uneasy mixture of the concrete and the formal."

The fifteen-year-olds in the study were able to deal readily with the abstract if they had the necessary information. They were able to handle formal thought comfortably with failures "likely to be in content and in fluency rather than in abstract quality per se."

The eighteen-year-old was a fifteen-year-old grown three years older. He had gained in experience, become more fluent, more elaborative, more philosophical. His ideas, however, were not substantially beyond those he could have held at fifteen. Of him Adelson and O'Neil write: "At times he is consciously, deliberately an ideologue. He holds forth."

Hirose (1972) administered a questionnaire containing thirty-two political-attitudes items to 543 Japanese high school and undergraduate students. He reported: (1) Despite a greater amount of political knowledge, older as compared to younger high school students displayed a more conservative attitude toward political matters; (2) political knowledge and radicalism both increased rapidly through the sophomore year in college and then became static at the sophomore level; and (3) the factor structure of political orientation was not affected by an individual's stage of development.

To what extent does knowledge accompany attitude and capacity during adolescence? A study by Jackson (1970) is interesting in that connection, assuming that interest and knowledge are related. Jackson studied political interests of children eleven through sixteen in Great Britain and the United States. His subjects showed little interest in political figures, preferring persons prominent in the entertainment world or persons depicted as heroes or heroines of fiction. When specifically asked to mention political figures, British children selected national figures, while Americans selected figures from different levels. Adolescent criterion for interest appears to be the fortuitous one of at-the-moment mention in the media. Of course, amount of information and interest is an individual matter depending upon individual variables. Musgrave (1971) examined the relationship between age, sex, social class, intelligence, and the development of political knowledge, attitudes, and values in 480 boys and girls aged twelve and fourteen. All variables bore positive relationships. Boys showed greater political knowledge than girls, and children with higher IQs showed more political knowledge, although it was not clear to what extent they were more critical in their use of the knowledge.

It would appear that family influence on political attitudes of adolescents has less than expected effects when voting behavior is taken as an indication of the effect. Connell (1972) notes that evidence does not support the conclusion that the primary source of political socialization is located in the family. Typical of studies supporting this position is one by

Blanchard and Scarboro (1973), who report that in a study of 118 eighteen- to nineteen-year-old college students voting for the first time, parental voting preferences were unrelated to the subjects' voting behavior.

The Importance of Conformity

An adolescent's attitudes are not necessarily fixed or unchangeable. Conformity, especially strong during the adolescent years, makes attitudes particularly susceptible to outside influences. As Barber (1968) notes, unless something inside a person drives him to seek the truth, his decisions will be made for him, even when he thinks he is making them. For example, Snyder (1969) reports that the social pressure of ridicule or unpopularity greatly accentuates the problem of ethical behavior. However, a person's expressed attitudes may be superficial or synthetic, and may serve to conceal his real feelings and values. Society expects conformity of its members and by one means or another seeks to enforce it. Many individuals conform, at least on the surface, because they feel they must or because they wish to avoid unpleasantness. One may not reject, with safety, mores that popular opinion holds sacred. The matter of conformity is even more important for the adolescent, since the adolescent peer group tends to be more intolerant of nonconformity than the adult group.

Conformity frequently confuses the adolescent. The groups with which he associates are inconsistent in their acceptance or rejection of various traits and attitudes. Honesty may be highly lauded in the school and church, but dishonesty may be the source of greatest admiration in the gang and sometimes, unfortunately, in the home. Loyalty to a teacher may involve disloyalty to peers. Courage may have a purely physical interpretation for some and a moral one for others. Sometimes an act that requires exceptional moral courage and abstinence may be interpreted as cowardice. Sometimes a seeming act of great courage is merely one of conformity by an individual too

cowardly to implement or stand up for his own values and ideals. A study of the effect of misinterpreted motives upon future adolescent behavior should yield some fascinating results.

Acceptance of certain attitudes and ideals as good is more than a matter of group or individual sanction. It is also a function of the section of the country or of the time in history in which one lives. Every schoolboy has heard the story of Sparta, where craft, guile, and deceit were among the most honorable attitudes and skills that boys training to be soldiers could learn.

As he goes through his daily life, an adolescent must somehow learn to apply a set of values that is both discriminative and flexible. At the same time, he must be able to recognize what values are completely unworkable, no matter who approves or disapproves of them. In the final analysis, an individual is the only person who may apply his values, and he alone must face others' reactions to their application, unless, of course, he involves others with him in his activities to the extent that they must share in the reactions such application calls forth. It is particularly difficult for an adolescent to deny the desirability of the values his peers hold. Insofar as these values conflict with those of parents or teachers, the adolescent may face adjustment difficulties; acceptance and approval by one side mean rejection and disapproval by the other.

Summary

Adolescence is a time of new attitudes and ideals that help to shape the adolescent's personality and adjustment to life. Such attitudes and ideals are individual matters and are the result of experience. "Characteristic" adolescent attitudes and ideals are unlikely, since individuals differ so greatly and have such diverse experiences. An attitude is a learned and consistent directional state of readiness to respond toward a given class of objects, activities, and concepts. Attitudes are parts of a system of moral values and may be taken as expressions of that system. A value is a defining process enabling an individual or a social group to make decisions as to what end, or means to an end, is desirable. A value may to some extent act as a need. A value judgment is an assessment of an individual or an activity in terms of its worth based on a system of values rather than its objective characteristics.

An ideal is an attitude or a series of attitudes toward one's own or others' behavior and motives that endeavors to have them embody perfection or at least represent the highest examples of their type. Every adolescent is confronted with a whole host of "sanctioned" attitudes and ideals that he is expected to possess or to acquire. A premium is placed on conformity, and the adolescent will often give lip service to what is expected of him in order to conceal his nonconformity and escape unpleasantness. The nonconforming adolescent may develop guilt feelings about his nonacceptance of attitudes and ideals that are sanctioned by adults.

Changing times bring changes in attitudes and in people's beliefs as to what is and what is not important. An activity or a point of view acceptable to one generation may not be as acceptable to another. It is usually difficult for one generation to appreciate the viewpoint of another.

It is more important for a youth worker to know the effect of given attitudes on an adolescent than it is for him to know they exist. It is also important to know ways and means of promoting "good" attitudes and of discouraging "bad" ones. In the final analysis, attitudes and ideals are individual rather than group matters and must be dealt with in that perspective.

One of the jobs of growing up is that of learning the social norms characteristic of the culture in which one is reared. However, attitudes, while they remain relatively stable over the life spans of most individuals, are susceptible to change in individual cases. Today's youth tend to be less traditional and more permissive in their orientation, though

here, again, individual differences occur in different classes of attitudes.

Society expects conformity of attitudes and tends to enforce it. One may not refuse to conform with impunity, and this is especially true of the adolescent, whose peer group tends to place an especially high value upon conformity. Unfortunately, the adolescent encounters many inconsistencies in his endeavors to conform.

The acceptability of attitudes is more than a group or an individual matter; it is a sectional and historical one as well. But in the long run, the adolescent must find values that satisfy himself as well as others.

The adolescent tends to be an idealist. His standards are apt to be high, and he tends to be intolerant of those who fail to meet them. He is likely to generalize on the basis of one case and may be severely disillusioned if those to whom he is closely attached display attitudes or conduct of which he disapproves. The adolescent needs to be guided to accept people as they are, while retaining his own integrity.

When one group within an advancing or changing culture perseverates in holding to old attitudes, difficulties of communication and adjustment occur. Of the various groups in the culture, adolescents and those past forty are most apt to perseverate in holding to their values, though they do so for different reasons.

An adolescent's attitudes are most likely to be favorable when he feels that he is an integral and contributing part of some enterprise, when he is not confronted by instances of negative reinforcement, and when he receives peer and significant adult reinforcement. Parents and other adults often fail to realize the great gap between many of their attitudes and prejudices and those of modern youth.

An individual's opportunities for social experiences and interpersonal activity exercise a facilitating and even an accelerating effect on moral development. It is even held that social participation is essential to normal moral development. Family relationships and parental child-rearing practices have also been considered of major importance in their effects upon children's moral development. Imitation is a basic means of acquiring attitudes and moral values.

A preadolescent's ideas on politics are at best vague and erratic, but as he enters the adolescent years and acquires capacity for formal thought, he is able to give reasoned and logical thought to political matters, although he still lacks practical experience enabling him to test reality. There is also the problem that few individuals operate continuously at their highest stage of cognitive capacity. There is, however, a considerable shift from year thirteen to year fifteen, after which an asymptote appears to be reached. An eighteen-year-old in his political beliefs and behavior is only a fifteen-year-old grown three years older. Of the eighteen-year-old it has been said, "he is consciously, deliberately an ideologue. He holds forth."

References

Adelson, J., and O'Neil, R. P. Growth of political ideas in adolescence: The sense of community. *Journal of Personality and Social Psychology* 4 (1966): 295–306.

Ahammer, I. M. Desirability judgements as a function of item content, instructional set and sex: A life span developmental study. *Human Development* 14 (1971): 195–207.

Barber, L. W. Unique patterns of catalyzers discovered from the use of an instrument designed to help college students recognize their own patterns in decision-making. *Character Potential* 4 (1968): 14–15, 51–62.

Beech, R. P., and Schoeppe, A. *A developmental study of adolescence*. Paper presented at the annual meeting of the American Psychological Association, Miami, 1970.

Bengston, V. L., and Lovejoy, M. C. Values, personality, and social structure: An intergenerational analysis. *American Behavioral Scientist* 16 (1973): 880–912.

Berger, R. Psychological structure of life-goals in adolescence. *Vita Humana* 5 (1962): 34–60.

Blanchard, E. B., and Scarboro, M. E. Locus of control and its prediction of voting behavior in college students. *Journal of Social Psychology* 89 (1973): 123–129.

Blumenfeld, W. S., et al. Youth's attitudes toward civil defence, fallout shelters, and homework. *Purdue Opinion Poll Reports*, no. 65, 1962.

Borelli, M., and Perron, R. Systemes de valeurs et representation de soi: Etude d'enfants de 8 a 14 ans appartenant a trois milieux socio-culturels. *Psychologie Francaise* 12 (1967).

Bradley, C. H. Inter-racial experience of youth in Baltimore in out-of-school life. *Journal of Educational Research* 57 (1963): 181–184.

Cattell, R. B. Fluctuations of sentiments and attitudes as a measure of character integration and of temperament. *American Journal of Psychology* 56 (1943): 195–216.

Connell, R. W. Political socialization in the American family: The evidence re-examined. *Public Opinion Quarterly* 36 (1972): 323–333.

Douvan, E. Sex differences in adolescent character processes. *Merrill-Palmer Quarterly* 6 (1960): 203–211.

Durkin, D. Children's concepts of justice: A comparison with the Piaget data. *Child Development* 9 (1959): 127–130.

Eames, T. H.; Douglas, H. B.; Guston, G.; and King, M. H. Attitudes and opinions of adolescents. *Journal of Education* 147 (1965): 1–43.

Englemann, W. Reifungsentwicklung und Reifungsveranderung in gefuhlsbetonten Wertungsbereich unsere Jugend. *Psychologische Rundschau* 13 (1962): 131–140.

Eppel, E. M., and Eppel, M. *Adolescents and morality: A study of some moral values and dilemmas of working relationships in the context of a changing climate of opinion*. New York: Humanities Press, 1967.

Erikson, E. H. Youth: Fidelity and diversity. *Daedalus* 91 (1962): 5–27.

Fleming, E. M.; Diagaria, D. F.; and Newth, H. G. R. Preferences and values among adolescent boys and girls. *Educational Research* 2 (1960): 221–224.

Fonzi, A. Successo e insuccesso come schemi di riferimento nella formazione di opinioni e atteggiamenti in adolescenti. *Rivista Psychologia Sozisle* 26 (1959): 221–233.

Garrison, K. C. A study of the aspirations and concerns of ninth-grade pupils from the public schools of Georgia. *Journal of Social Psychology* 69 (1966): 245–252.

Gilen, L. *Das Gewissen bei Funfzehnjahrigen: Psychologische Unferschungen.* Munster: Aschendorff, 1965.

Glasson, M. C. Making religion a force, not a form. *Character Potential* 3 (1965): 70–73.

Gorsuch, R., and Daly, B. Changes in ethical judgments of college students, 1958–1969. *Proceedings of the Annual Convention of the American Psychological Association* 5 (1970): 443–444.

Gorsuch, R. L., and Smith, R. A. Changes in students' evaluations of moral behavior 1969 vs 1939, 1949, and 1959. *Journal of Personality and Social Psychology* 24 (1972): 381–391.

Gottlieb, D., and Hodgkins, B. College student sub-cultures: Their structure and characteristics in relation to student attitude change. *School Review* 71 (1963): 266–289.

Hallworth, H. J., and Waite, G. A comparative study of value judgments of adolescents. *British Journal of Educational Psychology* 36 (1966): 202–209.

Hirose, H. Relationships between political knowledge and political attitudes in the process of political socialization. *Japanese Journal of Psychology* 43 (1972): 238–250.

Hjelle, L. A., and Clouser, R. Susceptibility to attitude change as a function of internal-external control. *Psychological Record* 20 (1970): 305–310.

Hoffman, M. L. Moral development. In Mussen, P. H. *Carmichaels' Manual of Child Psychology.* 3rd edition, ch. 23, pp. 276–277. New York: Wiley, 1970.

Hogan, R., and Dickstein, E. A measure of moral values. *Journal of Consulting and Clinical Psychology* 39 (1972): 210–214.

Hollander, J. Moral values: Personality and demographic correlates of attitudes toward crimes without victims. *Journal of Social Psychology* 87 (1972): 279–285.

Horowitz, H. Prediction of adolescent popularity and rejection from achievement and interests tests. *Journal of Educational Psychology* 58 (1967): 170–174.

Horton, R. E., and Remmers, H. H. Some ethical values of youth compared over the years. *Purdue Opinion Panel Poll No. 38*, vol. 13, no. 2, 1954.

Huntley, C. W. Changes in values during the four years of college. *College Student Survey* 1 (1967): 43–48.

Inhelder, B., and Piaget, J. *The growth of logical thinking.* New York: Basic Books, 1958.

Jackson, R. Children's politics and identification patterns: A comparative survey. *Educational Sciences: An International Journal* 4 (1970): 65–72.

Jones, E. E.; Gergen, K. J.; and Davis, K. E. Some determinants of reactions to being approved or disapproved as a person. *Psychological Monographs* 76 (1962).

Jones, M. C. A comparison of the attitudes and interests of ninth-grade students over two decades. *Journal of Educational Psychology* 51 (1960): 175–186.

Keasey, C. B. Social participation as a factor in the moral development of preadolescents. *Developmental Psychology* 5 (1971): 216–220.

Kerron, W. G. IES test patterns of accepted and rejected adolescents. *Perceptual and Motor Skills* 15 (1962): 435–438.

Kleiber, D. A., and Manaster, G. J. Youth's outlook on the future. *Journal of Youth and Adolescence* 1 (1972): 223–232.

Klieger, D. M., and Walsh, T. A. A pictorial technique for obtaining social desirability ratings from young children. *Psychological Reports* 20 (1967): 295–304.

Kniveton, B. An investigation of the attitudes of adolescents to aspects of their schooling. *British Journal of Educational Psychology* 39 (1969): 78–81.

Konopka, G. Formation of values in the developing person. *American Journal of Orthopsychiatry* 43 (1973): 86–96.

Kuranuki, M. On the moral judgment of children. *Japanese Journal of Educational Psychology* 16 (1968): 100–110.

LaVoie, J. Individual differences in resistance to temptation behavior in adolescents. *Journal of Clinical Psychology* 29 (1973): 20–22.

Lehmann, I. J. Changes in critical thinking, attitudes, and values from freshman to senior years. *Journal of Educational Psychology* 54 (1963): 305–315.

Livson, N., and Nichols, T. Social attitude configurations in an adolescent group. *Journal of Genetic Psychology* 91 (1957): 3–23.

Lorr, M.; Suziedelis, A.; and Tonesk, X. The structure of values: Conceptions of the desirable. *Journal of Research in Personality* 7 (1973) : 139–147.

McCue, K. W.; Rothenberg, D.; Allen, R. M.; and Jennings, T. W. Rorschach variables in two "study of values" types. *Journal of Genetic Psychology* 86 (1963) : 169–172.

McKinney, J. P.; Connolly, M.; and Clark, J. Development of a prescriptive morality: An historical observation. *Journal of Genetic Psychology* 122 (1973) : 105–110.

Morris, J. F. Symposium: The development of moral values in children. II. The development of the adolescent value judgments. *British Journal of Educational Psychology* 28 (1958) : 1–14.

Morrison, A., and Hallworth, H. J. The perception of peer personality by adolescent girls. *British Journal of Educational Psychology* 36 (1966) : 241–247.

Musgrave, P. W. Aspects of the political socialization of some Aberdeen adolescents and their educational implications. *Research in Education* 6 (1971) : 39–51.

Nichols, R. C. Personality change and the college. *American Educational Research Journal* 4 (1957) : 173–190.

O'Donnell, J. M., and Brown, M. J. The classical conditioning of attitudes: A comparative study of ages 8 to 18. *Journal of Personality and Social Psychology* 26 (1973) : 379–385.

Peck, R. F., and Galliani, C. Intelligence, ethnicity, and social roles in adolescence. *Sociometry* 25 (1962) : 64–72.

Podd, M. H. Ego identity status and morality: The relationship between two developmental constructs. *Developmental Psychology* 6 (1972) : 497–507.

Prince, R. Values, grades, achievement and career choice of high school students. *Elementary School Journal* 60 (1960) : 376–384.

Ramsey, C. E., and Nelson, L. Changes in values and attitudes toward the family. *American Sociological Review* 21 (1956) : 605–609.

Rim, Y. Values and attitudes. *Personality: An International Journal* 1 (1970) : 243–250.

Rousselet, J. Some aspects of the social ambitions of adolescents. *Enfance* 3 (1962) : 291–301.

Rousson, M. Facilitation et freinage dans le travail scolaire. *Enfance* no. 2 (1970) : 173–201.

Selman, R. L. The relation of role taking to the development of moral judgment in children. *Child Development* 42 (1971) : 79–91.

Sharples, D. Children's attitudes towards junior school activities. *British Journal of Educational Psychology* 39 (1969) : 72–77.

Simon, E. Suburbia: Its effect on the American Jewish teen-ager. *Journal of Educational Sociology* 36 (1962) : 124–133.

Snyder, C. Ego-weaknesses and problem areas of the 1967 Youth Congress delegates. *Character Potential* 4 (1969) : 37–41.

Sprinthall, N. A. A comparison of values among teachers, academic underachievers, and over-achievers. *Journal of Experimental Education* 33 (1964) : 193–196.

Stein, S. L. Changes in personal and interpersonal values by sex and occupational groups in grades 9 through 12. *Journal of Educational Research* 66 (1972) : 135–141.

Thompson, N. H. Decision-making by teenagers in six problem areas: The decision making studies: What do they mean for religious and character education? *Character Potential* 3 (1966) : 180–185.

Thompson, O. E. High school students' values: Emergent or traditional. *California Journal of Educational Research* 12 (1961) : 132–144.

Thompson, O. E. Student values in transition. *California Journal of Educational Research* 19 (1968) : 77–86.

Trenfield, W. G. An analysis of the relationships between selected factors and the civic interests of high school students. *Journal of Educational Research* 58 (1965) : 460–462.

Weinert, R. Vergleichsuntersuchung uber die Entwicklung der sittlichen Werthantlungen bei zwei Jugendgenerationen. *Zeitschrift für Experimentelle und Angewandte Psychologie* 14 (1967) : 651–702.

Wicker, A. W. Undermanning, performance and students' subjective experiences in behavior settings in large and small high schools. *Journal of Personality and Social Psychology* 10 (1968) : 255–261.

Wilson, W. C. Development of ethnic attitudes in adolescence. *Child Development* 34 (1963) : 247–256.

Wittenberg, R. M. Young people look at society. *Child Study* 37 (1959–1960) : 16–20.

Wright, D., and Cox, E. Changes in moral belief among sixth form boys and girls over a seven-year period in relation to religious belief, age, and sex differences. *Journal of Social and Clinical Psychology* 10 (1971) : 332–341.

Suggested Readings

Anderson, A., and Dvorak, B. Differences between college students and their elders in standards of conduct. *Journal of Abnormal and Social Psychology* 23 (1928–1929): 286–292.

Bell, R. R., and Buerkle, J. V. Mother and daughter attitudes to premarital sexual behavior. *Marriage and Family Living* 23 (1961): 390–392.

Borsedi, R. The neglected science of values. *Journal of Human Relations* 13 (1965): 433–445.

Clautour, S. E., and Moore, T. W. Attitudes of twelve-year-old children to present and future life roles. *Human Development* 12 (1969): 221–238.

Davis, W. C. Inventory of attitudes and ideals. *Personnel Journal* 41 (1962): 290–292.

Douglass, J. H. Today's youth and moral values. *Journal of Religion and Health* 8 (1969): 297–311.

Dressel, P. L., and Lehmann, I. J. The impact of higher education on student attitudes, values and critical thinking abilities. *Educational Record* 46 (1965): 248–258.

Freedman, M. B. *The college experience.* San Francisco: Jossey-Bass, 1967.

Goodman, P. *Compulsory miseducation and the community of scholars.* New York: Random House, 1962.

Graliker, B. V.; Fishler, K.; and Kock, R. Teenage reactions to a mentally retarded sibling. *American Journal of Mental Deficiency* 66 (1962): 838–843.

Joseph, T. P. Adolescents: From the views of the members of an informal group. *Genetic Psychology Monographs* 79 (1969): 3–88.

Keniston, K. Social change and youth in America. In Erikson, C., ed., *Youth: Change and Challenge,* pp. 161–187. New York: Basic Books, 1963.

Kirchner, J., and Hogan, A. Student values: A longitudinal study. *Psychology* 9 (1972): 36–39.

Kromboltz, J. D., and Verenhorst, B. Molders of pupil attitudes. *Personnel and Guidance Journal* 43 (1965): 443–446.

Lipset, S. M. American student activism in comparative perspective. *American Psychologist* 25 (1970): 675–693.

Malm, M. Junior high school period: Time for a unique educational program. *Teachers College Journal* 34 (1962): 46–50.

Mann, L.; Rosenthal, R.; and Abeles, R. P. Early election returns and the voting behavior of adolescent voters. *Journal of Applied Social Psychology* 1 (1971): 66–75.

Mauer, A. Adolescent attitudes toward death. *Journal of Genetic Psychology* 105 (1964): 75–90.

Merelman, R. M. The adolescence of political socialization. *Sociology of Education* 45 (1972): 134–166.

Orum, A. M. *The seeds of politics: Youth and politics in America.* Englewood Cliffs: Prentice-Hall, 1972.

Plant, W. T., and Minium, E. W. Differential personality development in young adults of markedly different aptitude levels. *Journal of Educational Psychology* 58 (1967): 141–152.

Reich, C. A. *The greening of America.* New York: Bantam, 1971.

Sanford, N. *Where colleges fail.* San Francisco: Jossey-Bass, 1967.

Schab, F. Cheating in high school: A comparison of behavior of students in the college prep and general curriculum. *Journal of Youth and Adolescence* 1 (1972): 251–256.

Suchman, E. A. The "hang loose" ethic and the spirit of drug use. *Journal of Health and Social Behavior* 9 (1968): 140–155.

Wallace, W. L. Peer influence and undergraduate aspirations for graduate study. *Sociology of Education* 38 (1965): 375–392.

Chapter Fourteen

Moral Development

Theories of Moral Development

Most theories of moral development, although making allowance for individual differences in the rate of progression, posit moral development as proceeding by means of an invariant sequence of qualitatively defined stages of structural development. In the beginning an individual perceives rules as external to the self but comes to identify the self with the rules and expectations of others. Finally, a differentiation is made between the self and conventional rules. Over the course of this development, rigidity and acceptance of authority yield to logic and a subjective interpretation of reality. Different theorists divide this progression into different numbers of stages, and some extend it over a longer formative period than do others. A few theorists endeavor to avoid description of the progression in stage terms, and there is some difference of opinion as to the most significant causal factors. All agree that the process is at least to some extent one of socialization, although some place more emphasis upon maturational factors than do others. All agree upon the great importance of morality in individual and interpersonal behavior.

At the present time the most comprehensive theories of moral development have been proposed by Piaget, Kohlberg, and Freud. Of these, the theory of Freud is historically the oldest and that of Kohlberg the youngest. Kohlberg's theory is derived from that of Piaget and makes a contribution to the study of adolescence by its explicit consideration of the post–twelve-year-old child. Piaget's cognitively based theory of developmental stages has attracted the greatest amount of quantitative research. The theory of Freud and the psychoanalytic school with their concepts of anxiety, guilt, and the superego has not resulted in a great deal of quantitative research as it is ordinarily conceived by psychologists working outside the psychoanalytic tradition, but it remains a vital force in psychiatric practice and offers an heuristic base for discussion for all those interested in the nature of human behavior.

The theories of Piaget, Kohlberg, and Freud are not the only theories of moral development extant, but they have been the most widely studied and accepted.

Piaget's Theory of the Development of Moral Judgment

Nearly a half-century ago Piaget (1932) in his trail-breaking book, *The Moral Judgment of the Child,* made the point that there is an orderly and logical pattern in the development of a child's moral judgments resulting in sequential changes over time in the bases upon which his judgments are made. In the beginning the child's moral judgments are made in terms of rigid interpretation of rules and regulations laid down by external authority, and if development is normal, the child's moral development ends with a state in which judgments are based on social considerations and flexible interpretation of rules. Although

Piaget uses stage terminology in speaking of the sequential nature of moral judgments, he indicates that individual differences in such judgments are extremely large at every age level, thus permitting considerable latitude in the interpretation of the boundaries of a stage.

Piaget's research was mainly concerned with four aspects of the development of moral judgments: (1) behavioral conformity to rules, (2) verbalized notions about rules, (3) moral attitudes more general than rule conformity, and (4) conceptions of justice. Piaget studied the development of rules by having children explain the rules of the game of marbles. General moral attitudes were studied by means of children's reactions to stories having a moral implication and by means of their attitudes toward the telling of lies. Conceptions of justice were studied by means of eliciting from children their ideas about how misdeeds should be punished, who would do the punishing, and how the punishments should be distributed among the members of a group.

Piaget reported the existence of four stages in the development of behavioral conformity to rules and of three stages in the development of verbalized notions about rules. At the first stage in the development of rule conformity the child is lacking in any conception of rules. He simply indulges in free play, although such play may gradually assume rituals quite private to himself. At the second stage, which appears between the third and fifth years, the childs' play behavior becomes imitative, and he adapts aspects of what be believes to be the rule-related procedures of his elders. Actually, his perceptions are incorrect, and his adaptations are in terms of his own private schemata. The result is that although he believes he is following what he sees, his play is egocentric; he may or may not apply any given rule, or his adaptation may have little to do with reality. At the third stage, appearing between the seventh and eighth years, although he still does not fully understand the rules and conformity to them, the child abandons his egocentric approach and genuinely tries to conform to the rules mutually agreed upon. This stage is marked by a real attempt at social conformity to rules, insofar as they are understood. Stage four usually begins in the preadolescent or early adolescent years, and in this stage the child fully understands the rules and seems fascinated by them to the extent of continually revising and readjusting them to deal with all kinds of possible situations that might arise.

The first stage of a child's verbalization of rules is really a period of preverbalization. For him rules are perceived and believed to be immutable. Insofar as the child is concerned, the rules have been laid down by higher authority (God, parents, older children, teachers, nature), and that is it. They have to be obeyed. At this stage children become upset at changes in rules or procedures to the point of active resistance to change. The comedy here is that the child is still at stage two or possibly three of behavioral conformity and is constantly violating the rules in which he so firmly believes without realizing his deviation. Finally, at stage three, appearing between the tenth and eleventh years, the child adopts the social and permissive attitude that rules may be changed if everyone concerned agrees. Higher authority is no longer seen as the sole arbiter, and the child perceives that rules, like everything else, are susceptible to change. In a real sense, the child becomes participative in the rule-making process and becomes one of the "elders" who can amend if not actually make the rules.

Where moral attitude is concerned, development is from an attitudinal state in which results are the sole criterion, with no consideration being given to antecedents and intent, toward a subjective attitudinal state in which antecedents and intent are definitely considered in making moral judgments. Younger children allocate seriousness in terms of magnitude. It is more serious and hence more wrong to drop and break two of anything, even if one doesn't intend to, than it is to drop and break one with malicious intent. The transition period during which motivation becomes a factor in making moral judgments occurs between the ninth and tenth years.

Where reaction to lying is concerned, a similar transition takes place. For younger children a lie is a lie no matter what the circumstances, whereas for older children the intention behind the lie is the criterion. In contrast to older children younger children interpret getting caught as the serious issue and feel that a lie is wrong because it is punished. Older children feel that a lie undetected and unpunished is just as serious as one detected and punished.

Piaget's research on conceptions of justice may be divided into findings on retributive, on immanent, and on distributive justice. Young children tend to believe that punishment for an offense should be both severe and directly in proportion to the seriousness of the offense (expiatory punishment). They ignore the nature or actual content of the offense. In contrast, by the time children become preadolescents or early adolescents, they tend increasingly to believe that punishment should be related directly to the nature of the offense entirely apart from its seriousness (punishment by reciprocity). Thus, older children avoid a concept of punishment for its own sake, taking the position that punishment by reciprocity would act as a vehicle to impress upon the offender both the nature and the consequences to others of his offense. Older children are also less likely to believe that punishment would be administered to the offender by acts of God or of nature (immanent justice). Younger children tend not to be surprised, indeed might well find their expectations fulfilled, at the possibility that an individual who committed an offense might suffer a direct retributive act by nature, such as being struck by lightning.

Where division of punishment among members of a group (distributive justice) is concerned, Piaget's research indicated a clear developmental progression. Children under seven or eight feel that this is the job of higher authority (parents, teachers, etc.) and that unequal treatment does not represent unfairness one way or the other but simply the way things are. In the middle years of childhood the child reverses himself and vigorously insists that everyone be treated alike under all circumstances. Children at this age, between eight and eleven, do use the concept of fairness and become upset if it is not strictly applied to all. At adolescence and even somewhat before, the child tends to test his egalitarian stance against reality and is willing to accept exceptions for cause. Still an egalitarian, his burgeoning knowledge of the world leads him to believe that exceptions are not necessarily unfair under certain conditions.

At the beginning of this discussion of Piaget's research, the point was made that while a stagelike developmental progression exists in the development of moral judgments, the actual stages are subject to broad interpretation and permit much scope for individual differences. While younger children are rarely if at all found to be operating at the level of the higher stages, older children may or may not be operating at the level at which they are presumably intellectually capable. Particularly at the time of interstage transition, as Markwalder (1972) and others point out, a considerable mixture of stages responses is to be anticipated. However, some individuals appear to be permanently fixated at early levels, while other preadolescents and adolescents seem to range freely across the whole gamut of the stages of moral development. Such individuals sometimes act quite immaturely in their judgments, and at other times they act more appropriately, at the highest level of which they are developmentally capable. For the older child who ranges freely over the developmental continuum in making his moral judgments, a crucial question has to do with the place on the continuum at which he is most customarily to be found. For example, although usually appropriately mature, how often does he regress, and are the regressions related to any particular subject matter? Are the regressions the rule rather than the exception with only occasional returns to more mature levels? There is also the problem, in interpreting a given adolescent's moral-judgment behavior, that certain environmental factors condition the normative progression of the stages. For example, Koenig et al. (1973) note that social class has a significant positive relationship to cognitive complexity and moral judgment. In their sample they demonstrated that their lower-class subjects, as compared to the middle-class children, were less cognitively complex and did tend to show less advanced moral judgments.

In general, Piaget's theory of the development of moral judgment visualizes two moralities in childhood, an early morality of constraint and a later morality of cooperation. The child's world of moral constraint is a highly objective world of absolute right and absolute wrong in which motives and personal-social contexts are not considered. In this world, justice is not tempered with mercy, and intent has no standing. What is done is done, and it is either right or wrong, good or bad—and punishment is rigidly, even harshly, applied. In this world right and wrong are determined by superior authority, and there is no room for questioning or for equity.

Following the morality of constraint, but seldom completely replacing it, is the morality of cooperation. The morality of cooperation grows out of mutual relationship among reference peers and finds its basis in the give and take of social interaction and shared respect. In the child's world of moral cooperation, motive and intent become important, and shades of right and wrong, of good and bad, are introduced. In this world rules that exist for social facilitation are considered in that light rather than as arbitrary givens. Equity becomes important as the child conceives moral judgment in beneficial rather than in victim-seeking terms. The move from the morality of constraint to that of cooperation is a move from a primitive to a civilized outlook.

The Validity of Piaget

Piaget's findings on moral development are provocative and have stimulated a great deal of research. How valid has such research proven them to be? For Piaget the underlying mechanism of the development of moral judg-ment involves the same cognitive processes underlying intellectual development. Rationality is the end product of both intellectual and moral maturity, and moral realism and intellectual realism can be viewed as parallel developments. Thus, it may be taken as a truism that growth in moral judgment cannot take place without an accompanying intellectual development. A number of investigators, including Abel (1951), Bobroff (1960), Harrower (1943), Johnson (1962), Lee (1971), Lerner (1937), and MacRae (1954), have noted the positive relationship between the maturity of an individual's moral judgments and his level of intellectual functioning.

Lee (1971) studied the growth of cognitive structures and moral judgment using as her sample 195 males aged five through seventeen in kindergarten through the twelfth grade. She hypothesizes that children's cognitive and moral development progresses sequentially and concomitantly from (1) the stage of preoperational thought, in which authority orientation forms the basis of moral judgments, to (2) the succeeding stage of concrete operational thought, when cooperation and reciprocity form the basis, to (3) the final stage of operational thought, when the orientation becomes ideological. Lee administered tasks to ascertain each child's level of cognitive functioning, using his cognitive performance as a means of predicting his level of moral judgment. Level of moral judgment was gained by means of responses to nine different morally conflicting stories. Lee writes: "These stories were designed to measure a child's centration on authority versus peer cooperation versus humanitarian acts."

Lee's findings furnish general support not only for Piaget's hypotheses that moral and cognitive development occur in a sequential series of stages, but also for his contention that their development is concomitant. Lee reports that, holding age constant, development of concrete operations can be predicted because it is related to a decrease in responses of an authority-reference character and is accompanied by increases in moral modes of conceptualization. An increase of "societal, idealistic modes of conceptualization" is best predicted by the advent of formal thinking.

Among others who have confirmed aspects of Piaget's theory, MacRae (1954) and Medinnus (1959) report that with increasing age acts are judged in terms of intentions rather than consequences. Bobroff (1960), Lerner (1937), and MacRae (1954) note that the dimension of unchangeability of rules is negatively correlated with age. Boehm (1962a) reports that with increasing age there is a tendency for children to define moral wrongness by reference to punishment. Harrower (1934) and Johnson (1962) report that with increasing age belief in expiatory justice gives way to a more restitutive justice. Buchanan and Thompson (1973) note that damage is the most important factor in moral decisions for younger children whereas intent is more important for older children. And finally, Medinnus (1959) and MacRae (1954) report that younger children believe in immanent judgment but older children substitute for this a belief in naturalistic causality.

A number of investigators, including Whiteman and Kozier (1964), Porteus and Johnson (1965), Kohlberg (1966), Boehm (1962b), and Bobroff (1960), indicate that aspects of moral judgment are positively related to intelligence. Abel (1941), Harrower (1934), Boehm (1962a), and Johnson (1962) report that aspects of moral judgment, such as objective responsibility, are related to socioeconomic class membership.

However, not all studies have confirmed Piaget's theory. American writers have criticized Piaget for overemphasizing maturational and underestimating environmental factors. He has not considered the possibilities of further moral development past age twelve, and the age norms he cites, based as they are on Swiss children, need some revision when applied in other cultures. Carlson (1973), in a study using Laotian children aged six to fourteen, tested the Piagetian view that the development of justice is related to mutual respect and solidarity among peers, while de-

velopment of subjective responsibility is intimately related to the amount and quality of child-adult interactions. Carlson's results indicate that developing subjective responsibility may be less related to adult constraint and that peer-group action may be less related to the development of justice than Piaget has suggested.

Armsby (1971) makes the point that Piaget's original story pairs do not clearly differentiate accidental from purposive behavior. Consequently, he feels that in order to make a valid judgment of the development of intentionality judgments, new moral-judgment stories are needed that clearly contrast an accidental with a purposive act. Accordingly, Armsby administered six revised moral-judgment story pairs clearly contrasting a purposive with an accidental act together with three standard Piaget story pairs to 740 Catholic and public school children aged six, eight, and ten. He reports two findings at variance with Piaget's results. First, intentionality judgments made by children occur at an earlier age than that postulated by Piaget. In the Armsby study a larger percentage of all children at six and eight made moral judgments based on intentionality than was true of the children reported by Piaget. Second, while an age progression does exist in the internalization of intentionality, there is no specific age at which the morality of constraint is succeeded by the morality of cooperation.

However, despite some disagreement, the consensus appears to be that the theoretical formulations of Piaget on the nature and course of moral development are indeed a valid but oversimplified picture of how moral development actually takes place. Moral development is a highly complex matter, and there would appear to be more dimensions involved than simple sequence from a morality of constraint to a morality of cooperation, however valid the assumption of the existence of that dimension may be. As Kay (1968) notes:

One may speak of this growth in terms of a changing attitude to rules; or to changing social relations; or as the corollary to a sequence of qualitatively different "morals"; or as a growth from a heteronomous to autonomous moral judgments. But even this further complexity cannot account for the research findings which followed.

Kohlberg's Theory of Moral Development

An extension and, to some extent, a revision of Piaget's findings on moral development have been accomplished by Kohlberg (1958, 1963, 1968), who began his research with a study of the development of moral autonomy in children, including in his sample adolescents in their sixteenth year. As a confirmed Piagetian, Kohlberg assumed (Kohlberg and Kramer 1969) that the development of autonomous morality was not completed until age twelve or thirteen and added sixteen-year-olds simply to allow for a few developmental laggards. Piaget's original research had included no children beyond their twelfth year, and Kohlberg's inclusion of older children opened new possibilities. A possibility actually bore fruit when an examination of his findings convinced Kohlberg that children had to travel a considerable distance beyond Piaget's autonomous stage to achieve moral maturity.

In his original study Kohlberg tape-recorded two-hour interviews with each of seventy-two boys. The boys, divided into three groups, aged ten, thirteen, and sixteen, were all from middle-class homes and all possessed relatively similar levels of mental abilities. The two-hour interviews were centered on discussions involving ten hypothetical moral dilemmas in which obedience to authority conflicted with the needs or well-being of others. In the interviews each boy was asked to select one of two acts as his most preferred solution for each of the ten dilemmas, and he was questioned about his reasons for making each choice. Kohlberg's interest in eliciting responses was not in their action content but in the quality of the reasons given for judgments made, as well as in the manner in which the conflict situation was defined. An analysis of the responses provided the basis for the formulation of a sequence of stages of moral reasoning.

Kohlberg proposed six developmental stages, each stage being defined on the basis of its position on some thirty moral attributes that had emerged from the analysis of children's responses. The attributes included those used by Piaget in his original 1932 research on moral development. Each of the six stages was ordered into one of three sequential levels of moral orientation, each level including two stages. Kohlberg's levels and stages are presented in Table 16.

Kohlberg's data generally support the assumptions that (1) each level of moral judgment must be attained before the individual can perform at the next higher level; (2) the attainment of a higher level of moral judgment appears to involve the reworking of earlier thought patterns rather than an additive process of development; and (3) moral development occurs as an invariant sequence and the sequence remains invariant no matter what the national or subcultural group happens to be.

In discussing his research Kohlberg (1966) makes the point that in moral development the increase and complexity of demands in childhood are significant factors in bringing about the transition from egocentricism to moral realism. However, there is no reason to believe that any individual can ever attain a cognitive-affective state entirely free of self-reference. Essentially, the self is the frame of reference with which man must view the world, and though he may become cognitively capable of subordinating personal reference in interpreting his environment, there is always the brake of the affective processes to prevent complete abandonment of egocentricism, and essentially, man is bound to turn to an egocentric position. However, the possibility of moral realism in adolescence is helpful in the adolescent's quest for identity, and it does give him an added tool in the necessary developmental task of testing reality.

Table 16 *Kohlberg's Levels and Stages of Moral Development**

I. Preconventional Level	II. Conventional Level	III. Post-conventional, Autonomous, or Principled Level
At this level of premorality the child responds to labels of good or bad and of right or wrong but makes his interpretation in terms either of physical or hedonistic consequences (reward, punishment, exchange of favors) or of the physical power of the label maker.	At this level of morality of conventional role-conformity, precedence is given to expectations of family, group, and nation regardless of consequences. Conformity is paramount. The child is loyal and desires to support, maintain, and justify authority with whom he identifies.	At this level of self-accepted principles, morality becomes a matter of sharing and of conformity to shared duties, rights, and standards. There is an effort to define moral values over and above what actually exists in authority and in one's affiliates. Control of conduct becomes internal, and it is perceived that there may be conflict between two socially accepted standards.
A. *Stage 1: Punishment and Obedience Orientation* An action is good or bad depending on its consequences and regardless of the human meaning or value of the consequences. The child avoids punishment and defers to power for its own sake, with no understanding of an underlying moral order that punishment or authority supports.	A. *Stage 3: Interpersonal Concordance, or "Good Boy–Nice Girl" Orientation* Good behavior pleases or helps others, and the child wants to be "nice" in that sense. Thinking about what is good behavior is stereotypic. For the first time behavior *begins* to be judged by intention.	A. *Stage 5: Social Contract Legalistic Orientation* A morality of contract, individual rights, and democratically accepted law has developed. Stance of the whole society becomes important in defining standards arrived at as a result of analysis and mutual decision. Rights are defined as general human rights, and there is believed to be a right to personal values and opinions. Rule of law is important but not in the sense of law and order; here is a concept of law that can be changed in terms of rational considerations of social utility.
B. *Stage 2: Instrumental Reactivistic Orientation* Right is what satisfies one's self and occasionally others. Reciprocity in in terms of "You help me, I'll help you," not in terms of loyalty, gratitude, justice. Elements of fairness, equal sharing, reciprocity are present, but in a physical, pragmatic way.	B. *Stage 4: Law and Order Orientation* A fixed order, rules, and maintenance of what is are desired. Emphasis is on respect for authority and doing what one is "supposed" to do.	B. *Stage 6: Universal Ethical Principle Orientation* Conscience is important, and right is determined on the basis of personal ethical principles with a rational basis. Moral principles are abstract and ethical and are of the order of the Golden Rule, the greatest good for the greatest number, or the categorical imperative, and are definitely not of the concrete moral rule order as are, for example, the Ten Commandments. Key words are *justice, reciprocity, equality, dignity*.

*Various writers have described Kohlberg's stages using different descriptive terminology and highlighting different aspects of the levels, orientations, and stages. At the present time no definitive names for either the stages or the orientations have been agreed upon. Table 16 represents a selected view from a number of different sources but in the main is based on statements made by Kohlberg (1968) and Kohlberg and Kramer (1969). A good non-Kohlberg source is to be found in Hoffman (1971).

A Comparison of Piaget and Kohlberg

While it is possible to outline the commonalities and differences of the theories of moral development outlined by Piaget and Kohlberg, when it comes to an evaluation of validity, it should be remembered that Kohlberg's theory is based upon and grows out of Piaget's and that Piaget's formulations were the subject of a major book published in 1932. On the other hand, aside from a dissertation in 1958, Kohlberg's hypotheses were first advanced in a journal article in 1963. Under the circumstances there has been comparatively little time to build and report a substantial body of research on Kohlberg's position. Piaget's theory has been and continues to be widely researched, as was previously indicated, and a considerable body of literature has been written on his views regarding the development of moral judgment. In general, Kohlberg accepts Piaget's basic cognitive developmental approach but criticizes aspects of its substance and has developed his own schemata of stages. Both men agree that there exists a developmental sequence in the determinants of moral or value judgments with subjective intent, as the child approaches adolescence, gradually succeeding objective outcome as the main criterion of moral judgment.

A Psychosocial Theory of Moral Development

A motivational theory of morality and character development unrelated to the work either of Piaget or Kohlberg has been advanced by Peck, Havighurst, et al. (1960). Their formulations grow out of the results of comprehensive community research, described in Chapter 15, performed by Havighurst and his associates extending over a period of several years and involving children from age ten through sixteen (Havighurst and Taba 1949; Havighurst et al. 1962). The theory of Peck and Havighurst is less stage oriented than is Piaget's or Kohlberg's, and it pays more specific attention to individual differences and the personality of the developing child. The theory is of particular interest to students of adolescence, since adolescents rather than younger children were used in the background research from which the theory evolved.

Peck and Havighurst propose a motivational theory of character structure and development, basing the theory directly upon the results of a longitudinal study of thirty-four children from their tenth to their seventeenth year. The study was conducted in a small Midwestern city. Peck and Havighurst see character as the product of learning and write that individual character is a "persisting pattern of attitudes and motives which produce a rather predictable kind and quality of moral behavior."

Peck and Havighurst obtained ratings of their adolescent subjects on thirty-five "moral traits." A factor analysis based on the intercorrelations of these traits produced three factors, which were named socialization, empathy, and autonomy. In addition they defined five character types: amoral, expedient, conforming, irrational-conscientious, and rational-altruistic. The first of these character types represents a person without concern for the morality of social living—or indeed for any morality whatsoever. The last four character types are explained in terms of the dimensions of socialization, empathy, and autonomy, and they represent the four reasons why a person's behavior may be in accord with the moral standards of his time.

Developmentally, the ideal outcome of moral growth is a moral maturity defined in terms of optimal placement on *each* of the five dimensional types. The practical outcome is conformity susceptible to explanation in terms of the same five dimensions.

Emergence of socialization, empathy, and autonomy are transition points followed by qualitative changes in the dynamics of social behavior. Before socialization a child is egocentric, impulsive, and undisciplined. After socialization, but before empathy, the child is excessively respectful of adult authority. An empathic but nonautonomous person places a greater priority on human needs than on the maintenance of rules, but his conduct remains closely tied to the expectations of his peer group. With autonomy, behavior may become independent of external controls. Early and middle adolescence is essentially a period of empathic behavior. It is only in late adolescence and in early adulthood that there can be much expectation of autonomous behavior.

The amoral person is completely egocentric. His game is immediate gratification, and others exist to serve his needs and desires. Impulse-ridden and weak in ego strength, he is without inner controls to restrain impulses. Fixated at this level, an individual suffers from inadequate but punitive feelings of guilt directed at himself as well as at society. An adolescent fixated at this level almost inevitably embarks upon delinquent behavior.

The expedient person, still egocentric, has internalized his need for self-gratification. Bowing to morality, he at the same time is willing to sacrifice others for his own self-gratification. Weak in ego strength and adapting to the easy way out, the expedient person readily accepts authoritarian solutions if they advance his self-centered desires. Superficially such a person appears to fit well into society. He may know the words of morality, but he does not know the tune.

The conforming person is internalized to obey. Of him Peck and Havighurst write: "He wants to and does conform to all the rules of his group. He wants to do what others do, and his only anxiety is for possible disapproval." The conforming person appears to represent the norm of humanity, and it is on this dimension that most persons are likely to be fixated. Peck and Havighurst note: "The unthinking conformer, who often does not want to think for himself, probably makes up the largest single group of Americans and perhaps of humanity everywhere." Remmers and Radler (1957) note that conformity is typical of the American teenager and it would appear that conformity is probably the model stage of the teenager.

The irrational-conscientious person is in an advanced stage of conformity. Weak in ego strength, he follows the dictates of his own internalized need for conformity without ever considering rational aspects. Literal-minded and rigid, such a person is impermeable in his compulsivity. Martyrs and mystics, uncomfortable people to deal with, are the stuff out of which the irrational-conscientious stage is composed.

Peck and Havighurst visualize the rational-altruistic person as the "highest level of moral maturity." The rational-altruistic person considers the welfare of others in all of his behavior, and he puts their welfare before his own. Cooperative, with a high sense of social responsibility, he applies moral principles situationally against the criterion of the welfare of others.

The orientation of Peck and Havighurst is Freudian, and they use such Freudian terminology as *ego strength* and *superego* in their discussions, but they are not operating strictly within the Freudian framework.

A Psychoanalytic Approach to Moral Development

In their study of moral development both Kohlberg and Piaget take, as has been previously indicated in this chapter, a cognitive developmental approach focusing on supposedly universal sequential stages of moral development. These theorists have emphasized the importance of cognitive development and socialization in moral development. A contrasting approach is the consideration of anxiety in moral development. Freud (1935) is a leading exponent of this last approach, indicating a sequence beginning with the child's anxiety about loss of parental love and moving on to the later anxiety over castration. In contrast to the cognitive approach, the psychoanalytic position deals primarily with questions of identification and guilt.

Freud posited the human mind as being made up of three functionally related systems, the id, the ego, and the superego. The id represents the basic sexual and aggressive instincts and their derivatives. The ego is the mediator between id and external reality. The superego is the governing process which represents the person's moral percepts and conscience. An individual starts life with the id as his entire psychological apparatus. Later in the developmental sequence, the ego and the superego differentiate themselves from the id as functionally separate processes.

The id is subordinate only to the pleasure principle, and the basis of its operation is a demand for immediate gratification. Id impulses are unorganized and undisciplined. At about the sixth month, as a result of environmental frustration of the developing individual, the ego begins to differentiate. The ego is the I or the self, and its area of responsibility includes feeling, perceiving, knowing, thinking, and choosing. The ego acts to control id impulses and to distribute psychic energy to promote maximum pleasure as it acts as a mediator between the id and the external environment. When the environment blocks id demands for immediate gratification, the child begins to differentiate between himself and external reality and id impulses, which reality gratifies as pleasure and thwarts as pain.

The superego differentiates from the id as a result of the Oedipal conflict and becomes operative between the fifth and sixth year. Although the superego is largely unconscious in its activity, it corresponds to what is known as conscience. The superego acts as a "never-sleeping censor" whose functional process is assessing the activities of the ego and the impulses of the id. The superego locates and punishes that which is immoral. It rewards with self-love and praise all moral acts, feelings, and thoughts.

In the pre-Oedipal period a child is amoral. What he does is for his own gratification, and he refrains from gratification only if the mediating ego makes it clear that consequences will represent environmentally induced pain. Anxiety and guilt become the weapons punishing superego transgressions. Malmquist (1968) makes the point that guilt emerges as an indication of the establishment of a delineated and functioning superego in its idealized and prohibitory aspects.

Blos (1968) notes that character formation is synonymous with adolescence. Blos sees character as consisting of functions with a homeostatic (equilibrium) mechanism that stabilizes ego identification, self-esteem, self-concept, and reactions to external stimuli. Blos posits four developmental preconditions as necessary for adolescent character formation: (1) relinquishment of infantile object ties, (2) assimilation of the residue from early childhood trauma, (3) ego continuity, and (4) sexual identity.

Recent years have witnessed an emphasis on defensive and adaptive ego functions in moral development. This view is expressed in Douvan and Adelson's (1966) interpretation of moral development during adolescence. They hypothesize that the more intact adaptive functions remain, "the more effective will control be; conversely, loss or failure of these functions will in most cases interfere with control. The loss of reality testing capacity ordinarily makes good control impossible to achieve." Douvan and Adelson note that the intensification of drives in adolescence may lead to failures in ego control by "activating super-ego forces," and explain: "The ego then defends itself not against the id but against the super-ego, using impulse-expression in a flight from guilt."

Ego theory attributes etiological primacy to family relations but in the context of social experiences outside the family. Sanford (1962) writes:

For values to be internalized they must be reflected on, and made the object of the individual's best efforts at judgment and decision making; they must find their way into the personality structure through the activity of the conscious and developed ego rather than through automatic conditioning or unconscious mechanisms.

Sanford (1962) has formulated curves to represent the development of ego maturity and impulse control that he inferred from the shape of the curves in the psychoanalytic literature, particularly the writings of Anna Freud. Figures 20 and 21 present estimated values

Figure 20   *Scales for the Development of Ego and Impulse Control*

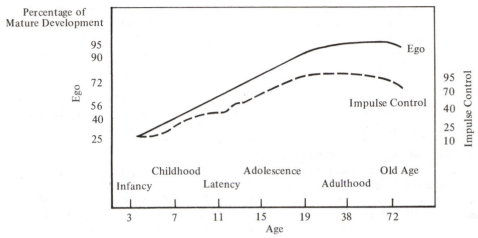

Source: Adapted from B. S. Bloom, *Stability and change in human characteristics* (New York: Wiley, 1964), p. 135, chart 1. Reprinted by permission of the publisher.

Figure 21   *Curves of Development for Selected Characteristics*

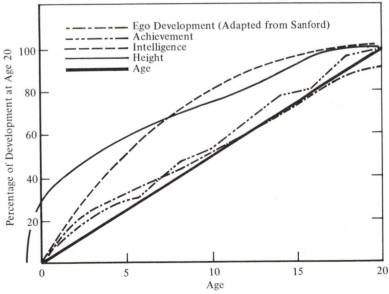

Source: Adapted from B. S. Bloom, *Stability and change in human characteristics* (New York: Wiley, 1964), p. 136, chart 2. Reprinted by permission of the publisher.

applied to these curves by Bloom (1964). From Figure 20 it will be noted that ego development reaches a practical plateau at about age twenty-five. About 40 percent of mature development is reached by about age seven. Approximately 80 percent of ego development is reached by age eighteen.

A Further Approach to Moral Development

An explanation of the nature of moral conduct and the development of moral character has been suggested by Hogan (1973). He defines morality, which he views as a product of biological and cultural evolution, as a methodology regulating and moderating social conduct. Hogan sees man as a rule-formulating and rule-following animal whose purposive social behavior occurs in a context of overlapping rule systems. Moral character can be explained by means of five concepts: moral knowledge, socialization, empathy, autonomy, and a dimension of moral judgment. Moral knowledge consists simply of knowing what is approved and what is disapproved. There are three kinds of moral knowledge: (1) specific injunctions related to specific acts, (2) moral principles consisting of general rules of conduct enabling an individual to choose between alternatives, and (3) comparison rules consisting of cognitive strategies enabling an individual to compare his behavior with an ideal norm. Socialization is the state of believing that the rules, values, and prohibitions of one's culture are personally mandatory. A person who does not take this position is regarded as unsocialized.

Empathy consists of willingness to consider the implications of what one does for the welfare of others. Autonomy involves the possession of an independent will and a habit of governing action by a personal sense of duty. Although they are conceptually independent, none of the five aspects of character function appears in isolation in the behavior of an individual. At any given moment in time, a person occupies a point on each continuum of each of the five dimensions. He may, for example, be high on three and low on two, or he may occupy any other combination of positions on the five continua. As an individual develops over the span of the three first decades, autonomy may, in combination with socialization and empathy, produce moral maturity. However, to find the process of moral maturity completed during the first two decades of life —and perhaps even well into the third—would be most unusual.

The Progression of the Stages

From the preceding discussion about the research of Piaget, Kohlberg, and others, we now know how moral judgment is assumed to evolve in childhood through the processes of socialization and cognitive development. Hence, given a child and information about his age, we should be able, using Piaget's or Kohlberg's stage theory, to state within a reasonable range of probability at what level he is capable of making moral judgments. But from stage theory we do not know for this same child to what extent this capacity actually will be applied in any given concrete or abstract situation. An individual cannot do what he is developmentally or cognitively incapable of doing, but equally there is no guarantee that he will always, frequently, or ever perform at his level of capacity. Developmental stage status is only one of a number of variables at work in the production of any given behavioral event. Speaking to this point in their study on the relationship at preadolescence of moral judgment and conformity, Saltzstein, Diamond, and Belenky (1972) write:

We assume that moral issues and reasoning may enter into the decision to conform or remain independent in a social influence situation. We do not assume that moral reasoning in the abstract and moral reasoning in concrete situations are perfectly correlated, or that the only factors involved in conformity-independence decisions are moral issues.

As a matter of fact, neither Piaget nor Kohlberg makes the assumption that the structures underlying nonverbal and verbal are identical. In his original work Piaget (1932) noted that an individual does not necessarily need to be able to function at the same structural level for all tasks. For example, the development of judgments of hypothetical situations could be progressing more slowly than development of judgments of concrete situations.

A considerable range in maturity of moral judgments even of late adolescents and young adults may be seen in data presented by Haan, Smith, and Block (1968). These investigators administered the Kohlberg Moral Judgment Scale to nearly one thousand subjects registered at either the University of California at Berkeley or San Francisco State College, or enrolled as Peace Corps Volunteers. None were freshman or graduate students. College subjects were drawn from a wide variety of campus groups, differing in opinion and attitude and ranging from activist to conservative. All three of Kohlberg's orientations and Stages 2 through 6 could be identified from the subjects' responses. The largest number of respondents gave responses falling into the conventional orientation of Stages 3 and 4. While there were more persons categorized under the more mature principled orientation than in the immature premoral, the numerical differences between these two stages were slight. Relatively few of these college and Peace Corps youth had attained Stage 6, lending some support to Kohlberg and Kramer's contention that Stage 6 is more characteristic of persons in the middle twenties than in the early twenties or late teens. The pile-up of cases at the conventional orientation level is unlikely to have represented lack of functional cognitive capacity in these college-age youth, but it does point up the fact that application, even hypothetical application, of moral judgments may be affected by numerous elements unrelated to developmental capacity. Birnbaum (1973) writes of the additive influence of a behavior episode judged as highly immoral. He asked undergraduates to rate hypothetical persons described by moral and immoral actions. Results indicate that a highly immoral deed appears to have an overriding influence

on overall judgment. If a person has committed one very bad deed, the tendency of the judge is to rate him as bad, with his good deeds having little influence. Moral judgment is presented by Birnbaum as a configural process.

Weiner and Peter (1973) asked three hundred children, aged four to eighteen, to make both moral and achievement judgments involving sixteen different situations. They reported that, in making both their moral and their achievement judgments, their subjects systematically made use of consequences of behavior as well as the intent or the level of ability or proficiency of the person being judged, although subjective intent tended to replace objective outcome as the child approached his twelfth year. However, after the twelfth year, judges returned to use of the earlier objective criteria. No differences were found on the basis of sex or race. The investigators were of the opinion that achievement striving is maintained primarily by social reward, and moral behavior is controlled by social punishment. Friedland and Carlson (1973) administered to a sample of 172 late adolescents a 112-item moral judgment questionnaire involving estimation of the badness of given acts. Severity of judgment was found to depend on both the social context and the behavior content of judged acts.

Summary

Most theories of moral development describe such development as proceeding by means of an invariant sequence of qualitatively defined stages. Within limitations, different individuals proceed through this development at different rates. Initially an individual perceives rules as external to self but gradually begins to internalize them. Over the course of moral development, rigidity and acceptance of authority yield to logic and a subjective interpretation of reality. The most comprehensive theories of moral development have been proposed by Piaget, Kohlberg, and Freud, although Kohlberg's theory is a direct derivation from Piaget's theory.

Piaget's influential theory proposes that there is an orderly and logical pattern in the development of a child's moral judgments resulting in sequential changes over time in the bases on which his judgments are made. The progression of moral judgment runs from a beginning marked by rigid interpretation of the rules to an end state in which judgments are based on social considerations and flexible interpretation of the rules. Piaget's research deals mainly with four aspects of moral development: (1) behavioral conformity to rules, (2) verbalized notions about rules, (3) moral attitudes more general than rule conformity, and (4) conceptions of justice. Piaget reported the existence of four stages in the development of behavioral conformity to rules and of three stages in the development of verbalized notions about rules. Where moral attitude is concerned, Piaget views development as proceeding from an attitudinal state in which results are the sole criterion, with no consideration being given to antecedents and intent, toward a subjective attitudinal state in which antecedents and intent are considered in making moral judgments. Piaget's research on conceptions of justice may be divided into findings on retributive, immanent, and distributive justice. The developmental progression is from retributive through immanent to distributive justice. While younger children are rarely to be found operating at the level of the higher stages, older children may or may not be operating at the level at which they are presumably capable.

In general, Piaget's theory of the development of moral judgment visualizes two moralities in childhood, an early morality of constraint and a later morality of cooperation, with the morality of constraint predating the morality of cooperation in the developmental progression. It is a truism that growth in moral judgment cannot take place without accompanying growth in intellectual development. Piaget's theory has been widely confirmed, although there are certain culture-based minor variations.

Kohlberg's theory is an extension and to some extent a revision of Piaget's findings.

Kohlberg proposes six developmental stages, each of the six stages being ordered into one of three sequential levels of moral orientation. Thus there are two stages occurring in each orientation level. Each level of moral judgment must be attained before the individual can attain at the next highest level. The attainment of a higher level of moral judgment involves the reworking of earlier thought patterns rather than an additive process of development. Finally, moral development occurs as an invariant sequence, and the sequence remains invariant no matter what the national or subcultural group.

Peck and Havighurst propose a motivational theory of character development. They see character as the product of learning and posit a persisting pattern of attitudes and motives that produce a predictable kind and quality of moral behavior. Developmentally, the emergence of socialization, empathy, and autonomy are transition points followed by qualitative changes in the dynamics of social behavior. Before socialization a child is egocentric, impulsive, and undisciplined. After socialization, but before empathy, he is excessively respectful of adult authority. With autonomy, behavior may become independent of external controls. Early and middle adolescence is a time of empathy, with the placing of emphasis on human needs rather than rules, but with conduct tied closely to the expectations of the peer group. Late adolescence is a time of autonomy.

The psychoanalytic approach of Freud proposes a sequence beginning with child's anxiety about loss of parental love and moving on to later anxiety over castration. In contrast to the cognitive approach of Piaget, the Freudian position deals primarily with questions of identification and guilt. In the Freudian system the superego stands for the conscience. Recent years have witnessed an emphasis on defensive and adaptive ego functions in moral development. A further theory of moral development is proposed by Hogan, who sees man as a rule-formulating and rule-following animal whose purposive social behavior occurs in a context of overlapping rule systems.

References

Abel, T. Moral judgments among subnormals. *Journal of Abnormal and Social Psychology* 36 (1951): 378–392.

Armsby, R. E. A re-examination of the development of moral judgments in children. *Child Development* 42 (1971): 1241–1248.

Birnbaum, M. H. Morality judgment: Test of an averaging model with differential weights. *Journal of Experimental Psychology* 99 (1973): 395–399.

Bloom, B. S. *Stability and change in human characteristics*. New York: Wiley, 1964.

Blos, P. Character formation in adolescence. *Psychoanalytic Study of the Child* 23 (1968): 245–263.

Bobroff, A. The stages of maturation in socialized thinking and in ego development of two groups of children. *Child Development* 31 (1960): 321–338.

Boehm, L. The development of conscience: A comparison of American children of different mental and socioeconomic levels. *Child Development* 33 (1962): 575–590 (a).

Boehm, L. The development of conscience: A comparison of students in Catholic parochial schools and in public schools. *Child Development* 33 (1962): 591–602(b).

Buchanan, J. P., and Thompson, S. K. A quantitative methodology to examine the development of moral judgment. *Child Development* 44 (1973): 186–189.

Carlson, J. S. Moral development of Lao children. *International Journal of Psychology* 8 (1973): 25–35.

Douvan, E., and Adelson J. *The adolescent experience*. New York: Wiley, 1966.

Freud, S. *A general introduction to psychoanalysis*. New York: Liveright, 1935.

Friedland, D. L., and Carlson, E. R. A factorial study of moral value judgments. *Proceedings of the 81st Annual Convention of the American Psychological Association, Montreal, Canada* 8 (1973): 317–318.

Haan, N.; Smith, M. B.; and Block, J. Home, personality, and political correlates of moral reasoning. *Journal of Personality and Social Psychology* 10 (1968): 183–201.

Harrower, M. E. Social status and moral development. *British Journal of Educational Psychology* 4 (1943): 29–33.

Havighurst, R. J.; Bowman, P. H.; Liddle, G. P.; Matthews, C. E.; and Pierce, J. V. *Growing Up in River City*. New York: Wiley, 1962.

Havighurst, R. J., and Taba, H. *Adolescent character and personality*. New York: Wiley, 1949.

Hogan, R. Moral conduct and moral character: A psychological perspective. *Psychological Bulletin* 79 (1973): 217–232.

Hoffman, M. L. Identification and conscience development. *Child Development* 42 (1971): 1071–1082.

Hollingshead, A. B. *Elmtown's youth*. New York: Wiley, 1949.

Johnson, R. A. A study of children's moral judgments. *Child Development* 33 (1962): 324–354.

Kay, A. W. *Moral Development*. New York: Schocken Book, 1968.

Koenig, F.; Sulzer, J.; Newland, V.; and Sturgeon, L. Cognitive complexity and moral judgment in middle and lower class children. *Child Study Journal* 3 (1973): 43–52.

Kohlberg, L. The development of modes of moral thinking and choice in the years ten to sixteen. Doctoral dissertation, University of Chicago, 1958.

Kohlberg, L. The development of children's orientations toward a moral order. *Vita Humana* 6 (1963): 11–33.

Kohlberg, L. Moral education in the schools: A developmental view. *School Review* 74 (1966): 1–30.

Kohlberg, L. Stage and sequence: The cognitive-developmental approach to socialization. In Goslin, D. A., ed., *Handbook of socialization theory*, pp. 347–380. Chicago: Rand McNally, 1968.

Kohlberg, L. *Stages in the development of moral thought and action*. New York: Holt, Rinehart and Winston, 1968.

Kohlberg, L., and Kramer, R. Continuities and discontinuities in childhood and adult moral development. *Human Development* 12 (1969): 93–120.

Lee, L. C. The concomitant development of cognitive and moral modes of thought: A test of selected deductions from Piaget's theory. *Genetic Psychology Monographs* 83 (1971): 93–146.

Lerner, E. *Constraint areas and moral judgment of children*. Menash, Wis.: Banta, 1937.

MacRae, D., Jr. A test of Piaget's theories of moral development. *Journal of Abnormal and Social Psychology* 49 (1954): 14–18.

Malmquist, C. P. Conscience development. *Psycho-

analytic Study of the Child 23 (1968): 301–331.

Markwalder, W. E. Stage mixture and cognitive development. *Southern Journal of Educational Research* 6 (1972): 219–225.

Medinnus, G. R. Immanent justice in children: A review of the literature and additional data. *Journal of Genetic Psychology* 94 (1959): 253–262.

Peck, R. F.; Havighurst, R. J.; Cooper, R.; Lilienthal, J.; and More, D. *The psychology of character development.* New York: Wiley, 1960.

Piaget, J. *The moral judgment of the child.* London: Kegan Paul, 1932.

Porteus, B. D., and Johnson, R. C. Children's responses to two measures of conscience development and their relation to sociometric nomination. *Child Development* 36 (1965): 703–711.

Remmers, H. H., and Radler, D. H. *The American teenager.* Indianapolis: Bobbs-Merrill, 1957.

Saltzstein, H. D.; Diamond, R. M.; and Belenky, M. Moral judgment level and conformity behavior. *Developmental Psychology* 7 (1972): 327–336.

Sanford, N. Developmental status of the entering freshman. In Sanford, N., ed., *The American college*, pp. 253–282. New York: Wiley, 1962.

Weiner, B., and Peter, N. A cognitive-developmental analysis of achievement and moral judgments. *Developmental Psychology* 9 (1973): 290–309.

Whiteman, P., and Kozier, K. Development of children's moralistic judgments—age, sex, IQ and personal experimental variables. *Child Development* 35 (1964): 843–850.

Suggested Readings

Andrews, J. The relationship of values to identity achievement status. *Journal of Youth and Adolescence* 2 (1973): 133–138.

Bandura, A., and McDonald, F. Influence of social reinforcement and the behavior of models in shaping children's moral judgments. *Journal of Abnormal and Social Psychology* 67 (1963): 274–281.

Barber, L. W. Teen-agers' effective use of lay-scientist skills in decision making. *Character Potential* 4 (1969): 34–36.

Benton, A. A. Productivity, distributive justice, and bargaining among children. *Journal of Personality and Social Psychology* 18 (1971): 68–78.

Birnbaum, M. P. Anxiety and moral judgment in early adolescence. *Journal of Genetic Psychology* 120 (1972): 13–26.

Durkin, D. Children's concepts of justice—a further comparison with Piaget's data. *Journal of Educational Research* 52 (1959): 252–257.

Erikson, E. Youth: Fidelity and diversity. In Erikson, E., ed., *Youth: Change and challenge*, pp. 1–23. New York: Basic Books, 1963.

Graham, D. *Moral learning and development: Theory and research.* New York: Wiley-Interscience, 1972.

Hogan, R., and Henley, N. Nomotics: The science of human rule systems. *Law and Society Review* 5 (1970): 135–146.

Hsieh, Chien-chi. Studies on the ability of moral judgment in adolescents. *Acta Psychologica* 3 (1964): 258–265.

Koenig, F.; Sulzer, J.; Newland, V.; and Sturgeon, L. Cognitive complexity and moral judgment in middle and lower class children. *Child Study Journal* 3 (1973): 43–52.

Kohlberg, L. The child as a moral philosopher. *Psychology Today* 2 (1968): 25–30.

Kohlberg, L. Development of moral character and moral ideology. In Hoffman, M. and L., eds., *Review of child development research*, vol. I. New York: Russell Sage Foundation, 1964.

McKechnie, R. J. Between Piaget's stages: A study in moral development. *British Journal of Educational Psychology* 41 (1971): 213–217.

Malmquist, C. P. Conscience development. *Psychoanalytic Study of the Child* 23 (1969): 301–331.

Markwalder, W. E. Stage mixture and cognitive development. *Southern Journal of Educational Research* 6 (1972): 219–225.

Post, S. C. *Moral values and the superego concept in psychoanalysis.* New York: International Universities Press, 1972.

Rest, J.; Turiel, E.; and Kohlberg, L. Level of moral development as a determinant of preference and comprehension of moral judgments made by others. *Journal of Personality* 37 (1969): 225–252.

Rettig, S., and Pasamanick, B. Changes in moral values among college students: A factorial study. *American Sociological Review* 24 (1959): 856–863.

Stephenson, G. M., and Barker, J. Personality and the pursuit of distributive justice: An experimental study of children's moral behavior. *British Journal of Social and Clinical Psychology* 11 (1972): 207–219.

Tapp, J. L., and Kohlberg, L. Developing senses of law and legal justice. *Journal of Social Issues* 27 (1971): 65–91.

Turiel, E., and Rothman, G. R. The influence of reasoning on behavioral choices at different stages of moral development. *Child Development* 43 (1972): 741–756.

Van den Daele, L. A developmental study of the ego-ideal. *Genetic Psychology Monographs* 78 (1968): 191–256.

Wiener, B., and Peter, N. A cognitive-developmental analysis of achievement and moral judgments. *Developmental Psychology* 9 (1973): 290–309.

Wright, D. *The psychology of moral behavior.* Harmondsworth, England: Penguin, 1971.

Chapter Fifteen

Character, Religion, and Values

The Meaning of Character

Acceptable attitudes, good values, and fine ideals in an individual result in his having what is called "good character." Peck and Galliani (1962) write that an individual's character is a "persisting pattern of attitudes and motives which produce a rather predictable kind and quality of moral behavior." They see the structure of character as the product of learning. Most people would wish to equate morality and character in that they believe that a person of good character is one who possesses and applies an "approved" moral code. Moral code in this sense is an accepted set of rules promulgated by society or a significant subgroup thereof and considered binding by all. The moral person or person of good character exemplifies in his behavior the letter as well as the intent of the rules.[1]

Unfortunately, the term *character* is elusive in meaning, and its interpretation varies widely from person to person. Ordinarily, the term is one of approval and is applied to a person whose system of values, conduct, and belief is in accord with that of the person using the term; it may also indicate that the course of action (or inaction) of the person categorized as having character is approved or admired. Lack of the approved traits and reactions or the presence of disapproved ones causes the individual to be designated as one who "lacks character" or has a "bad character." Occasionally a person who possesses an admired trait or point of view to a too great, an inconvenient, or a compulsive degree is designated as "too good" or "too honest." Often an adolescent is unable to judge the right time for the application of a given trait or point of view. Thus he may exercise it inappropriately, so that the ordinarily admired trait or ideal may become a liability.

The Relationship Between Attitudes and Character

The theory that attitudes influence conduct and character has been comparatively well established. Prescott (1938) lists the functions of attitudes held by an individual in determining his personality and character.

1. They supply the code or measuring rod by which the behavior of the individual and of others is judged.
2. They supply principles on the basis of which choices are made; when body conditions demand action, they determine what may and may not be done.

[1]Morality as it is understood by most people simply means conformity to the current social ideals finding acceptance in the culture in which they live or to those ideals finding acceptance in some significant reference group. Subcultural reference group ideals, however, may not find general acceptance if they are in conflict with those of the general culture. Activist youth, for example, accepting an activist group as highly moral, find general rejection because the ideal is often at variance with the ideal patterns of larger society. The modern world with all its complexities and conflicts offers scope for many conflicts of ideals situations, a fact that adolescents trying to test reality and to build a stable self- and world-view find quite disturbing and difficult to cope with.

3. They represent the crystallized meaning of accumulated experience, the *Weltanschauung* (philosophy of life) of the individual. This is the unifying or integrating thread that runs through and colors the interpretation of all experience, thus supplying unity and individuality.
4. They supply the basis for envisaging the future world and for projecting the place of the individual in that world. They become the bases for goals of behavior, for both short-term and long-term purposes that are, at the same time, social and personal.
5. To sum up all these functions is to say, in the terminology of Lewin, that attitudes determine the valences in most of the situations that we face in life.

Unfortunately, most studies that have attempted to establish the effect of attitudes upon conduct and character have been made with atypical children, particularly those with a record of juvenile delinquency or problem behavior. There is a paucity of studies dealing with nondeviating children. There is also the matter of cause and effect. The fact that two variables may show a high correlation does not guarantee that one causes the other, since a third unknown variable may cause both. Too, the attitude tests customarily used in such studies have limitations. A high score on an attitude test may have very little to do with a subject's actual behavior in a life situation.

Approaches to the Measurement of Character

As with intelligence, the approach to the measurement of character depends upon the definition of character. Different authorities will present different definitions or will emphasize different aspects. In practice, however, no matter what the definition, two approaches are ordinarily used in character measurement: The first is through the traits actually possessed by an individual, and the second, through the traits others attribute to him. Sometimes

results are the same; sometimes they differ, depending upon the extent to which the individual being studied may dissimilate and at times upon the observer's lack of social perception or adequate opportunity. This is particularly true insofar as we accept the idea that most samples of behavior, such as honesty or loyalty, are specific to the situation in which they occur. This idea, known as specificity of conduct, asserts that a person may be honest or loyal in one situation but just the opposite in another. There is no guarantee that a person will evidence the same amount and degree of any given "trait" in every situation itself. One would have to observe an individual under many different conditions at different times to gain a true picture of his consistency of conduct. Still, nearly everyone has some reputation among his associates, and it is partly upon the basis of this reputation that an adolescent is accepted or rejected in his peer group, approved of or disapproved of by adults, and revealed as needing or not needing specific character education.

The Prairie City Study: A Measurement of Character Reputation

In their study of sixteen-year-olds in Prairie City, Havighurst and Taba (1949) used four different measures, two with age-mates and two with adults, to obtain judgments on the character reputations of their subjects. Their first measure, used to secure the judgments of adults about the individual sixteen-year-olds in the study, was a 126-item check list of behavioral situations. Five "traits"—honesty, moral courage, friendliness, loyalty, and responsibility—appeared on the check list, each trait being represented in about 25 items. Typical items for the trait "Responsibility" were: "I'm usually late for appointments"; "When left in charge of a younger child, does not neglect it for something more interesting"; "Takes good care of school property." Teachers, employers, and youth-group leaders marked the check list for each sixteen-year-old they knew in the community. Numerical values were assigned to each item, and every subject was given a score on each of the five traits that was the median scale value of the items his raters had marked for him. Presumably, the reasoning behind the measure was that if one takes a wide sampling of more or less isolated situational instances of behavior and sums them up, a behavioral trend may emerge.

The second measure of character reputation reported by Havighurst and Taba (also used with adults) was a list of verbal sketches describing a situation that would be representative of a person who possessed to some degree the five traits listed above. A typical item was: "N is the sort of person whom everyone likes and who likes everyone. Boys and girls, young and old, are his friends. Wherever he goes he is smiling and greeting people, often stopping to do something to help them." Seven to ten situational descriptions were included for each of the five traits. Each sixteen-year-old received a numerical rating on each trait, which was computed by finding the median of the raters' reactions, a numerical value having been assigned to each situation.

The third measure, used among the subjects' age-mates, was a "Guess-Who" test consisting of paired word pictures purportedly representative of the five traits being measured. One member of the pair indicated the possession of the trait to a high degree; the other, to a low degree. Each trait was given approximately ten word pictures on the test. In each word picture the rater was to guess to whom, among the subjects, it was most applicable. Typical word pictures were: "Here is someone who never cheats in games"; "Here is someone who often cheats in games."

The last of the four measures, a portrait "Guess-Who" for age-mates, consisted of a paragraph for each trait describing a person who would rate high in the trait, and one describing a person who would rate low. It was believed that such a paragraph would "combine several manifestations of a trait." An

example of portrait paragraphs designed to measure moral courage follows.

Some boys and girls always let other people make up their minds for them. They will do things they know are wrong if other people do these things. They are afraid of what people will say. They will not stick up for the right if their friends are against them.

Some boys and girls always do what they think is right, no matter what other people think. They are not afraid to be unpopular. They look out for the rights of other people. They help everybody who needs help. They will speak up against teachers and other grown-up people if necessary.

Each rater placed the number that designated the paragraph before the name of the person he thought best described by the paragraph.

Table 17 presents the relationships among the character reputation measures. In general, the relationships among the five traits included in the Havighurst and Taba study are high. As might reasonably be expected, the relationship between ratings by adults and ratings by peers is not particularly high. Adults and adolescents do not have exactly the same interpretation of the meaning of any given individual's behavior, and their somewhat different values might lead to different judgments on the importance or unimportance of various kinds of behavior. Havighurst and Taba's major difficulty with the instruments of character reputation may be their apparent failure to recognize the fact that reputation for a given trait, even among persons equivalent in maturity status or in some other comparable category, may differ from group to group, and from person to person. People do not agree in their interpretations of others. They often do not see the same things, and their interpretations are made in terms of their own personalities, which may themselves present a fluctuating picture.

Questionnaires and Observations in Measuring Character

Another approach to learning about a person's character or system of values is to allow the

Table 17 *Product-Moment Correlations Between Character Reputation Instruments*

Trait	Check List and Character Sketch	Guess-Who and Portrait Guess-Who	Average Adult and Average Age-Mates	Check List plus Portrait Guess-Who Character Sketch plus Guess-Who
Honesty	0.51 ± 0.05	0.80 ± 0.03	0.78 ± 0.02	0.74 ± 0.03
Moral Courage	0.63 ± 0.04	0.68 ± 0.04	0.47 ± 0.05	0.69 ± 0.03
Friendliness	0.57 ± 0.04	0.46 ± 0.05	0.47 ± 0.05	0.66 ± 0.04
Loyalty	0.67 ± 0.04	0.72 ± 0.03	0.67 ± 0.04	0.74 ± 0.03
Responsibility	0.86 ± 0.02	0.70 ± 0.03	0.73 ± 0.03	0.80 ± 0.02
Average of Five Trait Scores	0.80 ± 0.02	0.76 ± 0.03	0.79 ± 0.02	0.86 ± 0.02

Source: R. Havighurst and H. Taba, *Adolescent character and personality* (New York: Wiley, 1949), p. 222. Reprinted by permission of the publisher.

person to reveal how he feels and what he believes. This may be done through the observation of his behavior, through a personal interview, or through the administration of various tests, questionnaires, and check lists. The questionnaire is commonly used because it is less time consuming.

In psychology, observational research is performed by trained observers who make systematic records of the behavior they observe, within the limits of an explicitly stated frame of reference. Since the observations are controlled and objective, they offer an advantage over the purely subjective approach, particularly as the experimental design ensures that crucial aspects of behavior will be systematically observed and objectively recorded. A classic study using observational methods was employed by Lippitt (1940) in his investigation of democratic and authoritarian group atmospheres.

The interview gains information by techniques ranging from the simplicity of a yes-no question to the complexity of a pattern of open-ended questions. A major difficulty with interview research is the amount of influence an examiner may exert on the examined, but many investigators feel that the interview's defects are more than made up by the flexibility

it permits the questioner in adapting his questions to the trend of the responses. Related techniques are sociometric measurements and the analysis of personal documents, which makes use of writings, diaries, and other personal productions of individuals as a means of assessing their attitudes. Runner (1937) used the personal-documents approach when he analyzed the diaries of two adolescent girls so that he might develop categories of interpersonal intimacy.

In the attitude questionnaire or scale, the individual is usually requested to approve or disapprove of a given act, situation, or point of view, in regard to himself or someone else. However, there are various alternative questionnaire approaches. Stereotype questionnaires have the examinee indicate which of a number of possible stereotypes he feels are descriptive of various persons, groups, things, or events. The situational questionnaire presents several situations representative of real life and asks the examinee to choose the alternative he feels is most appropriate for dealing with the hypothesized situation.

Moral emotion, as a measure of internal control, is indicated by research that has inferred moral characteristics of youth from their responses to transgressor stories. Bandura and Walters (1959) used this approach in their analysis of the relation between family socialization and strength of conscience in highly aggressive boys and normal boys. In the Bandura and Walters study, the desire to be like parents and strength of conscience were significantly associated with consistant discipline and the use of reasoning. And finally, social-distance questionnaires require the examinee to indicate which of various social relationships he would find acceptable in dealing with various ethnic, religious, racial, or other types of groups or persons.

Obviously, a great deal depends upon how a question is asked. In a Polish study of ideals, Flesznerowa (1963) found an apparent lack of ideals and values among students at the University of Warsaw, but he hypothesized that the type and style of his questionnaire confounded his results. In a rerun he received positive results when he rephrased the question in "contemporary language" suitable to the students' interests.

In their attempts to study the moral beliefs of adolescents, Havighurst and Taba (1949) designed two instruments, a questionnaire of student beliefs and a life-problems test. The questionnaire consisted of 109 statements on which the subject was to grade himself as agreeing, disagreeing, or undecided. Typical items included:

Some persons are naturally carefree and forgetful, and so they must be excused when they fail to complete assigned duties.

You should not say unkind things to another person, even if he greatly irritates you.

You need not feel obliged to keep a promise if you had to make it hurriedly or thoughtlessly.

If an employer asks you to do a job you think is wrong, you should refuse to do it, regardless of how good a job it is.

You should not tell even a close friend about family quarrels or difficulties.

Subjects were given three scores, a plus (desirable) score, a minus (undesirable) score, and an uncertainty score, on each of five traits,

in accordance with their AUD (agree, undecided, disagree) selections for each item.[2] The traits were friendliness, honesty, loyalty, moral courage, and responsibility.

The second measure of moral beliefs, the life-problems test, consisted of eight situations that described a conduct problem in various areas important to an adolescent. The conduct problem represented a situation in which the individual had to choose between conflicting values and to check the reason for his choice. An example follows.

Problem IV

Carl and Jim were friends and kept their books and coats in the same locker. Both boys were interested in reading a great deal and took out books from the school library. Carl had a job helping to check books out in the library. One day a new and interesting book for which there was a long waiting list disappeared. The librarian asked Carl to find out where the book was. Carl asked Jim about it, but Jim said he knew nothing about the book. Three days later Carl was cleaning out the locker and saw the book among Jim's things.

What should Carl do? (Check the statement you think is best.)
    A. Take up the problem with both Jim and the librarian.
    B. Give Jim a chance to return the book unnoticed.
    C. Let the matter pass.
Why?
    1. Both boys would have a clear conscience by clearing the matter with the librarian.
    2. By keeping quiet about having found the book, Carl would avoid telling a lie as well as embarrassing a friend.
    3. Carl's duty as a helper in the library is to see to it that irregularities about borrowing books are reported.
    4. One should not tell on a friend, even if it involves untruth.

In a further endeavor to study the moral values of the sixteen-year-olds in their study, Havighurst and Taba (1949) requested them to write essays on the topics: "The person I would

[2]An item analysis of the answers of adolescents to the 109 items on the questionnaire of student beliefs appears on p. 248 of Havighurst and Taba (1949).

like to be like"; "Where do I get my ideals"; and "My heroes." Each essay was rated on the basis of a scale "ranging from the selfish and materialistic to the altruistic and spiritual." After analyzing responses to the essays, the researchers reported that verbal statements of high ideals showed a positive but low relationship to good character reputation.

The Background of Character Measurement in Children

The inculcation of "moral character" traditionally has been an important foundation upon which the objectives of both secular and lay education have been erected. The importance of the "moral" individual as a parent and as a citizen was widely accepted. Psychologists recognized morality and its behavioral outcomes as at the heart of much that occurs in human relations and personal outlooks. The 1920s witnessed considerable interest in the study and analysis of children's character. Many facets of character were considered, but the most typical work of the period was the study of deceit in children and the development of cheating by students enrolled in various courses. Among the studies examining students' propensity to cheat were those by Persing (1926), Chamber (1926), Bird (1927), and Gundlach (1925). Gundlach's technique is representative of such studies. He gave a series of true-false questions to students seated at tables in pairs and observed the ensuing collusion. Bird administered an objective examination, noted identical errors, and after finding the number of identical errors due to chance, recorded the copying that had taken place. Chamber observed students through a concealed mirror while they were taking an examination. Persing graded papers too high and too low and recorded the names of individuals who reported that the grade they had been given was too high. Tests of this type appeared to serve little purpose other than that of recording who had cheated in a given situation. Consistency or the students' interpretation of the situation as one in which it was not immoral to receive help was not an issue in these four studies as the investigators had designed them.

One of the most comprehensive and ingenious studies of character of this early period, a study whose findings have been confirmed again and again and are as valid today as when they were first reported, was the Character Education Inquiry made at Columbia University by Hartshorne, May, and Shuttleworth (1928–1930). The major findings of this study, made nearly a half-century ago, have stood ever since. Certainly it has been for many years one of the most widely cited studies in the literature of developmental and educational psychology.

The Character Education Inquiry of Hartshorne et al. was an attempt to study various aspects of character, attitudes, conduct, and opinion through administration of many paper-and-pencil and situational tests. The investigators endeavored in many of their tests to place an individual in a situation in which he would be forced to display various attitudes and kinds of behavior without realizing that a test of such attitudes or behavior was being given. Whenever possible, the test simulated a real-life situation. For example, to measure "deceptive behavior," the subjects were given an examination in school. Their papers were then picked up and exact copies made by the experimenter that evening. The following day the papers were returned for self-marking and again picked up. Discrepancies between the original papers and the ones returned after self-grading were noted, with particular reference to changes that would give the subject a higher grade than he deserved. Another example of a situational test is that of a measure of honesty. Actual situations, such as games, in which the subject would use money or other material provided as part of the game were set up. The situation was so arranged that the subject could keep some of the money without apparent possibility of detection.

Still other tests included administration of questionnaires containing various personal questions about many specific acts of conduct that have universally wide approval but that are rarely carried out. Other questions included statements of socially disapproved acts that are commonly carried out by most people. The individual's answers were examined for consistency and truthfulness. It was felt that an individual who always claimed that he did the socially disapproved was probably engaging in deception.

Hartshorne et al. set up the following criteria for their tests.

1. The test situation should be as far as possible a natural situation. It should also be a controlled situation. The response should be as far as possible natural even when directed.
2. The test situation and the response should be of such nature as to allow all subjects equal opportunity to exhibit the behavior which is being tested. That is, there should be nothing about the test to prevent deceit, nor anything to trick a person into an act he would repudiate if he were aware of its import.
3. No test should subject the child to any moral strain other than that to which he is subjected in the natural course of his actual life situations.
4. The test should not put the subject and examiner in false social relations to one another. The examiner should guard against being deceptive himself in order to test the subject.
5. The test should have "low visibility," i.e., it should be of such a nature as not to arouse the suspicions of the subject.
6. The activity demanded of the subject should have real value for him whether he is aware of the values or not.
7. The test results should be clear and unambiguous. It should be clear whether the subject did or did not exhibit the behavior in question.
8. The scores should be quantitative showing the amount as well as the fact of deception.

Each test, therefore, should be flexible enough to include within its scope wide ranges of deceptive tendency.

The results of these studies were reported under three headings: studies in deceit, studies in service, and studies in the organization of character.

Hartshorne et al. report that neither deceit nor its opposite, "honesty," appear to be unified character traits, but rather are specific functions of life situations. They noted that a child may or may not cheat, lie, or steal in any given situation, depending upon any one of a large number of factors. Among these are the nature of the situation, its importance to the child, and the child's feelings at that particular time. Also important are the child's intelligence, age, home background, and other related factors. Most children will deceive in some situations and not in others. A child may display deceit on Monday and show exceptional honesty on Tuesday—or vice versa. A child may cheat on an arithmetic test but not on a spelling test.

The most common motive for cheating in a classroom situation appears to be the desire to do well. In general, lying, cheating, and stealing as measured by Hartshorne et al. appear to be correlated only slightly. The concomitants of deceit in the order of their importance appear to be: classroom association; general personal handicaps, such as emotional instability; relatively low intelligence; poor resistance to suggestion; and a limited or sterile cultural or social situation in the home.

According to these researchers, other things being equal, girls are neither more nor less deceitful than boys; older students tend to be slightly more deceitful than younger students; students who get good grades and who are more intelligent cheat less than do students who get poor grades and are less intelligent; and children from superior socioeconomic backgrounds cheat less than do children from inferior socioeconomic backgrounds. Cheating appears to be associated with factors such as bad discipline, unfortunate parental example, unstable home situations, and parental rejection. A child who is decently treated by his parents and his teachers is less apt to cheat than is one who is badly treated. Teachers who teach in a permissive, cordial, cooperative manner tend to encounter less cheating than do those who use more restrictive methods. Students in progressive schools appear to cheat less than do students in conventional schools. No general differences in deceptive behavior appear on the basis of religious affiliation; no apparent relationship exists between deceitfulness and membership in organizations purporting to teach honesty. There appears to be no relation between Sunday school attendance and deceitfulness, although children enrolled in Sunday school show a slight tendency to cheat less.

As a result of their studies in service, Hartshorne et al. conclude that "children vary enormously among themselves in their tendencies to be of service. The aggregate of habits peculiar to the child, which we label selfish or generous as the case may be, is learned in the course of his experience with others." In general, the most important factors in determining service behavior appear to be the extent of mutual friendship among children in the same classroom, satisfactory school adjustment, favorable home influence, sociability, stable emotional condition, and power to resist suggestion. Class loyalty appears to be as strong a motive for service behavior as recognition or greed, and greed appears to be about as prevalent as generosity. The tendency to be helpful is variable and often diminishes if the child becomes fatigued or if the situation requiring his assistance is repeated very often.

Hartshorne et al. believe that honesty, charity, cooperation, inhibition, and persistence are particular habits rather than general traits. Since tendencies within these areas of moral conduct are quite loosely organized, there is little relation among the several areas. Moral behavior appears to be specific and conditioned to a large degree by the external situation. On the other hand, many children show highly

consistent behavior, and while consistency of behavior is not necessarily associated with the more desirable behavior traits, the child who displays high consistency appears to be more highly integrated than one who does not. Hartshorne et al. note that, other things being equal, the integrated child tends to be the honest child. Theoretically, the ideal individual should not only show a high average performance on an attitude scale, he should also vary only slightly from this average. The hypothesis might be advanced that a child will tend to show greater consistency of behavior with advancing age throughout adolescence, although in any given situation his behavior may be at variance with that of his customary pattern. Hartshorne et al. advance the theory that if situations in which a child shows dishonesty were changed to remove the elements that excited dishonesty, then improved behavior would be the result.

Cheating

Since the Hartshorne study, there has been a steady stream of studies of cheating by adolescents and young adults, many of them offering direct confirmation of the Hartshorne specificity of moral conduct finding. Typical of these is a study by Harari and McDavid (1969), in which it is reported that situational factors are capable of significantly altering children's lying behavior. Both Leveque and Walker (1970) and Johnson and Gormly (1972) make the point that when children are given the opportunity to cheat they do, particularly when the chances of being caught are remote.

Steininger, Johnson, and Kirts (1964) report that the more anxiety and hostility provoking the situation in which an individual found himself, the more likely he would be not only to cheat and to justify cheating but to help others cheat as well. In a study made with Czechoslovakian children, Sipos (1964) reports that the occurrence of honest behavior is a collective expression of pupils directly influenced by a situation induced by the teacher.

As stress mounts, frustration tolerance declines and children tend to cheat, particularly when maximum performance beyond the child's ability is required. Thus, according to Sipos, the intensity of the stress situation is in direct relation to the degree of cheating. Steininger (1968), in a study of cheating among college freshmen, notes that the extent to which a student said that cheating was justified was a compromise between a negative attitude toward cheating in general and the need to defend it because situational pressures result in the temptation to cheat.

Pearlin, Yarrow, and Scarr (1967) report that children are most likely to cheat when their parents pressure them to succeed. Such parental pressure is often the result of high aspirations for the children coupled with limited resources. Pearlin et al. note that, in this case, cheating can be an unwitting result of striving after culturally valued goals under conditions of limited opportunity. Combining Sipos's and Pearlin's studies, one would have to conclude that a child of little ability from a high-aspiring home who is working under a restrictive, demanding teacher would almost have to cheat if the opportunity arose.

Vitro (1971) reports that when parental discipline is harsh, the result is a child more likely to cheat than one reared under more optimum conditions. He writes: "Incorporation of values and standards of morality is most favorable when parental discipline does not involve extreme techniques." However, Vitro reports that the problem of harsh discipline rests with the father rather than the mother.

Shelton and Hill (1969) and Smith, Ryan, and Diggins (1972) note that cheating is a response instrumental in the avoidance of aversive social consequences. Shelton and Hill (1969) report that cheating is influenced by achievement anxiety and knowledge of the performance of a peer reference group. However, achievement anxiety was only positively correlated with cheating when knowledge of reference-group performance was provided. Smith et al. (1972) report a potential loss of self-esteem as significantly related to cheating for both sexes.

Dienstbier and Munter (1971) hypothesize that it is not the emotional arousal per se that causes cheating but the interpretation of the meaning and significance of the arousal. Hetherington and Feldman (1964), Centra (1970), and Bonjean and McGee (1965) all note that the tendency to cheat and the specific type of cheating employed are reliably related to certain demographic, intellectual, and personality characteristics. Johnson and Gormly (1971) examined behaviorally measured cheating in relation to self-report data on academic activity, social participation, and future plans. They report that one-third of their subjects (ROTC upperclassmen) cheated on an assigned task. As compared to those who did not cheat, cheaters showed greater social participation.

There is some evidence that cheating is correlated with age, although the exact nature of the relationship is not clear. Jenison (1972) notes that older as compared to younger college students are more severe in their moral judgments about cheating. Henshel (1971), using a sample of Canadian girls, reports that older children show a stronger value-behavior relationship than younger ones with the incidence of cheating falling off in the upper as compared to the lower grades. An interesting related study is reported by Feldman and Feldman (1967), who note that male twelfth graders show a higher incidence of cheating than male seventh graders. More in conformity with Henshel's findings, Feldman and Feldman report that incidence of cheating among girls did not change from the seventh to the twelfth grade.

Other studies have pointed to sex differences in cheating behavior. For example, Johnson and Gormly (1972) report that females tend to cheat in response to consistently unfavorable self-perception while males were considerably more influenced by immediate situational factors. Jenison (1972) reports that females were more severe in their adverse judgments about cheating than were males.

Religion During Adolescence

Religion in one form or another permeates nearly all cultures. Western culture is no exception, with the result that religious faith and church membership play an important role. It is generally accepted that youth should receive religious training and possibly indoctrination, and that opportunities should be provided for them to participate in organized religion. Of course, some feel that religious training or even contact with organized religion is wrong and that youth should be allowed to accept or reject a religious point of view without guidance or help of any kind. However, people who have this point of view are in the minority, and the majority of youth reared in Western culture receive some sort of religious education, at least informally, if not through the offices of an organized church.

Whatever attitude prevails, a child will sooner or later have to accept or reject a religious point of view, join or not join a church, and organize or not organize his values with religion as a base. For the psychologist, several questions are of particular importance in this area. What are the religious beliefs of youth, and what is the developmental pattern of such beliefs as the child grows older? What religious needs do youth possess, what is their course, and what is the psychological effect of these needs? Practically, a further question might be added: What is the most effective means of promoting the proper religious and moral learning, and how can such learning be made an effective part of the individual's life? Here, of course, these questions must be answered with particular reference made to the adolescent years.

In "an attempt to explore the nature of religious beliefs held during the adolescent period, and to test by at least one type of evidence the hypothesis that adolescence is a period of increasing religious problems," Kuhlen and Arnold (1944) administered a questionnaire to 547 children and adolescents. The subjects consisted of three groups that averaged twelve, fifteen, and eighteen years of age, respectively. The questionnaire contained fifty-two statements that had to do with religious beliefs and eighteen problems that dealt with religious issues. A partial list of the results obtained is presented in Table 18. In general, there appear to be fairly large differences between twelve- and fifteen-year-olds in some areas. Kuhlen and Arnold report a tendency toward greater tolerance in attitudes toward both practices and beliefs with increasing age. More eighteen-year-olds than fifteen-year-olds and more fifteen-year-olds than twelve-year-olds agree that "Catholics, Jews, and Protestants are equally good," and that "It is not necessary to attend church to be a Christian." As children grow older, many appear to relinquish specific beliefs such as "Every word in the Bible is true," and "It is sinful to doubt the Bible." There is an increase in "Wonder About" statements. Kuhlen and Arnold note that "an analysis of responses of 'wondering about' particular beliefs and 'problems' did not substantiate the commonly accepted hypothesis that adolescence is a period of generally increased religious doubts and problems." They did feel that "the specific problems checked by the subjects indicated that many do have problems of a religious sort, want help (in fact, one of the greatest problems seemed to be getting such help), but are dissatisfied with conventional church services."

In discussing their findings Kuhlen and Arnold note that the fact that religious differences appear among their three age groups does not imply that such differences are a function of adolescence. They state:

It would seem more reasonable to assume that they are the result of accumulated experiences in combination with increasing intellectual maturity which makes the adolescent more capable of interpreting the environment of ideas and facts in which he is becoming increasingly immersed. Greater intellectual maturity might be expected to increase sensitivity to inconsistencies either among the beliefs and views and individual contacts, or between his already established beliefs

Table 18 *Changes in Specific Religious Beliefs During Adolescence, as Shown by the Percentage of 12-, 15-, and 18-Year-Old Children Who Checked Various Statements Indicating Belief, Disbelief, or Uncertainty (Wonder)*

Statement	"Believe"			"Not Believe"			"Wonder About"		
	12	15	18	12	15	18	12	15	18
God is a strange power working for good, rather than a person.	46	49	57	31	33	21	20	14	15
God is someone who watches you to see that you behave yourself, and who punishes you if you are not good.	70	49	33	18	37	48	11	13	18
I know there is a God.	94	80	79	3	5	2	2	14	16
Catholics, Jews, and Protestants are equally good.	67	79	86	9	9	7	24	11	7
There is a heaven.	82	78	74	4	5	5	13	16	20
Only good people go to heaven.	72	45	33	15	27	32	13	27	34
Hell is a place where you are punished for your sins on earth.	70	49	35	16	21	30	13	27	34
Heaven is here on earth.	12	13	14	69	57	52	18	28	32
People who go to church are better than people who do not go to church.	46	26	15	37	53	74	17	21	11
Young people should belong to the same church as their parents.	77	56	43	13	33	46	10	11	11
The main reason for going to church is to worship God.	88	80	79	6	12	15	4	7	6
It is not necessary to attend church to be a Christian.	42	62	67	38	23	24	18	15	8
Only our soul lives after death.	72	63	61	9	11	6	18	25	31
Good people say prayers regularly.	78	57	47	9	29	26	13	13	27
Prayers are answered.	76	69	65	3	5	8	21	25	27
Prayers are a source of help in times of trouble.	74	80	83	11	8	7	15	10	9
Prayers are to make up for something that you have done that's wrong.	47	24	21	35	58	69	18	17	9
Every word in the Bible is true.	79	51	34	6	16	23	15	31	43
It is sinful to doubt the Bible.	62	42	27	18	31	44	20	26	28

*Discrepancies between the totals of "Believe," "Not Believe," and "Wonder About," and 100 percent represents the percentages who did not respond to the statements. Differences of 8 or 9 will ordinarily yield a CR of 2.0, depending upon the magnitude of the percentages involved.

Source: R. G. Kuhlen and M. Arnold, "Age differences in religious beliefs and problems during adolescence," *Journal of Genetic Psychology* 65 (1944): 291–300. Reprinted by permission of The Journal Press.

and new learnings. Also with greater maturity the adolescent is more capable of abstract generalizations which might result in discarding some specific beliefs in favor of more general ones.

In discussing the practical value and applications of their study, Kuhlen and Arnold cite two obvious implications: First, those issues represented by statements that are increasingly wondered about as age increases may give clues as to appropriate topics for consideration in the teen years in both Sunday school classes and young people's groups. Second, beliefs discarded by children as they grow older may well be studied for their implications for teaching at earlier ages. Children's concepts regarding religion are more concrete and specific than are those of adults, the latter tending to be abstract and general. This change represents the normal growth of concepts. It would seem desirable that the specific and concrete beliefs taught to children be beliefs compatible with more abstract adult views, and not beliefs later to be discarded due to incompatibility.

Studies published since Kuhlen and Arnold's 1944 study have done little to change the picture presented by these investigators. Such elements as the ecumenical movement and new philosophical positions have been added, but for the mass of America's youth things have not changed very much. Young et al. (1966) report in a study of University of Texas students that as students proceed through the university they tend to favor organized religion less. Young et al. note, however, that this tendency must be interpreted in terms of such variables as sex, grade-point average, major academic field, religious preference, and frequency of church attendance. Strunk (1958) reports that those adolescents with a relatively affirmative self-report tend to score higher on religiosity than do less affirmative self-report scorers. Dutt (1965) and Garrity (1961) both point to the fact that girls tend to be more religious than boys, and Garrity reemphasizes the fact that older adolescents seem to have more questions than do younger adolescents.

Bealer and Willets (1967), in a research of the religious commitment of American youth, note that the label most applicable to teenagers' religious orientation is "hedging," since many manifest neither nihilism nor commitment. In a research study of the religious values of 4,005 youth from seventeen different colleges and universities, Roscoe (1968) reports that 73 percent expressed a belief in a personal God, and of these, 28 percent subscribed to the traditional Judeo-Christian biblical concept of God; 88 percent of the Catholics and 83 percent of the Protestants expressed a belief in a personal God. Of the three religious groups included in the sample, Jewish students were most liberal in their religious beliefs. Nearly a quarter of the students believed the Bible to represent the inspired word of God, while nearly two-thirds thought of it as an inspired book, historically unreliable but serving a valid religious purpose.

Chambers, Wilson, and Barger (1968) report that the need characteristics of college freshmen without religious affiliation differed from those with church affiliation on fifteen of sixty-seven picture identification measures of Murray's needs (discussed in Chapter 10). The investigators felt their data indicated the possibility of an inner need conflict on the part of the unaffiliated. The problems of personal adjustment of students without religious affiliation centered on poor perception of goals and conflicts over desires to be independent and to avoid responsibility for others. In a study of self-classified religious versus nonreligious college students, Mayo et al. (1969) report that religious males were significantly less depressed, less schizophrenic, and less psychopathically deviant than nonreligious males. Among females, those classifying themselves as nonreligious tended to possess higher levels of ego strength than was true of those classifying themselves as religious. Mayo's data, however, must be viewed in the light of their having been collected on the campus of a small Southern denominational university, where lack of religion might receive more social disapproval than would be true of a large metropolitan state university. In such a setting, the differences between religious and nonreligious students might well be less. It is impossible to separate attitudes and factors of personality from the milieu in which they exist. An adolescent without religious faith in a small-town high school would be more conspicuous and, hence, would need more ego strength to support his position, than would an adolescent in the more impersonal large-city high school where students become pretty much anonymous once outside the walls of their school building.

In any event, in the last few years America seems to have experienced a renewed interest in religion, at least insofar as increasing church attendance may be taken as evidence of religion. In such an atmosphere, the adolescent is confronted with more discussion of religion, and he encounters more people, including his parents, who express a positive and active interest in religion than has been true in the past quarter-century. When adults take a position regarding manners and morals, they generally expect younger people to follow in their footsteps. Yet the period of adolescence has often been characterized as a time of susceptibility to doubts about religious beliefs, and this at a time when parental expectations clearly point to acceptance. Such a situation may make the adolescent feel guilty about his own questions.

Brown and Pallant (1962) report that religious beliefs are susceptible to the same social influences that alter other attitudes and opinions. With this statement in mind, it is safe to say that adolescents acquire religious attitudes and ideals much as they acquire other types of attitudes and ideals. The most important source is their daily environment. If religion is stressed in the environment, and if it is presented in such a manner that it meets the adolescent's needs, then religion is likely to be an important force in his life. On the other hand, if religion is presented in such a manner that it is foreign to an adolescent's needs and aspirations, or if it is harsh and unreasonable,

then he is likely to reject it or ignore it as much as he possibly can. An adolescent who has accepted the religious beliefs of his parents in his early years may face anxiety and guilt feelings if he finds his beliefs and attitudes changing. It is particularly difficult for the adolescent to adjust when he encounters conflicting points of view toward religion and moral behavior, unless he has been so completely indoctrinated that he is unwilling to consider varying points of view. A child who has been thoroughly indoctrinated faces even more severe adjustment difficulties if he finds his attitudes toward religion changing. Studies seem to indicate that adolescence does not bring with it particularly great changes in religious beliefs and attitudes; the longer a child has retained his beliefs, the less likely he is to change. A completely new environment with viewpoints entirely different from those of the old environment may bring about changes in the individual, of course.

College has often been considered a source of radical changes in religious attitudes, and although studies do not appear to support this contention, there is evidence based on questionnaires and interviews that college students tend to become more liberal in their beliefs and attitudes about religion. Following college, a considerable stability of attitude about religion appears. Nelson (1956), in a study concerning students' religious attitudes in the years after leaving college, notes that "religious attitudes held in college tend to persist for at least 14 years."

Those interested in promoting religious attitudes and ideals during the adolescent years would do well to base their educational approach on an understanding of the nature of the adolescent period and the things that are important to adolescents. It is certain that discussion or warnings alone will have little effect. Weaver (1944) reports the following reasons why adolescents may not participate in activities of the church: unfriendliness or authoritarianism in church authorities, lack of interesting activities and meetings, and bickering among church-group members when a project was under way. If left to themselves, adolescents will frequently discuss matters of religion and religious philosophy, often at a surprising level of sophistication, in their efforts to work out a personal philosophy of their own.

Altruism

Altruism is both a point of view and a type of conduct based upon an attitude by an individual that he should consider the welfare of others without regard for his own welfare. Altruism is typical of other attitudes in that it develops as a result of socialization, but it is unlike other attitudes in that it is selfless. Cohen (1972) notes that as an organism man is hedonistic and reward-oriented, while cultures have evolved altruistic values as survival mechanisms. Thus, according to Cohen, altruism is a superorganic phenomenon that for a number of reasons is generally found in complex cultures with stable institutions that can produce the emotional development necessary to activate the culturally derived altruism in human behavior. Yet relatively few members of even the most advanced cultures develop any consistently applied body of altruistic attitudes. The selflessness that makes possible true altruism can only come when an individual has such a strong concept of self that he has developed enough ego strength to be able to step aside from it and, in a real sense, abandon it. But to abandon self completely is pathological. Perhaps the saving factor is that altruism within any individual is limited. If altruism should become too consistent over too many areas, we would have a picture of pathology. As a matter of fact, Latane (1970) and Morgan (1973) report that the application of altruism is situational and depends heavily upon the circumstances of the moment. Latane investigated the reactions of New York City passers-by to simple requests in a series of field studies using male and female undergraduates as requesters. Over 80 percent of the passers-by gave minor assistance (time, direc-

tion, or change), but this dropped to 34 percent when something as tangible as a dime was requested. Females were more likely to receive help than males, and males were more likely to give help than females. Requesters in groups were more likely to receive help; persons in groups were less likely to give help than single people. Latane was of the opinion that responses were probably mediated in part by the motives attributed to the requester, including the kind of person he appeared to be. In a review of the literature, Krebs (1970) notes that positive and negative affective states as well as states induced by the observation of models are found to influence the altruism of benefactors, and dependency and interpersonal attractiveness are found to influence the altruism-eliciting capacity of recipients. Effects are found for sex, age, ordinal position, social class, and nationality for benefactors and for friendship status, in-group affiliation, and social class for recipients. Thus, the application of altruism tends to be selective. Of course, the instances of altruism required in many of the altruism studies, as in the Latane study, are exceedingly minor and certainly not of the order of help that would be asked under such major circumstances as a general disaster or a serious accident.

To what extent is an adolescent capable of altruistic behavior? In general, it has to be said that the adolescent has not yet proceeded far enough along the channels of development to attain altruism at either a major or a consistent level. The adolescent is still struggling to build a concept of self and has not yet attained self-stability to the point where he is free to abandon self. He has yet to attain a sufficient degree of ego strength. Lowe and Ritchey (1973), in a study involving respondents' placing a stamp on an unstamped but addressed letter that had presumably been lost, report that older persons displayed a greater tendency to altruistic behavior. Of course, instances of altruism do occur in adolescence, but they are in minor matters and are often, in fact, self-serving rather than true examples of altruism. An example is offered in a study by Regan (1971), who notes that altruism often occurs after harm-doing as a means of expiating guilt. Of course, the possibility always exists in the case of any given individual that the development of maturity and of a stable self-concept has been accelerated as compared to the more normal developmental progression of his peers.

Conflicts in Attitudes and Values

In the process of developing a system of values and attitudes, an adolescent may find himself under pressure to make choices between conflicting alternatives. Such choice situations are most frequent when there is difference of opinion between parents and peers or between parents themselves. Frequently conflict will arise between social sanctions and the adolescent's own hedonistic tendencies. The inability of many adolescents to defer immediate gratification for future gains creates an area of potential conflict involving the school as well as parents. Adolescence appears to be a time of conflicting values. Konopka (1973) notes that while value formation is a birth-to-death process, the intellectual and emotional aspects come to a peak of activity during adolescence. The conflict of values between the emphasis on individual decision-making and equality in a democratic society and the authoritarianism of many institutions, such as the school, is a particular problem. As an idealist the adolescent assumes a perfect world but finds examples to the contrary on all sides. He hears of the equality of man but is a personal witness to racial bigotry, often in himself. He hears the religious position of compassion, faith, and charity but sees the abnegation of these things on the part of the very people, including his parents and teachers, who should stand for them most firmly. He learns the tenets of good government and hears the voices of the media label his government's leaders as transgressors and enemies of the very system they are elected to support. He witnesses cynicism and disregard for the rights and values of others on all

sides. Because he is still immature, lacks real experience of the world and its people, and is still trying to find out who he is and where he is going, he has great difficulty in resolving the value conflicts he witnesses. Because he is both young and an idealist, he tends to overreact and to generalize too broadly from single instances. Typically he either yields or becomes intolerant. If the former, he may enter a line of conduct leading to feelings of guilt and self-rejection. If the latter, he simply exacerbates his problem and encounters even more conflict. It is easy for the adolescent to miss the point that if there is much bad in the world, there is also much good.

Butter and Seidenberg (1973), in a study of specific value conflict areas and their influence on the level of moral development, asked one hundred undergraduates to submit an account of a recent personal moral conflict, the manner in which it was solved, and their reasons for decision. In the area of social relationships, the order of frequency of conflicts was 35 percent; in the area of honesty, 19 percent; in the area of sexual behavior, 14 percent; and in political-ideological attitude and action, 7 percent. Political conflicts were resolved on a more mature level than honesty or social conflicts, with sexual conflicts being resolved more maturely than were those of honesty. Results indicate that the area of conflict affects the moral maturity expressed in the conflict's resolution.

Modifying Attitudes and Judgments

To what extent can attitudes and moral judgments be modified? Is a child limited solely to his dominant developmental stage in making moral judgments, or is it possible for him to make judgments characteristic of a later stage? To what extent, when he has attained the highest stage of moral development, is it possible to modify an individual's attitudes and judgments? The present section is devoted to exploring answers to these questions, as well as to a discussion of the means of promoting proper and acceptable attitudes and ideals that will help adolescents make better adjustments in society as well as in their own personal lives. Further, the section will examine the reason for the validity of the attitudes and ideals that programs of character education endeavor to inculcate.

People interested in the welfare of youth often speak of character development as a desideratum of the adolescent period. It would be difficult to deny the validity of such a statement were it possible to be confident that "character development" really represented something that would be equally good for the individual and for society. Unfortunately, many people tend to conceive of character development in such a manner that one would hesitate to inflict it on either the individual or society. Hence, in evaluating the advisabilty of a program of character development, it is essential to know what the people who propose such a program mean by "good character."

Ordinarily, a society evolves a set of values and procedures that are held to be exceedingly important. Sometimes such values and procedures originate in attempts to protect and perpetuate the society in question. For example, most societies, modern and primitive alike, build a set of laws, rules, taboos, or folkways intended to punish the person who commits acts against the best interests of that society, or what the society conceives to be the best interests of the individual. The nature of such acts and the seriousness with which they are regarded vary from society to society and depend upon how important a threat the act may be to the society's security and substance. In the cattle-raising regions of the American West, horse stealing was once a most serious crime, punishable in the popular view by immediate death. In time of war the soldier who absents himself without leave has committed a crime that is far more serious, in terms of the punishment involved, than it would be in peacetime.

It is not the function of this discussion to either approve or disapprove of the values given currency in any society. Its function is to point out that many such values are highly artificial and exist because of the nature of the society itself. In another society, different, even opposite values might have currency, and the first society's values might be regarded as worthless, even perhaps vicious. But whatever a society's values, its members must conform or suffer serious consequences. In those cases in which a society has many conflicting values, or in which an individual tries to move in two spheres with mutually exclusive values, his problems of adjustment increase. It has been explained that an adolescent is often faced with the need to find approval in two such mutually exclusive spheres.

Whatever the source of the validity of the values held, parents and the various community agencies of education and recreation usually strongly desire to emphasize character development and the inculcation of a proper set of values in children's upbringing. That such a desire is in itself worthy is beyond question. A society composed of individuals of good character and high ideals and values is likely to function for the common good, and a child reared in such an environment will be a better person if he learns and accepts the society's values. Therefore, it is important that a program of character education actually attempt to inculcate these values and at the same time try to preserve the individual's integrity. A program of character education at variance with the values of the society in which it must exist, or one based upon a narrow, petty misconception of what good character is, cannot be condoned. This is especially true if the program does not consider the personalities and psychological welfare of the persons with whom it is dealing.

However, in implementing society's values it would be unwise to ignore the viewpoint and needs of the adolescents with whom one is dealing, if their viewpoint can be accommodated without destroying the structure one is trying to erect. Eames et al. (1965) reinforce this point when they write that teenage problems can best be dealt with if they are seen from the adolescent's viewpoint.

Given favorable circumstances, adolescent attitudes and moral judgments are susceptible to at least partial modification. Eisenman (1970) reports, for example, that moral judgments may be manipulated to be less severe. He administered a test of moral judgments under mitigating circumstances to five undergraduate classes. Two of the five classes then received instruction about the authoritarian personality while the remaining three received no such instruction. Following the instructional period, the test was again administered. It was found that students who were taught about the authoritarian personality made significantly less severe moral judgments. White and Minden (1969) report influence shifts toward a riskier or divergent attitude following small group discussion, and Baumgartel and Goldstein (1967) report shifts in values and needs as a result of instruction in a human relations course. The shift in this course was toward agreement with its mostly highly valued members. Berkowitz and Walker (1967) report the influence of peer consensus as a causal factor in attitude shifts, but Keasey (1973) warns that opinion and reasoning change are independent processes. Changes may be temporary simply as a means of reducing a disequilibrium state. When equilibrium is attained, the individual tends to return to his original attitude. Simon (1969) notes that the difficulty in teaching values is that they are not usually the outcome of direct verbal instruction but are implanted by natural nonverbal means, such as the modeling processes. Simon makes the point that some of the criteria that structure the teaching of values include social acceptance of the value, motivation for action, social reinforcement, and individual free participation in the choice.

Research accomplished by a number of investigators has shown that it is possible to shift children from their dominant style of moral reasoning to a developmentally later stage. However, in any individual case this possibility is dependent upon a number of contingencies. LeFurgy and Woloshin (1969)

classified thirteen-year-olds as either morally relativistic or morally realistic and exposed them to social influence procedures. Morally relativistic and morally realistic children of both sexes yield to peer influences in their responses to moral dilemma stories relating to Piaget's autonomous and heteronomous stages of moral development. However, the responsiveness to social influence of the morally relativistic children was of much shorter duration than was true of their morally realistic peers. Tracy and Cross (1973) exposed thirteen-year-olds to moral reasoning one stage above their initial stage before and after experimental treatment. They report striking differences for the experimental treatment at different levels of moral judgment. Children at the preconventional level shifted upward more than children at the conventional level. Social desirability was associated with the change, although socioeconomic status, intelligence, and role taking were not.

Fodor (1971) administered a test of moral development to 52 adolescent boys and then endeavored to get them to shift their position on a given moral issue. Those who resisted the efforts of the experimenter to the greatest degree received significantly higher moral-judgment scores than did those who at some point yielded to the experimenter's influence. Resisters viewed their mothers as having given them greater autonomy in their personal lives than was true of the mothers of the yielders. Lorimer (1971) examined the inducement of developmental advance in 130 adolescents of both sexes, using expository and film presentation conditions. Both types of treatment induced some change, but the pattern of change between groups differed. Lorimer interpreted this as indicative of the effects of the structure and content of the treatments interacting with the developmental level of the adolescents. Chaffee and Lindner (1969) note that a person's evaluation of an object changes as a function of its salience for him, its relationship with other objects, and the reduction of cognitive dissonance.

Burgess (1962), writing to parents, states:

What we have to do is to help our adolescent boys and girls find more of the real things, the things that need doing, the things that make sense to them. . . . To communicate true values parents must have true values. I would urge that we look beneath the surface of our opinions, our convictions, our fears and examine more thoughtfully and more honestly our own standards.

Burgess feels that adolescent "apathy" arises from disenchantment with adult standards.

The question then is whether or not it is possible to modify or guide an adolescent's existing attitudes and values in a desired direction. In answering this question, it should be borne in mind that individuals and situations differ and that the significance of an attitude to an individual will vary from attitude to attitude and from time to time. However, the psychological literature offers hope that, within limitations, it is possible to modify individual and group attitudes of adolescents as a result of outside experience.

Martin (1954) observed that values and standards are inculcated first, through the learning of behavior by imitation and reinforcement, and second, by the definition of values reached inductively from behavior. This means that values are acquired over a period of years, first from the parent or parent substitute, and later from other persons with whom the adolescent comes into contact—peers, teachers, and hero figures. When the individual learns to read, another very important source is opened to him.

Ausubel (1954), in discussing changes in values during adolescence, notes:

Values and goals are still acquired by intellectual satellization, that is, as by-products of subservience to others on whom the individual is dependent for derived status; but now personal loyalties have been transferred from parents to age-mates and such other parent surrogates as teachers, adult group leaders, and representatives of the church.

In general, it appears that attitudes and values adolescents hold grow out of their environments and the influences to which they have been subjected. So pervasive is the effect of environment that with increasing age adolescents' attitudes and points of view tend to conform more and more to those of the adults around them.

There has been much talk of the school's role in the education of children, and it has become popular to criticize what many have termed the overpreoccupation of the American school with "life adjustment." In the writer's opinion, schools in a democracy must prepare those placed in their charge for life in a democratic society, which means attention to a child's attitudes and values as well as mastery of the content and skills offered by the traditional academic curriculum. To add "life adjustment" does not mean that content and skills need be neglected. However, one criticism that can be leveled at the American school's interest in "life adjustment" is that too often it has meant solely social adjustment or participation and vocational training. The missing element has been moral training in attitudes and values as a really serious enterprise of the schools, the assumption being that this is an area for the home and the church. Yet the possibilities for influence by the school have been demonstrated again and again. For example, Krumboltz (1965) asked ninth graders to express the extent of their agreement with three statements attributed to one of three communicator groups. On the average, the 189 subjects agreed most readily with the statements when they were attributed to school counselors as compared to peers and parents. Of course, another school might not be as successful, but could this not be because it had abdicated its moral value role?

In discussing the implications of the Character Education Inquiry, Hartshorne, May, and Shuttleworth (1930) noted that it does little good for teachers or others to urge honest behavior by discussing standards and ideals of honesty, no matter to what degree such appeals are emotionalized. "Preaching" does not lead to the control of conduct and may result in unwholesome or undesirable effects. These investigators do not feel that the teaching of general ideas, standards, and ideals is either undesirable or unnecessary, but they do point out that prevailing "preaching" techniques are of no value and may be harmful. They believe that a character-education program should be based upon a careful educational analysis of situations in which deceit or dishonesty are likely to occur. Teachers and parents should then explicitly detail the nature of the direct or honest mode of response, so the child has an opportunity to practice direct methods of adjustment.

Hartshorne et al. recommended that an effort be made to show the child that deceit may be viewed in terms of personal relations and that honesty may be distinguished from dishonesty as a way of social interaction. He should be shown that social consequences must be considered in choosing the way he should behave in any given situation. They feel adults should make a real effort to understand why an individual acts as he does before blaming him on the basis of an arbitrary set of external values. They believe educators should be less interested in devices for teaching honesty or any other "trait" in isolation and more interested in constructing school experiences that will provide consistent and regular opportunities for successful use by both teachers and students of the forms of conduct that make for the common good. In summary, Hartshorne et al. feel that:

1. What is to be learned must be experienced.
2. What is to be experienced must be represented in the situation to which children are exposed.
3. If what is to be learned is some form of conduct or mode of adjustment, then the situations to which children are exposed must be opportunities to pursue interests that lead to the conduct to be learned.
4. This conduct must be carried on in relation to the particular situations to which it is the preferred mode of response.
5. A common and potent factor in such situations is the established practice and code of the group, which, by coloring the situation, may either hinder or assist the acquisition of desirable responses on the part of its members.
6. If standards and ideals, whether already in the possession of the group or not, are to function as controlling factors, they must become a part of the situation to which the child responds, and they must assist in the achievement of satisfactory modes of adjustment to those aspects of the situation that are independent of these standards and ideals—they must be tools rather than objects of aesthetic appreciation.
7. The achievement of specific standards, attitudes, and modes of conduct does not imply their integration. Integration is itself a specific achievement.

Here a word of warning is in order. Nearly any experience that is vivid for the individual and that constitutes for him an intense emotional experience is likely to have profound effect upon his attitudes, values, and future behavior. And the direction of the effect may not always be as his mentor had planned. Unless proper precautions are taken, too strong an emotional appeal may have a disintegrating effect on the individual. Teachers and others who wish to guide adolescents' education and development are advised to make occasional and common-sense use of emotional appeals but to be careful of overdoing it, because some individuals are less capable of accepting and adjusting to sustained emotional appeal than are others. It should also be remembered that too frequent use of a motivating device decreases its effectiveness and may even produce reactions opposite to those sought.

Summary

A person who has acceptable attitudes, high ideals, and fine values is usually categorized as having a "good character." Character has been defined as the ability to identify one's own happiness with the happiness of others and to control those impulses that are contrary to one's own purpose.

Character may be assessed either in terms of traits held by an individual as revealed by tests he has taken, or in terms of the traits attributed to him by others. Many ingenious devices have been proposed for the measurement of character, and of these, various types of questionnaires have received the widest use.

The 1920s witnessed considerable interest in the study and analysis of character. Situational tests to measure truthfulness and honesty became popular. Some attempts were made to observe physiological changes in individuals who were being untruthful. Among the most comprehensive and ingenious of these studies was that of the Character Education Inquiry, which endeavored to study such aspects of character as deceit, desire for service, and personality organization by means of many pencil-and-paper and situational tests. The Character Education Inquiry advanced the theory of the specificity of human conduct and indicated that integration of character and consistency go hand in hand. The ideal individual was seen as one who would show a high average performance on an attitude scale and vary only slightly from that average. A person's "impulse-judgment" ability appears to be a significant factor in the excellence of his character.

Environmental factors such as the peer group, parents, institutions, and vicarious experience are important in shaping an adolescent's attitudes. Of these, parental and peer-group influences are the most significant. The adolescent generally will tend to be more influenced by those he likes and by those who use good techniques than by those he dislikes or who use poor techniques in attempting to guide him.

A considerable amount of research on cheating behavior has been accomplished, most of it in direct confirmation of the studies of Hartshorne et al. Situational factors are capable of altering childrens' lying and cheating behavior. In general, it would appear that when children

are given an opportunity to cheat, they do, and the more anxiety and hostility provoking the situation, the greater the likelihood of cheating. Usually an individual indulging in cheating behavior will tend to justify it because of the circumstances that gave rise to it. Incorporation of values and standards of morality is most favorable when parental or other discipline does not involve harsh or extreme techniques.

Cheating is a response instrumental in the avoidance of aversive social consequences such as failure, peer or adult rejection, or loss of self-esteem. It is not the emotional arousal that causes cheating but the interpretation of the meaning and significance of the arousal. The tendency to cheat and the specific type of cheating employed are reliably related to certain demographic, intellectual, and personality characteristics.

Religious attitudes are formed and discarded in much the same manner as other attitudes. Changes in attitudes toward religion occur during adolescence, but they are not particularly radical. The attitude of most American youth toward religion has been termed "hedging," since many of them evidence neither nihilism or commitment. Most believe in a personal God and see the Bible as a valid outline of religious faith but do not accept the Bible as being historically accurate. In general, the need characteristics of individuals with religious affiliation differ from those of persons without such affiliation, and there is some evidence that adjustment patterns may also differ. The problems of personal adjustment of students without religious affiliation centered on poor perception of goals and conflicts over desires to be independent and to avoid responsibility for others.

Altruism is an attitude that considers the welfare of others without regard to the welfare of the individual having the altruistic attitude. True altruism can only come when an individual has such a strong concept of self that he has developed enough ego strength to step aside from the self and abandon it. Altruism is a mature end product of the developmental process. It is doubtful if most adolescents have been able to acquire a level of maturity making possible true altruism.

Conflict between opposing values is a not infrequent occurrence in adolescence instigated in relationships with parents and peers as well as by the adolescents' own feelings about right and wrong. The conflict of values in a democratic society is sometimes hard for an immature and inexperienced person to deal with. Value conflicts, however, are most frequently to be found in the area of interpersonal relationships.

In changing and developing attitudes in teenagers, adults will be most successful if they permit the adolescent to participate in making decisions. This offers him an opportunity to test himself and to feel that he is a responsible person.

Character education is necessary and desirable in rearing an adolescent, but it must encompass the good of both individual and society. It should recognize the importance of individual differences and should not be narrow and authoritarian. Teachers who hope to promote proper character education should be less interested in devices for teaching "traits" and more interested in promoting proper habits by offering consistent and regular opportunities to practice the behavior desired.

References

Ausubel, D. P. *Theory and problems of adolescent development.* New York: Grune and Stratton, 1954.

Bandura, A., and Walters, R. H. *Adolescent aggression: A study of the influences of child-training practices and family interrelations.* New York: Ronald, 1959.

Baumgartel, H., and Goldstein, H. W. Need and value shifts in training groups. *Journal of Applied Behavioral Science* 3 (1967): 87–101.

Bealer, R. C., and Willets, F. K. The religious interests of American high school youth: A survey of recent research. *Religious Education* 62 (1967): 435–444.

Berkowitz, L., and Walker, N. Laws and moral judgments. *Sociometry* 30 (1967): 410–422.

Bird, C. The detection of cheating in objective examinations. *School and Society* 25 (1927): 261–262.

Bonjean, C. M., and McGee, R. Scholastic dishonesty among undergraduates in differing systems of social control. *Sociology of Education* 38 (1965): 127–137.

Brown, L. B., and Pallant, D. J. Religious belief and social pressure. *Psychological Reports* 10 (1962): 813–814.

Burgess, H. S. Adolescent apathy. *Parent-Teacher Magazine* 57 (1962): 14–16.

Butter, E. J., and Seidenberg, B. Manifestations of moral development in concrete situations. *Social Behavior and Personality* 1 (1973): 64–70.

Centra, J. A. College freshman attitudes toward cheating. *Personnel and Guidance Journal* 48 (1970): 366–373.

Chaffee, S. H., and Lindner, J. W. Three processes of value change without behavioral change. *Journal of Communication* 19 (1969): 30–40.

Chamber, E. V. A study of dishonesty among the students of a parochial secondary school. *Pedogogical Seminary* 33 (1926): 717–728.

Chambers, J. L.; Wilson, W. T.; and Barger, B. Need differences between students with and without religious affiliation. *Journal of Counseling Psychology* 15 (1968): 208–210.

Cohen, R. Altruism: Human, cultural or what? *Journal of Social Issues* 28 (1972): 39–57.

Dienstbier, R., and Munter, P. O. Cheating as a function of the labeling of natural arousal. *Journal of Personality and Social Psychology* 17 (1971): 208–213.

Dutt, N. K. Attitudes of the university students toward religion. *Journal of Psychological Research* 9 (1965): 127–130.

Eames, T. H.; Douglas, H. B.; Guston, G.; and King, M. H. Attitudes and opinions of adolescents. *Journal of Education* 147 (1965): 1–43.

Eisenman, R. Teaching about the authoritarian personality: Effects on moral judgment. *Psychological Record* 20 (1970): 33–40.

Feldman, S. E., and Feldman, M. T. Transition of sex differences in cheating. *Psychological Reports* 20 (1967): 957–958.

Flesznerowa, E. Z badan nad wzorem osobowos-

ciowym wspolczesne mlodziezy. *Psychologia Wychowawcza* 6 (1963) : 403–413.

Fodor, E. M. Resistance to social influence among adolescents as a function of level of moral development. *Journal of Social Psychology* 85 (1971) : 121–126.

Garrity, F. D. A study of some secondary modern school pupils' attitudes towards religious education. *Religious Education* 56 (1961) : 141–143.

Gundlach, R. A method for the detection of cheating in college examinations. *School and Society* 22 (1925) : 215–216.

Harari, H., and McDavid, J. W. Situational influences on moral justice: A study of "finking." *Journal of Personality and Social Psychology* 11 (1969) : 240–244.

Hartshorne, H.; May, M. A.; and Shuttleworth, F. K. *Studies in the organization of character.* 3 vols. (1, *Studies in deceit*, 1928; 2, *Studies in service and self-control*, 1929; 3, *Studies in the organization of character*, 1930). New York: Macmillan, 1928–1930.

Havighurst, R. J., and Taba, H. *Adolescent character and personality.* New York: Wiley, 1949.

Henshel, A. M. The relationship between values and behavior: A developmental hypothesis. *Child Development* 42 (1971) : 1997–2007.

Hetherington, E. M., and Feldman, S. E. College cheating as a function of subject and situational variables. *Journal of Educational Psychology* 55 (1964) : 212–218.

Jenison, L. M. Student and faculty attitudes toward academic dishonesty offenses. *College Student Journal* 6 (1972) : 137–141.

Johnson, C. D., and Gormly, J. Achievement, sociability, and task importance in relation to academic cheating. *Psychological Reports* 28 (1971) : 302.

Johnson, C. D., and Gormly, J. Academic cheating: The contribution of sex, personality, and situational variables. *Developmental Psychology* 6 (1972) : 320–325.

Keasey, C. B. Experimentally induced changes in moral opinions and reasoning. *Journal of Personality and Social Psychology* 26 (1973) : 30–38.

Konopka, G. Formation of values in the developing person. *American Journal of Orthopsychiatry* 43 (1973) : 86–96.

Krebs, D. L. Altruism: An examination of the concept and a review of the literature. *Psychological Bulletin* 73 (1970) : 258–302.

Kuhlen, R. G., and Arnold, M. Age differences in religious beliefs and problems during adolescence. *Journal of Genetic Psychology* 65 (1944) : 291–300.

Latane, B. Field studies of altruistic compliance. *Representative Research in Social Psychology* 1 (1970) : 49–61.

LeFurgy, W. G., and Woloshin, G. W. Immediate and long term effects of experimentally induced social influence in the modification of adolescents' moral judgments. *Journal of Personality and Social Psychology* 12 (1969) : 104–110.

Leveque, K. L., and Walker, R. E. Correlates of high school cheating behavior. *Psychology in the Schools* 7 (1970) : 159–163.

Lippitt, R. An experimental study of the effect of democratic and authoritarian group atmospheres. *Iowa Studies in Child Welfare* 16 (1940) : 43–195.

Lorimer, R. Change in the development of moral judgments in adolescence: The effect of a structured exposition vs. a film and discussion. *Canadian Journal of Behavioral Sciences* 3 (1971) : 1–10.

Lowe, R., and Ritchey, G. Relation of altruism to age, social class, and ethnic identity. *Psychological Reports* 33 (1973) : 567–572.

Martin, W. E. Learning theory and justification: The development of values in children. *Journal of Genetic Psychology* 84 (1954) : 211–217.

Mayo, C. C.; Puryear, H. B.; and Richey, H. G. MMPI correlates of religiousness in late adolescent college students. *Journal of Nervous and Mental Disease* 149 (1969) : 381–385.

Morgan, W. G. Situational specificity in altruistic behavior. *Representative Research in Social Psychology* 4 (1973) : 56–66.

Nelson, E. Patterns of religious attitude shifts from college to fourteen years later. *Psychological Monographs*, vol. 70, no. 424, 1956.

Pearlin, L. I.; Yarrow, M. R.; and Scarr, H. A. Unintended effects of parental aspirations: The case of children's cheating. *American Journal of Sociology* 73 (1967) : 73–83.

Peck, R. F., and Galliani, C. Intelligence, ethnicity, and social roles in adolescence. *Sociometry* 25 (1962) : 64–72.

Persing, K. M. Morals and chemistry. *Educational Review* 72 (1926) : 164–168.

Prescott, D. A. *Emotion and the educative process.* Washington: American Council on Education, 1938.

Regan, J. W. Guilt, perceived injustice and altruistic behavior. *Journal of Personality and Social*

Psychology 18 (1971): 124–132.

Roscoe, J. T. Religious beliefs of American college students. *College Student Survey* 2 (1968): 49–55.

Runner, J. R. Social distance in adolescent relationships. *American Journal of Sociology* 42 (1937): 428–439.

Shelton, J., and Hill, J. P. Effects on cheating of achievement anxiety and knowledge of peer performance. *Developmental Psychology* 1 (1969): 449–455.

Simon, S. B. Promoting the search for values. *Educational Opportunity Forum* 1 (1969): 75–84.

Sipos, I. The influence of an induced frustration situation on the stability of honest behavior in pupils. *Ceskoslovenska Psychologie* 8 (1964): 16–23.

Smith, C. P.; Ryan, E. R.; and Diggins, D. R. Moral decision making: Cheating on examinations. *Journal of Personality* 40 (1972): 640–660.

Steininger, M. Attitudes toward cheating: General and specific. *Psychological Reports* 22 (1968): 1101–1107.

Steininger, M.; Johnson, R. E.; and Kirts, D. K. Cheating on college examinations as a function of situationally aroused anxiety and hostility. *Journal of Educational Psychology* 55 (1964): 317–324.

Strunk, O., Jr. Relationship between self-reports and adolescent religiosity. *Psychological Reports* 4 (1958): 683–686.

Tracy, J. J., and Cross, H. J. Antecedants of shift in moral judgment. *Journal of Personality and Social Psychology* 26 (1973): 238–244.

Vitro, F. T. The relationship of classroom dishonesty to perceived parental discipline. *Journal of College Student Personnel* 12 (1971): 427–429.

Weaver, P. Youth and religion. *Annals American Academy of Political Science* 236 (1944): 152–161.

White, W. F., and Minden, N. J. Risky-shift phenomenon in moral attitudes of high school boys and girls. *Psychological Reports* 25 (1969): 515–518.

Young, R. K.; Dustin, D. S.; and Holtzman, W. H. Change toward attitude toward religion in a southern community. *Psychological Reports* 18 (1966): 39–46.

Suggested Readings

Aronfreed, J. *Conduct and conscience: The socialization of internalized control over behavior.* New York: Academic Press, 1968.

Beck, C. M.; Crittenden, B. S.; and Sullivan, E. V. *Moral education: Interdisciplinary approaches.* Toronto: University of Toronto Press, 1971.

Blanchard, E. B., and Scarboro, M. E. Locus of control, political attitudes and voting behavior in a college-age population. *Psychological Reports* 30 (1972): 529–530.

Blume, N. Political variables related to young Republican and young Democratic club activities. *Journal of College Student Personnel* 13 (1972): 239–246.

Boehm, L. The development of conscience: A comparison of upper-middle-class academically gifted children attending Catholic and Jewish parochial schools. *Journal of Social Psychology* 59 (1963): 101–110.

Burchard, J. D. A methodology for conducting an experimental analysis of cheating behavior. *Journal of Experimental Child Psychology* 10 (1970): 146–158.

Carey, R. G. Influence of peers in shaping religious behavior. *Journal for the Scientific Study of Religion* 10 (1971): 157–159.

Conley, W. H. Do adolescents have faith? *Catholic Social Journal* 69 (1969): 4, 5, 8, 10.

DeBord, L. W. Adolescent religious participation: An examination of sib-structure and church attendance. *Adolescence* 4 (1969): 557–570.

DeVries, D. L., and Ajzen, I. The relationship of attitudes and normative beliefs to cheating. *Journal of Social Psychology* 83 (1971): 199–207.

Drapela, V. J. Personality adjustment and religious growth. *Journal of Religion and Health* 8 (1969): 87–97.

Easten, D., and Hess, R. D. Youth and the political system. In Lipset, S. M., and Lowenthal, L., eds., *Culture and Social Character*, pp. 226–251. New York: Free Press, 1961.

Easten D., and Hess R. D. The child's political world. *Midwest Journal of Political Science* 6 (1962): 229–246.

Greenstein, F. *Children and politics.* New Haven: Yale University Press, 1965.

Knowlton, J. Q., and Hamerlynck, L. A. Perception of deviant behavior: A study of cheating. *Journal of Educational Psychology* 58 (1967): 379–385.

Lindenauer, G. G. Teaching students responsibility. *Journal of Emotional Education* 9 (1969): 128–134.

Mackey, J. A. Moral insight in the classroom. *Elementary School Journal* 73 (1973): 233–238.

Miller, D. R., and Swanson, G. *Inner conflict and defense.* New York: Holt, 1960.

Pang, H. Religious attitudes of students. *Psychological Reports* 22 (1968): 344.

Rau, L. Conscience and identification. In Sears, R. R.; Rau, L.; and Alpert, R. *Identification and child rearing.* Stanford: Stanford University Press, 1964.

Roskens, R. W., and Dizney, H. F. A study of unethical academic behavior in high school and college. *Journal of Educational Research* 59 (1966): 231–234.

Schab, F. Honor and dishonor in the secondary schools of three cultures. *Adolescence* 6 (1971): 145–154.

Sutker, P. B.; Sutker, L. W.; and Kilpatrick, D. G. Religious preference, practice, and personal sexual attitudes and behavior. *Psychological Reports* 26 (1970): 835–841.

Turiel, E. Adolescent conflict in the development of moral principles. In Solso, R. L., ed., *Contemporary issues in cognitive psychology: The Loyola Symposium.* Washington: Winston, 1973.

Ward, C. D., and Barrett, J. E. The Ecumenical Council and attitude change among Catholic, Protestant, and Jewish college students. *Journal of Social Psychology* 74 (1968): 91–96.

Chapter Sixteen

Development of Responsibility in Adolescence

The Nature of Responsibility

In the developing adolescent a personality pattern involving a cluster of traits representing willingness to profit by experience and to accept responsibility for oneself and others represents a major developmental task. The attainment of such a sense of responsibility is essential if the adolescent is to become a socially useful person and of maximum use to himself. There are in actuality two quite different kinds of responsibility. One, the more basic of the two, is interior responsibility, which involves accepting responsibility for oneself in the sense that one should take care of oneself, be self-dependent, and assume the responsibility for becoming the person one conceives oneself to be. Interior responsibility represents the implementation of a kind of caretaker impulse.

The other, the more obvious, is exterior responsibility and involves responsibility to other people, to institutions, and so on. It consists partly in taking upon oneself the function of seeing that something gets done and done well, and it is obviously an attribute of leadership. It leads to the role of the instigator, the mover. Exterior responsibility implies involvement and may have as its origin either extrinsic or intrinsic motivation. Extrinsically motivated exterior responsibility is simply an extension of inward responsibility to exterior objects or affairs with an extrinsic rather than intrinsic focus. Thus, the adolescent accepts exterior responsibility as a means of bolstering the self. It is a kind of self-aggrandizement in which

the individual seems to say, "I have accepted this responsibility because it shows me and everyone else what kind of person I really am."

Intrinsically motivated exterior responsibility in its ultimate expression is selfless—that is, aggrandizement of the self is not involved. The individual does what he does for its own sake, although an incidental outcome may be self-actualization. In many ways it is analogous to Sullivan's last stage of selfless love and represents the attainment of a level of maturity that ordinarily does not occur until the later stages of adolescence. Of course, there are various levels of responsibility. In the earliest levels, characteristic of the behavior of preadolescents and early adolescents, a task is embarked upon merely because it has to be done. Johnnie mows the lawn because that is his job and it is now time to do it. In addition to task orientation at this level, there is also the implication of reward or parental approval if the task is accomplished and of disapproval or even punishment if it is not done. Johnnie may still be regarded as responsible if he can be depended upon to get the task done on time, no matter what his reason for being dependable. In contrast, Mark, although he dislikes disapproval and fears punishment, cannot be depended on to get the task done on time and indeed may not start it at all. Mark is not dependable. He lacks responsibility. A further feature of this level of responsibility is that the dependable adolescent does not require initial urging or in-process supervision while his less dependable peer needs both. It may well be that this early level of responsibility might better be called dependability, with the term *responsibility* reserved for the later, more mature stage of responsibility.

In the later stage of responsibility the individual examplifies dependability in its best sense but acts as his own task setter and extends his motivation beyond mere task accomplishment. The assumption of responsibility is for this individual a means of self-actualization, but, more, it exemplifies what might be called a social conscience. The task is voluntarily assumed and embarked on for the good of others or to further an enterprise that exists or should exist for the common cause. This level of responsibility is a basic attribute of positively oriented leadership. It is also a basic attribute of those who wish to help others and who are prepared to bend every effort to do so. The productive work of the world is carried out by persons capable of this level of responsibility. In high school such persons are to be found in positions of sports and activity leadership, and they are in the forefront of social-service activities such as a "clean up your neighborhood" campaign. One danger of this level of responsibility is that it may get out of control, and responsibility becomes interference in the affairs of others, leading to social rejection and its attendant emotional upset.

In contrast to responsibility, irresponsibility may be observed in superficiality, lack of emotional control, and a unilateral striving for ease, pleasure, and one's own way either at the expense of or with total disregard for higher values, the rights and preferences of others, or even of the demands of reality. The sociopath, with his complex of abnormal attitudes toward the social environment, represents an extreme of irresponsibility. Society, at a level less extreme than sociopathy, is accustomed to accepting irresponsibility on the part of younger children, but as the child proceeds into adolescence, society's tolerance rapidly dwindles. This becomes particularly true in the modern era as legal responsibilities such as suffrage and the right to enter upon contractual relationships are extended downward into the teen years.

As a matter of fact, it is probably fair to say that the assumption of responsibility, whether intrinsically or extrinsically motivated, is necessary for self-actualization. If this is true, then failure to assume personal responsibility represents disequilibrium and may well be a contributing factor in many neurotic and psychotic episodes. The concept of responsibility can be related to many aspects of psychic performance, including creativity. It can be placed as basic to the progress of civilization. As responsibility declines, people become more irresponsible, more self-centered, more hedonistic, more crime-prone, and less self-dependent. Lack of responsibility is a social as well as a personal disorder. The closing years of the Roman Empire knew it well. Modern writers such as Wheelis (1958) and McLuhan (1964) have described its symptoms in our times. The need to inculcate a sense of responsibility during adolescence is a recurring theme throughout this book.

Development of Responsibility

How does an individual become a responsible person? In the first place, as Meyer and Wacker (1970) indicate, the child has to have reached a developmental stage at which responsibility is cognitively possible. This involves development over a considerable length of time during which the child learns concepts of cause and effect, relates these concepts to himself and his environment, and finally internalizes a set of positive values regarding himself and his role as a responsible person. The development of personal responsibility should be considered as the development of a set of meanings and values having utilitarian as well as moral implications.

First, let us consider the growth of an understanding of cause and effect as a developmental variable. As he comes to grips with causality, the individual develops increasingly sophisticated attributions of cause of responsibility for the things that happen around him. In 1932, in *The Moral Judgment of the Child,*

Piaget delineated children's conceptions about rules, judgments, and related matters, and from this emerged statements about the progressive stages of moral development.[1] At a later date Heider (1958), using Piaget's stages as a base, proposed five levels of causality or attribution in ascending sequence from the most primitive to the most advanced. It is believed that children in the course of moral development progress from a very primitive undifferentiated attribution of the responsibility for, or the cause of, what happens to them or their environments to an advanced and highly differentiated attribution of responsibility. Theoretically, an adolescent normally should be progressing through the high levels of attribution and an adult should have achieved the highest level. Heider's levels are as follows:

Level 1 An individual is responsible if he is connected with an event in any way, whether or not he is present. A friend of a losing baseball pitcher is responsible for the loss of the game; a person passing a burning house is responsible for the fire. Objective causal connections are ignored.

Level 2 An individual is responsible for any of his acts whether or not he intended their consequences. If a child runs late at night from a curb into the side of a passing car, the driver is responsible.

Level 3 An individual is responsible for what he does if the consequences are foreseeable. It makes no difference whether or not he had foresight. The issue is that of the prudent man who *should* foresee.

Level 4 Given intention, an individual is responsible for acts to which the motive leads. Intention is the key to responsibility.

Level 5 If there is consensus, an individual shares responsibility for his act. That is, an individual is only partially responsible for an act, no matter what it is, if there is consensus that the act is justified. The environment as coercer is a sharer of responsibility.

[1]See the discussion in Chapter 14.

Shaw and Sulzer (1964) attempted to test the validity of the assumption of age-related progression through Heider's five levels. For subjects they used male and female second graders aged six to nine, and college students of both sexes aged nineteen to thirty-eight. Results, which produced no sex differences, only partially supported Heider's expectations. It would appear that children, as compared to late adolescents and adults, are indeed relatively undifferentiated where attribution of personal and environmental responsibility are concerned, although the differences between populations were not as great as expected. There was little support for the idea that coercion or provocation would mitigate attribution. The investigators write: "Adults (and late adolescents) seem to take circumstances into account when given credit but not when placing blame. Children, on the other hand, seem to reduce blame when the negative outcome is provoked." It would appear from this study that while age differences in sophistication of attribution do exist, attribution of responsibility is not purely a maturational variable, but is influenced by environmental circumstances. Shaw and Sulzer write: "It may be that children attribute responsibility on different bases for peers and adults. They apparently are more sophisticated or 'objective' when adult actors and activities are concerned but are more 'subjective' in evaluating peers." In a further study Shaw (1968) used as subjects a group of younger adolescents, aged eleven to sixteen, and reports that "adolescents do consider the structural and outcome variables in attributing responsibility to others for their actions." In other studies Shaw and Reitan (1967) and Shaw, Briscoe, and Garcia-Esteve (1968) indicate no essential differences in levels of attribution of responsibility between adolescents and adults except at Level 3 where adolescents tended to attribute relatively little responsibility for foreseen but intended positive outcomes. It is Shaw's contention that such a difference is an indication of the adolescents' tendency to set high standards for themselves as well as for others, an observation in line with Hurlock's (1968) hypothesis of the adolescent as reformer.

Of especial importance in considering the developmental nature of attribution of responsibility is a finding reported by Shaw (1968) and by Shaw, Briscoe, and Garcia-Esteve (1968) that cross-cultural differences exist in attribution. They reported that mainland Americans as compared to Puerto Ricans attributed greater responsibility for intentional outcomes, whether or not they are justified. Shaw (1968) notes that this finding "appears to be consistent with the hypothesis that attribution of responsibility is influenced by the child-rearing practices of the culture in which the individual resides."

Developmentally, then, it would appear that while maturational factors affect young children's attribution of responsibility where adolescents are concerned, environmental experience replaces maturation as the central issue. Whether he does or not, there is no maturational reason why an adolescent cannot operate at the highest of Heider's five levels if his experiential background is appropriate. That being true, it follows that there is no reason why an adolescent may not attribute responsibility to himself as a self-meaning to the point where he begins to assume a set of identities characteristic of a responsible person and to exemplify them in his role behavior. Given Piaget's stage of operational thought as a characteristic of the adolescent period, it should be possible for the adolescent to conceive of himself as a responsible person in abstract terms to the point that responsibility for self and others becomes internalized as part of his value system.

Facilitation and Responsibility

What sequence of events would appear to be facilitative in the development of responsibility? Probably first of all the adolescent needs to develop or to have developed a sense of personal control over the events of his environment. As a matter of fact, there has been considerable interest, as an explanatory behavior variable, in the extent to which an individual believes that his reinforcements (that is, what happens to him as a result of what he does) are contingent upon his own behavior or whether they are independent of it. Persons seeing results as stemming from their own efforts have been called "internals," while those who believe agents outside themselves are the causal agents are called "externals."

It may be assumed that the normally developing child increasingly gains mastery over his environment with increasing age. That being true, the child would more and more come to feel that events were under his control and that chance was less and less a factor in dealing with the environment. Penk (1969) tested this hypothesis with a group of seven- to eleven-year-olds and reports confirming evidence of a "significant relationship between levels of verbal abstraction and internal-external control." DiStefano et al. (1971), using a sample of adolescents, report a significant linear relationship for external-internal controls as a function of increasing age. Hence, it might be expected that a normally developing adolescent as he increases in age will increasingly come to see environmental rewards as susceptible to internal controls.

An adolescent's externality-internality status should have implications not only for his general personality style but for his role behavior in most of the enterprises in which he engages. Certainly, expectation of success or failure as a direct result of one's own efforts can be expected to produce a different pattern of behavior than an expectation that one's efforts are irrelevant in the face of controlling circumstances. McGhee and Crandall (1968) state the internality expectation for school performance when they write:

It seems probable that the degree to which a child believes that his own behavior is responsible for his academic successes and failures will affect his instrumental effort to attain these goals. The child who feels that success or failure is a consequence of his own behavior should show greater initiative in seeking intellectual rewards and greater effort and persistence in intellectual tasks and situa-ations. Put conversely, the external child, who feels that his rewards and punishments are given to him at the whim or design of other people or circumstances, has little reason to exert effort in an attempt to increase the probability of obtaining reward and avoiding punishment.

Research studies in general confirm the school performance hypothesis, although there are some differential aspects. In two studies, using subjects from elementary through high school, McGhee and Crandall (1968) report that the high-internal child consistently attains higher academic performance scores, although there is greater consistency of prediction for grades received than for achievement-test scores. Since grades usually represent teachers' per-ceptions of a child's entire performance rather than just test results it may have been that the grades were reflections of the internal child's effort. Digman (1972), in a study re-lating school achievement (as represented by grade-point average) to eleven personality traits, reports industriousness and intelligence as most centrally related to grade-point aver-age. Coleman et al. (1966), in a nationwide study of black and white children in grades six, nine, and twelve, reports internality as responsible for more of the variance of the black children's achievement scores than any other situational or personal variable included in the study. In the case of white children in-cluded in the study, externality stood as the second most predictive variable of achieve-ment performance. Crandall, Katkovsky, and Preston (1962) found that high-internal boys but not girls tended to spend more free time playing in activities of an intellectual nature and showed greater drive in carrying out those activities.

A concluson to be drawn from the foregoing discussion on attribution of responsibility and internality is that an adolescent, to be charac-terized as responsible, must be able to attribute responsibility at higher levels of conceptualiza-tion, must have internalized responsibility as a self-meaning, and must be internal in the

sense that he believes events can be changed and new conditions brought about as the result of his own efforts. Studies in the development of responsibility in children and adolescents have also pointed to the importance of child-rearing practices and parental relationships, willingness to delay immediate gratification for future gains, and the development of internal controls. Meyer and Wacker (1970), using as subjects a group of nine- to eleven-year-old boys, studied the development of a sense of responsibility for success and failure as it re-lated to parent-child interaction. They report that responsibility was more likely to develop to a higher degree in a family whose child-rearing practices were permissive than in those where practices were restrictive. A high degree of child responsibility in permissive families was correlated with the extension of appropriate independence at intermediate ages. On the other hand, in restrictive families the child's assumption of responsibility was rela-tively less, no matter at what age training for responsibility took place. In general, maternal expectations were more important than pa-ternal prohibitions in responsibility assump-tion. The investigators concluded that the optimum age at which independence could be extended was specific to the developmental age of the child, as well as to the child-rearing practices of his parents. Smith (1966), ana-lyzing the personality profiles of high school seniors of both sexes in relation to their fathers' occupations, found that children from professional home backgrounds were higher in "responsibility" as well as in "emotional stabil-ity" and "ascendency."

There can be little doubt that both impulsive-ness and desire for immediate gratification are highly related to responsibility. Mischel and Metzner (1962), in a study in which subjects were allowed a choice between a smaller im-mediate reinforcement or a larger reinforce-ment promised at a later time, note that willingness to postpone gratification is posi-tively related to social responsibility and nega-tively to delinquent behavior. Spivack and Levine (1971) presented a task involving increasing tension to a matched pair of groups of adolescents, one rated as impulsive and one as not impulsive. Impulsive adolescents were found to be less tolerant of physical discomfort and less willing to carry a task to completion. The authors speculate that an understanding of the mechanism determining tolerance for physical discomfort may contribute to an understanding of the mechanisms determining self-control—and by analogy, since self-control and deferment of gratification are logically related, to willingness to assume responsibility.

In psychological literature dealing with deferred-gratification research, writers have customarily linked deferment of gratification and socioeconomic class. Remmers, Horton, and Lysgaard (1952) and Schneider and Lysgaard (1953) report that upper socioeconomic children tend to accept deferred gratification as a way of life. Such an attitude defers present satisfaction for future pleasure or gain, such as saving for something to be used later, studying now for future use, deferring sexual relationships, and withholding judgment and immediate punitive action.

Straus (1962) and Stacy (1965) point to the fact that need deferment is functional for social mobility in the United States. And here, at the very beginning, we find the lower-class adolescent penalized in his hopes of social mobility by his very upbringing. Kohn (1959) reports working-class adults as usually more concerned with the immediate consequences of their children's actions than are middle-class parents, while the latter place greater emphasis upon the inculcation of abstract moral principles whose application is future as well as present oriented. Even in immediate family relationships, as Ansari and Ghose (1957) note, higher-class children begin earlier to repress and sublimate basic emotions. Thus, reared in a milieu that emphasizes the attainment of immediate as compared to long-term values, the lower-class adolescent must often look outside his family for support and reinforcement of long-term plans requiring denial of immediate satisfactions. For example, upwardly mobile youth need to find someone outside their family to give support and direction to their college plans. Ellis and Lane (1963) report that the best source for such outside support is the teacher. This does not mean that the lower-class family necessarily opposes an adolescent's further education; on the contrary, it may actively desire it. It is simply that the immediate as compared to the longer-term outlook is a conditioning factor that makes it more difficult for the lower-class youth to implement his plans. When active family support is given, it usually stems from the mother. Bennett and Gist (1964), using a sample of 800 urban high school students, found that maternal influence appeared to be stronger and more effective at lower-class levels, regardless of the child's sex. Ellis and Lane (1963), in a study of 194 lower-class-origin students at Stanford, note that it is the mother more often than the father whose reaction to the family's status in life is the catalyst for upward mobility. But even when upward mobility does occur, it brings its penalties. For example, in a study of 327 female college students, Hass (1966) reports that first-generation middle-class students (that is, from lower-class parents) were significantly more hostile on most measures than were second-generation middle-class students (that is, from middle-class parents).

In interpreting the preceding discussion on social class and deferment of gratification, it should be kept in mind that the statements are normative statements and do not rule out individual deviations. History bears ample witness to the presence of such deviations. Also, the research was performed in the 1950s and 1960s. As we proceed through the 1970s, it still seems to represent the situation, but new trends are discernible that may alter the picture to some extent if they continue. One new factor is that an appreciable number of white middle-class youth appear to be rejecting at least elements of the way of life of their parents and are refusing to follow patterns of behavior and education that will enable them to retain middle-class status after their parents' money is exhausted. Their number is not as large as the publicity they receive would indicate, nor is it certain whether this attitude will endure into adulthod. But whether or not it endures, the fact remains that some youth are denying themselves at a critical time in their lives the education and experiences necessary for eventual assumption of professional and other jobs needing high levels of skill and long periods of training. Obviously, if society is to be maintained either as we now know it or at any level of technical efficiency in some other system, someone will have to step into the gap being left by these downwardly mobile youth.[2]

The discussion to this point may have given the impression that acceptance of responsibility, with its frequently attendant necessity to defer gratification, is necessarily unpleasant. Actually, while it does have its unpleasant aspects, deferment may introduce compensatory pleasant fringe benefits. For example, Phillips (1966) reports that in a college setting the greater the frequency with which social gratification was deferred, the greater was the expression of satisfaction with the academic side of college. But balanced against this compensatory benefit were both a lower state of mental health and a lower level of satisfaction with the social side of college. The answer, in child rearing as well as in school practice, is to avoid single-minded concentration on one aspect of an individual's life at the expense of all others. Specific education for responsibility need not eliminate all other aspects.

Inculcation of Responsibility

What specific things can a teacher or parent, bearing in mind what has already been said,

[2]The argument has been advanced that such downwardly mobile youth are in effect more responsible than those who bow to the demands of middle-class culture and that they are humanity's hope for the future. The argument goes that their responsibility assumes the character of living what is defined as a personally meaningful life and, in some cases, of helping to convince a materialistic culture of the error of its ways. In some cases this may well be true, but in general the writer does not find the argument convincing, although he sometimes sympathizes with some aspects of it.

do to promote assumption of responsibility in an adolescent? Probably most efficacious of all is simply to induct the adolescent into responsibility by giving him responsibility, that is, to allow him maximum autonomy and independence just as early as he can assume it.

This giving of responsibility should not be a chance affair but should come as the result of careful parental planning. Parents might well ask: "How soon can we possibly permit Johnnie to do this or that?" and "What opportunities can be deliberately provided that will permit him to act independently and to acquire experiences that will promote his maturity and self-reliance?" As Campanelle (1965) notes, parents should help the adolescent accept responsibilities and develop self-direction. They should serve as consultants as well as be available in time of need. The schools, of course, should do likewise. Unfortunately, most parents tend to underestimate their adolescent's stage of development and his desire and capacity for independence and autonomy; they become too protective or restrictive for the boy's or girl's "own good." As has been said, an inexperienced, immature person needs certain protections and gradual inductions, but it is equally true that experience does not come if it is permanently withheld. The responsibility given adolescents during war shows the possibilities of accelerating maturity.

Parents and others might be more successful in dealing with adolescents' values and attitudes if they would include the adolescents in decision-making processes and deliberately give them training in making valid decisions for themselves. Sanford (1967) notes that the development of full social responsibility requires experience in social action or in actions helpful to other people. As Sanford sees it, an adolescent needs this participative experience in order to test the adequacy of his judgments and to familiarize himself with the limits of what he can do. And, of course, he needs support in carrying out the decisions arrived at if they are to maintain. Newcomb (1963) notes that a recently changed attitude is likely to persist if one of its behavioral expressions is the selection of a social environment that supports the changed attitudes.

Lindenauer (1969) describes a program for teachers to show students what responsibility is and how to assume it. He advises breaking the teaching process down into four steps through which students proceed at their own rate. His steps, which involve giving students responsibility for themselves by giving them responsible roles in the educative decision-making process as well as in its implementation are (1) acceptance of students as coplanners by the staff, (2) personal involvement of staff with students, (3) student recognition of rules and limits, and (4) active cooperative participation by the students in the ongoing process of their education. Lindenauer's suggestion is, of course, quite reminiscent of the move for student involvement in the planning aspects of higher education.

Some parents and teachers will wish to stop short of family and school participative responsibility as a method of training for responsibility. This is unfortunate since it reduces them to a less holistic didactic or presentation-of-example approach in place of the more applied "laboratory" approach of participation and experiences.[3] Too much has been written on verbal reasoning and on modeling as vehicles for behavior and attitude change to allow review here, but a study of Staub (1972) is indicative. He explored the relative effectiveness of verbal communication and of modeling as a means of changing children's attitudes and related behaviors. Using 267 seventh-grade boys and girls as subjects, Staub studied the effects of both verbal communication and modeling on his subjects' willingness to delay gratification by choosing delayed rewards as compared to immediately available smaller rewards. In this experiment modeling consisted of the behavioral example, without verbal exchange, of a model. Verbal persuasion consisted of giving subjects reasons for delaying gratification. In general, verbal persuasion did promote positive attitudes toward gratification delay on the part of girls, but was less successful with boys. On the other hand, modeling increased gratification delay on the part of boys, but not of girls. The authors conclude that verbal persuasion is a useful agent of behavioral change and that it appears to get better general results than does modeling. It is interesting that the change techniques had greater effects on attitudes than on behavior. As might be expected, a temptation actually present is harder to resist than a hypothetical one. It is clear from Staub's experiment that content of a verbal communication is important and is most successful when it is directed at the subject's rather than at the communicator's preferences. Staub makes the point that while a verbal communication containing reasons in favor of delaying gratification was successful, one "containing the description of the favorable attitudes and feelings of the communicator toward delaying gratification had no effect on delay behavior." In general, psychological research has offered confirming evidence for Staub's findings. Hoffman (1970), in reviewing the literature on the development of morality in children, notes that reasoning with children has good chances of success when it includes a description of the possible consequences of the child's actions.

Parents and others dealing with adolescents should be encouraged to know that verbal persuasion can be effective with children, as in Staub's study, in the eleven- to thirteen-year age range. However, they should know that it is best to rely on concrete cause-and-effect arguments and to avoid such statements as "because it would please me." Older children who have entered the stage of operational

---

[3] Some of the arguments against participative responsibility have their own validity. Some parents claim that it complicates their personal lives and that family living is less efficient and perhaps less pleasurable with participative responsibility, and others say they are simply abdicating their responsibility as parents or that children will become "masters in their own homes." Some schools feel that children or adolescents lack the experience or motivation to be allowed planning participation. They feel that as experienced educators they are capable of running the school and are paid to do so without interference from those who come to them to learn. And some children find responsibility too demanding, preferring not to be given responsibility.

thinking are capable of dealing with more hypothetical reasons, but with their more well-defined emancipative drives, they can be expected to be even less impressed with the communicator's preferences. Still, a great deal depends on the communicator and the history of his relationships with the child. Staub's finding on the lesser effectiveness of modeling is based upon the presence of the experimenter. Very different results might have been obtained from different modeling approaches. As a matter of fact, there is reason to believe that modeling under proper circumstances can be an effective agent of change. In the area of responsibility, there is no reason why a parent might not use both modeling and verbal persuasion and then allow the child to implement the hoped-for behavior change or growth by placing him in situations where he actually has responsibility.

Summary

Willingness to assume responsibility is a developmental task of adolescence. There are two quite different kinds of responsibility: interior responsibility and exterior responsibility. Interior responsibility represents an internal caretaker need, while exterior responsibility involves responsibility to others. Intrinsically motivated responsibility is selfless in its ultimate expression, in that aggrandizement of the self is not involved.

There are various levels of responsibility, ranking from task orientation to focus upon benefit to others. Dependability is one outcome of responsibility with self-dependability representing the most mature level of dependability. The highest level of responsibility assumption is a basic attribute of positively oriented leadership as well as of those who wish to help others. In contrast to responsibility, irresponsibility is characterized by superficiality, lack of emotional control, and a unilateral striving for ease, pleasure, and one's own way, either at the expense of or with total disregard for higher values, the rights and preferences of others, or even the demands of everyday reality.

For an individual to be capable of responsible behavior, he must have reached a stage at which responsibility is cognitively possible. The development of personal responsibility should be considered as the development of a set of meanings and values having utilitarian as well as moral implications. Heider has proposed five levels of causality for attribution of responsibility in ascending sequence from the most primitive to the most advanced. At the lowest level, an individual is seen as responsible if he is connected with an event in any way. At the highest level, an individual shares responsibility for his act if there is consensus. However, cross-cultural differences exist in the attribution of responsibility, a situation that apparently arises because of differences in child-rearing practices in different cultures. There is no reason why an adolescent may not attribute responsibility to himself as a self-meaning to the point where he begins to assume a set of identities characteristic of a responsible person and to exemplify them in his role behavior.

In optimum development of responsibility, an adolescent needs to acquire a sense of personal control over the events of his environment, a situation that occurs with increasing age as the individual learns that chance is less and less a factor in dealing with the environment. Hence, a normally developing adolescent as he increases in age will increasingly come to see environmental rewards as susceptible to internal controls. Other things being equal, the high-internal-control child is more likely to display responsibility and to attribute responsibility properly than is the externally controlled child or one whose internality is less well developed. An adolescent, to be characterized as responsible, must be able to attribute responsibility at higher levels of conceptualization, must have internalized responsibility as a self-meaning, and must be internal in the sense that he believes events to be changed and new conditions brought about as the result of his own efforts.

Both impulsiveness and desire for immediate gratification are highly related to responsibility, with ability to defer gratification and restrain impulsivity acting as foundations in responsibility assumption. On the whole, middle-class youth have demonstrated a greater tendency to be able to defer gratification, but it should be understood that it is not inevitable that a given middle-class individual will be able

to defer, any more than it is that a lower-class individual will be unable to defer.

The most efficacious means of inducting an adolescent into responsible behavior is to provide him with responsibility. He should be given a maximum of autonomy and independence just as early as he can assume it. Teachers and parents would do well to provide educative and child-rearing experiences that provide increasing opportunities for the exercise of responsibility.

References

Ansari, A., and Ghose, B. A study of family attitudes of children with contrasting socioeconomic backgrounds. *Educational Psychology* (Delhi), 4 (1957): 90–102.

Bennett, W. S., Jr., and Gist, N. P. Class and family influences on student aspiration. *Social Forces* 43 (1964): 167–173.

Campanelle, T. Achieving emotional independence in adolescence. *National Catholic Conference Journal* 9 (1965): 165–170.

Coleman, J. S.; Campbell, E. O.; Hobson, C. J.; McPartland, J.; Mood, A. M.; Weinteld, F. D.; and York, R. L. *Equality of educational opportunity.* Washington: Government Printing Office, 1966.

Crandall, V. J.; Katkovsky, W.; and Preston, A. Motivational and ability determinants of young childrens' intellectual achievement behaviors. *Child Development* 33 (1962): 643–661.

Digman, J. M. High school academic achievement as seen in the context of a longitudinal study of personality. *Proceedings of the annual convention of the American Psychological Association* (1972), pp. 19–20.

DiStefano, M. K.; Pryer, M. W.; and Smith, C. E. Comparisons of normal adolescents, psychiatric patients, and adults on internal-external control. *Journal of Clinical Psychology* 27 (1971): 343–345.

Ellis, R. A.; and Lane, W. C. Structural supports for upward mobility. *American Sociological Review* 28 (1963): 743–756.

Hass, K. Social correlates of hostility in a college sample. *British Journal of Social and Clinical Psychology* 5 (1966): 200–206.

Heider, F. The *psychology of interpersonal relations.* New York: Wiley, 1958.

Hoffman, M. Moral development. In Mussen, P. H., ed., *Manual of child psychology.* New York: Wiley, 1970.

Hurlock, E. B. The adolescent reformer. *Adolescence* 3 (1968): 273–306.

Kohn, M. L. Social class and parental values. *American Journal of Sociology* 64 (1959): 337–351.

Lindenauer, G. G. Teaching students responsibility. *Journal of Emotional Education* 9 (1969): 128–134.

McGhee, P. E., and Crandall, V. C. Beliefs in internal-external control of reinforcements and academic performance. *Child Development* 39 (1968): 91–102.

McLuhan, M. *Understanding media: The extensions of man.* New York: New American Library, 1964.

Meyer, W. V., and Wacker, A. Origin of perceived self-responsibility as a function of age for independence training. *Archiv fur Psychologie* 122 (1970): 24–39.

Mischel, W., and Metzner, R. Preference for delayed reward as a function of age, intelligence, and length of delay interval. *Journal of Abnormal and Social Psychology* 64 (1962): 425–431.

Newcomb, T. M. Persistence and regression of changed attitudes: Long-range studies. *Journal of Social Issues* 19 (1963): 3–14.

Penk, W. E. Age changes and correlates of internal-external locus of control scale. *Psychological Reports* 25 (1969): 856.

Phillips, D. L. Deferred gratification in a college setting: Some costs and gains. *Social Problems* 13 (1966): 333–343.

Piaget, J. *The moral judgment of the child*. New York: Harcourt, Brace, 1932.

Remmers, H. H.; Horton, R. E.; and Lysgaard, S. Teen-age personality in our culture. *Purdue Opinion Panel*, report of poll no. 32, 1952.

Sanford, N. The development of social responsibility. *American Journal of Orthopsychiatry* 37 (1967): 22–29.

Schneider, L., and Lysgaard, L. The deferred gratification pattern: A preliminary study. *American Sociological Review* 18 (1953): 142–149.

Shaw, M. E. Attribution of responsibility by adolescents in two cultures. *Adolescence* 3 (1968): 23–32.

Shaw, M. E.; Briscoe, M. E.; and Garcia-Esteve, J. A cross-cultural study of attribution of responsibility. *International Journal of Psychology* 3 (1968): 51–60.

Shaw, M. E., and Reitan, H. T. Attribution of responsibility and sanctioning behavior in different occupational groups. *Research Report* no. 4, NSF Grant GS-647, University of Florida, 1967.

Shaw, M. E., and Sulzer, J. L. An empirical test of Heider's levels in attribution of responsibility. *Journal of Abnormal and Social Psychology* 69 (1964): 39–46.

Smith, P. M., Jr. Personality rating of students whose fathers are professional or non-professional workers. *California Journal of Educational Research* 37 (1966): 793–810.

Spivack, G., and Levine, M. Tolerance for discomfort among impulsive adolescent boys. *Perceptual and Motor Skills* 33 (1971): 898.

Stacy, B. G. Some psychological aspects of intergeneration occupational mobility. *British Journal of Social and Clinical Psychology* 4 (1965): 275–286.

Staub, E. Effects of persuasion and modeling on delay of gratification. *Developmental Psychology* 6 (1972): 166–177.

Straus, M. A. Deferred gratification, social class, and the achievement syndrome. *American Sociological Review* 27 (1962): 326–335.

Wheelis, A. *The quest for identity*. New York: Norton, 1958.

Suggested Readings

Bandura, A., and Walters, R. *Social learning and personality development*. New York: Holt, Rinehart and Winston, 1963.

Carlson, J. S. Moral development of Lao children. *International Journal of Psychology* 8 (1973): 25–35.

Clifford, M. M. How learning and liking are related: A clue. *Journal of Educational Psychology* 64 (1973): 183–186.

Cohen, L.; Reid, I.; and Boothroyd, K. Validation of the Mehrabian need for achievement scale with college of education students. *British Journal of Educational Psychology* 43 (1973): 269–278.

Crandall, V. V.; Katkovsky, W.; and Crandall, V. J. Children's beliefs in their own control of reinforcement in intellectual academic achievement situations. *Child Development* 36 (1965): 91–109.

Davis, W. C., and Phares, E. Parental antecedents of internal-external control of reinforcement. *Psychological Reports* 24 (1969): 427–436.

Felker, D. W.; Stanwyck, D. J.; and Kay, R. S. The effects of a teacher program in self-concept enhancement on pupils' self-concept, anxiety and intellectual achievement responsibility. *Journal of Educational Research* 66 (1973): 443–445.

Fisbbein, M., and Ajzen, I. Attribution of responsibility: A theoretical note. *Journal of Experimental Social Psychology* 9 (1973): 148–153.

Gutkin, D. C. An analysis of the concept of moral intentionality. *Human Development* 16 (1973): 371–381.

Hall, H. V. Effects of direct and self-reinforcement as a function of internal-external control. *Perceptual and Motor Skills* 37 (1973): 753–754.

Heibrun, A. B. Parental model attributes, nurturant reinforcement and consistency of behavior in adolescents. *Child Development* 35 (1964): 151–167.

Hovland, C. L., and Janis, I. J. *Personality and persuasibility*. New Haven: Yale University Press, 1959.

Hyman, R. T. Individualization: The hidden agenda. *Elementary School Journal* 73 (1973): 412–423.

Katkovsky, W.; Crandall, V. J.; and Good, S. Parental antecedents of children's beliefs in internal-external controls of reinforcement in intellectual achievement situations. *Child Development* 28 (1967) : 765–776.

Krebs, D. L. Altruism—An examination of the concept and a review of the literature. *Psychological Bulletin* 73 (1970) : 258–302.

MacDonald, A. P., Jr. Internal-external locus of control: Parental antecedents. *Journal of Consulting and Clinical Psychology* 37 (1971): 141–147.

Mischel, W. Theory and research on the antecedents of self-imposed delay of reward. In Maher, B. A., ed., *Progress in experimental personality research.* New York: Academic Press, 1966.

Nowicki, S., and Roundtree, J. Correlates of locus of control in a secondary school population. *Developmental Psychology* 4 (1971): 477.

Nowicki, S. and Segal, W. Perceived parental characteristics, locus of control orientation, and behavioral correlates of locus of control. *Developmental Psychology* 10 (1974): 33–37.

Schneider, F. N. When will a stranger lend a helping hand? *Journal of Social Psychology* 90 (1973) : 335–336.

Solomon, D.; Houlihan, K. A.; and Parelius, R. J. Intellectual achievement responsibility in Negro and white children. *Psychological Reports* 24 (1969) : 479–483.

Wilson, S. R. Psychosomatic symptoms and reactions against the university. *Journal of College Student Personnel* 13 (1972): 551–555.

PART FIVE

The Psychobiology of Adolescence

Chapter Seventeen

Physical Growth

The Relation of Physical Growth to Adolescent Psychology

Since an individual or group can be understood mainly in terms of its developmental history, whether that history be biological, social, or psychological, it is desirable now to examine the relation of physical growth and development to adolescent psychology. An individual is a combination of what has happened to him in the past. His present self has been molded and shaped by past events. He will succeed and adjust to the present insofar as his past has given him the qualities and experience that will permit him to do so. And to the extent that the past has presented him with an anomaly—biological, social, or psychological—then to that extent will his adjustment be more difficult in the present.

If physical and physiological changes during adolescence were merely a matter of changing structure and function, one could simply describe and record them and then pass on to other topics. However, actual structural or functional change is only the beginning from which evolve social behavior, attitude toward self and others, and the entire constellation of values that give meaning and guidance to an adolescent's life. An individual's rate and direction of maturing may have significant effects upon his social acceptance and status, upon the efficiency of his participation in various activities, and in all probability, upon his emotional adjustment, insofar as a deviate physical status may make him conspicuous or prevent him from doing the things he feels are important.

But the matter is a reciprocal one. If social and psychological events are conditioned by physical growth, physical growth in its turn may be affected by social and psychological events. Growth is more than an internally engendered individual affair. It is also an affair of the environment and the culture and is thus influenced by them. The expenditure of energy and the reserves from which any given individual expends his energy are examples. Physical growth is an energy-consuming process. Individuals who expend undue amounts of energy, or those who, for other reasons, do not process sufficient energy to meet cultural demands, have available only a minimal reserve for the processes of growth. Writing on the subject, Garn (1954) notes:

The middle-class child, reared by moderately authoritarian and relatively apprehensive parents (by global standards), is protected from over-exertion. His play periods are timed, naps are enforced, and care is taken to insure uninterrupted slumber. Children of the lower classes, on the other hand, are treated in more permissive fashion, with less emphasis on rest and a more lenient attitude toward bedtime. Therefore, though the caloric intake may be comparable in the two groups, the caloric expenditure is not. And the difference, caloric intake minus caloric expenditure, represents the energy reserve available for tissue maintenance and growth. In some cultures even less attention is paid to rest. An African settlement or a Balinese village may operate on a 24-hour schedule with events of interest all the while.

There, uninterrupted sleep may be a rarity for the children, with the cat-naps alternating with participation in the village night-life. Such practices further increase the energy expenditure, leaving a minimal reserve for the process of growth. Besides, the temperature of the home may play an important role. Energy metabolism and temperature are inversely related. As the temperature falls, considerable energy is utilized in maintaining body temperature and in insensible shivering. Under these circumstances the high October-through-April temperatures of the American household (which distress visiting Europeans so markedly) may have a hothouse effect on the children, allowing the maximum usage of the energy intake for growth.

Thus, physiological and physical changes have wide repercussions in terms of the social and psychological behavior and the attitudes toward self and environment they engender. And to some extent cultural factors relate to the course and direction of physical growth. Hence, the student of adolescent psychology needs to know as much as he can about physical development so he may be more adequately qualified to understand and interpret the psychological behavior of the individual and the group.

Many exceedingly difficult problems confront the psychologist who wishes to investigate the facts of human development. In the first place, the process of differentiation and development is highly complex. Second, unlike the physical scientist, the psychologist working in the field of human growth finds it particularly difficult to control his observations and the many variables that have an impact on physical growth. Finally, there is the variability to which the quantitative measures of human growth are subject owing to the very nature of growth and differentiation.

The Concept of a Physical Self

One of the more visible aspects of the adolescent period is the accelerated rate of growth and change that occurs just prior to puberty and continues, at a lessening rate, through the middle teens. We are all familiar with the child who grows several inches during a brief summer vacation. We have all noted the comparatively sudden appearance of secondary sex characteristics. To the adult observer, such sudden growth spurts and transitions are sometimes startling and often, unfortunately, humorous. To the adolescent the changes are seldom humorous; they are often startling and even disquieting. If one has been five feet tall and has grown accustomed to that height, it takes more than a little equanimity to grow accustomed to the six extra inches that come fairly suddenly. This is especially true as one's trousers or skirts become far too short and as wrists tend to extend naked below the ends of one's sleeves. It is particularly unfortunate that such acceleration of growth comes at a time when the adolescent is in process of arriving at a satisfactory concept of self and when he may well be emotionally upset as he endeavors to learn new roles and to cope with the new status and experiences the advent of puberty has thrust upon him. But, difficult as such growth acceleration may be for the normally developing adolescent, the problem is compounded if the growth represents a marked deviation from what is happening to the rest of the peer group, as, for example, excessive overall growth or excessive growth of some significant part, such as the breasts or the penis. Such deviation may result in loss of self-esteem, undue self-consciousness, and even in unwholesome adaptations or efforts at compensation.

It is characteristic of human beings to have a concept of physical self, including a body image. The idea of a body image, first developed by Schilder (1935) and elaborated by Kolb (1959) and Schonfeld (1963), posits the body image as evolving from internalized psychological factors, cultural influences, concepts of the ideal body, and an individual's personal perception of his body appearance and its functional ability. In a real sense the body may be thought of as the symbol of the self.

When physical changes or additions occur that require radical revision in one's physical self-concept, it is usually difficult to adjust to the new physical actuality as well as to the new physical self-concept that actuality involves. An adult who finds himself putting on weight, balding, losing youthful good looks, or accumulating physical disabilities is in somewhat the same situation as the adolescent who is also undergoing physical changes that appear to be out of control. Perhaps it is more difficult for the adolescent to adjust to physical change than it is for the adult, because the adolescent is less apt to be prepared for the changes or to recognize their true meaning. There is also the additional factor that the adolescent's values may be such that he overestimates the importance of physical things and is less willing to accept the changes than an adult would be.

Consider, too, the pathetic case of the person who refuses to accept changed physical reality or who is sincerely unaware that personal physical changes have occurred, even though they are apparent to every casual observer. Such an individual may persist in playing a role formerly permitted by his earlier physical status, or may continue to visualize himself in terms of his former physical status. We often hear the phrase, "Act your age." Sometimes we see an older adolescent or even an adult attempting to wear clothing or assume activities much more appropriate to an earlier age. Such behavior is often noticed in adults nearing middle age who still persist in thinking of themselves as "younger" men or women. It is not easy for an adult to visualize himself as being as old as his contemporaries. We tend to be "young at heart," if not in physical fact. However, growing older is not uniformly resisted by adolescents. A case in point is the eagerness with which boys scan their faces, hoping for a crop of whiskers to shave. It is not necessarily growing older that is disturbing; it is sudden growth changes and unforeseen disadvantages or changes conflicting with one's aspirations that provide the disturbing element. It is a truism that many people spend the first half of their lives wishing they looked older and the second half wishing they looked younger.

As the child endeavors to cope with such self terms as *self-control, self-denial, self-pity, self-reliance, self-respect,* and *self-reproach,* asking him to talk about the location of his own "self" is always interesting. Gesell and his coworkers (1956) asked subjects in their long-term study of children the following question: "If you had to locate your self at some point or place within your body, where would that place be?" In reporting some of the answers Gesell writes:

One 10-year-old replied quite interpretively, "In my fingers because I do more things with them." Brain, head, and mind were answers at all ages. The 11-year-old combined concepts such as "head and hands," "eyes and ears," "brain and heart." A 12-year-old more comprehensively replied with, "all of me." Thirteen, true to form, reflected intently and tended to emphasize thinking: "The way I think and my brain." Fourteen stressed emotion: "If in school some teacher reads good poetry I feel it right here," said one, pointing precisely to the epigastric region. Another said, "In your heart and soul and what you feel you can't locate it. It's in you, but it's not physical." Still another respondent, aged fifteen, pleased us with a developmental comment, "I suppose my brains is myself and about the center of most everyone. I suppose when I was little I used to say my stomach." Sixteen found the question "tough" or "funny." He could not answer with ease because he did not wish to separate any part from the whole. He tended to identify himself with his whole body. One boy replied, "It's located in the face—the most characteristic thing—the whole difference between people. That is what you think of when you think of others." Several significantly responded, "All parts."

The fact that one's own body is always an important element in the development of self-concepts may be observed in an infant. One of his tasks is that of separating his own body from his surroundings and recognizing it and its parts as his. The body, once closely defined as part of oneself, remains a source of interest and exploration throughout childhood and into

adolescence. This interest is perfectly natural
and is in no sense morbid or bad. It is simply
part of growing up and recognizing oneself as
oneself. If the child grows up in an environment in which physical things such as strength,
endurance, appearance, or health are held to be
important, then interest in the body will tend
to be even greater.

Preoccupation with Physical Changes

The already heightened awareness and body
focus of the adolescent becomes even more
acute as his or her body attracts attention and
possibly comments from adults and peers. This
becomes particularly true when sex desires
from and toward members of the opposite sex
become an issue. Such accentuation of the
adolescent's interest in bodily things may take
several forms, among them an increased interest in the opposite sex, in personal appearance
and development, in strength and endurance,
and in personal health. Of the foregoing ac-
centuations, possibly one of the most common,
and one which is most apparent to the observer,
is interest in members of the opposite sex.

With such changes of interest in the physical
aspects of sex, adolescents tend not only to
become interested in the physical presence of
others, but to think of their own bodies from
the viewpoint of others who may observe them.
There is a change from an egocentric preoccupation with one's body for its own sake, to a
preoccupation with one's body as it relates to
others. Motives are often mixed in a given individual, or they may vary from individual to
individual. The adolescent has conflicting desires. On the one hand, he wants to look well,
to attract, to display; on the other, he wants to
hide those physical attributes of which he is
ashamed. The latter attitude is, of course, built
upon misunderstanding, but it is real enough
when it exists. Many a girl whose breasts are
beginning to develop refuses to stand erect
when asked to recite in front of her class; she

slouches or slumps so that she will be less
"revealing." Other girls glory in their physical
changes and go to extreme lengths in wearing
tight clothing and other attention-attracting
devices to parade their new maturity. Both
attitudes are unhealthy, or at least the result
of misconception, and they may be attributed
to faulty education about the true meaning of
physical change. Parents and teachers may do
their adolescent charges considerable service if
they prepare them for physical change, explain
its meaning, and guide them toward an understanding of what may and what may not be
done. The problem of first menstruation for
girls or of first ejaculation for boys is often
one with which the individual is totally un-
prepared to cope. There may be unnecessary
misunderstanding, fear, or revulsion if the individual has not been properly prepared.

It should not be supposed that boys adjust
to physical changes any more easily than do
girls. Tight clothing that a boy feels is too
revealing, or the possibility of erotic arousal
and possible erection are a constant source of
worry to many male adolescents.[1] One boy
avoided reciting before his tenth-grade class to
the extent of playing truant whenever he
thought it likely that he would be called upon
to recite. In a discussion with the school
psychologist, he said that he was easily aroused
sexually and often experienced erection. He
was in constant terror lest this fact be noted,
particularly by members of the opposite sex.
There are a number of cases in which both
boys and girls have worn tight clothes, bands,
or supporters over what they considered to be
too prominent sex organs. There are also cases
in which artificial padding has been added as
an aid to too frugal nature. Sometimes a kind
of exhibitionism in dress or manner sponsored

[1]Of course a great deal depends upon the clothing styles
of a particular era. If styles and social acceptance demand
a form of exposure, the problem, for some, may be lessened
but for others it will be accentuated. As the 1970s proceeded, tight blue jeans for both sexes and no bras for
girls were considerably more revealing than the looser
clothing of the 1950s and early 1960s. We can at least be
certain that styles will continue to change and what is
true today will not be true tomorrow.

by the culture in advertisements, "style," or in other ways shows an exaggerated preoccupation with the physical self. A crowded beach can be a good observation post to witness examples of such exhibitionism. Perhaps the penchant in the United States and in some parts of western Europe for sun-bathing, although it has several origins, is in part a further example of physical self-preoccupation.

But sex is only one aspect of physical growth. Adolescents also find themselves preoccupied with their appearance and body functions. Such preoccupation sometimes occur for sex-attraction reasons, but sometimes for other reasons, one of the most common of which is to appear well and to stand revealed to others in accordance with one's self-concept. Physical preoccupation may be highly exaggerated, and if the actuality departs too far from the ideal concept, the adolescent may make intense efforts to improve reality. If improvement fails, then the next step may be pronounced feelings of insecurity, inferiority, and anxiety. At times it seems that an adolescent cannot let himself alone.

Facial features are particularly trying to adolescents. Unfortunately many adolescents have skin eruptions, pimples, blackheads, or skin blemishes of one kind or another. Such a condition is not inevitable and is often unnecessary. But that is not the issue. These skin eruptions and blemishes are a considerable source of embarrassment to them. There is a superstition (and it is only a superstition) that a person with facial eruptions either masturbates a great deal or is subject to one of the so-called social diseases, such as gonorrhea or syphilis. When an adolescent places such an interpretation upon his acne or skin blemishes, and when he feels that others are doing the same, it is little wonder that he will go to extreme lengths to rid himself of his "stigma." Clarence is an extreme case in point. As a high school sophomore, Clarence suffered emotionally from a particularly bad case of acne, pimples, and blackheads. One day he shaved his face closely with a safety razor. The results were severe.

Because they feel that appearance is so important, adolescents tend to devote a great deal of time to their faces. Parents of teenage girls know the long hours they spend before a mirror in their bedrooms, and in the bathroom too. Boys are not at all averse to looking in a mirror. Sometimes the reaction is one of great satisfaction and self-conceit, but more often some feature is settled upon as "impossible." Edward felt that his lips were too thick and for many months went about with them firmly compressed. Dave felt his curly hair was a severe cross to bear and continually pestered his mother to allow him to have it chopped close to his head so he could train it to grow straight. On the other hand, Joe felt his slightly curly hair made him look romantic and fell into the habit of assisting nature with a curling iron. To heighten the illusion he grew sideburns and tried, without much success, to start a mustache. Joe, of course, represents the present trend in which long hair and "assistance to nature" are becoming increasingly the fashion among many male adolescents. Some members of the new generation, emulating Samson, view long hair as a masculinity symbol.

Apparent anomalies of growth are also disturbing. The adolescents' difficulties include a changing voice, fuzz or miniature whiskers that misguided parents will not allow to be shaved, too rapid development of some parts of the body (long legs or big feet), too much fat, too slight a build, freckles, and dozens of other items. Almost any anomaly of development represents a potential source of embarrassment to the individual, if not of actual rejection by his peers.

Growth Curves

As explained previously, adolescence is a time of growth and differentiation. In some areas of development, it is just as much a time of cessation of growth or the initial attainment of maturity. For most of the growth processes, rapid growth in infancy and early childhood is succeeded by a plateau or period of slow growth until just before pubescence. At that time there is usually a spurt of rapid growth, succeeded by less rapid growth and gradual deceleration of the growth curve until middle or late adolescence. In late adolescence most growth curves cease or reach an asymptote, or, in the case of mental development and physiological capacity, start the long slow decline that lasts throughout maturity. In a few cases, such as the thymus, the decline starts earlier and is extremely rapid. Various studies have revealed overall patterns of growth, and one may speak of general curves of growth, as, for example, in weight, and even describe their course and general nature. Several figures that illustrate the course of growth will be given in this chapter.

In its ordinary presentation, a *growth curve* is a conventional age-size plot, with time as the horizontal coordinate and a measure of length, weight, or surface as the vertical. Such a curve characteristically shows an initial rapid rise that later falls off to a slope of zero. As reported in the literature, such a curve is used for illustrative purposes and presents an average picture of growth among the population it represents. Unfortunately, such illustrative curves, although they do give a "smoothed" picture of the course of growth, are inaccurate pictures of the growth of any individual whose growth curve involves points of inflection not paralleled by the curve of population growth. There are great individual differences due to both heredity and environment, and these differences are to be found not only in persons, but also in groups. To understand individual variations, one may think of growth in terms of timing. Everyone is growing, but some, proceeding at a more rapid rate than are others, will experience growth phenomena at an earlier chronological age than will their contemporaries of equal age. The curve of growth for any individual will include a series of discrete phases mediated by one or more of various growth-stimulating hormones, with structural linear growth being limited by epiphysial

union. In considering the growth curves presented in this text, the reader must understand that "typical" growth curves and average growth curves represent trends for a given population and lack validity as a representation of a single individual's growth. However, even a deviate individual will have a certain amount of company—we may think of groups of individuals who are homogeneous with respect to a given growth factor. Such individuals may be considered together and contrasted to other individuals who are homogeneous in another growth factor. Dearborn (1938), Shuttleworth (1938, 1939), and others in the Harvard Growth Study divided their sample into a number of different homogeneous groups in respect to the advent of the first menstruation. In their analysis of data, they considered each of these homogeneous groups as a separate and distinct population. Jones (1939), Bayley (1943a, 1943b), and others in the California Growth Study dealt with early- and late-maturing samples based on skeletal age. Other investigators have used similar devices.

Types of Growth Curves

It should not be assumed that there is any one standard curve for every aspect of growth. Different organs and different parts of the body grow and develop at different rates of speed, and their growth curves may take different forms. Loevinger (1966) notes that developmental processes may be represented by five different models based on rate, terminal status, terminal age of changes, monotonicity, and effects of disturbances in growth. Loevinger's models are shown in Figure 22. In the first four, the scale of growth is represented on the ordinate, and age is represented on the abscissa.

In Model I the final growth attained is the same for everyone, although different individuals proceed at different rates and reach the terminal level at different ages. Skeletal development follows the course of Model I. In Model II, rates also differ, but terminal age

Figure 22   *Loevinger's Models Representing Developmental Processes*

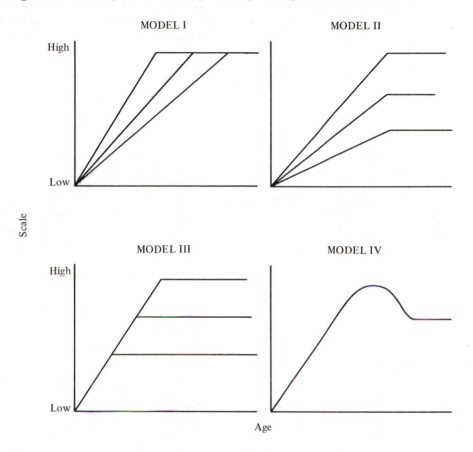

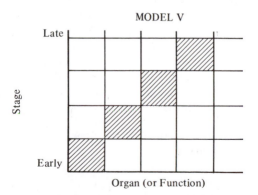

Source: Adapted from J. Loevinger, "Models and measures of developmental variation," in J. Brozek, ed., *The biology of human variation, Annals, New York Academy of Sciences* 134 (1966): 585–590, graphs on pp. 586–588. Reprinted by permission of the publisher and the author.

for growth is constant to the extent that adult differences may be predicted in childhood. With some minor variations, development of intelligence follows the course of Model II. In Model III, rate is the same for everyone, but terminal ages differ. Differences in adulthood reflect the age of cessation of growth. Loevinger (1966) writes:

To the extent that this model holds, early childhood differences for constant age are small and are not predictive of adult differences. This model has a special virtue. When it can be combined with a Model I process, giving essentially the percentage of adult growth achievement, then it again becomes possible to predict adult status. Height is determined by both Model II and Model III processes. Height differences in childhood are predictive of adult height differences, but the prediction can be improved by taking skeletal age into account, hence, predicting age of growth termination.

Model IV represents growth curves such as that of the thymus gland, for which the maximum value does not occur in adulthood. A common element of Models I through IV is that, as Loevinger points out, moderately severe growth disturbances may be compensated for so that they generally affect neither the unfolding pattern of growth nor the attainment of final adult status. Model V presents a situation in which growth disturbances do affect the pattern. In Model V, successive stages in development are defined by the predominance in the developing organism of different organs, organ-systems, or functions. If a disturbance in growth or an environmental insult (Selye 1956) does occur, its effect is on the organ predominant at that moment, the change effected is permanent, and the change will be reflected in all subsequent patterns. If an intact organ is necessary for future development of other organs or processes, then the developmental effects are obviously far reaching and irreversible.

Growth, as Tanner (1955) points out, is a form of motion over time. It may be measured over the life span of an individual in terms of distance traveled (at seventeen a boy may have attained six feet in height) or in terms of

velocity or rate of growth at any point or at a series of points (a sixteen-year-old may have attained his greatest velocity in his fourteenth year when he added nine centimeters to his height, as compared to his thirteenth year when he added seven, his fifteenth year when he added five, and his sixteenth year when he added two centimeters).

Thus, there are two ways in which to present growth data in the form of curves. The first, and the most familiar, is the distance curve. Such a curve is a picture of accumulation and/or decrease, showing as it does over sequential time the gross amount of growth that has occurred at each point on the curve. As one looks at the curve of increment, one may see how much growth has occurred and what the amount of accumulation of that growth has been at any point in the developmental sequence. Figure 23 is an example of a distance curve.

The second is a velocity curve, which depicts the rate of growth at any time, rather than its accumulation. It is sometimes desirable to know how fast growth is occurring at one time in the developmental sequence as compared to another time, and a velocity curve is used for this purpose. Figure 24 is an example of a velocity curve. In comparing the two curves, we notice that, as growth proceeds over the developmental sequence, each point on the distance curve represents simply an accumulation of all that has gone before, with the trend of the curve steadily upward[2] until a maximum point is reached. On the other hand, the velocity curve ignores accumulation as such and shows how fast the increment is occurring at any specified period of time as contrasted to any other time. Typically, velocity curves present a zigzag picture over their course. In general, curves of velocity yield more information in relating morphological to

[2]Obviously, growth may attain a plateau, or it may show decrements in which the trend is toward smaller or less, rather than toward more. In such cases, the curve will trend downward after a certain point. For example, in older persons there is a slight tendency toward decline in height. One whose maximum height may have been five feet seven inches may eventually measure five feet six inches. Here we will see a decline in the curve.

Figure 23 *A Distance Curve of Linear Growth in Height*

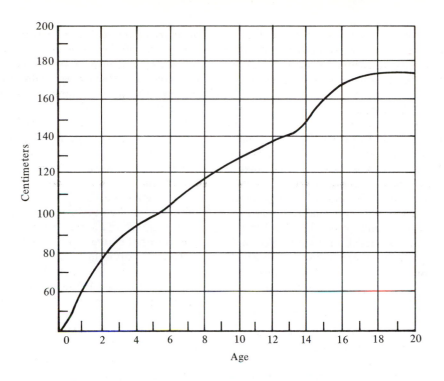

Figure 24 *A Velocity Curve of Linear Growth in Height*

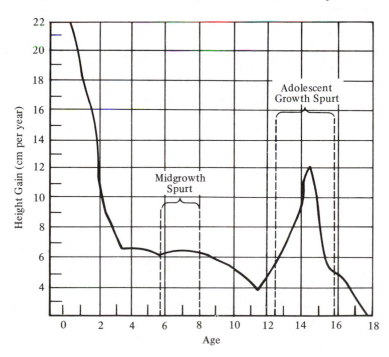

physiological circumstances than do distance curves, although the latter are most frequently encountered in the literature. A distance curve is essentially one of synthesis, while a velocity curve is analytic.

Physical growth ordinarily has been studied by means of growth increments in the various organs of the body, both internal and external, which may be measured by any one of three methods. First and most common is linear measurement of the length and width of growth increments or dimensions. Such linear growth may be most clearly observed and compared in measurements of standing height and sitting height. Second is areal or cross-sectional measurement, which concerns itself with areal increments or increases in body mass or volume. Such measurements most commonly include the area of various surfaces of the body, chest dimensions, and girth of arms, legs, hips, and so on. Third is ponderal measurement, which is concerned with growth in body or single organ weight and mass. Overall weight is an example of such measurement; it is concerned to a considerable extent with deposits of fatty tissue.

It is interesting to note that there are rather specific differences in growth patterns when they are considered from the aspect of areal as compared to linear or ponderal growth. One of the most outstanding contrasts occurs in increases (in relative postnatal increments) that take place between birth and early maturity. For example, growth in stature, which is one-dimensional, is 3.5-fold—that is, an individual increases in height 3.5 times his height at birth. In surface area, which is two-dimensional, growth is sevenfold. And finally, in weight, which is three-dimensional, the increase is 20-fold.

Longitudinal and Cross-sectional Measurement

Data for curves of growth may be gathered by longitudinal or by cross-sectional means. In the cross-sectional study, each individual is measured only once and average (mean) values are computed for each age. Thus, at one time in history a group of twelve-year-olds may be measured for their mean value in some aspect of growth at the same time that a group of thirteen-year-olds, or fourteen-year-olds, or fifteen-year-olds, and so on, are being measured. The resulting curve of growth shows the average picture of age-growth differences as these groups of different individuals are being compared.

In a longitudinal study each individual is measured as he attains each age to be included in the study. The resulting curve presents a picture of the same individuals rather than of different individuals. Longitudinal and cross-sectional data both have their values, but they provide different information. Cross-sectional studies present information about the distance curve of growth, as, for example, the average weight or height attained at various ages. Cross-sectional data provide normative[3] and clinical standards for growth achieved by average or healthy individuals and may be used in assessing the relative status of any given individual as he is compared with the norms. However, as Falkner (1966) notes, cross-sectional data can be misleading in that "average" curves can conceal as much as they reveal. The fact of individual differences conditions the generalizations that can be made about the course of development, particularly as they are applied to any given person. For example, while there is a preadolescent growth spurt, within this are individual patterns in

---

[3]One studying psychology is often confronted with the terms *standard* or *norm*—useful descriptive terms giving scientists and practitioners a basis for analysis and comparison of individuals or a way to present an overview, but nevertheless terms capable of misinterpretation and misunderstanding. In using a norm, it is essential to remember that there is wide variation in growth patterns, in developmental status, and in emotional maturity among individuals of any given category. In other words, around every norm is a normal permissible range, and any child's position within the permissible range is more important than is his position with reference to the midpoint. We should ask not whether an individual deviates from the midpoint but whether he deviates from the range that is permissible.

time of onset, and the average curve does not tell us everything that may be happening to an individual as the individual patterns are smoothed out and spread over time in the curve. Figure 25, which presents individual curves of height for three boys, together with an average curve compiled for the three individual curves, illustrates the concealment possibilities of the average curve.

Longitudinal data are of particular value in tracing the growth history of a single individual over time and in determining idiosyncratic patterns of growth, as well as the permissible parameters of deviation that such patterns may display if they are to remain within the "normal" range. Cross-sectional data are of limited value, particularly in the construction of velocity curves. While one may estimate by means of cross-sectional data a mean velocity value from age fourteen to fifteen by subtracting the age fourteen mean from the age fifteen mean, the resulting figure is a crude one. As Tanner (1955) notes, if we are to assume the usual figure for year-to-year correlation in body measurements, "it takes twenty or more times as many subjects measured cross-sectionally to locate the mean increment with the same precision, or standard error, as it would using subjects followed longitudinally."

Cross-sectional studies have the advantages that they are relatively easy to perform, they can supply information quickly, larger samples can be used realistically, and they are less expensive. Longitudinal studies ordinarily take place over a period of no less than two years,

Figure 25 *Curves of Annual Gains in Height of Three Individual Boys (A, B, and C). Note: The lower line shows the mean annual gain of the three boys.*

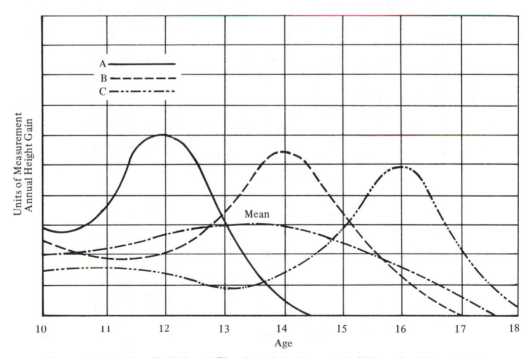

Source: Adapted from F. Falkner, "The physical development of children. A guide to the interpretation of growth charts and development assessments; and a commentary on contemporary and future problems," *Pediatrics* 29 (1962): 448–466. Reprinted by permission of the American Academy of Pediatrics.

and subjects may be lost as the study proceeds. Where the longitudinal study is of really long duration, there is the further possibility of lack of continuity in the research staff personnel. Before starting a longitudinal study, it is a good idea to run a preliminary cross-sectional pilot study.

Growth Curves for Height

One of the early complete seriatim measures in height, shown in Figure 26, was made by Count Philibert Gueneau de Montbeillard upon his son from 1760 to 1777 and published by Buffon in 1827. Montbeillard's distance curve of growth in height in the main describes the generalized height curve characteristic of all height data collected since that time. The curve shows four definite phases. There is a period of rapid growth in infancy and early childhood; a middle period from ages three to twelve or thirteen when growth is slow but constant; a period of marked acceleration around puberty from twelve to fifteen; and a final terminal period after fifteen, ending in a point of no further growth in early maturity. Such changes are even more striking when viewed graphically, as in Figure 27.

However, it is obvious that an accurate picture of trends in growth may not be sup-

Figure 26 *Montbeillard's Seriatim Measurements of the Stature of a French Boy, 1760–1777*

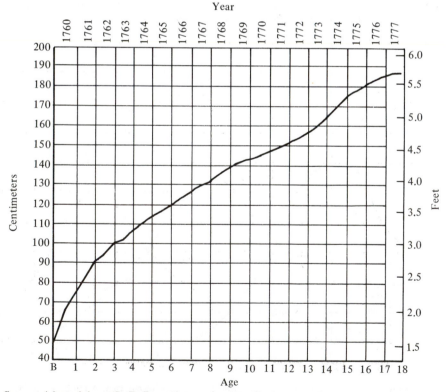

Source: Adapted from G. Buffon, *Oeuvres completes*, Paris, 1827. Cited in J. A. Harris, C. M. Jackson, D. G. Paterson, and R. E. Scammon, eds., *The measurement of man* (Minneapolis: University of Minnesota Press, 1930), p. 176. Reprinted by permission of the publisher.

plied by presenting data for one individual only, although consideration of the deviations of an individual's growth curve from the norm may reflect environmental conditions particularly affecting that person. From such deviations, when considered against the individual's life history, it is possible to make tentative generalizations about environmental effects upon the course of growth. For example, Rosenbaum (1959) reports the case of a tense, anxious, phobic man whose growth spurt was delayed until his seventeenth year. As a result of this case, Rosenbaum hypothesizes that psychological factors of a highly specific nature can inhibit growth in height in organically healthy children and adolescents.

There are significant deviations in the growth patterns and trends of boys as compared to those of girls, and of one boy as compared to another boy. The practice among investigators of human development has been to collect growth data on many individuals and to combine the data to form an average curve that will give an overall normative picture. In this way individuals who deviate widely from the norm will not be misinterpreted as being representative. Figure 28 presents the average standing heights of a group of south German boys and girls after a study by Pfuhl (1928). In a study such as Pfuhl's a comparatively homogeneous sample is presented, in that all the individuals represented are of

Figure 27 *Changes in Growth in Height from Birth Through Age 20*

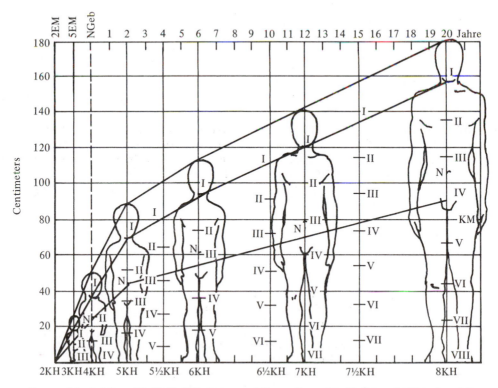

Source: Adapted from W. Pfuhl, "Wachstum und Proportionen," in K. Peter, G. Wetzel, and F. Heiderich, eds., *Handbuch der Anatomie des Kindes* (Munich: Bergmann, 1928), vol. I. Reprinted by permission of the publisher.

Figure 28   *Growth in Standing Height of Boys and Girls (South German Children of the Upper Social Stratum)*

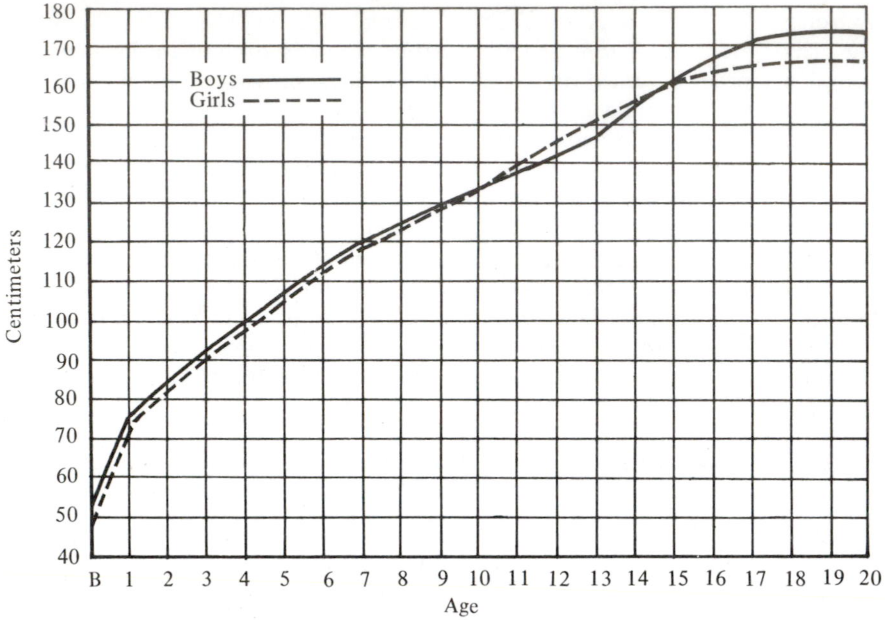

Source: Adapted from W. Pfuhl, "Wachstum und Proportionen," in K. Peter, G. Wetzel, and F. Heiderich, eds., *Handbuch der Anatomie des Kindes* (Munich: Bergmann, 1928), vol. I, p. 211. Reprinted by permission of the publisher.

German nationality and are from the same section of central Europe. Figure 29 presents the average heights of American boys and girls after a study by Shuttleworth (1939) from data collected in the Harvard Growth Study. Figure 30 depicts average heights of boys and girls from data presented by McCloy (1938).

Recent documentation, as Hale (1958) suggests, indicates that the rate of physical maturation of American youth has been accelerated in that the children of today are, among other things, taller and heavier than the children of previous generations. That such is indeed the case is demonstrated by studies such as those of Rauh, Schumsky, and Witt (1967). During March of 1963 these investigators measured the physical dimensions of 8,480 students selected at least to some extent

Figure 29   *Average Growth Trends in Standing Height of a Sample of 1,458 Boys and Girls from the Harvard Growth Study*
Source: Adapted from data in F. K. Shuttleworth, "The physical and mental growth of boys and girls ages six through nineteen in relation to their age of maximum growth," *Monographs of the Society for Research in Child Development* 4, no. 3, ser. 22 (1939). Copyright 1939 by The Society for Research in Child Development, Inc. Reprinted by permission of the publisher.

Figure 30   *Average Heights for Each Year of Age*
Source: Adapted from C. H. McCloy, "Appraising physical status: Methods and norms," *University of Iowa Studies in Child Welfare* 15 (1938). Reprinted by permission of the Institute of Child Behavior and Development.

Figure 29

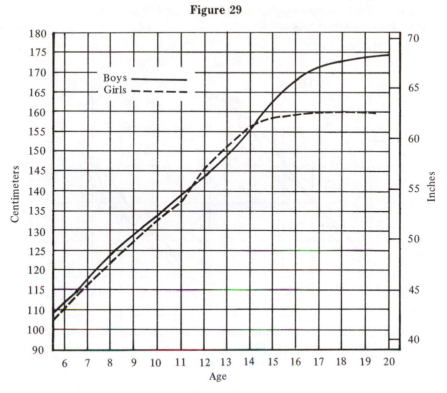

Figure 30

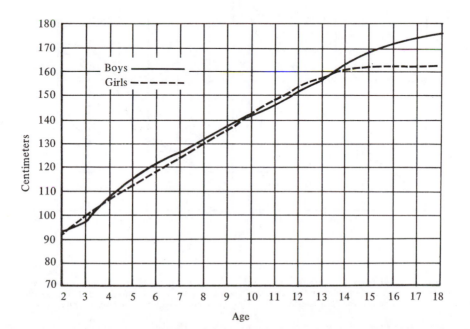

Figure 31   *A Comparison of Median Heights and Weights from Three Geographically Different Samples*

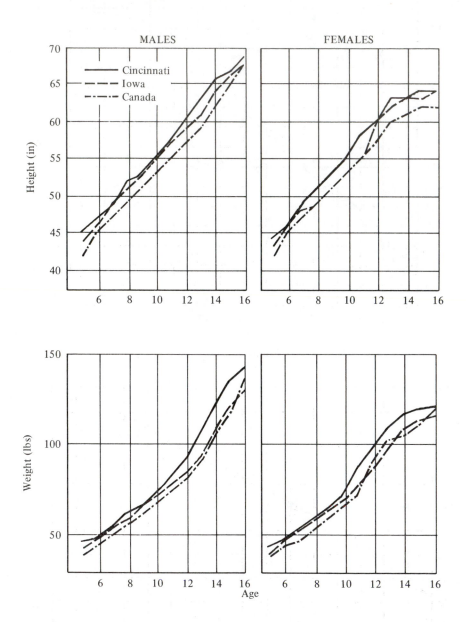

randomly[4] from kindergarten through the eleventh grade of the Cincinnati, Ohio, public and parochial schools. Results were compared with those previously reported by Stuart and Meredith (1946) of an Iowa longitudinal sample studied from 1930 to 1945 and by Pett and Ogilvie (1957) of a Canadian sample.

[4]There were 111,565 children attending the Cincinnati public and parochial schools. This population was reduced to a sample of 104,657 because, according to the investigators, there was a "need to eliminate some schools." From this sample of 104,657, 11,000 names were selected randomly for study, with all twelfth graders eliminated. Because of absence or transfer, 2,600 of the 11,000 had to be eliminated, leaving a sample of 8,480. Unfortunately, when subjects are not originally included or are later eliminated from a randomly selected sample drawn from the population used, there is always the question of whether the inclusion of these individuals would have significantly changed the results reported.

Rauh, Schumsky, and Witt report that the only discrepancy in trend among the three studies occurred in median weight after age ten, when the 1963 Cincinnati sample became increasingly heavier than the other two groups. With regard to median height and weight, the later Cincinnati sample was taller and heavier. However, despite these median differences, the course and form of the growth curves for the two samples had not changed. Apparently we can say that, unless some factor of geographical location was operating, present-day children tend to be on the average taller and heavier, although the nature of the linear and ponderal curves of growth remains unaltered. A comparison of the median heights and weights reported in these three studies is shown in Figure 31.

Figure 32 *Average Growth Trends in Standing Height as Related to Age at Maximum Growth (MG) for Boys*

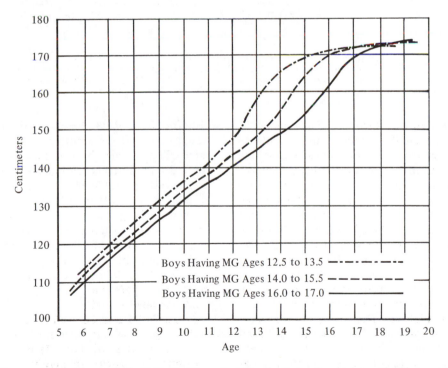

Source: Adapted from data in F. K. Shuttleworth, "The physical and mental growth of boys and girls ages six through nineteen in relation to their age of maximum growth," *Monographs of the Society for Research in Child Development* 4, no. 3, ser. 22 (1939). Copyright 1939 by The Society for Research in Child Development, Inc. Reprinted by permission of the publisher.

Figure 33   *Average Growth Trends in Standing Height as Related to Age at Maximum Growth (MG) for Girls*

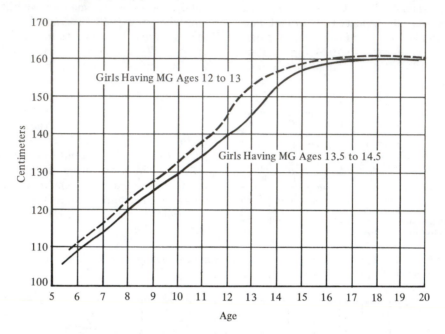

Source: Adapted from data in F. K. Shuttleworth, "The physical and mental growth of boys and girls ages six through nineteen in relation to their age of maximum growth," *Monographs of the Society for Research in Child Development* 4, no. 3, ser. 22 (1939). Copyright 1939 by The Society for Research in Child Development, Inc. Reprinted by permission of the publisher.

In contrast to the German sample shown in Figure 28, the usual American sample contains individuals who are less homogeneous in ethnic origins. An examination of the height curves reveals specific differences when boys are compared with girls. At birth, boys tend to be somewhat taller than girls and remain so until about age ten, at which time girls begin to forge ahead. From about eleven to fourteen, girls are taller than boys of the same age. But from shortly after fourteen, boys begin to forge ahead and maintain their superiority in height from then on. Nevertheless, this is only the average picture. There are always some boys who are shorter than some girls at all stages of development, and vice versa. There are also considerable differences in the ages at which different children have their growth spurts, or attain their maximum growth.

Figures 32 and 33 show growth trends as related to age at maximum growth for boys and girls. Thus, it may be seen that various factors of individual structure must be considered in interpreting a table of average heights. Bayley (1956) presents tables showing the percentage of mature height achieved by children of varying degrees of skeletal maturity together with prediction tables of ultimate height. Baldwin's (1921) presentation of the physical growth of children from birth to maturity has long been a standard reference in comparisons of linear and ponderal growth.

Figures 34 and 35 depict growth curves in height for boys and girls from data presented by Bayer and Bayley (1959). The curves present the growth in height of an average-size boy (or girl) who is maturing at an average rate, the growth of two boys (or girls)

Figure 34 *Growth Curves of Height by Age for Boys with Average, Accelerated, and Retarded Rates of Maturation*

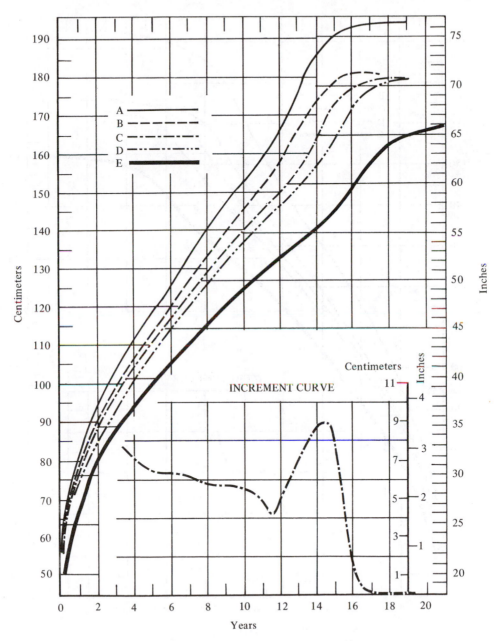

Source: Adapted from N. Bayley, "Growth curves of height and weight by age for boys and girls, scaled according to physical maturity," *Journal of Pediatrics* 48 (1956): 187–194. Reprinted by permission of The C. V. Mosby Company and the author.

Figure 35   *Growth Curves of Height by Age for Girls with Average, Accelerated, and Retarded Rates of Maturation*

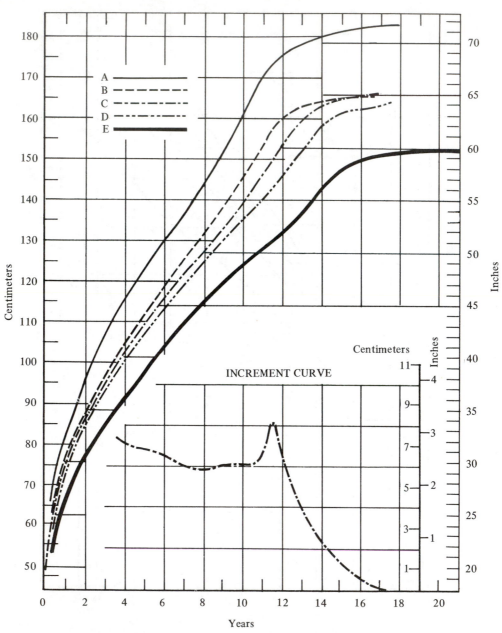

Source: Adapted from N. Bayley, "Growth curves of height and weight by age for boys and girls, scaled according to physical maturity," *Journal of Pediatrics* 48 (1956): 187–194. Reprinted by permission of The C. V. Mosby Company and the author.

who are maturing at accelerated rates, and of two boys (or girls) who are retarded in physical maturing. Taken together, the five cases presented by each of the curves shown in these two figures supply a not atypical picture of the individual growth patterns that are summed to produce a general growth curve.

As with Bayer and Bayley (1959), recent studies have shown a tendency to categorize subjects in terms of their maturity status and to present data in those terms (early, average, late maturing) as being more representative of true individual growth patterns. Figure 36 shows growth in height in terms of average yearly increments for early- as compared to late-maturing boys from Shuttleworth's Harvard Growth Study. Here we may observe that late-maturing children do not grow so fast as early-maturing children do in terms of increments per year, but their growth period

does extend over a longer period and continues after the growth of early-maturing children has ceased.

Another method of studying height changes has been in terms of annual increments, which present a picture of the relative velocity of growth for each year considered. A velocity curve is more informative than the one in Figure 24, which simply indicates the distance traveled. Velocity curves, as previously mentioned, are particularly useful in attempting to study relations between physiological and morphological aspects of growth. Annual increments of height are also more representative of the range of variability within a given group than are absolute heights.

Figure 37 represents, in terms of annual increments, the velocity of growth in height of Montbeillard's son, whose distance-growth curve appears in Figure 26. An examination of

Figure 36   *Average Yearly Increments of Growth in Standing Height for Early- as Compared to Late-maturing Boys and Girls. Note: Late and early categories determined by age at maximum growth.*

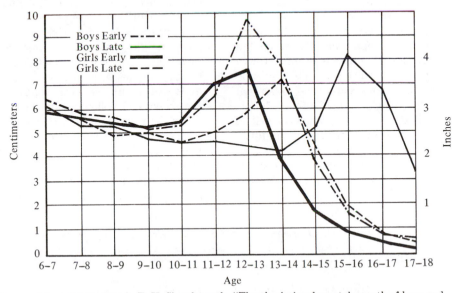

Source: Adapted from data in F. K. Shuttleworth, "The physical and mental growth of boys and girls ages six through nineteen in relation to their age of maximum growth," *Monographs of the Society for Research in Child Development* 4, no. 3, ser. 22 (1939). Copyright 1939 by The Society for Research in Child Development, Inc. Reprinted by permission of the publisher.

Figure 37   *Velocity of Growth in Height of a French Boy*

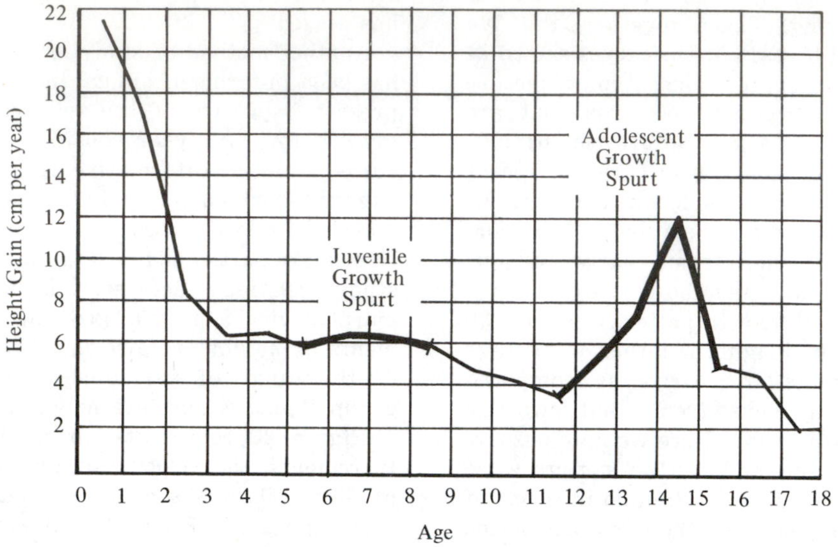

Source: Adapted from R. E. Scammon, "The First seriatim study of human growth," *American Journal of Physical Anthropology* 10 (1927): 333, fig. 1. Reprinted by permission of The Wistar Press.

Figure 37 reveals a more definitive picture of growth changes than is possible in Figure 26. Two growth spurts are shown, the greater one, known as the adolescent growth spurt, coming between thirteen and fifteen, and a lesser one, known as the juvenile or mid-growth spurt, between six and eight. The juvenile growth spurt has been noted by Robertson (1923), Meredith (1935), and Tanner (1947), but relatively little is actually known about it or its function. However, mothers of children between six and eight are well aware of it, as they have to let down trouser legs and skirts for their children to meet suddenly accelerated linear growth.

In girls the adolescent growth spurt usually occurs between the twelfth and fourteenth years, about two years earlier than in boys. Its magnitude is less for girls than for boys, its peak height velocity averaging about 3¼ inches as compared to 4 inches for boys. Prior to the adolescent growth spurt, boys and girls are about the same heights, but during the spurt and following it, the average boy is taller than the average girl. Figure 38 presents a comparison of the adolescent spurt in growth height for boys and girls. Figure 39 depicts the annual height increment of a group of boys and girls from Pfuhl's study. One of the most important things to observe about the

Figure 38   *Comparison of Adolescent Growth Spurt in Height of Boys and Girls*
Source: Adapted from J. M. Tanner, *Growth at adolescence* (Springfield, Ill.: Charles C. Thomas, 1955). Reprinted by permission of Blackwell Scientific Publications Ltd.

Figure 39   *A Comparison of the Annual Increments in Height of a Group of South German Boys and Girls*
Source: Adapted from W. Pfuhl, "Wachstum und Proportionen," in K. Peter, G. Wetzel, and F. Heiderich, eds., *Handbuch der Anatomie des Kindes* (Munich: Bergmann, 1928), vol. I, p. 211. Reprinted by permission of the publisher.

Figure 38

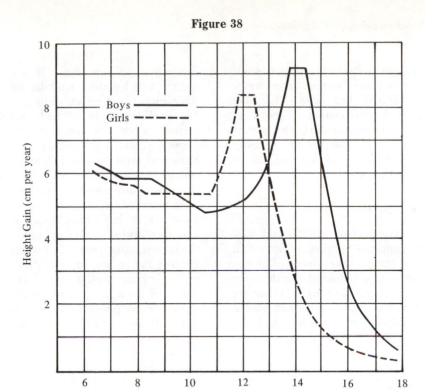

Figure 39

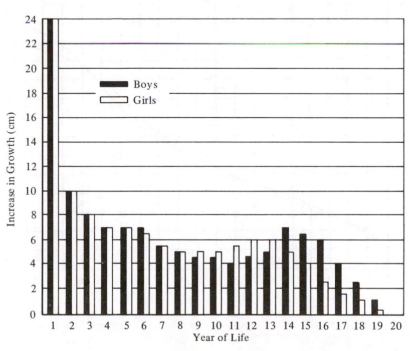

linear average height curve is the prepubescent growth spurt, which occurs at about age twelve for girls and thirteen for boys. The phenomenon of growth differences in boys as compared to girls, and particularly the earlier acceleration of girls, is also found in many other aspects of physical development, to be discussed later in this section.

Growth Curves for Weight

Height is only one aspect of growth and does not present a complete picture of physical status. There are many other aspects, but one of the most commonly considered, particularly in connection with height, is weight. When we say James is five feet tall, we do not give a very clear picture of James as he really is.

But when we say James is five feet tall and weighs two hundred pounds, we have a fairly clear picture of an exceedingly obese boy. As far as increments of body weight are concerned, much the same course of growth is presented as in the linear curves of growth. Boys and girls tend to follow the same general course of growth, but girls tend to be lighter than boys until prepuberty. In the early part of puberty, they become heavier than boys, after which boys once again become heavier and maintain their advantage of weight throughout maturity. The same prepubescent growth spurt occurs in both boys and girls, with girls averaging one to two years in advance of boys at that particular time.

Figure 40 presents growth in body weight from Pfuhl's (1928) comparatively homo-

Figure 40   *Growth in Weight of Boys and Girls (South German Children of the Upper Social Stratum)*

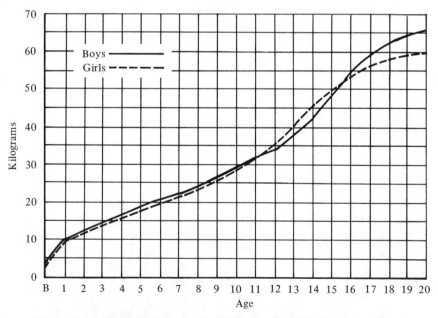

Source: Adapted from W. Pfuhl, "Wachstum und Proportionen," in K. Peter, G. Wetzel, and F. Heiderich, eds., *Handbuch der Anatomie des Kindes* (Munich: Bergmann, 1928), vol. I, p. 211. Reprinted by permission of the publisher.

geneous sample of south German youth. Figure 41 gives the average weight of an American sample of boys and girls from birth to maturity from Shuttleworth (1939). Figure 42 shows the growth trends in average body weight of ten groups of boys having different ages at maximum growth from the same study.

Figures 43 and 44 give data from Bayer and Bayley (1959) depicting growth in weight of boys and girls whose maturity is average, accelerated, and retarded. Here again, as with the data on height, age of maximum growth is an important factor in assessing a given individual's relative status. It should again be noted that average growth curves may present a most misleading picture. Figures 42, 39, and 36 should be studied together. Figure 45 presents still another approach to the analysis of

growth status previously discussed—annual increments in weight from Pfuhl's (1928) study. With weight, as with height, there are great individual differences. Any individual's height or weight cannot be predicted from his age; average heights and weights can be cited for any given age.

Linear and ponderal curves of growth present a number of similarities. Both tend to follow the same double sigmoid curve of growth, but in the case of ponderal growth there is a greater increase in rate and a number of minor variations preceding puberty.

There has also been considerable interest in the study of the growth of the various major organs of the body, entirely apart from the overall measurement of body stature and weight. The growth curves of the various

Figure 41 *Average Growth Trends in Weight of 1,458 Boys and Girls from the Harvard Growth Study*

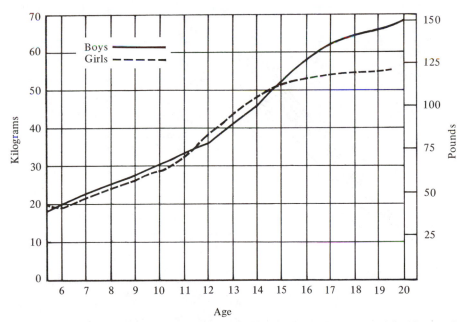

Source: Adapted from data in F. K. Shuttleworth, "The physical and mental growth of boys and girls ages six through nineteen in relation to their age of maximum growth," *Monographs of the Society for Research in Child Development* 4, no. 3, ser. 22 (1939). Copyright 1939 by The Society for Research in Child Development, Inc. Reprinted by permission of the publisher.

Figure 42   *Growth Trends in Average Body Weight of Ten Groups of Boys Having Different Ages at Maximum Growth*

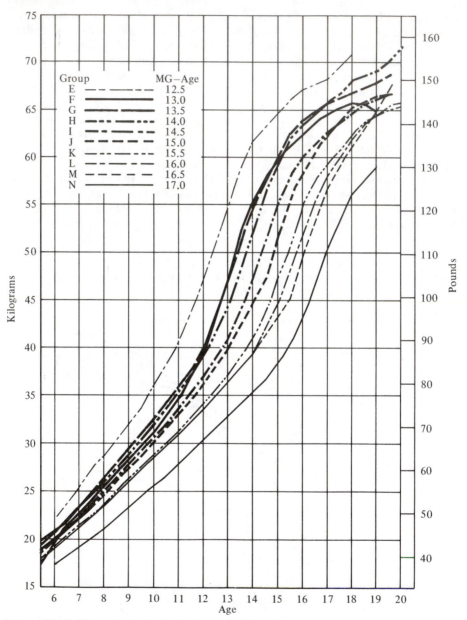

Source: Adapted from data in F. K. Shuttleworth, "The physical and mental growth of boys and girls ages six through nineteen in relation to their age of maximum growth," *Monographs of the Society for Research in Child Development* 4, no. 3, ser. 22 (1939). Copyright 1939 by The Society for Research in Child Development, Inc. Reprinted by permission of the publisher.

Figure 43 *Growth Curves of Weight by Age for Boys with Average, Accelerated, and Retarded Rates of Maturation*

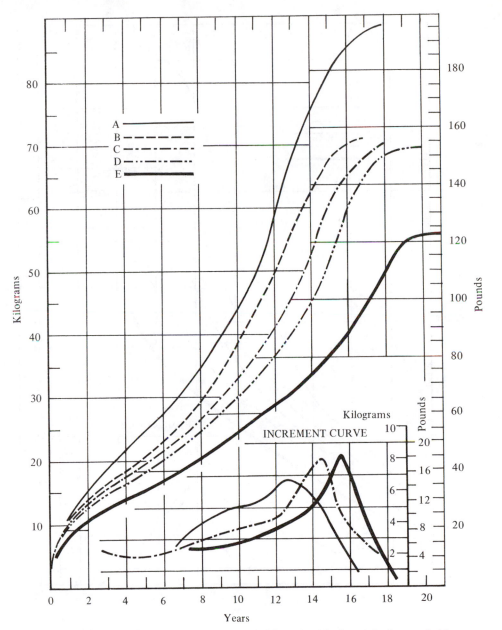

Figure 44　*Growth Curves of Weight by Age for Girls with Average, Accelerated, and Retarded Rates of Maturation*

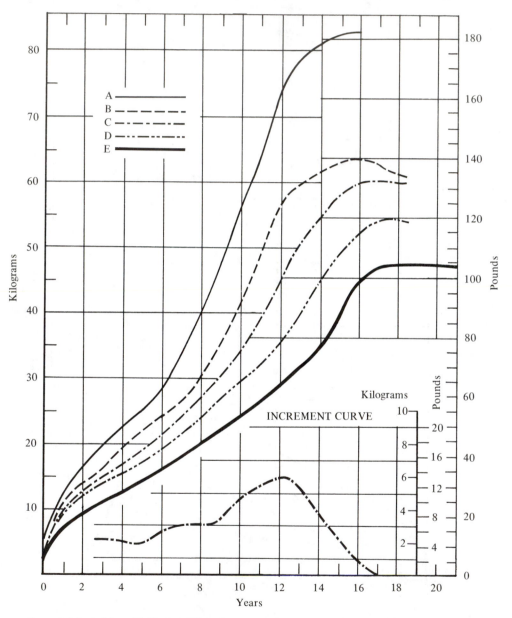

Source: Adapted from N. Bayley, "Growth curves of height and weight by age for boys and girls, scaled according to physical maturity," *Journal of Pediatrics* 48 (1956): 187–194. Reprinted by permission of The C. V. Mosby Company and the author.

Figure 45 *A Comparison of the Annual Increments in Weight of a Group of South German Boys and Girls*

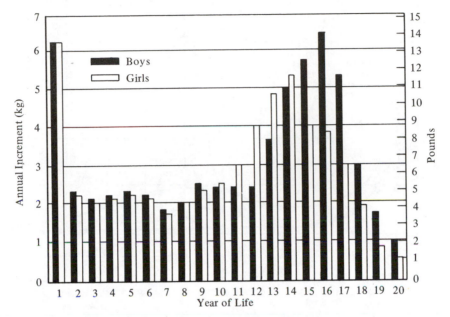

Source: Adapted from W. Pfuhl, "Wachstum und Proportionen," in K. Peter, G. Wetzel, and F. Heiderich, eds., *Handbuch der Anatomie des Kindes* (Munich: Bergmann, 1928), vol. I, p. 211. Reprinted by permission of the publisher.

organs are classifiable under four headings—lymphoid, neural, genital, and general—depending upon what class of organs is involved. Growth studies cited up to the present time have been in terms of some absolute unit of measurement like grams, centimeters, pounds, or feet, or in some relative form like percent of the magnitude at birth or at maturity. Another method is through study of the rate of growth. Rate of growth may be defined as the amount of increase in size per unit of time. Figure 46 shows the relative velocity of growth of the four types of tissue. The course of the neural, lymphoid, and genital curves of growth should be compared with the general curve of growth, which depicts the course of the overall exterior bodily dimensions. The figure shows the familiar infancy, early childhood, and puberty growth spurts, the regular but slow growth of middle childhood and adolescence, and the cessation of growth in early maturity. The general type of growth curve applies to all external linear dimensions of the body except the head and neck. Internally, it applies to the dimensions of the respiratory system, the skeleton and musculature, and weights of a number of the viscera, such as the kidneys, the spleen, and the pancreas.

Summary

Adolescence is a time of growth and physical change. Many physical changes occur comparatively suddenly, and frequently offer a striking contrast to the state of affairs which precedes the change. Such changes are often disquieting to the adolescent, but adults often think them humorous.

Figure 46   *Relative Velocity of the Four Basic Types of Tissue Growth*

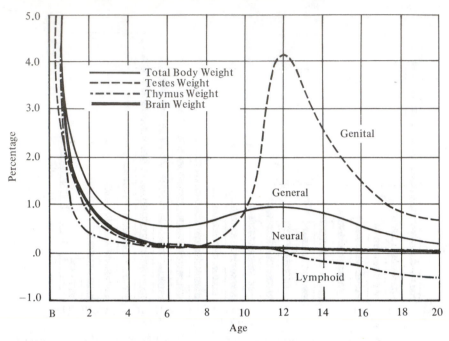

Source: Adapted from J. A. Harris, C. M. Jackson, D. G. Paterson, and R. E. Scammon, eds., *The measurement of man* (Minneapolis: University of Minnesota Press, 1930), p. 213. Copyright 1930 by the University of Minnesota, University of Minnesota Press, Minneapolis. Reprinted by permission of the publisher.

Most persons possess a fairly well-formulated self-image, and the body frequently acts as a symbol of the self. Hence, physical changes mean that either the self-concept must change or the new bodily form must be reconciled to the already existing self-concept. Neither alternative is easy, and many individuals find the reality of their physical selves exceedingly difficult to adjust to.

One of the infant's first tasks is to identify his body as his own, and childhood and adolescence tend to become a long series of explorations in this direction. Accentuation of interest in the body follows the attention of others to the body and its adornment, as well as the arousal or development within the individual of sexual desires. Such accentuation of interest may take any of several forms, including interest in the opposite sex, in personal appearance, in strength and endurance, and in physical health.

Interest in the opposite sex is one of the outstanding characteristics of the normally developing adolescent, and it leads to increased attention not only to one's own physical attributes but also to others' physical attributes. Such interests may cause the adolescent to display mixed motives. On one hand, he may wish to display his physical self for the admiration of others, and, on the other, he may wish to conceal physical attributes that cause embarrassment as a result of his new preoccupations and interpretation. In any event, the change is outward from egocentric preoccupation with one's body for its own sake to preoccupation with it as it relates to others. Adults could help their adolescent charges through a difficult adjustment period if they would make a real endeavor to prepare them for the changes they will soon experience.

Sex is far from being the only preoccupation of the adolescent. He also devotes a great deal of time to his personal appearance and his body functions, particularly as they bear on his concept of self. Insofar as the adolescent finds physical reality departing from his concept of his physical self, he may encounter feelings of insecurity, inferiority, and anxiety.

Skin blemishes, often neither inevitable nor necessary in adolescence, nevertheless are a trial to many teenagers. The significance of such blemishes is often misinterpreted, and extreme measures may be taken to remove them. Adolescents typically spend much time and effort on their faces and appearances, sometimes with startling results.

Any apparent anomaly of growth tends to be a trial to an adolescent, particularly if it places him at a physical disadvantage, or in a position of unfavorable contrast to his peers. Adolescents are particularly prone to ridicule or reject those age-mates who have physical anomalies or who deviate in some way from the physical norm. Such ridicule or rejection only accentuates the difficulties of an adolescent who may already be worrying about whether or not he is normal.

The course and direction of growth may be presented in the form of a curve, although there is no one standard curve of growth. Different parts of the body grow and develop at different rates, and curves for various parts of the body may take different forms. There are also wide individual variations in curves, although all curves follow certain nomothetic lines common to the race and proceed within certain outside limits.

An understanding of a group or of an individual comes partly as a result of the pertinent developmental history involved. This is so largely because an individual brings his past to the present, and his past becomes a limiting factor in his present activity and adjustment.

The content of human development is such that it makes controlled observation difficult and poses many methodological problems un-known to scientists in other fields. After some initial difficulties, quantification of data, with particular reference to the analysis of relationships, marked a great deal of the work in development after 1900. Of late there has been a recognition of the appropriateness of new problems and methods of approach and a turning toward more qualitative methods. Interest in personality and the social correlates of development has also increased noticeably in recent years.

Physical growth is ordinarily studied by means of one or a combination of three growth increments: linear, areal and ponderal. While there are general curves of growth, the growth curves for the three types of growth increments are not alike. This is particularly true of the percentage of total growth from birth to pubescence. Curves are also presented as velocity or as distance curves, the former being particularly applicable to longitudinal data. Developmental processes may be shown by five different models based on rate, terminal status, terminal age of changes, monotonicity, and effects of disturbance in growth.

In considering an individual's status, more than one dimension must be regarded. For example, height alone or weight alone would give an incomplete picture. Ordinarily, a height-weight relationship is used in estimating a person's physical status and in comparing him with the status of other persons. Usually comparisons are made on the basis of an average curve gathered by seriatim or cross-sectional measurements of a large sample. Most effective use of samples for comparative purposes presupposes a carefully selected and representative sample, that is, one that is neither too homogeneous nor too heterogeneous for the purpose at hand.

Some individuals deviate markedly from the normative picture, but such deviations may not be serious when the individual's complete physical and developmental picture is considered. There are specific sex differences in physical growth patterns, with boys, except at one point in the developmental sequence, having the advantage over girls. However, girls are typically advanced over boys in the developmental sequence during the middle years, which explains their temporary height-weight superiority in the early teens. Still, some boys are heavier and taller than some girls at all ages, and vice versa. It is impossible to consider the facts of physical growth and development without an appreciation of the role of individual differences.

References

Baldwin, B. T. The physical growth of children from birth to maturity. *University of Iowa Studies in Child Welfare*, vol. 1, 1921.

Bayer, L. M., and Bayley, N. *Growth diagnosis*. Chicago: University of Chicago Press, 1959.

Bayley, N. Size and body build of adolescents in relation to rate of skeletal maturing. *Child Development* 14 (1943): 47–90(a).

Bayley, N. Skeletal maturing in adolescence as a basis for determining percentage of completed growth. *Child Development* 14 (1943): 1–46(b).

Bayley, N. Tables for predicting adult height from skeletal age and present height. *Journal of Pediatrics* 28 (1946): 49–64.

Buffon, G. *Oeuvres completes*, vol. 12. Paris, 1827.

Dearborn, W. F.; Rothney, J. W.; and Shuttleworth, F. K. Data on the growth of public school children. *Monographs of the Society for Research in Child Development*, vol. 3, 1938.

Falkner, F. The physical development of children. *Pediatrics* 29 (1962): 448–465.

Falkner, F. General considerations in human development. In Falkner, F., ed., *Human development*. Philadelphia: Saunders, 1966.

Garn, S. M. Cultural factors affecting the study of human biology. *Human Biology* 26 (1954): 71–79.

Gesell, A.; Ilg, F. L.; and Ames, L. B. *Youth: The years from ten to sixteen*. New York: Harper, 1956.

Hale, C. J. Changing growth patterns of the American child. *Education* 78 (1958): 467–470.

Harris, J. A.; Jackson, C. M.; Paterson, D. G.; and Scammon, R. E., eds. *The measurement of man*. Minneapolis: University of Minnesota Press, 1930.

Jones, H. E. The adolescent growth study. I. Principles and methods; II. Procedures. *Journal of Consulting Psychology* 3 (1939): 157–159, 177–180.

Kolb, L. C. Disturbance of the body image. In S. Arieti, ed., *American handbook of psychiatry*. New York: Basic Books, 1959.

Loevinger, J. Models and measures of developmental variation. In Brozek, J., ed., *The biology of human variation*, pp. 585–590. Annals, New York Academy of Sciences, vol. 134, art. 2, 1966.

McCloy, C. H. Appraising physical status: Methods and norms. *University of Iowa Studies in Child Welfare*, vol. 15, 1938.

Meredith, H. V. The rhythm of physical growth: A study of 18 anthropometric measurements on Iowa City white males ranging in age between birth and 18 years. *University of Iowa Studies in Child Welfare*, vol. 11, no. 3, 1935.

Pett, L. B., and Ogilvie, G. F. The report on Canadian average weights, heights, and skinfolds. *Canadian Bulletin of Nutrition* 5 (1957): 1–81.

Pfuhl, W. Wachstum und Proportionen. In Peter, K.; Wetzel, G.; and Heiderich, F., eds., *Handbuch der Anatomie des Kindes*, vol. 1. Munich: J. F. Bergmann, 1928.

Rauh, J. L.; Schumsky, D. A.; and Witt, M. T. Heights, weight and obesity in urban school children. *Child Development* 38 (1967): 515–530.

Robertson, T. B. *The chemical basis of growth and senescence*. Philadelphia: Lippincott, 1923.

Rosenbaum, M. The role of psychological factors in delayed growth in adolescence: A case report. *American Journal of Orthopsychiatry* 29 (1959): 762–771.

Scammon, R. E. The first seriatim study of human growth. *American Journal of Physical Anthropology* 10 (1927): 329–336.

Schilder, P. The image and appearance of the human body. *Studies in the constructive energies of the psyche*. London: Kegan Paul, 1935.

Schonfeld, W. A. Body image in adolescents: A psychiatric concept for the pediatrician. *Pediatrics* 31 (1963): 845.

Selye, H. *The stress of life*. New York: McGraw-Hill, 1956.

Shuttleworth, F. K. Sexual maturation and the skeletal growth of girls aged six to nineteen. *Monographs of the Society for Research in Child*

Development, vol. 3, 1938.

Shuttleworth, F. K. The physical and mental growth of boys and girls ages six through nineteen in relation to their age of maximum growth. *Monographs of the Society for Research in Child Development*, vol. 4, 1939.

Stuart, H. C., and Meredith, H. V. Use of body measurements in a school health program: II.

methods to be followed in taking and interpreting measurements and norms. *American Journal of Public Health* 36 (1946): 1365–1386.

Tanner, J. M. The morphological level of personality. *Proceedings Royal Society of Medicine* 40 (1947): 301–308.

Tanner, J. M. *Growth at adolescence*. Springfield, Illinois: Charles C. Thomas, 1955.

Suggested Readings

Bayley, N. Growth curves of height and weight by age for boys and girls, scaled according to physical maturity. *Journal of Pediatrics* 48 (1956): 187–194.

Cheek, D. B. *Human growth*. Philadelphia: Lea and Febiger, 1968.

Crisp, A. H.; Douglas, J. W.; Ross, J. M.; and Stonehill, E. Some developmental aspects of disorders of weight. *Journal of Psychosomatic Research* 14 (1970): 313–320.

Dwyer, J., and Mayer, J. Psychological effects of variations in physical appearance. *Adolescence* 3 (1968): 353–380.

Falkner, F. The physical development of children *Pediatrics* 29 (1962): 448–465.

Forbes, G. B. Toward a new dimension in human growth. *Pediatrics* 36 (1965): 825–835.

Forbes, G. B. Growth of the lean body mass in man. *Growth* 36 (1972): 325–338.

Frisch, R. E., and Revelle, R. Variations in body weights and the age of the adolescent growth spurt among Latin American and Asian populations, in relation to calorie supplies. *Human Biology* 41 (1969): 185–212.

Frisch, R. E., and Revelle, R. The height and weight of adolescent boys and girls at the time of peak velocity of growth in height and weight: Longitudinal data. *Human Biology* 41 (1969): 536–559.

Frisch, R. E., and Revelle, R. Height and weight at menarche and a hypothesis of critical body weights and adolescent events. *Science* 169 (1970): 397–398.

Jaworski, A. A., and Jaworski, R. A. New teenage boy and girl growth charts for pediatric office use. *Clinical Pediatrics* 10 (1971): 410–413.

Katz, S. H.; Rivinus, H.; and Barker, W. Physical anthropology and the biobehavioral approach to child growth and development. *American*

Journal of Physical Anthropology 38 (1972): 105–118.

Linden, F. vander. The interpretation of incremental data and velocity growth curves. *Growth* 34 (1970): 221–224.

Miklashevskaya, N. N. Sex differences in growth of the head and face in children and adolescents. *Human Biology* 41 (1969): 250–262.

National Center for Health Statistics. *Height and weight of youths 12–17 years: United States*. Rockville, Md.: U.S. Dept. of Health, Education and Welfare, 1973.

Payne, I. R.; Rasmussen, D. M.; and Shinedling, M. Characteristics of obese university females who lose weight. *Psychological Reports* 27 (1970): 567–571.

Pett, L. B., and Ogilvie, G. F. The Canadian height-weight survey. In Brozek, J., ed., *Body measurements and human nutrition*. Detroit: Wayne University Press, 1956.

Sohar, E.; Scapa, E.; and Ravid, M. Constancy of relative body weight in children. *Archives of Disease in Childhood* 48 (1973): 389–392.

Tanner, J. M. Earlier maturation in man. *Scientific American* 218 (1968): 21–27.

Tanner, J. M.; Whitehouse, R. H.; and Takaishi, M. Standards from birth to maturity for height, weight, height velocity, weight velocity: British children, 1965. *Archives of Disease in Childhood* 41 (1966): 454–635.

Welch, Q. B. Fitting growth and research data. *Growth* 34 (1970): 293–312.

Wolanski, N. Basic problems in physical development in man in relation to the evaluation of development of children and youth. *Current Anthropology* 8 (1967): 35–60.

Wolanski, N. Genetic and ecological factors in human growth. *Human Biology* 42 (1970): 349–368.

Chapter Eighteen

Physiological Development

A Frame of Reference

These chapters on the physical and physiological aspects of adolescents attempt to describe the course and nature of growth and development, and to show the physiological and sociological effects of this growth. No one aspect of growth is held to be more important or more significant than any other, nor should it be believed that any one aspect of growth may be considered in terms of the psychological functioning of the organism without simultaneous consideration of the entire associated range of growth phenomena. If two aspects of growth appear together in time, then they are inseparable, and should not be considered apart from each other, although their relationship, aside from the fact that they appear at the same time, is often quite tenuous.

Growth, as it is ordinarily conceived and studied, and as it was discussed in the previous chapter, involves not only increment, or addition, and change in form; it also involves change in function and in status. It may represent increasing differentiation, new abilities, and the assumption of new tasks, as well as changes in area, height, and weight. However, the psychologist is particularly interested in growth as a functional change. He endeavors to study the effects of growth on the behavior of individuals and of groups, and in doing so tries to classify and describe behavior.

In this connection considerable variation will be shown in the behavior and growth patterns of different individuals, although such behavior and growth must occur within the limitations imposed by species and race. Thus, in referring to an individual, the psychologist must be careful to recognize that the person's behavior and development are unique to himself and may, within defined limits, deviate markedly from those of other persons. But in actual practice the psychologist does more than describe what an individual does; by implication he also describes what an individual does not do, or is incapable of doing. Further, his description is often comparative—that is, any given person is described as more or less like other persons. For example, Johnnie is described as taller than Freddie, and both as taller than average boys of their age. In reality, the psychologist's description of an individual and his behavior implies that other individuals act as frames of reference in the psychologist's thinking. This is particularly true when the psychologist's task moves from a simple listing of attributes or behavioral acts to an interpretation of those acts or attributes. An adolescent's behavior and the reasons for his behavior become significant and take on meaning when they are compared with the behavior of other adolescents of like status.

Therefore, the psychologist tends to be interested in classification and description. He seeks points of reference or rallying points around which he may organize, categorize, or interpret the phenomena of growth and behavior. Advent of puberty, period of most rapid growth, and period of awakening interest in members of the opposite sex are examples of possible reference points. Insofar as he may describe behavior in terms of such points of reference, or as such points enable him to see the relation of several behavioral acts or attributes that occur simultaneously, his task of behavior description and analysis becomes easier, or at least more orderly and meaningful.

For example, it may be discovered that with the advent of puberty a whole list of behavioral changes occurs. Such behavioral changes may be seen as interrelated because they all occur at the time of puberty, which becomes one of the reference points of adolescence. However, it is often misleading to consider any behavioral change as the cause of one that accompanies or follows it. One can only say that they all appear together at one point in time and that they are part of the whole picture as it is at that time. To say that an adolescent is pubescent is to say that the associated group of behavioral changes are also present; their presence thus becomes meaningful, and it is easier to understand the child's behavior and attitudes. Such reference points may often give the psychologist an opportunity to interpret the relationship of seemingly isolated aspects of growth and behavior. The descriptive term *adolescence* is one such reference point, although an exceedingly comprehensive one. *Adolescence* classifies the individual's psychological and growth status, and his behavior may be interpreted in the light of his status or stage. Unfortunately, there is too often a tendency to feel that the stage is primary and causes the behavior, rather than that the behavior causes the stage.[1]

An adolescent does not behave in any given way because he is an adolescent. He is an adolescent because his behavior takes on characteristics that are conveniently described as adolescent. Hence, the reference point is simply a way of classifying an individual whose behavior displays certain characteristics. Recognizing the reference point as a convenience, or as a mere descriptive label around which to arrange and describe behavior and attributes, will reveal the falsity of the assumption that behavior is due to a stage, such as adolescence, rather than that behavior is responsible for the stage.

Therefore, in his study of behavior and growth, the psychologist is tempted to seek as many descriptive points of reference as his data or his ingenuity may provide. In the case of growth phenomena, they are ponderal, areal, and linear growth, and the curve of growth is described in terms of acceleration and deceleration. Various curves are studied and relationships sought.

One of the more interesting growth phenomena is the sudden spurt in growth approximately following the tenth chronological year. This growth spurt appears in all individuals, although not at exactly the same time, and it tends to occur about one and one-half years earlier in girls than it does in boys. In order to understand the significance of this single phenomenon—the growth spurt—the student must seek other phenomena of growth or behavior that may occur just before, with, or just after the original phenomenon. A whole complex of changes seems to occur in close proximity to this growth spurt, some in interests and behavior, some in growth, and some in physiological function. For example, at this period there also occur changes in bodily proportions, the assumption of secondary sex characteristics, changes in the size of internal organs, changes in basal metabolism, and the maturation of the reproductive organs. Confronted by such a complex of changes, the question then becomes: To what extent are these phenomena related? Which are the precursors and which are the end results? Is there any opportunity here to make a new rallying point, or to postulate a "stage," so that behavior and growth may be described in terms of the rallying point, or at least as occurring before or after it?

[1] The word *cause* may be somewhat at fault since science more and more attempts to show relationship between measured phenomena, rather than causes in the old-fashioned sense. Some readers will prefer the term *functional* in the mathematical sense.

At this growth-change rallying point, a phenomenon that seems particularly significant in terms of its far-reaching behavioral effects is the physiological advent of puberty. Psychologists have recognized the practical importance of this point in the growth cycle by labeling children as pubescent or prepubescent, and by attributing many factors of their growth and behavior to their pubescent or prepubescent status. Here one aspect of change in developmental status is singled out as basic, and a great deal of growth and behavior is described in terms of this aspect, even as being characteristic of it. As a matter of fact, there can be little doubt that many things that prepubescents do or fail to do, and that pubescents do or fail to do, may be attributed to their physiological status. Yet to say that the gradual cessation of certain kinds of growth following puberty is caused by sexual maturity is to go beyond what is actually known. It would be as meaningless as to say that the linear growth spurt before puberty is the cause of puberty. In terms of growth it is best to think of pubescence as neither causal nor resultant, but as associated with the other changes, and as a convenient point of reference in describing and analyzing the associated changes. Certainly many changes occur together during this period, and there is good reason to say that puberty is a rallying point or time around which to describe and classify behavior that has occurred. But it is risky to say that any one of the associated changes taking place around the time of puberty is most important biologically. Still the psychologist likes to name his rallying point, so he tries to determine which of the specific associated changes appear to have the greatest behavioral repercussions. He selects one, in this case, the arrival of sexual maturity, and names it *pubescence*. But in reality his title of classification does not deny the importance of the other associated growth changes. He is simply using a semantic convenience as he talks of behavior at a time when a whole group of important changes have taken place.

The Advent of Puberty

One of the major physiological landmarks of adolescence, and one which forms a major demarcation point in the study of growth during the first twenty years, is the phenomenon of sexual maturity. The advent of puberty or sexual maturity has been the subject of numerous studies, some longitudinal and some cross-sectional. Kessen (1960), Tanner (1951, 1955), and Krogman (1955), in their discussions of studies of growth, note the paucity of longitudinal studies[2] as well as the mishandling of both cross-sectional and longitudinal research. Nondevelopmental psychologists such as Berg (1965) and Sanford (1965) have commented on the pressing need for well-ordered longitudinal research, although Bell (1960) notes that longitudinal research as such cannot be assumed to be a cure-all for all the problems confronting developmental research. Krogman (1955) writes:

The fact remains that most of our growth standards are distance standards, and moreover, embarrassingly limited to height and weight. And yet, most of our technics use distance standards as if they were standards of velocity. Examples of this are percentile ranking, the plotting of chronological age against dimensional age (as CA/WA), and the Wetzel Grid, which is log weight plotted against log height. Mere size relations can never substitute for increment as an evaluation of velocity.[3]

All this does not mean, of course, that well-conceived and properly interpreted longitudinal

---

[2]Typical of the longitudinal studies reported have been those of Jones (1944), Dearborn and Rothney (1941), Peskin (1967), Shuttleworth (1937, 1939), Meredith (1935, 1939), Greulich et al. (1938), Carlson (1965), Boas (1932), Muller (1950), Jones (1965), and Norval et al. (1951). Bayley (1965) and Stone and Onque (1959) have presented comprehensive listings of longitudinal studies. Among cross-sectional studies reported have been those of Zukowski et al. (1964), Crampton (1908, 1944), Schonfeld (1943), Minick (1966), Dimock (1937), Clements (1953), Kubitschek (1932), and Baldwin (1916), to mention only a few.

[3]See also Goulet and Baltes (1970) and Mussen (1960).

studies necessarily lack either validity or usefulness.

Puberty may be defined as that time in the life cycle when the reproductive organs attain functional maturity and the individual is potentially capable of reproducing his kind. But a consideration of puberty must recognize that it is a physiological process involving the organism as a whole. The ramifications extend over the adolescent's entire body and, in many cases, will have both emotional and social repercussions, particularly for girls. In discussing a broader "whole child" definition of puberty, More (1953) noted that such a definition introduces "a societal dimension, that of appearance . . . making it of wider effectiveness than the less inclusive question of maturation of genitals alone." Especially in girls, puberty is marked by the gradual appearance of secondary sex characteristics. A gradual change in figure occurs, which includes deposits of fat on the hips, development of the breasts, a widening of the pelvis, and the appearance of hair on the pubes and axillae. The advent of puberty is generally judged in girls by the appearance of first menstruation (menarche). Before first menstruation a girl is classified as prepubescent; following that time she is classified as pubescent. A difficulty in classifying an individual as pubescent or prepubescent has been that many investigators have sought their information by a simple questioning of the subjects involved, which tends to lead to the usual inaccuracies of data based on memory and willingness to cooperate.

Greulich (1944), in discussing the use of menarche as an index of maturity, speaks of the irregularity of the menstrual cycle in young girls and notes:

This should make one reluctant to attribute to the menarche itself the importance as a criterion of maturity which is commonly ascribed to it by writers on adolescence; for it seems probable that some of the same factors which are responsible for the marked irregularity of the early menstrual cycles in girls can operate to advance or retard the occurrence of the menarche itself.

He further states:

It would seem best to regard the menarche as neither a dependable criterion of maturity nor as necessarily the expression of any narrowly circumscribed state of sexual maturation. It is rather the reflection of a physiological state which may occur at different times during the pubertal period in different individuals, and which usually precedes by a considerable interval the attainment of the capacity to reproduce.

A perusal of some of the numerous studies of average age of first menstruation may give an impression of confusion and disagreement. However, differences in first age of menstruation may partly reflect the different samples used and the different report techniques adopted by various observers. The potential inaccuracy of self-reporting by subjects has already been cited. There is also the problem of the noncomparability of data if one investigator interpreted the thirteenth year to comprise twelve years and six months to thirteen years and six months, while another interpreted the thirteenth year to extend from thirteen years and no months to thirteen years and twelve months. Other limiting factors are the time in history, nutritional and socioeconomic status, geographical distribution, and homogeneity of groups.

Schaeffer (1906) placed the time of menstruation for 10,500 Berlin girls at an average of fifteen years seven months. Twenty-three years later, Neurath (1932) using a sample of central European girls, cites twelve to fourteen years. In a Dutch study van't Land and deHaas (1957) report that in a group of twelve-year-old girls 12 percent had started to menstruate. Schaeffer's results are so much at variance with later studies that one might well question the value of the techniques used in gathering information from the Berlin sample. One interesting study by Gould and Gould (1932) may throw some light on Schaeffer's results. The Goulds found that 680 daughters of 357 mothers tended to menstruate .38 years earlier than did their mothers. A secular trend may be operating to reduce the age of advent

Figure 47   *Secular Trend in Age at Menarche, 1850–1950. Note: Data on Norway from Kiil (1939, 1953); on Sweden and Finland from Backman (1948) and Romanus (1952); on U.S.A. (University of North Carolina entrants) from Mills (1950), 1950 value estimated; and on England from Wilson and Sutherland (1950).*

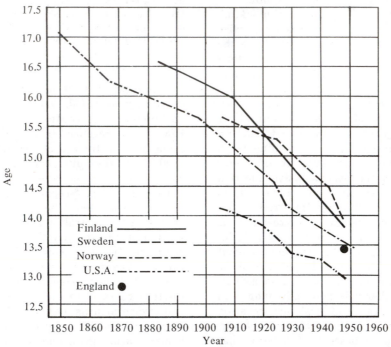

Source: Adapted from J. M. Tanner, *Growth at adolescence* (Springfield, Ill.: Charles C. Thomas, 1955). Reprinted by permission of Blackwell Scientific Publications Ltd.

of puberty in girls. Evidence to confirm this possibility is offered by Tanner (1955), who summarized data provided by various studies[4] extending from 1850 to 1950 and reports that the age of first menstruation has been decreasing by four to five months a decade for over a hundred years. Figure 47 presents a graphic picture of the secular trend reported by Tanner.[5]

What of the future? Tanner (1955) notes that there is no evidence that the trend has ceased or that girls are necessarily maturing at anything like the earliest possible time. However, Falkner (1966) is of the opinion that the secular trend is "an undulating trend over the centuries," that human biology does not in the long run permit "bizarre extrapolations," and that the secular trend will reach a plateau and level off when optimum conditions occur.

This raises the question as to the conditions that affect the advent of puberty. That environmental difference may have some effect is implied in a study by Engle and Shelesnyak (1934) of girls at a low socioeconomic level who lived at the Hebrew Orphan Asylum in New York City. They found that 250 girls in their study had an average first menstruation at 13.5 years, with a range of 11 to 16.3 years. In contrast, Shuttleworth (1937), in a study of

[4]See Kiil (1939, 1953), Backman (1948), Romanus (1952), Mills (1950), and Wilson and Sutherland (1950).

[5]Tanner also notes that as menarche has grown earlier, menopause has appeared later in life, suggesting a pituitary involvement in the evolution of these secular trends.

girls at a higher socioeconomic level who lived in Cleveland, Ohio, cites 12.5 as the average age of menarche. Thus, on the average, the Hebrew Orphan Asylum girls had their first menstruation at a somewhat later date than did the noninstitutional girls. A number of selective factors may have been operating other than socioeconomic status to cause the difference between the mean ages cited in the two studies, in which Jewish were compared to non-Jewish girls, although a number of other studies have cited similar relationships between onset of menarche and socioeconomic status. For example, in a study of 6,141 Israeli girls, Shilo and Goldberg (1965) report that daughters of unskilled workers had the latest onset, citing an average age of 13.33. In an earlier study Shilo (1960), using 2,832 Israeli girls, also cites a relationship between socioeconomic status and onset of menarche, reporting at that time an average age of 14.2 for girls from lower-income families and an average of 13.85 for girls from higher socioeconomic families. While both the Shilo studies agree in the socioeconomic-menarche relationship, the later study shows a rather large decrease in age. This may represent a secular trend, but it is also possible that the changing nature of the population in Israel may have introduced other significant selective factors. In his first study, Shilo (1960) reports an average age of 13.8 for onset of menarche for girls with Israeli-born fathers, as compared to an age of 13.5 for girls of Occidental-born fathers. However, in his second study, Shilo (1965) reports a reverse trend, with daughters of Israeli-born fathers having the significantly earlier age of 13.05, as compared to 13.14 for those with European- or American-born fathers. In the second study, however, while daughters of Asian- and African-born fathers still showed the latest onset of menarche, it had reduced to an average age of 13.35. The earlier age of menarche for daughters of Asian- and African-born fathers is of particular interest in indicating the possible importance of cultural or even racial factors in that other studies have cited later ages of

menarche for non-Occidental and non-Jewish populations. Tanner and O'Keefe (1962) report the mean menarcheal age of high-socioeconomic-status Ibo girls in eastern Nigeria was 14.1, with 95 percent of the sample being within the age range 11.2 to 17.0. Burrell, Healy, and Tanner (1961), in a study of 47,420 Bantu schoolgirls, report that the mean age of menarche for those from economically poor homes was 15.42 ± 0.04, while for girls from more prosperous homes, the mean age was 15.02 ± 0.03. In Burrell's sample the girls from poor homes showed more variability in age at menarche.

To return more specifically to socioeconomic status as a causal or selection variable, various studies opposing those cited in the foregoing discussion have discounted the existence of a relationship between socioeconomic status and menarche. For example, Henton (1958, 1961), in studies of both white and black girls, reports the absence of any significant relationship between socioeconomic status and age of onset of puberty, and Douglas and Ross (1964) report similar results in a study of 1,600 girls.

It was formerly believed that climate has a considerable effect upon the acceleration of sexual maturity. Children reared in warm climates were supposed to mature more quickly than did those reared in temperate or cold climates. As Donovan and ten Bosch (1965) note, this may well have been true in the eighteenth century and the early years of the nineteenth when, according to Kussmaul (1862), average ages at menarche in India were cited as ranging from 12 years 6 months to 13 years 5 months, as compared to 17 years in western Europe (Tanner 1962). But modern research has failed to verify the climate hypothesis as valid for the present era, and, indeed, available evidence appears to controvert it. Even in the early and middle years of the nineteenth century, a series of studies by Roberton (1831, 1844, 1845) took the position that climate was not operative. Many years after Roberton, Mueller (1932), in a study of Japanese girls, found that menarche does not occur any earlier than it does in their northern

Figure 48 *Cumulated Percentages: Adolescent Physical Development in the Female*

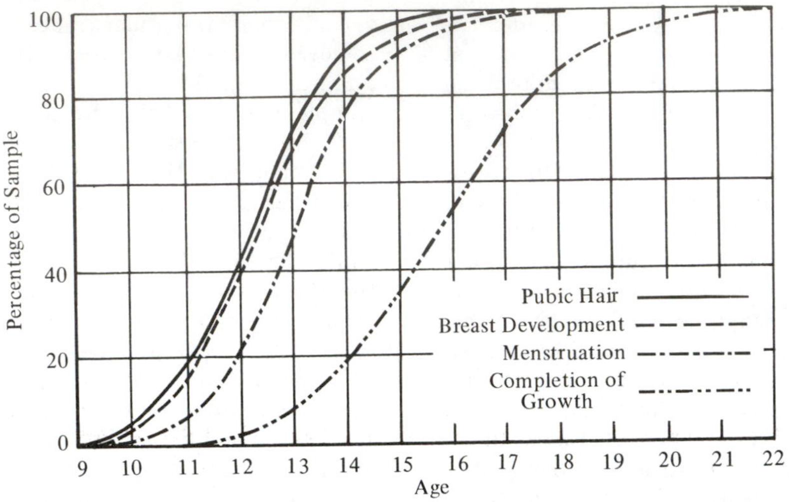

Source: Adapted from A. C. Kinsey et al., *Sexual behavior in the human female* (Philadelphia: Saunders, 1953), p. 124. Reprinted by permission of Paul H. Gebhard, Director, Institute for Sex Research, Indiana University.

European counterparts, and he notes that other observers have failed to find accelerated maturity among the natives of India, Egypt, or Japan. Ellis (1950) reports age of onset of menarche as similar for girls reared in temperate and tropical climates, and Levine (1953) reports the same similarity for temperate and cold climates. It is possible that in a number of these studies the important variable may have been race rather than climate, but Mills (1937), in a review of the literature on age of sexual maturity in relation to climate, wrote:

Nowhere on earth do girls mature so early as they do in the central part of North America.... Among the entering freshman class of 1935 at the University of Cincinnati, there were sixty-two girls seventeen years of age with a mean age of menarche of 12.9 years.... South toward the Gulf of Mexico, East toward the Atlantic coast, or Northeast into Canada, the menses tend to begin at later ages ... throughout South America the development of puberty is delayed about one year.

Montagu (1957) makes much the same point in a generalizing statement on this subject.

There is some evidence that genetic factors may have some bearing upon time of advent of puberty. Tisserand-Perrier (1953) notes that the average length of time between the onsets of first menstruation in pairs of identical twins was 2.2 months, as compared to 8.2 months for nonidentical twins, and Petri (1935) reports that the average difference between age of onset of first menstruation was under three months for identical twins, as compared to twelve months for fraternal twins and eighteen months for mothers, as compared to daughters.

On the whole, the general American standard for age at menarche seems to be close to the figure arrived at by Shuttleworth (1937) in his study of two hundred selected Cleveland, Ohio, girls—12.5 years, although there are many individual differences. In summing up present scientific evidence, Greulich (1944) writes: "There is a considerable body of evidence which indicates that good nutrition and a generally favorable environment tend, within limits, to hasten the onset of puberty and that, conversely, an inadequate diet, severe illness, or other unfavorable environmental conditions tend to retard it." Figure 48 depicts the cumulated percentages of menstruation and

Table 19 *Pubescent Status and Chronological Age of 1,406 Boys*

Chronological Age of Boys Between:	No. of Boys	Prepubescent		Pubescent		Postpubescent	
		No.	%	No.	%	No.	%
10 and 11	106	104	98	1	1	1	1
11 and 12	227	188	83	32	14	7	3
12 and 13	347	215	62	86	25	46	13
13 and 14	280	112	40	80	29	88	31
14 and 15	240	32	13	52	22	156	65
15 and 16	115	2	2	9	8	104	90
16 and 17	67	0	0	0	0	67	100
17 and 18	21	0	0	0	0	21	100
Not Given	3						

Source: H. S. Dimock, *Rediscovering the adolescent* (New York: Association Press, 1937), p. 209. Reprinted by permission of the publisher.

some associated aspects of physical growth after a study by Kinsey (1953).

First Ejaculation

A number of studies have endeavored to determine the age of onset of puberty in boys. The problem is difficult since the clear-cut line of demarcation provided by first menstruation in girls is missing, and the various physical or physiological landmarks by which the pubescent status of boys is determined tend to develop at different times. Dimock (1937), in a study of 1,406 boys in a summer camp, reported the average age of pubescence as 13 years 1 month, on the basis of the Crampton Criteria.[6] Of his 1,406 cases, 260 were pubescent. The 260 were from ten to sixteen years of age, with 1 percent in their eleventh year, 14 percent in their twelfth, 76 percent in their thirteenth, fourteenth, and fifteenth years, and 8 percent in the sixteenth year. Table 19 presents the pubescent status of the boys in Dimock's study.

Carey (1936), using the same Crampton Criteria for determining pubescent status of boys, reports that 49 out of 259 boys from eleven to eighteen years at St. Mary's Industrial School in Baltimore, Maryland, were pubescent. The mean chronological age of the pubescent group was 14 years 3 months, with a standard deviation of 12.1 months.

One of the most ambitious studies of the advent of sexual maturity in boys was that of Kinsey, Pomeroy, and Martin (1948). Kinsey fixes the time of the onset of puberty in boys as the date of the first ejaculation, although sufficient stimulation may bring it on earlier than usual. However, he also notes that age of "onset of adolescence must be recognized whenever there is any development of any physiologic or physical character that pertains to adolescence." He further notes: "When the year of first ejaculation coincides with the year in which the first pubic hair appears, and with the time of onset of rapid growth of height, and/or with certain other developments, there is no question that that year may

[6]The Crampton Criteria are described in Dimock (1937): so-called because of the pioneer study conducted by Crampton early in the century.... (a) Prepubescence is the total period of life before there are any signs of puberty; (b) pubescence is marked by the appearance of pigmented hair in the pubic region; (c) postpubescence is marked by a kink or twist in the pubic hair and a wrinkled scrotum.

These criteria are not so reliable in determining the pubescent state of a boy as would be the date of first nocturnal emission or microscopic evidence of the first secretion of spermatozoa. Crampton validated the criteria he employed, however, by some microscopic examinations of secretions and "in every case well-formed and mobile spermatozoa made their appearance in the months of transition to postpubescence."

Table 20   *Sources of First Ejaculation in Relation to Age of Onset of Adolescence*

Source of First Ejaculation	Percentage Depending on Each Source When Age at Onset of Adolescence Is:				
	8–11	12	13	14	15 & later
Masturbation	71.6	64.8	58.9	55.0	52.1
Nocturnal Emissions	21.6	28.2	35.6	38.9	37.1
Petting	0.0	0.3	0.6	0.3	2.2
Intercourse	0.6	1.4	0.9	0.9	3.2
Homosexual	2.6	3.2	1.2	2.0	2.2
Animal	0.3	0.3	0.2	0.3	0.0
Spontaneous	3.3	1.8	2.6	2.6	3.2
Total	100.0	100.0	100.0	100.0	100.0
N	306.0	722.0	984.0	650.0	186.0

Source: A. C. Kinsey, W. B. Pomeroy, and C. E. Martin, *Sexual behavior in the human male* (Philadelphia: Saunders, 1948), p. 300. Reprinted by permission of Paul H. Gebhard, Director, Institute for Sex Research, Indiana University.

be accepted as the first year of adolescence." Kinsey feels that in the cases in which physical development seems to be some years in advance of first ejaculation, it is better to determine the date of puberty by exterior physical changes rather than by the date of the first ejaculation. But in the Kinsey study, 85 percent of the cases reported simultaneous acceleration in physical development and first ejaculation.

While, aside from actual age of occurrence, much that has been said about the advent of puberty in girls in the previous section also applies to boys, it is particularly interesting to note that there appears to be a positive relationship between social or educational level and date of first ejaculation. In discussing this relationship, Kinsey (1948) writes:

In the male the age of first ejaculation varies by nearly a year between different educational (social) levels: the mean is 14.58 for boys who never go beyond eighth grade in school, 13.97 for boys who go into high but not beyond, and 13.71 for boys who will go to college. The differences are probably the outcome of nutritional inequalities at different social levels, and they are in line with similar differences in mean ages of females at menarche, where nutrition is usually considered a prime factor affecting variation.

Of course, so far as ejaculation is concerned, the young boy may hasten its first appearance by mechanical or other means. Table 20 from the Kinsey (1948) study presents sources of first ejaculation in relation to the age of onset of adolescence. The table shows that masturbation tends to be the primary source of first ejaculation for boys at all ages, with nocturnal emissions coming second, but the older the boy at onset of puberty, the less likely it is that masturbation will be his first source of ejaculation. As Kinsey notes, "boys who mature first more often act deliberately in going after their first outlet; the boys who mature last more often depend upon the involuntary reactions which bring nocturnal emissions."

In addition to first ejaculation, puberty is also marked, as the previous discussion has implied, by the gradual appearance of secondary sex characteristics. In boys, the larynx enlarges in size with an accentuation of the prominence called the Adam's apple; the voice changes; hair appears on the pubes, the axillae, and the face; and the external genitals are in a period of rapid growth. Greulich (1944), speaking of the pubescent changes in skin, hair, and cutaneous glands, writes that such changes "are, for the most part, a reflection of changes associated with the maturation of the repro-

Figure 49 *Percentage of Boys Becoming Pubescent in Each of the School Grades, 1 through 14*

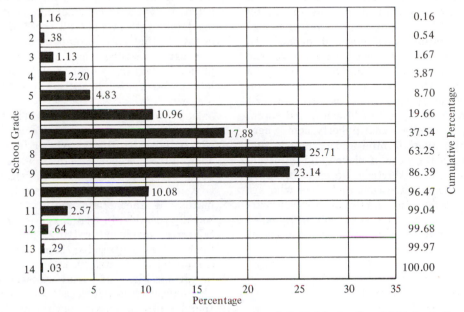

Source: Adapted from A. C. Kinsey, W. B. Pomeroy, and C. E. Martin, *Sexual behavior in the human male* (Philadelphia: Saunders, 1948), p. 187. Reprinted by permission of Paul H. Gebhard, Director, Institute for Sex Research, Indiana University.

ductive system. So intimate is the relationship between the integument and the reproductive system during this period of life that the former reflects rather accurately the development status of the latter." Stein (1924) notes that the shape of the hairline on the head may be taken as a secondary sexual characteristic. The hairline of immature boys, and of both girls and women, is in the form of an uninterrupted bowlike curve, whereas the hairline of the mature male has two wedge-shaped indentations, located at each side of the forehead and called *calvities frontalis adolescentium.* Greulich (1944) confirms Stein's findings to the extent that he found the wedges uniformly absent in young men classified as "hypogenital" or "hypogonadal."[7] On the other hand, they were sometimes absent or poorly developed in

[7]Hypogonadal is used to signify deficiency in functions of growth or development of the gamete-producing gland, e.g., the testis or ovary.

apparently normally developed men. Hence there is some question as to the accuracy of the calvities frontalis adolescentium as an accurate indicator of pubescent status.

Figure 49 shows the percentage of adolescent boys who become pubescent in each grade, after a study by Kinsey, Pomeroy, and Martin (1948). Inspection of the figure indicates the problem confronting teachers of the various grades, particularly the seventh through the ninth, who must deal with children who vary in stages of development, interests, and motivation. The problem becomes even more complicated by the fact that boys are considerably behind girls in sexual development, so that many more girls than boys will be pubescent in the eighth, ninth, and tenth grades, with corresponding differences in interests and attitudes. Here is a clear example of the difficulties arising from any system using chronological age as a grouping factor.

In summary, the time of the advent of puberty is a matter of individual growth, and individuals display wide variations. Such variations are determined to some extent by heredity, and to some extent by environmental factors, including nutrition and disease. In general, girls reach puberty before boys, the difference averaging from one to two years. As has been indicated, the exact age depends upon environmental factors, such as race, rate of anatomical growth, state of health, and so on. Girls will generally reach puberty somewhere between the ages of nine and seventeen and boys between the ages of eleven and eighteen. Thus, although at thirteen we may find boys who are already pubescent and girls who are still prepubescent, the number of thirteen-year-old boys who are pubescent will be smaller than the number of thirteen-year-old girls of the same status.

Social and Emotional Aspects of Puberty

The impact of puberty engenders social and emotional differences for boys as compared to girls, and on the average they tend to follow markedly different paths of self-concept, social interaction, and expectation, and physiological functioning as they attempt to achieve the series of adjustments that lead to adulthood. In his comparative study of adolescent boys and girls, More (1953) notes:

The advent of puberty in girls appears to be a relatively abrupt phenomenon, requiring emotional adjustments of an immediate nature. There is significantly less coordination of puberty with changes in emotional attitude for the boys. With them it seems to be a fairly indefinite process in comparison with girls.

Similar findings obtain for boys as compared to girls in the area of social adjustment. However, whether or not the age at which an individual adolescent attains puberty is earlier or later than that of the majority of his same-age peers is particularly important. Deviancy tends to have social and emotional aspects that go beyond the mere fact that the deviate is different in one category of development or behavior. Thus, in considering the deviate one must take into account all sorts of associated behaviors that may accompany deviancy. While the early maturer has various social and physical advantages over the later maturer, the late maturer also has certain advantages of his own.

In a comparison, made when they were thirty-three years of age, of a group of men who as boys had been early or late maturing, Jones (1957) reports that as adolescents, the early maturers were more physically attractive, more poised, more relaxed, and more matter of fact. Late maturers were more socially reactive, in that they were more eager, talkative, attention getting, and expressive. Such social expressive behavior, sometimes symptomatic of anxiety, may have advantages in various kinds of social transactions, but it also exposes the adolescent to possible rejection because he may appear overeager, subservient, intrusive, and even a nuisance. Jones, in this same study, did note that although the physical differences disappeared in adulthood, the pattern of personality differences distinguishing early and late maturers persisted. From this study we may gather that age of onset of puberty in boys does have implications for their personal adjustment. In this connection Mussen and Jones (1957) report that while early and late maturers did not differ in need achievement or in need for personal recognition, late maturers did display more negative concepts of self, more feelings of being dominated and rejected, more feelings of inadequacy, a more rebellious attitude toward their parents, and a greater prolongation of dependency needs. Early maturers, in contrast, were more self-confident, independent, and capable of playing an adult role in interpersonal relationships. Peskin (1967) writes that the length of a child's latency period acts as a regulator for the somatic changes to follow and may well exert a decisive influence on the impulse-control mechanisms of his personality during the second decade of life. However, an optimistic note is struck by Jones (1965), who, while acknowledging that the physically accelerated boy is socially advantaged in the peer culture and that the same pattern continues into adulthood, also points out that the late-maturing boy is active and explorative, with evidence of compensatory mechanisms. She also notes the tendency of the late-maturing boy to be insightful, independent, and impulsive in adulthood.

There is of course a broad spectrum of individual differences in the social effects of puberty on girls. For some girls physical maturity is much more important than it is for others. In a six-year longitudinal study of seventeen girls, More (1953) says the more physically mature girl is:

regarded by her peers as being warmer, more friendly, pleasant to be around, and emotionally stable than the less physically mature girl. The earlier maturing girl is seen as participating in peer life at a higher rate than her retarded sisters, and in so doing she earns a reputation for being relatively forceful, assertive, and bossy in group action. The earlier maturing girl tends to be well groomed, calm, and physically integrated. By contrast, the later maturing girl displays a higher degree of motoric tension to her peers. She is felt to be more quarrelsome, argumentative and demanding of attention than the earlier maturing girl.

A somewhat different picture was presented by Shipment (1964), who reports no differences between early- and late-maturing girls in emotional maturity or in performance upon a measure of timidity.

In contrast to girls, More (1953) notes that "broadly speaking," in the sample he studied, the order of physical maturation for boys lacked an important relationship to peer evaluations of social interaction variables.

A further interesting social-adjustment difference contrasts late-maturing boys and late-maturing girls. Faust (1960) reports that less developmentally mature (menarcheal age) girls in junior high school were characterized by a tendency to withdraw and to attempt to be inconspicuous in their groups, whereas more

mature girls received significantly high scores on such items as "grown-up" and "possesses older friends." Jones and Bayley (1950), on the other hand, note that late-maturing boys received higher than average ratings on behavior such as attention-getting, assurance in class, restlessness, and talkativeness. Jones and Bayley feel that such attention-getting mannerisms were attempts at compensation for inferiority by late-maturing boys, as a means of defending themselves against the anxieties caused by late development. Jones and Bayley (1950) also note that "grown-up" and "older" friends discriminate between early- and late-maturing boys in a Guess-Who test. In commenting on the Jones and Bayley study as compared to her own, Faust (1960) writes: "Both of these patterns seem to represent a perseveration of certain of the components of the respective, sex-appropriate, pre-adolescent pattern which was prestige lending for neither boys nor girls at this level." Stone and Barker (1939) also indicated level of maturity as a factor in friendship.

In discussing emotional maturation, More (1953) writes that the earlier-maturing girl is "different from her late maturing sister in factors of emotional maturation, of inner life, and psychological perspective both of herself and of the outer world." More (1953) reports the late-maturing girl as more preoccupied with a private fantasy life, more emotionally dependent, more inconsistent, and more governed in her behavior by pressures put on her by other people or events. As with social interaction, More sees less difference between early- and late-maturing girls. In relating the Mussen and Jones study with that of More, the reader may take the position that while puberty and its time of inception does have both social and emotional effects on both sexes, the effects are more far-reaching and dramatic for girls than for boys. In terms of social relationships, more mature children tend to be taller on the average and are more grown-up in appearance where secondary sex characteristics are concerned, and peer society usually sees these as prestige-building factors.

Douglas and Ross (1964) report, in a study of 1,700 boys and 1,600 girls, that some cultural factors appear to be involved in the age of onset of puberty. Measuring their sample at eight, eleven, and fifteen years of age, they found no relationship between age of onset of puberty and social class, but they did find the following intellectual and performance variables to favor the early maturers: (1) higher intelligence and reading scores, (2) long retention in school, and (3) better school performance. Differences in all three variables were most pronounced among boys whose parents could be categorized in the lower working class. Still, even in the cultural realm, individual differences cannot be ignored. Basing their study upon the single case of an exceedingly early maturing girl, Connor and McGeorge (1965) note that she presented a picture of good adjustment, with psychosexual adjustment appropriate to her age.

In considering the studies cited on physical maturation, the reader should remember that discussions of these matters are in terms of averages and tendencies. An individual child may well depart from the norm, and an extreme deviation in the advent of puberty, such as extremely early maturing, may place the child in a very difficult position where social expectation is concerned, to the point that he or she may encounter exceptional problems of social and emotional adjustment.

Endocrine Aspects of Adolescence

Puberty is part of the normal growth process and closely associated with all the other factors and phenomena of growth. One of these factors is the glands of internal secretion, which are of considerable importance in preparing an individual for sexual maturity, as well as in promoting other aspects of growth. Nathanson, Towne, and Aub (1941) note that the glands of internal secretion have three main functions: "to stimulate growth, to influence metabolic activities, and to regulate the physical metamorphoses of children." In speaking of their relations to growth they write:

Development in normal youth is essentially a problem of normal activity of the pituitary gland and the ability of the peripheral endocrine organs to respond to its stimulation. Laboratory and clinical evidence indicate that without the normal function of this particular endocrine organ, the otherwise normal peripheral glands such as ovaries and testicles remain quiescent and unstimulated. The problem, therefore, of normal sex differentiation in growth in childhood is essentially a problem of the stimulation of the peripheral glands by the secretion of the anterior pituitary gland. Alterations in puberty seem to be due usually to abnormalities of the anterior pituitary stimulation and much less frequently to abnormalities of the gonads, the adrenals, or other endocrine glands.

Shuttleworth (1939) advanced a somewhat controversial endocrine theory of growth, developed in connection with the Harvard Growth Study. He stated:

In brief, our theory is that the patterns of physical growth shown by different dimensions and different groups from conception to maturity are the resultant of a progressive balancing of endocrine factors, of the timing of endocrine stimulation, of factors peculiar to each dimension, of factors determining mature size, and of factors associated with sex. Each of these five factors represents an exceedingly complex set of forces, some of which operate persistently throughout the growth span, while others operate for only limited intervals and at different ages. None acts independently. All are inextricably entangled by their mutual action and interaction in a single continuous process. An observed growth pattern is the external manifestation of the constantly shifting balance of such underlying forces.

In general, it appears that some time before the onset of pubescence the anterior lobe of the pituitary gland produces a gonadotropic hormone (follicle-stimulating hormone, FSH, prolan A),[8] which tends to stimulate the growth of the immature gonads. Greulich (1944) states:

An inadequate production of gonadotropic hormone in the pre-adolescent child prevents the

[8]A hormone which produces accelerated sexual maturation. Injection of the pituitary gonadotropic hormone in immature animals tends to result in more rapid sexual maturation.

normal growth and development of the ovaries or testes, and, indirectly, that of the other reproductive organs as well, and results in a hypogonadal or hypogenital condition, in which the reproductive organs remain in an immature state and the various secondary sexual characteristics fail to develop properly. On the other hand, the presence of an excessive amount of this gonadotropic hormone in early life produces one type of precocious sexual development.

Thus, under the stimulation of the gonadotropic hormone, the gonads (ovaries in females, testes in males) accelerate their growth and the individual attains sexual maturity; at this point the gonads produce mature sperm and ova, as well as estrogenic (female) and androgenic (male) sex hormones.

In this connection Shock (1944) cites evidence that hormone secretion occurs prior to the time the gonads begin their accelerated growth, although it exists in relatively small amounts.

With advancing age and developmental status there is a general tendency for this hormone (the gonadotropic) to increase in amount from the undetectable level of early childhood to levels characteristic of the adult. Since castration in prepubertal boys leads to an immediate large output of gonadotropic hormone, it may be assumed that either the immature pituitary gland excretes some gonadotropic substance which is completely utilized by the immature gonad, or the immature gonad exerts on the pituitary some inhibitory effect which normally diminishes at puberty. Thus, there is no reason to believe that the onset of puberty in boys is characterized by a sudden secretion of the pituitary gland. A probable mechanism for the initiation of puberty is a gradual increase in pituitary secretion coupled with an increasing sensitivity of the gonads to the hormone.

In both boys and girls, estrogens and androgens (17-ketosteroids) may be traced in constantly enlarging amounts from the third year through puberty. Figure 50 presents age changes in the excretion of male and female sex hormones, after a study of Nathanson et al. (1941). Nathanson et al. (1941) write:

From three to seven years of age, both boys and girls excrete a small and constant amount of estrogens and 17-ketosteroids in the urine. There is very little difference between the sexes. From eight to eleven years of age there is an increased excretion of these sex hormones; 17-ketosteroids increase more rapidly in boys, estrogen in girls. About one and one-half years before the menarche, estrogen excretion becomes cyclic in girls; and the intensity of these cycles gradually increase. The appearance of estrogen cycles precedes the dramatic sexual development of girls before the menarche. No cycles are obvious in the excretions of girls before the menarche. No cycles are obvious in the excretions of boys. There is no cycle in 17-ketosteroid excretion in either sex. Boys, however, have a higher excretion, especially after eleven years of age when secondary sex characteristics begin to appear.

Nathanson et al. (1941) note that the period of small excretion of estrogens and 17-ketosteroids between three and seven years of age is a time when the body build of boys and girls is not particularly dissimilar. They note that the origin of these hormones is not fully established and "some of them may come from the adrenal cortex rather than from the ovaries and testes," although they do not rule out the possibility that the ovaries and testes may be factors in their formation. In discussing the prepubertal estrogen cycle in girls, they write:

The fact that both the 17-ketosteroids and the estrogens rise in both sexes, long before a cycle of estrogen appears in girls, indicates that the primary stimulation of the peripheral endocrine glands results in a constant secretion, and the cyclic secretion is superimposed on this initial change. In boys the physical changes of puberty accompany the simple continued elevation of androgen excretion, [while] in girls it is clear that the cyclic excretion of estrogens precedes the appearance of striking secondary sex characteristics.

Thus, it may be observed that both androgens and estrogens are excreted by both sexes, but that the excretion of androgen is more characteristic of males than of females, and the excretion of estrogens is more characteristic of females. However, an excessive secretion of the major hormone of the opposite sex by either a boy or a girl will tend to lead to at least a

Figure 50   *Age Changes in the Excretion of Sex Hormones*

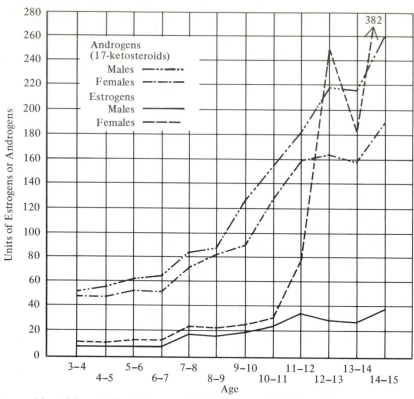

Source: Adapted from I. T. Nathanson, L. E. Towne, and J. C. Aub, "Normal excretion of sex hormones in childhood," *Endocrinology* 28 (1941): 851–865. Reprinted by permission of J. B. Lippincott Company and Mrs. J. C. Aub.

partial assumption of some of the secondary sex characteristics of members of the opposite sex. The drastic increase of the sex hormone appropriate to one's sex following the ninth year may be seen in the data presented in Figure 50, although androgen is secreted in relatively larger amounts than is estrogen.

The amount of hormones present at any point in the growth cycle of an individual, and, by analogy, the rate of activity of the glands from which the hormones are secreted, may be determined through quantitative analysis by measuring the amounts of pituitary, adrenal, and sex hormones to be found in the blood and urine. The methods used are still comparatively crude, and there now appears to be no accurate

way of determining the presence of sex hormones in the bloodstream, although it is possible to measure the amounts of the hormones secreted in the urine through chemical analysis.

Because this is a new field with uncertain techniques, there have been comparatively few studies in the determination of hormone levels in the urine, and even fewer attempts to correlate the information derived to the human growth sequence. Most of the studies have utilized animals or very small samples of available children. One of the more important studies in this area is that of Nathanson et al. (1941), who used 104 normal children and made a total of 1,100 hormone determinations.

Other Physiological Changes

In general, the rate of physiological maturation differs greatly for different physiological changes, and quite sudden changes may occur in the case of any individual. Particularly extreme variability is characteristic of many of the physiological functions during the adolescent period owing partly to the fact that the adolescent has failed, or has not had time, to learn to maintain a physiological equilibrium. Thus, in interpreting studies of adolescent physiological functioning, this variability should be constantly in mind.

Among the many physiological changes that occur during adolescence are those in circulation, pulse rate, blood pressure, and the chemical composition of the blood; changes in respiration and energy metabolism; and changes in the products of excretory function. As adolescence proceeds the pulse rate tends to diminish and, although an increase occurs with exercise, the amount of that increase is less. Early-menstruating girls and children who experience an early adolescent growth spurt have a pulse rate that is characteristic of more mature girls.

Blood pressure rises with age, although there is a tendency for a decrease in girls after age sixteen. Total respiratory volume increases during adolescence, with average vital capacity increasing about three times between ages six and sixteen. Basal metabolism tends on the average to diminish, following a metabolic acceleration at puberty. However, metabolic changes with age are greater and less variable for boys than for girls. A rapid decrease occurs with the beginning of menstruation.

Shock (1944) writes that many of the problems an adolescent has to deal with are those:

associated with the adjustments which the adolescent is called upon to make to an environment dominated by adults at a time when his own internal environment is in a state of flux. The unpredictable variations in the adolescent's behavior, so exasperating to adults, may often have a physiological basis. . . . Until the individual can reconcile his own internal environment with his social and cultural environment, some degree of conflict and psychological turmoil will likely prevail.

Such behavior may range from restless activity, resulting perhaps from an increased production of sex hormones within the adolescent, to the opposite picture of apathy and listlessness during periods of lowered basal metabolism. In either case, the adolescent must adjust if he is to escape periods of conflict, unrest, and seemingly erratic behavior.

For the most part, the outward manifestations of physiological change are acceptable enough in our culture for the average adolescent to adjust to them. One exception is acne, which often appears during adolescence and which tends not only to cause embarrassment to the adolescent himself but sometimes calls forth an unfortunate reaction of distaste from those with whom he comes in contact.

Summary

The phenomenon of growth is extremely complex, composed of many interrelated aspects, any one of which cannot be studied apart from the others if its real contribution to human behavior is to be understood. Therefore, psychologists have customarily selected stages, points of reference, or rallying points around which to arrange and interpret the interrelated variables of growth. For the psychologist one of the most significant rallying points is the advent of puberty.

Puberty is that time in the life cycle at which the reproductive organs attain functional maturity. Its advent is marked by first menstruation in girls; there is no clear-cut line of demarcation between the prepubescent and the pubescent boy. The average age at the advent of puberty appears to fall between twelve and thirteen for girls, and between fourteen and fifteen for boys. Environmental as well as internal physiological factors appear to influence the age at which puberty will occur in a given individual, although climatic factors are deemphasized in current thinking.

The advent of puberty is also marked in both sexes by the appearance of a series of secondary sex characteristics as well as by various behavior changes.

Puberty is closely associated with the growth and activity of the internal secretion glands, which tend to stimulate growth, influence metabolic activities, and regulate the physical metamorphosis of children. The anterior pituitary gland plays the most important role of all in promoting an individual's physical maturity. There is general agreement that the advent of sexual maturity is closely related to an increasing amount of hormone secretion.

Puberty brings with it interest in the opposite sex and new sex activities, which become inevitable and normal aspects of the adolescent's life. The student of the adolescent period of development must recognize the importance to the adolescent of the new experiences that accompany sexual maturity. Adolescent sexual activities and sexual desires often lead to emotional difficulties and guilt reactions. The adolescent is a sexually mature individual who has all the adult's biological sex drives, tensions, and needs for sexual release, but no socially approved means of securing direct relief. The form of sexual outlet an individual adopts will depend upon his social environment and his upbringing. The importance of proper sex information and education cannot be overemphasized.

The advent of puberty has different emotional and social implications for boys as compared to girls. For girls, puberty is a relatively abrupt phenomenon, making emotional demands of a more severe order than is ordinarily true of boys. The same situation obtains in the area of social adjustment to both peers and adults. In general, the early-maturing girl presents a better picture of emotional and social integration than does her late-maturing sister, although in this, as in all areas of behavior, there is a spectrum of individual differences. Late-maturing boys often present a more aggressive and restless picture than do those boys whose maturity is accelerated.

Among the many physiological changes, of either acceleration or deceleration, occurring during adolescence are changes in circulation, exemplified in pulse rate, blood pressure, and the internal composition of the blood; and changes in respiration and energy metabolism. One of the most important aspects of physiological development is the great individual variation and fluctuation that occurs. Curves of function cited are usually smoothed curves, which tend to obscure or compensate for the individual variations that make up the average curve. One main reason for such individual variation lies in the fact that the adolescent either has failed, or has not had time, to learn to maintain a physiological equilibrium. The adolescent is undergoing many physiological adjustments that were not necessary in childhood and that will have reached stability in adulthood. For this reason, adolescence may be regarded as a period of physiological learning.

References

Backman, G. Die beschleunigte Entwicklung der Jugend verfruhte Menarche, verspatete Menopause, verlangerte Lebensdauer. *Act. Anat.* 4 (1948) : 421–480.

Baldwin, B. T. A measuring scale for physical growth and physiological age. *15th Yearbook.* National Society for the Study of Education: Public School Publishing Company, 1916.

Bayley, N. Research in child development: A longitudinal perspective. *Merrill-Palmer Quarterly* 11 (1965) : 183–208.

Bell, R. Q. Retrospective and prospective views of early personality development. *Merrill-Palmer Quarterly* 6 (1960) : 133–144.

Berg, I.A. Cultural trends and the task of psychology. *American Psychologist* 20 (1965) : 203–207.

Boas, G. Studies in growth. *Human Biology* 4 (1932) : 307–350.

Burrell, R. J. W.; Healy, M. J. R.; and Tanner, J. M. Age at menarche in South African Bantu girls living in the Transkei Reserve. *Human Biology* 33 (1961) : 250–261.

Carey, T. F. The relation of physical growth to developmental age in boys. *Monographs for Research in Child Development*. Washington: Catholic University, 1936.

Carlson, R. Stability and change in the adolescent's self-image. *Child Development* 36 (1965) : 659–666.

Clements, E. M. B. Changes in the mean stature and weight of British children over the past seventy years. *British Medical Journal* 2 (1953) :897–912.

Connor, D. V., and McGeorge, M. Psychological aspects of accelerated pubertal development. *Journal of Child Psychology and Psychiatry* 6 (1965) : 161–177.

Crampton, C. W. Anatomical or physiological age versus chronological age. *Pedigogical Seminary* 15 (1908) : 230–237.

Crampton, C. W. Physiological age—a fundamental principle. *Child Development* 15 (1944) : 3–52.

Dearborn, W. F., and Rothney, J. W. M. *Predicting the child's development*. Cambridge: Sci-Art Publishers, 1941.

Dimock, H. S. *Rediscovering the adolescent*. New York: Association Press, 1937.

Donovan, B. T., and ten Bosch, V. *Physiology of puberty*. Baltimore: Williams and Wilkins, 1965.

Douglas, J. W. B., and Ross, J. M. Age of puberty related to educational ability, attainment, and school leaving age. *Journal of Child Psychology and Psychiatry* 5 (1964) : 185–196.

Ellis, R. W. B. Age of puberty in the tropics. *British Medical Journal* 1 (1950) : 85–89.

Engle, E., and Shelesnyak, M. First menstruation and subsequent menstrual cycles of pubertal girls. *Human Biology* 4 (1934) : 431–453.

Falkner, F. General consideration in human development. In Falkner, F., ed., *Human development*, pp. 10–39. Philadelphia: Saunders, 1966.

Faust, M. S. Developmental maturity as a determinant in prestige of adolescent girls. *Child Development* 31 (1960) : 173–186.

Gould, H. N., and Gould, M. R. Age of first menstruation in mothers and daughters. *Journal of the American Medical Association* 98 (1932) : 1349–1352.

Goulet, L. R., and Baltes, P. B. *Life-span developmental psychology*. New York: Academic Press, 1970.

Greulich, W. W. Physical changes in adolescence. In *Adolescence*, 43rd Yearbook of the National Society for the Study of Education, pp. 8–32. Chicago: University of Chicago Press, 1944.

Greulich, W. W.; Day, H. G.; Lachman, S. E.; Wolfe, J. B.; and Shuttleworth, F. K. A handbook of methods for the study of adolescent children. *Monographs of the Society for Research in Child Development*, vol. 3, 1938.

Henton, C. L. A comparative study of the onset of menarche among Negro and white children. *Journal of Psychology* 46 (1958) : 65–73.

Henton, C. L. The effect of socio-economic and emotional factors on the onset of menarche among Negro and white girls. *Journal of Genetic Psychology* 98 (1961) : 255–264.

Jones, H. E. The development of physical abilities. In *Adolescence*, 43rd Yearbook of the National Society for the Study of Education, pp. 100–122. Chicago: University of Chicago Press, 1944.

Jones, M. C. The later careers of boys who were early—or late—maturing. *Child Development* 28 (1957) : 11–128.

Jones, M. C. Psychological correlates of somatic development. *Child Development* 36 (1965) : 899–911.

Jones, M. C., and Bayley, N. Physical maturing among boys as related to behavior. *Journal of Educational Psychology* 41 (1950) : 129–148.

Kessen, W. Research design in the study of developmental problems. In Mussen, P. H., ed., *Handbook of research methods in developmental psychology*, chapter 2. New York: Wiley, 1960.

Kiil, V. Stature and growth of Norwegian men during the past 200 years. *Skr. Norske Vidensk Akad.*, no. 6, 1939.

Kiil, V. Menarch-alderen hos Skolepiker i Oslo og sammenhengen mellom menarche-alder og fysisk utvikling. *Statist. Kvartalshelft* 43 (1953) : 84–88.

Kinsey, A. C.; Pomeroy, W. B.; and Martin, C. E. *Sexual behavior in the human male*. Philadelphia: Saunders, 1948.

Kinsey, A. C.; Pomeroy, W. B.; et al. *Sexual behavior in the human female*. Philadelphia: Saunders, 1953.

Krogman, W. M. The physical growth of children:

An appraisal of studies 1950–1955. *Monographs of the Society for Research in Child Development,* vol. 20, 1955.

Kubitschek, P. E. Sexual development of boys with special reference to the appearance of the sexual characters and their relationship to structural and personality types. *Journal of Nervous and Mental Disease* 76 (1932): 425–451.

Kussmaul, A. Uber geschlechtliche Fruhreife. *Wurzb. Med. Zeitschr.* 3 (1862): 321–360.

Land, G. M. van't, and Haas, J. H. de. Menarche—leftijd in Nederland. *Nederland Tijdschrift Geneesk* 101 (1957): 1425–1431.

Levine, V. E. Studies in physiological anthropology. III. The age of onset of menstruation of the Alaskan Eskimo. *American Journal of Anthropology* 11 (1953): 252.

Meredith, H. V. The rhythm of physical growth. *University of Iowa Studies in Child Welfare* 11 (1935): 1–128.

Meredith, H. V. Stature of Massachusetts children of North European and Italian ancestry. *American Journal of Physical Anthropology* 24 (1939): 301–346.

Mills, C. A. Geographic and time variations in body growth and age of menarche. *Human Biology* 9 (1937): 43–56.

Mills, C. A. Temperature influence over human growth and development. *Human Biology* 22 (1950): 71–74.

Minick, M. A. Cortisol and cortisine excretion from infancy to adult life. *Metabolism* 15 (1966): 359–363.

Montagu, M. F. A. *The reproductive development of the female.* New York: Julian Press, 1957.

More, D. M. Developmental concordance and discordance during puberty and during adolescence. *Monographs of the Society for Research in Child Development,* vol. 18, 1953.

Mueller, H. Enkele waarnemingen omtrent den groei van het beenderenstelsel en omtrent de geslachterijkheid van Javaansche meisjes. *Mededeelengen van den Dienst de Volksgezondheid in Nederlandsch-Indie* 21 (1932): 48–63.

Muller, T. Die Korperproportionen und ihre veranderungen im Kleinkindalter. *Archive Julius-Klaus Stift,* Zurich 25 (1950): 375–468.

Mussen, P. H., ed., *Handbook of research methods in child development.* New York: Wiley, 1960.

Mussen, P. H., and Jones, M. C. Self-conceptions, motivations and interpersonal attitudes of late and early maturing boys. *Child Development* 28 (1957): 243–256.

Nathanson, I. T.; Towne, L. E.; and Aub, J. C. Normal excretion of sex hormones in childhood. *Endocrinology* 23 (1941): 851–856.

Neurath, R. *Die Pubertat.* Vienna: Julius Springer, 1932.

Norval, M.; Kennedy, R. L. J.; and Berkon, J. Biometric studies of the growth of children of Rochester, Minnesota. *Human Biology* 23 (1951): 273–301.

Peskin, H. Pubertal onset and ego functioning. *Journal of Abnormal Psychology* 72 (1967): 1–15.

Petri, E. Untersuchungen zur Erbbedingtheit der Menarche. *Zeitschr. Morph. Anthropologie* 33 (1935): 43–48.

Roberton, J. Period of puberty in women. *New England Medical and Surgical Journal,* 1831. (Abstracted in *American Journal of Science.*)

Roberton, J. On the alleged influence of climate on female puberty in Greece. *Edinburgh Medical and Surgical Journal* 62 (1844): 1–11.

Roberton, J. On the period of puberty in Esquimaux women. *Edinburgh Medical and Surgical Journal* 63 (1845): 57–65.

Romanus, T. Menarche in school girls. *Acta Genetic.* (Basel) 45 (1952): 33–47.

Sanford, N. Will psychologists study human problems? *American Psychologist* 20 (1965): 192–202.

Schaeffer, R. Uber Beginn, Dauer, und Erloschen der Menstruation: Statistische Mitteilungen uber 10,500 Falle aus der Gynaekologischen Poliklinik. *Monatschrift fur Geburtshilfe und Gynaekologie* 23 (1906): 169–191.

Schonfeld, W. A. Primary and secondary sexual characteristics: Study of their development in males from birth through maturity. *American Journal of the Diseases of Children* 65 (1943): 535–549.

Shilo, I. Sekar al hathalat haveset ben benot batey hasefer birushalayim (Survey on the age of menarche in school pupils in Jerusalem.) *Harefuah* 59 (1960): 305–307.

Shilo, A., and Goldberg, R. Sekar al hathalat haveset etsel naarot batey-hasefer be-Tel-Aviv (Survey of menarche among Tel Aviv school girls.) *Harefuah* 68 (1965): 161–163.

Shipment, W. G. Age of menarche and adult personality. *Archives of General Psychiatry* 10 (1964): 155–159.

Shock, N. W. Physiological changes in adolescence. In *Adolescence*, 43rd Yearbook of the National Society for the Study of Education. Chicago: University of Chicago Press, 1944.

Shuttleworth, F. K. Sexual maturation and the physical growth of girls aged six to nineteen. *Monographs of the Society for Research in Child Development*, vol. 2, 1937.

Shuttleworth, F. K. The physical and mental growth of boys and girls ages six through nineteen in relation to their age of maximum growth. *Monographs of the Society for Research in Child Development*, vol. 4, 1939.

Stein, R. O. Untersuchungen uber die Ursache der Glatze. *Wiener Klin. Wschr.* 1 (1924): 6–10.

Stone, A. A., and Onque, G. C. *Longitudinal studies of child personality.* Cambridge: Harvard University Press, 1959.

Stone, C. P., and Barker, R. G. The attitudes and interests of premenarcheal girls. *Journal of*

Genetic Psychology 54 (1939): 27–71.

Tanner, J. M. Some notes on the reporting of growth data. *Human Biology* 23 (1951): 93–159.

Tanner, J. M. *Growth at adolescence.* Springfield, Illinois: Charles C. Thomas, 1955.

Tanner, J. M., and O'Keefe, B. Age at menarche in Nigerian school girls, with a note on their heights and weights from age 12 to 19. *Human Biology* 34 (1962): 187–196.

Tisserand-Perrier, M. Etude comparative de certains processus de croissance chez les jumeaux. *Journal de la Génétique Humaine* 2 (1953): 87–102.

Wilson, D. C., and Sutherland, I. Further observation on the age of menarche. *British Medical Journal* 2 (1950): 862–866.

Zukowski, W.; Kmietowicz-Zukowska, A.; and Gruska, S. The age at menarche in Polish girls. *Human Biology* 36 (1964): 233–234.

Suggested Readings

Adams, P. L. Puberty as a biosocial turning point. *Psychosomatics* 10 (1969): 343–349.

Adams, P. L. Late sexual maturation in girls. *Medical Aspects of Human Sexuality* 6 (1972): 50–75.

Amundsen, D. W., and Diers, C. J. The age of menarche in classical Greece and Rome. *Human Biology* 41 (1969): 125–131.

Birnbaum, F. D., and Eskin, B. A. Psychosexual aspects of endocrine disorders. *Medical Aspects of Human Sexuality* 7 (1973): 134–150.

Bojlen, K., and Bentzon, M. W. The influence of climate and nutrition on age at menarche. *Human Biology* 40: 69–85.

Frisch, R., and Revelle, R. Height and weight at menarche and a hypothesis of critical body weights and adolescent events. *Science* 169 (1970): 397–399.

Ivey, M. E., and Bardwick, J. M. Patterns of affective fluctuation in the menstrual cycle. *Psychosomatic Medicine* 30 (1968): 336–345.

Kogut, M. D. Growth and development in adolescence. *Pediatric Clinics of North America* 20 (1973): 789–806.

Marshall, W. A., and Tanner, J. M. Variations in pattern of pubertal changes in girls. *Archives of the Diseases of Childhood* 44 (1969): 291–303.

Marshall, W. A., and Tanner, J. M. Variations in the pattern of pubertal changes in boys. *Archives of the Diseases of Childhood* 45 (1970): 13–23.

Root, A. W. Endocrinology of puberty. *Journal of Pediatrics* 83 (1973): 1–19.

Schachter, R. J., et al. Acne vulgaris and psychologic impact on high school students. *New York State Journal of Medicine* 71 (1971): 2886–2890.

Tanner, J. M. Growth and endocrinology of the adolescent. In Gardner, L. I., ed., *Endocrine and genetic diseases of childhood.* Philadelphia: Saunders, 1969.

Tanner, J. M. Human growth hormone. *Nature* 237 (1972): 433–439.

Thomas, J. K. Adolescent endocrinology for counselors of adolescents. *Adolescence* 8 (1973): 395–406.

Visser, H. K. A. Some physiological and clinical aspects of puberty. *Archives of the Diseases of Childhood* 48 (1973): 169–182.

Zacharias, L.; Wurtman, R. J.; and Schatzoff, M. Sexual maturation in contemporary American girls. *American Journal of Obstetrics and Gynecology* 108 (1970): 833–846.

Chapter Nineteen

Structural Growth and Physical Functioning

Hand in hand with physiological changes go changes in the body structure and proportions of children who are experiencing puberty. These physiological, anatomical, and structural changes are closely interrelated, and all have far-reaching emotional and social effects. A child's body structure and the course of his skeletal growth are the outward physical manifestations of himself that he presents to the world. Both adults and the child's peers, including members of the opposite sex, tend to judge him as a person by these manifestations, as they adhere to or depart from the norm. Therefore, an understanding of the course and nature of skeletal development and body form is essential in arriving at a thorough understanding of adolescent behavior and in interpreting certain classes of adolescent problems and facilitations.

Skeletal Analysis

The discussion in Chapter 17 noted the need to classify and compare adolescents according to some common reference point. Sexual maturity, commonly called pubescence, is one of the most useful of such reference points. A great many internal and external changes occur at about the time of puberty,[1] some just prior to its advent, some immediately following it. It is therefore possible to say that the sexually

mature person has proceeded further along the path of physical growth and development than has the sexually immature or prepubescent.

Chronological age has traditionally been the most popular means of classifying children.[2] Unfortunately, chronological age represents only one aspect of growth—an external one at that—and it does not provide a true physiological or physical picture of the individual. Individual differences within any given age range are so great that chronological age as such becomes meaningless as a comparative index, particularly if people of similar chronological age are compared. Young (1963) notes that skeletal and pubertal maturity, rather than chronological age, accounts for most of the variability among adolescent boys. For example, a thirteen-year-old boy may be sexually mature and much more developed physically than a fourteen-year-old boy, and a fourteen-year-old girl may have proceeded much further along the path of physical development than has a sixteen-year-old boy. Hence, there is general agreement that one's sexual maturity status offers a more useful frame of reference for comparing individuals than does chronological age.

[1]The onset of puberty is the earliest age at which an individual can bear or beget children.

[2]In popular thinking, chronological age is most often used to determine the individual's maturity as well as his legal and moral responsibility. We say, "He couldn't help it; he's only six." In many states sixteen is the legal age for obtaining a driver's permit. Eighteen was set as the minimum draft age in World War II. Minimum ages for marriage and for full responsibility have received legal sanction. An individual is not permitted to vote until he is eighteen. An individual may not be a United States senator before he is thirty, nor president of the United States before he is thirty-five.

However, one difficulty with using pubescence as a comparative reference point is the difficulty in determining exactly when its advent occurs. As already explained, menarche, or age at first menstruation, is commonly used as a means of classification of girls. Classification of boys is more difficult, but generally the stage of development of axillary hair, pubic hair, or secondary sexual characteristics is used to determine a boy's pubescent status. The Crampton Criteria, mentioned in Chapter 18, have been one method of arriving at an index of a boy's developmental age. However, the use of symptoms such as menarche or various exterior signs such as hair has been criticized as being undependable and involving processes other than the inception of physical maturity.

There are other ways, including skeletal age, dental age, and morphological age (size, height, etc.), to determine a boy's or girl's level of physical maturity. Shuttleworth (1939), in the Harvard Growth Study, classified children as early, average, and late maturing by determining the individual's age of most rapid growth (age of maximum growth) through an analysis of consecutive measurements made at stated intervals during his growing-up process. But Shuttleworth's method presupposes the existence of serial records that would not ordinarily be available unless a well-planned longitudinal study were in process. Stolz and Stolz (1951), in their analysis of the growth of adolescent boys, used age at maximum height velocity, and Nicholson and Hanley (1953) have used a percentage of adult height (usually 90 percent), but both these have value only in looking back and interpreting children who have been followed longitudinally throughout their growth period.

One of the more accurate methods for determining level of maturity may be that of skeletal analysis. In this method the progress or status of ossification is recorded by means of x-ray pictures. Skeletal analysis has the great advantage of providing a comparatively exact estimate of the individual's level of maturity at any point in his life span.

Two kinds of ossification occur in the human skeleton. One is intramembranous, and the other is intracartilaginous or endochondral. Intramembranous ossification occurs to a large degree during the prenatal months. Before the cranial bones form, an outer layer of skin, a middle fibrous membrane, and inner meningeal membranes cover the brain. The fibrous membrane eventually becomes the periosteum and the bone. It is composed of a matrix of fibers and cells or osteoblasts. As bone forms, a process of calcification takes place from various points of ossification. First, spicules radiate, become fibers, and then calcify. The bone network becomes thicker as the osteoblasts form new layers of bone. The bone increases in thickness as layer after layer of bone tissue is deposited under the periosteum. The result is layers of bone on the inner and outer surface, with a layer of soft tissue in between. When the child is born, intramembranous ossification is not wholly complete. Over the skull surface there are still a number of membranous areas called fontanels, which separate the various ossified sections. Further ossification of the skull consists of the gradual uniting of the ossified centers and the elimination of the fontanels.[3] Intramembranous ossification is not used as a means of identifying later stages of physical maturity because the process is completed too early and is difficult to study in living organisms.

The second type of ossification, intracartilaginous, is the type most commonly used in studies of physical growth. Intracartilaginous ossification begins shortly after the second month in utero, by which time the embryo's skeleton is pretty well preformed or finished in cartilage.

Bone formation consists of the ossification and joining of the cartilage cells composing the skeleton. Working simultaneously from

---

[3]For those students interested in the process of ossification and further definition of terms such as spicules, periosteum, osteoblasts, etc., an adequate textbook of anatomy is suggested. Among the many available texts are C. S. Francis and G. C. Knowlton, *Textbook of Anatomy and Physiology*, 2nd ed., Mosby; A. S. Romer, *The Vertebrate Body*, Saunders; or H. W. Ham, *Histology*, Lippincott.

various centers, groups of cartilage cells arrange themselves in rows, and lime is deposited
in the spaces between the cells. The lime deposits, which at first only separate the cells,
finally surround them completely. Such en-
circlement shuts off the cells' nutriment, causing them to atrophy and eventually to
disappear. In the meantime, a number of cells
grow from the membrane, or perichondrium,
that covers the cartilage. These new cells are
deposited in the space left vacant by the
atrophy of the cartilage cells.

The number of centers of ossification is not
uniformly the same for all bones. In the long
bones, ossification proceeds first from a center
in the body of the bone called the diaphysis
and from centers at each extremity called the
epiphyses. Ossification proceeds both inward
and outward—that is, it proceeds from the
epiphyses toward the diaphysis, and from the
diaphysis toward the epiphyses. In short bones,
ossification proceeds toward the surface from
a point near the center.

Thin layers of cartilage continue to develop
between the epiphyses and the diaphysis as
each new portion ossifies. When such cartilage
layers are no longer added, the bone has attained its growth. Ordinarily, the individual is
in his early twenties before such bones as the
sternum and hip bones finally unite to form
single bones. In females, this process takes
about twenty years to reach completion, but a
somewhat longer time is involved in males.

Modern investigators have generally accepted
skeletal X rays as valid indicators of maturity,
and there appears to be a consensus that the
wrist bones may be taken as representative of
general developmental status.[4] However, a
number of investigators have preferred to use
other sections of the skeleton in addition to the
wrist in order to form a composite index.
Sontag and Lipford (1943) developed a concept of "bone age" based on X rays of several
joints. The foot, knee, hip, and elbow can all

yield definitive information. Unfortunately, a
problem arises in finding a standard with which
to compare skeletal X rays. There have been a
number of attempts to formulate such standards, but those presently available do not
entirely agree, with the result that indexes and
ages computed by different systems are not
directly comparable. Consequently, each investigator has to decide which standard he
intends to accept in making his study. At the
present time the most usable sets of standards
are those proposed by Flory (1936), Todd
(1937), and Tanner et al. (1959, 1962) for the
wrist and hand; by Pyle and Hoerr (1955) for
the knee;[5] by Speijer (1950) for the wrist,
hand, and pelvis for a sample of Dutch children; by Hoerr, Pyle, and Francis (1962) for
the foot and ankle; and by Acheson (1954a,
1954b, 1957) for the pelvis and hip joint.
Todd's position was that maturation within an
individual can best be witnessed by the transformation of fibrous tissue into bone and
cartilage, that, in effect, osteogenesis in cartilage represents a process of ripening, which
can be identified and analyzed.

Todd's (1939) basic work was performed by
an x-ray study of a sample of over one thousand
children. His most intensive work was done on
the knee, the hand, and the elbow. The study
was conducted by having the children return
at intervals for examination, so that a series of
X rays was available for each child. He found
progressively diminishing variability in the
weight curves of both boys and girls. Between
the first and fifth years, he noted a "stable and
uniform character of progress." In the period
from five to thirteen, girls showed a "minor
progressive acceleration of female skeletal
maturation" between the ages of six and eight,
with a slowing up between eight and nine. At
nine the maturation of males tends to catch
up with that of females. At ten girls again
accelerate, and by the time they are thirteen

[4]Here we must differentiate technically between maturation and growth. Where ossification as representative of
maturation is concerned, we mean a change in form of the
biological and chemical make-up of the tissue. In contrast,
growth represents the formation of new tissue.

[5]Todd's (1937) standards for the wrist and hand were
published as an atlas of skeletal maturation. Part I, *The
Hand*, has been revised by Greulich and Pyle (1950, 1959)
and published as a radiographic atlas of skeletal development of the hand and wrist. Pyle and Hoerr's standards
for the knee are also a revision of Todd's original work.

they have arrived at a state of maturation not attained by boys until they reach their fifteenth year. There is a definite slowing down of skeletal maturation in girls following their thirteenth year, until, by the sixteenth to the seventeenth year, boys have again caught up with them. Todd notes that from seventeen on, "an increasing stabilization is significantly apparent and the years eighteen to twenty-two are remarkable for the uniform maturation of the skeleton in males and females which both keep to the same schedule."

Of course there are individual differences; Todd's figures are merely averages and present the normative picture. In writing of individual differences in development Todd states:

Such peculiarities as are shown in the female accelerations between six and eight years and between ten and sixteen years cannot occur without considerable scatter. It is therefore quite to be expected that we should find, as we do, a greater individual variability among girls than among boys ... [but] many girls show no greater progress than the boys and some are even retarded behind the boys.

Todd notes that there is considerably less variability among younger children than among children between ten and sixteen. Flory (1935) notes that "girls are ahead of boys at birth; they are about one year ahead at school age; they are approximately one and one-half years ahead at age nine; and about two years ahead of boys at the average age of onset of puberty."

The Todd and Flory results agree in the main, but their citations of average ages differ. Such differences may be due to sampling or to various other factors, which would not necessarily invalidate the overall picture offered by either study. In comparing the Flory and Todd methods, Pyle and Menino (1939) note:

Skeletal age ratings made according to the Todd Atlas show that the Fels Institute children[6] were

more delayed in bone growth than when they were rated according to the Flory Atlas.... The children as a group were always consistently less mature in skeletal age than either standard, but less than five percent of the children are retarded enough to suggest significant delay in their bone development.

In comparing the two systems Bayley (1943) notes that "Flory's criteria of development stress the carpal bones, as areas less subject to environmental effects (retardation due to illness, nutritive disturbances, etc.)." She states that, aside from these and certain other differences, "in points of view regarding the relative importance of various criteria of maturation ... the two standards are similar" and "both give finer gradations for the process of skeletal maturation than can be found in ... other clinical norms."[7] Later, Bayer and Bayley (1959) wrote:

The Todd method ... makes use of the fact that, after an osseous center has appeared, it changes its size and shape in a systematic fashion as the ossification gradually spreads through the cartilaginous parts of the skeleton. Therefore, x-ray pictures of the bones that are maturing at a normal rate show regularly increasing maturity in the configuration of these osseous centers and often, also, in the adjoining ends of the long bones. Thus, it is possible to select a series of standard films of a single area that represent the characteristic bony patterns at successively mature ages. One can then readily compare a patient's film with these standards for its assessment.

For her own work Bayley uses the Greulich-Pyle revisions of the Todd Atlas (*Radiographic Atlas of Skeletal Development of the Hand and Wrist,* 1959), although she proposes that the Pyle-Hoerr 1955 standards for the knee are a second choice sometimes useful as an additional area for appraisal. However, the knee tends to be a less reliable indicator of skeletal maturity.

---

[6]The Fels Research Institute for the Study of Human Development had for many years been engaged in a broadly based longitudinal study of many crucial aspects of the growth and development of a population of children.

[7]Bayley (1940) has criticized many of the available clinical norms, stating that they "have the same defect as mental-age scales, in that they are dependent on chronological age. This forces the average curve of growth in a straight line, failing to distinguish the periods of rapid and slow development."

Figure 51 *A Comparison of the Skeletal Development
of Boys and Girls at Various Ages*

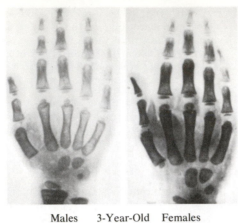

Males   3-Year-Old   Females   Males   6-Year-Old   Females

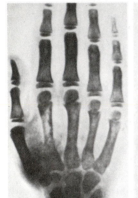
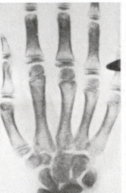
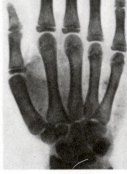

Males   9-Year-Old   Females   Males   12-Year-Old   Females

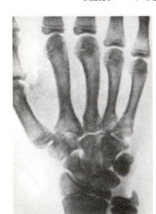
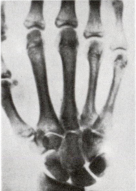
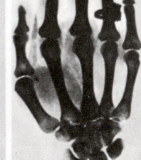

Males   15-Year-Old   Females   Males   17-Year-Old   Females

Source: C. D. Flory, "Osseous development in the hand as an index of skeletal development,"
Monographs of the Society for Research in Child Development 1, no. 3 (1936). Copyright 1936 by
The Society for Research in Child Development, Inc. Reprinted by permission of the publisher.

Figure 51 shows the skeletal development of the hand and wrist for boys and girls at various ages. Figure 52 shows the skeletal development of the knee. It is interesting to note that girls tend to mature on the average some two years earlier than boys, although there are large individual differences within each sex category; some boys are greatly advanced, some girls greatly retarded. In a study of the relationship between skeletal maturing and growth in the size of 177 early-, average-, and late-maturing girls, Bayley (1943a, 1943b) reports:

Early maturing girls, as a group, are relatively large and late maturing girls are small before thirteen years; while after this age their relative sizes are reversed. For their skeletal ages the late maturing girls tend to be larger than average at all ages. There is also a constant tendency for the early maturing girls to be small for their skeletal ages.

In boys, Bayley finds a different relationship between growth in size and rate of maturing. She writes:

For their chronological age early maturing boys are relatively large at all ages; late maturing boys are small between the ages of eleven and sixteen. When compared at the same skeletal ages, these differences disappear, with one exception—early maturing boys have relatively broad hips at all ages, especially as they grow older. The indexes of build show the late maturers to be characteristically slender-hipped and long-legged, while the early maturers are typically broad-hipped.

The body build indexes for girls generally do not reveal differences related to the rate of maturation, although at a given chronological age late maturers tend to be relatively narrow-hipped. Bayley does not feel that early or late maturing makes either boys or girls characteristically more or less masculine or feminine in terms of their national or racial characteristics.

Flory (1936), in speaking of the relationship between ossification and puberty writes:

Pubertal onset can be predicted fairly well by the appearance of the sesamoid bone at the distal end of the first metacarpal.[8] The sesamoid appears in girls' hands at about two years before first menstruation. This sesamoid appears after the ossification ratio has reached 100. Thus, first menstruation occurs after the ossification ratio is 100 or larger and after the sesamoid has appeared. Accelerated and retarded adolescence may be predicted therefore by these two means. Skeletal-months ratings have some value in predicting the onset of pubescence. A child who is accelerated in skeletal development is more likely to become pubescent earlier than an individual who is retarded in bony development. Skeletal-age ratings at age eleven correlate .647 ± .048 with first menstruation.

Advances in knowledge and technique have made early approaches seem relatively crude and unsophisticated. Such has been the case with skeletal analysis, where the need to rely upon simple pictorial standards characteristic of the early work is being gradually replaced by more advanced approaches, based on new knowledge about the ossification process. For example, it is now definitely recognized that there are irregularities in the ossification sequence and that some centers, even within a relatively restricted area such as the hand, are more informative than are others in judging the status of skeletal maturation.[9] Further, anatomic development does not proceed evenly, since discrepancies of several years may be found when comparing different parts of the body, as, for example, the hand and the foot. Acheson (1954a, 1957) has attempted to weigh different centers of ossification on the basis of the relative information they provide. Pyle and Sontag (1943) and Elgermark (1946) have studied the number and timing of various ossification centers, including the hip, knee and ankle, elbow, shoulder, and hand, and have provided tables summarizing their findings.

[8]A clearer understanding of the process of skeletal development as it pertains to the bones of the hand and the wrist may be gained if the student is familiar with the skeletal structure of these parts. Charts of skeletal structure may be found in sources such as B. Anson, *An Atlas of Human Anatomy*, Saunders.

[9]As early as 1937, Todd noted in his atlas that some centers of the hand apparently produced more information than did others, but he did not offer supportive evidence.

Figure 52　*Comparative Rates of Maturation in the Knee of Males and Females Developing at a Moderate Rate*

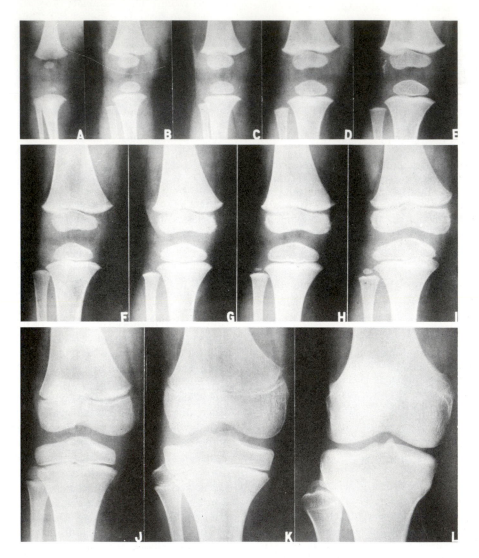

A.	Male, 40 Weeks	Female, 38 Weeks	G.	Male, 3 Years	Female, 2.3 Years
B.	Male, 6 Months	Female, 5 Months	H.	Male, 3.5 Years	Female, 2.7 Years
C.	Male, 9 Months	Female, 7.5 Months	I.	Male, 4.5 Years	Female, 3.5 Years
D.	Male, 12 Months	Female, 10 Months	J.	Male, 8 Years	Female, 6.2 Years
E.	Male, 18 Months	Female, 15 Months	K.	Male, 13 Years	Female, 10 Years
F.	Male, 2 Years	Female, 1.8 Years	L.	Male, 18 Years	Female, 15.5 Years

Source: From S. I. Pyle and N. L. Hoerr, *A radiographic standard of reference for the growing knee,* rev. ed. (Springfield, Ill.: Charles C. Thomas, 1969), p. 128, fig. 13. Courtesy of Charles C. Thomas, Publisher, Springfield, Illinois. Reprinted by permission of the publisher and S. I. Pyle.

Obviously the picture of general maturational status would be yielded by a sampling of the whole skeleton, although limited skeletal parts could be selected for the most efficient supply of information for specific purposes. As Garn, Silverman, and Rohmann (1964) write:

A . . . complication in bone-age assessment is the developmental discrepancy that can occur between one anatomical area or region of the body and a second region or area. Although skeletal development does proceed much as a whole . . . discrepancies of one or two years or even more may be observed when comparing the hand or lower arm to the foot or lower leg. . . . Depending on whether the hand is advanced relative to the leg or vice versa, use of a system involving the hand alone obviously can yield erroneous estimates of skeletal completion and residual growth . . . if the subject of concern is a particular bony area, that bone is more informative than the hand alone or the shoulder, elbow, and hand in combination. Conversely, if skeletal status as a whole is the subject of concern, a general sampling is clearly indicated.

Garn and associates,[10] using the serial radiographs gathered over a period of nearly four decades of subjects in the Fels Longitudinal Studies, have worked out a series of correlation matrices providing interrelationships at onset of ossification for each of fifty-two bony centers of the hand and foot. Using these centers as a starting point Garn et al. were able to locate nineteen centers with intercorrelations large enough that their predictive value was high, and they have suggested the "usefully-high predictive values" of these nineteen centers in skeletal analysis.

In the Garn intercorrelation tables it was found, in agreement with studies by others, that correlations were higher for girls than for boys and that the short bones of the fingers and toes provided higher correlations than did the wrist and ankle round bones. Garn, therefore, suggests that round bones should not be used in assessing skeletal maturation and that

some of the short bones, as well as the radius, ulna, tibia, and fibula, have so little predictive value that they could be eliminated from consideration. However, although the Fels Institute investigators have been interested in skeletal ossification for some time, their work is still such that a usable set of standards for the entire developmental sequence has yet to be formulated. Research at Fels is currently investigating the pattern of ossification in the knee, hip, shoulder, and elbow. Preliminary results indicate that hand-foot, knee-elbow, and shoulder-hip furnish the highest correlations for the onset of ossification. An interesting aspect here is that the genetically determined program for skeletal maturation ex utero is best revealed by the proximal and distal centers.[11]

Some question has been raised about the possible harmful effects of penetrating radiation resulting from the use of X rays in skeletal analysis. Modern technology and world atomic programs have made it more essential than ever to provide maximum protection when X rays are used, but X rays used in gaining pictures of the chest, long bones, soft tissues, and so on do not use radiation to the danger point unless used to excess. Adequate safeguards may be provided against the possibility of genetic mutations involving the progeny of the subject. Garn (1959) writes:

Besides the use of filters, and insistence on high-speed films and intensifying screens, radiation can be limited to the part involved, through the use of cones with adjustable lead diaphragms. The area of irradiation can further be reduced by aperture plates shaped to fit the plate proportions. Moreover, accidental direct gonadal radiation can be avoided by the use of lead-rubber flaps and shields. . . . The aim of all of these precautions is to minimize gonadal radiation to a point where it does not add appreciably to the natural background radiation. Even in a longitudinal growth study, continued on through adulthood, total gonadal doses can be kept far below the present recommended tolerances of 10r during the reproductive period.

[10]Garn and Rohmann (1959, 1960a, 1962); Garn, Rohmann, and Applebaum (1961); Garn, Silverman, and Rohmann (1964); Garn, Rohmann, and Robinow (1961).

[11]The reader may wish to relate this point to the Chapter 3 discussion of Gesell's theory of the course of development.

The reader will understand, of course, that modern x-ray apparatus and techniques are very complicated and must be used only by properly trained persons. Under no circumstances should an untrained person use x-ray apparatus; the inherent dangers, for both operator and person being x-rayed, are too great.

Bodily Dimension Relationships

While height and weight in relation to peers are commonly used to furnish estimates of a child's growth progress, such measures can furnish only a partial picture of a child's actual status. A more adequate picture is provided by measures of the relative proportions of the different parts of the body which go to make up body form or body build. Wide differences will be found in skeletal build and in the proportions of the body and its extremities. A person may be tall and thin, tall and fat, short and fat, or short and thin. Some persons are well muscled, others are not. Some have a large skeletal framework with broad shoulders, a combination that enables them to carry a great deal more weight gracefully than would be possible for one of equal size who had a more "delicately" structured framework. Individuals display considerable differences in leg length, trunk length, hip width, and, of course, in the ratios that exist between these various dimensions.

The man in the street recognizes differences in build and is even able to cite their effects upon an individual's life. He is perfectly correct in his observations and assumptions, for difference in body proportions is one of the major ways in which individuals deviate from the norm. As we know from earlier discussions, such deviant individuals may find their differences a source of maladjustment and the cause of much emotional involvement. This is particularly true in adolescence when the body assumes such great importance. A keen adolescent version of individual differences was heard at a basketball game when one teenager was overheard saying to another, "Oh, you know

the type—a forty-year-old businessman who has let himself go to pot." This is not a recognition of individual difference, but a rejection of a type that is recognized and more or less contemptuously categorized. We may assume that the teenager's opinion was of little interest to the forty-year-old businessman, but if the older man were to take the teenager's opinion seriously—that is, if the opinion affected important aspects of his life—he might well become emotionally involved and might even experience adjustment difficulties. During wartime many "old" men over thirty who find themselves in the ranks keenly experience this kind of rejection. Many a parent who finds his adolescent son or daughter ashamed of his physical appearance will experience the same feeling of rejection on a small social scale. The adolescent who deviates along unacceptable lines, surrounded by his peers and dependent upon them for acceptance and social and psychological security, suffers far more under the rejection some physical anomaly brings.

Classifications of Body Build

Domey, Duckworth, and Morandi (1964) note the many technical problems and unsolved methodologies involved in the development of body-type classification. They write:

What measurement should be used; what are the best measures; how should certain lengths be defined? Can objective data and the prediction of formulas be generalized for both sexes, all races, all ages? How do "objective" measures of physique correlate with "subjective" ratings of body type? What is the relation of structure to performance?

The first problem is that any classification system must recognize that nature does not provide neatly discrete categories of human physique. Considering the many body parts involved, it becomes obvious that any "type" is a compendium of various elements that introduce endless possible permutations and combinations. Although a classification system categorizes in terms of a series of explicitly stated types, it must recognize that the types are not "pure," and it must have ample scope for combinations of types and for interpolations between types. However, a workable classification system becomes more possible if, following a principle of parsimony, a relatively few aspects of the physique can stand surrogate for the rest and permit a meaningful description of the body as a whole. Then a scaling system for classification of individual constitutional differences is not impossible. But a great deal of preliminary research is necessary before a sufficiently parsimonious system can be assembled. The scientific worker endeavoring to evolve a body-type classification works in a specific domain whose elements are susceptible to exact measurement, in contrast to someone trying to classify personality types. Trouble begins when, having formulated an objective body-type classification system, the scientist tries to correlate it with more subjectively defined classifications such as personality.

There have been many attempts at classification of body build, ranging from Hippocrates's tall, thin, or *habitus phthisicus* and the stocky, obese, or *habitus apoplecticus* types and Galenus's attempts to relate the four "humours" to variations in physique to the somatotypes and measurement ratios of such present-day workers as Sheldon. Most of the schemes have assumed a continuum ranging from a tall, more or less slender type at one end, through a normal intermediate type in the middle, to a relatively short, thickset type at the other end. One type of classification tries to categorize individuals on the basis of predisposition to various kinds of diseases or on the special importance in their physical make-up of some particular organ or body function. Hippocrates noted the tendency to increased incidence of tuberculosis in his *habitus phthisicus* class and to apoplexy in his *habitus apoplecticus* class. Still another type of classification is arrived at by setting up a ratio between two different body measures, usually with sitting or standing height as the denominator—for example, chest circumfer-

ence to height, head length to height, stem length to height, hip width to height, weight to height, or height to weight.

Rees and Eysenck (1945) and Eysenck (1959) have proposed a body index that assumes that the body is a rectangle that can be described by the two independent dimensions of height and width. Height times width gives total size, while division of one by the other provides a ratio representing shape. With the Rees and Eysenck method, if the obtained means and standard deviations from height and transverse chest width are evaluated, one can arrive at a description of the body's general size and shape.

Most common of all classification approaches are those that assign a series of descriptive categories along a continuum. Some of these approaches make the categories quite discrete, while others allow for a more defensible overlapping or "mixed typing" between adjoining categories. Classifications based upon such arbitrary more or less discrete categories differ markedly from those of the ratio type. Ratio-type categories are usually arrived at objectively and tend to be based on the presupposition that it is not useful or even defensible to define subjectively a series of relatively discrete categories placed along a continuum extending from one extreme to the other. Of course, it is theoretically possible to formulate a somatotypology based on ratio-descriptive statements that might be placed serially along a continuum.

One of the more ambitious schemes of physical description is that of Sheldon (1942), who uses male samples in his studies. He describes varieties of individual physical development as existing along one of three continua. He does not believe there are discrete physical types that can be rigidly classified; rather he feels that although any individual may be roughly classified as being primarily somewhere along the continuum of one type, he may to some extent occupy minor positions on the other two continua. The continua are called endomorphic, mesomorphic, and ectomorphic because Sheldon (1942, 1954) holds that the three germinal layers of the embryo, the endoderm, mesoderm, and ectoderm, produced three different kinds of tissue. The three body types result from the significantly different proportions in which these tissues occur in different physiques. Roughly speaking, the endomorphic person is rather fat; the ectomorphic, thin; and the mesomorphic displays exceptional bone and muscle growth.

According to Sheldon, in the mesomorphic type the body structure is tough, strong, hard, and well developed. The skin is thick, and the blood vessels are large. Mesomorphs are visualized as maintaining sturdy upright postures. In contrast, in the ectomorphic type the body is tall, tending toward fragility. The viscera and body structure are not well developed and the chest is relatively flat. The ectomorph is seen as being restrained in his movements. His posture tends to be stooped. Endomorphs are characterized by large, highly developed viscera, coupled with underdevelopment of the bone, muscle, and connective tissue. Endomorphs tend to obesity and softness of body composition.

Each person to be classified by the Sheldon system is rated from 1 to 7 on each of the three continua, since all three continua play a part in any individual's physical make-up. Somatotypes are classified in terms of a three-digit number. For example, we might find a given individual rated 4 in endomorphy, 3 in mesomorphy, and 2 in ectomorphy.[12] From a developmental point of view, the question arises as to whether there is an intersomatotype mobility involving, for example, changes due to nutritional factors or to aging. Sheldon feels that the somatotype is stable and relatively fixed from birth, and that the overall picture of an individual's general structure and weight development may be predicted in

[12]The number to the left always indicates the degree of endomorphy; that to the right, the degree of ectomorphy. The middle digit indicates the degree of mesomorphy. Number 1 indicates minimum preponderance and number 7 maximum preponderance. The extreme mesomorph would be 171, the extreme ectomorph 117, and so on. For all practical purposes, no individual could ever be rated 777 or even 616. Ordinarily the sum of the three component digits would not exceed 13 or be less than 9.

advance. As a matter of fact, this is still a controversial point, and only future experimentation can render a definite decision. At the present time there is evidence indicating that a greater amount of intersomatotype mobility exists than Sheldon is so far willing to accept.

As might be expected, there has been considerable criticism of the Sheldon system. For example, Meredith (1940) questions the definitions Sheldon furnished for his continua, and Humphreys (1957) is of the opinion that the scale is more ipsative (individual) than normative and that the "arm chair" choice of type restricts the information available.

The Course of Bodily Growth

A marked prepubescent spurt is observed in the growth of many bodily dimensions, a spurt characterized by sexual differentiation in the earlier and more rapid growth of girls. For example, in girls there is greater growth in hip width, accompanied by sex differences in the distribution of fatty deposits and the appearance of secondary sex characteristics. Despite a slow start, boys soon exceed girls in shoulder width; this fact is partly responsible for the greater strength boys commonly have, since their larger bony framework provides greater leverage for muscle operation.

As previously explained, the current tendency is to present growth data in terms of late-, average-, and early-maturing boys or girls rather than in terms of either sex alone. This is done because quite different developmental rates and sequences have been found in individuals whose rates of maturity are markedly accelerated. Various investigators have reported some tendency for mesomorphic and ectomorphic states to be related to rate of maturation, although the relationship appears neither very large nor even very definite. Dupertuis and Michael (1953) note that mesomorphs tend to grow faster and mature earlier. Tanner (1955) reports a progressive decrease in mesomorphy from latest- to earliest-maturing groups with, conversely, a progressive increase occurring in ectomorphy. Richey (1937) reports that late-maturing boys have the least weight for their heights at maturity, the weight-height relationship being taken as an indication of ectomorphy. Bayley (1943) reports that late-maturing boys display a tendency to be long-legged and narrow-hipped, two common characteristics of the ectomorphic person. On the other hand, Reynolds and Wines (1951) report that ectomorphic individuals display a tendency toward earlier sexual maturation than do mesomorphs. Livson and McNeill (1962), in a partial replication of the Dupertuis and Michael study, report somewhat equivocal results. While their findings agree with those of other investigators where general direction of differences in maturation rates of ectomorphs as compared to mesomorphs are concerned, they also note that "it is clear that, whatever may be the effect of somatotype, it does not operate as a continuous function over the full range of either component." Hence, within any group of mesomorphs or of ectomorphs we find considerable variability, although the maturation rate variability of ectomorphs is significantly more homogeneous.

Body Type and Temperament

There has always been considerable interest, particularly among laymen, in the relation between temperament and body build. Even among psychologists interested in the scientific study of behavior, an "easy" approach to measuring psychological and intellectual status has long been an attractive will-o'-the-wisp. Since the last century, when workers attempted to classify human beings into types, investigators in medicine, psychology, sociology, and education have endeavored to find correlates between types and temperament, personality, and intelligence. Sugarman and Haronian (1964) report that there are cultural stereotypes associated with body type and that the adolescent views himself in terms of these

stereotypes. An individual's sophistication about his own body concept was highest in mesomorphs and lowest in endomorphs. Sugarman and Haronian consider level of sophistication-of-body concept a measure of the degree of feelings of satisfaction or esteem of the individual for his own body. Hyperobese children were particularly liable to hold a negative self-concept. However, a study by Kagan (1966), using younger children, indicates that where sex-role standards for body build are concerned, the stereotypes do not operate in the early years, no matter how much they may be of concern later, as adolescence approaches. Apparently concern about one's body type is another potential problem offered by the advent of puberty.

Still, research results extending over the past fifty years have shown that the relationships are either uniformly low or nonexistent. A typical study in this area is one by von Zerssen (1965), who endeavored to correlate anthropometric measurements after the Sheldon system with performance on a temperament test. Von Zerssen reported that although the temperament dimension correlates significantly with the mesomorphic component, the relationship between temperament and physique is not high enough to permit temperament diagnosis by means of somatotyping. However, it should be remembered that in any given case differences in build may have emotional repercussions, particularly if a given individual's pattern of development departs markedly from the norm, so that his social relations cause him embarrassment, or if his particular build denies or restricts his participation in the normal activities of his peers. But this is a matter of a combination of the environment, the group, and the physical and personal organization of the individuals involved. Of all the studies that have attempted to find relationships between physique and temperament, the one that seems most to bear out many of the old beliefs about body build and temperament is Sheldon's (1942). Sheldon reports comparatively high correlations between certain aspects of temperament and his body-build classifications. But here again all the evidence is not yet in, and our best stand is that it is not body build as such that is important in temperament, but the more or less fortuitous relationship a given individual may work out or be required to submit to in his particular environment or culture. And this, of course, varies from individual to individual and can hardly be predicted too far in advance —and certainly not on the mere evidence of body type or ratio alone.

Physical Ability and the Culture

Any discussion of physical development, and particularly of anatomical growth and body build, leads to consideration of physical efficiency, including strength, physical fitness, physical coordination, health, and motor development.

Physical prowess is essential for many tasks of everyday living, although it tends to be considerably more important to boys than to girls. The typical adolescent boy in our society is expected to fit the "manly," physically active, physically adept stereotype of boyhood. He is a fugitive from the term *sissy*. He is supposed to do all things "regular" boys do. He stands to gain prestige and social acceptance through athletic ability in competitive sports. A boy is expected to be good at sports and to have both the inclination and the stamina to indulge in a program of steady physical activity.

If the young boy lacks any of these attributes, he must seek other means of finding social approval and acceptance, but no matter what these other means may be, he is always exposed to criticism or even contempt when he comes into contact with those who are athletically more successful. This does not mean that a boy must of necessity be a stellar athlete to find acceptance. He may deviate considerably from a norm of great physical prowess, as most boys do, but his deviation may go only so far; physical activity and interest must appear to some degree in his activities. He may compensate strongly in other directions if he lacks physical ability, but such compensations have their limitations, and overcompensation may even militate against him.

On the other hand, our culture ordinarily neither expects nor requires athletic ability in girls, no matter how much it may require of them in physical attraction. As a matter of fact, an adolescent girl who displays exceptional athletic ability may find herself in a less favored social position among both adults and her peers than would her less athletic sister. Of course, there are certain boy-girl sports in which a girl may gain considerable acceptance, providing she is not too good. Among these are tennis, swimming, skating, bicycling, walking, and golf. However, occasionally a girl who attains exceptional skill in a sport—a national figure-skating contestant or one who wins a place on an Olympic team or otherwise demonstrates outstanding ability—may be accepted on the basis of her prominence as a public figure. However, the average adolescent boy, or even one who has considerable skill, might find a problem in masculine-feminine role relationship in dealing with a girl so far removed from the female stereotype. A great deal would depend upon the girl's skill in handling the relationship.

Studies extending over a considerable number of years have indicated the close relationship between physical fitness and social acceptability during the adolescent years. Yarnell (1966) reports a positive relationship between popularity and physical fitness, and between physical strength and athletic ability. Thrasher (1927), in his classic study of Chicago gangs, points out the importance of athletic skill in combination with "gameness" and daring to the boy who hopes to be a leader among his peers—a situation that is still true today but is by no means confined to gangs. Bower (1940), in a study of the popularity of seventh- and ninth-grade boys, found popularity significantly related to strength and physical ability as judged by a series of track events. Cowell (1935) notes the lesser social acceptability of "fringers" in playground activities and the tendency in such children to withdraw as lack of participation leads to more and more social rejection. Of course, not all children in such situations withdraw. Some may display considerable aggression and turn their attention elsewhere, sometimes toward constructive activities, sometimes toward activities that may lead to overt problem behavior. On the basis of their past histories of athletic participation, Werner and Gottheil (1966) separated 340 U.S. Military Academy cadets into two groups designated as athletic participants and as athletic nonparticipants. They found that a significantly larger proportion of the participants as compared to the nonparticipants, graduate. But even among athletes there are differences. A high level of proficiency and success appears to be a differentiating factor. LaPlace (1954) reports that major-league baseball players are better able to adjust to occupations requiring social contacts and tend to display more initiative than do minor-league players. Still another factor is the type of sport involved. For example, Thune (1949) reports that weightlifters tend to be strong and dominant individuals as compared to those who participate in regular team sports.

This discussion of the relationship of physical fitness and participation to social acceptability might lead to the assumption that increasing either physical fitness or successful sports participation would result in social acceptability gains. There is some evidence that might be interpreted to support this assumption, but so many confounding factors are involved that it is impossible to make such a generalization with security.

Most of the available studies purporting to show improved social relationships over time as a result of a physical-fitness or sports program have included a situation in which a specific effort was made to improve social relationships over and beyond the usual activities of the actual sports or fitness program. The result is, of course, that one does not know whether the program, the social behavior effect, or some combination of the two is really causal. For example, Skubic (1949) reports a doubling in the volume of social interaction over a six-week period in women's physical-education classes, but notes that emphasis was placed on early mutual acquaintance.

Physical Fitness and Personality

As Cureton (1964) notes, the:

interrelatedness of physiological and psychological states has long been an assumption in our interpretation of physical fitness data, each test being considered in light of both its psychological and physiological implications.... The pattern of personality traits associated with specific physical fitness is slowly emerging from our studies with adults and young men.

Various investigators, including Werner and Gottheil (1966), Tillman (1965), Slusher (1964), Cureton (1964), Spangler and Thomas (1962), Merriman (1960), and Seltzer and Gallagher (1959), have indicated personality differences between individuals who were fit or were athletes and those who were not. Merriman (1960) administered a personality test (California Psychological Inventory) and a test of motor ability (Phillips JCR Test) to 808 high school boys and reports that the upper motor-ability group differed significantly from the lower motor-ability group in greater poise, ascendency, and self-assurance. Werner and Gottheil (1966) report that college athletes differed significantly on seven of the sixteen Cattell PF Test from nonparticipants.[13] Cureton (1964) reports the administration of the PD test to forty-one British and American former Olympic champions. The athletes differed from the nonathletes on four factors, the athletes having greater ego strength (freedom from neurotic tendencies), being more dominant, more outgoing, and showing less guilt proneness or susceptibility to worry. Betz (1956), also using the PF test, reports a positive correlation between achievement on physical-performance measures (Schneider index and a swimming test), and negative correlations between dominance, adventurousness, sophistication, radicalism, control of general behavior, and the length of an "all-out" treadmill run.

Seltzer and Gallagher (1959), on the basis of interviews, categorized 358 boys into three

[13]The PF test measures general intelligence and fifteen personality factors including ego strength, dominance, and guilt proneness.

groups: (1) those of stable personality, (2) those well adjusted but exhibiting minor problems (restlessness, excessive sensitivity, inability to express feelings), and (3) weak or inflexible personalities (instability, insecurity, inability to adjust to stress, moodiness, lack of competitiveness, purposelessness). The boys in Group 3 (N = 26) were most disproportionate in physical structure (small chest girth relative to height, broad faces relative to chest girth). In contrast, the Group 1 boys (N = 85) contained few individuals who were disproportionate in physical structure.

Therefore, correlations between personality and physical status and performance do exist, but it need not be concluded that all differences are necessarily in favor of the athletes or those who are ostensibly physically fit. For example, Slusher (1964) reports that while Minnesota Multiphasic Personality Inventory scores for athletes were lower on femininity as compared to nonathletes, they were higher in hypochondriasis. Individual personalities tend, to some extent, to relate to the roles they play in life, and it is not surprising to find personality differences between persons of any performance categories with both positive and negative aspects characterizing both groups.

However, it appears that physical ability is important in promoting all-around adjustment and social acceptance for any adolescent boy, and to a lesser extent and in more limited areas, for any adolescent girl. It is not the only factor operating, of course, but it is a central one. Therefore, it would be logical to expect every school to have a comprehensive program of physical assessment and remediation.

The Place of Athletic Competition

A serious question arises in regard to the advisability of competitive athletics for high school youth. Competitive athletics have been advocated as a means of stressing the importance of physical fitness and of inducing children to participate in sports, so that they may gain desirable athletic skills. It is held that competition is an important part of life

and can best be taught to children during their formative years by means of an organized interscholastic athletic program. Sports are viewed as a preparation for life, and we encounter such statements as, "The battles of England are won on the playing fields of Eton." Competitive effort is further seen as a release for the "natural" energy and the "high spirits" of youth.

All this sounds very well, but research, although it does not rule out the advantages of organized and closely supervised athletic programs, seems to indicate that they are only one means to the end of physical fitness and that they should be embarked on with great caution and with many safeguards. Brindley (1953) notes that "a child can best be developed in respect to posture, coordination, strength and control, and emotional balance by a process of gradual training during the years of physiological immaturity, not by forced development of special skills." Johnson (1956), in a study of exercise that utilized fifty-nine junior high school boys, reports that when placed under competitive conditions, they worked harder, but their output was not significantly greater than that of the control group of boys who were not proceeding under competitive conditions. Johnson further reports that the competitive group exhibited a slower recovery from heart and blood-vessel strain as compared to the control group. Moreover, 37 percent of the boys in the competitive group developed nausea during either the exercise or the recovery period as compared to only one case in the noncompetitive group. Such nausea may well have been due to anxiety and other emotional factors engendered by the competitive situation. Langer (1966) reports that anxiety with both chronic and acute antecedents was the most significant factor related to college varsity football performance, but better performers were able to control the anxiety level under stress conditions. However, sometimes such outward control exacts an internal or a later behavior toll.

Reichert (1958) quotes a study of Cleveland junior high school boys that indicated that the children participating in highly competitive interscholastic athletics failed to gain as much in lung capacity, height, and weight as did a comparable group of boys in the same school who took part in a standard physical education program and in intramural athletics. Fait (1958), in a comparison of two groups of junior high school boys, reports no differences between the group that participated in interscholastic activities and the group that did not, except for a greater growth in height in the nonparticipators.

Parents and teachers worry about possible injuries in competitive sports. Advocates of athletic competition argue that both injuries and emotional disturbances are insignificant under intelligent and well-trained adult supervisors. In answering this point, Reichert (1958) writes:

Preadolescent and adolescent children are at a vulnerable age. During this age there are periods of rapid growth, with temporary maladjustments and weaknesses. For example, bone growth at this age is more rapid than muscle development, so that temporarily the bones and joints lack the normal protection of covering muscles and supporting tendons. During these periods the child is particularly susceptible to dislocations of joints and to bone injuries, especially the epiphyses. These are injuries which can cause permanent damage and can interfere with normal growth.

Lowman (1947), in a poll of four hundred orthopedists, reports that 75 percent felt that interscholastic competition was not advisable for young adolescents, particularly where body contact was involved. The remaining 25 percent qualified their answers but did indicate the possibility of harmful effects. The Joint High School Football Injury Study of 1949 indicated that strenuous competition involving fatigue, violent and sustained exercise, and bruising body contact tended to place an overload on immature hearts, lungs, and kidneys, with effects that might not become manifest until weeks or even years later.

One of the more disadvantageous outcomes of an interscholastic centered program has been the practice of training elementary and junior high school children long before they are physically ready, so that a selected few

may "come up" to high school prepared to act as sparring partners for the exclusive varsity squad. Innovators of this particular type of exploitation have even claimed that their "feed-in" or "farm" system encourages popular participation. However, the fact is that its aim is highly selective, with the result that children are excluded who most need participation in a reasonable program on their own level. An athletic program should not be aimed, in their case, at inferior proficiency in one overemphasized sport, but should encourage the development of all-around ability and minimal skills for those who need them most. Unfortunately, in the varsity-centered school there is too often no time, staff, or money to devote to the interests of these people. This is in no sense to be taken as an attempt to indict interscholastic sports, which have a rightful and, if sanely managed, beneficial effect in an educational program. It is rather an indication that a sane, well-rounded program free of exploitation is needed for everyone in a reasonably operated school system. Schools might inaugurate athletic programs permitting wide participation for fun and health instead of concentrating on a highly specialized program of competitive interscholastic sports oriented firmly toward the Armageddon of a "tough" schedule. A competitive interscholastic program picks boys who are good at sports and may relegate the rest to the spectators' bench or, for two or three, to the cheerleaders' megaphone. Fortunately, good modern physical education practice has been toward deemphasizing the one-team sports and stressing schoolwide remedial and intramural practice.

Measures of Strength

Various measures of strength are commonly used in studying the developmental patterns and the physical efficiency status of individuals and of groups. Aside from their scientific use in the study of human development, such measures find applied use as indexes of physical fitness in physical education programs and assessment of physical status.

Two types of strength are ordinarily considered in studies of physical growth: dynamic strength and static dynamometric strength. Dynamic strength is measured by either lifting or propelling the whole weight of the body, or by performing various complex athletic acts other than those that test coordination and reaction time. Measures yielded include the time for running various short distances, the distance an individual can jump vertically or horizontally, the number of times he can chin himself, or the distance he can throw an object.

Static dynamometric strength is measured by squeezing, pulling, pushing, or lifting various kinds of spring dynamometers. Measures yielded include the strength of right or left grip, pull or thrust using both hands or arms, leg lift, and back lift. Many different kinds of dynamometers are available for measuring manual strength. Among them are the adjustable hand-size Smedley, and the elliptical Collin. The strength of various muscle groups may be measured by the Universal dynamometer, while the Martin can be used primarily to measure arm and leg muscle groups.

Probably the most common strength measures are those for the right or left grip. Various investigators have included grip measures in their studies of growth trends in strength. Developmental measures of strength of grip have yielded quite similar curves for both boys and girls just before fourteen, although, age for age, boys are somewhat stronger. At fourteen a differentiation begins and continues to increase more sharply with greater maturity. The greatest relative increase in strength of grip comes for boys between fourteen and seventeen, after which the increase begins to decelerate. For girls the greatest increase comes between twelve and thirteen, after which deceleration is more rapid than it is for boys.

Ability to play a game is not ordinarily included in studies of growth and development. Psychologists interested in game participation usually study the number of times a game is indulged in over a given period of time. Data are then analyzed on the basis of categories, such as age, socioeconomic status, or sex. Psychologists who make comparative studies of strength also divide their subjects on the basis of sex, age of reaching a given physiological or physical status, chronological age, socioeconomic status, or intelligence, so that they may then compare and contrast the data gathered.

Strength normally increases rapidly during the first twenty years of life, but at varying rates from year to year. In general, it is particularly accelerated following the sixth year.

Various measures of strength other than grip are available. How do the curves of growth for such measures relate to those for grip? Here again is the phenomenon of the general curve of growth. Not only do the various measures of strength tend to show similar curves of growth, there are also high correlations between the course of development of strength and the development of other physical features. Certain interesting features must be considered in a study of the growth of strength. Strength, it must be remembered, is an end product of the functioning of certain body parts; it is not an entity in its own right. As such, it differs from the physical dimensions of height, weight, and body build discussed earlier. For example, height and weight are tangible things whose existence may be perceived by the observer. They exist at any given moment without effort by their possessor. Strength, on the other hand, is a potential that exists only when it is called into use. It depends upon other tangible physical features, through which it operates and without which it would remain nonexistent. Such physical features include the skeletal framework, the body weight and musculature, the body's neural organization, and finally, its general state of physical tonus or health. Hence, to consider the growth of strength in its proper perspective one must also consider the growth of all the aspects of the body, tangible and intangible. Under the circumstances, it is no wonder that strength bears a specific relation to all these aspects, particularly to weight. For example, Meredith (1935) found that strength of grip and weight both displayed marked acceleration when the boys he studied reached thirteen.

Therefore, since strength may be thought of as a function potential depending upon various factors in addition to muscle size, it is reasonable to expect that knowledge of the anatomical growth of an individual's muscles alone would not yield a proper index of his strength. As a matter of fact, because of the accelerated general growth of the body around the time of pubescence, it has been found that strength tends to increase faster than does the anatomical growth of muscle. Sex differences in the growth of strength are partly due to differences in weight, musculature, and the skeletal framework of boys as compared to girls, but such differences may also be due partly to the more frequent and vigorous use of the muscles, which results from the greater physical activity of boys in our culture. In this connection it is interesting to note that at the age when differences in strength between boys and girls begin to increase markedly, most girls are entering upon a more feminine cultural phase, during which their activities assume a more sedentary character than do those of boys. While most girls are now antitomboy in their attitudes, boys are still in the phase in which physical prowess is held to be preeminent.

Summary

There is a consensus that an individual's relative maturity status offers a more useful frame of reference than does his chronological age. There are various indexes of maturity status, including sexual maturity, but the most definitive is that of anatomic age, which is determined by the analysis of skeletal development, or the degree of skeletal ossification, through a standardized analysis of X rays of the wrist bones or other selected skeletal parts. As compared to girls, boys exhibit the same general retardation in development that they tend to show in other variables of development. In general, there is a close positive relationship between sexual and skeletal maturation.

A number of methods for the measurement of skeletal analysis are available, but the methodology proposed by Todd and by those who have revised his system have had the greatest currency. At the present time the reliance upon simple pictorial standards that characterized the early work is being gradually replaced by more advanced approaches. Newer findings about the process of ossification indicate irregularities in the ossification sequence and the fact that some centers, even within a relatively restricted area such as the hand, are more informative than others in judging the status of skeletal maturation. Discrepancies of several years may be found when comparing different parts of the body.

In addition to height and weight, it is important to consider the growth of smaller segments of the body and also the relative proportions these various parts bear, one to the other. Some parts of the body grow at a much faster rate than do other parts. Psychologically, maladjustments and emotional involvements may occur in individuals who depart too far from the normative picture of their peers, although this is not inevitable.

Classification of body build is traditionally determined by assuming a continuum ranging from a tall, more or less slender type at one end, through a normal intermediate type in the middle, to a relatively short, thickset type at the other end. Points along the continuum are selected as representative of the various relatively different types indicated by the classification system. A second means of classification involves computation of an index number arrived at by setting up a ratio between two body measures. There are other methods of classifying body build, but the ratio method has been of particular interest because of its seeming objectivity, compared to most of the more subjective continuum methods. One of the more ambitious present-day schemes of physical description is that of Sheldon.

Attempts at "typing" individuals seem to be more popular than scientific and tend to find small acceptance among developmental psychologists. It is believed that a descriptive approach to physical status that uses a continuum is superior to one which uses a number of discrete categories.

Currently, the tendency is to minimize chronological age in presenting growth data and to substitute instead the concept of late- and early-maturing individuals. As in the case of height and weight, there are very specific sex differences in relative bodily proportions. This is particularly true in areas such as hip and shoulder width and fatty deposits. The mesomorphic and ectomorphic states appear to be related to rate of maturation, but the relationship seems neither very large nor even very definite. In general, mesomorphs tend to grow faster and mature earlier, although there is considerable variability within any given body-type classification.

The relation of body build to temperament has been studied with considerable interest, but the findings are generally inconclusive. A given cultural attitude may overemphasize certain aspects of build and may cause emotional and adjustment difficulties for individuals who depart from the accepted cultural pattern.

In modern American culture, physical prowess and athletic ability and interest are expected of boys; their absence in any given individual may lead to adjustment problems. The boy who is a good athlete finds that a social premium has been placed upon his skill and ability. Girls are frequently neither expected nor encouraged to display physical prowess or to assume the role of an athlete. In fact, overemphasis by any girl on athletic ability may lead to serious problems of adjustment and nonacceptance. Thus, for boys, physical ability appears important in promoting all-around adjustment and social acceptance, and for girls it is less important past a minimum point. Therefore, it is exceedingly important, particularly for boys, that schools provide schoolwide participation programs to promote proper skills for all children enrolled who are physically able to participate. Unfortunately, such ideal programs are usually lacking, and present recreational trends encourage spectatorship rather than participation.

Various measures of strength form one method of studying developmental patterns and the physical efficiency status of individuals and groups. Two types of strength are ordinarily considered in studies of physical growth: dynamic strength and static dynamometric strength.

Strength normally increases rapidly during the first twenty years of life, but at varying rates from year to year. In general, it is particularly accelerated following the sixth year. Measures of right and left grip strength are most commonly reported.

Strength, in terms of its actual existence, is only the end product of the functioning of certain parts of the body; it is not an entity in its own right. It must usually be thought of in terms of potential—something that, on any given occasion, may or may not be called into being. In terms of correlations, strength appears to be most closely related to weight. Activity leads to the development of strength; the lesser activity of girls as compared to boys partially explains differences in strength, although differences in build and skeletal structure are more important.

There appears to be no overall general or central motor ability, although numerous factors are common among the various motor functions. In developmental sequences, strength develops earlier in the lower extremities than in the appendages of the upper half of the trunk. No relationship has been found between strength and intelligence. It does appear profitable to analyze strength data in terms of late or early maturation, since sexual maturity shows a positive correlation with strength.

An adolescent's strength and physical fitness status are more than physical phenomena; they have far-reaching implications for his social and emotional adjustment. Deviation from the stereotype may evoke social disapproval, at least partial exclusion from peer activities, and emotional ridicule and rejection of problems brought about by the child's physical self.

References

Abernathy, E. M. Correlations in physical and mental growth. *Journal of Educational Psychology* 16 (1925): 458–466, 539–546.

Acheson, R. M. The Oxford method of assessing skeletal maturity. *Clinical Orthopediatrics* 10 (1954): 19–39a.

Acheson, R. M. A method of assessing skeletal maturity from radiographs: A report of the Oxford Child Health Survey. *Journal of Anatomy* 88 (1954): 498–508b.

Acheson, R. M. The Oxford method of assessing skeletal maturity. *Clinical Orthopediatrics* 10 (1957): 19–39.

Bayer, L. M., and Bayley, N. B. *Growth diagnosis*. Chicago: University of Chicago Press, 1959.

Bayley, N. Skeletal x-rays as indicators of maturity. *Journal of Consulting Psychology* 4 (1940): 69–73.

Bayley, N. Size and body build of adolescents in relation to rate of skeletal maturing. *Child Development* 14 (1943): 47–90a.

Bayley, N. Skeletal maturing in adolescence as a basis for determining percentage of completed growth. *Child Development* 14 (1943): 1–46b.

Betz, R. A. Comparison between personality traits and physical fitness tests of males. Master's thesis, University of Illinois, 1956.

Bower, P. A. The relation of physical, mental and personality factors to popularity in adolescent boys. Doctoral dissertation, University of California, 1940.

Brindley, E. D. Interschool athletics for elementary school youngsters. *Journal of School Health* 23 (1953): 209.

Cowell, C. C. An abstract of a study of differentials in junior high school boys based on the observation of physical education activities. *Research Quarterly* 6 (1935): 129–136.

Cureton, T. K. Physical training produces important changes, psychological and physical. In *Sport Medicine*. Helsinki: International Symposium of Medicine and Physiology of Sports and Athletics, 1953.

Cureton, T. K. Improving the physical fitness of youth. *Monographs of the Society for Research in Child Development*, vol. 29, no. 4, 1964.

Damon, A.; Bleibtreu, H. K.; Eliot, D.; and Giles, E. Predicting somatotype from body measurements. *American Journal of Physical Anthropology* 20 (1962): 461–473.

Domey, R. G.; Duckworth, G. E.; and Morandi, A. J. Taxonomies and correlates of physique. *Psychological Bulletin* 62 (1964): 411–426.

Draper, G. *Disease and the man*. London: Kegan Paul, 1930.

Dupertuis, C. W., and Michael, N. B. Comparison of growth in height and weight between ectomorphic and mesomorphic boys. *Child Development* 24 (1953): 203–214.

Eichron, D. H. A comparison of laboratory determinations and Wetzel grid estimates of basal metabolism among adolescents. *Journal of Pediatrics* 46 (1955): 146–154.

Elgermark, O. The normal development of the ossification centres during infancy and childhood. *Acta Paediatrica* 33 (1946): 9–30.

Eysenck, H. J. The Rees-Eysenck body index and Sheldon's somatotype system. *Journal of Mental Science* 105 (1959): 1053–1058.

Fait, H. Statement read before Annual Meeting of American Association for Health, Physical Education, and Recreation, April, 1956. Cited in J. L. Reichert, Competitive athletics for preteenage children, *Journal of the American Medical Association* 166 (1958): 1701–1707.

Flory, C. D. Sex differences in skeletal development. *Child Development* 6 (1935): 205–212.

Flory, C. D. Osseous development in the hand as an index of skeletal development. *Monographs of the Society for Research in Child Development* 1, no. 3 (1936).

Garn, S. M., and Rohmann, C. G. Communalities of the ossification centers of the hand and wrist. *American Journal of Physical Anthropology* 17 (1959): 319–323.

Garn, S. M. and Rohmann, C. G. Variability in the order of ossification of the bony centers of the hand and wrist. *American Journal of Physical Anthropology* 18 (1960a): 219–229.

Garn, S. M., and Rohmann, C. G. The number of hand-wrist centers. *American Journal of Physical Anthropology* 18 (1960b): 293–299.

Garn, S. M., and Rohmann, C. G. X-linked inheritance of developmental timing in man. *Nature* 196 (1962): 695–696.

Garn, S. M.; Rohmann, C. G.; and Applebaum, B. Complete epiphyseal union of the hand. *American Journal of Physical Anthropology* 19 (1961): 365–372.

Garn, S. M.; Rohmann, C. G.; and Robinow, M.

Increments in hand-wrist ossification. *American Journal of Physical Anthropology* 19 (1961): 45–53.

Garn, S. M.; Silverman, F. N.; and Rohmann, C. G. A rational approach to the assessment of skeletal maturation. *Annales de Radiologie, Paris* 7 (1964): 297–307.

Garn, S. M.; Silverman, F.; and Sontag, L. W. X-ray protection in studies of growth and development. *American Journal of Physical Anthropology* 15, no. 3 (1957).

Greulich, W. W., and Pyle, S. I. *Radiographic atlas of skeletal development in the hand and wrist.* 1st ed. Palo Alto: Stanford University Press, 1950.

Greulich, W. W., and Pyle, S. I. *Radiographic atlas of skeletal development of the hand and wrist.* 2nd ed. Palo Alto: Stanford University Press, 1959.

Hoerr, N. L.; Pyle, S. I.; and Francis, C. C. *Radiographic atlas of skeletal development of the foot and ankle.* Springfield, Ill.: Charles C. Thomas, 1962.

Humphreys, L. G. Characteristics of type concepts with special reference to Sheldon's typology. *Psychological Bulletin* 54 (1957): 218–228.

Johnson, B. L. Influence of pubertal development on responses to motivated exercise. *Research Quarterly* 27 (1956): 182–193.

Jones, H. E. Relationships in physical and mental development. *Review of Educational Research* 9 (1939): 91–102.

Kagan, J. Body build and conceptual impulsivity in children. *Journal of Personality* 34 (1966): 118–128.

Klineberg, O.; Asch, S. E.; and Block, H. An experimental study of constitutional types. *Genetic Psychology Monographs* 16 (1934): 140–221.

Langer, P. Varsity football performance. *Perceptual and Motor Skills* 23 (1966): 1191–1199.

LaPlace, J. P. Personality and its relationship to success in professional baseball. *Research Quarterly* 25 (1954): 313–319.

Livson, N. and McNeill, D. Physique and maturation rate in male adolescents. *Child Development* 33 (1962): 145–152.

Lombroso, C. *L'uomo deliquente.* Torina, 1889.

Long, E., and Caldwell, E. W. Some investigations concerning the reaction between carpal ossification and physical and mental development. *American Journal of the Diseases of Childhood* 1 (1911): 113–138.

Lowman, C. L. Vulnerable age. *Journal of Health and Physical Education* 18 (1947): 635.

Meredith, H. V. The rhythm of physical growth: A study of 18 anthropometric measurements on Iowa City white males ranging in age between birth and 18 years. *University of Iowa Studies in Child Welfare,* vol. 11, no. 3 (1935).

Meredith, H. V. Comments on the varieties of human physique. *Child Development* 2 (1940): 301–309.

Merriman, J. B. Relationship of personality traits to motor ability. *Research Quarterly* 31 (1960): 163–173.

Nicholson, A. B., and Hanley, C. Indices of physiological maturity: Derivation and interrelationships. *Child Development* 24 (1953): 3–38.

Parnell, R. W. *Behavior and physique: An introduction to practical and applied somatometry.* London: Arnold, 1958.

Paterson, D. G. *Physique and intellect.* New York: Century, 1930.

Pyle, S. I., and Hoerr, N. L. *Radiographic atlas of skeletal development of the knee.* Springfield, Ill.: Charles C. Thomas, 1955.

Pyle, S. I., and Menino, C. Observations on estimating skeletal age from the Todd and Flory bones atlases. *Child Development* 10 (1939): 27–34.

Pyle, S. I., and Sontag, L. W. Variability in onset of ossification in epiphyses and short bones of the extremities. *American Journal of Roentgenology* 49 (1943): 795–798.

Rees, W. L., and Eysenck. H. J. A factorial study of some morphological and psychological aspects of human constitution. *Journal of Mental Science* 41 (1945): 8–21.

Reichert, J. L. Competitive athletics for pre-teen-age children. *Journal of American Medical Association* 166 (1958): 1701–1707.

Reynolds, E. L., and Wines, J. V. Physical changes associated with adolescence in boys. *American Journal of the Diseases of Children* (1951): 529–597.

Richey, H. G. The relation of accelerated, normal, and retarded puberty to the height and weight of school children. *Monographs of the Society for Research in Child Development* 2, no. 1 (1937).

Seltzer, C. C., and Gallagher, J. R. Body disproportions and personality ratings in a group of adolescent males. *Growth* 23 (1959): 1–11.

Sheldon, W. H. *The varieties of temperament: A*

psychology of constitutional differences. New York: Harper, 1942.

Sheldon, W. H.; Dupertuis, C. W.; and McDermott, E. *Atlas of men.* New York: Harper, 1954.

Sheldon, W. H.; Stevens, S. S.; and Tucker, W. B. *The varieties of human physique.* New York: Harper, 1942.

Shuttleworth, F. K. The physical and mental growth of boys and girls ages six through nineteen in relation to their age of maximum growth. *Monographs of the Society for Research in Child Development,* vol. 4 (1939).

Skubic, E. A study in acquaintanceship and social status in physical education classes. *Research Quarterly* 20 (1949): 80–87.

Slusher, H. S. Personality and intelligence characteristics of selected high school athletes. *Research Quarterly* 35 (1964): 539–545.

Sontag, L. W., and Lipford, J. The effect of illness and other factors on appearance pattern of skeletal epiphyses. *Journal of Pediatrics* 23 (1943): 391–409.

Spangler, D. P., and Thomas, C. W. The effects of age, sex, and physical disability upon manifest needs. *Journal of Counseling Psychology* 9 (1962): 313–319.

Speijer, B. *Betekenis en Bepaling van de Skeletleeftijd* (Summary and Atlas in English). Leiden: Sijthoff, 1950.

Stolz, H. R., and Stolz, L. M. *Somatic development of adolescent boys.* New York: Macmillan, 1951.

Sugarman, A. A., and Haronian, F. Body type and sophistication of body concept. *Journal of Personality* 32 (1964): 380–394.

Tanner, J. M. *Growth at adolescence.* Springfield, Ill.: Charles C. Thomas, 1955.

Tanner, J. M., and Whitehouse, R. H. *Standards for skeletal maturity, part I.* Paris: International Children's Center, 1959.

Tanner, J. M.; Whitehouse, R. H.; and Healy, M. J. E. *A new system for estimating the maturity of the hand and wrist, with standards derived from 2,600 healthy British children. Part II: The scoring system.* Paris: International Children's Center, 1962.

Thrasher, F. M. *The gang.* Chicago: University of Chicago Press, 1927.

Thune, J. B. Personality of weightlifters. *Research Quarterly* 20 (1949): 296–306.

Thurstone, L. L. Factor analysis and body types. *Psychometrika* 1 (1946): 15–22.

Tillman, K. Relationship between physical fitness and selected personality traits. *Research Quarterly* 36 (1965): 483–489.

Todd, T. W. *Atlas of skeletal maturation, Part I: The hand.* St. Louis: Mosby, 1937.

Werner, A. C., and Gottheil, E. Personality development and participation in college athletics. *Research Quarterly* 37 (1966): 126–131.

Yarnell, C. D. Relationship of physical fitness to selected measures of popularity. *Research Quarterly* 37 (1966): 286–288.

Young, H. B. Aging adolescence. *Developmental Medicine and Child Neurology* 5 (1963): 451–460.

Zerssen, D. von, Eine biometrische Uberprufung der Theorien von Sheldon uber Zusammenhange zwischen Korperbau und Temperament. *Zeitschrift fur Experimentelle und Angewandte Psychologie* 12 (1965): 521–548.

Suggested Readings

Biller, H. B., and Liebman, D. A. Body build, sex-role preference, and sex-role adoption in junior high school boys. *Journal of Genetic Psychology* 118 (1971): 81–86.

Clifford, E. Body satisfaction in adolescence. *Perceptual and Motor Skills* 33 (1971): 119–125.

Dreizen, S.; Spirakis, C. N.; and Stone, R. E. A comparison of skeletal growth and maturation in under-nourished and well-nourished girls before and after menarche. *Journal of Pediatrics* 70 (1967): 256–263.

Espenschade, A. The contributions of physical activity to growth. *Research Quarterly* 31 (1960): 351.

Felker, D. W. Social stereotyping of male and female body types with differing facial expressions by elementary age boys and girls. *Journal of Psychology* 82 (1972): 151–154.

Hansman, C. F., and Maresh, M. M. A longitudinal study of skeletal maturation. *American Journal of the Diseases of Children* 101 (1961): 305–321.

Hewitt, D., and Acheson, R. M. Some aspects of skeletal development through adolescence: II.

The interrelationship between skeletal maturation and growth at puberty. *American Journal of Physical Anthropology* 19 (1961): 333–334.

Hopkins, B. Body-build stereotypes in cross-cultural perspective. *Perceptual and Motor Skills* 37 (1973): 313–314.

Johnston, F. E. The concept of skeletal age. *Clinical Pediatrics* 1 (1962): 133–144.

Lerner, R. M. The development of stereotyped expectancies of body build-behavior relations. *Child Development* 40 (1969): 137–141.

Lewis, V. G.; Money, J.; and Bobrow, N. Psychologic study of boys with short stature, retarded osseous growth, and normal age of pubertal onset. *Adolescence* 8 (1973): 445–454.

Malina, R. M. Exercise and an influence on growth. *Clinical Pediatrics* 8 (1969): 16–26.

Malina, R. M. Skeletal maturation studied longitudinally over one year in American whites and negroes six through thirteen years of age. *Human Biology* 42 (1970): 377–390.

Mochizuki, M. A study about the relationship between the mental tempo and body types. *Journal of Child Development* 5 (1969): 6–14.

Sloan, A. W. Physical fitness and body build of young men and women. *Ergonomics* 12 (1969): 25–32.

Staffieri, J. R. Body build and behavioral expectancies in young females. *Developmental Psychology* 6 (1972): 125–127.

Stone, G. P. Appearance and the self. In Rose, A. M., ed., *Human behavior and social processes: An interactionist approach*. Boston: Houghton Mifflin, 1962.

Thomson, A. M. The evaluation of human growth patterns. *American Journal of the Diseases of Children* 120 (1970): 398–403.

PART SIX

The Adolescent and Society

Chapter Twenty

The Adolescent and the Culture

Many writers, instead of looking mainly at the adolescent himself in terms of his own inherent attributes *as* an adolescent, prefer to seek in the culture of the day an explanation for adolescent behavior and attitudes. They then try to relate this to the inherent aspects of being an adolescent, but the focus is primarily from without. Of course, eventually one must turn the focus upon the adolescent himself. To understand in any meaningful way the impact of society upon the adolescent, one needs to know something of the nature of the adolescent as a person in order to judge what are likely to be the behavioral outcomes of cultural influences. If the adolescent cannot be understood apart from the culture in which he lives, neither can the impact of the culture be understood without a prior understanding of the psychological bases of adolescent behavior. It has been the purpose of the chapters preceding this one to present the necessary psychological background. It is the purpose of the chapters in this section to consider the most probable impact of the culture on a functioning human being during his adolescent years.

Following Mead's (1928, 1930) studies, the point has often been made that an adolescent is a product of his culture. As such, his actions and thoughts reflect the culture as he has experienced it, actually or vicariously. Therefore, the culture's structure is seen, aside from physical-maturation aspects, as both molding the adolescent's perceptions and determining the nature of the problems he faces. A culture may be particularly problem producing, or it may be particularly facilitative. That being so, one must understand the culture if one is to understand its products. A great many of the generalizations about adolescence are culture bound—in analyzing and interpreting adolescence in a culture one must anchor the generalizations to the culture. This chapter will describe the nature of the American culture as a socioeconomic matrix for the rearing of adolescents.

Starting in the 1940s and 1950s, and gaining in scope and volume during the 1960s, writers on adolescence such as Jennings (1964), Parsons (1962), Potvin (1964), Friedenberg (1962), and Goodman (1960) have been analyzing the American culture in terms of its effects on adolescence. They have largely arrived at the conclusion that it is a culture fraught with problems for child rearing. The view that the period of adolescence in America is one of tension, alienation, and rebellion is particularly prominent in sociological literature. As Matza (1961) notes, "Whatever the difference of opinion regarding the source, there seems to be a general consensus that something requires explaining, and this something usually turns out to be youthful rebellion."[1]

---

[1]The impact of modern culture is not confined to America, as may be seen in discussions (among others) of Israel by Golan (1958) and Blumental (1958), of Germany by Spiel (1966) and Hochheimer (1966), of Italy by Cervini (1966), of Finland by Kaila (1958), and of Puerto Rico by Trent (1965). All over the Western world the rising rebelliousness of youth is perceived and commented upon.

The Nature of Modern American Society

Let us look specifically at the structure of American culture to see if we can identify some aspects that are potentially problem-producing where adolescents are concerned. This look does not assume that the areas identified necessarily produce insurmountable problems for children one way or the other— they simply present cultural situations that are part of the American adolescent's life and produce the problems and sources of stress that characterize the context in which he is being reared. What is America like?

In considering the organization and structure of a culture, the general categories of social behavior, moral values and attitudes, communication, economics, politics, and technology are convenient. One looks at these descriptively, in terms of major trends, seeking especially the overridingly important changes in progress. Of particular significance is the culture's perception and evaluation of itself and its concept of its objectives and their likelihood of attainment.

In American culture, the industrialization and high level of productivity are impressive. This industrialization has grown rapidly, extending over the past century, as America has moved from a predominantly rural-agricultural to a predominantly urban-industrial civilization. This changeover is still in progress as the rapid growth of the sciences and of their technical application has provided increased knowledge and ability to manipulate men and their environments. Hand in hand with industrialization has been the growth in the organization and functions of government. Few aspects of American life are not directly affected by the operations of government, both local and national. A third factor of basic importance in shaping the culture, as Parsons (1962) notes, is a complicated legal system that stands as an intermediary between the governmental and nongovernmental aspects of American society.

Thus, we can isolate four defining aspects of American culture: (1) increasing industrialization and productivity, (2) an expanding and ubiquitous government, (3) increasing advances in scientific discovery and application, and (4) a complicated intermediary legal system. All this adds up to an exceedingly complex society with many ramifications and regimentations in the daily affairs of its people. However, it is the by-products of these four defining aspects that directly affect the behavior of American adolescents.

The first by-product is sheer size, with all the problems of impersonality size can bring. One no longer has effective face-to-face relationships with significant persons. It is easy for the individual to feel lost, unimportant, powerless, unwanted. There are American high schools today whose student bodies exceed five thousand and whose faculties alone outnumber the children in some of yesterday's fair-sized secondary schools. Yet the example of the high school is only a case in point. As a nation we have grown to worship bigness, to welcome it and foster it as a nation, while we simultaneously retreat from it to seek refuge in our private lives. The adolescent perceives the bigness-privacy dichotomy, and he also perceives his family's relative anonymity and powerlessness to effect changes outside its immediate circle. Increasing technology and governmental activity make the individual less important, and the adolescent himself can easily feel powerless and noninvolved. That there are counterforces is not always apparent, since the negative aspects are the ones that are always highlighted.

Second is the rapidity with which change takes place. As Keniston (1962) points out, such rapid flux means that "little can be counted on from generation to generation ... all technologies, all institutions and all values are open to revision and obsolescence." It is difficult to adjust, to feel a sense of continuity, and to communicate across the generations. Yet, as with bigness, we as a nation welcome the change and abandon the old ways, even as we regret the changes. There is a certain nostalgia in America underlying the unremitting drive toward the new. Even among adolescents is to be found nostalgia for something they never knew, represented by a move to collect mementos of the past. Many antique and junk stores cater to this adolescent interest in collecting trophies of the past to display in their rooms or simply to store away in the manner of collectors of any age. Actually, a society in flux has less effect on the adolescent than might be supposed, since the changing times are his times and he is a denizen of them. Most of his problems in this area arise from his dealings with adults who are uneasy, bewildered, or actively resistant to change. Of course, change brings uncertainty, and this must sometimes be dealt with by the adolescent, but he tends to interpret a change as for the better, since he has relatively little stake in continuity. Still, youth does have conservative tendencies, and change may come too fast for him, or he may be influenced by his elders. Szczepanski (1959) reports that in Israel it is becoming harder and harder for adolescents to adjust to the rapidly changing culture and that revolutionary ideas have little appeal. It may be that Israel offers youth a more meaningfully participative role in an emerging economy and that they feel they have a stake in the continuity of the enterprise. Generalizations across cultures must be made with extreme caution.

Third, with industrialization and the growth of the sciences and their applications, a whole host of concomitant phenomena have appeared on the American scene. The machine is master, and the economy revolves around it. Nothing is sweeter to the ear of most American male youth than the roar of a hot rod or the tuning up of a Go-Kart.[2] Among the aspects of American culture fostered by our industrialized economy are:

1. Urbanization with its attendant problems, such as crowding and slums, gangs and delinquency, and impersonality.
2. The mobility of families and persons that makes the United States a nation on the

move in living, in recreation, in job change, and in nearly every activity of life, including marriage and divorce.
3. An educational system designed to meet the needs of our expanding economy and technology that has prolonged youth's time in school, and has broadened the attendance base, while paying more attention to mediocrity than to excellence, yet has paradoxically fostered the stresses of selection-exclusion.
4. A continuing process of mechanization and automation that tends to restrict progressively employment opportunities for youth and often provides jobs that devalue the education youth have attained.
5. An affluent society in which youth's increasing purchasing power is pandered to by an advertising-manufacturing enterprise that is developing huge special markets for youth.
6. A type of family organization in which meaningful productive membership, a supportive kinship, and extended family relationships are being eroded.
7. Vast differences in economic and social opportunity.
8. As Soskin, Duhl, and Leopold (1966) point out, the entrusting of a large share of the education of adolescent males to the care of women and the isolation of youth from any practical apprenticeship in adult male society.

Historical Changes in the Society

Technological and social changes are not the only ones to be considered. Since the environment in which a child develops is also a matter of history, the impact of American culture upon adolescence must be evaluated against the backdrop of the times. In the 1930s this backdrop was the Depression; in the 1940s, World War II and the new world that followed, with its reassessment of man; in the 1950s, Korea, recessions, and the acceleration of technology and science; and in the 1960s, Vietnam and a

[2]Sometimes called a "whizzer," it is essentially a flat platform with four wheels, a seat, and a steering wheel. The engine is about three horsepower. It is capable of 65 to 100 mph on a race track built for the purpose.

world in flux, with the very future of mankind hanging in the balance. Each of these periods presented special problems for adolescence.

The Depression of the 1930s extended adolescence and accentuated its problems by making early marriage, economic independence, freedom from dependence on adults, and planning for a future career almost impossible for large numbers of the population. The matter of marriage was particularly dramatic, for not only was an appropriate sexual adjustment delayed, but deferred marriages tended to continue, often for years, the period of economic and social dependence upon parents. Even when marriage did occur, newly wedded couples were sometimes forced to live with their parents, and this prolonged an unhealthy period of dependence. The same situation also existed in the period of prosperity following World War II, when the high cost of living and the stringent housing shortage made living with their parents inevitable for many newlyweds. But as prosperity continued into the 1950s and 1960s, higher wages and increased opportunities counteracted high living costs, with the result that the adolescent entered upon his golden age of affluence. Thus, many of the financial barriers to emancipation of the 1930s and 1940s were dispersed. Johnny could and did get married in the 1960s, and he did not have to live with his parents, although they and his working wife often footed the bill, particularly if Johnny was seeking higher education. The occasional recessions were not enough to turn the tide. Of course, several million adolescents and their families never did enter the period of affluence. For them, except for the examples of conspicuous consumption about them, the 1950s and 1960s must have seemed little different from the 1930s, at least in opportunities and the economics of living. The 1970s have opened new vistas of disaster with inflation, recession, and unemployment living side by side in a period of the greatest general affluence this nation has ever known. Contrasts are shocking, and the road ahead is not at all clear. It is an age

of stress and uncertainty—not a comfortable age in which an adolescent might easily find security and an affirmation of values.

Some of the wartime and affluency-period accelerations had good effects, but many of them added new problems or brought on cultural changes that called for considerable adjustment by both adolescents and adults. As Boll (1944) and others noted, many adolescents found full adult status thrust upon them long before they were able to cope with the problems such status posed. For example, many adults were unwilling to accept youthful workers on an equal basis, and their resentment often took the form of denying the adolescent worker the status to which his duties entitled him. Adolescents soon found that being "tolerated" was a disagreeable substitute for being ignored.

Younger adolescents also found themselves confronted by new, though perhaps less dramatic, problems. Still confined to the traditionally nonemancipated role of the early teenager, they felt even more keenly the wartime restrictions placed upon them. They felt they were entitled to greater participation in the exciting and restless life about them. The period was characterized by a great rise in sex delinquency. Families migrated to parts of the country new to them, homes were broken by the war, and open parent-youth conflict became more common.

The plight of youth in Germany after World War II furnishes another example of the influence of a historical period on typical problems of adolescence. Defeated, without hope or prospect of immediate future, forced to accept adult responsibilities earlier than before, and laboring under many deprivations, youth developed under different conditions from those experienced by boys and girls of similar age in Canada or the United States. McGranahan (1946) sums up their situation in the postwar period when he notes that they presented a "picture of inconsistency and confusion." The idealism and sentimentality so typical of German youth of the past century, as described by Becker (1946), had disappeared, to be replaced by a cynicism and self-interest, which marked a complete revolution in outlook.

Yet, the historical picture for Germany has once again changed, and today we find the youth of West Germany with a new status and a viewpoint that, except for certain aspects peculiar to Germany's present-day position in the world, is not unlike that of many American youth. As Lewis (1959) points out in writing of a survey made of the opinion of German youth, "only one in ten of the youngsters proved to have an inkling of what had happened in their parents' generation and the role of the man who had led them. The other children replied automatically, 'Hitler was the one who built the autobahns'; 'Hitler was the one who wiped out unemployment.' "

Another example is the effects of desegregation of schools upon personally involved individual adolescents of both races when their school life became the focal point of a public and legal controversy. Obviously, other aspects of the movement for racial equality, including race riots, freedom marches, and sit-ins, all affect adolescents seeking to understand who and what they are and to relate the resulting self-construct to the society in which they live.

Space and the nature of this text have not permitted more than a most superficial account of some of the highlights of American culture, but the discussion may have brought out the complexity of the culture in which today's adolescents are being reared. This complexity is so great that it is virtually impossible to isolate any one cultural aspect and say that this and this alone is causal. When we do locate causal components, we are nearly always confronted with the interaction of a multiplicity of variables.

The Teenager and Society

The teenager is essentially an activist, and an activist with much physical energy and drive. He is a great holder of values and is reluctant to countenance deviation from these values by anyone. He tends to differentiate sharply between good and bad, permissible and nonpermissible. His distinctions are clear-cut, brooking no middle ground. Above all, he is impatient. All this makes him the ideal revolutionary. The prospect of martyrdom, if not its actuality, appears attractive, and he is eager to espouse causes he sees as his and in which he feels personally involved. Add to this the fact that he is a minority figure and perceives himself as dominated by adults and shut out by them from the "important" things and decisions of life. His perception is generally quite true, yet at the same time, paradoxically, the adult world, by adopting a "cult of youth," places youth on a pedestal and denigrates itself. That this tendency to overadmire youth and the things of youth is not confined to the United States is evident from an examination of the newspapers and magazines, the advertisements, the mass-valued activities, the musical interests, the fashions, and so on of France, England, Germany, Italy, and doubtless of other European countries. The influence of the student movement in South and Central America and in the Near East is a further example of adult domination by youth. Yet the paradox is always there: the adult world admires, imitates, and is influenced, yet it withholds and excludes and does not admit to full membership; hence, the arousal and partial sanction of the teenager's activist tendencies.

Matza (1961) notes that youth's vulnerability to a variety of deviate patterns seems to take three forms in America: delinquency, radicalism, or bohemianism. Delinquency, guided by a "celebration of prowess, manifests a spirit of adventure, disdain of work, aggression." Its outlets are victimization and status offenses. Radicalism is "guided by an apocalyptic vision, populism, and evangelism." For youth, the "radical enterprise consists of mundane political activity that, to its participants, seems extraordinary as a result of unconventional definitions of politics." Bohemianism (or "beat") finds commitment to three things, "romanticism, expressive authenticity, and monasticism." Its manifestation may be either frivolous or morose and its "enterprises cluster around unconventional art and unconventional personal experience."

To Matza's three patterns might be added withdrawal, noninvolvement, and various mass movements not strictly categorizable as delinquent, radical, or Bohemian. The reaction of noninvolvement, retreat, or unwillingness to commit oneself was so prevalent following the middle 1950s that it became a subject of discussion, even in such a popular-appeal source as the *Saturday Evening Post* (see Gallup and Hill 1961, on the "cool generation"). This attitude of noninvolvement and disinterest known as "cool"[3] is usually accompanied by overtones of anxiety about the future. "Cool" may, among other things, stand as one symptom of alienation. It may also be a defensive pose of a child trying to conceal his inexperience or misunderstanding.

In the 1960s, however, Matza's stance of Bohemianism and rebellion succeeded the stance of cool, and the youth of that era became an involved generation whose often emotional outbursts were the very antithesis of cool. The 1970s seem to be a transition period. The cool attitude has not returned but many youth do express attitudes of noninvolvement. Bohemianism, still with us, is less popular, and overt rebellion for the moment seems passé. The scene seems to be one of marking time, of waiting. Covert rebellion and passive rejection are definitely present but do not appear to be major issues of conflict with the older generation. One manifestation of rejection may be in the clothing and way of confronting the world adopted by the youth of the 1970s. If the generation of the 1950s was cool and the generation of the 1960s involved, then many of their elders would call the generation of the 1970s the sloppy generation. It is hard at this point

to predict the generation of the 1980s. If the generation of the 1970s is indeed a transition generation, the question becomes: Where is the transition leading?

The preceding discussion shows that youth can be both activist and highly reactive to their environment. And while youth are capable of positive and adjustive action, they are also vulnerable to various forms of deviate behavior. In rearing adolescents the problem seems to be one of acceptably channeling youth's energies and activities in directions that will be of greatest perceived personal value to them in the present as well as in the future. However, channeling should be of such a nature that it will yield maximum benefits to the nation as well as to society at large. It is reckless of adults to forget in rearing children that today's adolescents are tomorrow's controlling adults. If the job of child rearing has not been well done, eventually society and the nation will suffer cruelly, if indeed they can endure in any civilized fashion. The responsibility of those charged with rearing youth is clear. It is a task that cannot be ignored, for the consequences of failure will lead future man down strange and unhappy roads.

However, society must look to itself as well as to the child. Various writers, such as Heath, Maier, and Remmers (1958), make the point that teenagers appear to absorb the values of the culture and reflect back in their behavior the culture's attitudes. Aquinas (1958) believes that adolescents are a "prototype of the adult world in which they live."

Some writers are of the opinion that a leading problem in adolescent development within modern culture is that the very culture in its outlook and actual behavior is itself adolescent. Thus, we have a case of the immature leading the immature. Huizinga (1971) takes this position and notes that in Western civilization the play attitude of the adolescent toward life has become a permanent aspect of the whole culture. This adolescent attitude of play is characterized by: (1) lack of personal dignity, (2) lack of a sense of decorum, (3) lack of re-

---

[3]The word *cool* entered popular adolescent jargon with the significance of not showing emotion, as in "keep your cool." Lately it has taken on the connotation of *sophisticated*.

spect for opinions of others, (4) excessive concentration on self, (5) weakening of judgmental and critical ability, and (6) a semiserious attitude toward life. Huizinga feels that confusion of play and seriousness is one of the most important aspects of the malady of our time. He calls this puerilism—a community attitude leading to behavior more immature than the actual level of its critical and intellectual faculties. Lauterbach (1970) describes a permissive, child-centered United States culture that has developed infantile and adolescent fixations in the national thinking process, manifest in illusions of omnipotence and short-range thinking. Gardner (1957) makes the point that in present-day America we are thrusting our adolescents into a group of societies that are beset with the same problems as those characterizing the adolescents themselves. Gardner sees America as in reality a whole host of societies that are showing evidence of a lack of set values and standards. American society has become increasingly less stable and given to capricious and unpredictable behavior. For Gardner, all of this adds up to a national adolescence, which makes it difficult for the adolescent to solve his conflicts in regard to social morality in a society that is itself conflicted.

Friedenberg (1959), who sees adolescence as primarily a social process whose main outcome is the formation of a clear and stable self-identification, feels that the trend of American culture is the antithesis of that which would allow a child to achieve a self-identification that would bring him to terms with himself. As Friedenberg interprets it, American culture is hostile to clarity and vividness and impedes the formation of any fidelity of self-image. According to him, adults possess an inner hostility to youth, and their behavior reflects it. Adolescents confronted by the soft ambiguity of the culture and veiled adult hostility can only conform or rebel, but either way leads to emotional problems, making adolescence "more difficult, more dangerous, and more troublesome" to the adolescent as well as to everyone else. Friedenberg writes of his hypothesized influence of the culture: "It makes adolescence rarer. Fewer youngsters really dare go through with it; they merely undergo puberty and simulate maturity." His conclusion is that "adolescence as a developmental process is becoming obsolete," as the culture denies the developing individual the maturity-determining personal integration that "results from the conflict between a growing human being and his society." Hence Friedenberg's term, *the vanishing adolescent.*

There can be no doubt that values are changing in America today, some for the better and some for the worse. Some of the value changes are undoubtedly facilitative of adolescent adjustment, and some are not, but during its transition stage even an eventually facilitative change may cause conflict and difficulty in adjustment for all concerned. Zube (1972), in an analysis of a popular family magazine (*Ladies Home Journal*), studied shifts in value orientation in American society from 1948 to 1969. In general, the shift is from future to present and from doing to being. Zube listed three trends as particularly significant:

1. Morality as a rather permanent, inflexible set of standards is becoming a more fluid concept which each person defines for himself.
2. Psychological explanation for behavior is increasingly used to justify the behavior.
3. The importance of mental health for the good of family and society is giving way to concern with psychological adjustment to meet the needs of the individual.

Erikson (1967) states that "the fabric of traditional authority has been torn so severely in the last decades that the reestablishment of certain earlier forms of convention is all but unlikely."

A number of writers have pointed to such changing values in American society as being at the heart of adolescent maladjustment and unrest. Such changes are viewed as creating conditions that potentially can result not only in maladjustment but in overt resistance and, at some periods in history, in open rebellion. Settlage (1970) observes that rapid social change, leading to a lack of convictions regarding values in society, has made the role of parents more difficult. Among the problems encountered by the modern-day adolescent in his socialization process are (1) difficulties in accepting challenges, (2) devotion to activities not requiring a competitive effort, (3) regressive retreats into self, and (4) escape through experimentation with drugs. Settlage proposes that there is a need for a more intensive study of "intrapsychic processes of normal adolescence" with special consideration to familial, subcultural, and cultural factors.

Snopik, Rabovitch, and Tausk (1969) also examined the effects of adolescence on behavior in the context of a society undergoing rapid change, in this case in Argentina. They report that typical reactions during adolescence are greatly exacerbated by lack of stability in social values. They see two crisis points: (1) when the family-derived conventional ideals are found to be in conflict with the requirements of change, and (2) when newly developed personal ideals come in conflict with the realities of a competitive society. These investigators note that the conflicts can be so severe that there is the possibility of psychotic disintegration unless there is worked out a gradual adaptation to social reality. They also point to the possibility of the adoption by the adolescent of a set of ideals based on rebellion and rejection. On a more optimistic note, Arasteh (1969) believes that man is compelled to form a new style by means of the disintegration of unsuitable values and reintegration of desirable values. He feels that youth cannot mature by means of an unrealistic psychosocial moratorium but needs to create a new communal superego through action. Arasteh sees the action as adapting itself differently in different cultures: for example, in politics for Afro-Asian youth, in economic development in Israel, and in the arts and humanities in the West.

Adolescent Tension in American Culture

Given that adolescent tension does exist on a wide scale in America and that its results may be seen in adolescents' vulnerability to various behavior deviations, we may assume that it does not occur without cause. We may further assume that a search for the causes is worthwhile. As we saw in Chapter 3, many psychologists, particularly of the psychoanalytic variety—and to a lesser extent of the neo-Freudian—look for answers within the biological organism and hold that tension is built into the process of development. Sociologists, on the other hand, look to the environment, as do many psychologists, particularly those who view learning as basic to behavior. In this chapter we accept the hypothesis that adolescence in America is a period of stress and examine the cultural context for causes of tension as, in Chapter 3, we examined the biological nature of man for the same purpose. Assumption of the existence of stress can be justified by the drumfire of discussion on the "problems" of adolescence in the popular and scientific literature and on the evidence of the juvenile courts, daily newspapers, teachers, parents, and others concerned with adolescence.

Of course, the reader may still wish to question the validity of the assumption and to ask whether we have given the dog a bad name. Is the emperor really clothed? We shall turn to this question at the end of the chapter, but for the moment we shall let the assumption of stress and tension stand. What, then, are the possible causal factors?

Davis (1940, 1944), over a quarter-century ago, noting the rebelliousness of youth as compared to the greater docility reported in primitive societies, wrote two articles trying to explain the reasons. He saw three as particularly important. First, parents and children live together, but since the parents' attitudes were largely shaped during their own childhood, and since changes in the culture have been rapid, friction is inevitable. Second, the domination of modern society, industry, and education by the principle of merit produces tension as it furnishes grounds for controversy over who shall receive scarce rights and prerequisites. And third, as compared to adolescents, adults are more realistic because they have more at stake in the ongoing system and see the necessity of making compromises to preserve the social order. Adolescents, outside the establishment, do not feel responsible for it or for its defects, which often leads to their fluctuation between idealism and cynicism, both of which seem unreasonable or at least unrealistic to adults.

Wolfenden (1970) makes the point that youngsters have always suffered from strain and stress in growing up. While some feel that today's affluence serves to ameliorate the strain, others feel that the modern way of life as contrasted to older ways simply serves to increase the strain. Manifestations of such differences are to be found in (1) the "focus on youth" attitude, (2) personal problems partly generated by a passion for sincerity and honesty, (3) the loss of conventions and other simple guides to behavior, and (4) the revolutionary ethos of "smash the system." Wolfenden concludes that the unhappiness behind a desire to smash has its roots in a profound disillusionment with internal domestic and national policies and deep concern about great causes. Hughes (1969) claims the events of the 1960s —wars, riots, and assassinations—convinced many young Americans that society is sick. Hughes feels that evidence of society's malfunctioning is tangible and irrefutable, but at the same time there is something neurotic in the mental set that sees sickness all around us. He would say to youth that in spite of pressures for quick answers and slipshod methods there is no excuse for panic—the liberal temper of mind has not lost its relevance.

Erikson (1970) feels that youth will not be seduced into easy revolutionary answers. He notes that youth in advanced industrial cultures today tend to reject the status quo yet are disillusioned with the long-range results of all known revolutionary movements. The condition is one of confused rebellion, which may be characterized as a revolt of the dependent. Prugh (1969) writes that society "is seriously conflicted, currently torn and temporarily faltering in its coping capacities." Agreeing with writers such as Beck (1958), he sees the core problem as being "the imbalance between our rapid technological advances and our relative lack of progress relations." He feels that youth are "reasserting the dignity of individual human beings and the importance of human values by demanding different priorities." Prugh sees the solution in new mechanisms for communication and shared responsibility.

Some writers, such as Grace and Lewellyn (1959), Meissner (1961), and Potvin (1964), point to the culturally determined ambiguity of youth's position as the major source of tension. In a study of 1,278 high school boys, Meissner reports that as the boys grew older they indicated significant increases in depression, sadness, dissatisfaction with their life situation, feelings of not being understood, and feelings of loneliness.

The ambiguity of the period of adolescence and the adolescent's lack of understanding of what is required of him are recurring themes in the literature on adolescence. Some discussions attribute these characteristics of the period to the fact that an adolescent is suspended between childhood and adulthood and his culture permits him to be in neither one nor the other. Under the circumstances, adolescence is an ambiguous period because of its location in the developmental sequence. Chapter 3 included a discussion of Lewin's marginal man, Erikson's moratorium of adolescence, and Anna Freud's idea of the adolescent mourning for his lost childhood. Others, like Friedenberg, claim that the culture itself lacks clarity and is in no position to define anything to anyone, with the natural result that the adolescent has picked up the same malaise in his self-identification attempts. Still others, as, for example, Potvin, take the stand that the period is ambiguous because the adolescent's role has not been defined for him, but they do not assume the culture's inability to do so. Potvin writes that "conflicting demands create a conflict situation," which leads to dissatisfaction and alienation on the part of youth. The result is collective behavior grounded on "generalized beliefs which redefine their role." Such collective mobilization could follow productive channels, but, as Potvin sees it, the fundamental generalized beliefs on which mobilization is based become almost magical in nature. The resulting behavior tends to consist of crazes based on wish fulfillment and hysteria, mass movements designed to force on adults acceptance of the adolescent's values, and hostile outbursts by adolescents built upon the feeling that some adverse agent is causing their anxiety. Potvin feels that parents and society are equally to blame and that the solution involves the attempt by both to redefine the ambiguous situation. Friedenberg (1962) writes, "Adults unconsciously insist that teenagers vicariously act out what they themselves ambivalently fear and the adolescent becomes the favorite rebel without a cause—causeless because society seemingly asks so little of him, merely that he 'grow-up,' finish school, and get on the payroll."

Coleman (1972) examined the current and changing roles of the school, the family, and the work place in the development of youth into young adults. Owing to changes in these institutions, adolescents are shielded from responsibility, held in a dependent status, and kept away from productive work—all of which makes their transition into adulthood a difficult and troublesome process. Coleman suggests that adolescents be provided with a variety of skills so that they can more effectively make the transition into adulthood. He suggests that the school be confined to the provision of intellectual skills only, on the assumption that other skills can be more effectively learned through active participation in the occupational institutions of society.

McCleary (1970) notes that the technological emphasis of modern society leads the young to think that the solution to social problems is equally amenable to immediate solution. He writes:

We have actually extended the rivalry between father and son (of the growing-up period) into a much later age than is healthy and by so doing we are setting up situations so complicated, frustrations so intense and hostility so guilt-ridden that no decent boy can turn on his self-sacrificing parents—he must make the system the target for his violence.

Szczepanski (1959) applies much the same reasoning to Israeli youth, whose adjustment to the rapidly changing culture has become harder and harder as the adolescent period has been prolonged.

Other writers have taken other stands. Sorokin (1956) speaks of the conflict engendered by puritanical repression of sexuality and the stimulation provided by a sex-obsessed culture. Parsons (1942) points to adults' overemphasis on performance; Sexton (1965) and Bornemann (1958) speak to the problems of coming to terms with a technological and crisis-ridden world; Mussen and Beytagh (1969) speak of the transition from an agricultural to an industrial way of life; and Beck (1958) speaks of the general rootlessness of society.

Martin Essex says of adolescence that for the first time in the eons of man's history adolescents are not an economic asset to their parents, the point being that valuelessness presents a problem in self-view leading to problem behavior.[4] This is possibly an oversimplification, but substituting or adding the trait of adolescent dependence may make the generalization more meaningful. Further, there may be special cases of adolescents who have less value than others; even in the past there were some cases in which adolescents were relatively valueless, as with a rich man's overprotected son. But there is a countereffect in modern culture. Youth is valued in this youth-worshipping culture, and while an individual may be valueless as a contributing family member, he can garner self-esteem from being a member of a highly valued class.

[4]Personal communication from Martin Essex (1970).

Reading the bulk of the literature, we find emphasis upon the discontinuous and negative aspects of the culture. Are there no other views? A number of writers have, indeed, emphasized the positive side, although their number is not large. Rosen (1967) notes that modern times have been characterized as an "age of anxiety" representing a period of insecurity, frustration, and uneasiness in which familiar guidelines have begun to disintegrate and the future seems ominous. He makes the point, however, that this experience is neither new nor unique. Man has survived his own past and can be expected to do equally well with his future. Toussieng (1968), in a discussion of the ego identity problems of youth today, makes the point that between the extremes of rigid conformity and identity diffusion or lack of commitment lies a new identity that is flexible, adaptable, and responsive to the changing world.

It may even, to some extent, be a positive value that modern technology gives an adolescent time to grow up and be involved, to have, in effect, a moratorium. Eisenstadt (1962) makes the point that it is the only time permitting full identification with the ultimate values and symbols.

Time and the Adolescent

Perhaps one of the greatest of all developmental changes is that of the perception of time. The very young have no perception of time at all, even when they are apparently able to manipulate the verbal symbols of time. They live in a world of now and not now. As they progress through middle childhood, they can manipulate and understand the abstractions of space-time, but still without any real reference to self—probably because the self is itself, in their view, still amorphous and little considered. In adolescence the situation is different because the self is now being considered in formal terms, has become of deep personal concern, and all aspects of the environment have to be considered in terms of the self. Time

is no exception, but there is still a qualitative difference between the adolescent and the adult in his consideration of time. Developmentally, during adolescence time is seen as a limitless ocean upon which one floats almost in a state of suspension. In contrast, maturity sees time as a rushing stream down which one is propelled with increasing velocity toward a certain, and as one grows considerably older, early end. Writers have suggested the feeling of velocity with metaphors of a fleeing thief, a galloping horseman, and a rushing stream. The contrasting metaphors of the still sea or the Rock of Gibraltar are expressions of adolescence, not of maturity. In a real sense, the adolescent sees himself as immortal, and horizons are of little personal concern as he floats on his still sea. And this is properly so, for in such a situation one can dream, can feel that there is time to build oneself and to accomplish all one wishes. The long summer vacations would be the most valuable of all educative experiences if the adolescent could somehow release himself from the conformity-inducing pressures of his culture and get to know himself as a person. Actually, the adult concept of a vacation is an escape from time—or was, until the pressures of "recreation" and the "traveler's schedule" returned it to the world of work.

Unfortunately, the adolescent's time is being eroded by all the pressures of his culture, particularly the school, the mass media, the necessity for vocational decision, and perhaps the pressure of the Puritan ethic. (It may be that adults unconsciously envy children their concept of time and want to deprive them of it, rationalizing their motives, of course.) The pressure starts in middle childhood, and the contemplation of a nine- or ten-year-old's schedule would appall any reasonable person. Up at 7:00 for a hasty breakfast, which must be finished in time to meet the 7:55 bus, to arrive at school at 8:22, to begin a school day conpartmentalized by a continuous series of periods announced (and ended) by the ringing of bells. Immediately after school—unless there is a scheduled extracurricular activity—he must catch the bus home in time for the piano lesson, the paper route, or some other activity, with the favorite TV program to be watched at 6:00 sharp, followed by dinner, then the meeting of the Cub Scouts. And so it goes through the week.

Despite this previous conditioning, the adolescent is not so amenable to this robbery of time, or rather, the adult-disapproved ones are not. The "good" adolescents, on entering high school, become even more involved as they begin (physically at least, though perhaps not mentally) the sequence of activities school and society lay out for them. The daily schedule of the Big-Man-About-the-Corridors is exceeded only by the Big-Man-About-Campus. Both are reminiscent of the promising junior executive in industry on his way up. It is getting to the point where one can see children only by appointment. Exaggerated? Possibly, but readers might like to take a group of children of different ages and analyze their daily activities as they are scheduled over a period of a week or a month. Perhaps we shall succeed, eventually, in changing the adolescent's concept of time, but the victory will be a hollow one, for we shall have taken away one of the most psychologically important devices he has for self-integration.

Alienation

Alienation is a syndrome consisting of attitudes of egocentricity, distrust, pessimism, anxiety, meaninglessness, powerlessness, and normlessness. It is a state of estrangement between the self and the objective world, or between different parts of the personality. It represents the breakdown of the individual's sense of attachment to society. The alienated person feels alone, cutoff, unwanted, unloved, and unvalued. As Jackson (1973) points out, a number of discussions of alienation (Bay 1967, Flacks 1967, Keniston 1967) have indicated that social-adaptive behavior and social attitudes and self-attitudes reflect the integration, or lack of it, of the individual with the roles and mores of society. Bickford and Neal

(1969) report that high alienation in each of its major forms (meaninglessness, normlessness, social isolation, powerlessness) is associated with low degrees of knowledge that would tend to alleviate the causes of the alienation. Tolor and LeBlanc (1971) examined correlations between alienation status and various personality variables. They reported positive correlations between alienation and external locus of control ($r = .59$ to $.75$), negative affect states of anxiety ($r = .21$), hostility ($r = .24$), and depression ($r = .19$). The alienated person is difficult to cope with and often incites social rejection. Ziller (1969) suggests that the processes leading from exclusion to the alienation syndrome may be a self-fulfilling prophecy mediated by reduced social reinforcement. Ziller defines the alienation syndrome as consisting of low self-esteem, low social interest, and high self-centrality. While alienation cannot be said to be the position of the majority of the adult public, it is presently prevalent enough to be considered one of the defining characteristics of the modern era.

Does alienation among adolescents represent a normative trend, a transitory phenomenon, or a deviant aspect of psychological development among present-day adolescents? Opinions differ. Berman (1970) sees alienation as an inevitable and necessary state during adolescence, which in most cases can be resolved as soon as adulthood is reached. He views it as a mental process by means of which an essential psychic and physical distance from parents is achieved. The adolescent uses alienation in this sense as a defense against past relationships no longer appropriate in the world he now visualizes. Thus, as a child goes through adolescence, he needs to establish a new order of things by abandoning his childish relationship to his parents and to society. Such a need and its implementation lead to a transitory state of alienation. Although common to all adolescents, it can be pathological in some cases.

Whether or not alienation is a universal attribute of adolescence, there is evidence that the state of mind of many present-day adolescents could easily lead to the assumption of an attitude of alienation. Meissner (1961), even before the prevalence of the present alienation picture, administered a questionnaire to 1,278 high school boys, and reported significant increases with age of feelings of loneliness, depression, sadness, and dissatisfaction with their situation. More than one half were worried, moody, and depressed over studies, and many felt they were misunderstood by parents, friends, and teachers. Propper et al. (1970) found that dimensions of the alienation syndrome (egocentricity, distrust, pessimism, anxiety, and resentment) among Catholic parochial school males were comparable to those reported for predominantly Jewish public high school males. These authors speak of startling commonalities among adolescent populations differing in social class and religious affiliations.

However, it is possible to generalize too broadly from specific individuals or groups and assume that more adolescents have been infected by the alienation syndrome than is actually the case. The possession of one or more attributes of the alienation syndrome does not necessarily equal alienation, nor can alienation be expected to be the cause of every deviation. Pileggi (1969) writes: "There is a tendency . . . to lump peaceful student dissenters, political activists, radicals, old-fashioned rowdies, drug pushers, muggers, and vandals all in the same pot." Jackson (1973) reports that with a group of 290 eighteen- to twenty-one-year-olds of both sexes, powerlessness and self-abasement were not age-sex differentiated but that young males were dissatisfied with their powerless status and young females were dissatisfied with their self-abasing attitudes.

The Causes of Alienation

Alienation is seen by some as a result of the times in which we live. Noshpitz (1970) makes the point that in a caricatured and exaggerated form the adolescent is representing "some of the essential disappointment and frustration his parents and surrounding adults experience in their culture-coping attempts. The adults feel alienated; their offspring dramatize it." Noshpitz feels that adolescents are fleeing from forms of magical pressure applied by ads, politics, and certain versions of patriotism in an affluent and overstimulating society in which they are cheated by being cut off from the sources of energy the culture is producing. Williams (1970) sees the adolescent's alienation from society, peers, and his own affects —particularly as in the hippie movement— as resulting from a major deficit in family values, a deficit that is simply a reflection of the broader values of society. According to Williams, the deficit takes the form of child-rearing practices lacking emphasis on close personal relationships with parents or other children in a close one-to-one relationship. In the meantime, the culture's values, such as achievement and productivity, are emphasized, with little corresponding reinforcement given to experiences with other children of empathic closeness and mutuality. Then at adolescence the child finds himself confronted with inner and social expectations of developing a trusting, loving relationship with others. But the adolescent lacks experience and lacks resources to accept the relationship. Hence, the alienation and, in some cases, the hippie route.

Others have also found a source of alienation in early family relationships. Wise (1970) notes that the really seriously emotionally disturbed adolescents tend to have a history of traumatization in relationships with their mothers in their early years. The picture is one of mutual parent-child rejection. Paulson et al. (1972) compared early family relationships of a group of alienated or antiestablishment youth (N = 116) with those of a group of establishment youth (N = 94). Mean age of the groups was twenty. In general, the non-alienated youth recalled a family life characterized by emotional maturity and a positive intrafamily harmony. In contrast, the alienated recalled events involving parental irritability, family discord, and lack of rapport with the mother. Teicher (1972), in a description of the clinical picture presented by a group of older male adolescents, reports that they possessed in common depression, isolation, estrangement, and passive defiance of parental standards. All felt ambivalent toward domineering and forceful mothers, and all desired a relationship with passive distant fathers. A major characteristic of them all was frantic attachment to a girl.

Hanssen and Paulson (1972) note that among alienated youth the mother tends to be dominant, but among nonalienated youth the tendency is for the father to be dominant. In general, the homes of alienated youth show greater instability. The authors conclude that alienated young people are protesting a "slipping" morality. Klein and Gould (1969), using college women as subjects, hypothesize parental identification as a factor in the etiology of alienation. Nonalienated girls identify to a greater extent with their mothers, whereas alienated girls identify with neither parent. Nonalienated girls have a more positive perception of their mothers, whereas alienated girls perceive their mothers in negative terms. Alienated girls see no differences in the way their parents brought them up, whereas nonalienated girls perceive appropriate sex-role differences in their parents' child-rearing practices. As the result of an alienation scale given to 263 adolescents, Rode (1971) writes: "Individually, alienated adolescents of both sexes perceive their parents and particularly their mothers as hostile, non-accepting, and as exercising control through psychological means such as the instilling of persistent anxiety."

Any aspect of the current scene, even though transitory, may set off a wave of alienation. The Vietnam draft was one such aspect, Watergate and Chappaquiddick others. Shepard (1972) makes the point that lack of perceived status recognition within a status structure promotes social psychological withdrawal from the status structure, although any deprivation can trigger alienation. Phillips and Szurek (1970) hypothesize that in American society the satisfaction associated with early successful learning is reduced and distorted so that subsequent and continued learning is affected. The result is frustration leading to rebellion, alienation, and overconformity. Hickerson

(1966) notes that economically deprived children are also deprived of an equal opportunity to develop their talents and abilities in school. Hence, the school experience for these people leads to alienation.

Unwin (1969) sees adolescent protest as arising from frustration at an extension of the adolescent period by a generation "biologically more mature, intellectually superior, and socially and politically more informed." He hypothesizes that viewing youth problems as caricatures of "adult dilemmas and excesses" may help in the identification of "those aspects of their protest which have validity."

How Alienation Works

Alienation appears to take one or the other of two approaches: aggression or withdrawal. We see in the hippie movement an example of withdrawal and in the case of some psychotics an even more dramatic example of withdrawal. Youth engaged in rebellious political activity and protests represent the aggression side. If the paradigm of frustration-aggression-withdrawal holds, then we would say that political activity expressed in activist terms represents aggression following frustration. By the same token, if aggression does not work we can expect withdrawal, either of the hippie or psychotic order, and we might even find submission to the establishment, a state of affairs that would certainly receive social reinforcement. Nagaraja (1972), using a sample of fifty college and fifty high school students, studied the psychopathology of rebellious political behavior. All of Nagaraja's subjects were idealistic and saw themselves as the hope of the nation. All possessed a superego deficiency and were compulsively antiauthoritarian. However, despite these commonalities, rebellion appears to be a highly personal matter, with its form and depth depending on a multiplicity of variables, including age, intelligence, early childhood adaptive mechanisms, ego organization, and various other environmental influences.

Unwin (1969), speaking of depression in alienated youth, notes that dyssocial behavior "is an attempt to escape conscious knowledge of the inevitable disillusionment, disgust, and depression" after finding the "discrepancy between the values, ideals, and ethics inculcated by society and the actual practices of society." Ray and Sutton (1972) note that in an Australian sample general alienation was related to neuroticism, thereby confirming other studies done elsewhere indicating that many deviating people tend to display the alienation syndrome. In an experimental situation, Gould (1969) reports that high-alienated students conformed to a significantly greater extent than did low-alienated students. He also noted a significant tendency for high-alienated individuals to be first-born or only children.

Youth Rebellion Movements

Not all individuals handle alienation in the same manner, even when their alienation is of equal strength. Some lead relatively normal lives, while others embark upon an overt course of action in which they make a direct attack upon the system they reject. Such overt action may take the form of aggressive activity directed at a specific institution or its representatives, as in the case of the youth who promulgated the campus riots of the late 1960s. The other overt form of protest is one of withdrawal and nonattack, except in terms of personal example of rejection. This last approach is best exemplified in the hippie movement, also of the late 1960s. Today, neither the hippies nor the college rioters exist in exactly the same form they previously did, but overt approaches to alienation are still present in one form or another.

The hippie movement, as Allen and West (1968) point out, was built around the drug experience. Drugs provided a social ritual for these highly alienated people, a focus of guiltless law breaking, and a means of relieving undesirable forms of anger and aggression. However, the counterculture that these people represented was not, as Diez de Rio (1972) notes, political, economic, or religious. It was instead a form of embryonic expression, a manner of being. Adler (1968) feels that the personality configuration and values that emerged

within the hippie movement were quite like those emerging in any time of social crisis and transition when old behavior controls and values were no longer adequate and new ones had yet to emerge. The personality style of the hippie emphasized self-actualization, immediacy, and intuition as means of trying to adapt to the transition period in which he was living. Adler (1969) draws a parallel with Paris youth of the 1830s, when antiestablishment behavior and drug use among the young became as great an issue as in America in the 1960s.

A number of reasons have been advanced for the hippie movement. Wolman (1972–1973) proposes that the phenomenon of youth rebellion was a reaction to institutions that prolong adolescent dependence on society. Those who rebel are expressing their rights to independence and self-determination. Wolman is of the opinion that since colleges are institutions that prolong dependence, it is natural that they should be the sites of many rebellious outbreaks. Bonino (1970), in a study of Italian youth, agrees with Wolman in noting that a fundamental cause must be sought in conditions of social exclusion that characterize the adolescent, and particularly the student, in present-day society. Schneemann (1970) sees the hippie propensity as arising from lack of adequate family atmosphere and familial interpersonal relationships. Hostility, which results from the lack of adequate parental figures, becomes displaced and takes the form of antisocial behavior. Distler (1970) theorizes that there is more than the usual developmental generational conflict between parents and their adolescent children. The conflict in the case of the hippie is exacerbated by a clash between cultural patterns. It is a case of a culture that values achievement, rationality, goal-directedness, and individual responsibility versus one that values feelings, intimacy, sensory experience, and self-exploration. Langman, Block, and Cunningham (1973) report that parent-child conflict seems to have reduced the degree of identification with parental values and created subsequent predispositions for alternative values regarding politics, work, religion, and lifestyle.

Normality Versus Deviation

Most cultural-causation writers seem concerned primarily with the negative aspects of the culture that produce problems. Few seem to have dealt with the more positive facilitative aspects, and most of their research and commentary, as Bettelheim (1962) points out, concern males rather than females. The discussions of Goodman (1960) and of Friedenberg (1959), for example, have to do almost entirely with male youth. Yet there are many facilitative aspects for rearing adolescents in the American culture, and there is no great discrepancy between the number of adolescent females as compared to adolescent males. These same writers have also tended to emphasize deviate subgroups and to generalize from them to the entire adolescent population. One reads about "the adolescent culture," the "teenager," and so on, as though there were only one group.

Adelson (1964), basing his view upon the results of extensive semistructured interviews with some one thousand boys between the ages of fourteen and sixteen and two thousand girls between the ages of twelve and eighteen, advanced the idea that social scientists base their interpretation of the modern adolescent upon "two conspicuous but atypical enclaves of adolescence, drawn from extreme and opposing ends of the social-class continuum, and representing exceptional solutions to the adolescent crisis." In actuality, he feels, the majority of adolescents are of more benign status and fit neither of these extremes. One extreme he calls the Visionary-Victim, who is seen as "distinguished by a purity of moral vision which allows him to perceive or state the moral simplicity hidden by adult complication," while at the same time he is "victimized by adult corruption," he is neglected, exploited, and betrayed by adults too busy to bother with him. He is both passive and powerless and finds his prototypes in Salinger's Holden Caulfield and Franny Glass. Adelson calls the antitype, the other extreme, the Victimizer, and conceptualizes him as "leather-jacketed, cruel, sinister, and amoral." Evil, yet omnipotent, "he is the

nemesis-hero of a new genre of fiction and film." Adelson believes that these two extremes have emerged because the adolescent has come to occupy "a particularly intense place in American (and in European) thought and feeling" and has, in effect, "come to weigh oppressively on the American consciousness." Not so many years ago the adolescent was not interpreted in such extreme terms. He was a figure of fun, a kind of Henry Aldrich or Andy Hardy and, as such, was seen as callow, enthusiastic, flighty, and sometimes moody. Or, conversely, he was seen in a harmless Werther-like role of sensitivity, sentimentality, and overemotionality. In either role he was really outside the mainstream of adult preoccupation and, while often exasperating, was not really taken seriously.

But how does Adelson interpret the normative adolescent of his interviews? He sees the average adolescent as avoiding overt conflict with his family, although there well may be unconscious conflicts. He feels that the real disagreements tend to be on "token issues, teen issues," not on really serious matters. Further, he feels that the American adolescent receives much behavioral freedom but doesn't see the adolescent achieving emotional or even ideological freedom to any great extent. Finally, Adelson discounts the peer group as a stage for the confrontation of the self, and instead emphasizes its role as a place where an adolescent may display sociability and learn social skills but, perhaps, become quite stereotyped and undifferentiated in his reactions to others. Certainly, Adelson found little trace of an intense concern with philosophical issues on the adolescent's part. He sums up the matter by writing: "In all likelihood, the degree of tension and disorder has always been more apparent than real. It is always more likely that passion, defiance, and suffering will capture the fancy, and that the amiable, colorless forms of adaptation will be ignored." Offer, Sabshin, and Marcus (1965) provide supporting evidence for Adelson in a report of a study of a selected group of eighty-four model adolescent boys, aged fourteen to sixteen, from two suburban high schools. These subjects showed almost complete absence of psychopathology, but exhibited flexibility of affect expression and conflict, had good object relations with adults, felt a part of a larger cultural environment, and showed awareness of its norms and values.

Adelson's view does not constitute a theory of the nature of adolescence; rather, it describes what he found in one sample and constitutes a warning that one may make too great an issue of the period, become an alarmist, and overinterpret on the basis of deviate individuals. He does not deny that there are problems in adolescence or that deviancy exists. Of course, where society is concerned, the deviate does cause a problem and has to be dealt with. Additionally, in science we often approach normality by way of deviancy as a way of understanding normality. As Adelson points out, the danger is that we will interpret deviancy as the normal situation. Lebovici (1966), a French psychiatrist, speaking on the same topic, notes:

The French literature mentions a "crisis of adolescence," and Anglo-American authors speak of a "critical transition period." Without a doubt, the crisis concept is interesting from a psychological point of view, for it clearly demonstrates the importance of the changes in personality organization during this period. But it entails the risk of exaggeration of the more noisy aspects of this maturation and the difficulties they may provoke.

It is well that attention has been called to the lack of deviancy in the majority of American youth, but it should be recognized that individual problems can exist without giving rise to deviate behavior. Not everyone resorts to maladaptive problem behavior, delinquency, Bohemianism, alienation, or some other extreme simply because he has a problem or finds the world and himself difficult to manage. Some adolescents have learned to endure or to sublimate, some cope and work effectively within parameters, some dissemble, and some have even embraced the culture eagerly and feel in tune with its objectives. Of course, some children have managed to avoid overt problem behavior by internalizing their tensions and have in effect fed emotionally upon themselves. Such internalization may sooner or later result in the appearance of neurotic or psychotic symptoms, and internalizing children may be more seriously in need of help than are aggressive children. Fortunately, as is also true of children who express their problems in deviancy, these seriously internalizing children do not constitute the majority of adolescents.

Most children encounter and pass through their adolescence showing from time to time evidence of unrest, impatience, tension, or inappropriate behavior. Most will exhibit varying levels of difficulty in coping with their environments now and then, but they have a lot to learn about themselves as well as about the world, and the learning context is not easy. Without doubt, the American culture is highly complex, and it presents problems to inexperienced children who are trying to come to terms with the world, build a secure and reliable concept of self, and relate that self to others. Therefore, we would expect children as they come of age in the second decade of life to encounter problems and at times even considerable stress. But we need not "cry havoc and let loose the dogs of war" whenever we consider an adolescent, and we need not feel that in America he represents some kind of deviate individual with a serious problem requiring immediate aid.[5]

Summary

Cultural causation has been a popular theme of writers on adolescence. The adolescent as a physically vigorous activist is highly reactive to his environment and reflects in his behavior

[5]Some would say that all deviate children have been manipulated by adults for their own purposes and comfort, and possibly some have. But such a generalization represents an oversimplication and, when universally applied, this writer rejects it. He also disagrees with the position that all "good" children have simply internalized to the point at which they are in trouble emotionally. Adolescents are simply human beings proceeding through a time of life that offers some unique problems, but it also offers many that are common to all humanity.

what he finds there. What he finds seems to be a whole series of situations that produce tension and to these he may react by various forms of deviancy, such as delinquency, radicalism, Bohemianism, or withdrawal. Society needs to channel youth's interests and activities so they are meaningful and productive if a good job of child rearing is to be accomplished.

Causes of adolescent tension have been described as consisting of lack of understanding between adolescents and their parents, overemphasis on performance, lack of realism in adolescents, the ambiguity of their status, the rootlessness and lack of clarity of society, and the problems posed by a technical and crisis-ridden world. But most of all, a conflict between the generations seems to be the basic difficulty. Focal points of this conflict include changes in the times, intrinsic physical differences, adults' concepts of what should be done, educational practices, adult envy of youth and "stealing" of their ways, and adult construction and conduct of a world that adolescents feel is not theirs and that they often regard as poorly managed. Adult stereotypes govern a great deal of adult-adolescent interaction, and since most stereotypes are not wholly true, the results do nothing to improve intergenerational relationships.

A major developmental change is that of the perception of time. Developmentally, during adolescence time is seen as a limitless ocean upon which one floats almost in a state of suspension. But his time is being eroded by all the pressures of his culture, including the demands of the school, the mass media, the necessity for vocational decision, and the pressures of the Puritan work ethic. Gradually, as he approaches maturity, the adolescent accepts these demands and pressures as part of his life and comes to perceive time in the adult terms of a rushing stream.

Alienation is a syndrome consisting of attitudes of egocentricity, distrust, pessimism, anxiety, meaninglessness, powerlessness, and normlessness. It is an estrangement between the self and the objective outer world. Alienation is related to an individual's personality structure as well as to the events and conditions of his daily life. There is some difference of opinion as to the extent to which alienation represents a normative trend in adolescence. Causal factors include family relationships, withholding of adult role, political and social conditions, and the inconsistencies and the supposed "attitude" of the establishment. Whether or not alienation is a universal attribute of adolescence, the fact remains that conditions today offer a background ripe for the development of attitudes of alienation. Studies have indicated that a fair number of adolescents have been infected by the alienation syndrome. Alienation takes one or the other of two approaches: aggression or withdrawal. Youth engaged in rebellious political activity represent the aggressive side, while those who have espoused the hippie movement represent withdrawal from overt attack. The hippie movement was built around the drug experience and represents a way of life, rather than a movement of political and economic ideology and action.

There is a tendency to overgeneralize about adolescents, basing the generalizations upon deviancy and dramatic episodes. Yet the average adolescent does not display deviancy, and his method of coping with his environment, while certainly not problem-free, does not present the picture of great stress, parental rejection, and deviancy that the literature might lead one to expect.

As a culture, America is characterized by industrialization, the growth of science and technology, big government expanding its activities into all areas, and a complicated intermediary legal system. Among the by-products of these characteristics are a general bigness leading to lack of privacy and regimentation, rapid social change, mechanization, urbanization, family and personal mobility, an educational system focused on industry, an affluent society, socioeconomic discrepancies, and a less cohesive family.

The environment in which a child develops is also a matter of history, and an evaluation of the impact of American culture upon adolescence must be made against the backdrop of the times.

References

Adelson, J. The mystique of adolescence. *Psychiatry* 27 (1964) : 1–5.

Adler, N. The antinomian personality: The hippie character type. *Psychiatry* 31 (1968) : 325–338.

Adler, N. Paris had its hippies in the 1830's: They drove the establishment mad. *California's Health* 27 (1969) : 7–11.

Allen, J. R., and West, L. J. Flight from violence: Hippies and the green rebellion. *American Journal of Psychiatry* 125 (1968) : 364–370.

Aquinas, T. Youth and its psychological problems. *Journal of Social Therapy* 4 (1958) : 26–31.

Arasteh, R. The rebirth of youth in the age of cultural change. *Acta Paedopsychiatrica* 36 (1969) : 327–345.

Bay, C. Political and apolitical students: Facts in search of theory. *Journal of Social Issues* 23 (1967) : 76–91.

Beck, B. M. The adolescent's challenge to casework. *Social Work* 3 (1958) : 89–95.

Becker, H. *German youth: Bond or free.* New York: Oxford University Press, 1946.

Berman, M. Sex and the Jewish teenager. *Religious Education* 65 (1970) : 415–421.

Bettelheim, B. The problem of generation. *Daedalus* 91 (1962) : 68–96.

Bickford, H. L., and Neal, A. G. Alienation and social learning: A study of students in a vocational training center. *Sociology of Education* 42 (1969) : 141–153.

Blumental, H. E. *Psychological problems of the adolescent immigrant in Israel of today.* Jerusalem: Ministry of Labor, Department for Vocational Education, 1958.

Boll, E. S. Britain's experience with adolescents. *Annals of the American Academy of Political and Social Science* 236 (1944) : 74–82.

Bonino, S. Ricerca sul movimento studentesco degli Instituti Medi Superiori nella citta de Pinerolo. *Rivista di Psicologia Sociale e Archivio Italiano di Psicologia Generale e del Lavoro* 37 (1970) : 211–244.

Bornemann, E. Jugendprobleme unserer Zeit. *Psychologische Rundschau* (1958) : 77–104.

Cervini, C. La "questione giovanile" oggi. *Difesa Sociale* 45 (1966) : 64–77.

Coleman, J. S. How do the young become adults? *Center for Social Organization of Schools Report, Johns Hopkins University,* no. 130 (1972).

Davis, K. Sociology of parent-youth conflict. *American Sociological Review* 5 (1940) : 523–535.

Davis, K. Adolescence and the social structure. *Annals of the American Academy of Political and Social Science* 238 (1944) : 8–16.

Diez de Rio, I. Youth culture and adult society. *Revista del Instituto de la Juventud* 42 (1972) : 51–96.

Distler, L. S. The adolescent "hippie" and the emergence of a matristic culture. *Psychiatry* 33 (1970) : 362–371.

Eisenstadt, S. N. Archetypal patterns of youth. *Daedalus* 94 (1962) : 28–46.

Erikson, E. H. Memorandum on youth. *Daedalus* 96 (1967) : 860–870.

Erikson, E. H. Reflections on the dissent of contemporary youth. *Daedalus* 99 (1970) : 154–176.

Flacks, R. The liberated generation: An exploration of the roots of student protest. *Journal of Social Issues* 23 (1967) : 52–75.

Friedenberg, E. Z. *The vanishing adolescent.* New York: Dell, 1962. (Original publication, Boston: Beacon Press, 1959.)

Gallup, G., and Hill, E. The cool generation. *Saturday Evening Post,* December 1961.

Gardner, G. E. Present day society and the adolescent. *American Journal of Orthopsychiatry* 27 (1957) : 508–517.

Golan, S. Al beayot hanoar beyamenu. *Ofakim* 12 (1958) : 167–176.

Goodman, P. *Growing up absurd.* New York: Random House, 1960.

Gould, L. J. Conformity and marginality: Two faces of alienation. *Journal of Social Issues* 25 (1969) : 39–63.

Grace, H. A., and Lewellyn, L. W. The no man's land of youth. *Journal of Educational Sociology* 33 (1959) : 135–140.

Hanssen, C. A., and Paulson, M. J. Our anti-establishment youth: Revolution or evolution. *Adolescence* 7 (1972) : 393–408.

Heath, R. W.; Maier, M. H.; and Remmers, H. H. Youth's attitudes towards various aspects of their lives. *Purdue Opinion Poll Reports,* no. 51 (1958).

Hickerson, N. *Education for alienation.* New York: Prentice-Hall, 1966.

Hochheimer, W. Zur Rolle von Autoritat und Sexualitat im Generationskonflikt. *Psyche* 20 (1966) : 493–519.

Hughes, H. S. Emotional disturbance and American social change, 1944–1969. *American Journal of Psychiatry* 126 (1969) : 21–28.

Huizinga, J. Puerilism. *Psychoanalytic Review* 57 (1970–1971) : 632–638.

Jackson, D. W. Alienation and identity-role diffusion in late adolescence. *Journal of Psychology* 83 (1973) : 251–255.

Jennings, F. G. Adolescents, aspirations, and the older generation. *Teachers College Record* 65 (1964) : 335–341.

Johnson, J. J. The hippie as a developmental task. *Adolescence* 4 (1969) : 34–42.

Kaila, K. Psychiatry and higher education in Finland. *American Journal of Psychiatry* 114 (1958) : 1023–1027.

Keniston, K. Social change and youth in America. *Daedalus* 91 (1962) : 145–171.

Keniston, K. The sources of student dissent. *Journal of Social Issues* 23 (1967) : 108–137.

Klein, E. B., and Gould, L. J. Alienation and identification of college women. *Journal of Personality* 37 (1969) : 468–480.

Langman, L.; Block, R. L.; and Cunningham, I. Counter-cultural values at a Catholic university. *Social Problems* 20 (1973) : 521–532.

Lauterbach, A. Psychocultural roots of America's self-image. *American Journal of Psychotherapy* 24 (1970) : 627–642.

Lebovici, S. Adolescent modes of adaptation. *Preliminary Notes for the Sixth International Congress for Child Psychiatry.* Edinburgh, Scotland, 1966.

Lewis, F. What German youth knows about Hitler. *The New York Times Magazine,* June 7, 1959, pp. 72–74.

McCleary, R. D. The violence of the privileged in the U.S.A. *International Journal of Offender Therapy* 14 (1970) : 81–85.

McGovern, G. The child and the American future. *American Psychologist* 25 (1970) : 157–160.

McGranahan, D. V., and Janowitz, M. Studies of German youth. *Journal of Abnormal and Social Psychology* 41 (1946) : 3–14.

Matza, D. Subterranean traditions of youth. *Annals of the American Academy of Political and Social Science* 338 (1961) : 102–118.

Mead, M. *Coming of age in Samoa.* New York: Morrow, 1928. (Paperback edition, Mentor, 1949.)

Mead, M. *Growing up in New Guinea.* New York: Morrow, 1930. (Paperback edition, Mentor, 1953.)

Meissner, W. W. Some anxiety indications in the adolescent boy. *Journal of General Psychology* 64 (1961) : 251–257.

Milner, E. Extreme cultural discontinuity and contemporary adolescent behavior: A relational analysis. *International Journal of Social Psychiatry* 15 (1969) : 314–318.

Mussen, P., and Beytagh, L. A. Industralization, child-rearing practices, and children's personality. *Journal of Genetic Psychology* 115 (1969) : 195–216.

Nagaraja, J. The belligerent youth: Clinical study. *Child Psychiatry Quarterly* 5 (1972) : 9–12.

Noshpitz, J. D. Certain cultural and familial factors contributing to adolescent alienation. *Journal American Academy Child Psychiatry* 9 (1970) : 216–223.

Offer, D.; Sabshin, M.; and Marcus, D. Clinical evaluation of normal adolescents. *American Journal of Psychiatry* 121 (1965) : 864–872.

Parsons, T. Age and sex in the social structure of the United States. *American Sociological Review* 7 (1942) : 604–616.

Parsons, T. Youth in the context of American society. *Daedalus* 91 (1962) : 97–123.

Paulson, M. J.; Lin, T.; and Hanssen, C. Family harmony: An etiologic factor in alienation. *Child Development* 43 (1972) : 591–603.

Phillips, I., and Szurek, S. A. Conformity rebellion and learning: Confrontation of youth with society. *American Journal of Orthopsychiatry* 40 (1970) : 463–472.

Pileggi, N. Revolutionaires who have to be home by 7:30. *Phi Delta Kappan* 50 (1969) : 561–569.

Potvin, R. H. Adolescent behavior and American society. *Catholic Educational Review* 62 (1964) : 19–24.

Propper, M. M.; Kiaune, V.; and Murray, J. B. Alienation syndrome among male adolescents in prestige Catholic and public high schools. *Psychological Reports* 27 (1970) : 311–315.

Prugh, D. G. Youth's challenge and our response: Are we a sick society? *American Journal of Orthopsychiatry* 39 (1969) : 548–552.

Ray, J. J., and Sutton, A. J. Alienation in an Australian university. *Journal of Social Psychology* 86 (1972) : 319–320.

Rode, A. Perceptions of parental behavior among alienated adolescents. *Adolescence* 6 (1971) : 19–38.

Rosen, G. Emotion and sensibility in ages of anxiety: A comparative historic review. *American Journal of Psychiatry* 124 (1967) : 771–784.

Schneemann, N. Gedanken zur Entstehungsgeschichte des Gammlers anhand einer Analyse des

Struwwelpeters. *Zeitschrift fur Psychotherapie und Medizinische Psychologie* 20 (1970): 213–223.

Settlage, C. F. Adolescence and social change. *Journal of the American Academy of Child Psychiatry* 9 (1970): 203–215.

Sexton, V. S. The adolescent in the affluent society of the sixties: A sketch. *National Catholic Guidance Conference Journal* 9 (1965): 143–155.

Shepard, J. M. Alienation as a process: Work as a case in point. *Sociological Quarterly* 13 (1972): 161–173.

Snopik, S.; Rabovich, J. C.; and Tausk, J. R. Crisis adolescente y cambio social. *Revista Argentina de Psicologia* 1 (1969): 61–66.

Sorokin, P. *The American sex revolution.* Boston: Sargent, 1956.

Soskin, W. F.; Duhl, L. J.; and Leopold, R. L. Sociocultural aspects of adolescence. *Preliminary Notes for the Sixth International Congress for Child Psychiatry.* Edinburgh, Scotland, 1966.

Spiel, W. Psychodynamische Gedankengange zur Reifungskrise der Pubertat. *Praxis der Psychotherapie* 11 (1966): 126–135.

Szczepanski, Y. Hanoar boalam shel yamenu. *Ofakim* 13 (1959): 205–212.

Teicher, J. D. The alienated, older, isolated male adolescent. *American Journal of Psychotherapy* 26 (1972): 401–407.

Tolor, A., and LeBlanc, R. F. Personality correlates of alienation. *Journal of Consulting and Clinical Psychology* 37 (1971): 444.

Toussieng, P. W. Hangloose identity, or living death: The agonizing choice of growing old today. *Adolescence* 3 (1968): 307–318.

Trent, R. D. Economic development and identity conflict in Puerto Rico. *Journal of Social Psychology* 65 (1965): 293–310.

Unwin, J. R. Dissident youth. *Canada's Mental Health* 17 (1969): 4–10.

Weiner, I. B. The generation gap: Fact or fancy? *Adolescence* 6 (1971): 156–166.

Williams, F. S. Alienation of youth as reflected in the hippie movement. *Journal of the American Academy of Child Psychiatry* 9 (1970): 251–263.

Wise, L. J. Alienation of present-day adolescents. *Journal of the American Academy of Child Psychiatry* 9 (1970): 264–277.

Wolfenden, J. Students' strains and stresses. *British Journal of Psychiatry* 116 (1970): 577–585.

Wolman, B. B. The rebellion of youth. *International Journal of Social Psychiatry* 18 (1972–1973): 254–259.

Ziller, R. C. The alienation syndrome: A triadic pattern of self-other orientation. *Sociometry* 32 (1969): 287–300.

Zube, M. J. Changing concepts of morality: 1948–1969. *Social Forces* 50 (1972): 385–393.

Suggested Readings

Ashby, M. A. The wave of student unrest and implications for the secondary-school counselor. *Canadian Counsellor* 7 (1973): 16–23.

Beelick, D. B. Sources of student satisfaction and dissatisfaction. *Journal of Educational Research* 67 (1973): 19–22.

Chabassol, D. J. The measurement of some aspects of structure in adolescence. *Journal of Educational Research* 66 (1973): 247–250.

Erikson, E. H. Reflections on the dissent of contemporary youth. *International Journal of Psychoanalysis* 51 (1970): 11–22.

Ewing, D. B. The relations among anomie, dogmatism, and selected personal-social factors in asocial adolescent boys. *Journal of Social Issues* 27 (1971): 159–169.

Farnsworth, D. L. Dilemma of the adolescent in a changing society. *Psychiatric Annals* 3 (1973): 87–100.

Gottlieb, D., ed., *Youth in contemporary society.* Beverly Hills: Sage, 1973.

Graubard, S. R., ed., Youth: Change and challenge. *Daedalus* 91 (1962): 1–289.

Hamid, P. N., and Lloyd, J. Temporal perspectives and alienation. *Perceptual and Motor Skills* 37 (1973): 139–145.

Keniston, K. *The uncommitted: Alienated youth in American society.* Harcourt, Brace & World, 1960.

McNassor, D. Social structure for identity in adolescence: Western Europe and America. *Adolescence* 2 (1967): 311–334.

Mays, J. B. *The young pretenders: A study of teen-age culture in contemporary society.* New

York: Schocken Books, 1968.

Milner, E. Extreme cultural discontinuity and contemporary American adolescent behavior: A relational analysis. *International Journal of Social Psychiatry* 15 (1969): 314–318.

Minvchin, S. Adolescence: Society's response and responsibility. *Adolescence* 4 (1969): 455–476.

Nordberg, R. B. *The teen-ager and the new mysticism.* New York: Richards Rosen Press, 1973.

Propper, M. M., and Clark, E. T. Alienation: Another dimension of underachievement. *Journal of Psychology* 75 (1970): 13–18.

Schiamberg, L. B. *Adolescent alienation.* Columbus: Charles E. Merrill, 1973.

Solnit, A. J.; Settlage, C. F.; Goodman, S.; and Blos, P. Youth unrest: A symposium. *American Journal of Psychiatry* 125 (1969): 1145–1159.

Steinitz, V. A.; King, P.; Solomon, E.; and Shapiro, E. Ideological development in working class youth. *Harvard Educational Review* 43 (1973): 333–361.

Stroud, J. The betrayed generation. *Mental Health* 26 (1967): 9–11.

Thomas, L. E. Clothing and counterculture: An empirical study. *Adolescence* 8 (1973): 93–112.

Wallace, A., and Wheeler, M. Youth development program: Help for alienated youth. *School Counselor* 21 (1973): 61–62.

Waters, C. W. Comparison of protesting and nonprotesting students. *Psychological Reports* 33 (1973): 543–547.

Weiner, I. B. Perspectives on the modern adolescent. *Psychiatry* 35 (1972): 20–31.

Chapter Twenty-one

Intergenerational Conflict

The Meaning of a Generation

Of a given adolescent it may be said, "He is a typical member of his generation," or, "He feels about things the same way the rest of his generation do." What is a generation? Who are its members and who are excluded? What does it mean to be a member of a generation? Klecka (1971) speaks of a generation as a set of individuals who have been socialized in the same manner as the result of common exposure to the events of a particular period in history. Thus, a generation consists of those persons who were born and grew up during relatively the same historical time span. Such persons are characterized by a tendency to make evaluations or interpretations at least partly in terms of the experiences they had while growing up. Mannheim (1970) speaks of the unity of the generation as growing out of the similarity of location of a number of individuals within a social whole, together with a tendency toward certain definite modes of behavior, feeling, and thought. To belong to a generation represents having a sense of identity with its members in their common exposure and reaction to social and intellectual events.

Of course, generations overlap, but an individual may find some means of defining his own generation in terms of a stage of life, as "those of us who were teenagers at the same time," or "those of us who went to college in the 1960s," or "those of us who grew up during Vietnam." In this sense an individual could simultaneously perceive himself as belonging to several event-centered generations, but in actuality the perception of belonging to a generation usually extends over the events encompassed during a given span of years. Sometimes a specific line of demarcation is made, as in the case of those who are under and over thirty years of age. Most adolescents would define a generation in terms of chronological age or, occasionally, in terms of child-adult interpersonal function. Where identity of feeling is concerned, an adolescent could perceive himself as a member of a generation other than that represented by his own age cohort, although such identification would be relatively rare. In terms of generational identification most adolescents are peer centered.

That relationships between the generations present difficulties is obvious, but not all relationships are necessarily ones of conflict, although the seeds of conflict are certainly present. The crux of the matter seems to be the way in which the generations interpret each other, together with the social and economic conditions that color the interpretations.

Adults, looking at an adolescent, may say, "He speaks for his generation—he is what youth is like today." And then, depending upon their optimism or their pessimism and perhaps upon their insight, they may say, "Something is wrong," or, "Kids today are all right," pointing out a conspicuous example of a "good"[1] adolescent or group of adolescents whose behavior apparently meets their expectation of what youth should be like. The criterion for

[1] If there are "good" adolescents, must there not then be "bad" ones? The use of the term *good* is revealing.

such judgments is, of course, the culture as these adults have experienced it, or as, perhaps, they have wishfully hypothesized it, using an earlier culture as their reference point. Or the observing adult may say hopefully, "It will be all right in the end," meaning that when the adolescent grows up he will be like the adults the observer knows and approves of and unlike those he disapproves of. In any event, the criteria applied are not those of the adolescent, and the adult feels justified in assuming the role of a judge who approves or disapproves of someone as good, bad, or all right on the basis of his own criteria. Perhaps more serious, in most such evaluations, no question is asked as to what criteria the adolescent is applying, except in the form of the question, "What's the matter with you?" and to that no answer is expected or given. Perhaps the adolescent doesn't know and really thinks nothing is the matter, or that what is the matter is the adult; perhaps he is resigned, afraid, or inarticulate; perhaps he knows the question is rhetorical; or perhaps he is in as little position to explain historical, economic, and social change to his elders as they are to hear it.

One difficulty is that the culture is not static; it changes and evolves, and as one considers the evolution over several generations, one is surprised at how great the changes are. Sometimes they are slow and almost imperceptible; at other times they are sudden and dramatic. But, whether slow or sudden, the changes occur, and one generation is never a carbon copy of the succeeding one. When the changes are slow, in a period of relative stability, it is easier for one generation to cope with the next; but when the changes are sudden, the gulf between them widens and communication, if it does not break down altogether, becomes increasingly difficult. Today the culture is in a state of flux in nearly every aspect of its structure and values. Never in man's history have major changes come so fast and affected so many areas of living. A modern generation has difficulty in understanding the changes within its own generation, let alone in attempting to understand intergenerational differences.

However, when the change is recognized by the older generation and perhaps even accepted by it, there is a better possibility of at least one-way communication, in that the older generation has some basis for "understanding" its juniors. Unfortunately, communication is not two-way even then because the younger generation is too busy understanding itself to be interested in or able to engage in a dialogue with its elders about understanding them. When it comes down to it, why should they? Theirs is the present world, and tomorrow is theirs, at least until they in turn encounter a new generation, an eventuality not in the minds of most adolescents.

Sources of Conflict

There are many potential sources of adolescent-adult conflict, although none of them inevitably leads to dissension in every case. As he moves through the teens, the adolescent is faced by a number of developmental tasks that he must meet, and some of these bring him into direct conflict with his elders. It may even be said that successful meeting of the developmental tasks sets up a situation fostering intergenerational conflict. It is quite possible that the adolescent who avoids or does not successfully meet developmental tasks is less apt to perceive a generation gap, although he may find himself isolated from those of his peers who have successfully met the developmental tasks. Johnson (1969) notes that the youth social-deviation movements (beatnik, hippie) represent developmental task striving. Such youth seek an identity by a self-definition setting themselves apart from their elders with a related assertion of a right to affirm themselves as individuals. Count (1967) contends that "conflict is a normal and essential function in adolescent growth and within defined limits, beneficial." As Count sees it, within such defined limits adult-adolescent conflicts may be stimulated, encouraged, and managed for creative, constructive purposes.

A further cause of differences between generations has to do with the relative and sometimes incorrect perceptions that each has of the other. Bengtson and Kuypers (1971) make the point that expectations each generation has concerning generational interaction are rooted in the developmental stakes each has in the other. For the middle generation, the backdrop for perceiving generational relations concerns the establishment and maintenance of continuity over time. Experienced conflict arises from their anticipation that youthful emergence, unless guided and controlled, will create disruptive discontinuity. The younger generation, concerned about individuation, change, and emergence, fear that middle-generation influence will inhibit their development. Anderson (1973), in a study of thirteen-year-olds and their parents, notes that both generations had faulty perceptions of the attitudes of the opposite generation and that such faulty perceptions formed the basis for opposition or conflict. One of the problems may be a matter of communication. Wood et al. (1971), in a study of thirty-five-year-olds as compared to nineteen- and twenty-year-olds, makes the point that different-generation dyads do not communicate as effectively as same-generation dyads. Just because there is some conscious intent on the part of parents in their child-rearing practices does not mean that the adolescent will understand what those intentions are. Inadequate communication may obscure intentions. Christantiello (1969) suggests that the adult is at least equally at fault when a communication gap occurs between adult and adolescent. He feels that where communication is concerned, adults have often allowed themselves to become cold, inflexible, and immobile.

Macey (1972) makes the point that the fact of a difference between the generations was recognized long before the modern era. Both the Old and New Testaments inform us that "your old men shall dream dreams; your young men shall see visions." (Joel 2:28 and Acts 2:17) When these biblical words were written and for a long time thereafter, it was still pos-sible to envisage the close family unit with a division of labor and a mutuality of understanding where old men might indeed dream dreams. The living-together context as well as division of labor will have much to do with the range and seriousness of intergenerational conflict. The cohesive family unit with defined divisions of labor for the governance of intergenerational relations was true of biblical times. But the modern family is less cohesive; the division of labor either does not exist or is unclear, and the intergenerational relationships are both ambiguous and inconsistent.

Freudenberger (1969) points to the emotional and environmental deprivation as well as communication deficiencies within families as causes of conflict. Atkins (1970) focuses attention on the familial conflicts associated with the succession of generations that reach a peak of disturbance with the emergence of the adolescent, who must overcome both internal psychological and external actual obstacles to self-realization.

Both Assagiolo (1973) and Levine and Shaiova (1971) point to the perennial struggle between authority and independence as a source of intergenerational conflict. Speaking of adult-youth authority relationships, Levine and Shaiova note that equality and rationality are crucial points in the relationships. They feel that the new-found freedom of youth has led to the collapse of social and adult authority.

Munns (1971), in writing of the generation gap, notes that one causal problem may be lack of common ground between adults and adolescents. He makes the point that the mental development of youth is not complete in the teens. They do not think, as Piaget and Kohlberg have indicated, as adults do, with the result that communication and mutuality of understanding can become very difficult to attain. Muzio (1970), in a study of eleven- to fifteen-year-olds, feels that the conflict situation is exacerbated by the desire of the young adolescent to differentiate himself from the adult, whose responsibility frightens him.

Entirely apart from the culture are intrinsic differences of age that place obstacles in the way of adolescent-adult relationships. We must consider the adolescent's viewpoint as he thinks of and has to deal with parents and adults generally—and for that matter, we could well consider the viewpoint of any person as he has to deal with persons appreciably older than himself. Essentially, except for certain special individuals, we are all most interested in those of our own generation and normally find ourselves most comfortable and most in accord with their attitudes and ways. This is largely true of the middle-aged person considering the senior citizen, and of the adolescent considering the middle-aged. The generations may live together side by side, they overlap to some extent, but they are not of each other, and the differences, small as they sometimes appear, tend to outweigh the congruencies. For the adolescent the older person is the purveyor of manners and customs that constrain his youth. They represent an attitude toward life and a philosophical position against which he is in revolt. The adolescent tends to be, as he sees it, more romantic and at the same time more realistic in terms of the present day. He feels he is more au courant, more "with it." That his philosophy and attitudes will one day seem as conventional, as dull, and as outmoded to a new generation as those of the old generation now appear to him is something he can hardly be expected to grasp with any degree of conviction. Youth is more vigorous than age and has more stamina over the long run, and they are certainly willing, physically, to burn the candle at both ends, something most adults have to do sparingly, if at all. Youth is more spontaneous than age. Naegele (1962) writes of:

an industrial society in which adults must so frequently maintain public life by reasoning, planning, calculating, or scheming. In contrast (despite so many adult attempts at persuasion to the contrary), youth still stands for spontaneous, free, and unself-conscious activities, for a willingness to express enthusiasms as well as to have them.

A further difficulty in assessing the relationship between generations is the fact that America as a culture has become schizoid. Perhaps, as no other country has, we have deified our youth. We not only look upon ourselves as a young nation; as adults we see ourselves as young and fiercely hold to the trappings, points of view, and activities of youth. We try to conceal our age, we dress young, we act young. Our recreations are so often the recreations of youth, and we value those things we see as youthful. Yet we as adults are the players in the game rather than youth itself. We reject the young while we emulate them. In fact, in this culture one problem for adolescents seems to be that of finding something that is uniquely their own—a ground upon which adults cannot, will not, intrude. Yet adolescents no sooner adopt a new dance, a new form of dress or speech, or a new activity than adults take it over, sending youth back to something different. Of course, the one thing youth really have that adults do not is the actuality of youth. This is the soft spot in the armor of the youth-focused adult, and here youth can flaunt their status. They clearly have something adults do not have, which adults by their own actions admit they desire. Here, at this focal point of difference, youth often organize their rebellion. How can they be expected to reject something not rejected by their elders? Yet adults in turn complain about and, often, it seems, fear youth because they appear to lack respect for their elders. Should we be surprised?

But the problem goes deeper. America is not really a young nation, and as a nation it has accepted responsibilities even as, in the world of work, its adults have had to accept them. In its international relations, particularly in its system of aid and counsel for underdeveloped countries, America cannot play its youthful role. As Naegele (1962) notes: "American society . . . finds itself collectively constrained to advance its self-image from one of youth to a less chronologically specific and more demanding conception of a 'large and powerful nation.'" This is hardly a youthful stance and provides another area for mixed motives and ambivalence among adults that is part of the atmosphere in which adolescents must pursue their quest for understanding and self and cultural identification.

Friction between youth and older persons sometimes occurs when youth perceive that the older generation has tried to build a world that is not theirs and has committed them to an enterprise with which they do not wish to be identified. As Erikson (1962) has observed, youth are antihistorical, and all this commitment is a link with the historic past—the making of a world whose values and activities modern youth see as not theirs and which for them lacks meaning. To be involved means being involved in something maintained and created by a past generation. This becomes all the more a focal point of dissension when youth feel that the older generation has botched the job and violated the fidelity that is so important to youth.

During time of war, of course, youth, as Eisenstadt (1962) notes, is emphasized, and at least some aspects of maturity are accelerated. During World War II, and to a lesser extent during Korea and Vietnam, the process of prolonged economic dependence and deferred adult status was reversed. In the early 1940s and 1950s, and in the middle 1960s, many an adolescent in his late teens found himself in a position of responsibility and authority that would not ordinarily have been his in civilian life until middle or late maturity.

The case of John Ames might be taken as an example. John entered the armed forces, was commissioned, and piloted a bomber over Vietnam. He married before leaving the United States and had one child. John, a boy in his late teens, was well trained to perform competently a technically difficult and dangerous task. Entrusted as he was with a plane worth millions of dollars and the lives of his crew, he was given responsibility and status that made him a trusted member of the adult community. Had John been born ten years sooner, he might, at the same age, have been living in his home town, his chief responsibility an after-school part-time job, and his main hope that of taking the family car occasionally, without too many lectures on the fact that he was too young to drive it. He might have been going on occasional and tentative dates with the not uncommon paternal admonition to be home early.

In the last twenty-five to thirty years, we have been engaged in three youth-consuming conflicts—World War II, Korea, and Vietnam —not to mention the ever-present cold war and various brush-fire incidents. Perhaps it is not unnatural for youth to feel sometimes that they are being used.

Differences and Similarities Between Generations

There are characteristically many dissimilarities of opinion and point of view between the adolescent and adult generations. Most such differences cause few if any serious conflicts, although many of them may cause misunderstanding and minor irritations. In some cases, however, the differences become a major issue and serve to bring about a real generation gap. Whether a difference will become a major issue depends upon the individuals involved and the past history of their relationship. It is unlikely that most single differences of opinion or attitude will lead to major or prolonged dissension, but it is true that the effect of minor differences may be cumulative and result in major conflict.

Fengler and Wood (1972) investigated value differences among three generations and examined variations by sex, education, religion, and urban-rural residency. A college student, his parents, and one grandparent were interviewed from each of seventy-three three-generation families. Respondents were asked to state their reactions to a series of fifty statements covering eight major contemporary issues. Fengler and Wood report wide differences between student and parent generations and between parent and grandparent generations on six of the eight issues. The investigators conclude that age consistently contributes to the explanation of generational differences in values, even when controls on nonage variables are applied. Lerner, Pendorf, and Emery (1971) administered a twenty-nine-item questionnaire to adolescents (mean age 16.1) and adults (mean age 44.1) containing items on such contemporary issues as drug use, police and military authority and power, sexual behavior, and religion. Significant attitudinal differences between the generations obtained in 89.5 percent of the items. The investigators hypothesize, as a result of their study, a generation gap in political-social attitudes. Munns (1972) studied the relationship of adolescents' values to those of their parents and peer group as perceived by the adolescents themselves. They concluded that the adolescents viewed themselves somewhat like their fathers in theoretical, social, political, and religious values, but closer overall to their peer group than to either parent.

Payne, Summers, and Stewart (1973) also investigated both the scope and the uniqueness of generation value differences across three generations consisting of undergraduates, their parents and their grandparents. They administered an eighty-five-item questionnaire that indicated "how bad" the respondents would feel if they were to indulge in each of the behaviors described in the questionnaire.[2] Questionnaire responses were factor analyzed, and the results were assessed under the three following factor headings.

Factor I Conventional morality (as reading obscene literature or being unpatriotic).

Factor II Personal failure (as cheating on an examination and being caught or making promises to others and not keeping them).

Factor III Embarrassment (as having unexpected guests when your house is messy or failing at something you have tried hard to do).

Where conventional morality was concerned, each of the generations differed significantly

[2]Each item consisted of a brief description of a type of behavior such as "lying about one's past in order to get a job." Respondents indicated on a 7-point scale, ranging from not at all bad to extremely bad, how badly they would feel if they were to indulge in the type of behavior described.

(p < .01) from the others. Students indicated a lower level of negative affect than did parents, who in turn indicated that they would feel less negative affect than grandparents. The difference between parents and grandparents, however, was less than between parents and students. Obviously, the greatest gap of all was between students and grandparents.

Where personal failure was concerned, students and their grandparents did not differ at all, and while parents were more negative than either students or grandparents, the differences were not statistically significant. It is probable that parents are more involved in the economic struggle of breadwinning where failure has serious repercussions. Parents and grandparents did not differ significantly on the embarrassment area, but students were significantly different from both in the smaller number of situations they would find embarrassing. Figure 53 depicts the mean factor scores plotted across generations.

Thus, the students were on the whole less severe in their judgments of situations involving conventional morality and embarrassment, but a different ordering emerged for personal failure. Lerner et al. (1972) administered to high school students and their parents a questionnaire pertaining to such contemporary topics as drug use, sexual behavior, religion, and civil rights. They found that adolescent and adult groups differed on only 50 percent of the questionnaire items. Moreover, the differences in attitude appeared to reflect more a difference in intensity than in direction of attitudes.

Boshier and Taylor (1972) and Friedman, Gold, and Christie (1972) report studies indicating sons and daughters as being more liberal than their parents, although Boshier and Taylor indicate that parents are actually more liberal than their progeny estimate them to be.

LoSciuto and Karlin (1972) report finding more harmony than disharmony between high schoolers and their parents, and note that where there was disagreement, the issues were those of ordinary parent-child relationships

Figure 53 *Mean Factor Scores Plotted Across Generations*

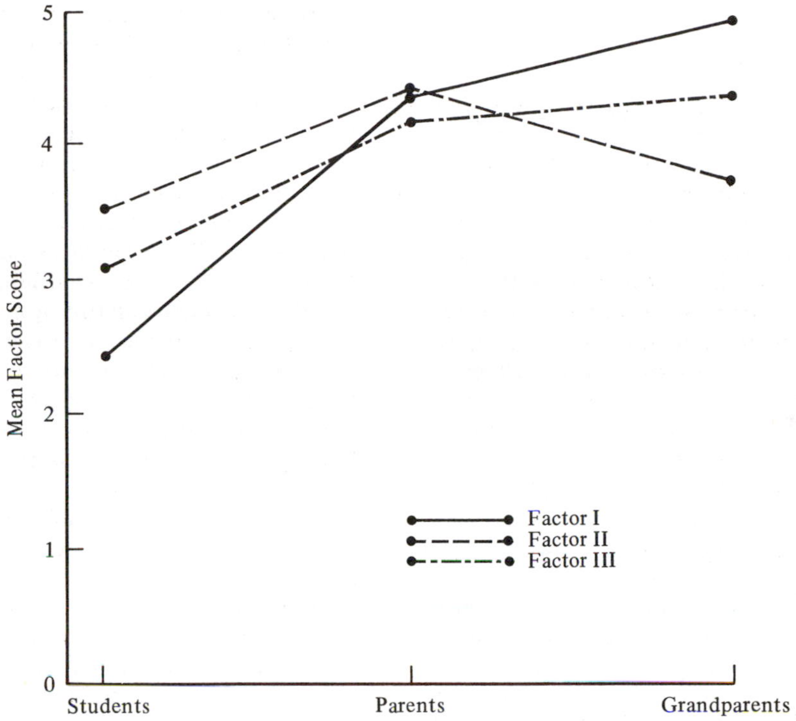

Source: Adapted from S. Payne, D. A. Summers, and T. R. Stewart, "Value differences across three generations," *Sociometry* 36 (1973): 26, fig. 1. Reprinted by permission of the American Sociological Association and the authors.

free of any particular philosophical bias. But they did find that those adolescents showing the greatest amount of disagreement with their parents spent as little time with them as possible and tended to reject such adult sources of values as religion. Lerner, Pendorf, and Emery (1971) report a similar value rejection and note that boys tended to be more dissident than girls, and that children in the upper grades were more dissident than those in the lower grades.

Yankelovich (1969) report large cross-generation differences in traditional values as well as in ideological and political beliefs. However, the gap was greatest between radical youth and their parents and less between conservative youth and their parents. In line with

this finding, Brunswick (1970) notes that youth who have a definite career goal and the means to implement it are closer to their parents in their basic values and attitudes.

According to Yankelovich (1969), a substantial majority of adolescents and their parents agree that (1) competition promotes excellence, (2) society benefits from authority, and (3) compromise leads to progress. But in the mechanics of daily living, as in the case of dress and grooming, there are basic disagreements, as is also true of certain matters of personal value choice such as religion and drug use. This last becomes particularly true when adolescents are away from home in college. In general, Yankelovich reports that youth are more aware of value differences than are their parents, but both (nearly 70 percent) feel that while a generation gap does exist, it has been exaggerated.

The Existence of a Generation Gap

From the available evidence can it be said that a serious generation gap really does exist in the perceptions of today's adolescents and adults? And insofar as a generation gap is perceived to exist, how objective is the perception? In an endeavor to answer these two questions, Ahammer and Baltus (1972) questioned groups of adolescents (ages fifteen to eighteen), adults (ages thirty-four to forty), and older people (ages sixty-four to seventy-four) on behavioral items enabling them to express reactions of desirability where they were concerned personally, and also to indicate how they felt the other two age groups would react to the items as desirable-undesirable. The investigators report no existing differences on the dimensions of nurturance and autonomy, but both adults and adolescents perceived older people as believing that nurturance was more and autonomy was less desirable. Adults felt that adolescents placed greater value on autonomy than the adolescents actually did. The investigators suggested that some perceptions of the generation gap are subjective rather than objective; that is, the perceptions are based on wrong assumptions about how another generation feels about certain kinds of behavior.

However, the fact of a generation gap between today's youth and the older members of society is widely accepted by the popular media of communications, by the man in the street, and by numerous professional writers and social scientists. It has been held that these differences are so great that they can be held to account, at least in part, for such quite diverse phenomena as drug abuse, campus unrest, and civil rights movements. Lorenz (1970) even goes so far as to take the position that rebelling youth is waging tribal war against the parent generation, thereby endangering

existing culture by demanding a complete break in its traditions. Hurlock (1966) sees today's youth as irresponsible, hedonistic, immoral, disciplineless, valueless, and without purpose.

In contrast to Lorenz's and Hurlock's positions, Venables (1965) sees the older generation as constituting a solemn meritocracy that under-values the less able and leaves no room for gaiety and nonsense. Venables sees the "tidy plans" of this meritocracy as inevitably breeding the rebellious young people "it deserves." Kunen (1968) sees a villainous "establishment" maliciously, or through sheer ignorance, inertia, incompetence, or insensitivity, neither recognizing nor making any effort to meet the legitimate demands of youth.

It has become fashionable at the present time to adopt the rhetoric of the generation gap and to assume differences in attitude and point of view on all kinds of problems involving the relationship of adolescents with their parents as well as with other adults. Such rhetoric enables both young and old to explain all kinds of perceived differences. As Petroni (1972) points out: "The under thirty and the over thirty are automatically presumed to occupy polar positions." Bengtson (1971) writes: "The generation gap is one of the clearest examples of intergroup perceptions defined by age," yet when it comes to individual perceptions he notes that the generation gap is perceived as greater for "people in general" then for "people in my family."

Yet for some, the rhetoric of the generation gap is not convincing and, as a matter of fact, definitive empirical evidence is lacking. Payne, Summers, and Stewart (1973) note that generation differences are hard to interpret.

> It is not always clear that the beliefs or attitudes which have been assessed constitute domains of serious conflict, nor is it clear in studies which do not involve parents and offspring whether the results can be attributed solely to generational differences.

Graff (1970) argues that while the adolescent rebellion is widely discussed and publicized, in reality most adolescents become very much like their parents in outlook. Those who are truly at odds with their parents are small in number. Graff feels that those adolescents who do differ and rebel often indulge in rebellious behavior to be part of the crowd and in order to have a good time.

Various writers argue that insofar as a generation gap does exist, it is narrow in scope. Such writers do not believe that the youth of today and their elders are in conflict over values and standards of behavior. These writers see differences as existing but feel that they are over minor matters such as preferences for music, clothing, and food. As Weiner (1971) notes, teenagers do in fact embrace a variety of uniquely teenage values, but the notion of a generation gap has often been fancifully over-generalized into a youth culture characterized by widespread disaffection, rebellion, immorality, and drug use. It is Weiner's position, a position with which this writer agrees, that the youth culture is in fact largely a superficial phenomenon and that most young people are psychologically stable, concerned with meaningful goals, and an integral part of their family and community. Disaffected youth do exist, but the highly alienated, promiscuous, drug-habituated adolescent is the exception rather than the rule and, when he is encountered, should be recognized as a psychologically disturbed individual in need of clinical attention.

In considering the generation gap and intergenerational conflict, two questions should be asked: (1) Who is in conflict? and (2) Who is rejecting what and upon what grounds? Are adolescents rejecting merely their parents and perhaps their teachers, or is the gap more pervasive? Are the children rejecting adult society in general with its array of social institutions, its ideologies, and its cultural values? Since the gap, insofar as it exists, is sociocultural in nature, we have to hypothesize that it includes more than parents and teachers, although the rejection will seldom extend to every aspect of adult culture, and it probably will be intermittent. It should be remembered that adolescents are seeking to define themselves and that

they test reality with assumptions that may well differ from day to day. What an adolescent accepts on Monday, he may more often doubt on Friday than would an adult with his more stabilized concept of self. In this sense, given a generation gap, the adolescent rather than the adult is permeable, and if the adult handles the situation well, he may effect changes in the adolescent's position. But this needs a stabilized and self-defined adult. If the adult has not reached such self-stabilization, he may be the permeable one whom the adolescent will change. And the uncertainty and the attacks on the validity of previous values in the present era have produced many uncertain and confused adults who lack self-stabilization and who, as a result, are easily led.

Summary

A generation consists of a set of individuals who were born and grew up together at the same time in history. They have been subjected to the same processes of socialization and are characterized by a tendency to make evaluations and interpretations at least partly in terms of the experiences they had while growing up. Generations overlap, but individuals usually find some event-centered means of defining their generational status. Most adolescents would define a generation in terms of chronological age. Conflict exists between generations, but not all, or even most, points of contact are conflict producing.

Developmental task achievement offers one potential source of intergenerational conflict. Further causes of conflict include the relative and often incorrect perceptions that different generations have of each other, lack of proper communication, division of labor and relative role, familial relationships, and the striving for independence of the younger generation. Other causes include lack of common ground between adolescents and adults and the desire of the adolescent to differentiate himself from the adult. Oftentimes, living side by side as they do, differences between the generations tend to be exacerbated, and small as they are, they tend to outweigh the congruencies. Friction between youth and older persons sometimes occurs when youth perceive that the older generation has tried to build a world that is not theirs and has committed them to an enterprise with which they do not wish to be identified.

There are characteristically many dissimilarities of opinion and point of view between the adolescent and adult generations, but whether a difference will become a major issue depends upon the individuals involved and their past history of relationship. Wide differences have been found to exist between parents and adoles-

cents, between parents and grandparents, and between adolescents and grandparents. In general, the younger generation tends to be more liberal than the older generation, although there are numerous points of similarity.

There has been considerable difference of opinion as to the existence and seriousness of a generation gap. Some observers feel that a deep and serious rift exists between the generations, while others believe that such a gap forms the exception rather than the rule. The rhetoric of the generation gap is such that many persons are convinced of its existence, and it is used as an explanation for all kinds of diverse situations affecting youth.

References

Ahammer, I. M., and Baltes, P. B. Objective versus perceived age differences in personality: How do adolescents, adults, and older people view themselves and each other. *Journal of Gerontology* 27 (1972): 46–51.

Anderson, B. E. Misunderstandings between generations: A general phenomenon? *Scandinavian Journal of Educational Research* 17 (1973): 1–10.

Assagiolo, R. The conflict between the generations and the psychosynthesis of the human ages. *Psychosynthesis Research Foundation*, no. 31 (1973).

Atkins, B. The oedipus myth, adolescence, and the succession of generations. *Journal of the American Psychoanalytic Association* 18 (1970): 860–875.

Bengtson, V. L. Interage perceptions and the generation gap. *Gerontologist* 11 (1971): 85–89.

Bengtson, V. L., and Kuypers, J. A. Generational differences and the developmental stake. *Aging and Human Development* 2 (1971): 249–260.

Boshier, R., and Taylor, A. J. The generation gap: Attitudinal differences between parents and their children in New Zealand. *New Zealand Journal of Educational Studies* 7 (1972): 130–140.

Brunswick, A. F. What generation gap? *Social Problems* 17 (1970): 358–371.

Christantiello, P. D. Vulnerability: A thaw in con-

gealed communication. *National Catholic Guidance Conference Journal* 13 (1969): 87–89.

Count, J. The conflict factor in adolescent growth. *Adolescence* 2 (1967): 167–181.

Eisenstadt, S. N. Archetypal patterns of youth. *Daedalus* 91 (1962): 28–46.

Erikson, E. H. Youth: Fidelity and diversity. *Daedalus* 91 (1962): 5–27.

Fengler, A. P., and Wood, V. The generation gap: An analysis of attitudes on contemporary issues. *Gerontologist* 12 (1972): 124–128.

Freudenberger, H. J. Treatment and dynamics of the "disrelated" teenager and his parents in the American society. *Psychotherapy: Theory, Research and Practice* 6 (1969): 249–255.

Friedman, L. N.; Gold, A. R.; and Christie, R. Dissecting the generation gap: Intergenerational and intrafamilial similarities and differences. *Public Opinion Quarterly* 36 (1972): 334–346.

Graff, H. The development of the adolescent. *Pennsylvania Psychiatric Quarterly* 10 (1970): 27–32.

Hurlock, E. B. American adolescents of today—a new species. *Adolescence* 1 (1966): 7–21.

Johnson, S. M., and Brown, R. A. Producing behavior change in parents of disturbed children. *Journal of Child Psychology and Psychiatry and Allied Disciplines* 10 (1969): 107–121.

Klecka, W. R. Applying political generations and the study of political behavior: A cohort analysis.

Public Opinion Quarterly 35 (1971): 358–373.

Kunen, J. S. Why we're against the Bigees. *Atlantic*, Oct. 1968, pp. 65–68.

Lerner, R. M.; Pendorf, J.; and Emery A. Attitudes of adolescents and adults toward contemporary issues. *Psychological Reports* 28 (1971): 139–145.

Lerner, R. M.; Schroeder, C.; Rewitzer, M.; and Weinstock, A. Attitudes of high school students and their parents toward contemporary issues. *Psychological Reports* 31 (1972): 255–258.

Levine, E. M., and Shaiova, C. H. Equality and rationality vs. child socialization: A conflict of interests. *Annals of Psychiatry and Related Disciplines* 9 (1971): 107–116.

Lorenz, K. The enmity between generations and its probable ethological causes. *Psychoanalytic Review* 57 (1970): 333–377.

LoSciuto, L. A., and Karlin, R. M. Correlates of the generation gap. *Journal of Psychology* 81 (1972): 253–262.

Macey, S. L. On dividing the lost: The delegation of power. *Yale Review* 61 (1972): 396–406.

Mannheim, K. The problem of generations. *Psychoanalytic Review* 57 (1970): 378–404.

Munns, M. Is there really a generation gap? *Adolescence* 6 (1971): 197–206.

Munns, M. The values of adolescents compared with parents and peers. *Adolescence* 7 (1972): 519–524.

Muzio, N. R. La valuazione di alcuni aspetti della personalità in soggetti dagli 11 ai 15 anni mediante il test del Bestiaire de Zazzo-Mathon. *Bollettino di Psicologia Applicata* 100–102 (1970): 247–260.

Naegele, K. D. Youth and society: Some observations. *Daedalus* 91 (1962): 47–67.

Payne, S.; Summers, D. A.; and Stewart, T. R. Value differences across three generations. *Sociometry* 36 (1973): 20–30.

Petroni, F. A. Adolescent liberalism: The myth of a generation gap. *Adolescence* 7 (1972): 221–232.

Venables, E. Proposed affinities in British-American perspectives of adolescence. *Journal of Marriage and the Family* 27 (1968): 148–155.

Weiner, I. B. The generation gap: Fact and fancy. *Adolescence* 6 (1971): 156–166.

Wood, R. V.; Yamauch, J. S.; and Bradac, J. J. The communication of meaning across generations. *Journal of Communication* 21 (1971): 160–169.

Yankelovitch, D. *Generations apart.* New York: Columbia Broadcasting System, 1969.

Suggested Readings

Berman, S. Alienation: An essential process of the psychology of adolescence. *Journal of the American Academy of Child Psychiatry* 9 (1970): 233–250.

Berrien, F. K.; Arkoff, A.; and Iwahara, S. Generation differences in values: Americans, Japanese-Americans, and Japanese. *Journal of Social Psychology* 71 (1967): 169–175.

Brown, W. N. Alienated youth. *Mental Hygiene* 52 (1968): 330–336.

Buys, D. J., and Schmidt, M. Student-father attitudes toward contemporary social issues: Replication with a matched sample. *Psychological Reports* 33 (1973): 271–272.

Elkind, D. Culture, change, and their effects on children. *Social Casework* 54 (1973): 360–366.

Erskine, H. The polls: Pacifism and the generation gap. *Public Opinion Quarterly* 36 (1972–1973): 616–627.

Freeman, H. R. The generation gap: Attitudes of students and of their parents. *Journal of Counseling Psychology* 19 (1972): 441–447.

Goldman, S. Profiles of an adolescent. *Journal of Psychology* 54 (1962): 229–240.

Gottlieb, D., ed., *Youth in contemporary society.* Beverly Hills, Cal.: Sage, 1973.

Hedlund, D. A. The sweet-and-sour bird of youth-culture. *Journal of the National Association of Private Psychiatric Hospitals* 4 (1972): 5–8.

Ingham, H. V., and Ingham, R. E. Variables in the conflict between the generations: India for comparison. *Social Psychiatry* 6 (1971): 153–157.

Jennings, F. G. Adolescent aspirations and the older generation. *Teachers College Record* 65 (1964): 335–341.

King, S. H. Coping and growth in adolescence. *Seminars in Psychiatry* 4 (1972): 355–366.

Kitano, H. H. L. Inter- and intra-generational differences in maternal attitudes toward child-rearing. *Journal of Social Psychology* 63 (1964): 215–220.

Klein, A. *Natural enemies: Youth and the clash*

of generations. Philadelphia: Lippincott, 1969.

Knox, W., and Kupferer, H. A discontinuity in the socialization of males in the United States. *Merrill-Palmer Quarterly* 17 (1971): 251–261.

Laufer, R. S. Sources of generational consciousness and conflict. *Annals of the American Academy of Political and Social Science* 395 (1971): 80–94.

Lerner, R. M., and Weinstock, A. Note on the generation gap. *Psychological Reports* 31 (1972): 457–458.

Mead, M. *Culture and commitment: A study of the generation gap*. Garden City, N.J.: Natural History Press, 1970.

Murray, J. B. The generation gap. *Journal of Genetic Psychology* 118 (1971): 71–80.

Mussen, P., and Beytagh, L. Industralization, child-rearing practices, children's personality. *Journal of Genetic Psychology* 115 (1969): 195–216.

Naegele, K. D. Youth and society: Some observations. *Daedalus* 91 (1962): 47–67.

Raphael, A. The adult and the teenager: A time for revision. *Catholic Educator* 40 (1969): 40–43.

Steinitz, V. A.; King, P.; Solomon, E.; and Shapiro, E. Ideological development in working-class youth. *Harvard Educational Review* 43 (1973): 333–361.

Waters, C. W. Comparison of protesting and nonprotesting students. *Psychological Reports* 33 (1973): 543–547.

Chapter Twenty-two

Family Attitudes and Relationships

The Psychological Function of the Home

The focal point of the adolescent's enforced role as a child is his home and family. The family, as Moulton et al. (1966) point out, provides for the child a socializing system in which he encounters a patterning of disciplinary and affectional behaviors. There can be no doubt, as numerous studies have demonstrated, that the experiences a child encounters in his family relationships are of crucial and lasting importance in his personality development. Mandelbaum (1969) notes that the family provides a framework within which the child may find roots, continuity, and a sense of belonging. Mandelbaum sees adolescence as recapitulating the attitudes of parents toward infancy. If the infant was able to learn trust, harmony, and a sense of identity, the transition to adulthood may be expected to be smooth. But if the parents have resisted the child's striving for autonomy, the adolescent may be expected to resort to rebellious methods as he attempts the transition into adulthood. McPherson (1970), in a study of the relationships of disturbed adolescents and their families, notes that there are consistent relationships between different patterns of familial behavior and the manifest style of problem expression exhibited by their adolescent sons and daughters. Lurie (1970) also reports that children's emotional impairment is related to family composition and functioning.

A study by Murphy (1963) offers a further example of the home's influence on a child's subsequent personal life. Murphy reports that college students who rated high in both autonomy and relatedness appeared to have parents who were autonomous, with inner-directed standards of behavior. In contrast, subjects rated low on autonomy and relatedness had parents who displayed no confidence in their children's ability to achieve autonomy.

As Debesse (1967) notes, when a child reaches adolescence, the home no longer is the sole influence as it was when he was a child, but it remains the "indispensable support" for his emotional development. As long as he is in contact with his family, the adolescent is deeply influenced by it, and it becomes an important determining factor in his "personal psychological space." Musgrove (1967) points to the continuing role of parents as "reference persons" even in late adolescence.

School and community contacts are only extensions of the home situation, which the adolescent has always before him. In the final analysis, the home represents the ultimate and definitive repository of adult authority where he is concerned. The importance of the home as a major factor in an individual's development has long been recognized by psychologists, social workers, sociologists, and others who work with youth and youth's parents.

Of the family's main functions, one of the least appreciated is its function as an educative agency for the culture in which it exists.

Parents have not only the opportunity, but also the duty, to offer their children the learning and experiences that will enable them to fit into their environments. As Fromm (1944) has indicated:

In order that any society may function well, its members must acquire the kind of character which makes them want to act in the way they have to act as members of the society or a special class within it. They have to desire what objectively is necessary for them to do. Outer force is replaced by inner compulsion, and by the particular kind of human energy which is channeled into character traits.

But in rearing adolescents, what is the problem of translating "outer force" into "inner compulsion"? The adolescent may be likened partly to an unbroken horse who is beginning to feel the application of the spur or the whip. He tends to resist and fight back, but gradually conforms and is accepted as a useful member of society, or he seeks conformity within a dissident group—such as the juvenile gang— where his new conformity is a gage flung in the face of the conformity he is denying. Sometimes his socially approved conformity, which may represent to him a kind of self-abnegation if he does not inwardly accept it, gets him by for many years. But it may eventually cause increasing maladjustment.

Whether they wish to or not, children tend to imitate their parents and to ingest within their own personality structure and their defense mechanisms and manner of coping with the world, the behaviors and attitudes they have witnessed in their parents. Miller and Swanson (1960) note that denial is related to severe parental discipline, a paucity of rewards, and unexplained and misunderstood parental requests. Reubush, Byrum, and Farnham (1963) report that males who exhibit low defensive reactions tend to have mothers who are approving, encouraging, and warmly affectionate, while high-defensive males have mothers who fail to respond to their sons' needs and are less supporting and acceptant. In a study of subjects drawn from the California

Guidance Study, Weinstock (1967) states: "Primitive mechanisms like denial, repression, regression, and doubt are closely related to similar behavior in the parent." However, Weinstock notes that adolescents, in contrast to younger children, who are "exposed to considerable family conflict during adolescence become better able to deal with both external conflict and their own impulses" in adulthood. This is, of course, a matter of degree. While reasonable conflict may serve a reality-experience training function, if carried to too great extremes, it can produce unfavorable results, particularly in adolescents whose emotional stability is low. Parents need not present a continual picture of artificial sweetness and light to their offspring, but neither should they present too complete a picture of dissension.

Two particularly important factors in family living and social life in the home as they affect the personality development of children are the home's patterns of family discord and of affection and acceptant companionability. Children coming from homes characterized by good as contrasted to bad patterns of family living are better adjusted and have a more rewarding home life. The home is of great significance in the personality development of children. It is the child's source of refuge and of support. It is the agency that defines him as an individual and is the agency in the best position to facilitate his development into effective adulthood.

Thus, the home may be viewed as having two roles: that of a status-defining agency, and that of an experience-defining agency. As a status-defining agency, the home identifies the child's status in society and the role he must play to maintain that status or perhaps to avoid that status, which is imposed on him by his family.

The family may educate in the mores and ideals of society and of its own place in society by telling about ideals, by showing family possessions that represent the kind of family it is, by telling family anecdotes, and by satisfying and reinforcing relationships with relatives. All these things include the child, and later the adolescent, as a member of a continuing family unit. His family membership provides a focus for personal pride in an ongoing enterprise of which he is a part. Such membership leads to a feeling of belonging, acceptance, and security in the child. He tends to perceive his family as a worthy and cohesive unit. It was fashionable not so long ago to deprecate ideals, discount traditions, and emphasize the "realities" of existence. There is serious question as to how "real" these "realities" were, but there can be little question that the newer approaches deprived society's educative forces of some of their most potent motivational devices to turn outer into inner compulsion.

In inculcating in the child some idea of the principles of "right" conduct, one difficulty confronting the family is that right conduct in one situation or period of life may not be right in another situation or period. Children have difficulty recognizing and accepting this. Riesman (1955) observes: "In each society . . . a mode of insuring conformity is built into the child, and then either encouraged or frustrated in later adult experience"—or, one might add, in a later phase of childhood. There is the further matter of conflicting agencies building sometimes mutually exclusive kinds of conformity. Is not part of the problem of rearing children helping them acquire the ability to recognize and cope with "illicit" agencies which are trying to build conflicting responses? Sometimes the problem involves fostering recognition that the agency is temporarily "illicit" or even not illicit at all, only not appropriate at the present time.

Good marital adjustment in the home fosters parental acceptance of children, while poor marital adjustment of parents leads to feelings of insecurity in the children and denies them the psychologically sound home environment needed for their optimum present and future social and emotional adjustment. The adolescent who encounters parental discord within the home tends by his reactive behavior to the situation to make matters in the home more difficult for his parents and himself, and to take his tensions outside as well. Ackerman (1962) notes that the adolescent irrationally acts out "among his extrafamilial relationships the conflicts and anxieties of his family, particularly disturbances existing in the relationships of his two parents."

In those aspects of an adolescent's life marked by conflict with adult authority, the home and the school both become restrictive or police agents, whatever their intentions to the contrary. But that is not to say that the home or school should refrain from any type of restrictive activity. After all, the adolescent does need guidance and help, and both school and home have not only a guiding function but a protective one as well. The crux of the matter here is the manner and method, and also the reason, used and accepted by a given home in protecting and guiding. A good home and a good school recognize an adolescent's need for independence and his strivings for emancipation, and aid and encourage him when it is possible. They allow him opportunities and means to work toward a more independent status and encourage him to assume responsibilities, make decisions, plan for his future, and, in short, assume adult status as early as he possibly can. This assumption of adult status does not come all at once; it is the product of years of gradually extended independence and self-reliance. The family that plans to allow its adolescent member maximum autonomy and independence just as early as he can assume it is doing the best possible thing to insure his maturity of outlook and to smooth the "difficulties" of the adolescent period.

Even though an adolescent in his striving for independence assumes the veneer of an adult, it is well to remember that he is still a child, though it is often a deadly insult to imply this to him. As a child it is important for his proper development that he have a sense of security, of belonging, and of being wanted. His home and parents are there if help is needed; they stand behind him and offer him support, security, and shelter when he needs it. That is the important psychological function of the home. But in providing such backing, parents should be careful to offer it subtly when needed. The parent's role is often a waiting one. The adolescent should feel free to explore the adult world, secure in the knowledge that in time of need he has somewhere to turn. Thus an adolescent's home furnishes a key to an understanding of the stage of his development toward adulthood, and indeed, to a proper understanding of the adolescent himself. But the nature of a home is a direct function of the activities and attitudes of the parents and other adults who inhabit it. Hence the youth worker who wishes to understand an adolescent's psychology should be aware of the psychology of the adults who live with him, including his father and mother, and every other adult who inhabits the same house, from siblings, relatives, and servants, to boarders and even guests. As Hader (1965) points out, the grandparent who lives with the family can serve a modulating function by virtue of his or her presence, concern, and potentially real position of objectivity and experience. Of course not all grandparents are capable of such thoughtful involvement, and their presence and attitude may have a pernicious influence in family relationships.

Parental domination is probably the leading block to the normal course by which the adolescent emancipate himself from parental control and eventually, or reasonably early, acquires the ability to take his place as a mature individual in the economic and social world.

The reasons for parents' dominating attitude are numerous, but very frequently the end result is the same. Typically, the adolescent tends to resent domination, and his struggle against it often becomes a struggle for ascendancy between himself and his parents. Many factors impinge on this struggle, among them his isolation from outside influences, the degree of independence he has been accustomed to in the past, the consistency of the dominance, and whether or not the dominance attitude comes from one or both parents. Perhaps the most important considerations are whether the ad-

olescent feels that the dominance is reasonable and whether he accepts or rejects his parents' motives.

When parental domination is harsh, unusual, or irregular, severe reactions by the adolescent are likely to follow. This becomes particularly true when the parents' attitude is overly protective or overly rejectant.

Emancipation and Dependence

A desire and often an overt striving for independence and emancipation are natural and common aspects of the adolescent period. Meissner (1965) notes significant shifts between the early and late years of high school. Such shifts are generally in the direction of alienation from parents and increased rebelliousness. We say that the adolescent wishes to emancipate himself from adult controls in order to assume what he considers his rightful and proper place in the world. The process of becoming independent of parental and other adult controls in favor of self-dependence and self-support is known as psychological weaning and may be thought of as both an attribute and a problem.

Certainly parents are in a particularly strong position to inculcate in their children dependency needs that over a period of time may become so demanding that the child, even when he attains adulthood, displays dependency behavior so excessive it interferes with his effectiveness as a person. Conversely, a parent may inculcate in his children feelings of independence that impel them to become effective, responsible, self-sufficient persons. But parental behavior may also formulate drives for independence in their children that are in effect a rejection of and a revolt against parents to the extent of fomenting maladjustive and even delinquent behavior. As in so many affairs of life, a golden mean appears to be the optimum situation. Parental behavior should lead to the inculcation of independent self-sufficiency and self-reliance that does not simultaneously obviate reasonable dependence upon parents in appropriate areas and acceptance of a healthy parent-child relationship.

Parents must make some difficult decisions in deciding upon how they will handle their adolescent's desire for emancipation. Duvall (1965) points out that they face real dangers in pursuing either alternative in at least the following six areas that cannot be avoided with modern-day teenagers: (1) firm family control or freedom for the teen-ager, (2) responsibility vested in teenagers or adults, (3) relative emphasis upon social activities or academic advancement, (4) mobility or stability for the family and the teenager, (5) open communication or respect, and (6) commitment to values beyond the moment and to causes bigger than self- or identity confusion. In arriving at their decisions parents must realize that they and their families exist in a changing world and as a result have to adjust their values and ways appropriately to meet the demands of the changing scene. Wilson (1963) has pointed to the presence of general sociological factors, such as social mobility, rising material standards, and growing skill in large-scale manipulation, that compel people to refocus their lives. Parents must realize that what was once true and proper may no longer be so. Adolescents are products of their time and as such their adjustment can be facilitated or disturbed by their family's approach. There are also the problems presented by the different sexes. In a study of four thousand adolescents ranging in ages from ten to nineteen, Adams (1964) reports that girls, perhaps because of the greater home-centeredness and protection characteristically offered them, expressed more home-centered problems than did boys. Boys' problems tended to cluster to a greater extent around school and financial matters.

Furthermore, the process of achieving emancipation is a problem that is important beyond adolescence. Its effects are present throughout a person's adult life. Psychological weaning does not have to occur. An adolescent may wish to become independent and may struggle toward that end without achieving his desire. When independence is denied and delayed long

enough, the adolescent may come to accept his unweaned status, and eventually even prefer it. In such cases, it is not uncommon for an individual vigorously to reject independence and, when something happens to his parents, find that he has accepted parental domination so long that he is unable to adjust to a world without it. Numerous cases are on record in which one or the other of a married couple insists upon living either with his or her parents or in the same block, or, as the greatest possible concession, at least in the same town. An unhappy marriage relationship is likely to result, since this engenders a situation in which an individual, presumably living as a mature adult, is unwilling or unable to cast off the earlier role of childish dependence upon parents. Parental interference in the couple's married life is likely to occur, and nothing is done to loosen the ubiquitous apron strings. Some parents find it exceedingly difficult to allow their children to be, or to think of themselves as being, grown-up and independent. They endeavor to continue their parent-held relationship. If, over a long period of time, parents are able to circumvent an adolescent's resistance and build up in him habits of invariable yielding to their parental domination, the adolescent will find that, as year succeeds year, it becomes increasingly difficult to accept the need to cope unaided and unprotected with a competitive world. Later, an individual finds that, although mature in years, he has neither the experience nor the skill to enter such competition, and his protected status becomes even more necessary to him. If the adolescent fights against the situation, he may find himself faced with instabilities, insecurities, adult-youth conflicts, and problems that are serious in proportion to the seriousness of blocks and inconsistencies provided by his environment.

McCord et al. (1962) studied the antecedents of dependent behavior in children and reported that lack of family cohesion and parental rejection of the child heightened the child's overt dependent behavior. Mussen and Kagan (1958), in a study with college students using retrospective techniques, note that a greater proportion of individuals classified as extreme conformist than of those classified as independents perceived their parents as harsh punitive, and rejecting. These investigators hypothesize that conformity is a personality variable inculcated in children in their early years as a result of parent-child relationships. Of course, some children resist and, in effect, engage in a kind of rear guard defensive action. Bath and Lewis (1962) report, in a study of 103 college women, that parent-child conflicts tended to increase in intensity the more severe and inconsistent the parental practices grew.

Sooner or later the dependent child encounters frustration of his dependency needs. These investigators note that the dependent boys in their study were subject to feelings of inferiority, abnormal fears, sexual anxieties, sadistic tendencies, and in adulthood were more likely to experience psychotic breakdown.

Sex differences play an important role in dependency behavior. Kagan and Moss (1960) report that dependency behavior inculcated in girls (ages six to ten) tended to endure into adulthood but dependency behavior in boys was less stable. It appears that dependency behavior violates sex-role standards for males and that boys, as they grow older, are under pressure to inhibit overt expression of their dependency feelings. Girls, on the other hand, are not placed by society under as great pressure to appear independent, although present trends regarding woman's role in the world may tend to place rewards on their inhibition of dependency behavior.

One difficulty with seeking independence, insofar as the adolescent is concerned, is the inconsistency of the whole process. Although the adolescent feels he is grown-up and wants to be so treated, he still has childish habits. His parents, on the other hand, may feel that he is growing up and should act more as grownups do; yet, from force of habit they continue to treat him as a child. Often an adolescent develops a whole series of grievances against his parents. How, then, can parents best promote their adolescent's emancipation without going too far too soon? There are several pos-

sibilities. The adolescent must be understood and accepted as a person, he must be allowed as much independence as he can accept without harm, and his home must be both acceptant and emotionally stable. Parents will be effective in guiding and developing an adolescent's potentialities as a participative member of society to the extent that they facilitate independence in an acceptant and emotionally stable atmosphere. A home characterized by frequent illness, fatigue, impatience, quarrelsomeness, or nervousness is tension producing and leads both to poor emotional adjustment and uncooperative behavior. A calm and happy home, on the other hand, tends to produce both good emotional adjustment and cooperative behavior. Peck (1958), in a study of a group of adolescents tested and interviewed at each age from ten to eighteen reports that ego strength occurred in association with a stable and warm family life and that superego strength was related mainly to the regularity and consistency of family life. Marzolf (1965) also reports that students' perception of self-assurance in their parents was especially related to the students' scores on the Ego Strength scale of the Cattell 16-Personality Factor Questionnaire.

But it is not enough for a parent to have an intellectual understanding of the problem involved. To change attitudes and patterns of behavior one must recognize them when they occur and understand that change is difficult to effect. Here the teacher and other youth workers face a major task in working with a parent to bring about a child's best adjustment. To be effective, professional workers must recognize symptoms of maladjustment and must know enough about the psychology of behavior to work with both adolescents and their parents, for complete success is difficult without the cooperation of all concerned.

Again, a warning is necessary to parents. Extremes can be exceedingly dangerous. The foregoing discussion has pointed out the need to promote independence, but there is danger that a child may be emancipated too early, or that emancipation may be too vigorously and even harshly promoted. Emancipation cannot be achieved overnight, and the wise parent will make it a gradual process over a period of time so that the adolescent will not lose his sense of security or misunderstand his parents' motives.

The preceding discussion has emphasized the adolescent's strong and relatively early desire for emancipation from adult controls. Further, problems of emancipation are frequently the basis of overt conflict between parents and their adolescent sons and daughters. However, an early desire for emancipation is a phenomenon of American culture and is not necessarily true of adolescents in other Western cultures. For example, Boehm (1957), in a comparative study of the earlier development of social independence in American as compared to Swiss children, notes that the American child's conscience becomes less egocentric and internalizes earlier than does the Swiss child's.

Child-rearing practices in America, by substituting peer for parent dependency and by promoting children's independence to the point where they regard it as a right given to co-equals, do much to promote further emancipation wishes that the children feel free to make explicit. One former European (Boehm 1957) observed that "middle-class American parents attempt to bring up children who will be independent of their parents, who will be accepted, practicing members of their own peer group." She states further:

The European who comes to the United States is surprised to find a more rapid social development in American children than he has been used to seeing in European children. In thought and action American children become independent of their elders at an earlier age than do European children. Not only do they depend less on adult guidance and judgment, but their consciences seem to mature earlier also.

In Europe there is a tendency to educate children to accept an omnipotent parent's goals. A child is expected to push himself to his limits, as in the French school system or in the English early preparation for examinations, regardless of the effect it may have upon his peer relationships. Which approach is psy-

chologically best? Such a question can be answered only in terms of the culture in which the event occurs. More important psychologically than whether early emancipation is good or bad is the relationship the parent builds with his child to facilitate the existing cultural concept and the consistency with which he promotes that relationship. Kinnane and Pable (1962) report in a study of 121 eleventh- and twelfth-grade boys that the work values these children exhibited were directly related to the work values their families held. The investigators felt their findings were strengthened by the fact that, with the exception of heuristic-creative type values, these work values were not significantly related to either school curriculum or intelligence.

Rejection

In terms of the aggression or withdrawal response it elicits from the adolescent, one of the more serious types of parental attitude is rejection. Obviously, there are various degrees of parental rejection, ranging from mild to severe, with severe or absolute rejection encountered less often than the milder forms. Ordinarily rejection is indirect, often taking the guise of nagging and excessive criticism, impatience or crossness, invidious comparison, inconsistency, or suspiciousness. The actively rejecting parent tends to display hostility, to threaten, to needlessly deny the child things it wants, or, in some cases, to be indifferent and to pay no attention. A characteristic of the rejecting parent is that he does not admit his rejection even to himself, and when his rejection is brought to his attention, he is usually most unwilling to admit or recognize his own feelings. Unfortunately the fact of, although not the reason for, the rejection is quite clear to the child involved.

Many different reasons are advanced for parental rejection, most of them firmly fixed in a highly emotional base. One basic reason is the fact that many children come to their homes as unwanted additions. There may have been too many previous children, in which case the parental reaction tends to be one of discrimination against the child in favor of his older brothers or sisters. The unwanted child may be the target of unusually severe discipline. He may also have to accept the discard clothing and toys of his older brothers and sisters without ever being permitted to have anything new of his own.

As has been indicated, the child in such a situation is usually quite aware of it, and he attempts to use every means at his disposal to gain the affection and security he lacks. When his efforts do not work, he may become resentful, bitter, and discontented, not only within his home, but outside it as well. His overt response may take the form of either withdrawal or aggression, but in both cases he will probably have trouble adjusting to the demands society will eventually make upon him, as an adolescent and as an adult. In his attempt to gain parental acceptance, he may continue to act like a child long after he has passed beyond that stage. Unfortunately, he may generalize from his parents to his teachers, his employers, and other adults, and view them as parent substitutes, continuing to behave with them in the same childish manner to gain their acceptance. Such a person is extremely difficult to get along with, and unless his motives are recognized and understood, he will receive scant sympathy from his teachers or other youth workers.

Rejection may result when the adolescent becomes a cause for conflict between husband and wife. One parent may resent the child because he feels that he was inveigled into having the child. The child may have unwanted attributes or be of the opposite sex from the one desired. If the parents are particularly selfish and immature, the child will represent too great an economic sacrifice. He may be forced to live with relatives who feel he is a burden; living with grandparents during wartime is an example. Finally, the adolescent's behavior may bring him into conflict with his parents. For example, Schulman, Shoemaker, and Moelis (1962) report that parents of children with conduct problems tend to be significantly more hostile and rejecting toward their children than are parents of children whose behavior follows more normal patterns.

Among the situations that cause conflicts between parents and their children are a basic age or birth-cycle differential between parent and child and the decelerating rate of socialization with advancing age. Younger people tend to be vigorous and noisy and to like continual companionship and activity. An older person tends to decrease the amount and scope of his physical and social activities as he ages. He usually needs groups of people less and prefers from time to time a period of "peace and quiet." In seeking such a period, he will frequently be at cross-purposes with his children, who want to "have the gang in and get something doing."

There is also the matter of changing mores. Things widely accepted in the modern world would once have been strictly taboo. Smoking is one example. The girl who smoked in the 1890s was branded as an immoral, loose woman, and the parent who permitted his daughter to smoke found himself disgraced. Here it is interesting to note that, since the growth of individual freedom and the relaxation of taboos in heterosexual relations, the modern adolescent has less severe reasons for conflict in this area with his or her parents. It is certainly easier for the modern girl to approach her mother on matters such as sex or smoking than it was for her mother to approach hers. But since we are talking in terms of the mean, a word of caution is appropriate. There are many families whose values and points of reference are still those of several generations ago. From such families little can be expected in terms of sympathy with, or acceptance of, modern values, mores, and relinquishment of the taboos and preconceptions of another day. Situations causing parent-child conflict may be considerably more severe in some societies than in others, depending largely upon the societal organization. The variables in any given society that enhance parent-child conflict are the rate of social change, the complexity of the social structure, the degree of cultural integration, the velocity of movement (vertical mobility) within the social structure, and the relation of this mobility to the culture's values.

Consequences of parent-child conflicts and rejection include many elements other than harsh treatment or lack of attention. They may range all the way from out-and-out physical abandonment through placing the child in an institution such as a reform school, a boarding school, a convent, or a military school, to various acts of deliberate omission such as failure to provide adequate clothing, allowance, or educational opportunity. However, despite the obvious nature of these extreme acts, authorities are nearly unanimous in affirming that repercussions are far more serious from withheld emotional acceptance than from withheld physical things.

The effects of rejection may take one of several forms. The rejected child or adolescent tends to present a clinical picture of insecurity and is forever trying to elicit evidences of welcome and affection from his parents and other adults. Siegelman (1965), in a study of parent-child relationships, reports that anxious and introverted males tend to come from families in which both parents are rejecting. Mussen et al. (1963), in a comparative study of Italian and American children, note that, regardless of locale, boys who receive insufficient parental affection tend to feel rejected and unhappy. The rejected child is an attention seeker and sometimes goes to extreme lengths to achieve his aim, including deliberate attempts to make his parents upset about him. The more overt or definite the rejection, the greater tends to be the child's reaction to it. Herron (1962), in a study of the personality test performance of accepted and rejected adolescents, reports the rejected adolescents as displaying a weak ego restricted in its integrative capacity by either impulse demands or superego limitations.

Modern living in small homes and apartments makes the lot of the rejected child more difficult, since he cannot find the isolation that large families and homes once offered. In-

creased family mobility also increases his difficulties. Families today are on the move, and as the family goes from community to community, many an adolescent finds himself parted from his friends and the familiar surroundings that would ease his adjustment to rejection. In a strange community an adolescent must either find some outlet in the community itself or fall back upon a closer association with the parents who reject him. Oftentimes an adolescent, rejected by his parents, turns to another adult or to a member of the opposite sex for support. Rejected adolescents tend to find mass movements particularly appealing. Such movements often select a popular singer as their ideal (the particular singer—Elton John, Stevie Wonder, Mick Jagger—is of little importance; some current figure is selected as the momentary ideal) ; or the movement may be built around drug use or some other anti-social activity.

The discussion on rejection has been confined to rejection by the parent, but the problem of self-rejection by the child as it relates to rejection by his parents also exists. Body image has often been used by psychologists as a means of judging an individual's self-esteem and self-acceptance. Body-image disturbances have been held to be an indication of self-rejection and, to some extent, of neuroticism and anxiety often leading to problem behavior. In an interesting study of two thousand youths with body-image disturbances, Schonfeld (1966) found patterns of both conscious and unconscious derogatory and rejecting parental attitudes toward youth. However, it is not to be supposed that active and overt parental rejection is the only etiological factor in body-image disturbance. Parents who use their children to solve their own problems and anxieties also tend to rear progeny who have difficulties in self-acceptance. In the study cited previously, Schonfeld also reported body-image disturbances in children of parents who attempted to solve their own psychopathology or their own attitudes toward each other through their children, who projected their own anxieties over their own inadequacies on their children, and who exhibited to their children parental concern over both physical and sexual development.

Heilbrun and Orr (1966) report, in a study of self-acceptance on the basis of level of aspiration on a discrimination task, that subjects with a history of maternal rejection possessed lower levels of self-esteem, with an associated tendency to set lower goals for themselves than did subjects whose mothers had been accepting.

The reader by now may have the impression that any evidence of overt or active rejection leads to problem behavior in children. The research evidence does not entirely confirm this point of view. Heilbrun and Gillard (1966) report that some positive overt attention, even if it means rejection or overprotection, produces better results than low maternal control or ignoring. Rosenberg (1963) notes that, while moderate amounts of parental interest are not associated with substantial differences in self-esteem, extreme parental indifference may be even more closely associated with low self-esteem than are punitive reactions from parents.

Overindulgence

Extremes of parental reaction tend to have unfortunate effects on adolescent behavior and development. Indulgence up to a point makes an adolescent's adjustment considerably easier and gives him a real sense of security, in creating a permissive atmosphere in which he may move toward personal independence and gradual emancipation. But when indulgence becomes overindulgence, or when overprotectiveness appears, the consequences tend to be unfortunate.

The adolescent whose home history is one of overprotection and overindulgence experiences greater difficulty than usual in adjusting to the outside world. His parents' overattentiveness has led him into the habit of expecting help and attention from others. In a real sense, such an individual has never relinquished the egocentricism of his early childhood, when he conceived of the world and everything in it as created especially for his benefit and exploitation. All his life he has been used to getting attention, and he thinks such attention is his by right. Outside the home he endeavors to make himself the pampered center of every situation he enters. Naturally, he does not always receive the attention he wants, and his reaction, aggressive at first, may change to withdrawal if aggression fails to work. Such individuals look to others for help at each stage of their development. In school the teacher is expected to assume the role of an indulgent parent and to act, in effect, as a parent surrogate. Out of school and employed, such an adolescent often makes a nuisance of himself, endeavoring to establish the same kind of relationship with the boss. Frequently he will try to assign a quasi-parental role to older boys or girls, and finally, in marriage, will expect the spouse to behave much like a parent.

The overindulged adolescent typically finds great difficulty in separating himself from his parents. Many newly married girls do not want their husbands to have jobs outside the town in which their parents live. They may insist upon living in the same block or even in the same house as their parents so they can continue to depend upon them, seek advice, and in general perpetuate the comfortable child-parent relationship. Householders unfortunate enough to be on the same telephone party line with such a mother-daughter combination can testify to the long hours spent on the phone discussing the minutiae of each other's day. The daughter receives advice on exactly how she ought to handle the day's work, her husband, and many other matters. On those rare occasions when an adolescent attempts to break away from such relationships, the parent usually resists and the adolescent has guilt feelings.

The reasons for an overprotective attitude in one or both parents are various. Essentially, the emotional needs of the parents themselves are one of the most powerful determinants of the attitude toward children. Some parents merely wish to be kindhearted or to protect their children from difficulties. Others attempt to conceal rejection or to gain a reputation as a good parent. Oftentimes overprotection stems from a parent who had an unhappy childhood and is determined to protect the child from similar unhappiness and frustrations arising out of marriage. The protection may take any of numerous forms. Often an adolescent finds himself the victim of a conflict between his parents. In such a conflict one parent may attempt, usually unconsciously, to enlist the child's support and affection by standing as his advocate against the other parent. In more extreme cases he may even encourage the child to resist authority in order to annoy his spouse. The normal result is problem behavior by the adolescent.

An unhealthy familial relationship may also arise between a child and a parent when the parent selfishly uses the child as an emotional substitute for disappointment in the actualities of marriage. The same sort of thing may occur in a home broken by death or divorce: The remaining parent may turn to the child for companionship and emotional security. Such an attachment may become pathological in its intensity, particularly if the child is so closely identified with his deceased parent that he becomes in effect a surrogate for him. The child is overprotected, and his efforts to break away are usually resisted so vigorously that he either succumbs or his revolt is accompanied by intense guilt feelings. Often the adolescent in such a situation is less and less able to associate satisfactorily with other people, particularly members of the opposite sex, and is isolated and unable to cope satisfactorily with the realities of adult life.

One of the most selfish and pernicious reasons for maternal overprotection prolonged out of all reason is the mother's fear of losing her role as "protector." This is particularly true of older women whose homes have become the center of their universe and the only source of real satisfaction in life. Many people, after marriage, devote themselves exclusively to their homes and their children. As year succeeds year, the mother may give up all outside activities until nothing is left for her but the home. Then, sometime in her forties, she finds that her children are growing up and are about to leave the home and fend for themselves. Since their departure would leave her nothing to do and would in effect remove her only real interest and motive for living, she may tend to tighten the apron strings, enlist sympathy, inspire guilt feelings, and in general resist the emancipative process. Her resistance will be even greater if her marital relations have been unsatisfactory and her devotion to her children has taken the place of devotion to her husband. Such a reaction is understandable, but it has an unfortunate effect upon the adjustment of the adolescent who must submit to it. Some adolescents will under such circumstances make real efforts to break away, and many succeed, but usually at the expense of real guilt feelings, particularly if they recount "all the things mother has done for them."

The child's ordinal position also may become a factor in parent overindulgence. The firstborn or the last-born is most likely to be treated with the greatest indulgence. The first-born child, especially, is often in the unfortunate position of being overaccepted by his parents. They adopt an unrealistically lenient attitude toward him, granting his every wish and permitting him to adopt the role of a tyrant in the family scene.

The Psychological Climate in the Home

Individual differences are found among homes and parents even as they are found among adolescents themselves. There is no such thing as a typical home, but homes can be classified according to various parental attitude patterns, and the probable effect of certain of these patterns upon the behavior and personality development of the adolescent can be studied. Homes, like adolescents themselves, show considerable variation. Some appear to be particularly good places in which to rear children, while others range all the way from indifferent to exceedingly unfortunate. Since the adolescent is closely bound to his home background, and since the home exerts a considerable influence upon his immediate behavior, as well as upon the course and nature of his general physical and psychological development, it is particularly necessary for the student of adolescence to have more than a superficial aquaintance with various types of homes and their effects upon the children reared in them. A knowledge of exactly what constitutes a good home as compared to a bad home, and the part each plays in a given adolescent's behavioral pattern, is a first step in understanding that adolescent and working effectively with him. In many cases one may conceptualize in terms of problem homes just as validly as in terms of problem children.

Unfortunately, any attempt to categorize homes or parents into types or kinds is exceedingly difficult because of the many variables involved. For example, one might take a rejectant type of home. Who is doing the rejecting, the mother or the father? Or both? What part is played by the brothers and sisters, if any? Are the adolescent's siblings rejecting and rejected? Are some of them accepted by the parents and others rejected? Are adult relatives living in the home, and if they are, what role do they play? Are there boarders or roomers? What is the role of the occasional guest in the home, or the "friend of the family"? What sources of security and affection does the adolescent have outside the home, and are these sources ever vigorously in conflict with the home? All the foregoing variables, and many more, have to be considered when a home is to be classified. Therefore, it is seldom possible to classify a home in some simple category, since the number of possible permutations and combinations is almost infinite. For instance, a rejecting father and an overprotective mother may be in the same home. Such a combination would tend to produce inconsistent discipline, parental conflict, and both rejectance and acceptance; yet, in view of the fact that other factors operate in a home, the home could hardly be classified only in terms

of parental behavior. But it seems safe to assume that of all the factors involved in the character of most homes, the single most important factor, one transcending all others, is parental attitude. Therefore, an attempt to classify types of individual parental reaction, together with their causes, seems indicated.

Various attempts have been made to describe and classify interpersonal psychological climates or aspects of the home. Such classifications usually consist of descriptions of the parental role in dealing with children. Among the systems proposed have been the following: (1) democratic versus authoritarian; (2) permissiveness-strictness; (3) love-hostility versus control-autonomy; (4) traditional-developmental; (5) discipline versus authority; (6) instrument (task oriented) versus expressive (social-emotional oriented); (7) warm-cold and possessive-detached; and (8) dominant possessive–ignoring. Of the classifications basic to an understanding of the dynamics of child-parent relationships, two continua, dominance-submission and acceptance-rejection, have proved to be particularly useful.

An especially useful home climate classification that has stood the test of time and considerable research is one proposed by Baldwin, Kalhorn, and Breese (1945). The three main categories of parent behavior they postulate are: *rejectant, acceptant,* and *casual.* Each of the three in turn may be reclassified into several subcategories, summarized in Table 21, depending upon the structure and background of the various attitudes and behavioral trends that are involved in making up each pattern.

Table 21   *Patterns of Parent Behavior*

Rejectant	Acceptant	Casual
1. Nonchalant	1. Democratic	1. Autocratic
2. Active	2. Indulgent	2. Indulgent
	3. Democratic-Indulgent	

Source: Summarized from information in A. L. Baldwin, J. Kalhorn, and F. H. Breese, "Patterns of parental behavior," *Psychological Monographs* 58, no. 3 (1945).

Baldwin et al. describe the *rejectant* parent as one who, in his relations with his son or daughter, is "consistently hostile, unaffectionate, disapproving, and emotionally distant." The rejectant parent finds it is "psychologically impossible . . . to be genuinely solicitous or democratic or understanding." The rejectant home is described as a maladjusted one characterized by conflict, quarrels, and resentment between parents and children, and remarkably lacking in "warm sociable relations either between members of the family or between the family and the outside world." Living in such a family setting, the adolescent discovers that his interests and desires tend to be ignored or considered unimportant, and insofar as he endeavors to bring them to his parent's attention, or endeavors to assert himself, he encounters arbitrary denials, coercion, and even actual physical punishment. The parent's attitude is one of "general resentment and hostility toward the child which reveals itself in expressions of disapproval and constant carping." The parent neither understands nor sympathizes with the child, nor does he make any attempt to do so. Fundamentally the child is unwanted in the home and is continually made to feel so. The parents may not fully realize the degree of their rejection, or the reason for it. They constantly tend to be irritable in dealing with their child, hence may be unreasonably harsh when the child becomes overtly annoying. As Baldwin et al. indicate, "Their hostility pushes them to frustrate the child needlessly or to ignore him when a friendly interest would cost them nothing."

The actual form of rejection the parents take may fall in either of two categories. The rejection may be active and overt, or it may take the form of ignoring or *nonchalance*. The *nonchalant-rejectant* parent ignores his children and has as little to do with them as he possibly can. Insofar as the child's welfare interferes with his own, the child must suffer. Typically, the adolescent reared in such a family is allowed an extraordinary amount of independence so long as he does not intrude upon the parents' activities or force himself upon them. Families able to afford it often send their child away to boarding school and breathe a sigh of relief when he is out of sight. They are happy to have him spend his holidays at a friend's home. In less favored families the adolescent tends to spend more time outside the home, usually keeping late hours and satisfying his need for security and acceptance by joining a gang that often includes a number of boys older than he is. This stay-away-from-home pattern also emerges with girls, often accompanied by a history of increasing sex delinquency. Unfortunately for all concerned, children cannot always ignore their parents. They must go to them for aid, sometimes to seek advice or permission, and sometimes because they need affection and want their parents to like them and do things for them. When this happens, the parent tends to feel that he is being intruded upon and that his comfort is being interfered with. Consequently he becomes annoyed and overreacts. Baldwin et al. note that such parents "usually adopt measures whose severity reflects their irritation at being bothered and their determination to settle the problem for once and for all." If, through delinquent behavior or some other problem activity outside the home, the adolescent's activities cost his parent time and money or public embarrassment, the punishment that follows is apt to be harsh indeed. At such times the nonchalant role is exchanged for one of active rejection.

However, there are some parents whose rejection is active from the beginning. They do not like or want their children, but they seem unable to leave them alone. They lay down rules, insist upon strict observance and obedience, and seem to exert every means in their power to make their children uncomfortable and themselves unreasonable. They use prescription as a means of avoiding situations that would make them uncomfortable or place them in the position of having to give any large amount of attention to their child. It is easier to have a rule than to make an explanation. The rules of the *active-rejectant* parent are often unnecessarily restrictive, and sometimes they seem to be laid down for no apparent reason other than a desire to be frustrating.

That such a home environment will produce a maladjusted child is almost a foregone conclusion. The only surprising thing is the number of adolescents who apparently can find affection and security elsewhere and can develop into adjusted adults despite their parents. In either the nonchalant-rejectant or the active-rejectant home, the adolescent is usually anxious to get away at the earliest possible opportunity and will frequently adopt stringent measures in his efforts to do so, ranging from running away to—in the case of girls, especially —premature or unwise marriages based on the conviction that almost any home will be better than their own.

Remembering that adolescents wish to be independent, the student of adolescence might wrongly assume that a rejectant home would accelerate emancipation and would serve a useful function in that way. The error in this reasoning will become clear if one recalls the fact that although it is desirable to facilitate emancipation, the good home also has the function of creating a psychological climate of security and acceptance. Such a home provides help willingly when it is needed and is always a refuge to which the adolescent may return for help and comfort.

Baldwin et al. call the second category of parent behavior *acceptant*. The acceptant parent may in turn be classified as *democratic, indulgent,* and *democratic-indulgent*. The democratic home is one in which good adjustment occurs without undue attention being given to the child. Freedom and democracy are valued and the parents' respect for the child's individuality leads them to use evaluative comments sparingly, sometimes to the point of seeming nonsuggesting, uncritical, and withdrawn. When evaluative comments are made, they tend to be approving. The democratic parent is an information giver so that a child may make his own decisions in the full light of consequences and alternatives. In the democratic home the child gets freedom, choice,

and information but relatively little guidance or evaluation for past behavior. Baldwin et al. speak of the democratic-acceptant parent as coldly objective rather than anxious but above average in affection and rapport.

An adolescent who lives in a home of this description has a much easier time in working out his emancipation and tends to feel less restricted by his preadult role. Independence is his for the asking, and he enters adulthood with considerable experience in making his own decisions and standing on his own feet. Unfortunately, he may have had little training in making his decisions wisely.

The indulgent-acceptant home is characterized by child-centeredness and a large amount of parent-child interaction. Rapport tends to be good, and the climate is one of general approval. The parents are anxious and devoted, but their warmth is not characterized by any great amount of understanding. The general parental attitude is one of high though affectionate emotion. The democratic-indulgent parent strikes "a happy mean between cold and objective democracy and indulgence."

The third category is that of the *casual* parent. The casual parent is one whose behavior appears to fit neither the patterns of acceptance nor that of rejection, although he does not occupy an intermediate position between the two. The casual parent is defined as one who tends to be "consistently mild and casual" in his emotional relationships with his children. He may be subclassified as *autocratic-casual,* or *indulgent-casual.*

The autocratic-casual parent uses autocracy as a means of control rather than as an expression of rejection and dislike. He tends to refrain from the extremes of autocracy frequently practiced by the rejectant parent, although his approach to control is emotional rather than rational. As autocrats autocratic-casual parents are neither cold nor efficiently autocratic. Baldwin et al. note that they fail to solve problems neatly and emotionally and tend to blunder through one crisis after another in order to arrive at makeshift solutions. Such parents feel that the parent's authority is superior to the child's on all occasions, but their behavior tends to fall into one of two patterns. One group, autocratic by policy, use old-fashioned discipline and assert their authority on every possible occasion. The other group tend to pride themselves that they are using "modern" methods of child rearing. They endeavor to be sympathetic and to understand their child's point of view, but although they do not go out of their way to be autocratic, they do resort to dictatorial commands when an important issue arises. The contrast between the two groups is between a deliberate policy of old-fashioned discipline and one of hit-or-miss expediency.

The indulgent-casual parent presents a generally mild picture. In common with the autocratic-casual parent the indulgent-casual parent seems to lack any persistent focus around which to build his reaction to every situation. He tends to react as the mood strikes him but the reaction is generally a kindly indulgent one that results in haphazard service to the child's wishes. No attempt is made to satisfy the child's every desire, nor is any attempt made to make a virtue out of being a "good" parent. On the other hand, the child is not begrudged time and attention. Baldwin et al. note that they are matter of fact and are indulgent only because they usually find it easier to give in than to deny.

Parents who know the effects of various types of family climate upon child behavior often endeavor to conduct their family environments to fit a theoretically desirable climate. But a psychological climate involves so much of the parent's personality and style of behavior that it is questionable to what extent such endeavors can be successful. On the other hand, the parent often misunderstands exactly what a given climate involves in the way of behavior. Conway (1966), for example, reports that parents and teachers both can frustrate the transition from adolescence to adulthood by equating democracy with objectivity and objectivity with permissiveness. The result is that what parents think is a democratic home is actually one characterized by permissiveness, which, in its egocentric effects, produces behavior that is the antithesis of democracy.

The Relative Roles of Mother and Father

While both parents are ideally necessary for the developing adolescent, it is interesting to examine the relative influence of the mother as compared to the father, and to ask which one tends to exert the greater influence on the child. The traditional opinion has been that the mother exerts the greater influence, possibly because of the greater amount of time she spends with the child. Yet recent research seems to indicate that the father's immediate influence upon his children and the effect of his influence upon their future attitudes and behavior are at least as great as the mother's, and some investigators report the father's role and influence as being even greater.

The relative primacy of the father's role is demonstrated in a study by Zunich (1962). Of 644 relationships between parental-attitude scores and student problems, Zunich reported ninety-two to be significant. Of these, thirty-eight were father-daughter as compared to twenty-nine mother-daughter, and fourteen of these were father-son as compared to eleven mother-son.

Alcorn (1962) asserts that while the mother is the central figure in the child's life until age ten, from ten to sixteen the father becomes at least equally important, with a strong possibility that his long-term influence surpasses the mother's. McNasser (1962) reinforced Alcorn's position by noting that the adolescent years require a strong masculine influence. McNasser deplores the fact that contemporary American culture concedes the dominant role to the mother and thus emphasizes a life of softness and ease, with aloofness toward the outside. This maternal attitude and its cultural sanction, he feels, produces a "fatherless generation" that secondary schools cannot handle. Heilbrun and Fromme (1965) report that identification with a more masculine father for boys and a more masculine mother for girls was associated with the best adolescent adjustment.

Findings such as these about the father's role in the family are at variance with the traditionally held belief that children view the father as the authoritarian figure who often encounters the brunt of an adolescent's emancipative efforts. In an earlier day this conception may have been true, but the role of women has been changing in modern times to the extent that the mother may well be assuming the direct punitive role. Such findings are quite in accord with Nash's (1965) point of view that American society is in effect matricentric. However, support for the traditional view comes from studies such as that reported by Vogel and Lauterbach (1963), indicating that problem sons had more idealized views of their mother's behavior and more hostile perceptions of their father's behavior. Johnson (1963) takes the position that sex-role learning for both males and females is dependent upon an adequate identification with the father. She sees sex-role learning as the internalization of a reciprocal role relationship wherein the father is the key parent.

A great deal has been written about the effects of the overindulgent, nonpunitive mother on her son's behavior. Comparatively little has been written about the corresponding effect of the nonpunitive father. There is some reason to believe that the father's nonpunitiveness may enchance either the son's aggressiveness or perhaps his masculinity traits by allowing a development free of masculine overdomination and denial. Hokanson (1961) reports a comparative study of male college students who displayed high test hostility as compared to a low-test-hostility group. He states that students who admitted strong feelings of aggressiveness on psychological tests perceived their fathers as having been significantly less punitive than their mothers, and less punitive then either parent of the low-test-hostility students.

Sex differences of the adolescents involved of course must be considered in arriving at a picture of relative parental influence. For example, Grinder and Spector (1965) report high school girls as more likely to see their mothers as more powerful, while high school boys, in contrast, perceive their fathers as occupying the power role.

It may be profitless to become overconcerned about the relative influence of mother and father. Ideally, both parents are present and play complementary roles in their children's upbringing. Landis (1962) reports the father as a more reliable index of family integration than the mother, and notes that "the relationship with both parents is an even more accurate index." Mueller (1966), in a study of 199 male and female college freshmen, reports that independent as compared to nonindependent individuals tend to perceive both, rather than just one, of their parents as strong.

Intrafamily Perceptions

Difficulties and misunderstandings in family relationships arise when various family members do not agree with one another. One problem of family living is that parents and their children so often perceive the same situation differently. This is further complicated in parent-adolescent dealings by the fact that a parent develops certain insights and expectations based on the child as he has been perceived over the years. But children change as they grow older. The younger child is home-centered, and his activities are carried on close to the home. His playmates, if not actually known to his parents, at least live in the neighborhood. With increasing age, a child's contacts widen, he meets new people and makes new friends, many of them unknown to his parents. His needs and interests change, and he desires to be independent. Usually the mother is the first person to notice these changes as she finds former methods of persuasion and discipline no longer effective.

Research investigators have often compared the attitudes of parents and children on various topics, the idea being that similarities and differences of opinion and attitude on crucial issues may furnish at least a partial picture of the kind of relationships obtaining in a given family. A further reason for such studies is the more general one of trying to learn the extent to which parents tend to influence their children—or perhaps the extent to which children influence their parents. Obviously differences or similarities of opinion or attitude on nearly any given topic may have no significance beyond revealing intergenerational differences, but just as obviously there are a few crucial topics where differences of opinion could well lead to family dissension. One might also assume, when a given set of parents and their children disagree over a significantly wide range of topics, that either the home exerts small ideological influence or, perhaps, that the differences represent the children's real effort to discount much that their parents and their homes stand for. But one should be especially cautious in generalizing from any single study in this area and should seek trends emerging from examination of a number of such studies.

As might be expected, studies report all kinds of parent-child differences of opinion as well as mutual misunderstandings and misperceptions. Middleton and Putney (1963), in a study of 1,440 students in sixteen American colleges, report as much deviation as conformity to parental political beliefs. Hebron and London (1964) report that the transitional age for attainment of greater independence of attitude in adolescent girls is located at the fourteenth and fifteenth years.

In a study with a group of adolescents, Hess and Goldblatt (1959–1960) conducted interviews and administered questionnaires in which they asked the subjects to describe themselves and then to indicate how they felt their parents would describe them. The same procedure was used with the parents. In general, both groups were moderately favorable in their descriptions of teenagers, but the teenagers

felt that their parents would underrate them, while the parents believed the teenagers would overrate their own capabilities and maturity. By and large, the adolescents perceived their parents more favorably than the parents perceived themselves. In discussing what seemed to be an apparent lack of communication and understanding between parents and their teenage children, Hess and Goldblatt felt that the difficulty might lie in the quite different meaning teenage behavior has for the two generations. Parents have long-range goals for their children, goals which cause them to overlook or underestimate the tensions and problems of growing up. But teenagers are faced with and are concerned about the immediate problems of maturing. Hess writes: "As the adolescent attempts to redefine himself, to move toward autonomy and establish an adult identity, his tendency to over-estimate adult competence may prove a useful spur. But his feeling that adults devalue his achievements and depreciate his efforts . . . complicate[s] the task of learning and internalizing roles."

Certainly, as van der Veen, Huebner, Jargens, and Neja (1964) point out, a person's perception of his family is of great importance in the family's adjustment. When parents mutually possess ideal concepts about their family and actually try to implement them in practice the whole family's adjustment tends to be good. Problems arise, as van der Veen et al. note, when parents perceive their family differently and when for some reason their behavior in the family is at variance with their ideal feelings. In the Hess study cited previously, it may well have been that the parents felt some guilt in a perception of their own inadequacy in being the parents they would ideally like to be. Such feelings are often encountered when parents discuss their relationships with their teenage sons and daughters. As Lidz (1963) has noted, the family's essential dynamic structure depends upon parental ability to form a coalition, maintain boundaries between generations, and adhere to appropriate sex-linked roles. This is indeed a large order, and it is not surprising that many parents feel inadequate to the task. The results of parental inadequacy may be seen in a study by McDonald (1962) in which he used a matched sample to compare the parents of normal and of emotionally disturbed children with respect to self-descriptions, attitudes toward self, and attitudes toward each other. McDonald used the Leary Interpersonal Checklist to gather data for the comparison. Parents of disturbed as compared to those of normal children (1) were more self-rejecting; (2) more frequently described their children as distrustful, self-effacing, or dependent; (3) were more frequently disidentified with their children; and (4) devaluated the personalities of their spouses and children more frequently. While McDonald recognized that some of these reactions may well have been due to the disruptive influence in the home of the disturbed children, his opinion was that various personality characteristics of the parents—for example, lack of self-acceptance—had existed prior to parenthood or marriage.

Summary

An adolescent is a human being whose basic reactions to blocking or fulfillment of his needs, desires, and drives are typically those of a human being at any age. He differs from people of other age levels primarily in his stage of physical development, his maturity status, the things in life he deems most important, and the peculiar problems his environment presents. Of the environmental problems, the adolescent in Western culture finds his relationship to adults one of the most difficult. Sexually mature and seeking independence and emancipation from adult and parental controls, he finds himself in a subordinate position that requires him to accept a child's role long after he feels he is capable of playing an adult's role and taking an adult's place in society. In a sense, his actual role is a conflicting one, for, as he grows older, he is sometimes expected to assume an adult's, and sometimes a child's, role. His response to his subordinate role is sometimes overtly aggressive and sometimes covertly so. At times his subordination becomes so much a habit and childish protection so comfortable that it is exceedingly difficult for him to attain social and emotional maturity. Long continued dependence may have unfortunate effects throughout his adult life and may, among other things, make it difficult or impossible to adjust to marriage. The competitive adult world becomes one to which he cannot properly adjust, as he continually seeks a parent surrogate upon whom he can depend. In short, even though an adult in years, he is still a child emotionally. On the other hand, an adolescent whose parents have aided the emancipation process or who has achieved independence and self-reliance during the adolescent period has a much better opportunity to function as a mature individual. It is the duty of parents and teachers alike to promote emancipation, to give the adolescent an opportunity to function as an independent person in as many areas as possible as early as possible. One basic difficulty here is that of striking a golden mean between denying an adolescent any help and being overprotective and overdominating.

The home is the focal point of the adolescent's enforced role as a child. The school and community in their relations with adolescents are in reality only extensions of the home. The home is important to the adolescent because it transmits and interprets his culture to him; it decidedly affects and molds his personality; it offers him security and affection if it is a good home; it operates as a status- and role-defining agency; and, finally, it is central in promoting his maturity and determining his future adjustment as an adult.

The school and the home both play a police function in child-adult relations. Though this policing is necessary to a degree, it should eventually lead to self-reliance if properly exercised. But an oversevere or unduly emphasized police function can result in problem behavior or undue submission and dependence. It is not unusual for a child to take his tensions outside the family circle and seek releases for his aggressions elsewhere if the family situation becomes too overpowering.

In general, American child-rearing practices, by substituting peer for parent dependency and by promoting the independence of children to the point where they regard it as a right given to coequals, promote further emancipation wishes that the children feel quite free to make explicit.

An understanding of a given parent's behavior involves knowing why he adopts the attitudes that he does. There are many different reasons for parental attitudes and reactions. They include turning to the child as a source of affection and security when the parent is not adjusted to the marital partner; overconscientiousness; resentment of the child's cost in time, money, and personal freedom; the child's physical status, particularly if he is sickly or weak; and the child's ordinal position, especially if he is the first- or last-born. Of all the parental reactions, rejection and domination, whatever their causes, are most far-reaching in effects. A rejected child presents a clinical picture of inferiority. He is forever seeking security and affection, and when he does not receive it from his parents, he is apt to turn to other sources. He typically feels isolated, and any situation in his environment that accents or increases his isolation worsens matters. Rejection is particularly difficult to deal with because its manifestations are usually indirect and its presence unrecognized or vigorously denied by the rejecting parent.

Research studies have demonstrated the home's influence upon adolescent behavior and attitudes both inside and outside the family setting. We can conceptualize just as validly in terms of problem homes as of problem children.

Since some homes show considerable individual differences, it is essential for the youth worker to have some concept of the various kinds of homes. Yet it is difficult to classify homes because of the many variables involved, although there is agreement that parental attitude is one of the most important of all.

The two factors basic to an understanding of parent-child relationships appear to be the variables of dominance-submission and acceptance-rejection, neither of which may be considered properly apart from the other. Baldwin et al., in attempting to classify types of parental attitude and behavior, offer three categories: rejectant, acceptant, and casual. Each category is in turn subcategorized. The rejectant parent is one who does not want his child and overtly shows it. His attitude may take an active, overt form, or it may be nonchalant and ignoring. Under the former, the child suffers strict rules, while under the latter he is allowed extraordinary freedom if he does not intrude upon his parents. In either case, intrusion tends to lead to severe punishment.

The acceptant parent falls into one of three categories. First is the indulgent parent, whose behavior is marked by child-centeredness and a great deal of child-parent contact with good rapport, though with overprotective tendencies. Second is the democratic parent, who is well adjusted where his child is concerned. The child does not receive undue attention but is given an opportunity to follow his own bent. Information rather than orders is given. Third is the democratic-indulgent parent, who tends to be more emotional about his child, but also tends to strike a happy medium between an indulgent and a democratic attitude.

The behavior of the casual parent is consistently mild and casual. There are two types of casual parents. One is autocratic-casual, in which autocracy is a means of control rather than a symptom of rejection and dislike. The other is indulgent-casual. Parents in this subcategory are haphazard but always mild in their relationships with their children. They do not make a fetish of self-sacrifice and do not go out of their way to indulge the child, nor do they, on the other hand, begrudge the time and effort the child costs.

Difficulties and misunderstandings in family relationships arise when various members of a family do not agree with one another. Where disagreements exist over a wide range of topics it may be assumed that either the home exerts little ideological influence or that the differences represent the children's effort to discount much that their homes stand for. Family problems are particularly apt to arise when parents perceive their family differently and when for some reason their behavior in the family is at variance with their real feelings.

A fairly important question in considering family behavior concerns the relative influence of the mother as compared to that of the father. Traditionally, it has been believed that the mother exerts the greater influence, but modern research indicates that the father's role and influence are at least as great, and during the middle teen years, possibly even greater. The ideal situation still remains one in which both parents are present and play complementary roles in the child's upbringing, even though the immediate impact of one parent differs from the other's.

References

Ackerman, N. W. Adolescent problems: A symptom of family disorder. *Family Process* 1 (1962): 202–213.

Adams, J. F. Adolescent personal problems as a function of age and sex. *Journal of Genetic Psychology* 104 (1964): 207–214.

Alcorn, B. K. Some psychological effects of paternal deprivation upon children from 10 to 16. *Journal of Educational Sociology* 35 (1962): 337–345.

Baldwin, A. L.; Kalhorn, J.; and Breese, F. H. Patterns of parental behavior. *Psychological Monographs*, vol. 58 (1945).

Bath, J. A., and Lewis, E. C. Attitudes of young female adults toward some areas of parent-adolescent conflict. *Journal of Genetic Psychology* 100 (1962): 241–253.

Boehm, L. The development of independence: A comparative study. *Child Development* 28 (1957): 83–92.

Conway, J. A. Protests, permissiveness, and the adolescent. *Child Study Center Bulletin*, University of Miami, Florida 2 (1966): 96–99.

Debesse, M. L'enfant et la famille. *Bulletin de Psychologie* 20 (1967): 1470–1474.

Duvall, E. M. Family dilemmas with teenagers. *Family Life Coordinator* 14 (1965): 35–38.

Fromm, E. Individual and social origins of neurosis. *American Sociological Review* 9 (1944): 380–384.

Grinder, R. E., and Spector, J. C. Sex differences in adolescents' perceptions of parental resource control. *Journal of Genetic Psychology* 106 (1965): 337–344.

Hader, M. The importance of grandparents in family life. *Family Process* 4 (1965): 228–238.

Hebron, M. E., and London, W. A study of stereotypes in the caretaking of English children. *British Journal of Educational Psychology* 34 (1964): 125–131.

Heilbrun, A. B., and Fromme, D. K. Parental identification of late adolescents and level of adjustment: The importance of parental-model attributes, ordinal position and sex of the child. *Journal of Genetic Psychology* 107 (1965): 49–59.

Heilbrun, A. B., and Gillard, B. J. Perceived maternal childbearing behavior and motivational effects of social reinforcement in females. *Perceptual and Motor Skills* 23 (1966): 439–446.

Heilbrun, A. B., and Orr, H. Perceived maternal child-rearing history and subsequent motivational effects of failure. *Journal of Genetic Psychology* 109 (1966): 75–89.

Herron, W. G. Test patterns of accepted and rejected adolescents. *Perceptual and Motor Skills* 15 (1962): 435–438.

Hess, R. D., and Goldblatt, I. The status of adolescents in American society: A problem of social identity. *Child Study* 37 (1959–1960): 21–23.

Hokanson, J. E. The effects of guilt arousal and severity of discipline on adult aggressive behavior. *Journal of Clinical Psychology* 17 (1961): 29–32.

Johnson, M. M. Sex-role learning in the nuclear family. *Child Development* 34 (1963): 319–333.

Kagan, J., and Moss, H. A. The stability of passive and independent behavior from childhood through adulthood. *Child Development* 31 (1960): 577–591.

Kinnane, J. F., and Pable, M. W. Family background and work value orientation. *Journal of Counseling Psychology* 9 (1962): 320–325.

Landis, J. T. A reexamination of the role of the

father as an index of family integration. *Marriage and Family Living* 24 (1962): 122–128.

Lidz, T. *The family and human adaptation*. New York: International Universities Press, 1963.

Lurie, O. R. The emotional health of children in a family setting. *Community Mental Health Journal* 6 (1970): 229–235.

McCord, W.; McCord, J.; and Verden, P. Familial and behavioral correlates of dependency in male children. *Child Development* 33 (1962): 313–326.

McDonald, R. L. Intrafamilial conflict and emotional disturbance. *Journal of Genetic Psychology* 101 (1962): 201–208.

McNasser, D. Fatherless generation. *Journal of Secondary Education* 37 (1962): 5–7.

McPherson, S. Communication of intents among parents and their disturbed adolescent child. *Journal of Abnormal Psychology* 76 (1970): 98–105.

Mandelbaum, A. Youth and Family. *Menninger Quarterly* 23 (1969): 4–11.

Marzolf, S. S. Parent behavior as reported by college students. *Journal of Clinical Psychology* 21 (1965): 360–366.

Meissner, W. W. Parental interaction of the adolescent boy. *Journal of Genetic Psychology* 107 (1965): 225–233.

Middleton, R., and Putney, S. Student rebellion against parental political beliefs. *Social Forces* 41 (1963): 377–383.

Miller, D. R., and Swanson, G. E. *Inner conflict and defense*. New York: Holt, 1960.

Moulton, R. W.; Burnstein, E.; Liberty, P. G.; and Altucher, N. Patterning of parental affection and disciplinary dominance as a determinant of guilt and sex typing. *Journal of Personality and Social Psychology* 4 (1966): 356–363.

Mueller, W. J. Need structure and the projection of traits onto parents. *Journal of Personality and Social Psychology* 3 (1966): 63–72.

Murphy, E. B.; Silber, E.; Coebho, G. V.; Hamburg, D. A.; and Greenberg, I. Development of autonomy and parent-child interaction in late adolescence. *American Journal of Orthopsychiatry* 33 (1963): 643–652.

Musgrove, F. University freshmen and their parents' attitudes. *Educational Research* 10 (1967): 78–80.

Mussen, P. H., and Kagan, J. Group conformity and perceptions of parents. *Child Development* 29 (1958): 57–60.

Mussen, P. H.; Young, H. B.; Gaddini, R.; and Morante, L. The influence of father-son relationships on adolescent personality and attitudes. *Journal of Child Psychology and Psychiatry* 4 (1963): 3–16.

Nash, J. The father in contemporary culture and current psychological literature. *Child Development* 36 (1965): 261–297.

Peck, R. F. Family patterns correlated with adolescent personality structure. *Journal of Abnormal and Social Psychology* 57 (1958): 347–350.

Riesman, D.; Glazer, N.; and Denney, R. *The lonely crowd*. Garden City, N. Y.: Doubleday, 1955.

Reubush, B. K.; Byrum, M.; and Farnham, L. J. Problem solving as a function of children's defensiveness and parental behavior. *Journal of Abnormal and Social Psychology* 67 (1963): 355–362.

Rosenberg, M. Parental interest and children's self-conceptions. *Sociometry* 26 (1963): 35–49.

Schulman, R. E.; Shoemaker, D. J.; and Moelis, I. Laboratory measurement of parental behavior. *Journal of Consulting Psychology* 26 (1962): 109–114.

Siegelman, M. College student personality correlates of early parent-child relationship. *Journal of Consulting Psychology* 29 (1965): 558–564.

Veen, F. van der; Huebner, B.; Jorgens, B.; and Neja, P. Relationships between the parents' concept of the family and family adjustment. *American Journal of Orthopsychiatry* 34 (1964): 45–55.

Vogel, W., and Lauterbach, C. G. Relationships between normal and disturbed sons' percepts of their parents' behavior and personality attributes of the parents and sons. *Journal of Clinical Psychology* 19 (1963): 52–56.

Weinstock, A. R. Family environment and the development of defense and coping mechanisms. *Journal of Personality and Social Psychology* 5 (1967): 67–75.

Wilson, R. Difficult housing estates. *Human Relations* 16 (1963): 3–43.

Zunich, M. The relation between junior high school students' problems and parental attitudes toward child rearing and family life. *Journal of Educational Research* 56 (1962): 134–138.

Zunich, M. Attitudes of lower-class families. *Journal of Social Psychology* 63 (1964): 367–371.

Suggested Readings

Armentrout, J. A. Siblings' concurrent perceptions of their parents' child-rearing attitudes. *Perceptual and Motor Skills* 30 (1970) : 782.

Barnett, J. Dependency conflicts in the young adult. *Psychoanalytic Review* 58 (1971): 111–125.

Biller, H. B. The mother-child relationship and the father-absent boy's personality development. *Merrill-Palmer Quarterly* 17 (1971): 227–241.

Boshier, R., and Thom, E. Do conservative parents nurture conservative children? *Social Behavior and Personality* 1 (1973): 108–110.

Diener, E. Maternal child-rearing attitudes as antecedents of self-actualization. *Psychological Reports* 31 (1972): 694.

Fischoff, J. The role of the parents' unconscious in children's antisocial behavior. *Journal of Clinical Child Psychology* 2 (1973): 31–33.

Grusec, J. E. Power and the internalization of self-denial. *Child Development* 42 (1971): 93–105.

Guardo, C. J., and Meisels, M. Child-parent spatial patterns under praise and reproof. *Developmental Psychology* 5 (1971): 365.

Harris, S. L., and Nathan, P. E. Parents' locus of control and perception of cause of children's problems. *Journal of Clinical Psychology* 29 (1973): 182–184.

Husband, P., and Henton, P. E. Families of children with repeated accidents. *Archives of Disease in Childhood* 47 (1972): 396–400.

Landau, R.; Harth, P.; Othnay, N.; and Sharfhertz, C. The influence of psychotic parents on their children's development. *American Journal of Psychiatry* 129 (1972): 38–43.

LaVoie, J. C., and Looft, W. R. Parental antecedents of resistance-to-temptation behavior in adolescent males. *Merrill-Palmer Quarterly* 19 (1973): 107–116.

Lukianowicz, N. Rejected children. *Psychiatria Clinica* 5 (1972): 174–186.

McKinney, J. P. The development of values—prescriptive or proscriptive? *Human Development* 14 (1971): 71–80.

McKinney, J. P.; Connolly, J.; and Clark, J. Development of a prescriptive morality: An historical observation. *Journal of Genetic Psychology* 122 (1973): 105–110.

Mlott, S. R. Some significant relationships between adolescents and their parents as revealed by the Minnesota Multiphasic Personality Inventory. *Adolescence* 7 (1972): 169–182.

Nelson, D. D. A study of personality adjustment among adolescent children with working and non-working mothers. *Journal of Educational Research* 64 (1971): 328–330.

Osofsky, J. D. The shaping of mothers' behavior by children. *Journal of Marriage and the Family* 32 (1970): 400–405.

Osofsky, J. D. Children's influence upon parental behavior: An attempt to define the relationship with the use of laboratory tasks. *Genetic Psychology Monographs* 83 (1971): 147–169.

Qadri, A. J., and Kaleem, G. A. Effect of parental attitudes on personality adjustment and self-esteem of children. *Behaviorometrics* 1 (1971): 19–24.

Slaughter, D. T. Parental potency and the achievement of inner-city black children. *American Journal of Orthopsychiatry* 40 (1970): 433–440.

Snyder, E. E., and Spreitzer, E. A. Family influence and involvement in sports. *Research Quarterly* 44 (1973): 249–255.

Soltz, V. The frightened parent syndrome. *Individual Psychologist* 6 (1969): 1–7.

Stinnett, N.; Talley, S.; and Walters, J. Parent-child relationships of black and white high school students: A comparison. *Journal of Social Psychology* 91 (1973): 349–350.

Wakefield, W. M. Awareness, affection, and perceived similarity of the parent-child relationship. *Journal of Genetic Psychology* 117 (1970): 91–97.

Chapter Twenty-three

Social Behavior and Conformity

The Importance of Social Behavior in Adolescence

An adolescent normally tends to attach great importance to the attitudes and opinions of others, especially those his own age. Adolescence is a time of expanding and urgent interest in persons of the opposite sex, both as persons and as biological organisms. It is a time of seeking an appropriate social role and satisfying social relationships that will accord with concepts of self. Above all else, it is a time when personal adjustment, both present and future, is closely related to social success and ability to play the social role in which the individual would like to see himself.

The complications the adolescent encounters in his social life are varied. He has recently passed through stages in social development during which both his accepted personal role and the role others expected of him were considerably different from the role he must now play. He is an individual without experience, still in fact a child, who finds himself in what is to him a rapidly expanding adult's world. He finds that he has new physical urges, new physical growth, new interests and values, and new concepts of self. He finds, unwittingly, that he has turned his back on much that used to be important to him. The process of growing up is difficult and strange, particularly in the relationships it brings with others, contemporaries or adults. The adolescent must finally emerge from his social explorations with mature and adequate social attitudes, stand-

ards, and skills if he is to find any degree of social adjustment as an adult.

Widening Social Relationships

Hollander (1964) writes: "The peer group is not a unitary source of influence, but one which varies in terms of age-level and the nature of the particular group of peers involved as well as the context and nature of their activity." He posits "at least three significant age-level distinctions": preschool, school, and adolescent.

A young child is essentially egocentric. He sees himself as the center of the universe. He is a person to be served and waited on, a person with little patience for anything that blocks his desires or sense of security. He is, above all, a person who has small regard for and less appreciation of the rights and feelings of others so long as he himself has his way. In a study of young children Gellert (1961) notes the extent to which they ignore the attitudes and behavior of their playmates, while Berenda (1950) reports on the minimum response to social pressures from their age-mates of children under seven as compared to the greater response of children in the seven to thirteen age group. Hunt and Synnerdale (1959) report on the lack of influence of social pressures on five- and six-year-olds.

Some individuals seem never to lose their egocentric attitude no matter what their age, perhaps because of faulty upbringing or because of unusual environmental circumstances.

But for the normally developing individual, the progress of true maturity may be measured in part by his growing awareness of, and interest in, other persons, together with an appreciation of their rights and desires and a willingness to subordinate personal wishes to the greater good of the greater number. Expanding the child's social consciousness as he moves toward maturity is an important training problem. The outcome represents the difference between a "spoiled," disagreeable, poorly adjusted child and a likable youngster who finds acceptable social adjustments. The first-grade teacher is continually confronted with the problem of heterogeneity in a group of young children: many come from homes in which, in varying degrees, they have exercised tyranny over their parents. Some have been exceedingly important persons in a home more or less centered around their desires and the promotion of their welfare, and their contacts with children who might "rival" them have been negligible. In the first grade such children do not understand that there are other people who are as important as they are. They do not realize that the wishes of others must be taken into consideration, sometimes at the expense of their own. During the course of the first school year an appreciation of the rights of others is gradually instilled. This process continues throughout the school years, with increasing social skills and abilities in working with others. Social competence comes from acquaintance with various rules of conduct and etiquette that must be gained partly through actual experience. Too, the child's constantly expanding social world brings him more and more in contact with persons to whom, as an individual, he means less and less. When he was a small child, his world was centered about his parents, with his mother usually playing the major role. Later he moved from this world to one that included his siblings and, gradually, an increasingly large and dispersed group of outsiders. As a child grows older, his circle of acquaintances widens week by week, and the continuing perfection and expansion of communication and the increasing mobility of all elements of the population have, over the past years, accelerated the rate and extent of that expansion.

An examination of the community location of a child's friends will illustrate. When he is very small, his friends consist of relatives and children who are brought to the house to visit. When he is able to go about a bit, he has a concentration of friends in the immediate vicinity of his home, but seldom anywhere else. A little later the friends will be somewhat more scattered, but all within the same or the adjoining block. By the time he enters elementary school, his friendships may extend for two or three blocks, but by the end of the first year he will know children scattered over most of the entire area served by his grade, although his best friends are most likely to be those living in his immediate neighborhood. This dispersing process accelerates with entrance into junior and senior high school, until a map of the dispersion of the adolescent's friends will show them spread rather widely over the community, and even outside it, although still with a strong concentration within the neighborhood. This condition will be particularly marked insofar as there are strong socioeconomic, racial, or national differences within the community.

In general, the experience of going to school is the most important social change a child will encounter between the preschool period and adolescence. Its ramifications will permeate and shape nearly all aspects of his life.

As his social contacts widen, like the ever-widening ripples caused by a stone thrown into a still pond, the child changes both psychologically and physically. New interests, attitudes, and values arise to replace the old. People take on new values and new meanings as they are fitted into the individual's pattern of psychological growth. To an elementary school child, adults tend to be more important as a class and are probably more venerated than they are later. Little differentiation is made on the basis of sex, though among boys, particularly, physical prowess is highly esteemed. Gradually the child tends to feel less closely related to adults in general. He may even harbor definite feelings of antagonism towards adults, although most adolescents have a well-defined tendency to idealize a number of aspects of adult life.

The prepubescent period is a time of vigorous social interaction, at least among like-sexed individuals, although there is some indication of heterosexual interests. Hollander (1964) writes of this group: "In the school years before adolescence, the child's peer group seems to serve as a supplemental agent of socialization to the family by providing for play activity. A transition to same-sex peer group composition also occurs in this stage." But in contrast to the adolescent period, the social interaction of the preadolescent period is exceedingly impersonal, characterized, one might say, by the law of the jungle. Preadolescents are learning the "game" of how to cope with and master others in social situations. It is not their role to work out close relationships or necessarily to give other members of their clique either consideration or mercy. The relatively greater amount of friendship fluctuation in middle childhood and preadolescence as compared to adolescence has been pointed out by Skorepa, Horrocks, and Thompson (1963). The preadolescent follows a highly egocentric survival-of-the-fittest approach in his social relationships. As Friedenberg (1959) put it, "I think most thoughtful adults, if they were obliged to sojourn among American eight-to-ten year olds, would want to be awfully careful which side of Alice's mushroom they nibbled."

How then, are adolescents different? Hollander (1964) writes:

The adolescent peer group appears to mark a difference both in its equality and its functions . . . it tends to incorporate a different "culture" often at variance with the adult culture and frequently in response to the particular pressures attending upon the ambiguity of adolescent status in our society.

Among themselves, at least, although not necessarily in their relationships with others, they are more sensitive, more discerning, and more personally involved with the other person —in effect more tender in their interpersonal relationships. Three and possibly four things seem to have happened on their transition into adolescence. First is the advent of puberty and the emotional difference the interpolation of sexual motivation brings about not only in same-sex but in intersexual relationships. Second is a new ability to look at the world in more theoretical, hypothetical terms as they arrive at the stage of formal thinking. Third, where in preadolescence the child learned the rules of the game of social intercourse with little self-reference, in adolescence he looks within; he is beginning to view himself as a person with a corresponding interest in others that impels him to see what they are like as persons. And fourth (though here one can be less certain, for the adolescent still has much to learn about social behavior), the basic rules of interpersonal behavior and of manipulation have been acquired and one can play the social game automatically without constantly having to refer to, or to learn, the basics. The finesse, of course, has still to come. But all this does not imply that adolescent social relationships simulate a sort of Garden of Eden. The jungle is still there—the competitiveness, the denigration of others, the occasional cruelty or heedlessness—but there is a difference, even if it is not consistently present. Perhaps the jungle has become more human, more humane, and man is beginning to take his place as a social creature, appreciating and being appreciated by others of his kind.

When puberty has come, and the social groupings are different, the first noticeable manifestation of the new era is the temporary abandonment or rather de-emphasis of the same-sex crowd of late childhood in favor of pairings of close friends of the same sex. Such pairings are complementary and offer an opportunity for the exchange of confidences as well as of long silences. It seems that such pairings represent the new interest in other people as people as the adolescent begins the struggle of becoming analytically interested in himself as a person, and as he endeavors to define himself. The pairings give him an opportunity to deal with and get to know well a person of his own age and sex who becomes, in effect, a laboratory in which he may really look at the other and try out on him (or her) his own ideas and perceptions. One might say that the adolescent has provided himself with a mirror. That the relationship has to some extent a tinge of the erotic is often implicit, although the manifestations seldom take an explicitly overt form. Certainly the erotic element is as little realized by the adolescent as it is likely to be condoned by the surrounding adults. Yet such covert eroticism is a natural aspect of the biologically and emotionally developing child. It helps to effect the transition in the processes of socialization from self-centeredness to other-centeredness, and parents, teachers, and other adults should not be worried or feel they are confronted with a potential situation to discuss with anyone, least of all the adolescent.

Competence and the Peer Group

Earlier it was stated that during adolescence competence is highly admired and demanded. The adolescent peer group provides a place to exercise such competence. In contrast to the peer groupings before the advent of puberty, the adolescent group engages in more complicated activities. Differential abilities are noted and likely to be valued and highly accepted if they produce competent behavior and if they appear to further the group's perceived needs and objectives. Technique, the smooth approach that gets results in relationships with adults, is at a premium and pays high rewards in social approval and support. Clumsiness is penalized, and many adolescents who do not recognize these peer-society facts of life and instead try to perpetuate the less sophisticated techniques of the preadolescent groupings are definitely neither appreciated nor approved. They may occasionally be used in baiting an adult or in making some point the group wishes made, but, having served their function, they are dropped or at best made uncomfortable as

they are endured. Of course adolescents still lack experience, their techniques do not always work, and they are not infallible in their judgments of people and situations. Still, the direction is clear.

Changes in Role During Development

One of the more difficult aspects of expanding social functioning for children is the seeming inconsistency they encounter as new behavior is expected of them and old behavior patterns are found to be unacceptable. It is not only a matter of how the child behaves himself, it includes the change in others' attitudes toward him. When such adult attitudes are inconsistent from one occasion to another, the adolescent's adjustment difficulties become even more pronounced. Social development is more than a matter of increasing social skills and ever-widening social contacts; it is concerned with group participation and the assumption of new roles in mingling with various groups. One of the most difficult social changes in adolescence is the need to exchange a passive for an active social role. As a child, the individual's physical presence was usually enough to insure inclusion in a play group, a schoolroom group, or some other children's gathering. The whole matter of group participation was transitory at best, since most child groups gather without any great degree of premeditation, unless it is on the part of a supervising adult; the groups are closely knit without enduring intragroup alliances. On the other hand, if the adolescent wishes to be included in a group, he usually finds he must do something so that his acceptance will be continued. In a social sense, the child group is natural and uncritical. It accepts what is there. The adolescent group tends to be hypercritical, snobbish, and highly artificial. Physical presence does not equal acceptance. With good reason, the adolescent has to worry about what others think. He who wishes to be accepted is on trial and must prove himself, often by assuming a role or an

attitude foreign to his inclinations. That he is
willing to assume such a role to gain acceptance is proof of the importance of the peer
group's good will, whereas to the younger child
the opinion of his peers is of comparatively
little significance. He feels that he is good
enough and expects others to accept him at his
own valuation. In any event, the small child is
"acting himself" in relations with peers, while
his older brother or sister is "covering up."

As children grow up, their social roles become more differentiated, some of them becoming quite compartmentalized and even mutually
exclusive, particularly as contacts widen. In the
child's play group, an individual can assume
many roles interchangeably—small children
tend not to specialize for any length of time.
But with the advent of relatively narrow
special-interest groups and formally organized
games, particularly in high school sports, roles
become quite differentiated and publicly emphasize certain personal qualities of each
participant. When the characteristic is one that
elicits admiration and social approval, such
specialization may be ego-sustaining, but when
the characteristic is less attractive, the adolescent may find himself committed to a distasteful role, with implications for an adverse
self-concept. Younger children tend to find a
great deal of satisfaction in large, relatively
formal, centralized groups such as the Boy or
Girl Scouts, but as adolescence proceeds such
groups become less attractive and are replaced by smaller specific-interest groups more
homogeneous in nature.

Consciousness of sex also becomes an important issue in a child's social development,
frequently taking the form of antagonism in
the years immediately preceding adolescence,
but succeeded by great interest and attraction
as adolescence proceeds. Conduct in relation to
others becomes an important issue. New codes
of adult or near-adult behavior must be learned
and adopted. Relationships with and conduct
toward other persons, particularly those of the
opposite sex, must be reappraised and changed
in line with the new attitudes and values that
have arisen.

As an adolescent approaches adulthood, he
is often placed in social situations in which he
must behave as an adult before he knows
exactly how to do so. He has developed a sense
of values that tends to overstress the social
importance of certain aspects of conduct or
appearance, and he may overreact if he cannot
meet the standards set by himself or his group,
either because of physical or monetary limitations. An adolescent girl preparing to go to a
formal dance offers a rich illustration of the
excessive importance placed upon trifles that
are often in reality both unimportant and not
noticeable to others. The adolescent has been
defined as an inexperienced child in an adult
situation.

A further complicating factor for some children is the accelerated social mobility presently
taking place in America. Ellis and Lane (1967)
report on the disproportionate share of isolat-
ing experiences and social strain encountered
by upwardly-mobile youth as they endeavor to
assume the role in the peer group demanded by
the status to which they or their parents aspire.

Anxiety and Social Role

Such problems of role definition and differentiation can become anxiety producing, and
many adolescents present a picture of more or
less generalized anxiety. Ausubel (1958)
speaks of a state of transitional anxiety occurring in the individual during periods of
psychological transition. This he sees as resulting from the threats to self-esteem inherent
in a situation in which a person is moving
from an accustomed state to one in which a
new state of equilibrium is sought. The situation of transition may be described as one of
aspiration for something yet to be attained.
Certainly adolescence, with its drive for
emancipation and definition of role, is an example of a transitional period when the individual is characterized by a status lower
than his aspirations. This threatens self-
esteem and hence leads to anxiety and frustration resulting in defensive behavior. For most
adolescents the defensive behavior is relatively

benign and represents an effort to cope within a socially approved framework. Some, however, as Iannaccaro (1962) notes, attempt to use aggressive defensive reactions and escape rather than compromise as a mode of adjustment to frustration.

The Adolescent's Concept of His Role

In peer-group society the quantity and quality of an individual's social relationships are conditioned by his self-concept. For example, Reese (1961) reports that acceptance by peers is related to an individual's self-oriented attitudes, while Goslin (1962) cites a tendency for the group to isolate children who perceive themselves differently than they are perceived by the group.

However, an adolescent's self-concept can be influenced by group attitudes and activities as they are brought to bear directly upon him. Gerard (1961) hypothesizes that an individual's knowledge of the opinions others hold of him would affect his self-view as manifested in his self-evaluation. Rosen et al. (1960), in a study of preadolescent and early-adolescent boys, present evidence indicating that a boy's desire to make a change in himself depends upon the extent that his peers dislike him and do not consider him a role model they wish to emulate. Rivlin (1959) reports that involvement with peer groups leads to greater self-confidence and a more favorable self-concept. He also noted that creative groups of adolescents are more sociable and more confident in interpersonal relationships than are less creative groups.

On the other hand, it is not necessarily true that an adolescent's self-image (insight) is such that he has a true picture of how others feel about him. Werdelin (1966) reports that adolescent's self-ratings showed considerable discrepancy between ratings made by both teachers and peers. This may, of course, be a problem of defense.

It should be pointed out that an individual in any group may have two roles, the role he actually plays and his conception of the role. The physician who makes his daily rounds, sees patients in his office, and does the myriad jobs that fall to the lot of the general practitioner is one example. That is his actual role. But it may be very different from the role as he interprets it. He may visualize himself as the crusader, the knight in white armor combating the forces of evil, a veritable benefactor of mankind.

So it is with the adolescent. He may see himself as playing an entirely different role from his actual one, and as long as he does not come up against an unpleasant reality too often, he may adjust quite comfortably. If reality becomes too difficult, he may take refuge in daydreaming, which makes any role possible. As he gains more and more satisfaction in fantasy and less and less in reality, he may resort increasingly to dreams and withdraw as much as possible from social participation. Adolescent daydreaming is not necessarily bad; indeed, it is quite normal and is to be expected. But when it begins to affect an individual's life to the point where he uses it as a continual and habitual retreat from reality, it is a symptom of serious underlying maladjustment. Adolescents who find great satisfaction in daydreaming may find little satisfaction in the social contacts of real life. They may even become reluctant to seek social experiences, even though they might be successful if they tried; it is so much easier to daydream.

As has been explained so often, individuals differ; individual differences in general and special abilities, in information, and so on, help define an adolescent's role in his group. The larger the group, of course, the more compartmentalized the role. The role an individual actually does assume depends upon his aptitude for it, or upon a series of circumstances that force a role upon him and make him continue it even against his will. There are many roles to be played in any group, some desirable, others very undesirable. Included are those of the leader, the buffoon, the cheerful follower, the troublemaker, the drudge, the lieutenant or second in command, the one who has the answers, the showoff, the gossip, the "good fellow," and many more. Observations of groups of adolescents at one of their after-school hangouts, on the playground, or in the school cafeteria or corridors will reveal many of the possibilities.

Several kinds of factors are influential in placing a person in a role, sometimes forced on the adolescent by the group, and sometimes voluntarily assumed and promoted by the individual himself. One such factor, physical or mental endowment, produces the bully, the athlete, the boy with glasses, the fat boy, the slow thinker, or the clever person with a plan. Personal possessions may give status: Examples are the boy who has an automobile, or coveted play equipment or facilities, or a big allowance, or a good-looking sister or brother. Another factor may be a personal relationship existing between an individual and a high-status member of the group: there are the "plain" friend of a popular girl or the "kid" brother or sister of the person with connections useful to the group.

However, the nature of the role and its status value depend upon the kind of group and the group's objectives. A role that gives low status in one peer group might provide high status in another. Too, the individual himself plays his part. The butt of ridicule in one group may lead an embarrassed and low-status group life, while another person in the same group may cleverly use the attributes that bring ridicule upon another person to bring social approval upon himself. An extremely fat girl in a high school senior class so anticipated jokes upon herself and so used her physical anomaly in her social contacts that she became popular and indeed was voted by her classmates as the one student most likely to succeed.

Whatever role an individual plays in a group, for him it is an exceedingly important one, even though the adult observer may consider the role and its consequences trivial and unimportant. The status a child has gained is one that has come from his own world and forms the basis of his peer acceptance. A role an adult might feel is subservient or inconsequential may actually be a great source of satisfaction to its player as he interprets it in the setting of group approval.

The adolescent's concept of himself is a rather tenuous and changing thing, but, like most people's concepts of themselves, it satisfies a specific need to bolster the ego. To gain security for the ego he assumes some role that may meet with social approval. If approval is not forthcoming, he must find either a new role or an excuse for the disapproved or low-status role he is forced to play. Consequently, it is exceedingly important that the adult provide an adolescent with every reasonable opportunity to bolster his ego. This may be accomplished partly by helping him assume socially approved roles that are ego-bolstering. It is a mistake to "show him up" or to make him feel embarrassed or insufficient because of his age or status.

Many youth workers wrongly assume that a physical anomaly or some other undesirable attribute may evoke social disapproval in the adolescent peer group. It may, of course, but it is not inevitable. Care should be taken to refrain from assuming that problems exist where there are none, or what is worse, creating them. The youth worker has the task of diagnosing or predicting difficulty or maladjustment and then doing something about it, but he should be exceedingly careful to handle the matter with circumspection and not try to remedy a problem that does not, or is not likely to, exist for a given individual. Many who work with adolescents have trouble in deciding what to say when a personal difficulty is known to exist. They should say nothing at all until sure that the adolescent is psychologically ready to receive the information and the person imparting it is able to suggest some positive means of alleviating the difficulty. If the adolescent is psychologically unready to receive personal information about himself, the youth worker, after assuring himself that the issue is important, should help that individual arrive at a point where he will be ready and able to know what he must do for his own best development. The need for a positive program must again be emphasized. One counselor told an adolescent that he "had a speech defect and ought to clear it up" if he "wanted to talk like a man," but he had no suggestions as to how it might be cleared up.

Problems of Self-appraisal

Adolescents tend constantly to question their social roles and frequently seek information that will enable them to play more effective ones. But the adolescent does not begin the social relations of adolescence without some previous background of experience—he brings to them the total of his past experiences. Many things in his past help him with his new problems, among them various skills such as dancing, games proficiency, knowledge of etiquette, and so on. On the other hand, he may find that some of the attitudes and skills that did him yeoman service as a child militate against him as an adolescent. An analysis of the social problems of concern to adolescents reveals that boys and girls have somewhat different problems, that there are socioeconomic differences, rural-urban differences, and a multitude of other differences. Some problems are common to most adolescents.

When adolescents discuss personal problems of immediate concern, the matter of heterosexual relationships often arises. This is to be expected of younger adolescents, for boy-girl relations are new to them; they are embarking on new experiences and have many questions. Parents and others who work with youth are seriously concerned about the source of their answers to these questions. To whom do they feel free to go? Some won't admit lack of knowledge and try to explore on their own. Some are embarrassed and refuse to place themselves in situations in which they do not know how to behave or what to say. Some ac-

quire more or less accurate information by comparing notes with their friends in the bull sessions continually going on among adolescents. Few, apparently, obtain any appreciable amount of information from their parents, and fewer still from the established curricula of our schools. Here indeed is a challenging area for adults who wish to help adolescents in their adjustment problems.

Often an adolescent is driven in his desire for anchorage to attach himself to an individual whom he idealizes and follows. Usually such a person, if near the adolescent's own age, is in the peer group to which the adolescent belongs. Sometimes he is not, in which case the individual who picks an outsider as his ideal may find himself in difficulty with his group.

Adults find it particularly hard to understand certain isolated aspects of an adolescent's behavior that may have little relation even to the "unreasonable" activities of other adolescents. In such cases it must be remembered that causes may be found for any type of behavior. An adolescent may fasten upon some isolated aspect of an admired adult's life and misinterpret it as he tries to imitate the model in his behavior.

"Stages" of Social Adjustment

In considering this matter of the progress of social development, it is extremely tempting to try to classify an individual's progress in terms of "stages" that are held to be common to all children. True, interests and behavior characteristic of an age level do exist, but they are not universal, nor do they necessarily hold from individual to individual or from environment to environment. There is a real danger inherent in categorizing social development specifically in terms of stages, since a stage is essentially a category whose limitations are biological. Yet popular thinking tends to make considerable use of the stage idea, such as the "gang stage," or the "girl-crazy stage." Comments like, "Well, after all he is fourteen and that's how fourteen-year-olds act," and "After all, he's a boy" are commonly heard. Of course, there is a grain of truth in these comments, for there are norms and even a most probable reaction. But the psychologist is too aware of the possibilities of individual deviation to accept them wholeheartedly.[1]

Since popular expectations about typical stage behavior do exist, the adolescent may get into trouble when he deviates from what is popularly considered normal behavior, that is, when his behavior is advanced or retarded compared with what people expect it to be. In psychology, it is preferable to obtain a normative picture and cite median behavior to be expected in any given situation, so deviations can be recognized. Then it may be possible to find in the deviations the symptoms that will indicate the true situation of the individual under observation.

The Peer Group as an Educative Experience

The influence of the peer group being what it is, it offers any culture or any educational system a powerful weapon with which to guide and mold the direction in which its youth goes. In America there is no really planned or concerted attempt on a national or state level to make any great use of the youth group, but such attempts have been made elsewhere. In Israel, in the cooperative living villages, maximum use has been made of peer relationships, and Bronnfenbrenner (1962) has pointed to the Russian educator's use of the guided child's group as the principal means of socialization. The Russian system emphasizes the group rather than the individual, even to the extent of punishing and rewarding on a group rather

than an individual basis. Such a system further enhances the group cohesiveness characteristic of adolescence in complex societies. Obviously there are gains, but this system also accentuates the problem of overemphasizing peer groupings and promotes the cleavage between the generations. A saving factor would be to broaden the age base of the group so that it would be less chronologically homogeneous and more representative of a cross-section of the population.

Teachers might do well to consider their own relationship to the peer society over which they nominally preside. In a consideration of the teacher in the high school social structure, Gordon (1955) notes that teachers who wish to be most effective in promoting learning must recognize the personal and social interrelationships of their students and adapt their approaches to the realities of that social structure. The difficulty here lies in the teacher's conflict between the concept of her role held by the peer group and the concept she and other adults hold.

Most adolescents, immersed as they are in the fascinating problems of their peer world, concerned with growing up and emancipation, and distracted by the nonacademic aspects of school life, tend to set lower academic standards for themselves than do their teachers. The result can be strained relations, promoted and perpetuated as the students reinforce their conceptions of the teacher's role by their interaction with each other. The teacher represents a taskmaster, the incarnation of the out-group adult world. His definition of authority is at variance with that of the students. It is not unusual for a teacher to lack insight into or to be unwilling to accept the informal student status system that causes the conflict. Such rejection often leads to student sanctions against the teacher or, where a number of teachers are involved, against the whole school. Yet the opposite approach on the teacher's part is not without its dangers. As a teacher becomes more aware of the peer status system and tries to be sympathetically involved, he tends to overemphasize students' particularistic

[1]This is not to say that orderly sequences of social as well as biological changes do not take place during development or that the changes may not be grossly grouped into "periods" of the developmental sequence. Such periods were discussed earlier in this chapter. The point here is that there are great individual differences in the developmental sequence and they must be considered. Further, popular categorization of aspects of development that oversimplify the situation are misleading if not wrong— for example, adolescence as the "foolish stage."

aspects, frequently at the expense of decent academic standards against which to judge the results of the learning experiences that are the primary reason for the school's existence. Thus, the teacher's role becomes especially difficult as he endeavors to inhibit simultaneously two potentially antagonistic but congruent worlds. However, the perceptive teacher may do much to create a favorable climate for good teacher-pupil relationships and for effective learning if he can properly balance his acceptance of the importance of peer status and his insistence upon the maintenance of acceptable standards of academic performance. Learning as an activity may be presented in such a manner that its intrinsic interest will not conflict with interpersonal peer-group affairs and attitudes.

With increasing age, the adolescent can find school a profitable and interesting learning experience, with consequent reduction of student-teacher tensions. But this condition depends upon many ifs: if he perceives the school as fulfilling real psychological and social needs, if it appears to present him with a worthwhile challenge at his ability level, if he can accept the student-teacher role relationship, and if his academic activities are within the limits the peer group sets. It is sometimes easier to effect changes through a peer group than through any of the individuals that compose it.

Many individual differences in social relationships may be observed. These are present in all aspects of behavior. The differences may exist between individuals or between groups. Group differences, like individual differences, may reflect the composition of the group, the reason for the group's existence, geographical or time factors, sex differences, socioeconomic differences, or dozens of other possibilities. The youth worker who finds an adolescent or a group of adolescents departing to any degree from the peer social norms is faced with potential social maladjustment. There is a serious question as to whether or not observed deviate interests and activities, even though they appear to give satisfaction, are in reality to the best interest of normally developing individuals, who must spend large parts of their working time and recreational life in the company of others. An adolescent who has developed the skills, interests, and attitudes that will be accepted by his age-mates, and who can and does participate widely with members of both sexes of his own age, is not only adjusting well to his present environment, but is also laying a substantial foundation for social adjustment and success as an adult. The fact that many adolescents are far from having made optimum adjustment is demonstrated by the numbers of young people who enter college without ever having been to a party, attended a dance, been on a date, or found successful and satisfying social experiences with others of their own age.

Because the adolescent is embarking on many new experiences, because he is undergoing sensations and changes that are strange and mysterious to him and assuming new values and new attitudes, and, above all, because he is not sure how to cope with his environment, he tends to feel insecure in many areas of his daily living. As a result he looks for an anchor to help him find a measure of security and ego defense. Most tempting of all possible anchors is the peer group—people in a similar situation —with whom he may either ignore his problems or imagine they do not exist. Furthermore, in the peer group he can "belong" and find the status he so badly needs. The peer group also offers a young person the experiences and the training for which he is striving. For that reason it is little wonder that the peer group becomes so important to an adolescent that exclusion from it or lack of adequate status within it often constitutes a traumatic experience. It also explains why the peer group tends to be self-centered, status-conscious, and hostile to any elements, such as adults, that may violate its integrity. Thus, we find the adolescent experiencing considerable emotional upset when his peer relations are not satisfactory. When he was a child he had strong emotional attachments, usually to his parents. With broadening social interests and greater physical-space mobility, the child develops new needs and transfers his emotional attachment to other persons—and becomes upset if they do not respond.   ⋅   ⋅

Peer-Group Advantages and Disadvantages

This raises interesting though controversial questions: To what extent is the peer group good for an adolescent, and to what extent is it really bad? Also, what are the implications for those interested in promoting the optimum growth and development of both boys and girls?

There seems to be general agreement that the peer group is good because it may give an adolescent security, an opportunity for status, and a feeling of belonging. It provides a chance for him to learn something of the rights of others among equals who are bent on their own interests and self-expression. It gives the adolescent a refuge from the adult world. Finally, the peer group acts as an agency of control and a place to learn. This last is of particular interest to parents, educators, and others who attempt to direct and guide adolescent behavior. The adult who wishes to maintain a constructive influence upon adolescent behavior must refer continually to age-mate opinions and methods of doing things. To overlook this fundamental fact is to alienate oneself from the adolescent and render him even more susceptible to his group's influences. It must always be remembered that it is dangerous to interpret adolescent behavior in terms of adult behavior or standards. One must try to place oneself in the adolescent's position—impossible for some adults.

In considering the good features of the peer group, the reader will probably have recognized that those same factors that make for good may have a reverse effect if the group's objectives are antisocial or otherwise undesirable. Since it is unlikely that all the viewpoints and activities adopted by any given group are in the best interests of its members, the results might be very unfortunate if such

a group should act as a vehicle of learning. In fact, much group intra-action only jells bad attitudes and ideas. Here again the parent or youth worker must move cautiously in trying for changes.

Another potentially unfortunate characteristic of the peer group is that it may wean an individual from his parents too early or serve to set up unfortunate tensions between parents and children. A child who has long been indoctrinated in love and respect for his parents will probably not ignore their wishes if they oppose his peer group, even though his intense desire to assert his own individuality impels him to do so. In such a case a conflict situation may be set up, particularly if adults are hostile toward the group.

But probably most serious of all are the psychological effects on the individual who is ignored or repulsed by the group, or who is given at best dubious status. Adolescents, like all children, are frank and cruel in their treatment of others, particularly those who constitute an "out" group. Some children, try as they may, simply do not have the qualities the peer group considers important. An individual who lacks certain attributes, even though a nominal member or associate of the group, may have difficulty unless he can find within the group a role in which his very unacceptability becomes an asset.

Lack of acceptance probably becomes most important when there is a great deal of emotional or ego involvement, when the individual's other resources are too limited to meet his needs, or when a given group represents the things the adolescent most wants. It is not uncommon for an adolescent, rejected by a highly desired group, to refuse to join another group in which he might find status. Fortunately, this is sometimes a temporary state of affairs, for adolescent values change rapidly and the thing that seems desirable today may be less so next week. On the other hand, the adolescent most apt to be permanently injured by peer-group rebuffs is the very insecure person. Such a person may have well-developed feelings of inferiority, and a rebuff may strike at the very core of his self-esteem and feelings of worth. It may perhaps confirm fears about himself that he has already developed, and his increased feelings of insecurity and inferiority may result in further and further withdrawal into himself so that he stops trying to find peer acceptance. This is one of the more severe things that can happen psychologically, although children will occasionally be found who use rejection experiences to redouble their efforts in the adult world, sometimes doing extremely well. However, this is rare enough, and the potentialities of nonacceptance are so severe, that an adult is on very insecure ground if he expects an adolescent to "rise above his difficulties" and succeed in spite of them. He may succeed, but the chances are very much against him. Helping the child find acceptance, and helping him gain skills and techniques that will promote acceptance, is a far more effective method of therapy.

It also happens that the peer-group member who was once accepted and popular because he had some attribute important at a given stage of development is rejected because the attribute is valueless later. Such an individual is bewildered at his nonacceptance; he tends to act even more as he did when he was accepted, which only alienates him further from the group. Most teachers are familiar with the high school group rejectee who was very popular in elementary or early junior high school. Then there is the overvigorous, boisterous, girl-hating boy who tries to carry that attitude from a gang of like-minded ten-year-olds up through the years of senior high when his group is definitely interested in girls and manners. Common to every college campus is that perennial nuisance, the old grad who returns to his campus on every occasion and who seems to have forgotten that he ever grew up. This kind of person usually fails to find acceptance among the college group to which he reverts emotionally, for behavior acceptable in one generation is not necessarily so in another. The best refuge for such rejectees or retarded personalities is a group of like-minded individuals that will tend to gain in cohesiveness as others disapprove of them.

Children who cannot find peer status in a given group may be helped in two concrete ways. One (possibly the best in terms of all-around adjustment) is for the youth worker to help the adolescent develop some skill that the group values and that he may use as a status-building or acceptance factor. The other is to help him find some other peer group in which he may find the security, acceptance, and experiences he needs. Another peer group should be found if possible. Recourse to a hobby or to the company of adults denies the individual the social acceptance and experience that is so vitally important to him. It is also well to make sure that the substitute group is not markedly different developmentally from the person in question, for association with a much younger group is unhealthy in terms of fitting an individual for social participation with his peers or equals. It may promote in him attributes he is unwilling to sacrifice later. An adolescent who has dominated a younger group over a period of time has difficulty in associating with any other group unless he can dominate it as he did his former associates. The bully is a typical example—the overgrown older boy who is held back in elementary school year after year and who is forced to associate with younger children when he could have found good social acceptance among his peers.

But it must not be supposed that every adolescent who is not a member of a peer group has of necessity been rejected. Some adolescents who might like to participate are unable to for one reason or another. The child on the isolated farm, cut off from all possibility of intercourse with his own age-mates, is one example. Another is the boy who has to work, and who, like Horatio Alger's heroes, has no time for play.

There is also the voluntary nonparticipator, the child who matures too rapidly and grows impatient with adolescent mores, perhaps viewing them with adult insight. He is apt to be unhappy and may enter actual adulthood with fewer real social skills than he should have. His attitude may also be a sham—an excuse for withdrawal or a case of sour grapes—and this possibility should usually be considered when an adolescent seems to feel superior to his age-mates as a class.

Conformity and the Peer Group

An attribute of adolescence usually considered characteristic is that of dependence upon and conformity to the opinions and behavior of the like-aged peer group. Adolescents typically seem to conform to the opinions, activities, and appearance of other adolescents. These young people are essentially conservative where their own age-mates are concerned, however much they may appear to depart from adult stand-ards of conduct, dress, or acceptance of values. If a certain kind of shoe, a particular kind of sweater or skirt, shorts, patched blue jeans, bib overalls, shirts hanging out of blue jeans, insect pins, a special hair style, or symbolic ribbons are generally worn by adolescent girls, then the girl who wishes to escape the op-probrium of being different must wear the clothing and adopt the affectations then in fashion. If by some chance her parents prevent her from following the ways of her age-mates, she is faced with what she perceives as an em-barrassing situation against which she is likely to struggle more or less overtly. Smucker and Creekmore (1972) point to the strategic im-portance of clothing in the socialization of high school students. To an adolescent the fact that "other kids are doing it" is a cogent and over-powering reason for doing a thing, and par-ents can alienate their adolescents by refusing to agree.

Boys are no exception to the rule. The same slang, mannerisms, way of dress, and attitude as that of "the gang" must be adopted by any adolescent boy who wishes to be accepted. The almost universal acceptance by a whole school's adolescent population of a fad such as yo-yos, bug pins, a type of dance, or some esoteric de-parture from normal speech illustrates the intragroup conservatism of adolescents. An adolescent often wants to be "different," but different in conformity to certain basic pat-terns of peer behavior, or in even more slavish conformity to the dictates and observances of an in-group that is trying to emphasize its differences from the outsiders. There is always the individual who becomes the leader and whose precept and example is followed by others, but except for this individual, who manages to master the peer group, most ad-olescents find they must either conform or be excluded. Even the leader, who can ignore and change peer-group customs and attitudes, can do so only to a limited extent, and must not often flout the accepted group mores and ob-servances lest he find himself rejected. As the norms of the family and the adult world dimin-ish in importance in the adolescent subculture, the norms of the peer group become of greater significance. And the greater the peer-group in-tegration and cohesion, the more it replaces the family in the socialization process. However, for those parents who make a real endeavor and whose child-rearing practices are not re-strictive, the peer group can be both a transi-tional and a facilitative source of learning.

Cultural Expectations

In considering peer affiliation and the primacy of the peer group, it is important to recognize the importance of group affiliation and inter-personal "adjustment" in American culture. Parents become worried if children are not participating and adjusting socially, and schools make an issue of group participation and acceptance even to the point of mentioning it on report cards. Such conditioning to believe in the importance of social relationships con-vinces most American adolescents and young persons that it is indeed essential to be in tune with the peer group, and many of them go a considerable distance in affirming the value of their social relationships. Bauer (1967) notes, in a study of undergraduate peer relationships in a Midwestern university, that two-thirds of the fourth-year students felt that social development had been the most valuable part of their college experience. Here the goal of satisfying social development supplants the goal of intellectual development, leaving the main academic enterprise as merely one of satisfying course requirements.

Thus the attitude of adults in America promotes adolescents' feelings that the peer group is important, but equally important is the fact that adults have also identified and expressed the idea that the peer group is a separate and potent entity in American culture. Certainly Americans pay a great deal of attention to the corporate existence of teenagers. We even have columns in our newspapers on "What Teen-Agers Think." All this tends to identify the adolescent, to himself and to adults, as a member of a special class and to set him off as something different, deserving special attention as a class. Yet this recognition, while it views adolescents as something other than children, still does not consider them as full members of the adult community. In effect, it gives them a cause and offers the peer group as a focal point of solidarity for expression and mutual reinforcement of themselves as an entity. The natural result is the formation of an adolescent subculture. Coleman (1961) writes: "The adolescent becomes . . . 'cut off' from the rest of society, forced toward his own age. With his fellows he comes to constitute a small society, one that has most of its important interactions within itself, and maintains only a few threads of connection with the outside society." Gottlieb, Reeves, and ten Houten (1966) note that such subcultural membership and reference leads the adolescent to seek goals "within his peer subculture even at the risk of social rejection from the adult referents." Schwartz and Merten (1967) write that youth culture is a genuinely independent subculture that gives adolescents their own world view, lifestyles, and moral standards. These writers feel that to understand the adolescent subculture it is necessary to begin by asking what meanings peer-group norms have for adolescents.

The Acceptance Stance of Peer Groups

One strong source of peer-group influence is its accepting stance in various matters of importance to adolescents in comparison to the more nonaccepting attitude of parents, teachers, and other adults. For example, Jones, Gergen, and Davis (1962) report a study in which college women in an introductory course in psychology were interviewed by experimenters who eventually told each subject that they were either negatively or positively impressed by her as a person. The subjects in the study were favorably impressed by an experimenter who approved of them as persons, but tended to discount an experimenter who expressed negative feelings about them. In general, subjects became more negative in their feedback after they had received negative feedback than they did after receiving positive feedback. As Jones and Thibaut (1958) had previously noted:

When someone else likes you this more or less automatically increases your potential power or control over his responses to you—if you know that a person likes you, you also tend to assume that he "will do things for you." On the other hand, to be liked by others is a comforting index of one's own worth or virtue.

Of course, it cannot be assumed that adolescents necessarily feel that their parents dislike them as persons (although some do feel that way, with cause), but they often do find their parents reacting negatively in matters important to adolescents, whereas they find their peers reacting positively. Hence, in these matters the adolescent turns to the peer group in preference to his parents, and his behavior feedback to the parents is often quite negative.

The Relative Primacy of Peer Groups

The preceding discussions show that the peer group is indeed important in an adolescent's life, and the quite valid generalization that adolescents tend to conform to peer values and judgments as well as to peer activities can be made. Students of adolescence have commonly held that the peer group has, in the adolescent's mind, an influence that bulks larger than practically any other aspect of his life, and certainly most adolescents belong to peer groups and spend a great deal of time in peer associations. Therefore, as the adolescent mingles more and more with his age-mates and participates in group activity with them, his feeling of belonging to the group becomes greater and greater and may transcend nearly everything else in importance.

Many have felt that the peer group demands and receives the adolescent's loyalty against all comers, and have cited evidence of adolescent conformity to group dictates. Certainly an adolescent subculture does exist, is influential, and has been created not only by adolescent needs but also by various cultural pressures and adult expectations. However, it is easy to oversimplify the nature and function of the adolescent subculture. The reader should be cautious in accepting generalizations about it, particularly those that hypothesize the ubiquity of its influence and the need to conform to its standards. Elkin and Westley (1955) contend that the peer culture's influence upon adolescents is not nearly as great as has commonly been assumed and that teenagers are not compulsively independent and rejecting of adult values and desires. As a result of a study conducted by interviews with forty middle-class Montreal teenagers, they reported that although a well-defined and clearly identifiable youth culture does exist, its influence is less dominant than are the accepted patterns of family authority and guidance. Snyder (1966), who also posits the existence of a youth subculture, agrees with Elkin and Westley in noting that it has a number of different dimensions and is not typically characterized by conformity in values and behavior. There is some question as to whether the adolescent subculture is merely a reflection of the larger adult culture or whether it is characterized by separate norms that particularly emphasize fun, popularity, and conformity.

Peer-conformity generalizations must be conditioned by the fact of individual differences. It is not surprising to find varying degrees of peer conformity in adolescents, when compared with the norm, extending from absolute conformity to absolute nonconformity. There is also a further limiting factor to the peer-conformity generalization. Situations differ, and some situations, particularly for some adolescents, are less conformity-inducing than are others. The real questions to be answered here are those about the nature of the adolescent whose peer-conformity propensities are less than those of his fellows and about the kind of situation that tends to produce peer nonconformity. Typically, answers to such questions are to be found in the individual's attitudinal-personality structure, in his past experiences and level of maturity, as well as in the various surrounding environmental conditions.

Individual Differences and Peer Primacy

Perhaps most important of all in assessing the relative effects of peer society is the fact that individual differences involve not only the characteristics of the individual being dealt with, but also what he brings to the peer group in terms of past experience. An individual adolescent's proneness to conform to peer pressures is a matter of personality and status. When an adolescent enters peer society, he brings with him an experiential background provided by his previous upbringing, and also the personal idiosyncracies that make up his personality pattern.

Marston and Levine (1964), using a sample of college students, report that their subjects could be categorized as interaction-, task-, and self-oriented, and that their personal orientation determined the role they would assume in group relationships. Task-oriented persons tended to prefer friends whose orientation was centered around cultural and intellectual matters; self-oriented persons less frequently tended to be officers of extracurricular organizations; and interaction-oriented persons more frequently tended to belong to fraternities and sororities and were more apt to indulge in group discussions. Solomon (1961), in a study of 372 Michigan high school students, reports that in making decisions parents were often "surprisingly uninfluential," and while peers "exerted moderate influence," most influential of all were the individual child's "impulses" and "values." McGhee and Teevan (1967) report that high-need-affiliation high school students conform significantly more than do those whose need affiliation is less, while Tuddenham (1959) reported that lesser conformity is associated with higher status. Tuddenham (1959) also reports the same association with higher competence and higher education.

Individual differences in conformity behavior may also be a matter of stage of development. Piaget (1954) notes that social development, as manifested by learning the "rules of the game," follows an orderly sequence of stages that is curvilinear in order. The child is uninfluenced by rules at first, but gradually begins to learn and follow them until, by the time he reaches the eleventh or twelfth year, the rules are internalized and used pretty much completely. Following such internalization, Piaget sees the adolescent as creating and codifying many of his own rules, with a corresponding need to conform less than does the preadolescent or perhaps even the early adolescent, who has yet to internalize. Conformity in the sense used here is represented by behavior in accordance with social customs and norms. Following Piaget's line of reasoning, one would expect the adolescent to have erected defenses against conformity, which would make him less apt to conform to peer-society norms than would his preadolescent brother.

Costanzo and Shaw (1966), in a study using ninety-six subjects ranging in age from seven to twenty-one, confirmed the hypothesis that conformity to pressure from peers is a non-linear function of age. They write, "from the preadolescent to the adolescent period of development, the amount of conformity to ex-

ternal social pressure increases," whereas conformity decreases after adolescence and through early adulthood. Costanzo and Shaw's results are shown in Figure 54. There is some discrepancy in these findings as compared to Piaget's statement, yet considering the rather nebulous definitions of adolescence and national differences in the samples upon which the findings were based, it is likely that the differences are more apparent than real.

A study by Iscoe, Williams, and Harvey (1963), while it confirmed the findings of Costanzo and Shaw where girls are concerned, found a difference (although a nonsignificant one) between the sexes in ages of attainment of maximum conformity. For four age groups consisting of 256 males and females of both sexes (seven-, nine-, twelve-, and fifteen-year-olds) maximum conformity was attained at age twelve for girls as compared to age fifteen for boys. Two reasons might be considered for this discrepancy. One involves the later attainment of puberty in boys, which may be causal in conformity-behavior needs. Costanzo and Shaw write:

With the onset of pubescence, the child becomes acutely aware of his social peers and relies upon them for many of his external behavior patterns (i.e., ways of behaving, "code between buddies," clubs, gang age, etc.). Therefore, the child at the pubescent stage displays much uncertainty with his own judgment, and mirrors the behavior of his peers.

The other possibility is a boy's greater difficulty with self-concept.

This writer takes the position that in judging the likelihood of conformity one must consider self-concept status as well as chronological age and high prestige pressures. It might be hypothesized that the less established or secure the self-concept, the greater the need to conform. Hence, adolescents who are particularly conforming may well be those who are having difficulty with self-concept. Of course, this does not deny the influence of situational

Figure 54 *Mean Conformity as a Function of Age*

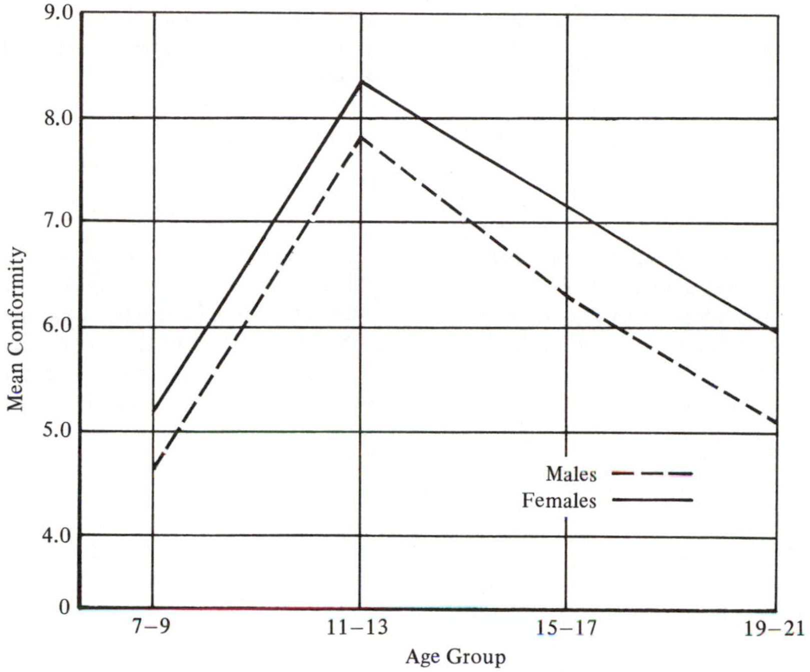

Source: Adapted from P. R. Costanzo and M. E. Shaw, "Conformity as a function of age level," *Child Development* 37 (1966): 967–975, fig. 1. Copyright © 1966 by The Society for Research in Child Development, Inc. Reprinted by permission of the publisher.

factors or of various kinds of individual differences other than self-concept status, age, and sex.

Situational Influences upon Conformity

Where peer-conformity generalizations are concerned, there is also the further limiting factor that situations differ and some situations induce less peer conformity than others. Brittain (1963) studied situation limitations with a sample of adolescent girls to whom he presented hypothetical dilemmas involving conflicting parent-peer expectations. He found that whether a given adolescent will be peer or parent conforming when confronted with parent-peer cross-pressures depended upon the alternatives given him. They tend to be parent conforming in making certain kinds of choices and peer conforming in making others.

No adolescent enters adolescent peer society without a previous history of family interaction, and it is fair to assume that the quality of this interaction may be the reason for the relatively greater or smaller social influence of the family in contrast to the adolescent peers. In a study of changes in family and peer orientation of children between the fourth and tenth grades, Bowerman and Kinch (1959) report that although as children become increasingly involved in peer activities they become increasingly oriented to the peer group, their actual acceptance of the norms and values of the peer group tends to be both situational and a question of individual differences. For example, according to Bowerman and Kinch, if the adolescent's family adjustment is good, his propensity to conform to peer demands, at least in some areas, is less than if the family adjustment is poor.

Hollander (1964) notes that the family and the peer group are both anchorages in the process of socialization and that together they are mediators of social forces. He writes that adolescents are not necessarily "unselective in their acceptance of peer standards as against those of parents," and adds, "it is not . . . a matter of the adolescent peer group having its own way . . . social influence is not an either/ or affair."

The presence of siblings is a factor often overlooked in assessing the family as an antecedent in the formation of an adolescent's peer-conformity propensities. In a study of college women, Schmuck (1963) reports that an individual's siblings affected the kind and amount of conformity he displayed in peer relationships. Girls with a sister displayed defiance more frequently than did those with a brother. Brittain (1966), using ninth- and tenth-grade girls, identified each girl as tending toward peer conformity or toward parent conformity by means of a structured paper-pencil instrument presenting a series of dilemmas that forced the respondents to make either peer or parent choices. In agreement with Schmuck's findings, he reports that for girls peer orientation tends to be a function of age and sex of siblings. Girls who had older sisters tended to be more peer conforming, while those with younger brothers were least peer conforming.

Further Situational Factors

When we speak of the influence of the peer group we must ask: Which peers? Obviously, some peers exert more influence than others. For example, Keislar (1959) reports that high-achievement peers were imitated significantly more frequently, hence were more influential, than were low-achievement peers. Of course, while we could say that the peer group, because of its younger age, common interests,

and need for mutual support, could be a general factor, some younger persons do not share common interests with some groups but do have a great deal in common with others. Some adolescents find that the only things that draw them to an available local peer group are the adult expectation that they will be drawn and their common age, coupled with the adult tendency to close some activities to them, leaving the peer group as the principal social outlet.

Further, in judging any given adolescent's conformity status, we must beware of the false positive. An adolescent may use the group to achieve an end, with the result that the conformity he displays may be simply a technique to manipulate the group for his own ends. Thus what appears to be conformity may actually be a planned use of the group for his own purpose. Such an adolescent conforms or does not conform, depending upon his perception of what the peer group can do for him if he appears to go along with them. Such use of peers may be cynical, but it can be very effective.

Sex Differences in Peer-Group Influences

There appear to be definite differences in the effects of the peer group upon boys as compared to girls. Boys in their striving for emancipation find especial support in the peer group, with the result that it earns their loyalty. But girls, whose cultural role provides less drive for emancipation, have less need for group support. Here we see a difference in the developmental tasks facing boys and girls. The female adolescent needs to develop interpersonal skills and find love. In contrast, the male adolescent needs to accept the cultural stereotype of achievement if he is to attain achievement and independence, thus meeting cultural expectations. Here the girl can find that the best-friend relationship in the smaller group context serves her purposes as adequately as would the more impersonal large-group constellation, in fact more adequately, since the interpersonal relationships in the smaller groupings can be closer. As Douvan and Gold

(1966) note: "The two sex groups use social relationships differently to support and express ... central concerns."

Summary

An adolescent normally places great importance upon his interpersonal relationships, particularly when his peers are involved. However, his inexperience and limited background lead to complications as he attempts to devise and implement a social role.

The developing individual moves from an early egocentricity toward a growing interest in others. Such progress is characterized by an ever-widening circle of acquaintances and social experiences that give rise to new interests, values, and attitudes. But this process is gradual. As late as preadolescence, the child, while typically interacting vigorously with his fellows, is doing so on a highly impersonal self-centered basis in a same-sex format. Friendships are less important and fluctuate more extensively than in adolescence. Puberty introduces greater personal interest in and acceptance of others, especially those of the opposite sex. During adolescence, building upon the previously acquired basics of social behavior, the child can be more interpersonally effective. In adolescence there is a de-emphasis of the same-sex crowd of preadolescence in favor of pairings in which two individuals have an opportunity to know each other.

The adolescent peer group provides an arena for the exercise of the competence so highly admired by adolescents. Activities become more complicated, and different abilities come into their own as social roles become more differentiated. Adolescent groups tend to be smaller than those of the preceding years, and the individual's ability (or lack of it) to cope with his various social roles becomes more obvious. Roles become more active, and the opinions of others become increasingly important in social interaction. The problem of lack of experience in what are increasingly becoming adultlike situations remains.

Problems of role definition and differentiation can become anxiety producing as social situations present a threat to self-esteem. Adolescents tend to conform to the opinions, activities, and appearance of other adolescents. Such conformity leads to a de-emphasis of the norms of the family and the adult world, particularly as the peer group is cohesive. Yet there are limits to the primacy of the peer group and the conformity it can demand. Teenagers seem not to be compulsively independent and rejecting of adult values and desires, and while a youth subculture does exist, its influence is often less dominant than are accepted patterns of authority and guidance. The amount of conformity tends to be situational and a matter of individual differences. The quality of previous family interaction is important in determining a given adolescent's conformity status. By the time he becomes an adolescent a child may have learned to erect defenses against conformity and to have become relatively selective in his conforming behavior, to the point where conformity to pressure from peers is a nonlinear function of age. In any event, in judging the likelihood of conformity in any adolescent, it would be well to consider self-concept status as well as chronological age and high prestige pressures.

Youth workers who wish to help adolescents with their social development and acceptance problems should do so only after careful analysis of the situation and its needs, and then only on the basis of a positive program. It is a mistake to criticize without offering constructive remedial suggestions. It is equally a mistake to criticize before the individual concerned is psychologically ready to receive the criticism.

The group role is a means whereby an adolescent may boost his ego, a necessary state of affairs, since the typical adolescent's changing environment and lack of experience tend to make him feel insecure. The peer group becomes a means of gaining security and anchorage. Under the circumstances, it is little wonder that acceptance is important and rejection upsetting or even traumatic. When reality is not satisfying, the adolescent tends to seek recourse in daydreams or fantasy. Daydreaming, as a retreat from reality and a substitute for experience, may become harmful if carried to extremes. On the other hand, daydreaming is not an atypical situation in adolescence and if not carried to extremes tends to be harmless. Daydreaming as a habitual substitute for experience or effort, or as a retreat, may have unfortunate implications.

Adolescents are continually interested in questions pertaining to sex and heterosexual relations. Sources of information are sketchy, and in the realm of sex information particularly the adolescent usually has to seek the inaccurate knowledge of his contemporaries. Here parents and youth authorities have a responsibility they often do not meet.

The adolescent will frequently idealize an older person, sometimes one in his own peer group, sometimes one outside it. If the idealized person is outside the peer group, friction often develops, particularly if the adolescent tries to emulate his ideal or to impose him on the peer group.

On the whole, the influence of the peer group is good in that it offers security and an opportunity to learn, and promotes emancipation. It may have bad effects since it is influential enough to jell bad habits and attitudes. It may accelerate psychological weaning unduly and set up unfortunate child-parent conflicts. Nonacceptance in the peer group may have extremely bad emotional effects, which present serious problems for children who lack the attributes for acceptance.

An adolescent who is self-centered finds nonacceptance by a given peer group difficult to adjust to. Acceptance in one group often becomes so important that acceptance by other groups is rejected even when offered. The more insecure the individual, the more far-reaching the rebuff. This may lead to withdrawal and retreat from reality, although it may occasionally inspire an individual to increased effort. Sometimes a person acceptable to his peers at one stage of his development is unable to keep pace with developmental

changes in his age-mates' interests and attitudes, and continues his formerly accepted behavior, only to find that it has become unacceptable to more mature individuals. Such a person may seek recourse to younger persons with whom his behavior will be acceptable. However, long-continued association with younger children makes for unfortunate habits, difficult to relinquish.

Some adolescents do not participate in peer activities because they do not wish to do so; they may have matured rapidly and gained considerable maturity of insight. In terms of true later adjustment, these people tend to be unfortunate. There is always the possibility that lack of interest may be a pose to cover fear, failure, or inexperience. Some adolescents miss peer participation because they have to work or are geographically isolated.

The adolescent faces many pressures to participate actively in peer society and to conform to peer-group examples and pressures. These include cultural expectations that peer-group affiliation is both normal and beneficial and that peer nonparticipation is maladjustive and undesirable. American adults are very conscious of their children's social behavior and acceptability, to the point of incorporating "soial adjustment" as a necessary and meaningful objective of education. They are also very conscious of the teenager as a sort of corporate entity and have so promoted this concept that the adolescent is offered a focal point of solidarity for expression and mutual reinforcement.

A strong source of the influence of the peer group is its accepting stance in various matters important to adolescents, in comparison to the more nonaccepting attitudes of adults.

A major question in understanding adolescents concerns the extent to which the influence of the peer group overrides that of other factors in the adolescent's life. Earlier research seemed to indicate the relative primacy of the peer group, but later investigations have indicated that peer-group primacy statements must be limited by both situational and individual difference factors. Therefore, ignoring conditioning factors in assessing peer-group influence leads to an oversimplification of the nature and function of the adolescent subculture.

Where individual differences are concerned, any given adolescent's proneness to conform to peer pressures is a matter of personality and status. There is also the matter of the individual's stage of progress through the developmental sequence of his first twenty years. Conformity to pressure from peers seems to be a nonlinear function of age. Throughout preadolescence the amount of conformity to external social pressure increases, but with the advent of puberty it begins to decrease.

Further, in judging the likelihood of conformity, one must also take into consideration the self-concept status.

Where situational factors are concerned, the availability of alternatives is an important conformity-determining factor, as is the quality and quantity of previous parent-child interaction. The better a child's adjustment to his family is, the less is his susceptibility to peer pressures. The presence of siblings is also important. Another factor with a bearing upon conformity is socioeconomic status.

References

Ausubel, D. P. *Theory and problems of child development.* New York: Grune and Stratton, 1958.

Bauer, E. J. Student peer groups and academic development. *College Student Survey* 1 (1967): 22–31.

Berenda, R. W. The influence of the group on the judgments of children. New York: King's Crown Press, 1950.

Brittain, C. V. Adolescent choices and parent-peer cross-pressures. *American Sociological Review* 28 (1963): 385–391.

Brittain, C. V. Age and sex of siblings and conformity toward parents versus peers in adolescence. *Child Development* 37 (1966): 709–714.

Bowerman, C. E., and Kinch, J. W. Changes in family and peer orientation of children between the fourth and tenth grades. *Social Forces* 37 (1959): 206–211.

Bronfenbrener, U. Soviet methods of character education: Some implication for research. *American Psychologist* 17 (1962): 550–564.

Coleman, J. *Social climates in high school.* Publication no. OE33016. Washington, D.C.: Dept. of Health, Education, and Welfare, 1961.

Costanzo, P. R., and Shaw, M. E. Conformity as a function of age level. *Child Development* 37 (1966): 967–975.

Douvan, E., and Gold, M. Modal patterns in American adolescence. In Hoffman, L. W., and Hoffman, M. L., eds., *Review of child development research*, vol. 2, pp. 469–528. New York: Russell Sage Foundation, 1966.

Elkin, F., and Westley, W. A. The myth of adolescent culture. *American Sociological Review* 20 (1955): 680–684.

Ellis, R. A., and Lane, W. C. Social mobility and social isolation: A test of Sorokin's dissociative hypothesis. *American Sociological Review* 32 (1967): 237–253.

Friedenberg, E. Z. *The vanishing adolescent.* Boston: Beacon Press, 1959.

Gellert, E. Stability and fluctuation in the power relationships of young children. *Journal of Abnormal and Social Psychology* 62 (1961): 8–15.

Gerard, H. B. Some determinants of self-evaluation. *Journal of Abnormal and Social Psychology* 62 (1961): 288–293.

Gordon, C. W. The role of the teacher in the social structure of the high school. *Journal of Educational Sociology* 29 (1955): 21–29.

Goslin, D. A. Accuracy of self perception and acceptance. *Sociometry* 25 (1962): 283–296.

Gottlieb, D.; Reeves, J.; and ten Houten, W. D. *The emergence of youth societies.* New York: Free Press, 1966.

Hollander, E. P. Individuality and social identity: Extra-familial agents of social influence on children. *Final Report to the National Institute of Child Health and Human Development*, Grant HD00887. Buffalo: Dept. of Psychology, State University of New York, 1964.

Hunt, R. G., and Synnerdale, V. Social influences among kindergarten children. *Sociology and Social Research* 43 (1959): 171–174.

Iannaccaro, E. Studio dei modi di reasione alla frustrazione in funzione di certe variabili familari in un gruppo di adolescenti. *Contributi dell'Instituto di Psicologia* no. 25 (1962) : 374–387.

Iscoe, I.; Williams, M.; and Harvey, J. Modification of children's judgments by a simulated group technique: A normative developmental study. *Child Development* 34 (1963) : 963–978.

Jones, E. E.; Gergen, K. J.; and Davis, K. E. Some determinants of reactions to being approved or disapproved as a person. *Psychological Monographs*, no. 521, 76, no. 2 (1962).

Jones, E. E., and Thibaut, J. W. Interaction goals as bases of influence in interpersonal perception. In Taguiri, R., and Petrullo, L. eds., *Person perception and interpersonal behavior*, pp. 151–179. Stanford: Stanford University Press, 1958.

Keislar, E. R. Experimental development of "like" and "dislike" of others among adolescent girls. *Child Development* 32 (1961) : 59–66.

McGhee, P. E., and Teevan, R. C. Conformity behavior and need for affiliation. *Journal of Social Psychology* 72 (1967) : 117–121.

Marston, A. R., and Levine, E. M. Interaction patterns in a college population. *Journal of Social Psychology* 62 (1964) : 149–154.

Piaget, J. *The moral judgment of the child.* New York: Harcourt, Brace, 1932 (Basic Books edition, 1954).

Reese, H. W. Relationship between self acceptance and sociometric choices. *Journal of Abnormal and Social Psychology* 62 (1961) : 472–474.

Rivlin, L. G. Creativity and the self-attitudes of sociability of high school students. *Journal of Educational Psychology* 50 (1959) : 147–152.

Rosen, S.; Levinger, G.; and Lippitt, R. Desired change in self and others as a function of resource ownership. *Human Relations* 13 (1960) : 187–193.

Schmuck, R. Sex of siblings, birth order position, and female dispositions to conform in two-child families. *Child Development* 64 (1963) : 913–918.

Schwartz, G., and Merten, D. The language of adolescence: An anthropological approach to the youth culture. *American Journal of Sociology* 72 (1967) : 453–468.

Skorepa, C. A.; Horrocks, J. E.; and Thompson, G. G. A study of friendship fluctuations of college students. *Journal of Genetic Psychology* 102 (1963) : 151–157.

Smucker, B., and Creekmore, A. M. Adolescents' clothing conformity, awareness and peer acceptance. *Home Economics Research Journal* 1 (1972) : 92–97.

Snyder, E. E. Socioeconomic variations, values, and social participation among high school students. *Journal of Marriage and the Family* 28 (1966) : 174–176.

Solomon, D. Adolescents' decisions: A comparison of influence from parents with that of other sources. *Marriage and Family Living* 23 (1961) : 393–395.

Tuddenham, R. D. Correlates of yielding to a distorted group norm. *Journal of Personality* 27 (1959) : 272–284.

Werdelin, I. Teacher ratings, peer ratings, and self-ratings. *Educational Psychology Inter.* 11 (1966) : 1–19.

Suggested Readings

Allaman, J. D.; Joyce, C. S.; and Crandall, V. The antecedents of social desirability response tendencies of children and young adults. *Child Development* 43 (1972) : 1135–1160.

Berman, A. L. Social schemas: An investigation of age and socialization variables. *Psychological Reports* 28 (1971) : 343–348.

Clausen, J. A. The organism and socialization. *Journal of Health and Social Behavior* 8 (1967) : 243–252.

Estes, B. W., and Rush, D. Social schemas: A developmental study. *Journal of Psychology* 78 (1971) : 119–123.

Feffer, M. Developmental analysis of interpersonal behavior. *Psychological Review* 77 (1970) : 197–214.

Feldman, R. A. Normative integration, alienation and conformity in adolescent groups. *Adolescence* 7 (1972) : 327–341.

Gecas, V.; Thomas D. L.; and Weigert, A. S. Social identities in Anglo and Latin adolescents. *Social Forces* 51 (1973) : 477–484.

Gough, H. G. Scoring high on an index of social maturity. *Journal of Abnormal Psychology* 77 (1971) : 236–241.

Greenberger, E., and Sorenson, A. B. Toward a concept of psychosocial maturity. *Center for Social Organization of the Schools Report*, no.

108. Baltimore: Johns Hopkins University, 1971.

Harper, D. G. The reliability of measures of sociometric acceptance and rejection. *Sociometry* 31 (1968) : 219–227.

Helper, M. M. Message preferences: An approach to the assessment of interpersonal standards. *Journal of Projective Techniques and Personality Assessment* 34 (1970) : 64–70.

Insel, P., and Wilson, G. D. Measuring social attitudes in children. *British Journal of Social and Clinical Psychology* 10 (1971) : 84–86.

Jurovsky, A. The functionality of interpersonal proximity in adolescents. *European Journal of Social Psychology* 1 (1971) : 95–96.

Kolsin, S.; Koslim, B.; Pargament, R.; and Bird, H. Children's social distance constructs: A developmental study. *Proceedings of the Annual Convention of the American Psychological Association* 6 (1971) : 151–152.

Levin, A. Y.; Dubno, P.; and Akula, W. G. Face-to-face interaction in the peer nomination process. *Journal of Applied Psychology* 55 (1971) : 495–497.

Mehrabian, A., and Ksionzky, A. Categories of social behavior. *Comparative Group Studies* 3 (1972) : 425–436.

Nias, D. K. The structuring of social attitudes of children. *Child Development* 43 (1972) : 211–219.

Poveda, T. G. A perspective on adolescent social relations. *Psychiatry, Washington, D.C.* 35 (1972) : 32–47.

Powell, E. R., and Wilson, C. S. Peer concept and sociometric analysis of a small group. *Psychological Reports* 25 (1969) : 452–454.

Rockway, A. M. Cognitive factors in adolescent person perception development. *Developmental Psychology* 1 (1969) : 630.

Rodgers, R. R.; Bronfenbrener, M.; and Devereux, E. C. Standards of social behavior among school children in four cultures. *International Journal of Psychology* 3 (1968) : 31–41.

Sermat, V. Is game behavior related to behavior in other interpersonal situations. *Journal of Personality and Social Psychology* 16 (1970) : 92–109.

Smith, H. W. Some developmental interpersonal dynamics through childhood. *American Sociological Review* 38, (1973) : 543–552.

Teichman, Y. Emotional arousal and affiliation. *Journal of Experimental Social Psychology* 9 (1973) : 591–605.

Tognoli, J., and Keisner, R. Gain and loss of esteem as determinants of interpersonal attraction. *Journal of Personality and Social Psychology* 23 (1972) : 201–204.

Chapter Twenty-four

Adolescent Groups and Group Membership

It has been seen that the peer group is, within limitations, one of the great motivating forces of adolescence. An adolescent's relationship to his peers and his participation in their activities is usually one of the most important things in his life. His ego involvement is often such that exclusion can seem a major tragedy, while acceptance can bring feelings of security and happiness. Under the circumstances, it is appropriate to consider the make-up and nature of the adolescent peer group.

The Study of the Group

Since the early 1900s American psychologists and sociologists have shown much interest in children's group behavior and peer relationships. Indicative of the interest is the large amount of research accomplished over these years on children's interpersonal behavior and on the attributes of their formal and informal groups. As a matter of fact, the importance of group membership and adjustive social behavior designed to meet expected social norms has become a preoccupation of American culture, to the point where many consider it an obsession. For instance, educators and parents have implemented this preoccupation in the American educational system to such an extent that group membership and cooperation, teamwork, and other like matters have become a major concern of both the curricular and extracurricular programs of the schools. Some years ago, in an inquiry into the objectives of education in the state of New York, it was explicitly stated that the inculcation of social competence was a major aim of the New York state educational system. The situation in New York and elsewhere, despite occasional side excursions inspired by such events as Sputnik, has remained essentially the same in the intervening years since the New York report was made.[1] To be socially "out" is held by many to be more unfortunate than to be intellectually "out." Novels such as Sinclair Lewis's *Babbitt* are insightful discussions of the American propensity—and their relevancy extends far beyond the time in which they were written. Under the circumstances, it is not strange to find the culture's preoccupation reflected in its social scientists' research activities. In any event, whether one holds the culture's social-adjustment interest to be good or bad, social behavior of children is a valid and fruitful area of scientific inquiry.

As early as 1904 Terman reported on suggestibility in children and, in experimentally constituted groups, examined attributes of stability and of leadership. In 1909 Cooley wrote: "The general fact is that children, especially boys after their twelfth year, live in fellowships in which their sympathy, ambition and honor are engaged even more often than they are in the family."

Interest mounted in the years following Cooley's statement, but in the 1930s the pace, as represented by the research studies ac-

[1]Obviously, the inculcation of social competence is not the only objective of the schools, particularly in an age presenting so many technical innovations and demands. It is nevertheless a major and ubiquitous objective.

complished, really quickened. The 1930s also saw substantial improvements in data-collection techniques as well as advances in the sophistication of theory underlying group research. The 1940s brought a decrease in the amount of research on children's groups, but the 1950s and 1960s saw a return to the quantity produced in the 1930s, a trend which has continued into the 1970s. However, after a certain amount of research has been accomplished in a given area, further efforts are apt to reach a point of diminishing returns or perhaps to produce a plateau of some duration before a new breakthrough occurs. Such seems to be the present situation in children's group research. The research produced in the period following 1950 has depended heavily upon previous research and, despite its quantity, has added relatively little to already existing information and theory. In his discussion of childhood peer-relationship research initiated after 1940, Campbell (1964) writes:

The debt of such research to earlier work is frequently quite evident: it is apparent in definition of research problems, in methods employed, and in conceptualization and theory underlying research. Research and theory since 1940 have been not so much new as they have represented a refinement and an extension of [the] earlier period.

The Nature of the Group

Any group, except as a historical notation or matter of record, has no material existence apart from the individuals who compose it. Hence, the psychology of the group must be approached through the common psychology of its members. This writer previously noted (1966):

The group is the artifact, and its individual members with their human motives and behavior are the group's composers and creators. Increase in the size of the group adds only problems of logistics and communication. It adds nothing else of basic importance. Yet, having emphasized this truth, we must go on to observe that man is shaped and influenced by his context, and as a member of a group he does not act alone. He is as much

influenced by the group consensus as by his own perception. We may even say that the group consensus becomes the individual's perception, and he is no longer free to test reality. But, though these appear paradoxical elements, the individual still acts as an individual in the light of what the group consensus has taught him. His individual psychology is operative even as he responds to the influence of his group, but he is chained by the point of view and reinforcements of his culture.

Although the group can be nothing more than the joint efforts and relationships of those who compose it, such conjoining produces a situation that becomes more than the mere summing of each member's personal idiosyncrasies. At times a group seems to have a life of its own, and the adolescent peer-group member appears, at least superficially, a different person in his association with the group than he is when away from it.

Essentially, we witness in the group's behavior an interaction effect among its members' personalities, and since most groups have an implicit if not explicit purpose, the group gives a direction and focus to the behavior it arouses and sponsors. People are not really different in a group situation, they are simply behaving in a permissive—or restrictive— atmosphere that encourages or inhibits aspects of personality and attitudes already present. Without doubt, the group stimulates its members, offers them social facilitation, and often provides a stage upon which they can act out their aggressions and test their self-concepts. But the group does not have the same effects upon all its members. Nothing about the group cancels out the fact of individual differences. And by the same token, we cannot generalize from one adolescent group to another with complete confidence, for groups differ among themselves just as much as do the individuals who compose them. However, we can predict with some accuracy a group's future behavior if we know enough about its past activities. What a group has done is a strong determiner of what it will do.

Actual participation in a group's activities does not mean that an adolescent either belongs to or is accepted by the group. One may be a participant without being psychologically a member. To be really a member of a group is a two-way street involving, on the one hand, acceptance by the members and, on the other, an emotional sense of belonging. To be a participant without really being accepted may be emotionally stressful for the adolescent who really wants to belong, and it may elicit from him various kinds of defensive or propitiating behavior that makes him seem quite "unlike himself." Adults are sometimes deceived by an adolescent's group participation into believing that he is actually an accepted group member.

The foregoing discussion shows that with all the permutations and combinations of interaction and personal individual differences involved, all adolescent peer groups cannot be alike. And different groups exist for different reasons. In a given school, institution, or neighborhood there are many groups of one kind or another. To work adequately with such groups, the youth worker must be able to define the nature of the adolescent group he is dealing with, in order to adapt his methods and techniques to that particular group.

Adolescent groups may be ephemeral, or they may be long-lived with considerable continuity and vitality of program and activity. They may have considerable internal "we" feeling and group cohesiveness, or they may lack these qualities and seem to exist mainly to promote the members' individual efforts. Such a group may be said to exist on an "I" basis, with every member seeking only his own interests; he would be perfectly willing to exploit or abandon the group, whichever appeared best to promote his own ends. Whether a group is primarily "I" or "we," and whether or not it possesses continuity and vitality, depends upon its purposes, the members' acceptance of the purposes, the reasons and methods that called the group into being, the needs of the individual members and the extent to which the group serves those needs, and finally, the methods of control exercised by the group's own leaders as well as those exercised by its various adult supervisors, if there are any.

The Classification of Groups

When we consider an adolescent group or, for that matter, any group, we have to ask ourselves several questions. First, what is the group trying to achieve? Is it embarked upon the attainment of some specific task? Is it primarily concerned with personal relationships among its members? Second, in what setting does it function? Third, what are its relationships to adults and to other adolescent groups? Fourth, what is its structured organization, its size, and its affiliations? Is it formal or informal, a separate entity or a subunit of a larger whole? Does it have a leader, did he emerge, or was he appointed or elected, and what is his role? Fifth, what are the interpersonal relationships of its members, and how do they conceive of the group? What is its level of cohesion? Sixth, of what kinds of people is the group composed? What are their motivations and backgrounds? How old are the members, and what has been their previous socialization experience? Seventh, how long has the group existed, how often does it meet, and in what stage of development is it? And eighth, what alternative groups do its members have access to?

Most classifications of groups are not comprehensive enough to include all the above factors. Those using a standard group classification have to add the missing elements they believe will best serve their purpose. However, the answers to the eight questions proposed are all significant in any thoroughgoing interpretation of a group and its activities.

Groupings of individuals may be classified as *pairs*, as *primary groups*, as *extended primary groups*, or as *secondary groups*. *Pairs*—which include such intimate groupings as mother and child, husband and wife, lover and sweetheart, and two close friends—may be categorized as unisexual or heterosexual, depending on whether both members of the pair are of the same or of different sex. The *primary group*, the most typical of all adolescent groupings, is characterized by face-to-face association, small numbers, unspecialized purpose, comparative intimacy, and relative permanence. The home, the spontaneous play group, and the old-fashioned neighborhood group are examples.

The *extended primary group* is an organized face-to-face intimate group, limited in some degree by special purpose and by the fact of organization. Boy Scout troops, college fraternities and sororities, luncheon clubs, and so on are examples. They have many of the characteristics of primary groups and in fact may perform many of the functions of primary groups, yet organization and the limitations of special purpose give them some of the characteristics of secondary groups. *Secondary groups* are groups wholly lacking in intimacy of association and usually in most of the other primary and extended primary-group characteristics. Crowds and assemblages (audiences and mobs), communities, corporations, nations, as well as attention, interest, and purpose groups are examples.

In the more formal atmosphere of the secondary and extended primary groups, the pattern of interpersonal relations is predetermined. In the formal group the individual's role is largely defined as the group is guided along previously established lines. In the informal atmosphere of the intimate pair and primary groups the members' individual characteristics determine the group's structure. In such a setting a member's role is dependent to a greater degree upon group interactions.

This classification implies that any individual is simultaneously a member of a great many different groups of varying degrees of importance to him, and that in each he may play a good many different roles. But for the adolescent the really important groups, psychologically, are the first three, the more intimate face-to-face personal association groups that form an integral functioning part of his everyday life. In discussing adolescent primary groups, Phelps and Horrocks (1958) write:

A large portion of adolescent social life is organized around small informal groups. Such groups are the providing ground for the teen-ager's widening perception of his social role and the exploration of techniques to implement that role. The informal group plays a much more important part in the life of the adolescent than do formally organized groups and may be thought of as a focal area of experience in the process of coming of age. Observation of informal adolescent groups leads to the conclusion that while the group is more or less ephemeral in its membership and continuity it does center around certain commonalities possessed by its members. Membership is usually exclusive in that some youth are excluded or are made to feel uncomfortable when participating in the group's activities. An understanding of adolescent behavior would be advanced by an analysis of the kinds of activities and attitudes important in the formation and perpetuation of such groups with particular reference to those things which contrast one group to another as well as to the commonalities which bind them all together as part of the larger adolescent age peer society.

In their study of conformity and deviation in adolescence, Sherif and Sherif (1964) used the term *reference group* and described it as "the group with which the individual identifies or aspires to belong," thus viewing the group in terms of the attitudes of a member or prospective member rather than in terms of structure. Also ignoring structure, Lewin and Lippitt (1938, 1939) classified groups in terms of their psychological atmosphere and method of procedure when they set up an experiment on the comparative influence of groups proceeding autocratically, democratically, and in an atmosphere of laissez faire.

It should be remembered that any group must function in an environment and that the environment has much to do with shaping and directing the nature of the group and setting its direction and limitations. Two given quasi-primary groups—for example, two troops of Boy Scouts—may be entirely different due to the opportunities the milieu offers or withholds for group participation to the activity facilitation, and to the need for internal loyalty.

Youth agencies tend to classify groups in terms of function or habitat, such as a recreation group, an older boys' group, and so on. A more commonly used classification is that of the gang, the clique, and the crowd. The last two classifications seem particularly meaningful because rather specific developmental social differences separate them.

Developmental Stages of Groups

Groups appear to develop in a series of identifiable stages over their existence, from inception until breakup. Tuckman (1965) has proposed four developmental stages through which groups pass, unless they are terminated before they reach the fourth stage. Tuckman's first stage occurs while the group is forming and consists of a period of orientation accomplished primarily through testing. During this time the boundaries of interpersonal and task behaviors are identified, and identity relationships with leaders and with other members are established. In the adolescent group this stage is an opportunity for each member to endeavor to establish himself in terms of his self-concept and, incidentally, to test the validity of that concept against reality. Gradually, roles are defined, alliances and interrelationships are roughed out. This is a crucial time for each member, because initial impressions held by peers are those most likely to shape subsequent actions. The child who enters a new group with a background of previous successful socialization and a well-formulated self-concept is at a decided advantage. Reese (1966) reports that acceptance by peers is definitely associated with more positive self-oriented attitudes.

Tuckman's second developmental stage is one "characterized by conflict and polarization around interpersonal issues, with concomitant emotional responding in the task sphere." He speaks of this phase as a period of "storming" and notes the background of resistance to group influence and task requirement. For the adolescent, it is a time of resistance to an unsatisfactory role that may have been allocated to him and a time when his reality testing may lead to self-concept modification. It is also a time when surrender of one's own inclinations

for those of the group is resisted. In some cases the emancipation-seeking youth feels that the group is becoming a kind of suppressing parent figure. If the group has a specific task to achieve, imposed from without, this is also a time of resistance to the need to "get on with the job."

During the third stage, according to Tuckman, resistance is overcome, cohesiveness develops, the group roles are adjusted to, and new standards evolve. This is the period of "norming," and the group assumes an identity mutually bolstering to all its members. It is during this stage that most adults make their interpretation of adolescent groups as they see the group presenting to the outer world the attributes of the self-satisfied in-group. Actually, all is not as smooth as it may appear, in that problems of definition and of growing accustomed to allotted roles remain.

Tuckman calls the fourth and final stage that of performance and sees it as a time when "interpersonal structure becomes the tool of task activities." During this stage, structural and role issues have been pretty well resolved, to the point that they support the group's endeavors. In a real sense the group is becoming more relaxed as it finds security in its continuity. Greater role flexibility is even possible. But within this solidification of structure of the adolescent group are the seeds of the group's own destruction, for the group as a unit tends to be less adaptive to new departures at a time when the adolescents who compose the group are changing so rapidly. The result is a tendency to break away from the group, or to regress back to the second stage as the group is reformulated.

Tuckman (1965) points out that his model of group development is quite in accord with developmental theory generally, particularly as it fits the developmental sequence of human behavior, as a child moves from his earliest years into those of maturity. For example, in Tuckman's first stage the group is new and therefore unsure and uncertain, with a corresponding need to depend upon an authority figure. This state is analagous to that of infancy and that of the young child first encountering rules. In the second stage the group is no longer new, and its members are reacting emotionally and negatively both to the group as such and to the tasks it is imposing. Tuckman draws an analogy between the second stage and that of the young child who, having passed through an obedient stage, now exhibits rebelliousness. In the third stage the group members, having overcome their emotionality, are now more sensitive to one another or more willing to cooperate. This third stage is mirrored in a child's personal development as he proceeds through the middle period of socialization. And finally, in the fourth stage, since the group has become functional, interpersonal problems are not an issue as the group attempts a realistic appraisal and solution of the tasks before it. In the personal development sequence such "marriage to reality" and interdependence are characteristic of the mature human being.

The Clique

Following their twelfth year, it becomes common to hear children speak of "our crowd" or "our set." This is the period of the clique, which may be defined as a small participation group of intimately interacting associates who agree upon exclusion of others from their group and who possess similar characteristics of social status and interests. Laponska (1962), in an analysis of 487 essays written by high school boys and girls, reports the gradual displacement over the high school years of separatism, antagonism, and egoism, and their replacement by cliques.

Cliques bring together children who are similar in background, skills, values, and attitudes. While individual friendships may transcend the restriction of similarity, studies or discussions, such as Havighurst et al. (1962), Coleman (1961), and Hollingshead (1949), have indicated that cliques are generally composed of individuals from the same social class. Hollingshead (1949) notes that:

The clique is integrated around two types of factors: first a commonly shared set of likes and dislikes which tie the members together and which separate them from other groups; and second, standing in the community or class. Although members of different cliques may be enemies in a social sense, they commonly work together when an issue involving class interests is at stake.

The unified front of rival fraternities or sororities on a college campus is a case in point. Thus, the clique may sometimes be a large group with which there is identification but not very much association, although ordinarily the clique is a more highly personal unit. However, Spaulding (1966) notes that strong attachment to primary and quasi-primary groups carries over into a stronger attachment to larger groupings or organizations to which the primary groups are attached or with which they are associated.

Most cliques are composed of small groups consisting of dyads, triads, or sextets held together by the personal satisfactions that the members gain from one another's company. Clique members stand in groups of two or three outside a classroom and just talk. They wait together for the bus, do things together, and on the whole seem to find their justification in one another's presence and small talk. While the clique is a definite group with a definite code, and common opinions and tastes, these matters are never formulated, and there is seldom any semblance of organization. If for some reason they formally organize, the organization soon disintegrates. The clique forms a situation in which the adolescent may relax and be someone. There is no way of applying for membership—a clique member may bring around a friend who becomes gradually accepted, but just as often the prospective addition fails to be accepted. Teachers or parents may punish a member of the clique, order him to stay away, tell him the other members of the group are not good for him, but it will rarely make any difference—the group will still get together. A clique will often set a pattern for achievement, in that a member who exceeds the group's pattern will find himself talked down, while if he fails to come up to the group's level, it is made clear that he must conform. Thus, where school behavior is concerned, a clique may be either a positive or a negative influence. Friendship cliques form an important device for adjustment to high school. The clique helps adolescents in solving practical problems, in sifting and clarifying ideas, and in gaining status.

Hollingshead (1949), in his study of 259 cliques in Elmtown, notes that they may be divided into three clique types on the basis of function: school, recreational, and institutional. In discussing the three types he writes:

School cliques are composed of either boys or girls who associate with each other around the school. Their membership can be seen between class periods during the last quarter hour of the lunch hour, or immediately after school, participating in the activity of the moment. There are 106 school cliques which have from two to nine members for boys, two to twelve for girls; the modal size for both sexes is five members. Recreational cliques function in various situations away from school. Their members are only slightly different from the school cliques, but in a typical recreation clique some members of the school clique are missing. The place of the missing boy or girl may be taken by a person who belongs to another school clique, but for recreational purposes this person participates with a clique with which he does not associate around school. Sometimes a large school clique splits into two recreational cliques. They range in size from two to seven members and have a modal membership of four for both the boys and the girls. Institutional cliques are seen in specific nonschool situations such as Sunday School, young people's meetings at the churches, Boy Scouts, and Camp Fire Girls. Thirty-three institutional cliques are known to exist, thirteen of boys, and twenty of girls. They are smaller than the others, ranging from two to five members each. The modal membership is three for the boys and four for the girls.

Cliques tend to set barriers to meet particular situations. They may be uni- or bisexual, formal or informal, age graded or not, but there is usually a strong emotional involvement. On the emotional side, cliques are characterized by the presence of close friendships and willingness to render mutual assistance, and by cohesiveness in the presence of outsiders.

Some writers in the field of adolescence use the term *crowd*, while others do not. For those who do not, *clique* is used as an all-inclusive term. Those who use the term *crowd* refer to a large clique or to a more or less loosely united group of cliques. *Crowd*, used in the sense of an expanded clique or a series of cliques, is a useful term that describes adequately certain aspects of larger adolescent group behavior. In general, the heterosexual crowd is a development of adolescence, and together with boy-girl pairs, is characteristic of late adolescence and early maturity.

The Activities of Clique and Crowd

We have described adolescent peer-group relationships, discussed the relative influence of adolescent peer society, and outlined the different forms assumed by adolescent groups. But we must go a step further. Obviously the life of any group must occur in an environmental context that cannot but help limit, control, or facilitate what takes place. Thus, an understanding of the dynamics of any adolescent group depends upon a knowledge of the conditioning situational factors involved. Campbell (1964) lists five situational factors that influence both group and individual functioning: (1) the actual physical setting and structure of the environment, (2) the conditions obtaining in the physical setting, (3) the clarity of the members' perception of what the group is trying to do, (4) the reward structure the group provides, and (5) the group's social structure. When confronted with the activities of an adolescent crowd or clique, the most helpful initial step is to assess the clique in terms of its environment and membership before endeavoring to understand or forecast its behavior.

A surprisingly large amount of the adolescent's social and recreational life is built around the local high school athletic contests—football in the fall and basketball or hockey in the winter are the most popular sports with the spectator-adolescents; the games offer an opportunity to cheer the team (and, incidentally, to see them play), and also an opportunity in the winter to be away from home in the company of one's peers. The home games are good dating and party opportunities; also, for those who are "too young" or not acceptable to (or even afraid of) the opposite sex, there is the possibility of attending in unisexual pairs or groups. Considerable license is allowed after the game, and the adolescents tend to wander about town in a gala mood, particularly following a victory. The local soda fountains teem; there is fast driving along local roads and a fair amount of parked-car petting or necking (adolescents have new names for this activity at frequent intervals—*smooching, making out*, and so forth—and adolescent bull sessions include much discussion as to the exact areal limitations of the word used). In some communities, adults contribute to the general frenzy and the town becomes known as a football or a basketball town.

But even in communities where athletics are not the major focus of attention, adolescent group life proceeds apace. After school, from about three to five, the soda fountains nearest the high school are fairly crowded with groups of girls, pairs of girls, a boy-girl pair on a Coke date (Coca-Cola is the most popular beverage), and mixed groups of boys and girls. There are also occasional solitary boys, but not often groups of boys. Here the events and personalities of the school day are discussed, and the boys indulge in considerable horseplay. Many of the girls take packages of cigarettes from their purses and puff furiously—a circumstance that would horrify many of their parents, who are not yet aware that their daughters have taken up smoking. There are usually one or two particularly popular hangouts whose proprietors cater to the school crowd. These people are the repositories of many confidences and sometimes serve as sources of information on high school athletics,

personalities, teachers, and other more forbidden topics. Here, as elsewhere, clique groupings are observed.

Yet in any community a great deal of self-organized constructive activity is carried on by informal groups of adolescents, especially in relation to science, mechanics, hunting, fishing, and the like. One group of boys may be engaged in the cooperative construction of a high-fidelity phonograph, another in the operation of an amateur short-wave radio station, another in the study of the theory and problems of rocket propulsion, and still another in some social-service community effort. Numerous adolescents are in business for themselves, their endeavors ranging from paper delivery, clerking, and lawn care to more ambitious cooperative business enterprises. Many adolescents of both sexes find the more academic extracurricular activities of their school, like the school paper or the yearbook, a productive outlet for their energy and service interests.

Visiting is a popular pastime among high school girls, although boys, probably partly because they are less restricted, tend to spend much less time at home or at a friend's home, preferring instead to wander about town, or perhaps to visit a nearby town. In contrast to the high school youth, the out-of-school youth tends to spend even more of his leisure hours away from home. He usually works, and the daytime hours available to students are closed to him. In his leisure time he tends to want to "do something," and that usually means seeking recreation somewhere in the community, rather than having friends visit at home. Then too, he is often nearer emancipation, and home ties may be weak to the point at which the home is no longer the base of his activities. His group activity tends to follow the pattern of the mixed or unisexual clique on an evening of fun, or the bisexual pair showing exclusive courtship behavior.

There are considerable differences, based on socioeconomic position, in the nature of the visit to another adolescent's home. Hollingshead (1949) notes, in the Elmtown study, that upper- and middle-class girls tend to visit in groups as compared to two or three individuals in class IV. (Class I is the "upper" class; class V, the "lower" class.) Typically, the class II girl's life is oriented around the clique, as is that of the class III girl to a lesser extent. Time at home is spent with members of the clique, discussing clique affairs, deciding on future plans, eating snacks from the refrigerator, playing records, discussing boys and clothes, or just gossiping. When alone, the class II or III girl spends a great deal of time "fixing up" and conducting interminable conversations over the telephone with clique members whom she may have seen only a few moments before the telephone conversation began. Hollingshead adds: "The class IV girls' families do not have so many telephones, few have record players or records, and kitchen raids and spontaneous parties are not allowed in most of the homes. Thus, the home visits tend to be on a smaller scale and to take the form of discussion between close friends." In contrast, class V "clique and recreational contacts occur on the street, in a tavern, or in a hangout rather than in the home."

Dancing, though frowned upon by parents in some religious denominations, is popular with adolescent groups, particularly among the upper and middle socioeconomic divisions. Opportunities for dancing may occur at school or a country club, at local dance halls or hotels, at private parties, or in soda-fountains, depending pretty much upon the individual's socioeconomic status and, of course, on the clique with which he is most closely identified. In general, upper-class children tend to have access to more organized recreational facilities conducted under more ideal conditions than do lower-class children—a situation quite apparent to anyone who observes the nature and location of their group activities.

Group Continuity and Cohesiveness

In assessing the nature and influence of any given adolescent group, it is important to learn something of its continuity as well as the extent of its cohesiveness. Hagstrom and Selvin (1965) list indicators of cohesiveness: (1) the degree to which members choose friends from within the group, (2) verbal expression of satisfaction with the group, (3) participation in group activities, willingness to remain in the group when alternatives exist, and (4) consensus on values relevant to the group's activities. As a result of factor analysis of nineteen possible indicators of group cohesiveness, Hagstrom and Selvin (1965) report that two dimensions are necessary for the interpretation of various aspects of group behavior and individual behavior in groups, namely, social satisfaction and sociometric cohesion. In discussing group behavior they note that groups containing large numbers of friends are not groups that are of necessity highly attractive to members.

To the youth leader or teacher, continuity and group cohesiveness are important if the group is to last long enough and have an active enough program to serve acceptable training or social purposes and satisfy its members' emotional needs. Parents, youth workers, and others interested in youth should promote group activities and help young people form peer organizations that may promote useful social and developmental ends. This is particularly important for organizations like the Boy Scouts, who hope through their organized program to meet the needs of youth and to offer them a substantial social and personal training program. However, if a boy leaves the Scouts at fourteen or fifteen, and if during his time of membership he attends only occasional meetings, the Scouts can hardly be expected to have any great or enduring amount of influence on him. The same is true of other program organizations such as the Girl Scouts, Camp Fire Girls, Boys' Club, YMCA, YWCA, and the various other organizations that cater to youth. Schoolteachers frequently complain that the six and one-half hours a day during which youth is under the school's direct supervision is hardly enough time to influence them to a desirable degree. Church leaders have long decried the comparatively brief time they have to work with the young people of their denominational groups.

What are the elements that go into the making of internal group solidarity? In a study of adolescent boys made in 1937 but still applicable to today's youth, Dimock classified fifty-five different groups as to type of program or agency and computed the average friendship index and its range for each of four main categories, on the assumption that a high friendship index was an indication of a high degree of group cohesiveness. Neighborhood groups, usually spontaneously formed and without adult supervision, had the highest average friendship index, considerably higher than did the YMCA, church, and Scout-sponsored groups; the category including the Scouts and school social clubs (Hi-Y) was superior to the church and special-interest categories. There seemed to be fewer individuals in the Scouts and the neighborhood groups who lacked acceptability than in either the church or special-interest groups; in the latter two, the program itself was apparently more important than the personal liking of members for one another. The Scout troop in this case gave the boys more varied things to do, and thus tended to involve them in a series of different activities; in this way, they had a better chance to know one another and to do things together. In such a group an individual would have several opportunities to display his skill and thus build up his acceptability. If he were not good at one thing, he might be good at something else. In the single-interest group this would not be true. A person who lacked skill in the main business at hand would not be able to seek recourse to some other activity within the group. Thus the multiple-purpose group seems to have greater cohesiveness than the single-purpose group. In general, a group that has outside opposition, or has been called into being by conflict, shows greater cohesiveness than one that has not.

Dimock, in his study of the reasons for group cohesiveness, concluded that:

The manner in which the group is formed or its membership selected is the decisive factor in determining the degree of its cohesiveness. . . . When boys themselves exercise primary initiative and responsibility in determining who and how many shall belong to a particular group, there seems to be a strong tendency for the group to be relatively small and markedly cohesive. The size of the group, then, is the result of the membership selection process rather than the friendship index being the result of size.

Dimock found "no general tendency for group cohesiveness to be associated with the age of the members of the group within the age range ten to seventeen." He stated the hypothesis that "young children are more casual and restricted in their friendship than adolescents . . . also . . . groups of young men would likely tend to be less cohesive than groups of adolescents."

He further noted that "there is a distinct tendency for the friendship indices of groups to decrease as the number of members increases" and that "small groups are by no means necessarily cohesive yet cohesive groups are almost invariably small. Cohesiveness is apparently a determiner of size rather than size being a condition of cohesiveness."

Normally an inverse relationship exists between group cohesiveness and authoritanism-autocracy by the group leader. Cohesion rests upon member interaction, dependence, sentiment, and the various informal relationships that obtain among the members as they engage in a common task. In this view, the leader is best seen as an involved group *member* whose job it is to keep the group moving while at the same time he remains a working and interacting member of it. However, the behavior of people is a function of their personalities and needs systems, and in some groups basic personality types require more authoritarian approaches if cohesiveness is to be maintained. This is particularly true where the situation has brought together people whose dependency needs are satisfied by a strong leader. Such a situation will often be found in the teenage delinquent gang.

This discussion has stressed male groupings, but much that is true of male groups is also true of female groups, although there are a number of specific differences. Girls' groups are not usually as well organized as boys', but their admission-exclusion decisions are on a more highly personal basis, and they tend to operate without an identified leader. In contrast, boys' groups usually have a designated leader, and they tend to operate under rather specifically structured rules of a relatively impersonal nature. Boys' groups also tend to be more task oriented than do those of girls. But for either boys or girls, as Hormann and Timaeus (1961) report, the coherence of group structure increases with age.

However, it would be a mistake to assume that the only differences between groups are on the basis of sex, objectives, or developmental status. Adequate comparative studies have not been made, but there is no reason to suppose, for example, that there may not be greater differences between peer groups segregated by socioeconomic level, or by rural or urban location, than there are between sex groups within any one of these categories.

There is probably no infallibly accurate means of indicating what causes a group's program to be vital and interesting to its adolescent members. Nor is there any way of knowing what will insure the perpetuation of the group and the continued participation of its members. Part of the answer probably lies in the personal intragroup relations that exist among the members. Dimock notes that:

Boys who have a substantial acceptability status and a number of friends in the group participate in its activities twice as much and continue as members twice as long as boys whose status and friendship are negligible. Spasmodic attendance and heavy membership mortality may be attributed largely to those boys who have virtually no friends in the group to which they belong.

The Group Leader

Of all the roles adolescents may assume in the group, the one that has received the largest amount of attention has been that of the leader. This is appropriate because the leader's position is a responsible one; upon him often rests the nature and direction of the group's activ-

ity. Often it is possible, by studying a group leader, to predict what the group will do, or, at least, to be in a better position to understand and interpret the group's activity. Since society must depend heavily upon its leaders, it is exceedingly important for those interested in human behavior to endeavor to isolate some of the factors that go into the making of leaders and to study the process of leadership itself. For those interested in the training and guidance of youth, it is important to recognize potential or actual leaders and to do everything possible to guide their growth and development along socially desirable lines, to the end that society may profit by their leadership. The great difficulty here, of course, lies in being able to identify the qualities that make a good leader.

The quest for the attributes of the good leader has occupied the time of many people and much space in psychological and other literature. Most of the early studies or discussions tried to find the attributes or the typical personality or character traits of leaders per se, on the assumption that a leader in one situation would be a leader in any situation. A more modern and accurate view is that leadership tends to be situation specific. Qualities of leadership required in one situation may be inapplicable or even disadvantageous in another. For example, an adolescent displaying accepted leadership in a group of his intellectual equals might not function as such if he were placed in a duller group, or at least limitations might be placed upon the acceptability of his leadership. In an unpublished study conducted with Ohio State University freshmen and sophomores, the writer found that a gifted person selected as a group leader for a group of his intellectual equals tended not to be selected as leader if placed in a group with a lower intelligence level, unless the group was engaged in preparing a report or a project requiring academic skill, in which case the bright student usually found himself in a position of acknowledged leadership. A fruitful approach to the study of leadership during adolescence might be to observe the kind of behavior adolescents expect their chosen leaders to display, with an analysis of how this behavior is permitted to differ from age level to age level as the adolescent proceeds on his course toward maturity.

Probably the most dramatic difference between the child leader and the adolescent leader is the method of control the leader may use successfully. In childhood, the group tends to place a premium upon the aggressive, dominant leader who bosses them about. With increasing maturity the person who wishes to assume leadership prerogatives must be more subtle in his techniques. There is a tendency to place a premium upon cooperativeness and to rebel against the individual who becomes a full-fledged leader before his ninth or tenth year, in the sense that his leadership is "situational" and his peers do not expect him to lead all group activities, as is true of the adolescent. The adolescent leader must also be representative of the kind of people he is leading and must fall within the pattern of their mores. The adolescent group, unlike the children's group, is likely to resist the person who deviates too greatly.

In general, it can be expected that the most successful adolescent group leader, and by the same token the most successful adult youth-group leader, is one who exercises his control subtly without trying to dominate the group. In other words, the most acceptable leader insofar as adolescents are concerned is the individual who recognizes the needs of the group and the individuals who compose it, and endeavors to meet those needs without attempting undue aggressive domination.

Summary

The study of group structure and of the behavior of individuals in groups has been a long-time interest of American social scientists —an interest that reflects the preoccupation of the American culture with group social behavior. However, the group has no existence apart from the members who compose it, and the psychology of the group must be approached through the common psychology of its members. Essentially, in the group's behavior we witness an interaction effect among its members' personalities, and since most groups have an implicit if not explicit purpose, the group gives a direction and focus to the behavior it arouses and sponsors. But nothing about the group cancels out the fact of individual differences.

Actual participation in a group's activities does not mean that an adolescent either belongs to or is accepted by the group. Generalizations about adolescent group participation must be made with considerable caution. Different groups exist for different reasons.

Groups may be classified under various headings, but no existing classification can successfully include and define all aspects of any given group. Groups may be roughly classified as intimate pair groups, primary groups, extended primary groups, and secondary groups. Other classifications have been in terms of references, of central figures, of atmosphere and method of procedure, and of habitat. Commonly used classifications are those of the clique and the crowd.

Groups appear to develop in a series of identifiable stages over their existence, from the time of their inception until their breakup, and in this sequence of stages they approximate the pattern of ontogenetic development. Sequential developmental stages through which groups pass have been described as the stages of orientation, storming, norming, and performance.

The adolescent crowd develops somewhat later than the clique and usually grows from it. The crowd has been defined as a large clique or as a more or less loosely united group of cliques. The crowd is less personal than the clique, but selection is still made on the basis of homogeneity, and its membership tends to be highly restricted. The crowd is more characteristic of later adolescence and maturity than it is of early adolescence.

Clique and crowd activities include playing, talking, and eating together. The kind of clique is important since cliques vary in type, and generalization may be inappropriate.

Some writers see a trend toward the formalization of adolescent group activities, but the majority of adolescents still confine most of their activities to informal as compared to formal groups. The lower the socioeconomic class, the less the likelihood of formal clique organization.

Most popular among group activities are watching and celebrating high school athletic contests, sitting and talking in soda fountains or other gathering places, going to movies, visiting, and dancing. In all these activities, but more especially in dancing and visiting, considerable differences can be observed between boys and girls still attending school and those out of school and between socioeconomic classes.

In promoting solidarity and cohesion there are no infallible rules that will apply to all groups, since groups tend to vary so widely. In general, a group with a high intragroup index of friendship will tend to be more cohesive, to have a more vital program, and to last longer than one with a low friendship index. An adolescent will like his group and keep participating in its program if he sympathizes with its purposes and mores. The group must offer him security and fulfill some need so that he may participate without undue strain. Yet to be acceptable to the group he must conform to its beliefs and usages.

Spontaneously formed groups tend to be more cohesive than artificially formed ones.

The multiple-purpose group tends to have more cohesiveness then the single-purpose group. Group size appears to be more important in group cohesiveness—more so than age, although advancing age or preadolescence appears to make for less intragroup cohesion. Definite sex differences appear in the solidarity patterns presented by male and female groups, although there are numerous similarities.

Leadership constitutes one of the more important group roles. The welfare of the group as well as the nature and direction of its activity often rests upon the shoulders of its leaders. Since the welfare of society also depends upon the excellence and ability of its leaders, it is important to insure that adolescents who exhibit leadership qualities are encouraged and helped to develop along socially approved lines. Schools should be particularly alert to the personal adjustment needs of their school leaders.

Early researchers endeavored to isolate universally applicable characteristics of leadership, under the assumption that a leader in one situation would be a leader in any situation. Later research does not accept this point of view and tends to endorse the principle of the specificity of leadership.

Successful adolescent leaders use methods of control different from those used by child group leaders. The leader who takes into account his group's wishes and needs is most successful. His methods must be comparatively subtle and must not depart too markedly from acceptable adolescent patterns of behavior.

References

Campbell, J. D. Peer relations in childhood. In Hoffman, M. L. and Hoffman, L. W., *Review of Child Development*, vol. 1, pp. 289–322. New York: Russell Sage Foundation, 1964.

Coleman, J. S. *The adolescent society.* Glencoe, Ill.: Free Press, 1961.

Dimock, H. S. *Rediscovering the adolescent.* New York: Association Press, 1937.

Hagstrom, W. O., and Selvin, H. C. Two dimensions of cohesiveness in small groups. *Sociometry* 28 (1965) : 30–43.

Havighurst, R. J.; Bowman, P. H.; Liddle, G. P.; Matthews, C. B.; and Peirce, J. V. *Growing Up in River City.* New York: Wiley, 1962.

Hollingshead, A. B. *Elmtown's youth.* New York: Wiley, 1949.

Hormann, H., and Timaeus, E. Altersabhangigkeit einiger Gruppenstrukturen bei Oberschulerinnen. *Psychologische Rundschau* 12 (1961): 93–99.

Horrocks, J. E. Foreword to Sherif, M., *In common predicament*. Boston: Houghton Mifflin, 1966.

Laponska, R. O. Stosunkach spolezynch miedzy dziewczetami i cholpcami w klasach koedukacyjnch (Social relations between boys and girls in coeducation classes). *Psychol. Wych.* 5 (1962): 20–31.

Lewin, K., and Lippitt, R. An experimental approach to the study of autocracy and democracy: A preliminary note. *Sociometry* 1 (1938): 292–300.

Lewin, K.; Lippitt, R.; and White, R. Patterns of aggressive behavior in experimentally created "social climates." *Journal of Social Psychology*

10 (1939): 271–299.

Phelps, H. R., and Horrocks, J. E. Factors influencing informal groups of adolescents. *Child Development* 29 (1958): 69–86.

Reese, H. W. Attitudes toward the opposite sex in late childhood. *Merrill-Palmer Quarterly* 12 (1966): 157–163.

Sherif, M., and Sherif, C. W. *Reference groups*. New York: Harper & Row, 1964.

Spaulding, C. B. Relative attachment of students to groups and organizations. *Sociology and Social Research* 50 (1966): 421–435.

Tuckman, B. W. Developmental sequence in small groups. *Psychological Bulletin* 63 (1965): 384–399.

Suggested Readings

Baron, R. A. Reducing the influence of an aggressive model: The restraining effects of peer censure. *Journal of Experimental Social Psychology* 8 (1972): 266–275.

Cusick, P. A. Adolescent groups and the school organization. *School Review* 82 (1973): 116–126.

Daugherty, R. A., and Waters, T. J. Closure flexibility, field dependence and student leadership. *Perceptual and Motor Skills* 29 (1969): 256–258.

Deb, S. Representation of personality through role playing in small groups. *Behaviorometrics* 1 (1971): 3–10.

Goodman, N. Adolescent norms and behavior: Organization and conformity. *Merrill-Palmer Quarterly* 15 (1969): 199–211.

Haythorn, W. W. The composition of groups: A review of the literature. *Acta Psychologica* 28 (1968): 97–128.

Kemper, T. D. Reference groups, socialization and achievement. *American Sociological Review* 33 (1968): 31–45.

Larsen, K. S. Dogmatism and sociometric status as determinants of interaction in a small group. *Psychological Reports* 29 (1971): 449–450.

Lindsay, J. S. On the number in a group. *Human Relations* 25 (1972): 47–64.

Lorber, N. M. Measuring the character of children's peer relations using the Ohio Social Acceptance Scale. *California Journal of Educational Research* 24 (1973): 71–77.

Lott, A. J., and Lott, B. Some indirect measures

of interpersonal attraction among children. *Journal of Educational Psychology* 61 (1970): 124–135.

Lynch, A. Q. Perception of peer leadership influence. *Journal of College Student Personnel* 11 (1970): 203–205.

MacLeod, A. R., and Knill, W. D. Students council leadership. *Alberta Journal of Educational Research* 14 (1968): 203–208.

Miller, J. G. Living systems: The group. *Behavioral Science* 16 (1971): 302–398.

Moerk, E. L. Effects of personality structure on individual activities in a group and on group processes. *Human Relations* (1972): 505–513.

Moscovici, S., and Zavalloni, M. The group as a polarizer of attitudes. *Journal of Personality and Social Psychology* 12 (1969): 125–135.

Napier, R., and Gershenfield, M. K. *Groups: Theory and experience*. Boston: Houghton Mifflin, 1973.

Nash, R. Clique formation among primary and secondary school children. *British Journal of Sociology* 24 (1973): 303–313.

Pasternack, M., and Silvey, L. Leadership patterns in gifted peer groups. *Gifted Child Quarterly* 13 (1969): 126–128.

Rothaus, P.; Davis, R. T.; and Banker, C. A. Participation in adolescent autonomous groups. *Journal of Genetic Psychology* 114 (1969): 135–142.

Schmuck, P., and Schmuck, R. Classroom peer relationships: What can the school psychologist do? *School Psychology Digest* 2 (1973): 4–12.

Solomon, R. W., and Wahler, R. G. Peer reinforcement control of classroom problem behavior. *Journal of Applied Behavioral Analysis* 6 (1973) : 49–56.

Sugarman, B. Social norms in teenage boys' peer groups: A study of their implications. *Human Relations* 21 (1968) : 41–58.

Trow, W. C.; Zander, A. E.; Morse, W. C.; and Jenkins, D. H. Psychology of group behavior: The class as a group. In Lightfoot, A., ed., *Inquiries into the social foundations of education.* Chicago: Rand McNally, 1972.

Wagner, H. The increasing importance of the peer group during adolescence. *Adolescence* 6 (1971) : 53–58.

Zander, A.; Fuller, R.; and Armstrong, W. Attributed pride or shame in group and self. *Journal of Personality and Social Psychology* 23 (1972) : 346–352.

Chapter Twenty-five

Vocational Development

The Problem

The moratorium of youth ends at graduation from high school. Up to that time, no one expects most adolescents to have an occupation, expect for part-time jobs, as long as they remain in school. But commencement day changes the role, and the adolescent who does not volunteer for military service is expected to get a job and move toward economic self-sufficiency or continue on in some institution of higher or technical learning so that he can eventually enter the job market. Girls, particularly those whose families are of higher socio-economic status, are not under quite the same pressure as boys, but for both the days of childhood are definitely over.

Remmers and Radler (1957) note that six months after leaving school one-third of the new graduates plan to be employed, although in actuality a larger percentage than that will be on the job before this time is up. Yet in a national survey of a stratified sample of high school boys and girls, Remmers and Radler report that over 50 percent do not seem to have given much thought to their future. Of the 40 to 50 percent who do admit to having thought of the future, more than half wonder for what work they are suited and nearly as many have a question about how much ability they have. About 42 percent do not know what occupation to consider, nor do they really seem to know what their interests are. Despite this lack of information, Remmers and Radler note that less than a third ask questions of practical vocational significance, such as, "What kind of training do different jobs require?" and, "What fields are overcrowded?"

Youth tend not to be as concerned about their vocational future as the immediate nature of the problem in the later years of high school warrants, but society is beginning to recognize that the new nature of the American labor force makes vocational choice and preparation a crucial issue. Every state that participated in the 1960 White House Conference on Children and Youth recommended "vocational programs in high schools which do not have them now, or their expansion and improvement where they already exist." One state recommended a "planned program of work in the home, school, and community which will give children experience in the responsibilities of a job assignment. . . . There should be something of work experience on a graduated scale available to every child as he matures."

The American labor force will increase from about 73.5 million persons in 1960 to some 100 million in 1980. Because of the changing age pattern in this country, younger persons may be expected to become a larger proportion of the work force during these decades. Such an increase and the emphasis upon the younger worker pose a national problem as well as a personal one for every individual adolescent who enters or who must prepare to enter the labor force during the last quarter of the present century.

The Necessity of a Vocation

Aside from occasional chores or part-time work to earn spending money, children are happily free from the need to earn their own living. Of course, some are required to find minor jobs and contribute to the family expenses, but in the main few children do not realize that, in an emergency, they may rely upon their family or those who are responsible for them. Nor does society expect children to have jobs or to support themselves; it is enough that they attend school and find acceptable means of amusement.

An adolescent is nearing the close of childhood; sooner or later he begins to realize that he must one day be responsible for his own living. Moreover, he finds that society's leniency to him as a vocationless child has been replaced by an assumption that as an adult a considerable portion of his time will be spent in some remunerative employment.

As he meets more and more people he finds that, in American culture, almost the first thing one wishes to know about a new acquaintance is his occupation and how good he is at it. He finds that success tends to be judged largely in terms of income and that people are quite interested in other people's incomes.

Adolescent boys, in particular, spend a great deal of time asking one another about their plans after graduation. Vocational guidance counselors preach the gospel of thinking about one's lifework, and parents, especially, are vitally interested in their children's vocational future. It is not unusual for parents to press their adolescent sons and daughters to "make up their minds" or to announce that the adolescent involved is "going into" some occupational field selected by the parent.

As a result of all these pressures, the adolescent begins to consider job possibilities and to plan for his vocational future. Sometimes this planning activity arises out of his own interests, but just as frequently it is the result of a desire to do the accepted thing and to conform to what is expected of him. As stated previously, the typical adolescent tends to be a conservative person who conforms closely to the patterns established and carried out by the other adolescents he knows. If the others are thinking about their vocational futures he tends to do likewise, or to feel somewhat guilty and left out if he does not.

However, incentives other than adult pressure or peer-group conformity urge an adolescent to consider his vocational future. One of the most important of these is the adolescent's desire for personal freedom and economic independence. This is part and parcel of every well-adjusted adolescent's desire for emancipation from parental and other adult controls. As a member of a family the adolescent occupies an inferior position. He is expected to do as he is told. He must obey certain restrictions, such as coming home at a given hour, doing chores, obeying family rules, and following parental dictates in his choice of friends and activities. If he disobeys, he may be punished, denied certain activities, or submitted to a humiliating calling down. His money expenditures are controlled, and he must usually appeal to his parents, either for permission to spend money he has saved or for grants in addition to his allowance, which all too often is doled out at irregular intervals or as charity. Under the circumstances, with rebellion impossible or unwise, he looks forward to the time when he may earn his own money. As an independent wage earner he could spend as he pleased and in some measure be financially independent of his parents, consequently, free of their control. Thus, he feels that he could do as he wished. But earning money means securing a job, which in turn means selecting some occupation. Hence, the additional incentive of emancipation from parental control serves as a motivating factor in the adolescent becoming interested in his vocational future.

Another motivating factor is the marriage incentive, possibly of greater interest to girls during the adolescent years than to boys, although late adolescence finds boys becoming more and more concerned about marriage.

There is an increasing tendency for people, particularly men, to marry even younger today than was formerly the case. The issue therefore becomes important for the older adolescent. Even though he does not actually marry during this period or even pick the girl he will eventually marry, he may decide several different times that he has found the "right girl" (or, in the case of girls, "the right boy"). Each time this happens, marriage and its responsibilities are considered and may even exert a strong attraction. But to be married means to assume financial responsibility, which again comes as the result of a job. Thus, another incentive is added.

For many adolescents, particularly those who are somewhat immature, the desire for emancipation, for marriage, for an occupational future, or even for conformity to peer mores, takes the less constructive form of daydreaming, delinquency, or efforts short of seriously considering an occupational choice. But on the whole, the more constructive approach is to consider one's future, or the attainment of objectives such as emancipation, in vocational terms. An immature individual who unduly postpones an occupational decision only increases the total span of his own immaturity, for dependence upon others does not diminish until some vocational decisions are made, not perhaps in terms of a full-fledged decision as to the complete course of one's occupational future, but in terms of trying to secure some kind of job at least temporarily. Unfortunate indeed is the adolescent who postpones this important decision too long. Jennie is a case in point.

Jennie was the younger of two daughters born to well-to-do parents. When Jennie was eight years old her older sister died, with the result that her parents became overprotective and indulged Jennie's every whim. The mother was particularly anxious to keep her daughter near her and was terrified at the thought of the day that the girl would be old enough to leave her home and her mother's protection. Under the circumstances, she decided to post-

pone the event as long as possible and, in effect, to increase her daughter's dependence. Jennie, although of average intelligence, was not very successful in school and failed several grades.

When she was sixteen, she was still in the seventh grade, and her mother decided to withdraw her from school on the pretext of ill health, although as a matter of fact Jennie was unusually healthy. Her parents decided not to let her attempt to secure employment until she had "recovered" her health. Jennie remained at home for the following four years to "recover" and help her mother with the housework. When she was twenty, she enrolled in a local business school to learn typing but abandoned the idea after a month on the excuse that her eyes bothered her. She then secured a job through her father's influence as a clerk in a local department store but was fired after only a week. She told her mother that her department head and the other workers did not understand her and were unsympathetic. Her mother sympathized with her, and Jennie returned to helping her mother with the work about the house.

In the meantime, Jennie had had no social life. Her mother felt that she was too young to have dates, and there was little or no opportunity to meet other girls. The family owned an isolated camp where they stayed every summer, and during the winter her parents always accompanied her to the movies and all her other recreations. When Jennie was twenty-eight, her father started bringing a bachelor business associate, some twenty years older than Jennie, to the house. Jennie promptly fell violently in love with him, and for the following eight years it was the custom for him to eat with the family one or two evenings a week. Occasionally they would go to a movie or a baseball game, but always accompanied by Jennie's parents. When Jennie was about thirty-five, the man was transferred to another city and proposed marriage, but Jennie and her mother felt that it would be unwise for Jennie to leave home. By the time Jennie was forty-five, her father had retired, and both parents were aging rapidly; Jennie was soon to face

the tragedy of being left alone, an excessively dependent woman with no friends, no social ability, and no occupational skills or plans. Luckily for her, and unlike many others in like circumstances, she would have enough money to support herself so that she would have no economic problems. Her other problems were legion.

Failure to make some kind of vocational decision is also expensive in time and effort. The adolescent who does not make such a decision may enter the wrong curriculum and spend considerable time there, only to find later that much of it has been wasted. Nearly every personnel department in industry or business is familiar with the employee who, prior to his selection of a vocation, pursued a course of study that contributed little or nothing to his vocational future. Every college counselor is familiar with the student who, after several years of college work, makes his vocational decision and finds he must start all over, frequently at the loss of several years' time.

At this point, a specific warning is necessary to the vocational counselor, parent, teacher, or other person who is responsible for helping young people make their occupational decisions. Despite the undoubted pressures upon the adolescent to select his future occupation, and despite the possibilities of wasted time and effort if vocational decisions are not made, the youth worker will err if he pushes an adolescent too hard to make a decision before he is ready, and before he has sufficient information to make a proper choice. It is also wrong to press an individual to the point where he will feel guilty if he cannot decide. The proper approach is to provide information and services to the adolescent who is trying to find a vocation, and to open possibilities to one who has not considered the problem. It is a mistake to force a decision, and equally a mistake for the counselor or parent to forget that in the last analysis the decision is the adolescent's own, one which he may have to live with for the rest of his life. It is better for the adolescent to defer making a decision than to make one prematurely.

Aspirations

To what extent do adolescent youth really want to get ahead? Many have believed that the desire to get ahead is confined to the middle and upper classes, and that the children of the lower classes, except for a handful of anomalies, have no real desire for advancement, and to that extent seem not to share in the American tradition. Hollingshead (1949) writes, as a result of his Elmtown study, that lower-class children "have limited their horizons to the class horizon, and in the process have unconsciously placed themselves in such a position that they will occupy the same levels as their parents." However, there is evidence on the other side. In a study of culturally disadvantaged children (165 boys, 139 girls) in the New York City public schools, Clark (1965) reports that 30 percent of the boys and 85 percent of the girls in his study expressed professional and white-collar aspirations. Riccio (1965) compared a sample of high school age migrants from the southern Appalachian region with natives from a metropolitan region (Columbus, Ohio) for level of occupational aspirations, role models, and cultural conformity. His two samples consisted of ninety-seven males each, of equated intelligence, drawn from grades nine to twelve. He found no significant differences on Haller's Occupational Aspiration Scale and in their responses to the question: "Which people in the world would you most want to be like?"

But levels of aspiration are relative. One difficulty in assessing the level of desire to get ahead in any individual teenager is presented by the different value systems held by the various subgroups within the culture and the different interpretations they may place on what getting ahead really involves. The matter may be less one of a lack of desire to get ahead and more one of the relative worth of the various different outcomes that prompt one to get ahead. Obviously, the prestige hierarchy of occupations is not the same for all social strata. Not everyone sees professional and managerial occupations as the finest thing to which to

aspire. For lower-class boys a skilled job or ownership of a small business may represent just as fine an achievement as does a professional or managerial job to a middle- or upper-class boy. After all, absolute level of achievement is only one of the many factors that contribute to that highly individual thing, a feeling of personal success. The lower-class boy actually may have stronger impulses to get ahead than an upper-class boy. The idea has been advanced that the more unsatisfactory an individual finds the present, the more he is motivated to effect changes in the future, and that the lower class is characterized by a "deep, all-pervading" drive to provide a future superior to the present. The matter of exactly what represents improvement remains. The upper-class boy may simply wish to maintain his present family level without ever having any real experience of what he is avoiding by not going below that level. The lower-class boy may find an advance in conditions above his level such an improvement that he is immensely satisfied, though his new level is still below the upper-class boy's maintenance level. Thus for one, success may represent a simple maintenance of the same level, and for another, success may come only with a radical change for the better. It would be most unfortunate if everyone could interpret success only as standing above everyone else.

In a study of occupational aspirations, Empey (1965) administered a questionnaire to approximately one-tenth of all male seniors in the public high schools of the state of Washington. The social-class level of each senior was determined by a combination of occupational prestige scales. In his study Empey attempted to analyze occupational aspiration by measuring it from both a relative and an absolute standard. When an absolute standard was used, the aspirations of lower-class subjects were compared with those of upper-class subjects. In this manner an individual's actual occupational choice and his socioeconomic status were considered in determining his level of aspiration. In a discussion of his findings Empey wrote:

The absolute occupational status aspirations of male high school seniors from the middle and upper classes are significantly higher than those of seniors from the lower classes, and ... the relative occupational status aspirations of lower-class seniors indicate that they prefer and anticipate having significantly higher occupational statuses than their fathers.

A study by Sewell, Haller, and Straus (1956) using Wisconsin high school seniors of both sexes also indicates that values specific to different status positions are important influences on levels of educational and occupational aspiration. Thus it would appear that it is rare for an adolescent from any walk of life not to want to get ahead (or to maintain a level that places him ahead). Lower-class youth do not limit their occupational aspirations to the class horizon, but their aspirations tend to be less lofty than are those of children in the upper strata.

On the other hand, socioeconomic status is not the sole determinant of occupational aspiration. Many forces press upon a child during his developmental period, and while their range and scope may be restricted—or enlarged—by environmental factors such as socioeconomic status, the experiences these other forces provide must be considered. One such force is the interpersonal relations existing within the family. Crites (1962) studied the relationship of parental identification to vocational interest development and reports that a son's identification with both his parents significantly affects the patterning of his interests, although his identification with his father is the more important. As a matter of fact, as Cohen (1965) points out, fathers are more likely to consider a son's vocation, whereas mothers tend to consider the son's status.

In a study of family interpersonal relations, Dynes, Clarke, and Dinitz (1956) administered an aspiration scale and an index of parent-child interaction in questionnaire form to 350 college students. They report: "Unsatisfactory interpersonal relationships in the family of orientation were significantly related to high aspirational levels and satisfactory relationships were related to lower aspirational levels." Those whose aspirations were "high" reported experiencing feelings of rejection more often than did the "low" aspirers. High aspirers, as compared to low aspirers, felt less attachment to their parents, felt that their parents had shown more favoritism toward one child in their family, and were of the opinion that their childhood was less happy. But the high and low aspirers did not differ significantly in the frequency with which they had confided in their mothers or in the amount of conflict with either their fathers or their siblings.

One cannot escape the importance of certain personal aspects of an individual in considering his vocational aspirations. For example, Korman (1967) reports a study in which he found support for the hypothesis that high self-esteem students are more likely to choose those occupations they perceive as requiring their high abilities than are those with low self-esteem. Little (1967), in a study of 4,186 male noncollege graduates of a Wisconsin high school seven to eight years after their graduation, notes that levels of occupational attainment corresponded closely to levels of occupational aspiration, but high scholastic achievement in high school did not substantially escalate level of occupational attainment in any group.

Determinants of Occupational Choice

It is unprofitable to survey adolescent vocational interests apart from the factors that underlie and determine them. From the long-range point of view, it is more profitable to know why adolescents choose the vocations they do, and to learn what factors have influenced their selection, than it is to know what choices actually are made. Details and specific choices will change with the times and other environmental factors, but basic causes, needs, desires, and drives will tend to remain relatively constant. Curiosity and the desire to do well, to master the environment, or to better one's condition are fairly universal aspects of our culture; but the forms these aspects take in terms of interests or vocational selections show a quite considerable variation.

In general, the factors that determine vocational choice are environmentally engendered.[1] A vocational selection or interest represents the environment's impact on an adolescent's personality organization and the peculiar structure of his interests, needs, and desires. The consensus of the numerous studies investigating factors underlying vocational choice seems to be that parental advice or example and social prestige are among the most important factors that cause adolescents to choose their vocations. Certainly an adolescent's family plays an important role not only in determining the nature of his occupational choices but also in the plans he will make to carry them out. For example, Werts (1968), in a comparison of fathers' occupations and sons' career choices of 76,015 individuals at each high school grade level, found that sons tended to have different career choices depending on their fathers' occupations. However, despite the large amount of research available, there is some disagreement as to the exact nature and even the direction of such influence.

Closely related to parental influence is social prestige, which usually plays an important part in vocational selection. Economic pressures and the desires and expectations of friends and relatives impel an adolescent to select occupations fairly high on the socially approved list, occupations that usually endow their practitioners with social status. The adolescent's family is an important underlying factor here. The higher the family is in socioeconomic status, the more apt the adolescent is to wish to enter an occupation on at least as high a socioeconomic level as that of his parents. Vigod (1972) reports that the higher a child's socioeconomic status the higher will be the status of his expected occupation. It is com-

---

[1]Obviously some vocational choices are determined by the individual's physical make-up. As the physical make-up is undoubtedly in some measure inherited, from this viewpoint at least, certain nonenvironmental factors are significant in vocational choice.

paratively rare to find an adolescent expressing interest in an occupation lower in social status than that of his parents. The particular socioeconomic level desired is, of course, a comparative matter, since the son of a professional man may want to enter the professions, business, or military life, while the son of a man lower on the socioeconomic scale may be willing to settle for an occupation that represents for him and his family a considerable social advance over that of his parents.

Whether or not parental influence is healthy is a matter of some controversy. Although it may be assumed that an adolescent who is making a vocational choice needs his parents' support and encouragement, comparatively few parents have either the training or the objectivity to give their children adequate and good counsel about their vocational careers. Adolescents who follow family advice and decisions about their occupational future are unlikely to seek advice from counselors and, if they have accepted family advice, to consider other occupational possibilities. It is natural for parents to overestimate general ability or to underestimate the existence of a special aptitude and discourage its development. On the other hand, there is always the chance that a parent may overestimate an aptitude or hopefully imagine the existence of an aptitude that is entirely absent. Too frequently a parent (although he may deny it vigorously) is more interested in himself than in his son or daughter when he gives vocational advice. He may be overinterested in material things to the exclusion of the adolescent's own needs, interests, and abilities, or he may identify himself so closely with his offspring's future success that he gives advice as to what he would do, or what he wishes he could have done. In this way he hopes to experience vicariously through his child's success those things he himself missed, or those things in which he failed. The point of reference here is wrong for giving vocational advice—it is the child, not the parent, who has to live with the vocation selected. We are all familiar with the parent who wants to "give my child those things I missed."

"Those things" may be the last things in the world an adolescent wants or should have.

Yet some parents often can give good advice, based not only on a wealth of experience, but on an adequate knowledge of their child. The adolescent's task is to recognize both good and poor advice and take or leave this as he makes his choice. Unfortunately, few adolescents can make such a distinction: oversubservience to parental mandate may lead to submissive acceptance of parents' advice, or a struggle for emancipation from parental intervention may cause rejection of almost any advice they may offer. The most desirable state of affairs, of course, is for parental advice to be available and to be used with other selective factors, so long as it does not become the determining factor. Tasks for the vocational counselor are to help the adolescent use all the available factors in his choice, to protect him from overemphasis, and to aid him in arriving at a decision based on the facts and realities of his situation.

The most dangerous parental reaction of all is a plea for the adolescent's sympathy. The feeling that one must perpetuate the family stake in an enterprise is often a powerful incentive that influences extremely unwise vocational decisions.

There is evidence that occupational choice is at least in part determined by the personal characteristics of the person making the choice. Meir and Friedland (1971) report a positive correlation between occupational preference ranking and extrinsic needs, while Elder (1968) reports a relationship of interest level and need for achievement. Kunert (1969) investigated the personality-vocational choice relationship by means of the Vocational Life Patterns Q-Sort and noted that the motivational, personality, and self-concept descriptions of the VLP Q-Sort do distinguish among students registered in schools of law, medicine, theology, and engineering. Nugent (1968), in a study using the Kuder Vocational Preference Record, notes that vocational choice is an integral part of total personality development and that vocational maturity tends to relate to total maturity. Arbuthnot and Gruenfeld (1969) report that field-dependence–independence is predictive of educational and vocational interest, and Bodden and Klein (1972) report a significant positive correlation between cognitive complexity and occupational choice.

A number of investigators have pointed to the relationship between self-perception and vocational choice. Typical of the studies is one by Korman (1969), who reports that self-esteem operates as a moderator in the vocational choice process in that high self-esteem individuals are more likely to seek self-fulfillment than are low self-esteem individuals. Hollander and Parker (1972) report that occupational choices for adolescents were based in part on the degree of positive relationship between their self-descriptions and various occupational stereotypes. In this same connection Greenhaus (1971) reports that high self-esteem individuals tend to look at their own needs and relevant attributes in determining satisfaction with their occupational choice, whereas low self-esteem individuals tend to look more toward external cues. Resnick, Fauble, and Osipow (1970) report a positive relationship between vocational crystallization and self-esteem.

Vocational Measurement

Psychological tests provide the research investigator and the vocational counselor with an objective source of information about an individual's intelligence, special abilities, and general and specific interests. Those who advocate the use of psychological tests in occupational counseling assume that an individual may be matched with his attributes on the basis of a composite of test scores. They feel that if the match is made correctly, there is a high probability that the individual will be in an occupation in which he will be successful and in which he will like the tasks he must perform. No one test will present a complete picture, although a number of differential

batteries such as the Guilford-Zimmerman Aptitude Survey, the Flanagan Aptitude Tests, and the Differential Aptitude Tests are omnibus measures combining a number of tests into one battery.

The interest inventory is of particular interest in occupations research as well as in occupational counseling. The vocational interest inventory is typically a questionnaire or check list that the student fills out so that his answers may be classified under various headings and a profile of his interest preferences compiled. There are a good many different inventories of this type, all using more or less similar approaches, but revealing considerable differences when their theoretical bases are examined. There are a number of available interest inventories, but the Strong Vocational Interest Blank and the Kuder Preference Record[2] are among the better known and may be regarded as representative. The Kuder Preference Record is a self-scoring device which presents the examinee with lists of activities by threes. The examinee is to indicate which of the three activities in each group he most prefers and which he least prefers. A typical group of activities in the test is: (a) play a guitar, (b) draw a map, and (c) visit a museum. The vocational form of the Kuder (Form B) consists of nine scales: mechanical, computational, scientific, persuasive, artistic, literary, musical, social service, clerical, and masculinity-femininity, each of which yields a separate score. Form C includes the same nine scales plus two more, outdoor and verification.

The Strong Vocational Interest Blank consists of listings of occupations, hobbies, school subjects, kinds of people, and other matters for which respondents record their reaction as "like," "dislike," or "indifferent." The examinee's responses are compared with responses of persons judged successful in their own occupational fields. The women's form provides for scores in twenty-nine occupations,

---

[2]One form of the Strong is for men and one is for women. The Kuder comes in three forms: vocational, occupational, and personal.

plus a masculinity-femininity score. The men's form provides scores for forty-eight occupations under six major headings, plus scales for interest maturity, masculinity-femininity, occupational level, and specialization level.

Strong feels that anyone engaged in a particular occupation has a characteristic pattern of likes and dislikes that differentiates him from persons following other occupations. In a discussion of his test, Strong (1963) writes:

The Vocational Interest Blank is an aid in determining which way a person should go—what occupation he will enjoy. But whether he will do the work poorly or well is another matter. Performance is a reflection of ability, motivation, and character. So far there is no thorough-going establishment of the relationship of performance and interest. Such studies as we have indicate a low correlation between the two.

Obviously, an adolescent does not have enough knowledge to respond to interest inventories except in terms of his own limited experiences and whatever inaccurate imagination he can conjure ("Which of the following five occupations interests you most?" or "Would you rather go swimming in Jamaica or ice fishing in Greenland?"). A counselor really has to accompany an interest test with an intelligence test and perhaps one or more aptitude tests to gain a satisfactory reading.[3]

Ability and Vocational Choice

A number of studies have considered the relationship between occupation and test intelligence and have reported the presence of a hierarchy of occupational structure closely related to intelligence, whether the classification is based on the subject's occupation or his father's. Those engaged in professional occupations or whose fathers were members of a profession rank highest in intelligence, with clerical and business groups following, and farmers and unskilled workers lowest.

The most important single criterion of an individual's ability to succeed or fail in any given occupational endeavor seems to be level of mental ability. The vocational counselor in his endeavors to guide and counsel young people about their occupational future usually starts with an assessment of the individual's level of intelligence. But a given degree of mental ability is no guarantee that a particular individual will succeed in any occupation for which he has the intellectual capacity. It is merely an indication that, other things being equal, he has the capacity to succeed, at least insofar as intelligence is concerned. His actual success will depend upon an often unforeseeable combination of fortuitous circumstances, motivation and drive, educational opportunity, special aptitude, and many other factors. Conversely, however, it is known within certain limits that an individual with too low a general mental ability will be unable to succeed in certain occupations requiring a high level of mental ability, both in training and on-the-job practice. Great motivation and intense application will sometimes permit a less intelligent individual to overachieve to the point where he may surpass a more intelligent individual, particularly when the latter's motivation and application are deficient. But in an equal competitive situation, the less intelligent person will always have a difficult, if not an insurmountable, problem. Frequently the guidance worker will advise a less intelligent individual to avoid certain occupations, not because he would be unable to make his way if he showed great effort, but because success for him would come only at the expense of excessive, unwise mental and emotional strain, with mediocrity in his occupation more than a possibility, while the more intelligent person would have a comparatively easy time.

However, a high level of mental ability is not necessarily the best guarantee of success

---

[3]Further information about the nature of the various measures used in vocational advisement, including intelligence and aptitude tests, interest tests, and omnibus tests, may be found in J. E. Horrocks and T. L. Schoonover, *Measurement for Teachers;* J. E. Horrocks, *Assessment of Behavior;* or any other standard textbook in psychological measurement.

in any occupation. In numerous occupations a high level of mental ability is not only unnecessary; it may even be a real detriment. For example, if routine work, like ordinary assembly-line work, is required, or if simple directions must be followed day after day without need for either independent thinking or creativity, the less intelligent person makes the more efficient and better-adjusted worker. There are also many occupations in which a specialized ability is the most important factor, such as in certain types of mechanical work, some aspects of musical or artistic work, and salesmanship. In some of these fields a high level of mental ability is also required, but in many it is not. It is the job of the vocational counselor, teacher, or other youth worker to help an adolescent select the type of work his particular level of mental ability will permit him to do most effectively and which will provide him the maximum adjustment and happiness in life.

The student of adolescence must know something about the relationship of vocational choice to mental ability. In general, the typical adolescent bases his vocational interests on factors other than intellectual capacity, although past unsuccessful experiences may make some types of occupational classification distasteful to the person with inferior mental ability. But usually occupations are selected on the basis of very little information, and an individual will signify his interest in an occupation because he has misinterpreted what that occupational choice involves. An adolescent who wishes to become a surgeon usually overlooks the drudgery of medical school, the long years of preparation, and the disagreeable aspects of the job. He sees instead the gleaming operating theater, the mysterious masked figures in green, the brilliant manipulation of instruments before an admiring audience, and the glamour of screaming sirens in the night. By the same token, the prospective nurse sees the "cool hand on the fevered brow" and ignores the hard work, the disagreeable duties, the irascible patient, and the routine and red tape of the hospital.

Theories of Vocational Development

Since career choice is one of man's most significant tasks, as well as a central developmental task of adolescence, and since the career once selected—or in many cases reselected—is a major preoccupation of most people's lives, it is not surprising that a number of major theories of career development, as well as a number of minor studies,[4] have been advanced. Among the major theories are those of Roe, Super, Holland, and Ginzberg et al. These theories will be presented in the following sections, with some research background to provide the reader with an idea of the nature of vocational development.

Roe's Theory of Career Choice

A number of years ago, Roe (1951a, 1951b, 1953) investigated the developmental backgrounds and personalities of research scientists in various fields. Her major conclusion was that crucial differences exist between social and physical scientists, the real area of difference being in their interpersonal transactions and in their approach to others generally. She hypothesized that these transactional differences were a result of the child-rearing practices these scientists had encountered in their upbringing. Starting upon this base, Roe evolved a theory of careers built upon a combination of needs theory and canalization of psychic energy after the pattern of Maslow (1954) and Murphy (1947), plus certain ideas about the later-life effects of the way an individual was reared (1956, 1957).

According to Roe, every person receives a genetic endowment that drives him to expend his energy in specified directions, although this expenditure is not wholly voluntary, since every child encounters both frustrations and satisfactions of the needs that underlie his motivations. In the course of his developmental sequence, as the child expends his psychic energy,

[4]Hershenson and Roth (1966), Simon (1966), Kuviesky and Bealer (1966), Korman (1966), Gross (1967), Morris (1966).

it combines with his experiences to eventuate in a style of life designed to enable him to satisfy his system of needs. This lifestyle becomes the child's manner of dealing with all the aspects of his environment, including the choices he has to make throughout his life. One of his most important choices is the selection of a career. By examining an adolescent's accomplishments, one may presumably infer the vocational motivations that impel him to take action.

However, motivations have early origins. As a result of his early childhood experiences, a child, according to Roe, tends to be motivated either toward or away from persons, and it is this motivation that she found important in her early studies of personality differences between research scientists in different fields. Theoretically, a person in a service occupation would tend to come from an overprotective home characterized by loving care, whereas a scientist would tend to come from a rejecting home which is characterized by a cold psychological climate.

The vocational implication of Roe's theory is that, given high need intensity and a specific set of child-rearing experiences, an individual should do well in an occupation that satisfies his needs and demands a personality for which his childhood experiences were appropriate. Only two factors could block this vocational appropriateness: one, an intelligence not suitable for the job; and the other, the lack of socioeconomic assets with which to enter the occupation. In a later formulation of the Roe theory, Roe and Siegelman (1964) attempted to identify more explicitly the role of needs in interests and the kinds of childhood experiences having repercussions in later life.

Theories are interesting, but their adequacy and explanatory value comes in the confirmatory research that follows their formulation. To date, Roe's theory has not held up very well when applied to vocational development; some investigators have had difficulty with the needs, some with the child-rearing hypotheses, and some with both. For example, Hagen (1960), Utten (1962), Switzer (1962), Crites (1962), and Brunkan (1965) could not offer confirmatory evidence, while Grigg (1959), Kinnane and Pable (1962), and Levine (1963) report only partial confirmation. Green and Parker (1965) also report partial confirmation but found an interesting reversal. Using retrospective reconstructions of childhood experiences by adolescents, Green and Parker report that girls' experience with cold parental relationships led to non–person-oriented career choices, while boys' experience with warm and supporting parents led to person-oriented career choices. On the other hand, girls from warm, acceptant parental homes do not make person-oriented occupational choices, nor do boys from cold parental environments make non–person-oriented choices. The basic trouble with such a study concerns the accuracy of the adolescent's retrospective report of his childhood experiences.

Shappell, Hall, and Tarrier (1971) developed an inventory based on Roe's model and Maslow's need categories and tested high school sophomores and seniors. The seniors received higher mean scales than sophomores on twelve of thirteen scales. The investigators concluded that the closer proximity of seniors to employment increased their need expectations, and maturation does have an effect on the durations and intensity of psychological needs.

Super's Developmental Theory of Vocational Behavior

One of the most comprehensive theories of career choice is the developmental self-concept theory of vocational behavior proposed by Super. Super's position (1953, 1957, 1963a, 1963b, 1963c) is that an individual selects an occupation that gives him the greatest scope for self-expression, thus making a concrete effort to implement the self-concept he has erected over the years. In engaging in vocational choice as self-concept implementation, the individual is naturally limited by the stage of development he has attained as the various choices are made, but the external environment and the various opportunities available (or unavailable) also operate as limiting factors to the point that many individuals are blocked in self-realization through vocational choice. Obviously, each stage of the developmental cycle presents parameters to vocational choice. An early adolescent's vocational decisions would be different from those of a late adolescent, and the latter's would in turn be different to some degree from those made in later maturity. As Super interprets it, the child's observation of and identification with parents and other adults whom he has seen working are extremely important in his development of his vocational self-concept.

Super believes that different vocational behaviors can best be viewed in terms of the developmental stage of the person making the choice, with that person's attempts to implement his self-concept. But the individual's manner of adjustment at any stage in his developmental sequence predicts his manner of adjustment at a subsequent stage. An optimistic aspect of Super's theory is that any individual possesses within himself the capacity for success and satisfaction in quite a wide variety of occupational endeavors, although ability factors will obviously close some to him. Every person has a constellation of interests and abilities, and some occupations are more adapted to particular constellations than are others. In choosing occupations a real attempt should be made to relate interests and abilities to occupations, since research has proved that maximum satisfaction is gained when occupation and interest-ability are matched. But such matching sometimes requires an adjustment in self-concept—another aspect of the reality-testing principle.

Super postulates two major stages in vocational development: the exploratory and the establishment. The exploratory stage has three sequential substages: tentative, transition, and uncommitted trial. The establishment stage has two substages: the committed trial and the advancement. In passing through these stages each individual must achieve the following five developmental-vocational tasks:

1. *Crystallization*. The individual formulates ideas about work that fit him as a person and are in accord with his self-concept. This typically occurs between the fourteenth and eighteenth years.
2. *Specification of a vocational preference*. Here the individual narrows his choice and takes the first steps to bring about his entrance into occupation. This usually occurs between eighteen and twenty.
3. *Implementation of a vocational preference*. During this period, which usually comes between twenty-one and twenty-four, training and perhaps some employment occurs.
4. *Stabilization,* between twenty-five and thirty-five, involves settling down to the job and demonstration that the career choice was an appropriate one.
5. *Consolidation,* which occurs after age thirty-five, represents the period of advancement and attainment of status.

Super indicates that a person's vocational maturity may be assessed by the approximation of his own vocational behavior and that of the norm for his age group and circumstances.

Individuals exhibit their own peculiar circumstances of vocational development, which may be identified and recognized as regular and predictable when the individuals are studied intensively. Among identified career patterns are four major possibilities:

1. *Stable*. Here the individual makes his career choice quite early, and the decision is permanent. Careers in medicine and in the priesthood are typical examples.
2. *Conventional*. Here the individual tries several possibilities, with one eventually leading to a permanent choice.
3. *Unstable*. The individual following this pattern tries a number of jobs, each leading to stability for a time, only to be given up for another trial effort. Such a person's career is a never-ending succession of beginnings and endings, with only age or circumstances over which he has no control ending the succession in a final choice.

4. *Multiple Pattern.* This is simply a situation, such as that occurring in domestic service, where the individual moves over a horizontal range of stable-level jobs as he changes employers from time to time.

To understand the dynamics of Super's theory, one must understand Super's position that even a well-integrated individual constantly tests reality as he develops and encounters new experiences. Thus, we see the person over his life span as a continually developing entity readjusting and making changes as experience indicates the necessity. And this constant readjustment goes on in all the areas of living, including career choice and performance. Decisions about vocations have to be made in terms of self-concept. The adolescent has many ways of testing reality and adjusting his concept of self, possibly one of the most fruitful being that of role playing. A great deal of such role playing has large implications for vocational choice as it takes place in formal and informal group situations, as Hadley and Levy (1962) note. The reader may remember that the writer in an earlier chapter spoke of the peer group as providing a stage upon which an adolescent can play out his roles under trial conditions.

Where research has been concerned to date, the Super formulations have stood up well. Brophy (1959), Englander (1960), Norell and Grater (1960), Blocher and Schutz (1961), Stephenson (1961), Warren (1961), Morrison (1962), Anderson and Olsen (1965), and Oppenheimer (1966) have all studied aspects of the self-concept formulation. Super and Overstreet (1960), Montesano and Geist (1964), Gibbons (1964), Gibbons and Lohnes (1965), and Dilley (1965) have studied the vocational maturity aspect; and O'Connor and Kinnane (1961) and Kinnane and Gaubinger (1963) have dealt with the work-values aspect. Of course, continuing work is being done by Super and his associates (Super et al. 1963).

A particularly interesting study in the Super theory area was performed by Starishev-

sky and Matlin (1963), who propose the existence of two occupationally oriented languages, psychtalk and occtalk. The first, psychtalk, represents the language in which the individual thinks of himself. For example, "I am tall." The second, occtalk, involves expressions of educational and occupational intent, as, for example, "I am going to be a lawyer." These two languages have various self-concept meanings as they are used. For example, "I am going to be a nurse" may mean, "I am a compassionate, socially minded person who wants to help those in distress." Another person saying, "I'm working too hard" may be reflecting in a form of psychtalk the fact that he is ambivalent and really doesn't want to make a vocational commitment in occtalk; his psychtalk sets up a possible escape hatch.

Holland's Theory of Vocational Behavior

Holland has proposed a descriptive theory of vocational behavior that views occupational choice as merely an extension of an individual's personality as he endeavors to organize his life along lines compatible with the kind of person he is. According to Holland (1959, 1962, 1966), occupational titles are reference points individuals can use in projecting their self-views and their conceptions of the world of work. A counselor who allows an individual to indicate his reactions, pro and con, to a list of occupational titles can get a summary picture of his "modal personal style."

As Holland sees it, people have a series of stereotypes about the work world, and even though their knowledge of occupations is limited, their stereotypes are self-revealing and become in effect a kind of projective test of personality. As a means of obtaining a stimulus situation that will enable persons to reveal their stereotypes, Holland has devised a Vocational Preference Inventory (1958) of three hundred occupational titles, capable of yielding various subscores for a more adequate analysis of a respondent's interests.

Holland states that the work world may be divided into six different vocational environments, to which everyone must adjust and for which it is necessary to develop appropriate skills. Each environment can represent a style of life and a way of dealing with the world, and people's selection of a style identifies their modal personal orientation. The environments are:

1. *Realistic.* This is a highly active orientation emphasizing physical skill and masculinity. It is a concrete orientation toward skill and aggression, de-emphasizing social skills, interpersonal behavior, and verbality.
2. *Intellectual.* This is the thinking orientation preferring to deal with ideas rather than people. Persons with this orientation find their flair in understanding rather than in dominating or in persuading. They like to organize and integrate.
3. *Social.* Social relationships are the basis of this orientation. In contrast to the Realistic and Intellectual orientations, these people seek out others. They tend to avoid the intellectual and the physical striving aspects of life.
4. *Conventional.* This is the other-directed orientation that sets great store by the rules and regulations, identifying with power and status. Self-controlled, these people prefer to live in a structured world.
5. *Enterprising.* This is the orientation of domination and manipulation seeking status through interpersonal manipulation (artful dealing) and verbality.
6. *Artistic.* The orientation of emotional and artistic expression that emphasizes the primacy of the self and its products. Antagonistic to structure and with little self-control or real social interest, the focus is upon the self and its products. People of this orientation prefer a world in which they can exemplify the inner life of artistic expression.

Holland is not a developmentalist and does not describe the developmental origins of the orientations in a person's life, but presumably they result from the usual experiences of the early years and their amplification and extension in adolescence. His interest is in an individual's present status, and he simply indicates that, given one of the six orientations, the individual will seek an occupation to match it. Obviously the more an individual knows about himself (self-knowledge) and the world of work, the more likely he is to select an occupation making a good match.

Partially confirmatory research on Holland's theory, which is actually more a descriptive statement than a full-blown theory such as Super's, has been performed by a number of investigators, including Stockin (1964), Schutz and Blocher (1961), Osipow, Ashby, and Wall (1966), Johnson and Moore (1973), Lee and Hedahl (1973), Eggenberger and Herman (1972), and Wakefield and Daughtie (1973). More work remains to be done with this theory, especially on the etiology of the orientations, before it can be anything other than an insightful descriptive observation with useful "practical" applications in vocational counseling.

An Interdisciplinary Theory of Choice

The interdisciplinary theory of Ginzberg et al. (1951) was proposed by an interdisciplinary team (economics, psychiatry, psychology, sociology) interested in formulating a statement to describe the dynamics of occupational choice. As Ginzberg et al. view it, vocational choice involves four significant variables:

1. *Reality variable.* An individual is in a position in which he has to respond to the expectations and pressures of society, his peers, and other significant figures in making his vocational decision.
2. *Education variable.* The nature and amount of an individual's education either present or withhold opportunities for his vocational choice.
3. *Emotional variable.* An individual's emotional responses to his environment cannot

help but condition and influence the occupational choices he makes.

4. *Individual values variable.* As the individual matches his values to those he sees in the various occupations, the quality of his occupational choice is affected.

According to Ginzberg et al., occupational choice is a sequential, nonreversible process that occurs over a sequence of four stages, each of which has several substages. As he passes through the stages, an individual, confronted by conflicts between what he wishes and what is possible, has to make compromises. During the first, or fantasy, stage, children make all kinds of arbitrary choices in all areas of behavior, and insofar as young children give any consideration to occupational choice, they do so with a complete lack of reality orientation.

The second stage is the tentative stage, during which the child asks himself what he would like to do and when, while simultaneously finding out what he can do. In this time he finds that ability is a limiting factor and that some activities have greater extrinsic value than others. The substages of this period are those of interest, capacity, value, and transition.

During the third, or realistic, stage, the individual tries to find ways of making good his still tentative choices, and in doing so he finds that he is encountering and testing reality. From this emerges a relatively clear vocational pattern, realistically tested. The two substages of the realistic period are the periods of exploration and crystallization. The fourth, or specification, stage is the period in which the individual makes his choice and enters either his occupation or advanced training for it.

The developmental timetable for these four stages is an individual matter and shows considerable variation among individuals, but in general the fantasy stage ends sometime between ten and twelve, and the exploratory aspect of the tentative stage usually ends somewhere about seventeen or eighteen. The

crystallization aspect usually occurs between nineteen and twenty, although children from lower socioeconomic backgrounds tend to move through the realistic stage faster than do those who are more fortunately endowed. As these writers see the processes, the four most important aspects contributing to the adequacy of vocational choice are reality testing, development of suitable time perspective, ability to defer gratifications, and the ability to compromise in carrying out vocational plans. Ginzberg et al. note that people can usually be categorized as work oriented or pleasure oriented, and as active or passive problem solvers. As he goes through the successive stages, the developing individual tends to identify with a changing series of adults to receive reinforcement from the various identifications he makes.

Research on the interdisciplinary theory has been performed by a number of people, including O'Hara and Tiedeman (1959), O'Hara (1959), Davis, Hagan, and Strouf (1962), and Tucci (1963). Studies generally support the broad outlines of the hypotheses advanced by Ginzberg et al., but, as with most stage theory, there is some question as to the exact sequence, nature, and timing of the stages. There may even be some question as to whether stage identification and description may not be too artificial a way of describing the human behavior sequence.

Vocational Choice and Employment Opportunities

The realism of a student's vocational interests and his eventual selection of an occupation as the one he most prefers are vitally important to him in his general personal adjustment, achievement, and success in life. If he chooses wisely, in the full light of the facts on his abilities and interests, his chances of good adjustment and a satisfactory and rewarding adult life are greatly enhanced. But if he selects unwisely, either above or below his true capacities, he is more apt to be unhappy, bored, and frustrated. The intelligent boy who could have assumed leadership or made creative contributions, who finds his working life bounded by a routine, uninteresting job that offers no challenges, will either be unhappy or will find his satisfaction outside the hours he spends at work, relegating work to a vacuum he endures day after day. On the other hand, the boy who has entered an occupational field in which he is unable to succeed or at least to rise above a level of mediocrity, is equally unhappy. Vocational decision is therefore a most important aspect of an adolescent's life.

One of the difficulties encountered in choosing a vocation is the lack of available jobs in many occupational fields. Some occupations are so overcrowded that even the best qualified have difficulty finding employment. A trained person who cannot find an opportunity to make use of his training is in a most unfortunate position. Yet the facts of the case seem to be that young people give little thought to job availability in selecting their occupations. Hutson (1962) in 1961 replicated a study he had made in 1930 in which career choices of high school students were compared with IQ estimates and reasons for career choice (N in 1961 = 2,744 children in twenty-four schools). He notes that in both 1930 and 1961 the preponderance of choices for professional occupations was discouraging—38 to 65 percent, depending upon high school level and sex. Hutson concludes that students choose occupations with very little regard for their aptitudes and feels that 1961 adolescents demonstrated that they were entrenched in the fantasy stage of vocational selection. A study performed by Bradley in 1943, although made some years ago, is worth citing because of its comprehensive nature and the applicability of its findings to the present situation. Bradley, using a sample of 930 subjects, compared high school pupils' avowed vocational interests and actual employment opportunities in the United States. Despite the fact that 61.1 percent of the people are gainfully employed in agriculture and mechanical and industrial arts, only 8.8 percent of high school youth in the study indicated

interest in entering these fields. On the other hand, 61.7 percent indicated their interest in entering the field of professional service, a field in which only 4.4 percent of the population are gainfully employed; 29.7 percent wished to enter the business and clerical field, an area in which only 14.1 percent of the population find gainful employment. Bradley's study clearly indicates the discrepancy between occupational aspiration and the reality of jobs available.

Summary

Vocational planning is a major problem of late adolescence. The child or younger adolescent, sheltered by both parents and society, tends either to give little thought to his occupational future or to think of it unrealistically in terms of immediate play interests. The older adolescent is faced with a considerable number of environmental factors that tend to make him interested in his vocational future. But in considering his future occupation, he is beset by many pitfalls that make a wise decision particularly difficult. It is the vocational counselor's responsibility to help an adolescent to make his vocational plans, always keeping in mind that readiness is an important factor. The boy or girl involved should not be unduly rushed, although long-deferred vocational decisions may have unfortunate results.

Youth's vocational aspirations tend to be high and are particularly conditioned by the socioeconomic level of the parents. An unpleasant today offers added incentive to try to make the future better—a reason why the aspirations of lower-class children impel them to move upward on the social scale, while the upper-class adolescent looks for a way to maintain the level to which his family has accustomed him. But whatever his walk of life, it is rare for an adolescent to be uninterested in getting ahead. However, differences will be found in what any given child interprets as "getting ahead."

Measurement of interests is an important aspect of the vocational counselor's job. The interest inventory is the most popular of the various means available. Profiles of an individual's interests may be made from the inventory scores.

Still, interests as such are less important than are the bases for these interests. Details and superficial selections may change, but basic causes, such as curiosity and mastery, tend to remain comparatively stable. Factors that determine vocational choice are environmentally engendered. Parents and family are usually most influential, followed by friends and professional acquaintances, in that order. Sons of higher-income parents are more apt to want to follow in their fathers' footsteps than are the sons of lower-income parents. Social prestige is usually an important element in adolescents' vocational choices. But whatever the adolescent's final decision, face-to-face advice is greatly superior in influencing choice, compared to information from other sources.

Unfortunately, parental vocational advice is often unwise. It is often based upon highly emotional feelings and tends to omit the facts. Too often, such advice is based on self-gratification or projection. In general, children who follow family vocational advice tend to know less about their vocational choices than do children who have made their choices by other means. Nevertheless, the counselor would do well to make use of parents whenever possible in his vocational counseling program.

An individual's mental ability level is an important criterion of his probable vocational success in many occupations and is a good starting point for counseling. On the other hand, mere possession of a high level of mental ability does not guarantee success. The typical adolescent usually bases his vocational choice on factors other than mental ability, and, characteristically, he tends to select an occupation beyond his mental capacity. Announced interests and intelligence appear not to have any reasonable observable relationship, although more intelligent individuals are more likely to choose professional occupations. They tend to be more realistic and to make better occupational choices. The less intelligent adolescent has a narrower range of general interests to bring to his occupational thinking.

A number of major theories of vocational development and career selection have been devised, including those of Roe, Super, Holland, and Ginzberg. These theories provide a picture of the dynamics of vocational development and have offered considerable opportunities for research. Of the theories, Super's self-concept approach assumes more comprehensive proportions as a theory than do the others and has held up particularly well under confirmatory research.

Adolescents must be realistic in their vocational choice if future failure and dissatisfaction are to be avoided. Lack of realism exists generally in their vocational choices and is indicated particularly by the fact that so many adolescents indicate interest in professions in which openings are scarce, as compared to the few who indicate interest in the unskilled and semiskilled occupations in which so many spend their working lives. But in recent years there has been an increasing trend toward more realistic selections.

References

Anderson, T. B., and Olsen, L. C. Congruence of self and ideal-self and occupational choices. *Personnel Guidance Journal* 44 (1965): 171–176.

Arbuthnot, J., and Gruenfeld, L. Field independence and educational-vocational interests. *Journal of Consulting and Clinical Psychology* 33 (1969): 631.

Blocher, D. H., and Schutz, R. A. Relationships among self-descriptions, occupational stereotypes, and vocational preferences. *Journal of Counseling Psychology* 8 (1961): 314–317.

Bodden, J. L., and Klein, A. J. Cognitive complexity and appropriate vocational choice: Another look. *Journal of Counseling Psychology*

19 (1972) : 257–258.

Bradley, W. A., Jr. Correlation of vocational preferences. *Genetic Psychology Monographs* 28 (1943) : 99–169.

Brophy, A. L. Self, role, and satisfaction. *Genetic Psychology Monographs* 59 (1959) : 263–308.

Brunkan, R. J. Perceived parental attitudes and parental identification in relation to field of vocational choice. *Journal of Counseling Psychology* 12 (1965) : 39–47.

Clark, E. T. Culturally disadvantaged boys' and girls' aspirations to and knowledge of white-collar and professional occupations. *Urban Education* 1 (1965) : 164–174.

Cohen, E. G. Parental factors in educational mobility. *Sociology of Education* 38 (1965) : 407–425.

Crites, J. O. Parental identification in relation to vocational interest development. *Journal of Educational Psychology* 53 (1962) : 262–270.

Crites, J. O. An interpersonal relations scale for occupational groups. *Journal of Applied Psychology* 46 (1962) : 87–90.

Davis, D. A.; Hagan, N.; and Strouf, J. Occupational choice of twelve-year-olds. *Personnel and Guidance Journal* 40 (1962) : 628–629.

Dilley, J. S. Decision-making ability and vocational maturity. *Personnel and Guidance Journal* 44 (1965) : 423–427.

Dynes, R. R.; Clarke, A. C.; and Dinitz, S. Levels of occupational aspiration: Some aspects of family experience as a variable. *American Sociological Review* 21 (1956) : 212–215.

Eggenberger, J., and Herman, A. The Strong inventory and Holland's theory. *Journal of Vocational Behavior* 2 (1972) : 447–456.

Elder, G. H., Jr. Occupational level, achievement motivation and social mobility: A longitudinal analysis. *Journal of Counseling Psychology* 15 (1968) : 1–7.

Empey, L. T. Social class and occupational aspiration: A comparison of absolute and relative measurement. *American Sociological Review* 21 (1956) : 703–708.

Englander, M. E. A psychological analysis of a vocational choice: Teaching. *Journal of Counseling Psychology* 7 (1960) : 257–264.

Fromm, E. Individual and social origins of neurosis. *American Sociological Review* 9 (1944) : 380–384.

Gibbons, W. D. Changes in readiness for vocational planning from 8th to 10th grade. *Personnel and Guidance Journal* 42 (1964) : 908–913.

Gibbons, W. D., and Lohnes, P. R. Predicting five years of development in adolescents from readiness for vocational planning scales. *Journal of Educational Psychology* 56 (1965) : 244–253.

Ginzberg, E. Toward a theory of occupational choice. *Occupations* 30 (1952) : 491–494.

Ginzberg, E. *The nation's children. 2: Development and education.* White House Conference on Children and Youth. New York: Columbia University Press, 1960.

Ginzberg, E.; Ginsburg, S. W.; Axelrad, S.; and Herma, J. L. *Occupational choice: An approach to a general theory.* New York: Columbia University Press, 1951.

Green, L. B., and Parker, H. J. Parental influence upon adolescents' occupational choice: A test of an aspect of Roe's theory. *Journal of Counseling Psychology* 12 (1965) : 379–383.

Greenhaus, J. H. Self-esteem as an influence on occupational choice and occupational satisfaction. *Journal of Vocational Behavior* 1 (1971) : 75–83.

Grigg, A. E. Childhood experience and parental attitudes: A test of Roe's hypothesis. *Journal of Counseling Psychology* 6 (1959) : 153–156.

Gross, E. A sociological approach to the analysis of preparation for work life. *Personnel and Guidance Journal* 45 (1967) : 416–423.

Hadley, R. G., and Levy, W. V. Vocational development and reference groups. *Journal of Counseling Psychology* 9 (1962) : 110–114.

Hagen, D. Careers and family atmosphere: A test of Roe's theory. *Journal of Counseling Psychology* 7 (1960) : 251–256.

Hershenson, D. B., and Roth, R. M. A decisional process model for vocational development. *Journal of Counseling Psychology* 13 (1966) : 368–370.

Holland, J. L. A personality inventory employing occupational titles. *Journal of Applied Psychology* 42 (1958) : 336–342.

Holland, J. L. A theory of vocational choice. *Journal of Counseling Psychology* 6 (1959) : 35–45.

Holland, J. L. Some explorations of a theory of vocational choice: I. One- and two-year longitudinal studies. *Psychological Monographs*, no. 2, 76 (1962).

Holland, J. L. *The psychology of vocational choice.* Waltham, Mass.: Blaisdell, 1966.

Hollander, M. A., and Parker, H. J. Occupational stereotypes and self-descriptions: Their relationship to vocational choice. *Journal of Vocational Behavior* 2 (1972) : 57–65.

Hollingshead, A. B. *Elmtown's youth.* New York : Wiley, 1949.

Hutson, P. W. Vocational choices, 1930 and 1961. *Vocational Guidance Quarterly* 10 (1962) : 218–222.

Johnson, D. M., and Moore, J. C. An investigation of Holland's theory of vocational psychology. *Measurement and Evaluation in Guidance* 5 (1973) : 488–495.

Kinnane, J. F., and Gaubinger, J. R. Life values and work values. *Journal of Counseling Psychology* 10 (1963) : 362–366.

Kinnane, J. F., and Pable, M. W. Family background and work value orientation. *Journal of Counseling Psychology* 9 (1962) : 320–325.

Korman, A. K. Self-esteem variable in vocational choice. *Journal of Applied Psychology* 50 (1966) : 409–486.

Korman, A. K. Self-esteem as a moderator of the relationship between self-perceived abilities and vocational choice. *Journal of Applied Psychology* 51 (1967) : 65–67.

Korman, A. K. Self-esteem as a moderator in vocational choice. *Journal of Applied Psychology* 53 (1969) : 188–192.

Kunert, K. M. Psychological concomitants and determinants of vocational choice. *Journal of Applied Psychology* 53 (1969) : 152–158.

Kuviesky, W. P., and Bealer, R. C. A clarification of the concept "occupational choice." *Rural Sociology* 31 (1966) : 265–267.

Lee, D. L., and Hedahl, B. Holland's personality types applied to the SVIB basic interest scales. *Journal of Vocational Behavior* 3 (1973) : 61–68.

Levine, S. Occupation and personality: Relationship between the social factors of the job and human orientation. *Personnel and Guidance Journal* 41 (1963) : 602–605.

Little, K. J. The occupations of noncollege youth. *American Educational Research Journal* 4 (1967) : 147–153.

Maslow, A. H. *Motivation and personality.* New York : Harper & Row, 1954.

Meir, E., and Friedland, N. The relationship between intrinsic-extrinsic needs and occupational preferences. *Journal of Vocational Behavior* 1 (1971) : 159–165.

Montesano, N., and Geist, H. Differences in occupational choice between ninth and twelfth grade boys. *Personnel and Guidance Journal* 43 (1964) : 150–154.

Morris, J. L. Propensity for risk taking as a determinant of vocational choice. *Journal of Personality and Social Psychology* 3 (1966) : 328–335.

Morrison, R. L. Self-concept implementation in occupational choices. *Journal of Counseling Psychology* 9 (1962) : 255–260.

Murphy, G. *Personality: A bio-social approach to origins and structure.* New York : Harper & Row, 1947.

Norell, G., and Grater, H. Interest awareness as an aspect of self-awareness. *Journal of Counseling Psychology* 7 (1960) : 289–292.

Nugent, F. A. Relationship of the Kuder Preference Record Verification scores to adjustment: Implications for vocational development theory. *Journal of Applied Psychology* 52 (1968) : 429–431.

O'Connor, J. P., and Kinnane, J. F. A factor analysis of work values. *Journal of Counseling Psychology* 8 (1961) : 263–267.

O'Hara, R. P. Talks about self. *Harvard Studies in Career Development*, no. 14. Cambridge, Mass.: Center for Research in Careers, Harvard Graduate School of Education, 1959.

O'Hara, R. P., and Tiedeman, D. V. Vocational self-concept in adolescence. *Journal of Counseling Psychology* 6 (1959) : 292–301.

Oppenheimer, E. A. The relationship between certain self-construct and occupational preferences. *Journal of Counseling Psychology* 13 (1966) : 191–197.

Osipow, S. *Theories of career development.* New York: Appleton-Century-Crofts, 1968.

Osipow, S. H.; Ashby, J. D.; and Wall, H. W. Personality types and vocational choice: A test of Holland's theory. *Personnel and Guidance Journal* 45 (1966) : 37–42.

Remmers, H. H., and Radler, D. H. *The American teen-ager.* Indianapolis: Bobbs-Merrill, 1957.

Resnick, H.; Fauble, M. L.; and Osipow, S. H. Vocational crystallization and self-esteem in college students. *Journal of Counseling Psychology* 17 (1970) : 465–467.

Riccio, A. C. Occupational aspirations of migrant adolescents from the Appalachian south. *Vocational Guidance Quarterly* 14 (1965) : 26–30.

Roe, A. A psychological study of eminent biologists. *Psychological Monographs*, vol. 65, no. 14a (1951). (a)

Roe, A. A psychological study of eminent physical scientists. *Genetic Psychology Monographs* 43 (1951) : 121–293. (b)

Roe, A. A psychological study of eminent psychologists and anthropologists and a comparison with biological and physical scientists. *Psychological Monographs* 67, no. 2 (1953).

Roe, A. *The psychology of occupations.* New York: Wiley, 1956.

Roe, A. Early determinants of vocational choice. *Journal of Counseling Psychology* 4 (1957) : 212–217.

Roe, A., and Siegelman, M. The origin of interests. *American Personnel Guidance Association Inquiry Studies,* no. 1. Washington, D.C.: APGA, 1964.

Schutz, R. A., and Blocher, D. H. Self-satisfaction and level of occupational choice. *Personnel and Guidance Journal* 40 (1961) : 595–598.

Sewell, W. H.; Haller, A. O.; and Strauss, M. A. Social status and educational and occupational aspiration. *American Sociological Review* 22 (1956) : 67–73.

Shappell, D. L.; Hall, L. G.; and Tarrier, R. B. An application of Roe's vocational choice model. *School Counselor* 19 (1971) : 43–48.

Simon, J. B. An existential view of vocational development. *Personnel and Guidance Journal* 44 (1966) : 604–610.

Starishevsky, R., and Matlin, N. A. A model for the translation of self-concept into vocational terms. In Super, D. E. et al., *Career development: Self-concept theory.* CEEB Research Monograph no. 4. New York: CEEB, 1963.

Stephenson, R. R. Occupational choice as a crystallized self-concept. *Journal of Counseling Psychology* 8 (1961) : 211–216.

Stockin, B. S. A test of Holland's occupational level formulations. *Personnel and Guidance Journal* 42 (1964) : 599–602.

Strong, E. K., Jr. Rewarded versus new interest items. *Journal of Applied Psychology* 47 (1963) : 111–116.

Super, D. E. A theory of vocational development. *American Psychologist* 8 (1953) : 185–190.

Super, D. E. *The psychology of careers.* New York: Harper & Row, 1957.

Super, D. E. Self-concepts in vocational development. In Super, D. E., et al., *Career development: Self-concept theory.* CEEB Research Monograph no. 4. New York: CEEB, 1963a.

Super, D. E. Toward making self-concept theory operational. In Super, D. E., et al., *Career development: Self-concept theory.* CEEB Research Monograph no. 4. New York: CEEB, 1963b.

Super, D. E. Vocational development in adolescence and early adulthood: Tasks and behaviors. In Super, D. E., et al., *Career development: Self-concept theory.* CEEB Research Monograph no. 4. New York: CEEB, 1963c.

Super, D. E.; Crites, J.; Hummel, R.; Moser, H.; Overstreet, P.; and Warnath, C. *Vocational development: A framework for research.* New York: Teachers College, 1957.

Super, D. E., and Overstreet, P. L. *The vocational maturity of ninth-grade boys.* New York: Teachers College, 1960.

Super, D. E.; Starishevsky, R.; Matlin, N.; and Jordaan, J. P. *Career development: Self-concept theory.* CEEB Research Monograph no. 4. New York: CEEB, 1963.

Switzer, D. K.; Gregg, A. E.; Miller, J. S.; and Young, R. K. Early experiences and occupational choice: A test of Roe's hypothesis. *Journal of Counseling Psychology* 9 (1962) : 45–48.

Tucci, M. A. College freshmen and vocational choice. *Vocational Guidance Quarterly* 12 (1963) : 27–29.

Utten, A. C. Recalled parent-child relations as determinants of vocational choice. *Journal of Counseling Psychology* 9 (1962) : 49–53.

Vigod, Z. The relationship between occupational choice and parental occupation. *Alberta Journal of Educational Research* 18 (1972) : 287–294.

Wakefield, J. A., and Doughtie, E. B. The geometric relationship between Holland's personality typology and the Vocational Preference Inventory. *Journal of Counseling Psychology* 20 (1973) : 573–578.

Warren, J. R. Self-concept, occupational role expectation and change in college major. *Journal of Counseling Psychology* 8 (1961) : 164–169.

Werts, C. E. Career choice patterns. *Sociology of Education* 40 (1967) : 348–358.

Werts, C. E. Paternal influence on career choice. *Journal of Counseling Psychology* 15 (1968) : 48–52.

White House Conference on Children and Youth. *The states report on children and youth.* Washington, D.C.: Supt. of Documents, 1960.

Wolfbein, S. L. Education and employment. In Ginzberg, E., ed., *The nation's children,* vol. 2. White House Conference on Children and Youth. New York: Columbia University Press, 1960.

Suggested Readings

Ace, M. E.; Graen, G. B.; and Dawis, R. V. Biographic correlates of work attitudes. *Journal of Vocational Behavior* 2 (1972): 191–199.

Ansell, E. M., and Hansen, J. C. Patterns in vocational development of urban youth. *Journal of Counseling Psychology* 18 (1971): 505–508.

Banducci, R. Accuracy of occupational stereotypes of grade-twelve boys. *Journal of Counseling Psychology* 17 (1970): 534–539.

Barlett, W. E. Vocational maturity: Its past, present, and future development. *Journal of Vocational Behavior* 1 (1971): 217–229.

Brolin, D. Career education needs of secondary educable students. *Exceptional Children* 39 (1973): 619–624.

Campbell, D. P., and Holland, J. L. A merger in vocational interest research: Applying Holland's theory to Strong's data. *Journal of Vocational Behavior* 2 (1972): 353–376.

Cole, N. S. On measuring the vocational interests of women. *Counseling Psychology* 20 (1973): 105–112.

Crites, J. O. Methodological issues in the measurement of career maturity. *Measurement and Evaluation in Guidance* 6 (1974): 200–209.

Crites, J. O., and Semler, I. J. Adjustment, educational achievement, and vocational maturity as dimensions of development in adolescence. *Journal of Counseling Psychology* 14 (1967): 489–496.

Day, H. I. Intrinsic motivation and vocational choice. *Journal of Psychology* 81 (1972): 3–6.

Dinkmeyer, D. A developmental approach to career development. *Counseling and Values* 16 (1971): 28–33.

Dole, A. A. Factors in educational decisions among public school pupils. *Psychology in the Schools* 6 (1969): 73–79.

Eberlein, L.; Park, J.; and Mathieson, W. Self-ideal congruence in five occupational groups. *Alberta Journal of Education Research* 17 (1971): 95–103.

Herr, E. L. *Decision-making and vocational development*. Boston: Houghton Mifflin, 1970.

Hollander, J. Development of vocational decisions during adolescence. *Journal of Counseling Psychology* 18 (1971): 244–248.

Hollander, J. Differential parental influences on vocational interest development in adolescent males. *Journal of Vocational Behavior* 2 (1972): 67–76.

Nelson, J. I. High school context and college plans: The impact of social structure on aspirations. *American Sociological Review* 37 (1972): 143–148.

Pallone, N. J., and Hurley, R. B. Further data on key influences of occupational expectation among minority youth. *Journal of Counseling Psychology* 20 (1973): 484–486.

Sandem, C. A. Aspirations for college. *Personnel and Guidance Journal* 46 (1968): 462–465.

Seward, G. H., and Williamson, R. C. A cross-national study of adolescent professional goals. *Human Development* 12 (1969): 248–254.

Southworth, J. A., and Morningstar, M. E. Persistence of occupational choice and personality congruence. *Journal of Counseling Psychology* 17 (1970): 409–412.

Thompson, O. E. Occupational values of high school students. *Personnel and Guidance Journal* 44 (1966): 850–853.

Tseng, M. S., and Carter, A. R. Achievement motivation and fear of failure as determinants of vocational choice, vocational aspiration, and perception of vocational prestige. *Journal of Counseling Psychology* 17 (1970): 150–156.

Welsh, G. S. Vocational interests and intelligence in gifted adolescents. *Educational and Psychological Measurement* 31 (1971): 155–164.

Westbrook, B. W., and Parry-Hill, J. W. The measurement of cognitive vocational maturity. *Journal of Vocational Behavior* 3 (1973): 239–252.

Zytowski, D. G. *The influence of psychological factors upon vocational development*. Boston: Houghton Mifflin, 1970.

Author Index

Pederson, D. M., 93
Peel, E. A., 123
Pendorf, J., 460, 461
Penk, W. E., 116, 343
Peri, G., 115
Perkins, C. W., 103
Perkins, H. V., 95
Perl, R., 140n.
Perron, R., 288
Persing, K. M., 321
Peskin, H., 390n., 398
Peter, N., 311
Peterson, D. R., 57, 58
Petri, E., 394
Petroni, F. A., 462
Pett, L. B., 371
Pflaum, J., 66–67
Pfuhl, W., 367, 368, 376, 378, 379, 383
Phelps, H. R., 253, 515
Phillips, D. L., 346
Phillips, I., 446
Piaget, J., 91, 112, 113, 117, 118, 119, 120, 121, 122, 123, 124, 140, 244, 292, 299, 304, 306, 311, 342, 504
Pierce, J. V., 517
Piers, E. V., 103, 105
Pignatelli, M. L., 171
Pileggi, N., 445
Pilisuk, M., 103
Platt, J. J., 103, 104
Podd, M. H., 44, 287
Pomeroy, W. B., 394, 395, 396, 397
Porter, J. B., 68
Porteus, B. D., 303
Potvin, R. H., 433, 441
Powers, J. M., 104
Prescott, D. A., 208n., 316
Pressey, S. L., 177, 251
Preston, A., 344
Prince, R., 289n.
Project Talent, 178
Propper, M. M., 445
Prugh, D. G., 441
Pryer, M. W., 343
Pulver, S. E., 13
Puryear, H. B., 327
Putney, S., 483
Pyle, S. I., 410, 411, 413, 414

Quadrio, A., 115
Quereshi, M. Y., 141

Raban, R., 208n.

Rabovitch, J. C., 440
Radler, D. H., 307, 527
Ramfalk, C. W., 67
Ramsey, C. E., 283
Rasmussen, J. E., 45
Rauh, J. L., 368, 370
Ray, J. J., 447
Rees, W. L., 417
Reese, H. W., 494, 516
Reeves, J., 502
Regan, J. W., 330
Reichard, S., 140
Reichert, J. L., 422, 423
Reinert, G., 147n.
Reitan, H. T., 342
Remmers, H. H., 16, 283, 307, 345, 438, 527
Resnick, H., 534
Reubush, B. K., 468
Reuder, M. E., 67
Rewitzer, M., 460
Reynolds, E. L., 419
Riccio, A. C., 530
Rice, J. P., 177
Richards, T. W., 69
Richey, H. G., 327, 419
Riesman, D., 469
Rim, Y., 287
Ritchey, G., 329
Rivenbark, W. H., 92
Rivlin, L. G., 494
Roberton, J., 393
Roberts, R. J., 175
Robertson, T. B., 376
Robinow, M., 415n.
Robinson, F. P., 251
Robinson, N., 167
Rockway, A. S., 116
Rode, A., 446
Roe, A., 68, 536, 537
Rogers, C. R., 88, 163, 195
Rohmann, C. G., 415
Romanus, T., 392
Rongved, M., 103
Root, N. N., 35
Roscoe, J. T., 327
Rosen, G., 443
Rosen, S., 494
Rosenbaum, M., 367
Rosenberg, M., 101, 102, 476
Rosenblatt, B., 36
Rosenbluh, E. S., 170
Rosenzweig, S., 67
Rosler, H. D., 22

Subject Index

Abient needs, 196

Abstraction, increasing ability for, 116–117

Academic performance: self-evaluations and, 103; internality expectation for, 343–344

Acceleration, positive and negative, 142n.

Acceptance: parental, 480; by peer group, 499–501, 502

Accident-proneness, 266–267

Achievement, giftedness and, 173–178

Achievement anxiety, cheating and, 324

Achievement motivation, ego identity and, 44

Acne, preoccupation with, 359

Activities: needs contrasted with, 211; relationship to interests, 242–243; solitary, 264–266; of groups, 265–266, 518–520

Adaptive functions, in moral development, 308

Adient needs, 196

Adjective Check List, 172

Adjustment: stability of self-concept and, 96–97; giftedness and, 171, 172–173; needs and, 193, 217–218; success and, 249; religious affiliation and, 327–328; responsibility and, 341; alienation and, 446–447; perceptions of family and, 483–484

Adolescence: definition of, 3, 8–9, 12–14; changing nature of, 4; points of reference in, 4–5; description of, 8–9, 20–21; earlier descriptions and theories of, 9–11; modern interest in, 12; modern descriptions of, 14–23; proportion of population in, 23–24; concepts of adulthood, 47; as reference point, 389

Adulthood, adolescents' concepts of, 47

Adults: role in adolescent development, 6, 7; facilitation by, 19; stereotypes held by, 21–22; generalization of attitudes by, 278–279; hostility to youth, 439. *See also* Intergenerational conflict; Parents

Affection: sources of, 213; parental lack of, 475

Age: of puberty, 13, 391–395; at end of adoles-

cence, 13; PEN Inventory related to, 17–18; in stage theories, 22–23; developmental tasks related to, 41; of formal operations stage, 123; in computation of IQ, 135; of cessation of mental growth, 141–145, 146 (fig.); play and, 244; sex hormone excretion and, 401, 402 (fig.); as means of classifying children, 408; intergenerational conflict and, 457–459

Age differences: in personality structure, 58, 67, 68–69, 71–75, 77; in personality development, 62–64, 66; in self-disclosure, 92–93; in self-concept, 95–96; in conceptual behavior, 116–117; in interests, 251; in wishes, 260; in fears, 263; in attitudes, 284, 285, 291–292; in cheating, 324; in religious beliefs, 325, 327; in values, 459–460

Age grouping(s), 12; Gesell's characteristics of, 31–32

Aggression: frustration and, 203–204; as alienation, 446

Alienation, 444–445; causes of, 445–446; mechanisms of, 446–447; overt protest and, 447

Alloplastic drive, 39

Allport-Vernon-Lindzey Study of Values, 172

Altruism, 329–330

Ambiguity, culturally determined, 441–442

American College Testing Program, giftedness and, 173, 175, 174–175 (table), 176 (table)

American society: nature of, 434–435; historical changes in, 435–437; adolescent responses to, 437–440; adolescent tension in, 440–443; alienation from, 444–447; emphasis on youth, 458–459; emphasis on peer affiliations, 501–502

Anal stage, 33

Analytical-psychometric approach, 132

Androgens, 401–402

Anxiety: ego identity and, 44; sources of, 68; age related to, 69; creativity and, 164–165; in moral development, 307; competitive athletics and, 422; social role and, 493–494. *See also* Stress

565